𝒮

4

NOTABLE
SPORTS
FIGURES

4

NOTABLE SPORTS FIGURES

Dana Barnes, Editor

VOLUME 4 • T-Z

Appendix • Indexes

GALE®

Detroit • New York • San Diego • San Francisco • Cleveland • New Haven, Conn. • Waterville, Maine • London • Munich

Notable Sports Figures

Project Editor
Dana R. Barnes

Editorial
Laura Avery, Luann Brennan, Frank Castronova, Leigh Ann DeRemer, Andrea Henderson, Kathy Nemeh, Angela Pilchak, Tracie Ratiner, Bridget Travers

Research
Gary J. Oudersluys, Cheryl L. Warnock, Kelly Whittle

Editorial Support Services
Charlene Lewis, Sue Petrus

Editorial Standards
Lynne Maday

Permissions
Lori Hines

Imaging and Multimedia Content
Randy Basset, Dean Dauphinais, Leitha Etheridge-Sims, Lezlie Light, Dan W. Newell, Dave G. Oblender

Product Design
Jennifer Wahi

Manufacturing
Evi Seoud, Rhonda Williams

Library of Congress Cataloging-in-Publication Data

Notable sports figures / project editor, Dana R. Barnes.
    p. cm.
Includes bibliographical references and index.
ISBN 0-7876-6628-9 (Set Hardcover) -- ISBN 0-7876-6629-7 (Volume 1)
--ISBN 0-7876-6630-0 (Volume 2) -- ISBN 0-7876-6631-9 (Volume 3) --
ISBN 0-7876-7786-8 (Volume 4)
1. Sports--Biography. 2. Athletes--Biography. 3. Sports--History.
I. Barnes, Dana R.
GV697.A1N68 2004
796'.092'2--dc21
                                       2003011288

Contents

Introduction

Notable Sports Figures provides narrative biographical profiles of more than 600 individuals who have made significant contributions to their sport and to society. It covers sports figures from the nineteenth, twentieth, and twenty-first centuries who represent a wide variety of sports and countries. Lesser-known sports such as cricket, equestrian, and snowboarding are featured alongside sports like baseball, basketball, and football. *Notable Sports Figures* includes not only athletes, but also coaches, team executives, and media figures such as sportscasters and writers.

Notable Sports Figures takes a close look at the people in sports who have captured attention because of success *on* the playing field or controversy *off* the playing field. It provides biographical coverage of people from around the world and throughout history who have had an impact not only on their sport, but also on the society and culture of their times. Each biography features information on the entrant's family life, early involvement in sports, career highlights, championships, and awards. *Notable Sports Figures* also examines the impact that the subject had and continues to have on his or her sport, and the reasons why the individual is "notable." This includes consideration of the successes and failures, on the field and off, that keep the person in the public eye.

The biographies in *Notable Sports Figures* profile a broad variety of individuals. Athletes such as **Babe Ruth, Michael Jordan,** and **Martina Navratilova** are featured for their record-breaking accomplishments. **Jackie Robinson** and **Janet Guthrie** remain in the public consciousness because of their determination to cross racial and gender boundaries. Other sports figures have captured our attention by their controversial activities. Skater **Tonya Harding** continues to hold public interest not because of any medals won, but because of the scandalous attack on **Nancy Kerrigan.** Baseball player **"Shoeless" Joe Jackson** was one of the greatest players of his era, but he is remembered more for his complicity in the **"Black Sox"** scandal of 1919 than for his accomplishments on the field. Their lives, accomplishments, and reasons for the public's ongoing fascination with them are examined in *Notable Sports Figures.*

SELECTION PROCESS AND CRITERIA

A preliminary list of athletes, team executives, sportswriters, broadcasters, and other sports figures was compiled from a wide variety of sources, including Hall of Fame lists, periodical articles, and other biographical collections. The list was reviewed by an advisory board, and final selection was made by the editor. An effort was made to include athletes of varying nationalities, ethnicities, and fields of sport as well as those who have contributed to the success of a sport or team in general. Selection criteria include:

- Notable "first" achievements, including those who broke racial or gender barriers and paved the way for others

- Impact made on the individual's sport and on society as a whole

- Records set and broken

- Involvement in controversial or newsworthy activities on and off the playing field

FEATURES OF THIS PRODUCT

For easy access, entries are arranged alphabetically according to the entrant's last name.

- **Timeline**—includes significant events in the world of sports, from historic times to the present.

- **Entry head**—lists basic information on each sports figure, including name, birth and death years, nationality, and occupation/sport played.

- **Biographical essay**—offers 1,000 to 2,500 words on the person's life, career highlights, and the impact that the individual had and continues to have on his or her sport and on society. Bold-faced names within entries indicate an entry on that person.

- **Photos**—provide a portrait for many of the individuals profiled. Several essays also include an action photo.

- **Sidebars**—present a chronology of key events in the entrant's life, a list of major awards and accomplishments, and, as applicable, career statistics, brief biographies of important individuals in the entrant's life, "where is s/he now" information on previously popular sports figures, and excerpts from books and periodicals of significant events in the entrant's life and career.

• **Contact Information**—offers addresses, phone numbers, and web sites for selected living entrants.

• **Selected Writings**—lists books and publications written or edited by the entrant.

• **Further Information**—provides a list of resources the reader may access to seek additional information on the sports figure.

• **Appendix**—offers a glossary of commonly used sports abbreviations.

• **Indices**—allow the reader to access the entrants by nationality or sport. A general subject index with cross-references offers additional access.

We Welcome Your Suggestions. Mail your comments and suggestions for enhancing and improving *Notable Sports Figures* to:

The Editors
Notable Sports Figures
Gale Group
27500 Drake Road
Farmington Hills, MI 48331-3535
Phone: (800) 347-4253

Advisory Board

Contributors

Don Amerman, Julia Bauder, Cynthia Becker, David Becker, Michael Belfiore, Kari Bethel, Michael Betzold, Tim Borden, Carol Brennan, Gerald Brennan, Paul Burton, Frank Caso, Gordon Churchwell, Gloria Cooksey, Andrew Cunningham, Lisa Frick, Jan Goldberg, Joyce Hart, Eve Hermann, Ian Hoffman, Syd Jones, Wendy Kagan, Aric Karpinski, Christine Kelley, Judson Knight, Eric Lagergren, Jeanne Lesinski, Carole Manny, Paulo Nunes-Ueno, Patricia Onorato, Tricia Owen, Kristin Palm, Mike Pare, Annette Petruso, Ryan Poquette, Susan Salter, Brenna Sanchez, Lorraine Savage, Paula Scott, Pam Shelton, Ken Shepherd, Ann Shurgin, Barbra Smerz, Roger Smith, Janet Stamatel, Jane Summer, Erick Trickey, Amy Unterburger, Sheila Velazquez, Bruce Walker, Dave Wilkins, Kelly Winters, Rob Winters, Ben Zackheim

Acknowledgments

Photographs and illustrations appearing in *Notable Sports Figures* have been used with the permission of the following sources:

AP/WIDE WORLD PHOTOS:
1980 U.S. Olympic hockey team, photograph. AP/Wide World Photos./ Aamodt, Kjetil Andre, photograph. AP/Wide World Photos./ Aaron, Hank, photograph. AP/Wide World Photos./ Abbott, Jim, photograph. AP/Wide World Photos./ Abdul-Jabbar, Kareem, photograph. AP/Wide World Photos./ Abdul-Jabbar, Kareem, photograph. AP/Wide World Photos./ Agassi, Andre, photograph. AP/Wide World Photos./ Aikman, Troy, photograph. AP/Wide World Photos./ Akers, Michelle, photograph. AP/Wide World Photos, Inc./ Albert, Marv, photograph by Ron Frehm. AP/Wide World Photos./ Albright, Tenley, photograph. AP/Wide World Photos./ Alexander, Grover Cleveland, photograph. AP/Wide World Photos./ Allison, Davey, photograph. AP/Wide World Photos./ Alamo, Roberto, photograph. AP/Wide World Photos./ Anderson, George "Sparky," photograph. AP/Wide World Photos./ Andretti, Mario, photograph. AP/Wide World Photos./ Anthony, Earl, photograph. AP/Wide World Photos./ Armstrong, Lance, photograph. AP/Wide World Photos./ Armstrong, Lance, photograph. AP/Wide World Photos./ Ashe, Arthur, photograph. AP/Wide World Photos./ Ashford, Evelyn, photograph. AP/Wide World Photos./ Auerbach, Red, photograph. AP/Wide World Photos./ Autissier, Isabelle, photograph. AP/Wide World Photos./ Bailey, Donovan, photograph. AP/Wide World Photos./ Banks, Ernie, photograph. AP/Wide World Photos./ Bannister, Roger, photograph. AP/Wide World Photos./ Barton, Donna, photograph. AP/Wide World Photos./ Baugh, Sammy, photograph. AP/Wide World Photos./ Baumgartner, Bruce, photograph. AP/Wide World Photos./ Baylor, Elgin, photograph. AP/Wide World Photos./ Beckenbauer, Franz, photograph. AP/Wide World Photos./ Becker, Boris, photograph. AP/Wide World Photos./ Bedard, Myriam, photograph by Roberto Borea. AP/Wide World Photos./ Bell, Bert, photograph. AP/Wide World Photos./Bell, James "Cool Papa," photograph by Leon Algee. AP/Wide World Photos./ Bench, Johnny, photograph. AP/Wide World Photos./ Berra, Yogi, photograph. AP/Wide World Photos./ Biondi, Matt, photograph. AP/Wide World Photos./ Bird, Larry, photograph. AP/Wide World Photos./Bjoerndalen, Ole Einar, photograph. AP/Wide World Photos./ Blair, Bonnie, photograph. AP Wide World Photos./ Blair, Bonnie, portrait. AP/Wide World Photos./ Blake, Sir Peter, photograph. AP/Wide World Photos./ Bogues, Tyrone, "Muggsy," photograph. AP/Wide World Photos./ Bonds, Barry, photograph. AP/Wide World Photos./ Bonds, Barry, photograph. AP/Wide World Photos./ Borders, Ila, photograph by Nick Ut. AP/Wide World Photos./ Borg, Bjorn, photograph. AP/Wide World Photos./ Bossy, Michael, photograph. AP/Wide World Photos./ Bradley, William Warren, photograph. AP/Wide World Photos./ Bradman, Don, photograph. AP/Wide World Photos./ Bradshaw, Terry, photograph. AP/Wide World Photos./ Brock, Lou, photograph. AP/Wide World Photos./ Brock, Lou, photograph. AP/Wide World Photos./ Brooks, Herb, photograph by Gene J. Puskar. AP/Wide World Photos./ Brown, Jim, photograph. AP/Wide World Photos./ Brown, Jim, photograph. AP/Wide World Photos./ Brown, Mordecai, "Three Finger," photograph. AP/Wide World Photos./ Brown, Tim, photograph. AP/Wide World Photos./ Bubka, Sergei, photograph. AP/Wide World Photos./ Budge, Don, photograph. AP/Wide World Photos./ Butcher, Susan, photograph. AP/Wide World Photos./ Button, Dick, photograph. AP/Wide World Photos./ Campanella, Roy, photograph. AP/Wide World Photos./ Campbell, Earl, photograph. AP/Wide

World Photos./ Canseco, Jose, photograph. AP/Wide World Photos./ Capriati, Jennifer, photograph. AP/Wide World Photos./ Capriati, Jennifer, photograph. AP/Wide World Photos./ Carter, Cris, photograph by Michael Conroy. AP/Wide World Photos./ Carter, Vince, photograph by Chuck Stoody. AP/Wide World Photos./ Carter, Vince, photograph. AP/Wide World Photos./ Cartwright, Alexander Joy, photograph. AP/Wide World Photos./ Caulkins, Tracy, photograph. AP/Wide World Photos./ Chamberlain, Wilt, photograph. AP/Wide World Photos./ Chelios, Chris, photograph. AP/Wide World Photos./ Chun, Lee-Kyung, photograph. AP/Wide World Photos./ Clark, Kelly, photograph. AP/Wide World Photos./ Clark, Kelly, photograph. AP/Wide World Photos./ Clemens, Roger, photograph. AP/Wide World Photos./ Clemens, Roger, photograph. AP/Wide World Photos./ Clemente, Roberto Walker, photograph. AP/Wide World Photos./ Coachman, Alice, photograph. AP/Wide World Photos./ Coleman, Derrick, photograph. AP/Wide World Photos./ Colorado Silver Bullets (Samonds, Shereen, and former major league pitcher Phil Niekro), photograph. AP/Wide World Photos./ Comaneci, Nadia, photograph. AP/Wide World Photos./ Connors, Jimmy, photograph. AP/Wide World Photos./ Conradt, Jody, photograph. AP/Wide World Photos./ Cooper, Cynthia, photograph by David J. Phillip. AP/Wide World Photos./ Cosell, Howard, photograph. AP/Wide World Photos./ Courier, Jim, photograph. AP/Wide World Photos./ Cousy, Bob, photograph. AP/Wide World Photos./ Daly, Chuck, photograph. AP/Wide World Photos./ Davis, Terrell, photograph by Ed Andrieski. AP/Wide World Photos./ Dawes, Dominique, photograph by John McConnico. AP/Wide World Photos./ Dean, Dizzy, photograph. AP/Wide World Photos./ Decker-Slaney, Mary, photograph. AP/Wide World Photos./ Deegan, Brian, photograph. AP/Wide World Photos./ DeFrantz, Anita, photograph by Douglas C. Pizac. AP/Wide World Photos./ De La Hoya, Oscar, photograph. AP/Wide World Photos./ Dickerson, Eric, photograph by Bill Janscha. AP/Wide World Photos./ Dimaggio, Joe, photograph. AP/Wide World Photos./Disl, Uschi, photograph. AP/Wide World Photos./ Ditka, Mike, photograph. AP/Wide World Photos./Doby, Larry, photograph. AP/Wide World Photos./ Dolan, Tom, photograph. AP/Wide World Photos./ Dorsett, Tony, photograph by Bruce Zake. AP/Wide World Photos./ Dravecky, Dave, photograph. AP/Wide World Photos./ Durocher, Leo, photograph. AP/Wide World Photos./ Dyroen, Becky, photograph. AP/Wide World Photos./ Earnhardt, Dale, photograph. AP/Wide World Photos./ Edwards, Teresa, photograph. AP/Wide World Photos./ Egerszegi, Krisztina, photograph. AP/Wide World Photos./ Elway, John, photograph. AP/Wide World Photos./ Erving, Julius, photograph. AP/Wide World Photos./ Esposito, Phil, photograph by Kevin Frayer. AP/Wide World./ Evans, Janet, photograph. AP/Wide World Photos./ Ewbank, Weeb, photograph. AP/Wide World./ Fangio, Juan Manuel, photograph by Eduardo DiBaia. AP/Wide World Photos./ Faulk, Marshall, photograph. AP/Wide World Photos./ Favre, Brett. AP/Wide World Photos./ Fernandez, Lisa, photograph. AP/Wide World Photos./ Figo, Luis, photograph. AP/Wide World Photos./ Fisk, Carlton, photograph. AP/Wide World Photos./ Fittipaldi, Emerson, photograph. AP/Wide World Photos./ Fleming, Peggy, photograph. AP/Wide World Photos./ Flowers, Vonetta, photograph by Darron Cummings. AP/Wide World Photos./ Foreman, George, photograph by Charles Rex Arbogast. AP/Wide World Photos./ Forsberg, Magdalena, photograph. AP/Wide World Photos./ Foyt, A.J., photograph. AP/Wide World Photos./ Foyt, A. J., photograph by Dave Parker. AP/Wide World Photos./ Freeman, Cathy, photograph. AP/Wide World Photos./ Gable, Dan, photograph. AP/Wide World Photos./ Galindo, Rudy, photograph by Craig Fujii. AP/Wide World Photos./ Garcia, Sergio, photograph by Beth A. Keiser. AP/Wide World Photos./ Garnett, Kevin, photograph. AP/Wide World Photos./ Gehrig, Lou, photograph. AP/Wide World Photos./ Gibson, Althea, photograph. AP/Wide World Photos./ Gibson, Josh, photograph. AP/Wide World Photos./ Gonzales, Richard "Pancho," photograph. AP/Wide World Photos./Goolagong, Evonne, photograph. AP/Wide World Photos./ Goosen, Retief, photograph. AP/Wide World Photos./ Gordeeva, Ekaterina, photograph. AP/Wide World Photos./ Graf, Steffi, photograph. AP/Wide World Photos./ Granato, Cammi, photograph. AP/Wide World Photos./ Grange, Harold "Red," photograph. AP/Wide World Photos./ Grange, Red, photograph. AP/Wide World Photos./ Graziano, Rocky, photograph. AP/Wide World Photos./ Greenberg, Hank, photograph. AP/Wide World Photos./ Greene, Joe, photograph. AP/Wide World Photos./ Griese, Bob, photograph. AP/Wide World Photos./ Griffey, Jr., Ken, photograph. AP/Wide World Photos./ Griffey, Ken, Jr., photograph by Jay Drowns. AP/Wide World Photos./ Griffin, Archie, photograph. AP/Wide World Photos./ Gwynn, Tony, portrait. AP/Wide World Photos./ Hackl, Georg, photograph. AP/Wide World Photos./ Halas, George, photograph. AP/Wide World Photos./ Hall, Glenn, photograph. AP/Wide World Photos./ Hamilton, Scott, photograph. AP/Wide World Photos./ Hamm, Mia, photograph. AP/Wide World Photos./ Hardaway, Afernee, photograph. AP/Wide World Photos./ Hardaway, Tim Duane, photograph by Lee Wilfredo. AP/Wide World Photos./ Harding, Tonya, photograph. AP/Wide World Photos./ Harkes, John, photograph. AP/Wide World Photos./ Harwell, Ernie, photograph. AP/Wide World Photos./ Heiden, Eric, photograph. AP/Wide World Photos./ Henderson, Rickey, photograph by Kevork Djansezian. AP/Wide World Photos./ Henie, Sonja, photograph. AP/Wide World Photos./ Henie, Sonja, photograph. AP/Wide World Photos./ Hernandez, Luis, photograph. AP/Wide World Photos./ Hill, Grant, photograph. AP/Wide World Photos./ Hirsch, Elroy Leon, photograph. AP/Wide World Photos./ Hogan, Ben, photograph. AP/Wide World Photos./ Holdsclaw, Chamique, photograph. AP/Wide World Photos./ Holmgren, Mike, photograph. AP/Wide World Photos./ Hornsby, Rogers, photograph. AP/Wide World Photos./ Hornung, Paul, photograph. AP/Wide World Photos./ Howe, Gordie, photograph. AP/Wide World Photos./ Howe, Gordie, photograph by Dawn Villella. AP/Wide World Photos./ Hughes, Sarah, photograph. AP/Wide World Photos./ Hull, Brett, photograph. AP/Wide World Photos./ Indurain, Miguel, photograph. AP/Wide World Photos./ Irvin, Michael, photograph AP/Wide World Photos./ Jackson, Bo (Vincent), photograph. AP/Wide World Photos./ Jackson, Joseph "Shoeless Joe," photograph. AP/Wide World Photos./ Jackson, Phil, photograph by Tim Boyle. (c) Tim Boyle of AP/Wide World Photos./ Jackson, Reginald Martinez, photograph by Ray Stubblebine. AP/Wide World Photos./ Jansen, Dan, photograph. AP/Wide World Photos./ Jenner, Bruce, photograph. AP/Wide World Photos./ Johnson, Earvin "Magic", photograph. AP/Wide World Photos./ Johnson, Junior, photograph. AP/Wide World Photos./ Johnson, Michael, photograph. AP/Wide World Photos./ Johnson, Randy, portrait. AP/Wide World Photos./ Jones, Kevin, photograph. AP/Wide World Photos./ Jones, Marion, photograph by Michael Probst. AP/Wide World Photos./ Jones, Robert Tyre, Jr., photograph. AP/Wide World Photos./ Joyce, Joan, photograph. AP/Wide World Photos./ Joyner, Florence Griffith, photograph. AP/Wide World Photos./ Joyner-Kersee, Jackie, photograph. AP/Wide World Photos./ Kaline, Al, photograph. AP/Wide World Photos./ Karelin, Alexander, photograph. AP/Wide World Photos./ Kariya, Paul, photograph. AP/Wide World Photos./ Karsten, Ekaterina, photograph. AP/Wide World Photos./ Kelly, Jim, photograph. AP/Wide World Photos./ Kemp, Shawn, photograph. AP/Wide World Photos./ Kidd, Jason, photograph. AP/Wide World Photos./ Killebrew, Harmon, photograph. AP/Wide World./ Killy, Jean-Claude, photograph. AP/Wide World Photos./ Killy, Jean-Claude, photograph. AP/Wide World Photos./ King, Billie Jean, photograph. AP/Wide World Photos./ King, Don, photograph. AP/Wide World./ Kiraly, Karch, photograph. AP/Wide World Photos./ Kirvesniemi, Harri, photograph. AP/Wide World Photos./ Klug, Chris, photograph. AP/Wide World Photos./ Klug, Chris, photograph. AP/Wide World Photos./ Knight, Bobby, photograph. AP/Wide World Photos./ Koch, Bill, photograph. AP/Wide World Photos./ Korbut, Olga, photograph. AP/Wide World Photos./ Kostelic, Janica, photograph. AP/Wide World Photos./ Kournikova, Anna, photograph by Bill Kostroun. AP/Wide World Photos./ Kronberger, Petra, photograph by Michel Lipchitz. AP/Wide World Photos./ Krone, Julie, photograph. AP/Wide World Photos./ Kuerten, Gustavo, photograph. AP/Wide World Photos./ Kummer, Clarence, photograph. AP/Wide World Photos./ Kwan, Michelle, photograph. AP/Wide World Photos./ Ladewig, Marion, photograph. AP/Wide World Photos./ Lalas, Alexi, photograph. AP/Wide World Photos./ Lambeau, "Curley," photograph. AP/Wide World Photos./ LaMotta, Jake, photograph. AP/Wide World Photos./ Largent, Steve, photograph. AP/Wide World Photos./ Lasorda, Tommy, photograph. AP/Wide World Photos./ Latynina, Larisa, photograph. AP/Wide World Photos./ Laver, Rod, photograph. AP/Wide World Photos./ Lemieux, Mario, photograph. AP/Wide World Photos./ Lemon, Meadowlark (George), photograph. AP/Wide World Photos./ Leonard, Sugar Ray, photograph by Eric Risberg. AP/Wide World Photos./ Leonard, Sugar Ray, photograph. AP/Wide World Photos./ Leslie, Lisa, photograph. AP/Wide World Photos./ Lewis, Carl, photograph. AP/Wide World Photos./ Lewis, Lennox, photograph by Adam Nadel. AP/Wide World Photos./

Lewis, Lennox, photograph. AP/Wide World Photos./ Lieberman-Cline, Nancy, photograph. AP/Wide World Photos./ Lipinski, Tara, photograph. AP/Wide World Photos./ Lloyd, Earl, photograph. AP/Wide World Photos./ Lobo, Rebecca, portrait. AP/Wide World Photos./ Lopez, Nancy, photograph by Pat J. Carter. AP/Wide World Photos./ Loroupe, Tegla, photograph. AP/Wide World Photos./ Louganis, Greg, photograph. AP/Wide World Photos./ Louis, Joe, photograph. AP/Wide World Photos./ Madden, John, photograph by Aaron Rapopart. AP/Wide World Photos./ Maddux, Greg, photograph. AP/Wide World Photos./ Mahre, Phil, photograph. AP/Wide World Photos./ Maier, Hermann, photograph. AP/Wide World Photos./ Malone, Karl, photograph. AP/Wide World Photos./ Malone, Moses, photograph. AP/Wide World Photos./ Mantle, Mickey, photograph. AP/Wide World Photos, Inc./ Mantle, Mickey, photograph. AP/Wide World Photos./ Marino, Dan, photograph. AP/Wide World Photos./ Martin, Billy, photograph. AP/Wide World Photos./ Martin, Casey, photograph by John Kicker. AP/Wide World Photos./ Martin, Christy, photograph. AP/Wide World Photos./ Masterkova, Svetlana, photograph. AP/Wide World Photos./ Maynard, Don, photograph. AP/Wide World Photos./ Mays, Willie, photograph. AP/Wide World Photos./ McCray, Nikki, photograph. AP/Wide World Photos./ McEnroe, John Patrick, Jr., photograph by Richard Drew. AP/Wide World Photos./ McGwire, Mark, photograph by Tom Gannam. AP/Wide World Photos./ McKinney, Tamara, photograph. AP/Wide World Photos./ Mears, Rick, photograph. AP/Wide World Photos./ Messier, Mark, photograph. AP/Wide World Photos./ Meyers, Ann, photograph. AP/Wide World Photos./ Mikita, Stan, photograph. AP/Wide World Photos./ Mingxia, Fu, photograph. AP/Wide World Photos./ Moceanu, Dominique, photograph. AP/Wide World Photos./ Montana, Joe, photograph. AP/Wide World Photos./ Monti, Eugenio, photograph. AP/Wide World Photos./ Moore, Archie, photograph. AP/Wide World Photos./ Morgan, Joe (Leonard), photograph. AP/Wide World Photos./ Morris, Jim, photograph. AP/Wide World Photos./ Moses, Edwin Corley, photograph by Lennox McLendon. AP/Wide World Photos./ Moss, Randy, photograph by Jim Mone. AP/Wide World Photos./ Muldowney, Shirley "Cha Cha," photograph. AP/Wide World Photos./ Murden, Tori, photograph by Bob Jordan. AP/Wide World Photos./ Musial, Stan, photograph. AP/Wide World Photos./ Musial, Stan, photograph. AP/Wide World Photos./ Mutombu, Dikembe, photograph. AP/Wide World Photos./ Naismith, James, photograph. AP/Wide World Photos./ Namath, Joe, photograph. AP/Wide World Photos./ Namath, Joe, photograph. AP/Wide World Photos./ Navratilova, Martina, photograph. AP/Wide World Photos./ Navratilova, Martina, photograph. AP/Wide World Photos./ Neely, Cam, portrait. AP/Wide World Photos./ Newby-Fraser, Paula, photograph. AP/Wide World Photos./ O'Connor, David, photograph. AP/Wide World Photos./ Oerter, Al, photograph. AP/Wide World Photos./ Oh, Sadaharu, photograph. AP/Wide World Photos./ Ohno, Apolo Anton, photograph. AP/Wide World Photos./ Oldfield, Barney, photograph. AP/Wide World Photos./ Olsen, Merlin Jay, photograph. AP/Wide World Photos./ Olson, Lisa, photograph. AP/Wide World Photos./ O'Neal, Shaquille, photograph. AP/Wide World Photos./ O'Neil, Buck, photograph. AP/Wide World Photos./ O'Neill, Susan, photograph by Dennis Paquin. AP/Wide World Photos./ O'Sullivan, Sonia, photograph. AP/Wide World Photos./ Paige, Leroy Robert, "Satchel," photograph. AP/Wide World Photos./ Paige, Leroy Robert, photograph. AP/Wide World Photos./ Palmer, Shaun, photograph. AP/Wide World Photos./ Parcells, Bill, photograph by Bill Kostroun. AP/Wide World Photos./ Parra, Derek, photograph by Elaine Thompson. AP/Wide World Photos./ Paterno, Joe, photograph by Michael Conroy. AP/Wide World Photos./ Paterno, Joe, photograph. AP/Wide World Photos./ Patterson, Floyd, photograph. AP/Wide World Photos./ Payton, Gary, photograph. AP/Wide World Photos./ Payton, Walter, photograph by Fred Jewell. AP/Wide World Photos./ Pele, photograph. AP/Wide World Photos./ Perry, Gaylord, photograph. AP/Wide World Photos./ Pete Rose, photograph. AP/Wide World Photos./ Petty, Lee, photograph. AP/Wide World Photos./ Piniella, Lou, photograph. AP/Wide World Photos./ Pippen, Scottie, photograph by Tim Johnson. AP/Wide World Photos./ Podkopayeva, Lilia, photograph. AP/Wide World Photos./ Prost, Alain, photograph. AP/Wide World Photos./ Puckett, Kirby, photograph. AP/Wide World Photos./ Randle, John, photograph. AP/Wide World Photos./ Redgrave, Steve, photograph. AP/Wide World Photos./ Reece, Gabrielle, photograph. AP/Wide World Photos/Fashion Wire Daily./ Reese, Harold "Pee Wee," photograph. AP/Wide World Photos./ Retton, Mary Lou, photograph.

AP/Wide World Photos./ Rheaume, Manon, photograph. AP/Wide World Photos./ Rice, Jerry, photograph. AP/Wide World Photos./ Richard, Maurice, photograph. AP/Wide World Photos./ Richardson, Dot, photograph. AP/Wide World Photos./ Riddles, Libby, photograph. AP/Wide World Photos./ Rigby, Cathy, photograph. AP/Wide World Photos./ Riley, Pat, photograph by Mark Lennihan. AP/Wide World Photos./ Ripken, Calvin, photograph. AP/Wide World Photos./ Roba, Fatuma, photograph. AP/Wide World Photos./ Robertson, Oscar, photograph. AP/Wide World Photos./ Robinson, David, photograph. AP/Wide World Photos./ Robinson, Jackie, photograph. AP/Wide World Photos./ Rocker, John, photograph. AP/Wide World Photos./ Rodman, Dennis, photograph. AP/Wide World Photos./ Rodriguez, Alex, photograph. AP/Wide World Photos./ Roy, Patrick, portrait. AP/Wide World Photos./ Rubin, Barbara Joe, photograph. AP/Wide World Photos./ Ruud, Birger, photograph. AP/Wide World Photos./ Rudolph, Wilma, photograph. AP/Wide World Photos./ Russell, Bill, photograph. AP/Wide World Photos./ Ruth, Babe, photograph. AP/Wide World Photos./ Ryan, Lynn Nolan, photograph by Tim Sharp. AP/Wide World Photos./ Sabatini, Gabriela, photograph. AP/Wide World Photos./ St. James, Lyn, portrait. AP/Wide World Photos./ Sale, Jamie, and David Pelletier, photograph by Lionel Cironneau. AP/Wide World Photos./ Sampras, Pete, photograph. AP/Wide World Photos./ Sampras, Pete, photograph. AP/Wide World Photos./ Samuelson, Joan Benoit, photograph. AP/Wide World Photos./ Sanders, Barry, photograph by Rusty Kennedy. AP/Wide World Photos./ Sanders, Deion, photograph. AP/Wide World Photos./ Sanders, Deion, photograph by Rusty Kennedy. AP/Wide World Photos./ Sawchuk, Terry, photograph. AP/Wide World Photos./ Sayers, Gale, photograph. AP/Wide World Photos./ Schayes, Dolph, photograph. AP/Wide World Photos./ Schilling, Curtis Montague, photograph by Lenny Ignelzi. AP/Wide World Photos./ Schmeling, Max, photograph. AP/Wide World Photos./ Schmidt, Mike, photograph. AP/Wide World Photos./ Schmirler, Sandra, photograph. AP/Wide World Photos./ Schramm, Tex, photograph. AP/Wide World Photos./ Schumacher, Michael, photograph. AP/Wide World Photos./ Scott, Wendell Oliver, photograph. AP/Wide World Photos./ Scurry, Briana, photograph. AP/Wide World Photos./ Selanne, Teemu, photograph. AP/Wide World Photos./ Seau, Junior, photograph. AP/Wide World Photos./ Seaver, Tom, photograph. AP/Wide World Photos./ Secretariat, photograph. AP/Wide World Photos./ Secretariat, photograph. AP/Wide World Photos./ Seles, Monica, photograph. AP/Wide World Photos./ Selig, Bud, photograph. AP/Wide World Photos./ Sharp, Sterling, photograph. AP/Wide World Photos./ Shea, Jack, photograph. AP/Wide World Photos./ Sheffield, Gary, photograph. AP/Wide World Photos./ Shula, Don, photograph. AP/Wide World Photos./ Simpson, O. J., photograph. AP/Wide World Photos./ Smith, Tommie, photograph. AP/Wide World Photos./ Sosa, Sammy, photograph by Gary Dineen. AP/Wide World Photos./ Spinks, Michael, photograph. AP/Wide World Photos./ Spitz, Mark (Andrew), photograph. AP/Wide World Photos./ Sprewell, Latrell, photograph by John Dunn. AP/Wide World Photos./ Staley, Dawn, photograph by Rusty Kennedy. AP/Wide World Photos./ Starr, Bart, photograph. AP/Wide World Photos./ Staubach, Roger, photograph. AP/Wide World Photos./ Steinbrenner, George, photograph. AP/Wide World Photos./ Stengel, Casey, photograph. AP/Wide World Photos./ Stenmark, Ingemar, photograph. AP/Wide World Photos./ Stewart, Jackie, photograph. AP/Wide World Photos./ Stewart, Jackie, photograph. AP/Wide World Photos./ Stewart, Kordell, photograph. AP/Wide World Photos./ Stockton, John, photograph. AP/Wide World Photos./ Stojko, Elvis, photograph. AP/Wide World Photos./ Strawberry, Darryl, photograph. AP/Wide World Photos./ Strawberry, Darryl, photograph by Ron Frehm. AP/Wide World Photos./ Street, Picabo, photograph by David Longstreath. AP/Wide World Photos./ Street, Picabo, photograph. AP/Wide World Photos./ Strug, Kerri, photograph. AP/Wide World Photos./ Strug, Kerri, photograph. AP/Wide World Photos./ Suleymanoglu, Naim, photograph. AP/Wide World Photos./ Summitt, Pat, photograph. AP/Wide World Photos./ Suzuki, Ichiro, photograph by Eliane Thompson. AP/Wide World Photos./ Suzuki, Ichiro, photograph. AP/Wide World Photos./ Swoopes, Sheryl, photograph. AP/Wide World Photos./ Tarkanian, Jerry, photograph. AP/Wide World Photos./ Tarkanian, Jerry, photograph. AP/Wide World Photos./ Tarkenton, Fran, photograph. AP/Wide World Photos./ Taylor, Lawrence, photograph. AP/Wide World Photos./ Tendulkar, Sachin, photograph. AP/Wide World Photos./ Thomas, Frank, photograph. AP/Wide World Photos./ Thomas, Isiah, photograph by

Michael Conroy. AP/Wide World Photos./ Thomas, Isiah, photograph. AP/Wide World Photos./ Thomas, Thurman, photograph. AP/Wide World Photos./ Thompson, Jenny, photograph by Paul Sakuma. AP/Wide World Photos./ Thorpe, Ian, photograph by Russell McPhedran. AP/Wide World Photos./ Tomba, Alberto, photograph. AP/Wide World Photos./ Tomba, Alberto, photograph. AP/Wide World Photos, Inc./ Torrence, Gwen, photograph. AP/Wide World Photos./ Torvill, Jayne, and Christopher Dean, photograph. AP/Wide World Photos./ Trottier, Brian, photograph. AP/Wide World Photos./ Tunney, Gene, photograph. AP/Wide World./ Turner, Cathy, AP/Wide World Photos./ Tyson, Mike, photograph by Lennox McLendon. AP/Wide World Photos./ Tyus, Wyomia, photograph. AP/Wide World Photos./ Unitas, Johnny, photograph. AP/Wide World Photos./ Unitas, Johnny, photograph. AP/Wide World Photos./ Unser, Al, photograph. AP/Wide World Photos./ Vaughn, Mo, photograph. AP/Wide World Photos./ Ventura, Jesse, photograph. AP/Wide World Photos./ Vicario, Arantxa Sanchez, photograph. AP/Wide World Photos./ Vitale, Dick, photograph. AP/Wide World Photos./ Wagner, Honus, photograph. AP/Wide World Photos./ Waitz, Grete, photograph. AP/Wide World Photos./ Waitz, Grete, photograph. AP/Wide World Photos./ Walcott, Joe, photograph. AP/Wide World Photos./ Waldner, Jan Ove, photograph. AP/Wide World Photos./ Walton, Bill, photograph. AP/Wide World Photos./ Warne, Shane, photograph. AP/Wide World Photos./ Warner, Kurt, photograph by James A. Finley. AP/Wide World Photos./ Watters, Ricky, photograph. AP/Wide World Photos./ Webb, Anthony, "Spud," photograph. AP/Wide World Photos./ Webb, Karrie, photograph. AP/Wide World Photos./ Webber, Chris, photograph. AP/Wide World Photos./ Weber, Dick, photograph. AP/Wide World Photos./ Wehling, Ulrich, photograph. AP/Wide World Photos./ Weihenmayer, Erik, photograph. AP/Wide World Photos./ Weishoff, Paula, photograph. AP/Wide World Photos./ Weissmuller, Johnny, photograph. AP/Wide World Photos./ West, Jerry, photograph. AP/Wide World Photos./ West, Jerry, photograph. AP/Wide World Photos./ White, Reggie, photograph. AP/Wide World Photos./ Whitworth, Kathy, photograph. AP/Wide World Photos./ Wigger, Deena, photograph. AP/Wide World Photos./ Wilkens, Lenny, photograph. AP/Wide World Photos./ Wilkens, Lenny, photograph. AP/Wide World Photos./ Wilkins, Dominique, photograph. AP/Wide World Photos./ Wilkinson, Laura, photograph. AP/Wide World Photos./ Williams, Serena, photograph. AP/Wide World Photos./ Williams, Serena, photograph. AP/Wide World Photos./ Williams, Ted, photograph. AP/Wide World Photos./ Williams, Venus, photograph. AP/Wide World Photos./ Williams, Venus, photograph. AP/Wide World Photos./ Winfield, Dave, photograph. AP/Wide World Photos./ Witt, Katarina, photograph. AP/Wide World Photos./ Wooden, John, photograph. AP/Wide World Photos./ Wooden, John, photograph. AP/Wide World Photos./ Woods, Tiger, photograph by Dave Martin. AP/Wide World Photos./ Woods, Tiger, photograph by Diego Giudice. AP Wide World Photos./ Woodson, Charles, photograph. AP/Wide World Photos./ Woodson, Rod, photograph. AP/Wide World Photos./ Woodward, Lynette, photograph by Orlin Wagner. AP/Wide World Photos./ Wright, Mickey, photograph. AP/Wide World Photos./ Yamaguchi, Kristi, portrait. AP/Wide World Photos./ Young, Cy, photograph. AP/Wide World Photos./ Young, Sheila, photograph. AP/Wide World Photos./ Young, Steve, photograph. AP/Wide World Photos./ Zaharias, Babe (Mildred Ella) Didrikson, photograph. AP/Wide World Photos./ Zidane, Zinedine, photograph. AP/Wide World Photos./

ASSOCIATED FEATURES, INC.:
Dryden, Ken, photograph. Associated Features, Inc./ Esposito, Tony, photograph. Associated Features, Inc./ Hasek, Dominik, photograph. Associated Features./ Plante, Jacques, photograph. Associated Features./ Sakic, Joe, photograph. Associated Features.

BRUCE BENNETT STUDIOS, INC.:
Belfour, Ed, photograph. Courtesy of Bruce Bennett./ Bowman, Scotty, photograph. John Giamundo/B. Bennett./ Gretzky, Wayne, photograph. Courtesy of Bruce Bennett./ Gretzky, Wayne, photograph. Courtesy of Bruce Bennett./ Lefleur, Guy, photograph. Courtesy of Bruce Bennett./ Lemieux, Mario, photograph. Michael DiGirolamo/B. Bennett./ Lindros, Eric, photograph. Courtesy of B. Bennett./ Lindros, Eric, photograph. Courtesy of Bruce Bennett.

CORBIS:

Rose, Pete, photograph. (c) Stephen Dunn/Getty Images./ Russell, Bill, portrait. (c) Sporting News/Getty Images./ Sayers, Gale, photograph. Sporting News/Archive Photos, Inc./ Shoemaker, Willie, photograph. APA/Archive Photos, Inc./ Shriver, Eunice, photograph. Archive Photos, Inc./ Skobilikova, Lydia, photograph. (c) Hulton Archive/Getty Images./ Sorenstam, Annika, photograph by Steve Marcus. Archive Photos./ Starr, Bart, photograph. Sporting News/Archive Photos, Inc./ Sullivan, John Lawrence, photograph. (c) Hulton Archive/Getty Images./ Swann, Lynn, photograph. Sporting News/Archive Photos./ Thomas, Derrick, photograph by Susumu Takahashi. Reuters/Archive Photos, Inc./ Torre, Joe, photograph. Reuters/Ray Stubblebine/Archive Photos./ Tretiak, Vladislav, photograph. (c) Getty Images./ Trinidad, Felix Tito, photograph. (c) Gary M. Williams/Liaison Agency/Getty Images/ El Neuvo Dia./ Turner, Ted, photograph. Archive Photo/Malafronte./ Van Dyken, Amy, photograph. Reuters/Eric Gailard/Archive Photos./ Wenzel, Hanni, photograph. (c) Tony Duffy/Getty Images./ Williamson, Alison, photograph. (c) Mark Dadswell, Getty Images./

HOCKEY HALL OF FAME:
Blake, Hector, photograph. Courtesy of Hockey Hall of Fame./ Vezina, Georges, photograph. Courtesy of Hockey Hall of Fame.

THE LIBRARY OF CONGRESS:
Dempsey, Jack, photograph. The Library of Congress./ Rockne, Knute, photograph. The Library of Congress. Rudolph, Wilma, photograph. The Library of Congress./ Ruth, Babe, photograph. The Library of Congress.

BILLY MILLS:
Mills, Billy, photograph. Courtesy of Billy Mills./ Mills, Billy, photograph. Courtesy of Billy Mills.

NATIONAL ARCHIVES AND RECORDS ADMINISTRATION:
Thorpe, Jim, photograph. National Archives and Records Administration.

NATIONAL BASEBALL LIBRARY & ARCHIVE:
Chicago White Sox team, photograph. National Baseball Library & Archive, Cooperstown, NY.

NEW YORK KNICKS
Ewing, Patrick, photograph by George Kalinsky. The New York Knicks.

THE NEW YORK PUBLIC LIBRARY:
Washington, Ora, photograph by D. H. Polk. Photographs and Prints Division, Schomburg Center for Research in Black Culture, The New York Public Library, Astor, Lenox and Tilden Foundations.

PENSKE MOTORSPORTS, INC.:
Jackson, Joe, photograph. From The Image of Their Greatness: An Illustrated History of Baseball from 1900 to the Present, revised edition, by Lawrence Ritter and Donald Honig. Crown Trade Paperbacks, 1992. Copyright (c) 1992 by Lawrence S. Ritter and Donald Honig./ Penske, Roger. Photo courtesy of Penske Motorsports, Inc.

POPPERFOTO:
Patterson, Floyd, photograph. Popperfoto/Archive Photos./ Retton, Mary Lou, photograph. Popperfoto.

MITCHELL B. REIBEL:
Borg, Bjorn, photograph. Mitchell Reibel.

SPORTSPICS:
Petty, Richard, photograph. SportsPics.

UNITED PRESS INTERNATIONAL:
U. S. Olympic Hockey team, 1980, photograph. Courtesy of United Press International.

WIREIMAGE.COM:
Bryant, Kobe, photograph. Steve Granitz/WireImage.com.

Entry List

C

VOLUME 3

M

VOLUME 4

T

Timeline

776 B.C.
Greece's first recorded Olympic Games. Only Greeks are allowed to compete, and the games are limited to foot races of approximately 200 yards.

490 B.C.
According to Greek satirist Lucian, a courier named Pheidippides runs from the plains of Marathon to Athens, a distance of about 22 miles, with news of a Greek victory over the Persians. This becomes the inspiration for modern-day "marathon" races.

1457
Scotland's Parliament forbids "futeball and golfe" as their popularity is distracting men from practicing archery which is required for military training.

1552
Scotland's Royal Golf Club of St. Andrews begins. Its official founding comes 200 years later in 1754.

1702
Queen Anne of England gives approval for horseracing and introduces the idea of sweepstakes.

1744
First recorded cricket match in England. Rules of the game are codified in 1788.

1842
Alexander Cartwright invents baseball. Although the game has been played for many years, Cartwright writes down rules of play.

1863
The official rules for soccer are established by the Football Association in England.

1869
Princeton and Rutgers play the first college football game. Rutgers wins 6-4.

1874
British sportsman Walter Clopton Wingfield codifies the rules for lawn tennis.

1875
First running of the Kentucky Derby, won by Aristides.

1876
The National League (NL) is formed. The NL becomes the first stable baseball major league.

1877
The first Wimbledon tennis championship is won by Spencer Gore.

1891
Basketball invented by **James Naismith,** a physical education instructor at Springfield Men's Christian Association Training School. Naismith wrote the first 13 rules for the sport.

1892
"Gentleman Jim" Corbett defeats **John L. Sullivan** to win the first boxing championship fought with padded gloves and under the Marquis of Queensberry Rules.

1896
First of the "modern" Olympics are held in Athens, Greece. Competing are 311 athletes from 13 countries.

1900
The American League (AL) is formed. It soon joins the National League as a baseball major league.

Britain's Charlotte Cooper wins the first women's Olympic gold medal in women's tennis. Margaret Abbott wins the nine-hole golf competition, becoming the first American woman to win Olympic gold.

1903
The National Agreement calls an end to the war between the American and National baseball leagues. The agree-

ment calls for each league to be considered major leagues, the same alignment as today.

The first World Series is played. It features the Pittsburgh Pirates of the National League and the Boston Pilgrims of the American League. Boston wins the series 5-3.

1908
Jack Johnson defeats Tommy Burns to become the first African American to hold the world heavyweight boxing championship.

1911
First Indianapolis 500 is run.

Cy Young retires with a career record 511 wins. The trophy given annually to the best pitcher in each league is named after Young.

1912
Jim Thorpe wins three Olympic medals, one of them a gold medal in the decathlon. The medals are stripped from him in 1913 when it is discovered that he accepted a token sum of money to play baseball. The medals are restored and returned to his family in 1982.

1917
The National Hockey League (NHL) is formed. The new league contains only four teams.

1919
The **Chicago "Black Sox"** throw the World Series against the Cincinnati Reds in the biggest sports gambling incident of all-time. Eight players, including the great **"Shoeless" Joe Jackson,** are banned from baseball by commissioner Kennesaw Mountain Landis.

1920
The New York Yankees purchase the contract of **Babe Ruth** from the Boston Red Sox. "The Curse of the Bambino" prevents the Red Sox from winning a World Series since.

The National Football League (NFL) forms in Canton, Ohio. The original league has 14 teams.

1926
Gertrude Ederle becomes the first woman to swim the English Channel. Her time is nearly five hours faster than the previous five men who made the crossing.

1927
Babe Ruth of the New York Yankees hits 60 home runs in one season, breaking his own single-season record.

His total is more than 12 *teams* hit during the season. Ruth retires with 714 career home runs, also a record at the time.

1928
Ty Cobb retires from baseball with a lifetime .366 average that still stands as a record today. Cobb also retired with the career record for hits (4,189) and runs (2,246).

1930
Uruguay hosts and wins the first soccer World Cup. The event has been held every four years since.

Bobby Jones wins "Grand Slam" of golf by capturing the U.S. and British Opens and Amateurs.

1931
Knute Rockne dies in a plane crash. He finishes with a 121-12-5 record, a winning percentage of .881. Rockne led Notre Dame to five unbeaten and untied seasons.

1932
The Negro National League is formed. This is the first "major" league set up for African-American players.

Babe Didrikson Zaharias wins three gold medals at the Summer Olympics in Los Angeles, California. She sets new world records in the javelin throw and 80-meter hurdles.

1936
Sonja Henie wins the Winter Olympics gold medal for women's figure skating for the third consecutive time.

Jesse Owens wins four gold medals in track and field at the Summer Olympics in Berlin, Germany. Owens' feat comes as a shock to German dictator Adolf Hitler.

1937
Don Budge wins tennis's "Grand Slam." He is the first player to win Wimbledon and the Australian, French, and U.S. championships in the same calendar year.

1938
Helen Wills wins the final of her 19 "Grand Slam" singles tennis titles. She wins eight Wimbledons, seven U.S. Opens, and four French Opens.

The great **Joe Louis** knocks out German fighter **Max Schmeling.** The victory carries extra meaning as it also marks a win against Nazi Germany.

1939
The first baseball game is televised. The game features Cincinnati and Brooklyn.

On July 4, **Lou Gehrig** gives his famous farewell speech. He dies soon after from Amyotrophic Lateral Sclerosis (ALS), now called Lou Gehrig's Disease.

1941

Ted Williams of the Boston Red Sox hits .406. He is the last player to hit over .400 for an entire season.

Joe DiMaggio of the New York Yankees hits safely in 56 consecutive games. He breaks the record of 44 set by Wee Willie Keeler.

1943

The All American Girls Professional Baseball League is formed. At its peak in 1948 the league boasts 10 teams.

1945

Brooklyn Dodgers' executive **Branch Rickey** signs **Jackie Robinson** to a minor league contract.

1946

The color line in football is broken. Woody Strode and Kenny Washington play for the Rams and Marion Motley and Bill Willis join the Browns.

The Basketball Association of America is founded. Within three years it becomes the National Basketball Association (NBA).

1947

Jackie Robinson breaks the color barrier in baseball. This heroic ballplayer is subjected to harsh treatment from fans, fellow ballplayers, and even teammates.

1949

The Ladies' Professional Golf Association (LPGA) forms. **Babe Didrikson Zaharias** is a co-founder.

1957

Althea Gibson becomes the first African American to win Wimbledon and U.S. tennis championships. She repeats her feat the next year.

1958

Baseball's Brooklyn Dodgers move to Los Angeles and New York Giants move to San Francisco. The moves devastate long-time fans of each team.

What is now called the "greatest game ever played" is won by the Baltimore Colts in sudden-death overtime over the New York Giants 23-17. The game is widely televised and has much to do with the growth in popularity of football.

1959

Daytona 500 is run for the first time. It now is one of the most watched sporting events in the United States.

The American Football League (AFL) is founded. The league brings professional football to many new markets.

1960

Sugar Ray Robinson retires from boxing. During his career he wins the welterweight title once and holds the middleweight title five times. His lifetime record is 182-19.

Cassius Clay wins a gold medal in the light-heavyweight class at the Summer Olympics in Rome, Italy. Later, Clay throws his medal into the Ohio River as a reaction against the racial prejudice with which he is forced to contend.

Wilma Rudolph becomes the first American woman to win three gold medals in one Summer Olympics in Rome, Italy. She wins the 100- and 200-meter dashes and is a part of the winning 4 x 100 relay team.

1961

Roger Maris of the New York Yankees hits a single-season record 61 home runs. His record is tarnished by some observers because Maris plays a 162 game schedule while **Babe Ruth,** whose record he broke, played only 154 games in 1927.

1962

Wilt Chamberlain of the Philadelphia Warriors scores 100 points in a single game. He accomplishes this feat on March 2 against the New York Knicks. Chamberlain goes on to set another record when he averages 50.4 points per game during the same season and also leads the NBA in rebounding with 25.7 boards per game.

Oscar Robertson averages a triple double for an entire NBA season. He averages 30.8 points, 12.5 rebounds, and 11.4 assists per game.

1964

Cassius Clay scores a technical knockout of **Sonny Liston** to win the heavyweight championship. The victory is seen as a gigantic upset at the time. The day after his victory over Liston, Clay announces that he is a member of the Nation of Islam. He also announces that he is changing his name to **Muhammad Ali.**

1965

Star running back of the Cleveland Browns, **Jim Brown,** retires to pursue an acting career. He leaves the game holding the record for most career rushing yards, 12,312, in only eight seasons.

1966

The Boston Celtics win their eighth consecutive championship. No other major sports franchise has won this many consecutive titles.

Texas Western beats Kentucky 72-65 for the NCAA basketball championship. The champions feature an all-African American starting five while Kentucky starts five white players.

1967

First Iditarod dog sledding race held. The race begins as a 56 mile race, but by 1973 it evolves into a 1,152 mile trek between Anchorage and Nome, Alaska.

Charlie Sifford becomes the first African American to win on the PGA golf tour when he captures the Greater Hartford Open.

The first Super Bowl is played between the Green Bay Packers and Kansas City Chiefs. It is originally called the AFL-NFL World Championship Game.

1968

Bill Russell becomes the first African-American coach in any major sport. He leads the Boston Celtics to two championships as player-coach.

Americans **Tommie Smith** and John Carlos protest racism in the U.S. by raising black glove-clad fists on the medal stand after finishing first and third in the 200-meters at the Mexico City Olympics. The two are suspended from competition.

Eunice Kennedy Shriver begins the Special Olympics. The program grows into an international showcase for mentally challenged athletes.

The "Heidi" game becomes a piece of sports history as fans in the East miss the Oakland Raiders's thrilling comeback against the New York Jets. NBC decides to leave the game with 50 seconds left to start the movie *Heidi* on time at 7:00 p.m. ET. The network is barraged with calls complaining about the decision.

The American Football League (AFL) and National Football League (NFL) merge. The league retains the NFL name and splits teams into American and National conferences.

1969

Rod Laver of Australia wins the tennis "Grand Slam" for the second time in his career. He also won the Slam in 1962 as an amateur.

1970

Pele plays in fourth World Cup for his home country of Brazil.

On September 21, ABC's Monday Night Football debuts. The game features a contest between the Cleveland Browns and New York Jets. **Howard Cosell** and Don Meredith are the commentators.

1971

Gordie Howe, "Mister Hockey," retires from the NHL. At the time he holds career records for goals (801), assists (1,049), and points (1,850). Howe goes on to play seven more seasons in the World Hockey Association (WHA).

1972

Congress passes the Education Amendment Act, which includes Title IX. Title IX bans sex discrimination in federally funded schools in academics and athletics. The new law changes the landscape of college athletics, as more playing opportunities and scholarships are open to women.

Secretariat wins horse racing's Triple Crown, setting records for every race. He is the only horse to run under two minutes in the Kentucky Derby and wins the Belmont Stakes by a record 31 lengths.

Mark Spitz wins seven Olympic swimming gold medals. He sets the record for most medals won at a single Olympic Games.

Black September, an Arab terrorist group, kills eleven Israeli athletes held captive in the Olympic Village. The Games are suspended the following morning for a memorial service, after which, with the approval of the Israelis, they reconvene.

Out of respect to the Native American population, Stanford University changes its nickname from Indians to Cardinals. Other schools do the same, but professional teams do not.

1973

UCLA wins its seventh consecutive NCAA basketball championship. Coached by the legendary **John Wooden,** the Bruins during one stretch win 88 games in a row. UCLA goes on to win three more titles under Wooden.

Billie Jean King defeats Bobby Riggs in a "Battle of the Sexes" tennis match. Riggs, a self-proclaimed "male chauvinist," is 25 years older than King.

Running back **O.J. Simpson** of the Buffalo Bills becomes the first NFL player to ever rush for over 2,000 yards in a season. Simpson is the only player to accomplish this feat in 14 games.

The Miami Dolphins finish the NFL season with a perfect 17-0 record. The Dolphins close out their season with a 14-7 victory over the Washington Redskins in

Super Bowl VII. No NFL team before or since has finished a season with a perfect record.

1974

Hank Aaron breaks **Babe Ruth**'s career home run record. Aaron has to overcome not only history but racist attacks as he hits number 715 in Atlanta.

Muhammad Ali stuns the world with his eighth round knockout of **George Foreman** in "The Rumble in the Jungle." Ali uses the "rope-a-dope" strategy to wear out the much more powerful Foreman.

1975

Muhammad Ali defeats **Joe Frazier** in the "Thrilla in Manila." The victory was Ali's second in three fights with Frazier.

Pitchers Dave McNally and Andy Messersmith win their challenge to baseball's "reserve clause." Arbitrator Peter Seitz rules that once a player completes one season without a contract he can become a free agent. This is a landmark decision that opens the door to free agency in professional sports.

1976

Romanian **Nadia Comaneci** scores perfect 10s seven times in gymnastics competition at the Summer Olympics in Montreal, Quebec, Canada. This marks the first time that a 10 has ever been awarded.

Kornelia Ender of East Germany wins four Olympic gold medals in swimming. Her time in every one of her races breaks a world record.

1977

Janet Guthrie qualifies on the final day for a starting spot in the Indianapolis 500. She becomes the first woman to compete in the Memorial Day classic.

A.J. Foyt wins the Indianapolis 500 for a record-setting fourth time.

1978

Nancy Lopez wins a record-breaking five LPGA tournaments in a row during her rookie season. She goes on to win nine tournaments for the year.

1979

ESPN launches the first all-sports television network. The network now carries all the major professional and college sports.

1980

The **U.S. men's Olympic ice hockey team** defeats the heavily favored team from the Soviet Union, 4-3, in what becomes known as the "Miracle on Ice." The Americans go on to win the gold medal.

Eric Heiden of the U.S. wins five individual gold medals in speed skating at the Winter Olympics in Lake Placid, New York. No one before or since has won five individual events in a single Olympic Games. No other skater has ever swept the men's speed skating events.

The U.S. and its allies boycott the Summer Olympics in Moscow, USSR. The Americans cite the Soviet invasion of Afghanistan as the reason for their action.

1981

Richard Petty wins the Daytona 500. His win is his record-setting seventh victory in the big race.

1982

Louisiana State defeats Cheney State for the title in the first NCAA women's basketball championship.

Wayne Gretzky, the "Great One," scores 92 goals in a season. He adds 120 assists to end the season with 212 points, the first time anyone has scored over 200 points in one season.

Shirley Muldowney wins last of three National Hot Rod Association (NHRA) top fuel championships. Muldowney won 17 NHRA titles during her career.

1983

Australia II defies the odds and wins the America's Cup after 132 years of domination by the U.S. defenders. The New York Yacht Club had won 24 straight competitions.

1984

The Soviet Union and its allies (except Romania) boycott the Summer Olympics held in Los Angeles, California. Many believe this is in response to the U.S. boycott of Moscow Games in 1980.

Carl Lewis repeats **Jesse Owens**'s feat of winning four gold medals in track and field at the Summer Olympics in Los Angeles, California. Lewis wins the same events as Owens: the 100- and 200-meters, the long jump, and the 4 x 100m relay.

Joan Benoit Samuelson wins the first ever Olympic marathon for women. Her winning time over the 26.2 mile course is 2:24.52.

Dan Marino of the Miami Dolphins throws for 5,084 yards and 48 touchdowns, both NFL single-season records.

1985

On September 11, **Pete Rose** breaks **Ty Cobb**'s record for career hits when he gets his 4,192nd hit. Rose finishes his career with 4,256 hits. Unfortunately, Rose is banned from baseball after allegations of his gambling on the sport come to light.

1986

Nancy Lieberman is the first woman to play in a men's professional league - the United States Basketball League.

Jack Nicklaus wins his record 18th and final major championship at the Masters. During his illustrious career he wins 6 Masters, 4 U.S. Opens, 3 British Opens, and 5 PGA Championships.

1988

Greg Louganis wins gold medals in both platform and springboard diving. He is the first person to win both diving medals in two consecutive Olympics. Louganis wins despite hitting his head on the board during the springboard competition.

Florence Griffith-Joyner sets world records in both the 100- and 200-meter dashes.

Steffi Graf of Germany wins the "Golden Slam" of tennis by winning each of the "Grand Slam" events in addition to the Olympic gold medal. Graf retires with a record 22 victories in "Grand Slam" events.

1992

Jackie Joyner-Kersee establishes herself as the most dominant athlete in the five-event heptathlon, winning her second consecutive Summer Olympics gold medal in the event. Joyner-Kersee had set the world record at 7,291 points and held the next five highest scores.

Cito Gaston becomes the first African-American manager to take his team to the World Series. He is also the first to manage the world champions as his Blue Jays win the title the same year.

1993

Michael Jordan retires from basketball after leading the Bulls to three consecutive NBA championships. He says he is retiring to try to play professional baseball.

Julie Krone becomes the first woman jockey to win a Triple Crown horse race. She rides Colonial Affair to victory in the Belmont Stakes.

The Miami Dolphins defeat the Philadelphia Eagles 19-14, giving Dolphins coach **Don Shula** his 325th win. The victory moved Shula into first place on the all-time list, beating the record held by **George Halas** of the Chicago Bears.

1994

The husband of figure skater **Tonya Harding** hires two men to attack Harding's rival, **Nancy Kerrigan.** The men strike at the U.S. Figure Skating Championships in Detroit, Michigan. Kerrigan is knocked out of the competition, but still qualifies for the Olympic team.

Speedskater **Bonnie Blair** wins her fifth Winter Olympic gold medal, the most by any American woman. She won the 500-meters in 1988 then won both the 500- and 1000-meters in 1992 and 1994. Blair won a total of seven Olympic medals.

Pole-vaulter **Sergei Bubka** of the Ukraine sets the world record in the pole vault with a jump of 6.14 meters. Bubka holds the top 14 jumps of all-time in the event.

A baseball player's strike wipes out the end of the regular season and, for the first time since 1904, the World Series. The strike hurts baseball's popularity for years to come.

1995

Michael Jordan returns to the Chicago Bulls. He leads Chicago to three consecutive championships then retires again in 1998. Jordan retires as a five-time winner of the NBA Most Valuable Player Award and six-time winner of the NBA Finals MVP.

Extreme Games (X Games) are held for first time in Rhode Island and Vermont. The X Games and Winter X Games have been held every year since.

1996

Sprinter **Michael Johnson** wins a rare double at the Summer Olympics in Atlanta, Georgia. He wins both the 200- and 400-meter races, the first man ever to accomplish this feat at the Olympics.

Carl Lewis wins the long jump gold medal at the Summer Olympics in Atlanta, Georgia. It is the athlete's ninth gold medal, tying him for the most all-time with Finnish track legend Paavo Nurmi and Soviet gymnast **Larisa Latynina.**

Jackie Joyner-Kersee wins a bronze medal in the long jump at the Summer Olympics in Atlanta, Georgia. This brings her medal total for three Olympic Games to six, making her the most decorated female track and field athlete in U.S. history.

U.S. women capture the first-ever women's soccer Olympic gold medal.

Dan Marino retires. He leaves the game holding the NFL career record for yards (51,636) and touchdown passes (369).

1997

The Women's National Basketball Association (WNBA) is formed.

Tiger Woods is only 21 when he wins the Masters by a record-shattering 12 strokes. He also sets a record by shooting 18 under par.

1998

Team USA captures the first women's ice hockey gold medal at the Winter Olympics in Nagano, Japan.

Cal Ripken, Jr. breaks **Lou Gehrig**'s iron man record when he plays in his 2,632nd game on September 19.

1999

Vote-buying scandal rips the International Olympic Committee (IOC). Several IOC members are forced to quit because they took bribes from cities hoping to host the Olympics.

Wayne Gretzky retires with NHL records that may never be broken. He holds or shares 61 single-season and career records including the career records for most goals (894), most assists (1,963) and points (2,857). Gretzky also holds the single-season records for goals (92), assists (163), and points (215).

2000

New York Yankees win their 26th World Series. The win makes the Yankees the winningest organization in sports history.

2001

Tiger Woods becomes the first golfer to hold the championship for all four professional "Grand Slam" events when he wins the Masters. His accomplishment is not called a "Grand Slam" because all his victories do not occur in the same calendar year.

Roman Sebrle of the Czech Republic earns the title of "world's greatest athlete" by setting a world record in the 10-event decathlon. His final score is 9,026 points, making him the first man to surpass the 9,000 barrier.

Barry Bonds of the San Francisco Giants hits 73 home runs, a new major league single-season record. The next season he becomes only the fourth major leaguer to hit over 600 career home runs.

Michael Jordan returns to the NBA, this time playing for the Washington Wizards, a team in which he holds partial ownership. His 30.4 career scoring average is the highest of all-time.

2002

Brazil wins record fifth World Cup championship.

Coach **Phil Jackson** of the Los Angeles Lakers sets a record by coaching his ninth NBA champion. He won six titles as coach of the Chicago Bulls and three with Los Angeles. Jackson also tied **Scotty Bowman** of the NHL for most professional titles won as coach.

Hockey coach **Scotty Bowman** retires. He holds career records for most regular season (1,244) and playoff (223) wins.

Lance Armstrong wins the Tour de France cycling race for the fourth straight year. His victory comes only six years after doctors gave him little chance of surviving testicular cancer that had spread to his lymph nodes and brain.

Pete Sampras breaks his own record by winning his 14th Grand Slam tournament, the U.S. Open. He defeats rival **Andre Agassi** in the final.

Emmitt Smith of the Dallas Cowboys sets a new NFL career rushing record with 17,162 yards. Smith passes the great **Walter Payton** of the Chicago Bears.

Jerry Rice scores the 200th NFL touchdown of his remarkable career, the only man to reach this plateau. He ends the 2002 season holding the records for receptions (1,456), yards receiving (21,597), and touchdowns (202).

2003

Serena Williams wins four "Grand Slam" tennis championships in a row. She defeats her sister, **Venus Williams,** in the final of every event.

Jerry Tarkanian
1930-

American college basketball coach

Followed by controversy throughout much of his coaching career, Jerry Tarkanian put together one of the most enviable records in college basketball. Known by admirers and detractors alike as Tark the Shark, Tarkanian led his teams to four appearances in the National Collegiate Athletic Association's (NCAA) Final Four and one national championship during a collegiate coaching career that spanned nearly four decades. Before he stepped down as head coach at California State University, Fresno (commonly known as Fresno State) in March 2002, Tarkanian compiled an all-career win percentage of 80.3 percent, the fourth best in college basketball history.

More than 40 of the college players coached by Tarkanian went on to play in the National Basketball Association (NBA). He is perhaps best known for the 19 years (1973-1992) he spent as coach of the University of Nevada, Las Vegas (UNLV), a team that finished in the top 10 nine times under Tarkanian's guidance. His running battle with the NCAA stretched over more than two decades. Shortly after stepping down as head coach at UNLV, Tarkanian sued the NCAA, charging the athletic association had systematically tried to force him out of college basketball. Although the NCAA admitted no liability, the association settled the suit in 1998, agreeing to pay Tarkanian $2.5 million.

Tarkanian was born in Euclid, Ohio, on October 8, 1930. His mother, born Haigouhie Tarkhanian in Armenia, and her brother, Levon, had fled Turkish genocide in their native country. Later in Lebanon, she married a man with a last name similar to hers and moved with him to the United States, where she was known as Rosie. Tarkanian's father owned and operated a small grocery store in Euclid, and as a boy Jerry accompanied his father as he drove around town to make purchases. When Tarkanian was 11 years old, his father died, and his mother moved the family to Pasadena, California, where they lived with relatives. His only relief from the poverty of his youth was playing basketball and football.

Jerry Tarkanian

After high school Tarkanian enrolled at Pasadena City College but transferred to Fresno State University after winning an athletic scholarship. To supplement the meager stipend from his scholarship, he worked as an aide to Fresno State football coach Clark van Galder, who was to have a profound effect on Tarkanian's life. In his 1988 autobiography, *Tark: College Basketball's Winningest Coach,* written with Terry Pluto, Tarkanian wrote of van Galder: "He was an extraordinarily intense individual, and he demanded equal intensity from his players. How he got it was by becoming close with them, by forming an emotional bond. He would take me and my roommate Fred Bistrick, Fresno's quarterback, to the high school games with him. . . . We spent a lot of time with his family." When he became a coach himself, Tarkanian adopted much of the unorthodox coaching style of van Galder, forming a personal bond with his

Chronology

1930	Born in Euclid, Ohio, on October 8
1955	Graduates from Fresno State
1956	Earns master's degree in educational administration from University of Redlands
1956-57	Coaches basketball at San Joaquin Memorial High School in Fresno
1958	Coaches at Antelope Valley High School in Lancaster, California
1959-60	Coaches at Redlands High School
1961-66	Coaches at Riverside Junior College
1966-68	Coaches at Pasadena City College
1968-73	Coaches at Long Beach State College
1973-92	Coaches at University of Nevada, Las Vegas
1992	Coaches San Antonio Spurs
1995-2002	Coaches at Fresno State
2002	Named senior development consultant for Save Mart Center at Fresno State

Awards and Accomplishments

1964-67	Coaches Riverside Junior College to California Junior College Championship
1966-67	Coaches Pasadena City College to California Junior College Championship
1976-77	Coaches UNLV to NCAA Final Four
1979-80	Coaches UNLV to fourth place in National Invitational Tournament (NIT)
1983	Named Coach of the Year by United Press International
1986-87	Coaches UNLV to NCAA Final Four
1989-90	Coaches UNLV to NCAA Championship
1990-91	Coaches UNLV to NCAA Final Four
1995-96	Coaches Fresno State to NIT quarterfinals
1997-98	Coaches Fresno State to NIT semifinals

players rather than holding himself aloof as was more characteristic of coaches in that era.

Helps Coach High School Team

An unremarkable scholar, Tarkanian ran out of eligibility before he earned his degree from Fresno State. Years later he told the *Akron Beacon-Journal*: "It took me six years to get through college. I knew where the gym was and how to find every party. People would have said that it was a million-to-one shot that I'd ever graduate. They said I didn't belong in college." When his eligibility ran out, Tarkanian helped coach at Fresno's San Joaquin Memorial High School. After graduating from Fresno State, he joined the high school's staff as head basketball coach. Tarkanian coached at four California high schools before he was hired in 1961 by Riverside Junior College to lead its basketball team, which hadn't had a winning season in 11 years. Under Tarkanian's direction, Riverside's basketball team became the first in California to win three consecutive state junior college championships. It was during this period that he married Lois Huter, whom he'd met while both were students at Fresno State. The Tarkanians have four children: Pamela, Jodie, Danny, and George.

In 1966 Tarkanian took over as head basketball coach at Pasadena City College and worked the same sort of magic he'd produced at Riverside. In his very first year as coach, he led the Pasadena team to a state championship. The next stop in Tarkanian's coaching career was Long Beach State College, the first four-year college at which he'd coach. Beginning at Long Beach in 1968, he quickly acquired a reputation for his unorthodox recruiting and coaching style. He came under fire for what some saw as his heavy reliance on younger players as well as others who were less than stellar students. Tarkanian also attracted attention for flouting the unwritten rule that three of a team's five starting players should be white. This dramatic departure from racial

convention established Tarkanian in the black community as a coach who not only talked about equal opportunity but actually practiced it, according to Richard O. Davies, author of *The Maverick Spirit,* a book about controversial Nevadans. This reputation would pay great recruiting dividends later in his career.

Success at Long Beach State

In his five seasons at Long Beach State, Tarkanian compiled an impressive record of 122-20. The Long Beach State team never lost a home game while under his direction. In 1970 Tarkanian coached the Long Beach State squad into the NCAA Tournament, boasting that his entire first string was made up of former junior college players, a class of players that had long been considered second-rate material by coaches at other four-year colleges. It was at Long Beach that Tarkanian first developed the now-popular 1-2-2 zone defense. Of his defensive coaching skills, Wayne Embry, general manager of the Cleveland Cavaliers, explained to the *Akron Beacon-Journal*: "Tark is a hell of a coach. People think that all he does is roll out the balls and let them run. Forget it. He is one of the best defensive coaches in the country."

Tarkanian's troubles with the NCAA first surfaced during his tenure at Long Beach State. In 1972, shortly after the coach had written a column critical of the NCAA in a local newspaper, the giant athletic association launched an investigation into the college's basketball and football recruiting practices. In March 1973 Tarkanian took over as head basketball coach at UNLV. A month later, the NCAA submitted to Long Beach State an official inquiry listing alleged violations of NCAA rules. Supplemental allegations were submitted in August, September, and November 1973, and in January 1974 Long Beach State was placed on three years probation and penalized because of alleged rules violations. Tarkanian, now coaching at UNLV, denied the violations as they applied to Long Beach State's basketball program and protested that the findings were made without his participation in the hearing process.

Jerry Tarkanian, center

Stage Set for Further Conflict

The stage was set for further conflict with the NCAA even before Tarkanian accepted the coaching job at UNLV. The NCAA in November 1972 had announced an investigation into UNLV football and basketball. In February 1976 the athletic association submitted an official inquiry to UNLV officials, listing alleged violations of NCAA rules prior to and during Tarkanian's tenure. Most of the violations, according to the NCAA, were in the area of recruiting practices. Late that year UNLV officials, including Tarkanian, responded to the NCAA inquiry, denying that the alleged violations had occurred.

In his first season at UNLV, Tarkanian coached the basketball team to a winning record of 20-6. To better suit his second-season team, which had a number of players who were short by normal basketball standards but fast, he introduced a new playing style. As he recalled in his autobiography, "I figured that if we got the bigger teams running, it would take away their size advantage. Rather than work the ball around the perimeter, I wanted us to get the ball up the court as fast as possible and then take a quick jumper before the defense could set up. Speed would be the determining factor in the game. The team that got the rebounds would be the team that hustled for the ball more and reached it first." Tarkanian's new strategy required a man-to-man defense

rather than the zone defense he had popularized at Long Beach State.

New Strategy Begins to Click

Using the new strategy, Tarkanian's second season got off to a slow start, with the UNLV team losing its first three games. Once things began to click, however, the team, which came to be known as the Runnin Rebels, sailed to a 24-5 record for the season and made it to the second round of the NCAA tournament. The new playing style proved extremely popular with UNLV basketball fans, who said the new strategy created the energy of a high school game played with a lot more skill. Things got even better during the 1975-1976 season when the team ended the season, 29-2, and again advanced to the second round of the NCAA tournament.

Tarkanian's Runnin Rebels made it into the NCAA Tournament's Final Four on the strength of a 1976-1977 record of 29-3. In September 1977 the NCAA placed UNLV on two years probation, the penalties for which included a ban on postseason play for two years. At the same time the NCAA called for a two-year suspension of Tarkanian as coach, a sanction that was eventually blocked by the courts. The ban on postseason play remained in effect, however, so despite impressive records in both 1977-1978 (20-8) and

According to Michael Green, history professor at Community College of Southern Nevada, you can't assess Tarkanian without assessing Bob Maxson. To their mutual chagrin, they are historically inseparable.... They became embroiled in this terrible fight where neither man controlled his logic or emotion. In a sense, they destroyed each other. Robert C. Maxson, formerly senior vice president of academic affairs at the University of Houston, was brought to the University of Nevada, Las Vegas (UNLV), as its new president in 1984. His immediate mission was to upgrade the university's academic reputation, a goal that eventually brought him into conflict with Tarkanian

Rumors had long persisted that Tarkanian recruited students who were good basketball players but lacked the necessary skills to succeed academically. Although Maxson at first tried to make an ally of Tarkanian, any relationship the two might have developed was blown away by Maxson's decision in 1990 to replace Tarkanian supporter Brad Rothermiel with Dennis Finfrock as athletic director. Within two years, Tarkanian had stepped down as basketball coach, but Maxson was not far behind him, resigning in 1994.

Maxson in 1958 earned his bachelor's degree in education and psychology from the University of Arkansas at Monticello. He received a master's degree in education administration from Florida Atlantic University in 1967 and a doctorate in educational leadership from Mississippi State University in 1970. After leaving UNLV in 1994, he was hired to serve as president of California State University, Long Beach. Maxson is married to Dr. Sylvia Parrish Maxson, and the couple has two children, Todd and Kimberly.

1978-1979 (21-8), the UNLV team saw no postseason action during this period.

More Conflict

In August 1979 UNLV was restored to the full rights and privileges of NCAA membership after satisfying the penalties imposed by the association's Committee on Infractions. With a record of 23-9 for the 1979-1980 season, UNLV's basketball team advanced to the National Invitational Tournament (NIT), where it finished in fourth place. The following season was the weakest of Tarkanian's career at UNLV with a record of 16-12, but the Rebels bounced back in 1981-1982, ending the regular season with a record of 20-10 and advancing to the second round of the NIT. The Rebels record improved to 28-3 in 1982-1983, on the strength of which the team advanced to the second round of the NCAA tournament.

In 1984 UNLV recruited Dr. Robert Maxson from the University of Houston to serve as its new president and hopefully create for the school a reputation for academic excellence that would rival its glowing reputation as an athletic powerhouse. Although both Maxson and Tarkanian at first made an effort to get along, eventually the two clashed, particularly after Maxson forced Brad Rothermel to resign as athletic director and replaced him with Dennis Finfrock, no fan of Tarkanian.

Although his conflict with the NCAA continued throughout Tarkanian's tenure at UNLV, it seemed to have little effect on his effectiveness as a coach. The Rebels finished the 1983-84 season with a record of 29-6 and advanced to the third round of NCAA tournament.

The following season, UNLV made it to the second round of the NCAA tournament with a record of 28-4. In 1985-1986, the team finished the season with a 33-5 record and advanced to the third round of the NCAA tourney. Tarkanian's team returned to the NCAA Final Four at the end of the 1986-1987 season, during which it compiled a record of 37-2.

UNLV Rebels Clinch NCAA Championship

The UNLV Rebels continued to shine over the 1987-1988 and 1988-1989 seasons, advancing to the third and fourth rounds of the NCAA tournament, respectively. But greater glory lay ahead for Tarkanian's team which clinched the NCAA Championship in 1989-1990 after finishing the season with a record of 35-5. Despite NCAA attempts to bar the team from postseason play in 1990-1991, an agreement was struck to shift the postseason ban to the following year. This paved the way for another trip to the NCAA's Final Four. Despite a brilliant 26-2 record in 1991-1992, UNLV, abiding by its agreement with the NCAA, saw no postseason action. Part of the agreement struck with the NCAA called for Tarkanian to resign at the end of the 1991-1992 season. He stepped down in March 1992.

Tarkanian next gave NBA ball a try, signing on as head coach of the San Antonio Spurs. But his stint in pro basketball was short-lived, ending when Tarkanian was fired shortly after clashing with the team's owner. In 1995 he returned to his alma mater to coach the Fresno State Bulldogs. During his seven seasons as Bulldogs coach, the team compiled a winning record of 153-80. On March 15, 2002, Tarkanian stepped down as coach and accepted a position as senior development consultant with the university's Save Mart Center. In June 2002, Tarkanian revealed that he had been diagnosed with prostate cancer but expressed optimism that he would be cured.

Despite his long-running battles with the NCAA, Tarkanian will long be remembered as one of the winningest coaches in college basketball history. After Tarkanian left college basketball in March 2002, fellow coach Mike Krzyzewski of Duke told the Associated Press: "He's had an amazing career. Jerry had consistent high levels of success because his teams played hard defensively. He's one of the truly remarkable defensive coaches."

SELECTED WRITINGS BY TARKANIAN:

Winning Basketball Systems. Allyn & Bacon, 1981.
Winning Basketball. WCB/McGraw-Hill, 1983.
(With Terry Pluto) *Tark: College Basketball's Winningest Coach.* McGraw-Hill, 1988.
(With Don Yaeger) *Shark Attack: Jerry Tarkanian and His Battle with the NCAA and UNLV.* HarperCollins, 1992.

FURTHER INFORMATION

Books

"Jerry Tarkanian." *Complete Marquis Who's Who.* Marquis Who's Who, 2001.

"Jerry Tarkanian." *Newsmakers 1990,* Issue 4. Detroit: Gale Research, 1990.

"Jerry Tarkanian." *St. James Encyclopedia of Popular Culture,* 5 vols. St. James Press, 2000.

"Robert C. Maxson." *Complete Marquis Who's Who.* Marquis Who's Who, 2001.

Other

"Jerry Tarkanian (1930-): Tark the Shark." *Las Vegas Review-Journal.* http://www.1st100.com/part3/tarkanian.html (January 7, 2003).

"Jerry Tarkanian and the NCAA." Big John's UNLV Runnin Rebels Home Page. http://home.att.net/~rebels02/page21b_tarkncaa.html (January 6, 2003).

"Jerry Tarkanian: The Man Who Built UNLV." Big John's UNLV Runnin Rebels Home Page. http://home.att.net/~rebels02/pg21_tark.html (January 6, 2003).

"Jerry Tarkanian: Profile." Fresno State Online. http://gobulldogs.ocsn.com/sports/m-baskbl/mtt/tarkanian_jerry00.html (January 6, 2003).

"Robert C. Maxson." California State University. http://www.calstate.edu/PA/bios/prezbio/Maxson.shtml (January 7, 2003).

Sketch by Don Amerman

Fran Tarkenton
1940-

American football player

Few professional football players have burst upon the scene as spectacularly as Fran Tarkenton. In his very first pro game, Tarkenton came off the bench to toss four touchdown passes, leading his Minnesota Vikings team to a decisive 37-13 victory over the Chicago Bears. After eighteen seasons in the National Football League (NFL), Tarkenton left professional football with league records for passing attempts (6,467), completions (3,686), yards (47,003), and touchdowns (342). Tarkenton, who former Vikings coach Bud Grant once called "the greatest quarterback to ever play the game," was perhaps best known for his elusive scrambling ability. Inducted into the Professional Football Hall of Fame in 1986, Tarkenton topped the 1,000-yard passing mark in each of his eighteen seasons with the Vikings. If Tarkenton left the game

Fran Tarkenton

with any regrets at all, it may well have been his failure to win a Super Bowl during his career. He led the Vikings to the Super Bowl in 1974, 1975, and 1977 but lost all three championship games to their American Football Conference (AFC) opponents. Tarkenton's post-football career as a business entrepreneur, which rivaled his football years in its phenomenal success, was marred in the mid-1990s by government charges of financial fraud.

Born in Richmond, Virginia

He was born Francis Asbury Tarkenton in Richmond, Virginia, on February 3, 1940. The son of Dallas, a Methodist minister, and Frances Tarkenton, a homemaker, he attended high school in Athens, Georgia, where as a junior he led his football team to the state championships in 1955. During his senior year at Athens High, he was named all-state in not only football, but baseball and basketball as well. After graduation from high school, Tarkenton moved across town to study business administration at the University of Georgia in Athens. He also made a name for himself as starting quarterback for the Georgia Bulldogs football team. In his junior year, Tarkenton forever endeared himself to Bulldog fans by tossing a winning touchdown pass in the final seconds of the team's game against Auburn. He led the Bulldogs to a 1959 season record of 10-1 and the Southeastern Conference (SEC) title. As a senior, Tarkenton earned All-American and first team Academic All-American honors, as he captained the Bulldogs to a 6-4

Chronology

1940	Born in Richmond, Virginia, on February 3
1955	Leads Athens (GA) High School team to state football championship
1957-61	Attends University of Georgia
1961	Drafted by Minnesota Vikings of the NFL and Boston Patriots of the AFL
1966	Traded to New York Giants from the Vikings
1972	Returns to Minnesota Vikings and founds Behavioral Systems Inc.
1979	Retires from professional football
1979	Hired by ABC-TV as commentator on "Monday Night Football" and co-host of "That's Incredible"
1995	Sells KnowledgeWare at substantial loss
1999	Pays $100,000 in settlement of SEC fraud charges in connection with KnowledgeWare operation

Related Biography: Coach Wally Butts

Coach and athletic director at the University of Georgia for more than two decades, Wally Butts helped to shape the football careers of Hall of Famers Frank Sinkwich, Charley Trippi, and Fran Tarkenton. Perhaps more importantly, Butts instilled a sense of values and discipline in all the young men who passed through his football program at Georgia.

Born near Milledgeville, Georgia, on February 7, 1905, he was the only child of James Wallace Butts, who ran a dray service, and Anna Louisetta (Hutchinson) Butts. His mother died when he was only three, and he and his father moved to Atlanta, where young Butts was raised by a grandmother, aunts, and uncles. He developed into an outstanding football player and captained his football team at Mercer University in Macon, Georgia. After graduating from Mercer in 1928, Butts began coaching at Madison A&M University and later coached at Georgia Military College in Milledgeville and Male High School in Louisville, Kentucky.

In 1938 Butts was hired as an assistant by University of Georgia football coach Joel Hunt. The following year, Hunt quit, and Butts took over as head coach. Over the next twenty-two years, he built the University of Georgia's Bulldogs into a national football power. Perhaps his finest moment came in 1959 when his Bulldogs, led by All-Americans Tarkenton and Pat Dye, won the Southeastern Conference championship.

Butts left the University of Georgia in 1963, not long after a scandal erupted over a story in the *Saturday Evening Post* charging that he had colluded with legendary University of Alabama football coach Paul "Bear" Bryant to throw a game in 1962. Both Butts and Bryant sued the popular magazine, but only Butts' case made it court, where he was awarded libel damages of $3 million, a figure eventually pared down to just under $500,000. Butts launched a new career in the insurance business. He set up his own company in Athens, Georgia, and eventually became a millionaire, largely on the strength of business from Georgia alumni. In December 1973, Butts suffered a fatal heart attack while jogging on the city streets of Athens.

season record. Wallace Butts, Tarkenton's coach at Georgia, once said of his star quarterback: "Tarkenton has no superior as a field general and ball-handler."

Despite his impressive record at Georgia, Tarkenton was not selected until the third round of the NFL draft in 1961, and then by the newly-established Minnesota Vikings franchise. In the Vikings' debut game on September 17, 1961, Tarkenton threw four touchdown passes to lead the Vikings past the Chicago Bears, 37-13. In his first professional season, Tarkenton also established an NFL record for most consecutive completed passes with thirteen in the Vikings' 42-21 win over Los Angeles. For the season as a whole, he passed for a total of 1,997 yards and eighteen touchdowns. In the 1962 season, Tarkenton compiled a pass completion rate of only 49.5 percent—the lowest of his eighteen years in the NFL—with a total of 2,595 yards and twenty-two touchdowns, four of the touchdowns coming in the Vikings' November 4 game against the Pittsburgh Steelers.

Shines in Pro Bowl Play

In 1963, Tarkenton threw for 2,311 yards and fifteen touchdowns. The following season, he passed for a total of 2,506 yards and twenty-two touchdowns, winning himself a berth in the Pro Bowl as a reserve quarterback. He took MVP honors at the Pro Bowl when he completed eight of thirteen passes for 172, leading the West to a 34-14 win. After throwing for 2,609 yards and nineteen touchdowns in the regular 1965 season, Tarkenton was again tapped for the Pro Bowl. In 1966, what was to be his last season for the Vikings for six years, Tarkenton passed for a total of 2,561 yards and seventeen touchdowns.

Tarkenton had already earned the nickname of "The Scrambler" for his uncanny ability to elude tacklers and rush for yardage, but some of his improvisations on the football field left Vikings coaches unsettled and not altogether happy. Shortly after the 1966 season, he was traded to the New York Giants. In 1967, his first season with the Giants, Tarkenton passed for a total of 3,088 yards and

twenty-nine touchdowns. In 1968, he threw for 2,555 yards and twenty-one touchdowns, followed by 2,918 yards and twenty-three touchdowns in 1969. He passed for a total of 2,567 yards and eleven touchdowns in 1970 and 2,651 yards and eighteen touchdowns in 1971. Shortly after the 1971 season, the Giants traded Tarkenton back to the Vikings in exchange for Norm Snead, Bob Grim, Vince Clements, a first round draft pick in 1972 and a second-round selection in the 1973 draft.

Founds Behavioral Systems Inc.

Around this time, Tarkenton began to lay the groundwork for a career outside football. In 1972 he founded Behavioral Systems Inc., a motivational business. Drawing perhaps on some of the evangelical fervor of his childhood as the son of a minister, Tarkenton had always believed that almost anything could be accomplished by someone with the right combination of dogged determination and sufficient inspiration. Thousands of Americans paid handsome fees to hear Tarkenton deliver his messages of inspiration. Back at the helm of the Vikings for the 1972 season, Tarkenton threw for 2,651 yards and eighteen touchdowns, winning All-NFC honors from the *Sporting News* and United Press International. In 1973, his second season back with the Vikings, he threw for 2,113 yards and fifteen touchdowns, leading the team from the Twin Cities to an NFC Championship and the Super Bowl, where the Vikings fell to the Miami Dolphins, 24-7.

Career Statistics

Yr	Team	GP	Passing							Rushing			
			ATT	COM	YDS	COM%	Y/A	TD	INT	ATT	YDS	TD
1961	MIN	14	280	157	1997	56.1	7.1	18	17	56	308	5
1962	MIN	14	329	163	2595	49.5	7.9	22	25	41	361	2
1963	MIN	14	297	170	2311	57.2	7.8	15	15	28	162	1
1964	MIN	14	306	171	2506	55.9	8.2	22	11	50	330	2
1965	MIN	14	329	171	2609	52.0	7.9	19	11	56	356	1
1966	MIN	14	358	192	2561	53.6	7.2	17	16	62	376	4
1967	NYG	14	377	204	3088	54.1	8.2	29	19	44	306	2
1968	NYG	14	337	182	2555	54.0	7.6	21	12	57	301	3
1969	NYG	14	409	220	2918	53.8	7.1	23	8	37	172	0
1970	NYG	14	389	219	2777	56.3	7.1	19	12	43	236	2
1971	NYG	13	386	226	2567	58.5	6.7	11	21	30	111	3
1972	MIN	14	378	215	2651	56.9	7.0	18	13	27	180	0
1973	MIN	14	274	169	2113	61.7	7.7	15	7	41	202	1
1974	MIN	13	351	199	2598	56.7	7.4	17	12	21	120	2
1975	MIN	14	425	273	2994	64.2	7.0	25	13	16	108	2
1976	MIN	13	412	255	2961	61.9	7.2	17	8	27	45	1
1977	MIN	9	258	155	1734	60.1	6.7	9	14	15	6	0
1978	MIN	16	572	345	3468	60.3	6.1	25	32	24	-6	1
TOTAL		246	6467	3686	47003	57.0	7.3	342	266	675	3674	32

MIN: Minnesota Vikings; NYG: New York Giants.

Once again in 1974, Tarkenton led the Vikings to an NFC championship, but the team's luck was no better in Super Bowl IX, where it lost to the Pittsburgh Steelers, 16-6. Although Tarkenton was selected for the Pro Bowl, he did not play. In 1975, his 15th season in the NFL, he compiled a sizzling pass completion rate of 64.7 percent, the best of his career, throwing for 2,994 yards and 25 touchdowns. Tarkenton's performance powered the Vikings to another championship in the NFC's Central Division. The sports media heaped praise on Tarkenton for his brilliant year. He was named the NFL's Most Valuable Player by Associated Press, Newspaper Enterprise Association, *Pro Football Weekly,* and *Sporting News.* Additionally, *Sporting News* named him NFC Player of the Year; *Pro Football Weekly* dubbed him NFL Offensive Player of the Year; and both Associated Press and United Press International named him All-NFC.

In the 1976 season Tarkenton threw for 2,961 yards and seventeen touchdowns, winning the Vikings a return trip to the Super Bowl in January 1977. It was to be Tarkenton's final Super Bowl game, and, like the first two, it ended in defeat. In Super Bowl XI, the Oakland Raiders bested the Vikings, 32-14, although Tarkenton completed seventeen of thirty-five passes for 205 yards and a touchdown. At the end of the regular season, Tarkenton was named All-NFC by United Press International. In 1977, he suffered a broken leg in the Vikings' November 13 game against the Cincinnati Bengals, which kept him out of the final five games of the regular season as well as two playoff games. For the season as a whole, he threw for a total of 1,734 yards and nine touchdowns. In 1978, his final season, Tarkenton threw for 3,468 yards and twenty-five touchdowns, leading the Vikings to another NFC Central Division championship.

Retires from Pro Football

Shortly after the end of the 1978 season, Tarkenton announced his decision to retire from professional football. By this time, his business career was already well established. Between the early 1970s and the beginning of the new millennium, Tarkenton launched a dozen different businesses, and he's always had a passion for small business. It was when he ventured into business on a grander scale that Tarkenton eventually ran into trouble. His involvement with KnowledgeWare, an Atlanta-based software company selling customized applications to business mainframe operators around the world, started off on a positive note. But over time technology changed the face of business computer operations, replacing the mainframe with networked personal computers. Unfortunately KnowledgeWare didn't keep pace with these technological changes, and by mid-1994 the company was in deep trouble financially. By the end of 1994, Tarkenton, chairman and chief executive officer of KnowledgeWare, was forced to sell the company at a significant loss. The debacle not only cost Tarkenton money but some longtime business associates and friends. To make matters worse, the government eventually charged Tarkenton with carrying out a financial fraud scheme as CEO of KnowledgeWare. The former quarterback and six other former KnowledgeWare executives agreed in September 1999 to an agreement settling the case. They paid a fine of $100,000 and repaid more than $50,000 in incentive compensation. Under the terms of the settlement, they neither admitted or denied the charges.

Awards and Accomplishments	
1955	Led Athens High School football team to Georgia state championship
1959	Led University of Georgia Bulldogs to 10-1 record and SEC championship
1960	Earned AP All-American honors
1961	Threw for four touchdowns in first professional game for Vikings
1964	First of 9 Pro Bowl selections
1974	Led Vikings to Super Bowl VIII, where they lost to Miami Dolphins
1975	Led Vikings to Super Bowl IX, where they lost to Pittsburgh Steelers
1977	Led Vikings to Super Bowl XI, where they lost to Oakland Raiders
1978	All-NFC selection
1986	Inducted into the Pro Football Hall of Fame on August 2

Today Tarkenton is CEO of GoSmallBiz.com, an organization designed to help entrepreneurs run and grow their businesses. But he will forever be remembered as the Scrambler, one of professional football's most brilliant quarterbacks in history. Through eighteen seasons in the NFL, Tarkenton compiled a winning record, throwing for a total of 47,003 yards and 342 touchdowns, with a career pass completion rate of 57 percent.

CONTACT INFORMATION

Address: Fran Tarkenton, c/o GoSmallBiz.com, 3340 Peachtree Rd. N.E., Ste. 2570, Atlanta, GA 30326. Email: corp@gosmallbiz.com. Online: http://www.gosmallbiz.com.

SELECTED WRITINGS BY TARKENTON:

No Time for Losing, Revell, 1967.
(With Jack Olsen) *Better Scramble Than Lose,* Four Winds Press, 1969.
(With Brock Yates) *Broken Patterns: The Education of a Quarterback,* Simon & Schuster, 1971.
(With Jim Klobuchak) *Tarkenton,* Harper, 1976.
Playing to Win: Fran Tarkenton's Strategies for Business Success, Harper & Row, 1984.
(With Ted Tuleja) *How to Motivate People: The Team Strategy for Success,* Harper & Row, 1986.
(With Joseph H. Boyett) *The Competitive Edge: Essential Business Skills for Entrepreneurs,* Plume, 1991.
(With Wes Smith) *What Losing Taught Me about Winning: The Ultimate Guide for Success in Small and Home-based Businesses,* Simon & Schuster, 1997.

FURTHER INFORMATION

Books

"Fran(cis Asbury) Tarkenton." *Contemporary Authors Online.* Detroit: Gale Group, 2002.
"James Wallace Butts." *Dictionary of American Biography, Supplement 9: 1971-1975.* New York: Scribner, 1994.
Klobuchar, Jim. *Tarkenton.* New York: HarperCollins, 1976.

Periodicals

Klobuchar, Tim. "1961: Opening with a Bang." *Minneapolis Star Tribune* (September 3, 1998): 12C.
McEnrose, Paul. "The Scrambler: He Still Can Elude Adversity." *Minneapolis Star Tribune* (November 23, 1995): 1A.
Morris, Valeria. "Family Values." *CNNfn* (September 8, 1997).
Schlabach, Mark. "A Legend at Every Stop: Athens High, UGA, NFL." *Atlanta Constitution* (September 29, 1999): C3.
Walker, Tom. "Tarkenton to Pay $100,000 Settlement." *Atlanta Constitution* (September 29, 1999): C1.

Other

"About Us." GoSmallBiz.com. http://www.gosmallbiz.com/about/default.asp (October 20, 2002).
"Fran Tarkenton 1961-66; 72-78/Georgia." Minnesota Vikings. http://www.vikings.com/Alumni/FranTarkenton.htm (October 20, 2002).
"Fran Tarkenton: Biography." Football-Reference.com. http://www.football-reference.com/players/TarkFr00.htm (October 19, 2002).
"Fran Tarkenton: Biography." Pro Football Hall of Fame. http://www.profootballhof.com/players/mainpage.cfm?cont_id=100114 (October 19, 2002).

Sketch by Don Amerman

Lawrence Taylor
1959-

American football player

Lawrence Taylor lived on the edge. Quite possibly one of the best linebackers to play the game, Taylor starred for the New York Giants and set a new standard for how linebackers played the game. He brought about a new statistic (the sack), and was a dominant player whose personal life was plagued with substance abuse problems. His induction into the Hall of Fame, in 1999, was marked by controversy due to his problems with drugs.

Growing Up

Lawrence Taylor was born on February 4, 1959, in Williamsburg, Virginia. He grew up in a four-room

Lawrence Taylor

frame house on the outskirts of the restored colonial village. Hailing from a middle-class environment, Taylor was the middle brother of three, and his parents have remembered his early years as active ones. Taylor was physical even as a small child. "He liked to hit," his father Clarence told *New York Times Magazine*. His mother made Taylor spend hours working at chores around the house to keep him occupied, sweeping the floors, carrying in groceries.

At age nine, Taylor wrote down that he wanted to be famous and to be a millionaire before he reached 30. But he'd have to do it in some other way, because he was not a very diligent student, and although bright, he never turned on to what was offered him in the public education system.

Taylor wanted to play little league football, but his mother was worried about the dangers of the sport, so she signed him up for little league baseball, where he was an all-star for four summers in the position of catcher. As a catcher, just as he later did as a linebacker, he was able to survey all that was happening on the field. (In his later life he would say he loved the position of linebacker because "you control the game from there," much like the catcher does in baseball by calling the pitches and reading the field.)

Lawrence's high school coach, Mel Jones, had to do little to convince Taylor that football, not baseball, would be a great opportunity for him. He said that football was how he could earn a college scholarship, telling him that, "If you were black and from the rural South, you thought about football the way other kids thought about careers in law or medicine."

LT (as he came to be known later on with the New York Giants) continued to grow, and the summer between his junior and senior years in high school he grew five inches and added 30 pounds. That senior year of high school was as if a switch had turned on. "He was out to do something," Paul Raynes told the *New York Times Magazine*. "It was like he was saying 'I'm going to be great.'"

Limited College Opportunities

His late entry into football was one of the reasons he was largely skipped over by college recruiters. Only two recruiters spoke to him about college ball. The University of North Carolina offered him a scholarship, in spite of his poor grades, and Taylor wouldn't turn it down.

He entered college with the belief that he needed to raise hell, skip classes and get into trouble in order to survive. "I was trying to be a hoodlum," Taylor told the *New York Times* in 1984. He felt that by instilling fear into people, he could gain their respect. And for LT, that's what it was all about. But his social life followed him onto the field, and his first few years with UNC football were rather undisciplined. His inability to focus

Awards and Accomplishments

1981	East-West Shrine All-Star Team
1981	Japan Bowl All-Star Team
1981	Consensus All-American
1981	Atlantic Coast Conference Player of the Year
1982	NFL Player Association NFC Linebacker of the Year
1982	Associated Press NFL Defensive Rookie of the Year
1982	Bell Trophy (the season's top rookie)
1982-83, 1986	Associated Press NFL Defensive Player of the Year
1982-84, 1986	Seagram's Seven Crowns of Sports Award
1982-91	NFL Pro Bowl team
1983, 1985-86	NFL All-Pro Team
1983, 1986	United Press International NFC Defensive Player of the Year
1986	Professional Football Writers of America NFL Player of the Year
1989	Associated Press All-Pro Team
1989	United Press International All-NFC Team
1989	Professional Football Writers of America All-Pro Team
1989	All-NFL team
1994	NFL 75th Anniversary All-Time Team
1999	Pro Football Hall of Fame

Where Is He Now?

Inducted in the Pro Football Hall of Fame in 1999, Taylor continues to work at getting his life back on track, and, like most who have battled substance abuse problems, every day is a struggle. He has had parts recently in movies such as *The Waterboy* (1997), *Shaft* (2000), and *Any Given Sunday,* a 1999 film he had a larger part in. The movie starred Jamie Foxx and Al Pacino, and was, as Roger Ebert put it, "A smart sports movie swamped by production overkill." Oliver Stone directed the film, and Taylor has a strong supporting role. Taylor has also done voices for video games, one of the most recent is "Grand Theft Auto."

had him bouncing from noseguard to inside linebacker to outside linebacker.

The coaches finally saw where to put him and gave him a green light to make the inside linebacker position his own. They told LT to rely on his instincts, and he ended up with eighty solo tackles his junior year, forcing seven fumbles. Teams were scared, and the only team that season who tried to confront the menace that was Lawrence Taylor was Oklahoma, which used three men to block him.

As his college career wound down, he met and fell in love with Linda Cooley, a soft-spoken woman who admonished him for his constant belligerence. Taylor's close friends told him he would have to change his ways or risk losing the girl. And he did, proposing to Linda and then marrying her in 1982.

The Next Level

The New York Giants drafted Taylor as the second pick overall in the 1981 draft. He signed a six-year, $1.35 million contract with a $250,000 signing bonus. Taylor's entire time on the NFL field might itself be one long highlight. From the very first season, Taylor was more than impressive. He was voted All-Pro that first year, and he started in the Pro Bowl. In a 1981 article in the *Boston Globe,* Taylor's teammate and cornerback Terry Jackson said, "Lawrence is probably the greatest athlete I've ever been associated with."

He became the standard against which all other linebackers were compared. His intimidation of and subsequent racking up of quarterback sacks prompted the league to institute the "number of sacks" statistic, which prior to Taylor's entrance into the league had not been kept.

Searching for Greener Pastures

Upset with the overall performance of the Giants in the 1982 and 1983 seasons, Taylor shopped around for better deals with other teams. Though his contract with the Giants ran through 1987, and the team wouldn't trade him, he signed a deal with the New Jersey Generals, a USFL team, that would begin in 1988.

But the Giants counter-offered, and Taylor stayed with the team. In 1986, they would win their first ever Super Bowl, with Taylor playing an integral part. It would be the best season of his career, with 20.5 sacks and the winning of the coveted NFL's Most Valuable Player (MVP) award—only the second defensive player to ever win the award.

Sam Huff, who prior to LT's entrance into the league, was considered the ultimate linebacker, has said of Taylor, in a 1987 *Philadelphia Daily News* article: "He's fantastic. I've never seen anyone play the position better. He's so relentless...You've got to be a hell of a player to psyche out guys at this level, but Taylor can do it. When he wants to play, he's like some monster come down off a movie screen. He just tosses people around."

Off the Gridiron

Though he was a phenomenal success on the field, off the field Taylor's troubles would escalate. LT became well known in the New York media for complaining about the city and its pressures. This was not the relationship he wanted with the press when, with the success, money, and pressures of life in the NFL taking its toll, Taylor would sink into substance abuse.

He handled the pressures of success by turning to his old college habits—and then some. Drinking heavily ("Lawrence could put away a case in a night," friend Joseph Cale told the *Washington Post*), staying out late, and lacking discipline, his performance on the field, though still outstanding, looked, in the mid-eighties, to be slipping. Then word got out that Taylor was abusing cocaine.

Looking for Help

In the spring of 1986, Taylor checked himself into a rehabilitation program for substance abuse. The state-

Career Statistics

Yr	Team	GP	SACK	INT	TD
1981	NYG	16	-	1	-
1982	NYG	9	7.5	1	1
1983	NYG	16	9	2	-
1984	NYG	16	11.5	1	-
1985	NYG	16	13	-	-
1986	NYG	16	20.5	-	-
1987	NYG	12	12	3	-
1988	NYG	12	15.5	-	-
1989	NYG	16	15	-	-
1990	NYG	16	10.5	1	1
1991	NYG	14	7	-	-
1992	NYG	9	5	-	-
1993	NYG	16	6	-	-
TOTAL		184	132.5	9	2

NYG: New York Giants.

ment he issued at the time said: "In the past year, due to substance abuse, I have left the road I had hoped to follow both as a player and a public figure." When he emerged from treatment, he went on to have the best season of his career with the Giants, leading them to a Super Bowl victory. But Taylor would lead an on-again, off-again relationship with substance abuse.

Lawrence Taylor's off-the-field problems stirred up controversy when he was nominated for the Pro Football Hall of Fame in 1999. The *Washington Post* that year reported that some of the thirty-six media members who voted for the Hall of Fame were prepared "to bypass Taylor because of his legal troubles that include drug-related arrests and income tax problems." Taylor didn't help the situation by refusing to apologize about his past. But the guidelines for entrance into the Hall asked voters to consider only on-the-field accomplishments. Taylor was voted in.

Lawrence Taylor gained his reputation by doing things outside the lines. Though quite possibly one of the best linebackers to play the game, he's often referred to in the context of "drug abuse" or "breaking Joe Theisman's leg" (which happened in a now-famous Monday Night Football game). But Taylor is so much more than that. He starred for the New York Giants, setting new standards for how linebackers operated on the field. Taylor brought about the sack statistic, and he dominated the playing field. His personal life was plagued with substance abuse problems, yet because of his behavior off the field, his induction into the Hall of Fame and his reputation is one marked by controversy.

SELECTED WRITINGS BY TAYLOR:

(With David Falkner) *LT: Living on the Edge,* Times Books, 1987.

FURTHER INFORMATION

Books

Goodman, Michael E. *Lawrence Taylor (Sports Close Ups 2).* New York: Crestwood House, 1988.

"Lawrence Taylor." *Great Athletes,* vol. 7. Hackensack, N.J.: Salem Press, Inc., 2718-2720.

Liss, Howard. *The Lawrence Taylor Story.* Enslow Publishers, Inc., 1987.

Taylor, Lawrence, with David Falkner. *LT: Living on the Edge.* New York: Times Books, 1987.

Periodicals

Adande, J.A. "NFL Should Honor Taylor with Blitz of Attention Instead of Seemingly Low-Key Approach to Hall of Fame Induction." *Los Angeles Times* (August 7, 1999): 2.

Boston Globe (December 13, 1981).

Boston Globe (October 14, 1984).

Boston Globe (January 21, 1987).

Bradley, J.E. "LT and the Home Team." *Esquire* (December 1985): 306.

Contemporary Newsmakers 1987, Issue Cumulation. Detroit: Gale, 1988.

Delcos, John. "LT is winning the Battle With Time." *Football Digest* (April 1991): 44.

Ellenport, Craig. "The defense rests." *Sport* (January 1993): 48.

Huff, Melissa. "Football legend discusses addiction." Knight-Ridder/Tribune News Service (August 23, 1996).

Lieber, Jill. "Blitzed by himself. (Lawrence Taylor admits substance-abuse problem)." *Sports Illustrated* (September 19, 1988): 53.

Lieber, Jill. "Invincible? No, Just Real Mean." *Sports Illustrated* (January 26, 1987): 36.

Los Angeles Times (September 7, 1986).

Los Angeles Times (January 23, 1987).

Maske, Mark. "Taylor is Elected to Hall of Fame." *Washington Post* (January 31, 1999): D01.

Myers, Gary. "Phil Simms, Lawrence Taylor leave a gaping hole in Giants' heart." Knight-Ridder/Tribune News Service (July 13, 1994).

New York Times (August 2, 1985).

New York Times (March 21, 1986).

New York Times (January 4, 1987).

New York Times (March 25, 1987).

Philadelphia Daily News (October 9, 1986).

Philadelphia Daily News (January 16, 1987).

Philadelphia Daily News (January 21, 1987).

Shapiro, Milton. "Search and Destroy." *New York Times Magazine* (August 26, 1984): 18.

Simers, T.J. "Shame on 'Fame If Taylor Is Voted In." *Los Angeles Times* (January 26, 1999): 2.

Sports Illustrated (April 1, 1985).

Springer, Steve. "Tagliabue Gives His Vote to Taylor for Hall of Fame." *Los Angeles Times* (January 30, 1999): 6.

Stanton, Barry. "Interview: Lawrence Taylor." *Sport* (November 1985): 17.

Washington Post (April 6, 1986).

Washington Post (January 8, 1987).

Washington Post (January 14, 1987).

Washington Post (January 21, 1987).

Washington Post (February 27, 1987).

Washington Post (March 23, 1987).

Zimmerman, Paul. "Don't Cross This Line." *Sports Illustrated* (September 5, 1994): 50.

Zimmerman, Paul. "Terrific Tayloring." *Sports Illustrated* (September 17, 1990): 30-37.

Other

"Lawrence Taylor Pro Football Hall of Fame Induction Ceremony." http://www.bbwc.com/History/taylor-hof.html/ (November 10, 2002).

Sketch by Eric Lagergren

Sachin Tendulkar

Sachin Tendulkar
1973-

Indian cricket player

The "Super Natural," the "Willow Prince," "the King," and even "a god" are terms that have been used to describe Indian cricket batsman Sachin Tendulkar, yet he refers to himself as a normal person who is satisfied with being counted among the best batsmen in the world. A young prodigy, Tendulkar began playing cricket as a toddler and at age sixteen was selected to play on India's national team. In 2001 he became the first batsman to score a total of 10,000 runs in one-day cricket. He is an idol in his native India, where he lives humbly even though his salary and product endorsements have made him the world's wealthiest cricket player. Still at the top of his game in 2003, Tendulkar is sometimes compared to the great West Indian cricketer Vivian Richards and to Australian cricket legend **Don Bradman**, who died in 2001 at age 92.

Thirteen Coins

Sachin Ramesh Tendulkar was born April 24, 1973, in Bombay (now Mumbai), India. His father, Ramesh Tendulkar, was a language professor; he died in 1999. Sachin has two brothers and a sister. He began playing cricket at age 2 1/2, with his nanny in the family's backyard, using a broomstick for a bat. As he grew, he began playing street cricket with neighborhood children, and after watching the World Cup on television at age ten, he began to get serious about the game. Although left-handed, he learned to bat with his right hand as a youth. Street rules required players to bat with their nonpreferred hand to increase their chances of being eliminated. After the family moved close to Shivaji Park in Bombay, Sachin's game began to improve. At ages twelve and thirteen, he was practicing and playing school matches a total of twelve hours a day on some days. He once played fifty-four matches in a row. His coach, Ramakant Acherkar, encouraged Sachin to play his hardest by placing a rupee on top of one of his wicket stumps and offering the money to anyone who got Sachin out. If no one did, Sachin won the money. He still treasures thirteen of the coins he won in that way.

At age thirteen, Sachin scored his first century (100 runs) at school, and the following year he was invited to a net session with the Indian professional team. At age fifteen, he and a friend set a world record of runs (664) for his school, and at sixteen, Sachin was picked to play his first Test match for India against Pakistan. His father signed the papers for him, because Sachin was too young. By age seventeen, Sachin had toured New Zealand and England with the team. On the England tour he scored a match-saving 119 points, which made him the second youngest test century-maker ever. From there, his career has become better each year. On March 31, 2001, he became the first batsman to score 10,000 runs in one-day cricket, setting this record during a five-match

Chronology

1973	Born April 24 in Bombay (now Mumbai), India
1975	At age 2 1/2, begins hitting ball with a broomstick in his backyard
1983	Watches World Cup cricket match on television and becomes seriously interested in the game
1986	Scores his first century (100 runs) in his school, at age 13
1987	Is invited by captain of Indian team to a net session with the team
1988	With friend Vinod Kambli, sets world record of 664 runs for Shardashram School at inter-school tournament; at age 15, scores 100no (not out) in his first-class debut for Bombay team
1989	Scores 103no at one-day debut for Bombay team
1989-90	At age 16, is selected to play for India against Pakistan, making his international debut in One-Day Internationals (ODIs) and Test matches. On a tour of New Zealand, scores 88, just short of being the youngest century-maker in a test match
1990	Tours England and scores 119 in a match, making him the second-youngest test century-maker
1995	Signs first contract with WorldTel, for five-year commercial endorsements and marketing deal that will make him the world's richest cricket player
1996	Is appointed captain of Indian team—will serve until early 1998
1997	Daughter, Sarah, is born to Tendulkar and wife, Anjali, in October
1998	Makes 155 runs against Australia in Madras (now Chennai), India; meets 90-year-old Australian cricket master Sir Donald Bradman
1999	Begins having back pain in January—doctors later determine scar tissue in his lower vertebrae had become inflamed, but problem can be quickly corrected; bats in India's first World Cup match, against South Africa; flies home from match in England when father dies of cardiac arrest in mid-May; is again named captain of Indian team, in July; second child, a son, is born September 23
2001	Is invited to Bradman's 92nd birthday party, shortly before his death at 92; becomes first batsman to score 10,000 runs in one-day cricket, setting this record in third game of five-match series against Australia on March 31; re-signs with WorldTel; in November, is accused of tampering with cricket ball at match in Port Elizabeth, South Africa, and fined
2002	Pulls out of seven-match India-West Indies series with hamstring injuries; makes his thirtieth Test century, one more than Bradman; at end of November ranks third in international Test ratings, with 856 points and 58.46 average

Awards and Accomplishments

1992	Became youngest player to score 1,000 runs
1997	Voted Wisden Cricketer of the Year
1998	Received Rajiv Gandhi Khel Ratna Award, India's highest honor for achievement in sports, for the year 1997
1999	Received Padma Shri Award, bestowed by India's president, the nation's highest civilian honor
2001	On March 31, became first batsman to score 10,000 runs in one-day cricket
2002	On September 5, became youngest cricket player to play 100th Test match

Has broken the record for maximum centuries in International cricket (One-Day Internationals + Test matches)

Australian bowler **Shane Warne** once said Tendulkar gave him nightmares.

The 5'5" boyish star is mobbed by fans wherever he goes in India, except for his old neighborhood in Mumbai, where he still plays cricket with friends and is treated like a normal person. Every televised game he plays becomes a national event, and the details of his life are a national obsession. He is accustomed to the fuss but remains humble, in spite of the fact that he is the world's wealthiest cricketer and appears in about one-fourth of all Indian television commercials, so prolific are his endorsements.

Tendulkar is the first Indian to achieve such heights in both sports and media stardom. Over his career, he has helped to bring Indian cricket from a little-televised sport to a major national pastime. His talent and skill place him in the world annals of cricket, with the best of players from any country. Yet, he humbly said, in 1999, "I've never thought of myself as the best batsman in the world. My ambition was to be considered one of the best, and to stay there."

CONTACT INFORMATION

Address: c/o Mumbai Cricket Association, Wankhede Stadium, D. Road, Churchgate, Mumbai, India 400020. Fax: 022-2811795. Phone: 022-2817851. Email:mca @cricinfo.com. Online: http://www.tendulkar.cricinfo. com.

FURTHER INFORMATION

Periodicals

Joshi, Ruchir. "Bat out of Heaven: Many Factors Divide India, but Two Things Unite it: Cricket and a Star Named Sachin Tendulkar." *Time International* (April 29, 2002): 40.

Other

Brenkley, Stephen. "The Price of Being a God." CricInfo. http://www-usa.cricket.org/ (December 3, 2001).

series against Australia. He has broken the world record for maximum centuries in International cricket and continues to set records with every passing season. At the end of 2002 he was ranked third in the world in Test batting and was preparing for a forty-seven-day tour of New Zealand, after recovering from a hamstring injury.

India's Idol

For a country in love with the sport of cricket, Sachin Tendulkar has become a national treasure, idolized by millions. Cricket players the world over consider him probably the most complete batsman the game has ever seen. He is so skillful that there is practically no shot he cannot play. Bowlers dread facing him, because he is unflappable and succumbs to none of their tricks. Ace

CricInfo. "Sachin Tendulkar." http://www-usa.cricket. org/ (January 24, 2003).

CricInfo. "Sachin Wins Rajiv Gandhi Khel Ratna Award." http://www-usa.cricket.org/ (August 12, 1998).

CricInfo. "Tendulkar Conferred 'Padma Shri'." http:// www-usa.cricket.org/ (March 23, 1999).

Hughes, Simon. The Electronic Telegraph. "The Super Natural." http://www-usa.cricket.org/ (May 8, 1999).

"I Did Not Want to Be Indian Captain Says Tendulkar." Agence France Press. http://www-usa.cricket.org/ (July 30, 1999).

Lamb, Stephen. "Sachin Tendulkar: Masterful." CricInfo. http://www-usa.cricket.org/ (May 23, 2002).

LiveIndia.com. "Indian Cricket Test Records." http:// www.liveindia.com/cricket/ (January 27, 2003).

LiveIndia.com. "Profile of Sachin Ramesh Tendulkar." http://www.liveindia.com/cricket/ (January 27, 2003).

Longley, Geoff. "Tendulkar Finds Fatherhood 'Charming'." *The Christchurch Press* (New Zealand). http://www-usa.cricket.org/ (December 21, 1998).

Mumbai Cricket Association. http://www-usa.cricket. org/ (January 27, 2003).

"Ponting Overtakes Tendulkar in Test Batting Ratings." IndiaExpress Bureau. http://www.indiaexpress.com/ (November 25, 2002).

Ramchand, Partab. "A Different Sort of Century." CricInfo. http://www-usa.cricket.org./ (September 4, 2002).

Ramchand, Partab. "Tendulkar Will Be Back in Action Soon." CricInfo. http://www-usa.cricket.org/ (September 15, 1999).

Reuters News Service. "Tendulkar Greater Than Bradman, Says Gavaskar." http://www-usa.cricket.org/ (August 24, 2002).

"Tendulkar Re-Signs With WorldTel." CricInfo. http:// www-usa.cricket.org/ (May 17, 2001).

"Tendulkar, Zaheer Khan Fit for New Zealand Series." CricInfo. http://www-usa.cricket.org/ (November 23, 2002).

Vasu, Anand. "Former Cricketers Express Anger at Denness' Decision." CricInfo. http://www-usa. cricket.org/ (November 20, 2001).

Vasu, Anand. "Tendulkar Junior Born Yesterday." CricInfo. http://www-usa.cricket.org/ (September 24, 1999).

"World Cup Star Tendulkar Flies Home after Father's Death." Agence France Press. http://www-usa. cricket.org/ (May 19, 1999).

Sketch by Ann H. Shurgin

Derrick Thomas
1967-2000

American football player

Derrick Thomas

As a linebacker, Derrick Thomas was a presence feared by opposing quarterbacks. He possessed great quickness and unbelievable strength, and always found a way to bring down the ball carrier. Consistently at the top of his game, Thomas was a perennial selection for the Pro Bowl, and in ten seasons with the Kansas City Chiefs, became not only a dominant force on the field, but also a big part of the community through his generous giving and charitable work.

In what can only be described as a tragic loss, Thomas was paralyzed when his Suburban truck flipped on the icy roads near the Kansas City airport on January 23, 2000. He died only a few weeks later, on February 8, leaving an empty space both Kansas City and the Chiefs know they can never fill.

Growing Up

Derrick Thomas was born on January 1, 1967, in Miami, Florida. Chiefs fans know well the story of Thomas' childhood. When Derrick was 5, the North Vietnamese shot down his father, Robert James Thomas, an air force pilot, while he was piloting a B-52 Bomber. He was declared missing in action.

Edith Morgan, his mother, and Annie Adams, his grandmother, would raise Derrick. After his father was declared legally dead in 1980, Thomas rebelled. He was growing up in Miami's inner city, and he ended up getting into trouble. When he was fourteen,

Career Statistics

Yr	Team	Tackles				Misc/fumbles		Interceptions	
		TOT	SOLO	AST	SACK	FF	BK	INT	TD
1989	KC	75	56	19	10.0	3	0	0	0
1990	KC	63	47	16	20.0	6	0	0	0
1991	KC	79	60	19	14.0	4	0	0	0
1992	KC	67	54	13	15.0	8	0	0	0
1993	KC	43	32	11	8.0	4	0	0	0
1994	KC	71	67	4	11.0	2	0	0	0
1995	KC	53	48	5	8.0	2	0	0	0
1996	KC	55	49	6	13.0	4	1	0	0
1997	KC	34	30	4	9.5	3	0	0	0
1998	KC	42	35	7	12.0	2	0	0	0
1999	KC	60	54	6	7.0	2	0	1	0
TOTAL		642	532	110	127.5	40	1	1	0

C: Kansas City Chiefs.

Thomas was arrested by the South Miami police and sent to the Dade Marine Institute, a program run much like a boot camp. It was the last stop for juvenile offenders before they were sent on to prison, and although Thomas hated it, he said later that it was the best thing to happen to him. He told Jeffrey Flanagan of the *Kansas City Star* that getting caught made him stop "running with the wrong people. Instead of sitting around and throwing rocks at cars and buses, and trying to figure out what place to rob, I put all my energy into football."

After leaving the detention center, Thomas went on to earn all-league honors at South Miami High School, which in turn earned him a scholarship to the University of Alabama, a powerhouse in college football. Thomas became a star, amassing sixty-seven tackles in his junior season and compiling a school-record eighteen sacks. When he was a senior, he was presented the Butkus Award, given to the country's top linebacker. He graduated from the Crimson Tide with fifty-two sacks and seventy-four tackles, a new school record.

Roll Tide to Kansas City

Marty Schottenheimer had been brought in to turn around the Kansas City Chiefs organization that fared poorly throughout much of the 1980s. His first order of business was to draft Thomas, picked fourth overall by the Chiefs in the 1989 draft. Thomas made an immediate impact, recording ten sacks and fifty-five quarterback pressures. The Associated Press awarded him their Defensive Rookie of the Year Award, and he began a long series of Pro Bowl appearances, as well as winning the Mack Lee Award for best Chiefs Rookie.

Thomas helped usher in a new era for the Kansas City Chiefs. Throughout much of the nineties, the

Awards and Accomplishments

1988	Butkus Award; All-American
1989	Associated Press Defensive Rookie of the Year
1989-97	Pro Bowl
1991	Named Chiefs' Most Valuable Player
1993	Named NFL's Man of the Year
1993	Recipient of Veterans of Foreign Wars Hall of Fame Award
1993	Designated by President George Bush as "832nd Point of Light" for his charity work in Kansas City
1994	Named Chiefs' Most Valuable Player (second time)
1995	Receives Byron "Whizzer" White Humanitarian Award

Chiefs were playoff contenders, something fans hadn't seen in a long time. Thomas established a Chiefs record for sacks in only his second season (20), and forced many fumbles, helping turn the Kansas City defense into one of the best in the league. In 1994, his sixth season in the NFL, Thomas would become the Chiefs' all time sack leader with 72.5 sacks.

In his final four seasons, Thomas continued to exhibit the high level of play he was known for, though an injury to his left triceps prior to the 1997 season kept him out for four games. When he returned to the field, he did so with an arm brace, thus limiting his mobility and effectiveness.

Compounding his physical woes were the problems the Chiefs were having as a team. They couldn't seem to coalesce. Coach Schottenheimer seemed to have lost control of his players, and in a 1998 game against the Denver Broncos, Thomas, his frustrations mounting, racked up three penalties in one defensive series, earning him a one-week suspension. At the season's end, when the Chiefs failed to make the playoffs, Schottenheimer retired. Thomas planned to take some time off and then get ready for the next season.

Chronology

1967	Born January 1 in Miami, Florida, to Robert James Thomas and Edith Morgan
1972	Father's plane shot down by North Vietnamese on December 17
1980	Thomas' father declared legally dead
1981	Arrested for breaking into a store and sentenced to a school for troubled kids
1984	Earns All-League honors at South Miami High School
1985	Enters Alabama on scholarship to play with Crimson Tide
1989	Drafted fourth overall by Kansas City Chiefs
1990	Sets NFL single-game sack record by sacking Seattle QB David Krieg 7 times, forcing two fumbles
1990	Establishes the Third and Long Foundation, a charitable foundation focused on encouraging children to read and pursue their educational goals
1997	Injures left triceps tendon and is out for four games; still earns spot on Pro Bowl team by end of year
1998	Suspended for a week after being penalized three times in one defensive series in a game against Denver
1999	Playing as a pass-rusher, records only seven sacks
2000	Paralyzed on January 23 in car accident near Kansas City, Missouri
2000	Dies on February 8 from cardio-respiratory arrest

A Tragic End

Not wanting to miss the 1999 postseason, even if he could only to watch from the stands, Derrick Thomas, while driving to the Kansas City airport on January 23, 2000, was paralyzed when his truck flipped several times on the icy Interstate. He died only a few weeks later, on February 8.

Derrick Thomas was more than just a stellar athlete; he was an outstanding and giving human being. His Third and Long Foundation has helped hundreds of kids realize their educational goals and, like Thomas, overcome difficulty reading. His work off the field earned him the 1993 NFL Man of the Year.

The impact of Thomas' death was felt across the country, as fans mourned him for the loss of a great man as well as the tragic loss of a great football player.

FURTHER INFORMATION

Books

Newsmakers 2000, Issue 3. Detroit: Gale Group, 2000.
Oblender, David G. (ed.) *Contemporary Black Biography*, Volume 25. Detroit: Gale Group, 2000.
Sports Stars. Series 1-4. U•X•L, 1994-98.
Thomas, Derrick. *Forever a Chief: DT Always Giving Back*. Chicago: Triumph Books, 2000.

Periodicals

Chicago Tribune (February 9, 2000).
Football Digest (February 1995).
Jet (February 21, 1994).
Kansas City Star (February 9, 2000).
Los Angeles Times (February 9, 2000).

Mravic, Mark. "Chief concern." *Sports Illustrated* (January 31, 2000): 28-30.
New York Times (February 9, 2000).
Silver, Michael. "Derrick Thomas Remembered" (obituary). *Sports Illustrated* (February 21, 2000): 21.
Sporting News (January 17, 1994).
Sporting News (January 24, 1994).
Sporting News (January 31, 1994).
Sporting News (January 9, 1995).
Sporting News (January 15, 1996).
USA Today (February 9, 2000).
Washington Post (February 9, 2000).

Other

"Derrick Thomas (1967-2000)." CBS Sportsline. http://cbs.sportsline.com/u/football/nfl/legends/dthomas.htm (January 2, 2003).
"Derrick Thomas Remembered." Topeka Capital Journal Online. http://chiefszone.com/dthomas/ (January 2, 2003).

Sketch by Eric Lagergren

Frank Thomas
1968-

American baseball player

Immense and powerful, at six-feet five-inches tall and somewhere between 250 and 300 pounds (depending on the season), Frank Thomas is a giant menace to opposing pitchers, who start worrying about this powerhouse before he even steps to the plate. Thomas, known as "The Big Hurt" (a nickname that stuck when White Sox broadcaster Ken Harrelson said it in 1992 after watching him crush a home run over 450 feet) is truly one of baseball's great sluggers. Whether he goes by "Frank Thomas" or "The Big Hurt," the names show up time and again when the greatest right-handed batters in the history of baseball are discussed.

Growing Up

Frank Edward Thomas, Jr., was born on May 27, 1968, in Columbus, Georgia, to Frank Thomas Sr. and Charlie Mae Thomas. Frank's father was a deacon at the local Baptist Church, but he also worked for the city to bring in some extra money for the family. Thomas' mother worked in a local fabric factory, and although their kids grew up in a poor neighborhood, Thomas' parents raised him and his five brothers and sisters under strict rules to keep their kids out of trouble.

As a child, Thomas already showed the signs of being an outstanding athlete. Warned to avoid trouble,

Frank Thomas

Chronology

1968	Born May 27, in Columbus, Georgia
1977	Convinces father to let him play football in Pop Warner league (a league for twelve-year-olds)
1977	Younger sister Pam (two years old) dies of Leukemia
1986	Graduates High School and isn't drafted by any major league team
1986	Accepts scholarship to play football at Auburn
1987	Plays baseball for the U.S. Pan American Team and plays in Pan Am Games
1989	White Sox draft Frank Thomas with the 7th pick in the draft
1990	Called up to the Majors after spending a short time in the minors
1992	Crushes home run more than 450 feet
1992	Marries Elise Silver, daughter of a minor league baseball team owner. Frank and Elise will have two children
1993	Voted into his first All-Star spot
1993	Starts the Frank Thomas Charitable Foundation, which contributes to Leukemia Society of America
1994	Hits .452 in May, with twelve home runs; wins second straight American League MVP
1994	Major League Baseball season ends early on players strike, cutting short Thomas' phenomenal season
1996	Becomes the White Sox career home run leader
1997	Reaches base fifteen straight times, one short of major league record
2001	Injured during game against Mariners on April 27 and out for rest of season
2002	Renegotiates contract with White Sox after testy period in which it looked like Thomas might move to another team

he often participated in sports at the local Boys Club, playing baseball, basketball and football. He was good enough that they soon moved him up to play organized sports with kids two to three years his senior. Thomas was an imposing presence, large (some say chubby), and his reputation with a bat even then caused kids to panic. They'd "throw the ball behind him, over the backstop, all over the place," his dad recalled in a *Sports Illustrated* article. "They'd do anything to avoid pitching to him."

Not immune to pain, however, Thomas saw his two-year-old sister Pamela grow sick and die of leukemia when he was still a young boy. After he turned professional, he would establish the Frank Thomas Foundation, in 1993, to raise money to find a cure for the disease. The suddenness of his sister's death frightened Thomas, who, on Thanksgiving Day in 1977 vowed that, in Pamela's honor, he would become a professional baseball player.

Graduating Disappointment

While at high school in Columbus, Thomas honed his jump shot in basketball, excelled as a tight end on the football field (also kicking extra points and making every one), and led the baseball team to a state title two years in a row. His senior year Thomas batted .440 and was voted onto the all-state team.

Despite his power and prowess in baseball, however, when the 1986 draft was over, 888 players from high schools and colleges from around the country had been drafted—but not Thomas. He was devastated, claiming later on that he would have played anywhere, just to be able to get on the diamond. But he also realized later that it was one of the better things to happen to him, forcing him into college. He accepted a football scholarship to Auburn, a perennial collegiate powerhouse, where the time spent in the weight room increased his power, and the time spent learning the game at the college level helped turn him into "The Big Hurt" he is today.

Moving On Up

Thomas would leave the Auburn football team after only one season in order to concentrate on baseball. By his senior year (1989) he was voted the Southeastern Conference MVP in baseball, leaving the school with forty-nine career homers, a new record.

After a brief and dominating stint in the Chicago White Sox minor league system, Frank Thomas was finally called up to the big leagues on August 2, 1990. In those last few months of the season he would start at first base and bat .330, with 31 Runs Batted In (RBI), as well as hitting seven home runs.

Throughout the 1990s Thomas would exemplify a true power hitter, putting up impressive numbers year in and year out. In his first full season with the White Sox, he batted .318 and hit thirty-two home runs, with 109 RBIs. Though he was left out of the All-Star lineup that season, he finished third in MVP voting. In fact, he was

Career Statistics

Yr	Team	AVG	GP	AB	R	H	HR	RBI	BB	SO	SB	E
1990	CHW	.330	60	191	39	63	7	31	44	54	0	5
1991	CHW	.318	158	559	104	178	32	109	138	112	1	2
1992	CHW	.323	160	573	108	185	24	115	122	88	6	13
1993	CHW	.317	153	549	106	174	41	128	112	54	4	15
1994	CHW	.353	113	399	106	141	38	101	109	61	2	7
1995	CHW	.308	145	493	102	152	40	111	136	74	3	7
1996	CHW	.349	141	527	110	184	40	134	109	70	1	9
1997	CHW	.347	146	530	110	184	35	125	109	69	1	11
1998	CHW	.265	160	585	109	155	29	109	110	93	7	2
1999	CHW	.305	135	486	74	148	15	77	87	66	3	4
2000	CHW	.328	159	582	115	191	43	143	112	94	1	1
2001	CHW	.221	20	68	8	15	4	10	10	12	0	1
2002	CHW	.252	148	523	77	132	28	92	88	115	3	2
TOTAL		.314	1698	6065	1168	1902	376	1285	1286	962	32	79

CHW: Chicago White Sox.

Awards and Accomplishments

1989	SEC Most Valuable Player
1989	All-SEC Tournament Selection (baseball)
1990	Wins Baseball America's Minor League Player of the Year award
1991	Silver Slugger Award-American League
1993	Named American League MVP by unanimous vote; wins Silver Slugger Award
1994	Repeats as American League MVP
1997	Ted Williams Award-American League (most productive hitter)
1997	Wins first batting title with a .347 average
2000	Silver Slugger Award-American League

left off of the All-Star roster again in 1992, even though his numbers seemed to indicate otherwise (.323 with twenty-four home runs and 118 RBIs).

In 1993, Thomas made it to the All-Star game, but more importantly, his bat helped propel the White Sox to their first division title in ten years. With a batting average of .317 and a new White Sox record forty-one home runs, as well as 128 RBIs, Thomas was voted baseball's Most Valuable Player—only the tenth time in the history of the sport the MVP has been chosen by unanimous decision. He'd completed an impressive season, and he would only build on those numbers in 1994.

The Season That Could Have Been

The "what-ifs" about Thomas's 1994 season still echo in the halls of baseball statisticians. The year was shortened by a players' strike in mid-August, and through 113 games, Thomas had posted a .353 batting average and amassed thirty-eight home runs. He also had 101 RBIs, leading the league with runs scored (106), walks (109), slugging percentage (.729), and on-base percentage (.487). It was a truly impressive run,

capped by a May in which he averaged .452 at the plate while belting twelve home runs. Though Thomas would win a second MVP when the strike ended the season, one can only imagine what might have been. In fact, *Sports Illustrated* claimed that, barring the strike, Thomas might have broken **Babe Ruth**'s records for runs, walks, and extra-base-hits in a single season.

Getting Back On Track

In July of 1996, Thomas was injured for the first time, ending his consecutive games played streak at 346. It would be the beginning of some rocky times for Thomas, who in 1997 began to let disputes over his contract and outside interests in developing recording labels interfere with his concentration. Additionally, according to Gerry Callahan of *Sports Illustrated*, there was speculation that Thomas and his wife, Elise Silver, were going through some tough times in their marriage. Thomas, who tends to keep to himself and doesn't bother people with his brooding, told Callahan that, "All I'll say is, I'm a grown man with grown-up problems." His problems increased when he started putting on weight, and though he still compiled impressive statistics, they weren't the numbers Thomas was known for. The shadow of the outstanding player he had been loomed large. He wanted to, and would, get back to that spot.

The tough final years of the 1990s came to a head during spring training in 2000 when a shouting match erupted between Thomas and Sox manager Jerry Manual, involving, among other things, Thomas' refusal, due to a sore heel, to participate in the team's "shuttle run" drill. Though fans worried about what the argument might bode, Thomas and Manual let off some necessary steam, and Thomas went on to compile the numbers he was known for (.328, 43 home runs, 143 RBIs, 114 runs and 191 hits).

In the 2002 off-season, the White Sox exercised a "diminished skills" clause in Frank Thomas' contract. His 2001 season was riddled by injury, and to many, it looked as if the man who had a contract with the Sox through 2006 would now be a free agent. As fall wore on and winter approached, Thomas talked to several teams. But in early December, Thomas and the White Sox came to an agreement, albeit a rather complicated one.

The contract is chock full of options that, according to Scott Gregor of the *Daily Herald*, sound as if they were concocted "in an economic think tank." Thomas, who has been in the spotlight for over a decade, intends to remain in that spotlight, but this time for the right reasons—gaining his former prominence at the plate and putting up the numbers he's known for.

CONTACT INFORMATION

Address: Frank Thomas, c/o Chicago White Sox, 333 W. 35th St., Chicago, IL 60616.

FURTHER INFORMATION

Books

Contemporary Black Biography. Volume 12. Detroit: Gale Group, 1996.
Newsmakers 1994. Issue 4. Detroit: Gale Group, 1994.
Sports Stars. Series 1-4. U•X•L, 1994-98.

Periodicals

Baseball Weekly (April 16, 1997).
"The Big Heart." *Sports Illustrated* (August 8, 1994): 16.
Callahan, Gerry. "Hurt so good." *Sports Illustrated* (April 19, 1999): 60-64.
Cannella, S. "The Big Hurt: no 3. no more." *Sports Illustrated* (May 27, 2002): 96.
Nack, William. "Hurtin'." *Sports Illustrated* (March 13, 2000): 64-75.
Sports (April 1992).

Other

"Frank Thomas." http://www.baseball-reference.com/t/thomafr04.shtml (January 1, 2003).
"Frank Thomas." http://www.pubdim.net/baseballlibrary/ (January 1, 2003).

Sketch by Eric Lagergren

Isiah Thomas
1961-

American basketball player

When Isiah Thomas joined the Detroit Pistons in 1981, they were among the worst in the league, a disheartened group of guys struggling through each season. Thomas, however, transformed them into a proud, poised cohesive team. Under Thomas's direction—and attitude—the Pistons became known as the "Bad Boys" of the NBA. As their image deteriorated, their play improved. Thomas himself wore the smile of a gentleman, but underneath, he was more like a rugged outlaw, willing to do whatever it took to win the prize. For thirteen seasons, Thomas was the team's go-to guy: the one who could pour on the points when time was short and the odds were long. Once, Thomas scored sixteen points in the final ninety-four seconds of a game. Another time, he scored twenty-five points in a single NBA Finals quarter, setting an NBA record. Led by Thomas, the Pistons won back-to-back National Basketball Association (NBA) championships in 1989 and 1990. During his years with the Pistons, Thomas energized the city of Detroit and remains among the team's most beloved alums. He retired in 1994 as the Pistons' all-time leader in points (18,822), assists (9,061), steals (1,861), and games played (979)

Grew up in Grinding Poverty

Isiah Lord Thomas III was born April 30, 1961, in Chicago to Mary and Isiah Lord Thomas II. He was the ninth child born to the Thomases, who had come to Chicago to escape the racism that had plagued them during their childhoods in the South.

Isiah Thomas

Chronology

1961	Born April 30 in Chicago to Isiah Lord Thomas II and Mary Thomas
1979	Graduates from St. Joseph High School in Westchester, Illinois
1979	Represents United States in Pan American Games in Puerto Rico
1979	Joins Indiana Hoosiers basketball team coached by Bobby Knight
1981	Leads Hoosiers to the NCAA title
1981	Is the No. 2 pick in the June NBA draft, taken by the Detroit Pistons
1985	Marries Lynn Kendall
1987	Graduates from Indiana University on Mother's Day with a degree in criminal justice
1989-90	Leads Pistons to back-to-back NBA championships
1993	Purchases printing franchise American Speedy
1994	Tears Achilles' tendon, decides to retire
1994	Becomes part-owner and general manager of the Toronto Raptors
1997	Begins work as NBA analyst and broadcaster for NBC
1999	Buys controlling ownership of the nine-team Continental Basketball Association for $10 million
2000	Becomes head coach of the Indiana Pacers

Thomas grew up in the gritty ghetto of Chicago's West Side, where his mother ran the youth center at Our Lady of Sorrows Catholic Church. Because he was the youngest, Thomas's six brothers and two sisters called him "Junior."

Thomas's father worked at International Harvester, where he became the company's first African-American supervisor. Later, when the plant closed and he could only find work as a janitor, he became depressed and left the family.

Mary Thomas struggled to provide for her large family. The fridge was often bare, leaving the Thomas children to scrounge for food. In his book *The Fundamentals: Eight Plays for Winning the Games of Business and Life,* Thomas recalled that he spent his childhood trolling the streets with an empty belly, looking for loose change or fast-food wrappers with scraps of cheese still stuck inside. He shined shoes to earn money for food, then hoped he could make it home without being robbed.

As Thomas wrote in the book, "My earliest dreams were not-as you might imagine-fantasies of playing professional basketball. . . . My boyhood dreams were mostly about well-stocked refrigerators: huge refrigerators that were bursting at the hinges with mouth-watering roast chickens, heaping plates of spaghetti, and thick juicy steaks."

While Thomas's stomach may have been empty, his basketball skills were abundant and sprouted early on. When his older brother Larry played in a Catholic youth league, three-year-old Thomas provided the half-time entertainment. He'd slip on a jersey, which fit like a tent, then dribble around the court imitating the moves he'd seen. Just three, Thomas could already please a crowd.

Growing up, Thomas spent his days at a West Side pocket park playing basketball on the pockmarked courts. Thomas's brother, Lord Henry, was one of the neighborhood stars, and Thomas learned a lot of plays from him. For Thomas, going to the court became a way to block out the hunger, violence, and dangers that gnawed at him off the court.

In time, Thomas realized that his basketball skills might be his family's salvation-a way to drag his mother and siblings out of grinding poverty and into a safer neighborhood. The Thomas clan had been waiting for one of the boys to get a break, perhaps join the NBA. Thomas's brother Larry had been invited to try out for the Chicago Bulls but missed the chance by spraining his ankle. He then turned to the streets. Another brother, Lord Henry, lost his athletic potential to drugs. Now, it was up to Thomas to succeed. Thomas' brother, Larry, wanted to ensure Thomas' success, so he took him to the court day after day and drilled him on the fundamentals, all the while encouraging Thomas to stay out of trouble and shoot for his dreams.

As an eighth-grader, Thomas tore up the basketball courts. He impressed area coach Gene Pingatore so much that Pingatore secured financial aid for Thomas to attend St. Joseph High School, where Pingatore coached.

Awards and Accomplishments

1980	Named to the Associated Press All-Big Ten team, the first college freshman to receive the honor
1981	Led Indiana Hoosiers to the NCAA basketball championship; named tournament MVP
1982	NBA All-Rookie team
1982-93	Played in All-Star Game every season but his last
1984	All-Star game MVP
1984-85	Became first player in NBA history to average more than 20 points per game and make more than 1,000 assists in the same season
1984-85	Set NBA record with 1,123 assists
1985	Named Michiganian of the Year
1986	All-Star game MVP
1988	Set NBA Finals record for most points in a quarter (25), and most field goals in one quarter (11)
1989	Led Pistons to the NBA championship
1990	Led Pistons to the NBA Championship
1990	Named NBA Finals MVP
1996	Named to the NBA Greatest 50 Players of All Time Team
2000	Inducted into the Naismith Memorial Basketball Hall of Fame; uniform No. 11 retired by Pistons

A Mother's Courage: The Mary Thomas Story

Isiah Thomas's mother's life story was dramatized in a 1989 NBC-TV movie starring Alfre Woodard in the title role. The movie showed how the single mother worked to free her children from poverty as they came of age on the crime-riddled streets of Chicago's West Side. For the most part, Mary Thomas kept her children on the straight and narrow, making up with love what she lacked in money.

The movie depicts many telling events from Isiah Thomas' life, including the time Mary Thomas went to Mayor Richard Daley to complain that case workers wanted to move her family into a violence-plagued housing project-and she wasn't going to go. The movie also told about the time a gang showed up on the family's doorstep eager to recruit the Thomas boys. Mary Thomas, however, pointed her shotgun at them and threatened to blow them across the expressway. She explained that there was only one gang in that house, the Thomas gang.

The movie, and Mary Thomas' life, served as an inspiration to other mothers facing the same prospects she did. Originally broadcast as a "Magical World of Disney" Sunday night feature, the movie won an Emmy for Outstanding Children's Prime Time Program.

Throughout his life, Isiah Thomas always gave his mother credit for his success, and the movie shows why.

For Thomas, the move to the suburban, all-boy, nearly all white school was tough. Just getting there was an ordeal. To get to the Westchester, Illinois, school, Thomas rose at 5:30 a.m. for a one-and-a-half hour bus ride, which concluded with a long walk to the school's front door. Thomas knew the sacrifice was worth it if it would get his basketball skills noticed.

On the court, he regularly scored forty points a game. During his junior and senior seasons, Thomas led the St. Joseph Chargers to a 57-5 record, along with a disheartening second-place finish in the 1977-1978 Illinois state high school championship tournament.

Delivered Hoosiers a National Championship

Colleges across the United States courted Thomas, and he chose to play at Indiana University under coach **Bobby Knight**. At 6-foot-1, Thomas was small for a college player, and Knight nicknamed him "Pee Wee."

What Thomas lacked in stature, he made up for with his skills, particularly his supernatural ability to make shots against defenders who towered over him. During the 1979-1980 season, Thomas' freshman year, he escorted the Hoosiers to a 21-8 record and the Big Ten Championship. Leading his team in scoring (423 points), assists (159), and steals (62), Thomas was named to the Associated Press All-Big Ten team, the first freshman to receive the honor. Thomas was so popular at Indiana that classmates greeted him with standing ovations when he entered lecture halls following a game day.

His sophomore year, Thomas delivered the Hoosiers to the 1981 National Collegiate Athletic Association (NCAA) Tournament title game, where they beat the North Carolina State Tar Heels 63-50, with Thomas accounting for twenty-three of his team's points. Over the course of the tournament, Thomas scored ninety-one points and had forty-three assists in five games. He was named the tournament's outstanding player.

Thomas's terrific tournament play generated a lot of attention, and he landed on the cover of *Sports Illustrated.* He wondered if it was time to join the NBA. Thomas wanted to finish school, but he also wanted to get his mother out of the ghetto.

Thomas decided to turn pro. During the June 1981 NBA draft, the Detroit Pistons had the second pick, and they selected Thomas. Thomas signed a contract for $400,000 a year, which, coupled with his bonus, brought the total to more than $1 million. He immediately bought his mother a house in the suburbs. When Thomas quit college, his mother made him promise to finish his degree. Thomas took classes the next several off-seasons, graduating from Indiana with a degree in criminal justice in 1987.

Helped Pistons Rebound into Winning Team

When Thomas joined the Pistons, they were at the bottom of the league, lurching their way to a 21-61 record during the 1980-81 season. But with Thomas in the lineup playing guard during the start of the 1981-1982 season, the Pistons got off to an 8-5 record. During his first month in the big leagues, the twenty-year-old Thomas averaged twenty-one points per game. He added pizzazz to the Pistons' game, and attendance rose. The *Detroit News* proclaimed Thomas "Isiah the Savior."

Thomas finished the season averaging seventeen points per game for a total of 1,225 points. He handily

Isiah Thomas

made the All-Rookie and All-Star teams. The Pistons won thirty-nine games, their best finish in five years.

During the 1983-1984 season, Thomas led the Pistons to a 49-33 record. They faced the New York Knicks in the playoffs. The teams split the first four games of the series. During the fifth and deciding game, the Pistons were down 106-98 with just under two minutes to play. This is where Thomas showed his stuff. In ninety-four seconds, Thomas dropped in a lay-up, a three-pointer, five free throws, and three jump shots for sixteen points, tying the game at 114. The Pistons lost in overtime, but fans reveled in Thomas's play.

As Thomas gained star status on the court, he began using his name to help improve his community. Thomas wrote a weekly kids column for the *Detroit Free Press,* starred in an anti-drug film, and frequented inner-city schools, telling kids to stay in school and fight for their dreams. He also persuaded the mayor of Detroit to hold "No Crime Day" on September 27, 1986, so neighborhoods would be forced to focus efforts on dealing with crime, gangs, and drugs.

During the mid-1980s, Thomas realized that the Pistons needed a fresh image to help them compete. Though the Pistons had improved, other teams still thought of them as perennial losers. Over the next few years, Thomas helped redesign the team into the "Bad Boys" of the NBA. It was mostly a trick of perception, which worked. As the Pistons developed a more aggres-

sive image, their play improved. They also picked up better players, like **Dennis Rodman** in 1986. Finally, in 1988, the Pistons achieved their dream of making it to the NBA Finals, where they faced the defending champs, the Los Angeles Lakers and **Magic Johnson**.

The series was intense. Going into game six, Detroit led three games to two and needed one more victory for the title. The Lakers, playing at home, led 53-46 at the half. Thomas came out the second half determined to win. He scored a speedy fourteen points to put the Pistons back in the game, then promptly sprained his ankle. Thomas sat out thirty-five seconds, then insisted on going back in. Blocking out the pain, Thomas scored eleven more points for a third-quarter total of twenty-five, setting an NBA Finals record for most points scored in a quarter.

According to Ron Knapp's biography on Thomas, *Los Angeles Times* columnist Mike Downey wrote up Thomas' game this way, "He was out of this world. He was making shots off the wrong foot, off the glass, off the wall." Though Thomas scored forty-three points, Detroit lost 103-102, leaving the series tied at three games apiece. A gimpy Thomas suffered through the final game of the series as Detroit went down 108-105. Even though his team lost, Thomas became a champion of sorts. Fans were amazed with his skill and determination, which broke through even in the toughest moments.

Won Back-to-Back NBA Championships

The Pistons ended the 1988-89 season 63-19. They rolled through the playoffs, then knocked off the Los Angeles Lakers to win the NBA championship. That season, the Pistons exemplified basketball as a team sport. Their shared skills got them through. The Pistons were the NBA champs, yet none of the players stood out among the league's best. None of the team members made the All-NBA team, no one averaged at least twenty points per game, or was even among the league's top twenty in scoring. It had truly been a team effort. The Wheaties cereal company couldn't figure out who the team's star player was, so they put six of the Pistons on the front of the box.

The "Bad Boys" continued the 1989-1990 season looking like a championship team. They had a 25-1 record during a hot streak in January and February. With a season-ending record of 59-23, they again entered the playoffs and made it to the Finals, where they faced the Portland Trail Blazers. The Pistons were down ten points with only seven minutes left in the first game. Thomas once again hit his nerve to score twelve points in the last seven minutes, giving the Pistons a 105-99 win. Throughout the rest of the series, Thomas' play kept his team in the series. In game four, Thomas hit twenty-two points in the third quarter alone. The Pistons repeated as champs, with Thomas earning Finals MVP honors.

Career Statistics

Yr	Team	GP	PTS	FG%	3P%	FT%	RPG	APG	SPG	BPG	TO	PF
1981-82	DET	72	1225	.424	.288	.704	2.9	7.8	2.08	.24	299	253
1982-83	DET	81	1854	.472	.288	.710	4.0	7.8	2.46	.36	326	318
1983-84	DET	82	1748	.462	.338	.733	4.0	11.1	2.49	.40	307	324
1984-85	DET	81	1720	.458	.257	.809	4.5	13.9	2.31	.31	302	288
1985-86	DET	77	1609	.488	.310	.790	3.6	10.8	2.22	.26	289	245
1986-87	DET	81	1671	.463	.194	.768	3.9	10.0	1.89	.25	343	251
1987-88	DET	81	1577	.463	.309	.774	3.4	8.4	1.74	.21	273	217
1988-89	DET	80	1458	.464	.273	.818	3.4	8.3	1.66	.25	298	209
1989-90	DET	81	1492	.438	.309	.775	3.8	9.4	1.72	.23	322	206
1990-91	DET	48	776	.435	.292	.782	3.3	9.3	1.56	.21	185	118
1991-92	DET	78	1445	.446	.291	.772	3.2	7.2	1.51	.19	252	194
1992-93	DET	79	1391	.418	.308	.737	2.9	8.5	1.56	.23	284	222
1993-94	DET	58	856	.417	.310	.702	2.7	6.9	1.17	.10	202	126
TOTAL		979	18822	.452	.290	.759	3.6	9.3	1.90	.25	3682	2971

DET: Detroit Pistons.

Retired as Player, Became Coach

The Pistons fell apart during the 1993-94 season. Thomas appeared in his 12th All-Star game, but the Pistons ended the season 20-62. During the season's final home game, Thomas tore his Achilles' tendon. Rumors flew that the Pistons were interested in trading Thomas to the New York Knicks for a No. 1 draft pick. Thomas couldn't see himself playing for another team, so he decided to retire, though he later questioned the move.

As Thomas wrote in his book on the fundamentals, "I wish I'd given it more thought. . . . I think I had more basketball in me than I realized at that point, and since then I've thought that it wouldn't have been so bad to win a championship or two for New York and then hang up the sneakers."

Though he feels he may have retired prematurely, Thomas's statistics tell the story of a complete player. Thomas retired as the Pistons' all-time leader in points (18,822), assists (9,061), steals (1,861), and games played (979).

Thomas, however, did not leave the court. In 1994, he became part-owner and general manager of the Toronto Raptors. In 1997, he joined NBC as an NBA analyst and sportscaster, and in 1999, he purchased the Continental Basketball Association (CBA) for about $10 million. Thomas intended to boost interest in the nine-team league by adding Webcasts and lining up more sponsors. He dreamed of turning the CBA into an official minor league farm system for the NBA. With Thomas at the helm, the CBA became the only professional sports league in the hands of a minority owner.

In 2000, when Thomas became head coach of the Indiana Pacers, NBA rules forced him to put the CBA into a blind trust, and the league crumbled.

Thomas' time with the Pacers has been much more promising. In his first two seasons (2000-2001 and 2001-2002), Thomas coached the team to an 84-81 record. But he realizes, just as it took the Pistons years to build a championship team, it may take a few years for the Pacers. Once again, Thomas is chasing that dream of an NBA championship-this time as a coach.

He also devotes time to his family. In 1985, he married his college sweetheart, Lynn Kendall. They have two children, Joshua Isiah and Lauren.

Remembered as Inspiration to Others

Thomas will long be remembered for his brilliant shooting displays, particularly during post-season play. His 1988 record of twenty-five points in a single NBA Finals game quarter still stood in 2003.

Thomas's achievements, however, transcend the court. His success story continues to be an inspiration to youth growing up poor today. That Thomas moved from a life of stunting poverty into the basketball hall of fame is amazing. His story helps other children believe that they can do the same.

CONTACT INFORMATION

Address: c/o Indiana Pacers, 125 S. Pennsylvania St., Indianapolis, IN 46204. Fax: (317) 917-2599. Phone: (317) 917-2500. Email: PacersInsider@Pacers.com. Online: http://www.nba.com/pacers/news/fan_mail.html.

SELECTED WRITINGS BY THOMAS:

(With Matt Dobek) *Bad Boys,* McGraw-Hill, 1989.
The Fundamentals: Eight Plays for Winning the Games of Business and Life, HarperBusiness, 2001.

FURTHER INFORMATION

Books

Knapp, Ron. *Sports Great Isiah Thomas*. Hillside, N.J.: Enslow Publishers, Inc., 1992.

Rappoport, Ken. *Guts and Glory: Making it in the NBA*. New York: Walker and Company, 1997.

The Sporting News Official NBA Register, 2001-2002 Edition. St. Louis: The Sporting News, 2001.

Stewart, Mark. *Isiah Thomas*. New York: Children's Press, 1996.

Thomas, Isiah. *The Fundamentals: Eight Plays for Winning the Games of Business and Life*. New York: HarperBusiness, 2001.

Periodicals

Brown, Roxanne. "How to Save Inner-City Children from Gangs." *Ebony* (May 1990): 29.

Nance, Roscoe. "Looking Good Being Bad." *USA Today* (December 17, 2002).

Wertheim, L. Jon. "Nice Rebound." *Sports Illustrated* (November 18, 2002): 36.

Other

"Isiah Thomas Coach Info." NBA.com. http://www.nba.com/coachfile/isiah_thomas/?nav=page (January 5, 2003).

Sketch by Lisa Frick

Thurman Thomas
1966-

American football player

Thurman Thomas was a running back and pass receiver who, although short, was graceful and elusive on the gridiron. He was also powerful, breaking through the line and racking up yardage, becoming one of the premier offensive players in the National Football League (NFL). While playing with the Buffalo Bills, Thomas led the league in total yards for four consecutive seasons (1989-92), breaking the previous record held by **Jim Brown**. Thomas was also a key factor in propelling the Bills into four straight Super Bowls. Unfortunately, he was part of a Bills team that lost all four of those championships.

Growing Up

Thurman Thomas was born on May 16, 1966, in Houston, Texas, the only child of parents who would end up divorcing when he was four. His mother, Terl-

Thurman Thomas

isha, who would remarry eight years later, and claimed that Thomas was spoiled by relatives who constantly gave him what he wanted.

As a boy, Thomas was often the smallest one to participate in sports, and developed early on an attitude that compensated-or overcompensated-for what he lacked in size. He would later tell the *Pioneer Press* that people who made remarks about his stature getting in the way of his success "always motivated me toward doing something that I know I can do when other people say I can't."

Thomas was All-State running back and defensive back at Willowridge High in Missouri City, Texas (a suburb of Houston), and he played with a chip on his shoulder. He led his school to two state championship games and one state title. "I was raised in the ghetto and I have a tough attitude," Thomas told the *Washington Post*. "I'm not going to let anyone take advantage of me and I'm not going to take advantage of anybody else. I let people know how I feel. That's just the way I am."

By the end of high school, Thomas had rushed for just under 4,000 yards and forty-eight touchdowns. With his small stature, many college recruiters didn't look at him closely. Many told him that if he came to play for their teams, he could only play defensive back. But Thomas, determined to do what he was told he couldn't, sought out a school where he could carry the ball. Oklahoma State coach Jimmy Johnson—who would later go on to coach the Dallas Cowboys and the Miami Dol-

Chronology

1966	Born May 16 in Houston, Texas
1970	Parents divorce
1982	Put into starting lineup at Willowridge High School
1984	Finishes high school with 3,918 yards and 48 touchdowns
1984	Chooses Oklahoma State as college where he'll play football
1985	Gains 1650 yards, scoring 15 touchdowns and finishes 10th in Heisman voting as a sophomore
1986	Tears ACL in left knee during pick-up basketball game. Is out first few games of season
1989	Leads NFL in combined total yards, the first of four consecutive seasons
1991	Leads Bills to Super Bowl XXV, first of four consecutive trips (and four straight losses)
1991	Donates $30,000 to the United Negro College Fund and Buffalo chapters of YMCA and Special Olympics
1992	Establishes the Thurman Thomas Foundation, providing inner-city youth with scholarships to a local community college
1995	Thomas has 155 yards rushing in a game against the Steelers, proving to his critics that he's not getting too old to perform
1996	Quarterback Jim Kelly announces retirement, making Thomas think about his own NFL mortality
1997	Bills head coach Marv Levy retires at end of season, and Thomas sees the end of his career approaching
1999	Plays in only five games for the Bills. Leaves team at end of season
2000	Finishes career in Miami
2002	Heads up his business, Thurman Thomas Enterprises, based in Niagara Falls, NY

Awards and Accomplishments

1984	*Parade* magazine All-American Player of the Year
1984	Houston Touchdown Club's Texas Player of the Year
1984	Gator Bowl Most Valuable Player (as a freshman)
1985, 1987	College All-American
1989-93	NFL Pro Bowl Team
1991	Professional Football Writers Association Player of the Year
1991	NFL's Most Valuable Player
1991	*Sporting News* NFL Player of the Year
1991	United Press International AFC Offensive Player of the Year
1991	Miller Lite Player of the Year

phins—promised Thomas that he could run if he came to play for Oklahoma State. Thomas did, and went on to become one of the nation's premier runners.

Size Doesn't Matter

Thomas' NFL draft day was one that he thought he'd like to forget. At 5 feet 10 inches tall, Thomas was one of the smaller running backs in the draft. That fact, combined with a knee injury in his senior season, dropped him lower on the list, and he didn't go until the middle of the second round. ESPN, anticipating Thomas would go earlier, wanted to capture Thomas' reaction and sent a camera crew to his house. As Thomas watched the draft, and as player after player went before him, ESPN captured for a national audience Thurman Thomas' growing disappointment. Thomas later took a copy of that tape with him and watched it for motivation during his first few seasons in the NFL, vowing never to forget all of those teams that passed him up.

In spite of his physical hardship that rookie season, Thomas rushed for 881 yards on 207 carries on the season, even though he missed two games with a sore knee. He had found a home with Buffalo and a friend in head coach Marv Levy. Levy's famed "no-huddle" offense and the team's ability to keep the game moving quickly suited Thomas' style, and he became a versatile player, used as both a running back and a receiver. He would amass 1,913 yards in 1989, good enough to lead the league, and then repeat as league leader for the next three seasons.

With Thomas on their team, the Bills had a strong arsenal and began to compete for national championships. In four years prior to Thomas' arrival, the Buffalo Bills had a combined record of 15-40. But things started to click. They went 13-3 in 1990, making it into their first of four straight Super Bowls. Thomas had come off of a stellar season, rushing for 1297 yards, catching forty-nine passes for another 532 yards. Yet despite his combined effort for 190 yards in the title game, the Bills lost 20-19 in the final four seconds on a missed field goal. It would be an omen of bad things to come.

Thomas and the Bills compiled yet another winning season in 1991, going 13-3 again, and making it into Super Bowl XXVI. Thomas' combined yards for the season surpassed 2000, making him only the eleventh player in NFL history to do so, earning him the NFL's Most Valuable Player. But the Bills would lose the Super Bowl to the Washington Redskins.

For the next two seasons Thomas continued to excel on offense. 1992 was his best season, and he led the league in total yards gained, once more surpassing 2000 total yards, and once more making it into the playoffs and to Super Bowl XXVII. But the Bills would lose in a poor performance, getting hammered by the Dallas Cowboys, 52-17.

Thomas finished 1995 with the lowest totals of his career. The Bills would enter their fourth consecutive Super Bowl and hope to walk away with a victory and break whatever curse had been placed on them. But it was not to be.

Thurman Thomas struggled in 1996, though he surpassed 10,000 career yards and gained just over 1000 yards, becoming only the second player to do so in eight consecutive seasons. At the season's end, quarterback **Jim Kelly** announced his retirement, and Thomas started to think about his own NFL mortality.

The Bills picked up running back Antoine Smith in the 1997 draft, and that season, for the first time, Thomas failed to gain 1000 yards rushing. In 1999 he played in only five games for the Bills, and then in 2000 was traded to conference rival Miami, where he would retire at the end of the season.

Career Statistics

Yr	Team	Receiving				Rushing				Fumbles	
		REC	YDS	AVG	TD	ATT	YDS	AVG	TD	FUM	LST
1988	BUF	18	208	11.6	0	207	881	4.3	2	9	0
1989	BUF	60	669	11.2	6	298	1244	4.2	6	7	0
1990	BUF	49	532	10.9	2	271	1297	4.8	11	6	0
1991	BUF	62	631	10.2	5	288	1407	4.9	7	5	0
1992	BUF	58	626	10.8	3	312	1487	4.8	9	6	0
1993	BUF	48	387	8.1	0	355	1315	3.7	6	6	0
1994	BUF	50	349	7.0	2	287	1093	3.8	7	1	1
1995	BUF	26	220	8.5	2	267	1005	3.8	6	6	1
1996	BUF	26	254	9.8	0	281	1033	3.7	8	1	1
1997	BUF	30	208	6.9	0	154	643	4.2	1	2	2
1998	BUF	26	220	8.5	1	93	381	4.1	2	0	0
1999	BUF	3	37	12.3	1	36	152	4.2	0	0	0
2000	MIA	16	117	7.3	1	28	136	4.9	0	1	1
TOTAL		472	4458	9.4	23	2877	12074	4.2	65	50	6

BUF: Buffalo Bills; MIA: Miami Dolphins.

Where Is He Now?

Thurman Thomas and his wife Patti have two daughters, Olivia and Angelica. When he retired from professional football in 2000, Thurman Thomas began devoting much of his time to his business, Thurman Thomas Enterprises. Based in Niagara Falls, New York (just a short drive from Buffalo), Thomas remains close to the world of professional athletics. His company's mission is to provide guidance and training—in the form of seminars—to athletes and coaches of all levels, focusing on professional, semiprofessional and college athletes in "precarious or personally challenging situations." The company helps them make "well-informed choices" and their seminars are "designed to prevent adverse events that could lead to legal violations, negative press, and potential litigation."

Created A Loud Legacy

Often compared to other great running backs of his era, such as **Emmitt Smith** or **Barry Sanders**, Thomas felt unappreciated throughout much of his career, and he wasn't afraid to make those feelings known. His teammates knew he was volatile, but respected him nonetheless. "The thing about Thurman," Jim Kelly told the *Los Angeles Times*, "[is that] you never know what is going to come out of his mouth."

Thomas found himself irritated by the things the media focused on, such as his misplacing his helmet minutes before the start of Super Bowl XXVI and missing the first two plays of the game. "God, that stuff hurt," Thomas told *Sports Illustrated*. "To be remembered for losing my helmet in the Super Bowl? I've accomplished too much for that. People always remember the worst times."

Known as much for his mouth as for his abilities on the field, Thomas often spouted off in front of the press, however, giving them "the worst" to focus on. Combine that with a team that just couldn't win the Super Bowl, and in spite of his superior play, Thomas seemed destined to have bad raps placed upon him.

Despite the bad raps and the Super Bowl disappointments, Thurman Thomas is recognized as one of the greatest players of all time.

CONTACT INFORMATION

Email: tthomas@thurmanthomasenterprises.com.

FURTHER INFORMATION

Books

Newsmakers 1993. Issue 4. Detroit: Gale Group, 1993.
Sports Stars. Series 1-4. U•X•L, 1994-98.

Periodicals

Buffalo News (November 30, 2000).
Buffalo News February 28, 2001).
Buffalo News (November 5, 2002).
Los Angeles Times (January 18, 1991).
Los Angeles Times (October 4, 1992).
"Mistaken Identity." *Sports Illustrated* (February 1, 1993): 18.
Palm Beach Post (August 10, 2000): 1C.
San Francisco Chronicle (February 28, 2001): B8.
Seattle Times (October 5, 2000): D4.
Sporting News (October 5, 1992): 29-30.

Other

"Thurman Thomas Enterprises." Business Web site. http://www.thurmanthomasenterprises.com/aboutus.html (January 2, 2003)
"Thurman Thomas Web site." Official Web site. http://www.thurmanthomas34.com (January 2, 2003)

Sketch by Eric Lagergren

Jenny Thompson
1973-

American swimmer

With eight Olympic gold medals, the most ever awarded to an American woman, a stellar NCAA record, and world record-setting times in two events, Jenny Thompson was the most dominant American woman in swimming during the 1990s. Her career has been filled with many dramatic chapters, including medal-winning performances in relay events at three Olympic games and the failure to win an individual Olympic gold medal. In a sport dominated by young swimmers, Thompson has continued to improve her times and conquered the distractions of becoming a celebrity. Remarkably, Thompson is swimming into her thirties, having set her sights on the 2004 Olympics in Athens. She is also a medical student at Columbia University.

Thompson has said that she could swim before she could walk. It was one of several interests that her mother Margrid was determined to foster, despite the difficulties of raising four children as a single parent. When her daughter began swimming with the Seacoast Swimming Association, the family moved to Dover, New Hampshire so that Jenny could walk to practice. Margrid began a forty-mile commute back to her job in Massachusetts. In 1987 Jenny became the youngest U.S. gold medal swimmer ever at age fourteen, having won the 50-meter freestyle at the Pan American Games.

Thompson quickly earned a reputation for being strong and fast. She also became known for her competitiveness and passion for the American flag, which she wore on a bandana and other clothes. When she accepted a scholarship at Stanford University, Thompson wanted the experience to be about more than swimming and earned a degree in human biology. Many of the best American swimmers do not complete college in order to reap financial opportunities. This makes Thompson a standout in NCAA history with her nineteen individual and relay titles, and participation on four consecutive national championship teams.

Also during the early 1990s, Thompson broke a world record for the 100-meter freestyle with a time of 54.48 at the 1992 Olympic trials. At the 1992 Olympics in Barcelona, she won two gold medals: one in the 400-meter freestyle relay and one in the 400-meter medley relay. Thompson placed second to China's Zhuang Yong in the 100-meter freestyle despite swimming 54.84, amidst American suspicions that the Chinese team used steroids. Possible steroid use also colored the experience of having her 100-meter freestyle record broken by Le Jingyi of China at the 1994 World Swimming Championships. Just a month later, nine Chinese swimmers tested positive for drugs.

Jenny Thompson

Thompson broke her arm in May 1994 at a fraternity pool party, but recovered quickly after having it surgically repaired. She won two gold medals at the national championships that August and now had the 1996 Olympics in Atlanta, Georgia in sight. But when Thompson swam in the U.S. trials in Indianapolis, Indiana, she did not have the mental composure to qualify in any individual events. She agonized about performing well and suffered sleepless nights. In the process, however, she came to realize that gold medals and endorsement contracts were not why she was there. What Thompson loved was training, competing, and being part of a team.

Having been selected as a member of three U.S. relay teams, Thompson's discovery was reinforced at the 1996 Olympics. When she had to watch the 100-meter freestyle from the stands, the U.S. coach and Thompson's coach at Stanford, Richard Quick, sent her a note saying "Jenny, I love you very much. You'll always be my champion." In the 400-meter freestyle relay, Thompson swam with **Amy Van Dyken** and Angel Martino, two of her greatest rivals, to win the gold medal. Her anchor leg broke the Olympic record by .17 seconds. Thompson also was part of the victorious 800-meter freestyle relay team, which set another Olympic record, and earned a third gold medal by swimming in the preliminaries of the 400-meter medley relay.

Revitalized, Thompson won her first individual gold at a major international event in 1998, when she won the

100-meter freestyle at the World Swimming Championships. More medals came in the 100-meter butterfly, the 400-meter freestyle relay, and 400-meter medley. They combined to make her the first American to win four World Championship gold medals in one meet since **Tracy Caulkins** in 1978. At the 1999 Pan Pacific swimming championships, the swimmer set a new world record for the 100-meter butterfly with a time of 58.15, trumping a time that had been the record for eighteen years.

When Thompson entered the 2000 Olympics in Sydney, Australia, she had endorsement contracts with Speedo and the vitamin company Envion, as well as other swimming income. She proceeded to win three gold medals: the 400-meter medley relay, 400-meter freestyle relay, and 800-meter freestyle relay. Her time in the 100-meter freestyle earned her a bronze medal. She now had eight Olympic gold medals, more than any other U.S. woman.

Having long been focused on maintaining a well-rounded life, Thompson entered medical school at Columbia University in the fall of 2001. That put her in New York City on September 11, when she witnessed firsthand the terrorist attack on the World Trade Center. The experience convinced her to return to swimming in order to give something back to the sport she loves so well. She began combining the rigors of medical school with training and competing. Despite having taken more than a year off from swimming, Thompson soon proved her mettle by winning the women's 50-meter freestyle at the Pan Pacifics in August 2002. Just weeks earlier, she had been, at age 29, the oldest swimmer at the U.S. national summer championships; the youngest swimmers at the meet had not even been born when Thompson began swimming in national competitions at age twelve.

Thompson's new goal of helping other swimmers may send her to the 2004 Olympics in Athens, Greece. If she were to win yet another Olympic gold medal, it would tie her with **Mark Spitz**, **Carl Lewis**, and four other Olympic superstars. But that possibility is not what keeps Thompson in the pool. As an international champion since 1987, experience has taught her that other, equally important rewards can come from swimming. Her greatest joys have been the excitement of competing and the strong bonds with teammates, friends, and family that have been made in the process.

CONTACT INFORMATION

Address: c/o USA Swimming, U.S. Olympic Training Center, 1750 E. Boulder St., Colorado Springs, CO 80909.

FURTHER INFORMATION

Books

Great Women in Sports. Visible Ink Press, 1996.
Sports Stars. Series 5. U•X•L, 1999.

Periodicals

"Inside Olympic Sports." *Sports Illustrated* (August 30, 1999): 60.
McCallum, Jack. "Unflagging: Five-time gold medallist Jenny Thompson, 27, plans to undress her younger rivals in Sydney and become the most decorated U.S. woman Olympian ever." *Sports Illustrated* (August 14, 2000): 52.
Mulgannon, Terry. "A quick study." *Rodale's Fitness Swimmer* (January-February 1999): 24.
Nobles, Charlie. "Swimming; Thompson Attempting A Comeback." *New York Times* (August 12, 2002): D8.

"A Solitary Pursuit: It may be time for one of history's finest relay swimmers to stake her claim to individual glory." *Time* (August 7, 2000): 90.

"Thompson in Comeback." *New York Times* (August 28, 2002): D6.

Other

"For Olympic swimmer, attacks helped motivate a comeback." Associated Press File (August 29, 2002).

Stanford Cardinal Official Athletics Web Site. http://gostanford.ocsn.com/ (2003).

Sketch by Paula Pyzik Scott

Ian Thorpe

Ian Thorpe
1982-

Australian swimmer

Athletes in the men's competitive swimming arena typically reach their physical peak just after the age of twenty. Yet while only a teenager Ian Thorpe repeatedly set and broke a number of world freestyle records. His accomplishments left the sports world in awe, as he repeatedly won gold medals in international competition. The 200-, 400-, and 800-meter freestyle swims proved to be his personal domain. At age seventeen he was the youngest man on the Australian Men's Olympic team for 2000. His outstanding performance left observers to speculate that this was a mere glimpse of what he might accomplish at the Olympics in Athens in 2004.

Thorpe was born on October 13, 1982, near Sydney, in suburban Milperra. He is the second child and only son of Ken and Margaret Thorpe. His mother, a schoolteacher, placed great emphasis on the importance of proper speech, and Thorpe took her message to heart—even as a young child his articulation rivaled that of an adult, so much that Thorpe, "… Seemed more like a 21-year-old [than a child]," according to his second-grade teacher.

Thorpe's father, a gardener, was the son of a semi-professional cricket player, which some say is the de facto national sport of Australia. Although some consideration was given to steering young Ian Thorpe toward that sport, he was righteously clumsy and displayed little aptitude for the game. Ultimately he learned to swim instead.

Got His Feet Wet

Thorpe first took to the water as an eight-year-old, out of frustration from sitting on the pool deck and waiting for his sister, Christina, who was then a competitive swimmer. Eventually he jumped into the water spontaneously. A special buoyancy to Thorpe's body was evident very quickly; he had an innate feel for the water, so it seemed. Although he was hampered initially by an allergy to the chlorine in the pool, he outgrew the condition within a few years.

Swimming casually at first, at the Padstow swim club, Thorpe's talent was obvious to Doug Frost, the owner of the club and a professional coach. Frost identified Thorpe's talent and offered him a spot on the club's training squad.

Thorpe went into training at the age of nine, swimming initially less than two miles per week. He doubled his workouts at age ten, and added a third weekly session at age eleven. By age twelve, Thorpe was practicing five times weekly, and swimming between 9.5-11 miles every week. That year he began participating in the Australian junior national competition where he won an impressive nine gold medals at the championships in 1996.

After increasing his practice schedule to include daily workouts, at age thirteen Thorpe was swimming as much as eighteen miles per week. An all-A student at East Hills Boys Technology High School, in 1998 Thorpe was forced to choose between swimming and formal academics. Swimming then became the center of his life. He added intensive aerobics and endurance training to his regimen and at age fourteen increased his practice time to one session daily, adding a second daily session

Chronology

1982	Born October 13 in Milperra, New South Wales, Australia
1999	Breaks four world records at the Pan Pacific Championships in Sydney in May; sets and breaks the world 200-meter freestyle record at the same meet; records the fastest time ever in a lap of the 4x200-meter freestyle relay
2000	Breaks his own world record in the 400-meter freestyle; appears on *Friends*
2002	Hosts his own television show, *Undercover Angels*; replaces coach Doug Frost with assistant coach Tracey Menzies

Related Biography: Coach Doug Frost

Doug Frost is the owner of the Padstow Indoor Club, which he operates at his personal 25-meter indoor pool. He maintains a level three (highest) accreditation with the Australian Coaching Council and also with the Australian Swimming Federation (also level three).

In 1997 Frost joined the staff of Sutherland Aquatic Center outside of Sydney. That year he was named also to the staff of the Australian national team for the Pan Pacific Games. In 1998 he served on the national coaching staff for the World Championship Games. Frost maintains memberships on the board of the Australian Swimming Coaches and Teachers Association.

A forward-thinking, technology-driven sports professional, Frost was honored as the 1997 Australian Age Group Coach of the Year. In 2001 and 2002 he received back-to-back Coach of the Year honors.

It was at Padstow that Frost first had an opportunity to observe Thorpe in 1990. For the next twelve years he worked with Thorpe, initiating the swimmer into competition at age twelve. In 1996 Frost coached Thorpe to nine gold medals at the junior nationals. In 2002, after three Olympic gold medals and nearly a score of world records, Frost parted ways with Thorpe in what Thorpe described as an amicable split.

on a bi-weekly basis. Thorpe at that time was swimming as much as thirty miles every week. He expanded his training schedule once more, swimming as much as six hours per day and up to sixty-two miles per week. In those days he set a personal best of 4:10:66 in the 400-meter freestyle.

As Thorpe approached physical maturity, he developed a long, lanky, thick-chested frame and large thighs. This barrel-chested appearance—less broad in the shoulders and dramatically less narrow at the hips-distinguished him from his peers in men's competitive swimming. In time it became evident that his buoyant physique and instinctive flair for the fluid mechanics of the pool afforded him a competitive edge.

International Competition

Thorpe first attracted attention outside of the sports world when at age fourteen he became the youngest male ever to earn a spot on the Australian national swimming team. In 1997 he won second place at the Pan Pacific Games in Fukuoka, Japan, where he impressed the media with his quiet reserve and well-spoken ways.

Thorpe's athletic acumen improved as he matured. Barreling through the water and traveling at 3.1 meters per stroke, his talent was attributed in part to his expansive reach. At 6-feet-5-inches tall and 215 pounds, he is not only tall, but also sports unusually large feet, which at size seventeen are seven sizes larger than the average adult man. This disproportionate bigfootedness, according to some critics, is his greatest asset as an athlete. His long and flexible feet provide excellent propulsion in the water and—to Thorpe's dismay—are often compared to flippers. His kick, a six-beat stroke, works like a small propeller, which he synchronizes with his arms at a ratio of six kicks to one upper body stroke. He swims like a highly efficient machine. South African swimmer Ryk Neethling compared the volatility of Thorpe's wake to the inside of a washing machine. Said Neethling, who was quoted in Sydney's *Morning Herald,* "It can be hell out there behind him; it is so much more turbulent than normal."

With continued guidance from Frost and Don Talbot, the Australian national coach, Thorpe swam to a world championship in the men's freestyle in 1998 at age fif-

teen. He was the youngest world champion in history of that sport. The win generated public speculation about his Olympic potential for the Sydney games in 2000.

Thorpe stunned the world at the Pan Pacific Games in May 1999 in his native Sydney when at age sixteen he broke the world record in the 400-meter freestyle. Thorpe, with a time of 3:41:83, shaved very close to three full seconds from the old record. In the 200-meter freestyle that year he logged a world record time of 1:46:34 , which he personally bested at the same competition, to leave the world record at 1:46:00 by the end of the meet. In all, Thorpe set four world records in four days, including the fastest lap on record in the 4x200 freestyle relay. The Australians left with a total of thirteen gold medals and lauded Thorpe as their hero. "He could be the greatest swimmer we've ever had," Talbot was quoted by *Time*. "I have never seen anything like that," said former Olympian Randy Gaines, and Thorpe himself made no attempt to conceal his own amazement at the results of the competition.

In setting a world record at the new Olympic stadium at Sydney that year, Thorpe won a bonus prize of $16,000 for being the first to break a record in the new Olympic pool, which was built in preparation for the 2000 Olympics. Thorpe generously donated the money to cancer research and to a youth crisis prevention program. In part for his generosity, he was named Young Australian of the Year for 1999.

Australians love swimmers, and Thorpe as a sports prodigy attained near-superstar status, even before his first Olympic appearance. By the end of 1999, negotiations were underway for sponsorships and future endorsements. Banks, airlines, car manufactures, and others rushed to establish associations with Thorpe: Qantas, Adidas, Mazda, Sydney Water, and Omega, among others, joined his sponsorship team.

XXVII Olympiad

Thorpe in 2000, at age seventeen, became the youngest male ever to swim with the Australian Olympic team. At the Sydney Olympics that year, he was entered tentatively in six out of seven allowable events. Still growing and already 6-feet-4-inches tall by then, Thorpe weighed 200 pounds with an estimated body fat level of 7 percent, or 8 percent lower than the average male in his age group. In anticipation of Thorpe's Olympic performance, Dan Williams noted and reported in *Time* that Thorpe seemed to, "Move water like the moon.... [With] cartoon elasticity ... [and] the longest stroke in swimming, ... strangely beautiful and, to the competition, lethal."

In the 400-meter freestyle race that year, Thorpe broke his own world record for the second time in his career, finishing with a time of 3:40:59. He won gold medals with his team in the 4x100 and 4x200-meter freestyle relays. The 4x100-meter event, witnessed by a capacity crowd of 17,500 spectators, was an historic first-time win for the Australian team and marked the first Olympic loss ever for the United States in that event. Leigh Montville said of that race in *Sports Illustrated,* "Maybe the best [race] in history." He called Thorpe, "A jolt of high-voltage electricity that went through his sport and his country," and compared the teenager at once to Tom Sawyer and Ricky Martin. Swimmer Gary Hall Jr. of the losing U.S. team was quoted widely when he said, "I doff my swimming cap to Ian Thorpe!" Talbot meanwhile predicted that Thorpe might be the swimmer of the century.

In the only second-place finish of his Olympic experience that summer, Thorpe finished .48 seconds behind 22-year-old Pieter van don Hoogenband of the Netherlands in the 200-meter freestyle. At the final celebration, Thorpe was selected by his team to carry the Australian national flag into the Olympic closing ceremonies.

With his first Olympic competition behind him, Thorpe went on tour. Among the highlights of his travels he made a guest appearance at designer Giorgio Armani's runway show during a visit to New York and appeared on the *Jay Leno Show.* Thorpe went also to Washington D.C., where he met with then U.S. President Bill Clinton and the first family.

More World Records

At the Australian Open Championships at Hobart in 2001, Thorpe set new world records in the 200-meter and 800-meter freestyle and won national titles in the 100-meter, 200-meter, 400-meter and 800-meter freestyle. The four-race sweep had not been accomplished nationally since John Konrads accomplished the feat in 1959.

At the 2001 World Championships in Fukuoka, Thorpe claimed six medals, and set three world records. His performances sparked rumors of hall of fame glory when

---

Awards and Accomplishments

1997	Silver medal (400-meter freestyle) at the Pan Pacific Games
1998	Two gold medals at the World Championships; won four gold medals at the Commonwealth Games in Kuala Lumpur
1999, 2001-02	Named Australian Swimmer of the Year; named World Swimmer of the Year by *Swimming World*
2000	Three Olympics gold medals, and two silver; listed among *People*'s "Sexiest Men Alive: Awesome Aussies"
2001	Six gold medals at the World Championships; set three individual world records in the 200-meter, 400-meter, and 800-meter freestyles
2002	Received the American International Athlete Trophy; set a new world record in the 400-meter freestyle; won six gold medals at the Commonwealth Games in Manchester; won five gold medals at the Pan Pacific Games in Yokohama, Japan

At age 15, was the youngest male swimmer ever to win a world championship.

Thorpe has won eight gold medals, more than any athlete in the Federation Internationale de Natation Amateur.

---

he logged 1:44:06 minutes for the 200-meter freestyle, 3:40:17 in the 400-meter, and 7:39:16 in the 800-meter race. As Craig Lord wrote in *Swimming World,* "It is not so much the victory by which he is measured, but, instead, it is the margin of victory as this momentum-gaining Torpedo fires ten years ahead of his time!"

For the fourth time, in 2002 Thorpe broke his own world record in the 400-meter freestyle event, shaving .09 seconds from his 2001 record, to log a new time of 3:40:08. He added eleven gold medals to his collection that season, taking six golds at the Commonwealth Games in Manchester and an additional five at the Pan Pacific Games in Yokohama, Japan.

Amid a flurry of rumors, beginning in August of 2002, Thorpe announced plans to move to Europe, to train for the Athens Olympics in 2004. He confirmed also an amicable split from Frost, his personal coach, after a dozen years of resounding victories. Frost had brought the swimmer to seventeen world records and three Olympic gold medals during their one dozen years together as a coach-athlete team.

Thorpe announced further his intention to continue in training with Frost's assistant, Tracey Menzies, as his head coach. Menzies, who was named Rookie Coach of the Year in 2000, brought no other coaching credentials to the new job, leaving observers to question the validity of the coaching change after so much success with Frost. Australian champion Dawn Fraser, among others, expressed concern in particular over the unproven record of Menzies and suggested that Thorpe might have erred in judgment. Thorpe acknowledged the difficulty of making such a drastic decision. Regardless, he asserted a personal need for a change, citing an ebb of passion, and stated that he might retire from competitive swimming rather than continue to train with Frost. "I either had to make the change or walk away ... I was not enjoying myself," he said and was quoted on *SwimLine* on the World Wide Web.

Personal Glimpse

Truly an international hero, Thorpe speaks French fluently, and in the early 2000s was under consideration as a possible youth ambassador for the United Nations. He received the American International Athlete Trophy (formerly the **Jesse Owens** Award) in 2002.

As an honorary ambassador for tourism to Japan, he is ranked among the top three most recognized faces by the Japanese public, with his image appearing on Japanese buses and on giant video screens in bars. Too young to drink alcohol himself, Thorpe's personal interests veer toward child victims of terminal illness and other non-frivolous social causes. He is the co-founder the Ian Thorpe Foundation For Youth Trust, a program for children with life-threatening illness.

In addition to television guest appearances, Thorpe was seen as himself in a documentary, *Olympics Exposed with Andrew Denton*. A modest actor, Thorpe made a guest appearance on his favorite television show, *Friends;* the episode premiered on November 16, 2000. He is the host of his own cable television show, *Undercover Angels,* featuring Simone Kessell, Jackie O, and Katie Underwood. In keeping with Thorpe's deep sense of social consciousness, the format of the program provides a means of bringing succor to real people in need. His media manager, David Flaskas, stays busy reviewing and fielding offers for Thorpe, who after proving himself among the best swimmers in the world has yet to enter his prime.

CONTACT INFORMATION

Address: Office: Australian Swimming Inc., P.O. Box 940, Dickson, ACT 2602, Australia. Online: www.geocities.com/Colosseum/Field/8824/thorpe.html.

FURTHER INFORMATION

Periodicals

Morning Herald (Sydney, New South Wales, Australia), (August 28, 1999).
Newsweek (September 2000): 73.
Sports Illustrated (September 25, 2000): 44.
Swimming World (September 2001): 24.
Time (September 11, 2000): 76.
Time International (September 6, 1999): 54.
Time International (November 29, 1999).
Time International (September 25, 2000): 64.

Other

"How Doug Frost Prepared His Prize Pupil World Champion Ian Thorpe." www.geocities.com/dawler/prizepupil.htm (February 9, 2003).

"Late 9 News," *SwimInfo*. (September 12, 2002). www.swiminfo.com/lane9/news/4130.asp (February 9, 2003).
"Thorpe may be 'too big for his boots': Fraser." *ABC-News Online* (September 13, 2002). http://abc.net.au/news/2002/09/item20020913051326_1.htm (February 9, 2003).

Sketch by G. Cooksey

Jim Thorpe
1888-1953

American football and baseball player

Born in a cabin in Indian Territory (now Oklahoma), the Sauk (or Sac) and Fox Indian athlete Jim Thorpe began a climb to fame in 1907 as a college track-and-field and football star at Carlisle Indian Industrial School in Pennsylvania. He competed in the 1912 Olympic Games in Stockholm, Sweden, where he won gold medals in both the pentathlon and the decathlon. His medals were stripped from him, however, after a journalist reported that Thorpe had briefly played baseball for pay during the summers of 1909 and 1910, nullifying his status as an amateur athlete. Thorpe went on to a career in professional football and baseball. Widely acclaimed as the greatest all-around athlete of modern times, he had a natural gift that enabled him to excel at almost any sport he played. In addition to track, football, and baseball, Thorpe was adept at swimming, lacrosse, basketball, wrestling, golf, and tennis. His awards were many, including being named the Greatest Male Athlete of the Half-Century in 1950 and America's Athlete of the Century in 1999. His Olympic medals and titles were restored posthumously, in 1982.

Beginning on the Bright Path

James Francis Thorpe was born in a cabin in the Sauk and Fox Indian settlement of Keokuk Falls, near present-day Prague, Oklahoma, on the morning of May 28, 1888 (some sources say 1887). His father was Hiram P. Thorpe, the son of Irishman Hiram G. Thorpe and Noten-o-quah (Wind Woman) of the Sauk and Fox Thunder Clan of Chief Black Hawk. Thorpe's mother, Charlotte Vieux, was of French descent and of Potawatomi and Kickapoo Indian blood. She gave her son Jim the Indian name Wa-tho-huck, meaning "Bright Path" when she saw the path to the cabin illuminated by a ray of sunlight at dawn just after his birth.

Thorpe's father was a horse rancher and amateur athlete who taught his sons how to exercise as young boys.

He also taught them the value of fair play and good sports-manship, traits Thorpe would carry throughout his career as an athlete. Thorpe and his twin brother Charlie and their friends spent their free time fishing, trapping, playing fol-low-the-leader, and swimming. The boys also helped out with chores on the ranch. By the time Thorpe was fifteen he could catch, saddle, and ride any wild stallion.

In the spring of 1896, Charlie became ill with fever and shortly after died of pneumonia. The death of his twin left Thorpe with a deep emotional wound. His fa-ther enrolled him in the Haskell Institute, an Indian boarding school in Lawrence, Kansas, 300 miles away. There, Thorpe developed a love for football after watch-ing the varsity team practice. The team's star fullback made Thorpe a football from strips of leather stuffed with rags. Thorpe began to organize his own games and was soon good enough to play with the older boys.

When Thorpe received word that his father had been shot while hunting and was dying, the twelve-year-old walked 270 miles home, a trip that took him two weeks. By the time he arrived, his dad had recovered. However, his mother died from blood poisoning just a few months later. Thorpe returned to the ranch and attended nearby Garden Grove school for the next three years, playing baseball after school with friends.

Carlisle Indian

In 1904, Thorpe was recruited to attend the highly re-spected Carlisle Indian Industrial School in Carlisle, Pennsylvania. It was famous for its football team, the Carlisle Indians, which regularly beat the best Ivy League, military, and Big Ten college teams of the East. At 115 pounds and only 5'5 1/2" at age sixteen, Thorpe was too small to play on the varsity football team, but he won a spot on the tailor-shop team. Just as he was settling into Carlisle, however, Thorpe faced another tragedy: his father died of blood poisoning contracted while hunting.

One spring evening in 1907, the varsity track team discovered young Thorpe. It was the beginning of his track-and-field success as well as a relationship with track and football coach Glenn S. "Pop" Warner that would boost both their careers.

In the spring of 1908, Thorpe won a gold medal at the Penn Relays, with a jump of 6'1", and placed first in five events against Syracuse the following week. He went on to set a school record in the 220-yard hurdles, with a time of 26 seconds, a record he would later break by reaching his personal best time of 23.8 seconds.

By the 1908 football season, Thorpe weighed 175 pounds and was in great shape to start at left halfback. (Sources disagree about his later physical size. Some say he reached 5' 11" and 185 or 190 pounds, others say 6' 1" or 6' 2".) In what he later called the toughest football game of his life, he scored the only touchdown in a 6-6 tie against Penn State, a team loaded with all-American play-

Jim Thorpe

ers. The Indians finished the season 10-2-1, outscoring their opponents 212 to 55. Thorpe was named a third-team all-American by leading football authority Walter Camp.

By the spring track season of 1909, Thorpe was reaching his peak. He won six gold medals in one meet and dominated every other for the rest of the season. When summer came, he followed two teammates to Rocky Mount, North Carolina, to play minor-league baseball. He accepted the manager's offer of $15 a week as "meal money." At the time, this practice was common among college athletes, but most used pseudonyms in order to keep their status as amateurs. Thorpe was un-aware of the practice and used his own name. A few years later his lack of awareness would cost him dearly.

Thorpe left Carlisle and returned to Oklahoma during the fall of 1909. He worked on the family ranch, and then returned to North Carolina to play ball in the sum-mer. In Oklahoma he bumped into his former teammate and track coach, Albert Exendine, who encouraged him to come back to Carlisle. The 1911 football season, with Thorpe back on the team and in fine form, made nation-al headlines. Carlisle finished the season 11-1. Thorpe was named first-team all-American halfback, and his teammates elected him captain.

The 1912 Olympics

Thorpe's fame had followed him to the 1912 Olympics in Stockholm, Sweden, where he would com-

Chronology

1888	Born May 28 near Prague, Oklahoma; mother names him Wa-tho-huck, Sauk and Fox for "Bright Path"
1896	Twin brother, Charles, dies
1898	Is enrolled in Haskell Institute in Lawrence, Kansas
1901	Mother dies of blood poisoning
1904	Enrolls in Carlisle Indian Industrial School, Carlisle, Pennsylvania
1904	Father dies of blood poisoning
1907	Joins the Carlisle varsity track and football teams
1909-10	Takes time away from Carlisle to go back to Oklahoma; plays minor-league baseball at Rocky Mount and Fayetteville, North Carolina
1911	Reenrolls at Carlisle; is named first-team All-American by Walter Camp for season with Carlisle Indians football team
1912	Wins gold medals in the pentathlon and decathlon at Olympic Games in Stockholm, Sweden
1912	Named first-team All-American in football for second consecutive year
1913	Stripped of Olympic titles when news story breaks that he played baseball for pay in 1909-1910; gives back Olympic gold medals
1913	Leaves Carlisle and signs three-year contract with New York Giants pro baseball team
1913	Marries Carlisle sweetheart, Iva Miller; they will have a son and three daughters
1916-20	Plays halfback and serves as head coach for Canton Bulldogs pro football team, Canton, Ohio
1918	Son James, Jr., dies at age 3 after a sudden illness
1919	Leaves New York Giants baseball team after run-in with manager John McGraw
1920	American Professional Football Association is formed; Thorpe is named first president
1922-23	Organizes and plays for traveling Oorang Indians football team

1923	Marriage to Iva Miller ends
1925	Marries Freeda Kirkpatrick; they will have four sons
1926	Plays final season with Canton Bulldogs
1928	Plays token game with Chicago Cardinals on Thanksgiving Day; football career ends
1929-45	Works as laborer, movie extra, and lecturer
1932	After former fans raise money so he can attend, Thorpe takes seat next to Vice President Charles Curtis at Olympic Games in Los Angeles to a standing ovation by crowd of 105,000
1941	Marriage to Freeda Kirkpatrick ends
1945	Serves briefly in U.S. merchant marine; marries Patricia Gladys Askew
1948	Joins recreation staff of Chicago Park District and teaches track fundamentals to young people; is hired to prepare Israel's National Soccer Team for match against U.S. Olympic Soccer Team in New York
1950	Named Greatest Football Player of the Half-Century and Greatest Male Athlete of the Half-Century
1951	Movie about his life, *Jim Thorpe-All-American,* premieres in Oklahoma City and Carlisle
1953	Dies of massive heart attack on March 28 in Lomita, California; is buried in Mauch Chunk, Pennsylvania, which changes its name to Jim Thorpe
1963	Inducted as charter member of the Pro Football Hall of Fame in Canton, Ohio
1973	Amateur Athletic Union restores Thorpe's status as amateur for 1909-1912
1982-83	International Olympic Committee restores Thorpe's Olympic records and returns gold medals to his family
1999	U.S. Congress passes resolution naming Thorpe America's Athlete of the Century

pete against the best athletes of the time in both the pentathlon-introduced that year by the Swedes-and the decathlon, a grueling ten-event competition. During the pentathlon, he placed first in the running broad jump, with a leap of 23' 2.7". Although he had thrown a javelin for the first time only two months earlier, Thorpe placed fourth in this event. He finished first in the 200-meter dash, with a time of 22.9 seconds. His discus throw distance measured 116' 8.4", almost three feet ahead of the second place winner. In the 1,500-meter run, Thorpe paced himself, staying behind until the middle of the second lap, when he picked up speed. He had passed all other runners by the beginning of the fourth lap and easily finished first, with a time of 4 minutes 44.8 seconds. With a total score of 7, compared to 21 received by the second place winner, Thorpe won the gold.

Five days later, the long-anticipated decathlon began. The athletes competed in the pouring rain on the first day of the three-day event. Thorpe placed third in the 100-meter dash, second in the running broad jump, and then threw the shot put 42' 5 9/20", more than 2.5 feet further than the second place winner. On a beautiful second day, he placed first in the high jump, fourth in the 400-meter run, and first in the 110-meter hurdles with a time of 15.6 seconds, a time that would not be approached until the 1948 Olympics, when Bob Mathias completed the hurdles in 15.7 seconds. On the third day,

Thorpe placed second in discus, third in pole vault, third in the javelin throw, and then beat his pentathlon time in the 1,500-meter run, finishing in 4 minutes 40.1 seconds. He won the decathlon and the gold medal with a total of 8,412.95 points out of a possible 10,000. He finished almost 700 points ahead of Hugo Wieslander of Sweden, the silver medalist.

One of the most famous stories about Thorpe revolves around his acceptance of his second gold medal from King Gustav V of Sweden. As the king presented the medal and a bejeweled chalice as a gift, he grabbed Thorpe's hand and said, "Sir, you are the greatest athlete in the world." Thorpe answered simply, "Thanks, King."

By the time Thorpe and his fellow Olympians returned home, he was an international hero and celebrity, treated to ticker-tape parades in New York, Boston, and Philadelphia, and honored with banquets and parties. Bob Bernotas reported that the 24-year-old Indian was overwhelmed. "I heard people yelling my name, and I couldn't realize how one fellow could have so many friends," he said.

Greatest Football Season

The year 1912 brought Thorpe not only two Olympic gold medals, but it proved to be his greatest football sea-

---

Related Biography: Coach Glenn Scobey "Pop" Warner

"Pop" Warner was Carlisle's athletic director when nineteen-year-old Jim Thorpe began his career. Under Warner's guidance, Thorpe played his best years in football and won two gold medals in track at the 1912 Olympics.

The legend goes that Thorpe was watching the varsity track team practice the high jump. None could clear the bar, set at 5'9". Thorpe asked if he could try it, and the boys agreed. He cleared the bar on the first jump. Bob Bernotas, in his book *Jim Thorpe: Sac and Fox Athlete,* wrote that the next day, Warner called Thorpe into his office and said, "Do you know what you have done?" Thorpe replied, "Nothing bad, I hope." "Bad," Warner growled, "Boy, you've just broken the school record!" Warner put Thorpe on the team and assigned senior athlete Albert Exendine to train him; in time Thorpe broke all of Exendine's records.

Glenn S. Warner was born April 5, 1871, in Springville, New York. He earned a law degree from Cornell University in 1894. When Warner began playing football at Cornell, his teammates nicknamed him "Pop" because, at age 25, he was older than they were. He practiced law only briefly before beginning a lifelong career as a coach.

Warner was one of the first to use the single wingback attack and invented the double wingback formation. He is credited with developing the screen pass, reverse play, mousetrap, unbalanced line, rolling and clipping blocks, and others.

Carlisle closed in 1914, and Warner took over at the University of Pittsburgh. After nine years he joined Stanford University and became a renowned contemporary of the famed Knute Rockne, coach at Notre Dame. He went to Temple University in 1933 and then retired to Palo Alto in 1939, with a coaching record of 312 wins, 104 losses, and 32 ties in forty years. He died on September 7, 1954, at age 83.

Awards and Accomplishments

1908	Tied for first place in high jump at Penn Relays, taking home gold medal after flip of a coin
1908	Named third-team All-American by Walter Camp after first season as halfback with Carlisle Indians, who finished 10-2-1
1909	Wins six gold medals and one bronze in Lafayette-Carlisle track meet
1911	Selected first-team All-American by Camp after Carlisle Indians finish season 11-1, losing the one game by only one point
1912	Won gold medals in pentathlon and decathlon at fifth Olympiad in Stockholm, Sweden
1912	Won Amateur Athletic Union (AAU) All-Around Championship decathlon with 7,476 points, breaking old record of 7,385 points, in spite of being weakened by ptomaine poisoning and hampered by bad weather
1912	Named first-team All-American for second consecutive year after Carlisle Indians finish season 12-1-1, leading the nation in scoring, with 504 points
1920	Named first president of American Professional Football Association (APFA), which two years later was renamed National Football League (NFL)
1950	Selected by Associated Press polls as Greatest Football Player of the Half-Century and Greatest Male Athlete of the Half-Century
1951	Named to National College Football Hall of Fame
1951	Monument to Thorpe is erected in Carlisle, Pennsylvania
1953	Towns of Mauch Chunk and East Mauch Chunk, Pennsylvania, combine and are renamed Jim Thorpe, Pennsylvania
1955	NFL names its annual most valuable player award the Jim Thorpe Trophy
1958	Elected to National Indian Hall of Fame in Anadarko, Oklahoma
1961	Elected to Pennsylvania Hall of Fame
1963	Inducted as charter member of the Pro Football Hall of Fame in Canton, Ohio; life-size statue of Thorpe adorns lobby
1966	Portrait of Thorpe painted by Charles Banks Wilson unveiled in Oklahoma State Capitol; hangs alongside portraits of U.S. Senator Robert S. Kerr, Sequoyah, and Will Rogers
1973	House in which Thorpe's family lived from 1917 to 1923, in Yale, Oklahoma, opened as historic site by Oklahoma Historical Society
1975	Enshrined in National Track and Field Hall of Fame
1975	Portion of Oklahoma Highway 51 renamed Jim Thorpe Memorial Highway
1977	Named Greatest American Football Player in History in national poll conducted by *Sport Magazine*
1984	U.S. Government issues Jim Thorpe postage stamp
1996	Honored by Atlantic Committee for the Olympic Games by routing the Olympic torch relay through birthplace of Prague, Oklahoma
1996-2001	Named ABC's Wide World of Sports Athlete of the Century
1999	Named America's Athlete of the Century by a resolutions of the U.S. House of Representatives and Senate

---

son as well. He helped the Carlisle Indians to a season finish of 12-1-1. The team set a national record, scoring 504 points and allowing only 114. Thorpe scored 198 of those 504 points, setting an all-time record. Camp again named him a first-team all-American.

In a November 1912 game against the U.S. Military Academy at West Point, future five-star general and U.S. president Dwight D. Eisenhower played halfback and faced Thorpe. Bernotas wrote that Eisenhower later recalled, "On the football field there was no one like him in the world. Against us he dominated all of the action.... I personally feel no other athlete possessed his all-around abilities in games and sports."

AAU Strikes Blow

In January 1913, a reporter learned that Thorpe had played baseball for pay in North Carolina a few years earlier. By the end of the month, the story broke nationwide that Thorpe was a professional athlete and should not have been allowed to compete in the Olympics. The AAU demanded a letter from Thorpe, and he sent one, drafted with Warner's help, saying he "was not wise in the ways of the world and did not realize this was wrong." He said he only played baseball because he enjoyed it, not for the money, and that he hoped the AAU and his fans would "not be too hard in judging" him. However, the unyielding AAU erased Thorpe's records from the books and asked for his medals and awards

back. On Warner's advice, he returned them, and the AAU gave them to the second-place winners.

In spite of the disgrace, both national and international fans and the press were on his side throughout the ordeal. Their support helped him to go on with his career. Yet, the supposed misdeed haunted him for the rest of his life.

Professional Sports

In 1913, after receiving offers from six major-league baseball clubs, Thorpe left Carlisle and joined manager

Career Statistics

Yr	Team	AVG	GP	AB	R	H	HR	RBI	BB	SO	SB
1913	NYG	.143	19	35	6	5	1	2	1	9	2
1914	NYG	.194	30	31	5	6	0	2	0	4	1
1915	NYG	.231	17	52	8	12	0	1	2	16	4
1917	NYG	.193	26	57	12	11	0	4	8	10	1
	CIN	.247	77	251	29	62	4	36	6	35	11
1918	NYG	.248	58	113	15	28	1	11	4	18	3
1919	NYG	.333	2	3	0	1	0	1	0	0	0
	BSN	.327	60	156	16	51	1	25	6	30	7
TOTAL		.252	289	698	91	176	7	82	27	122	29

BSN: Boston Braves; CIN: Cincinnati Reds; NYG: New York Giants.

John McGraw's New York Giants. The easygoing Indian had trouble getting along with McGraw, and Thorpe performed better when away from the tough manager, farmed out to the minor leagues, and during a brief stint with the Cincinnati Reds. In 1919, McGraw supposedly called Thorpe a "dumb Indian" after he missed a signal and cost the team a run. Thorpe's pride got the better of him, and he went after McGraw. He was traded to the Boston Braves soon afterward for a final season in pro baseball. After leaving Boston he played minor league ball for the next nine summers, finishing his baseball career at Akron, Ohio, in 1928.

In the fall of 1915, Thorpe joined Jack Cusack's Canton (Ohio) Bulldogs pro football team. The team did so well with gate receipts that next season Cusack hired several all-American players. Thorpe stayed with the team each fall through 1920, while continuing to play pro baseball during the summers. In 1919 the Bulldogs ended the season undefeated, with an unofficial world championship.

After leaving the Bulldogs, Thorpe joined the Cleveland Tigers for one season and then became a part of the Oorang Indians, who spiced their games with Indian dances and hunting exhibitions. In 1924, at age thirty-six, he joined the Rock Island Independents and also played briefly with the New York Giants football team. He rejoined Canton in 1926 but played only a few games to please the fans. He played his final games with the Chicago Cardinals in 1928.

Thorpe excelled at every aspect of football: kicking, running, passing, and tackling. He was famous for his innovative body block, in which he rammed his big shoulder into a player's legs or upper body, often causing a fumble. He then grabbed the ball and ran for a touchdown. **Knute Rockne** often told the story about how he once tackled Thorpe, who said, "You shouldn't do that, Sonny. All these people came to watch old Jim run." The next time, Thorpe brought him down with his shoulder and ran forty yards for a touchdown before trotting back and telling him, "That's good, Sonny, you

let old Jim run." Dozens of other players told the same story over the years, with themselves as "Sonny."

Later Years

When his professional sports career came to an end, Thorpe was at a loss to find another. Living in the Los Angeles area, he emceed dance marathons and sporting events, worked as a painter and laborer, and acted bit parts in western movies. When the 1932 Olympics were to be held in Los Angeles, word got out that Thorpe lived in the city but could not afford a ticket to the games. Fans sent money so he could attend, and when he took his seat the crowd of 105,000 gave him a standing ovation.

In 1937 Thorpe became involved in a campaign to abolish the Bureau of Indian Affairs and then worked for a while as a public speaker, advocating better living conditions for American Indians.

Thorpe suffered the first of three heart attacks in 1942. In 1945 he was called to serve in the U.S. merchant marine. After World War II, Thorpe became a strong advocate of athletic programs for children. At age sixty, in exhibitions in San Francisco and New York, he kicked the football over the goal post from the fifty-yard line and punted the ball up to seventy-five yards.

The Greatest Athlete

In 1950, Associated Press polls of sportswriters and commentators elected Thorpe the Greatest Football Player of the Half-Century and the Greatest Male Athlete of the Half-Century. Thorpe was the first choice of 252 of the 391 journalists.

In 1951, a movie about his life, *Jim Thorpe-All-American,* premiered, starring Burt Lancaster. Thorpe had served as adviser on the film, showing Lancaster how to kick a football.

In 1951, Thorpe suffered a second heart attack. Although he quickly recovered from that attack, he had a third, massive, attack while eating lunch at home in Lomita, California, on March 28, 1953. He died soon af-

Jim Thorpe

Jim Thorpe-All-American

Although Thorpe sold the rights to his life story to Metro-Goldwyn-Mayer (MGM) for $1,500 in 1929, the planned movie, to be called *Red Son of Carlisle,* was never produced, as the Great Depression settled in on America. In 1949, as Thorpe's fame was undergoing a revival, Warner Brothers studios announced that it had purchased the rights to his life story from MGM and was planning to make the film. Unfortunately, Thorpe never realized any further money from the deal, because his original contract gave him no rights in the event of a resale.

The film, titled *Jim Thorpe-All-American,* premiered in August 1951, the month that Thorpe was inducted into the National College Football Hall of Fame. The film became a box-office hit. Written by Russell Birdwell and Frank Davis and directed by Michael Curtiz, the film stars, in addition to Lancaster, Charles Bickford as Pop Warner, Steve Cochran as "Peter Allendine" (a character based on Albert Exendine), and Phyllis Thaxter as "Margaret Miller" (a character based on Thorpe's first wife, Iva Miller).

The story, like most films, does not follow Thorpe's life in true detail. It portrays him as striving to be a success for his mother and taking up football to impress his girl at Carlisle. It plays down racial issues and becomes melodramatic when Thorpe struggles with a drinking problem and tries to find work in his later years. However, it ends with Warner bringing Thorpe the good news that Oklahoma will erect a monument to the great athlete.

terward. A front-page obituary in the *New York Times* called the loss of his Olympic medals a tragedy that should have long been rectified and said, "His memory should be kept for what it deserves—that of the greatest all-round athlete of our time."

After a Catholic funeral, Thorpe's body was supposed to have been buried in Oklahoma. However, his wife, Patricia, offered it to the economically struggling town of Mauch Chunk, Pennsylvania, if the town would change its name to Jim Thorpe. The people voted to do so, and to merge the neighboring town of East Mauch Chunk into the bargain. A large monument to Thorpe was erected, and his body was transferred to Pennsylvania.

Restoration of Medals

In 1973 the AAU finally restored Thorpe's amateur status for 1909-1912. In 1975 the U.S. Olympic Committee reinstated Thorpe, and in 1982, after a lengthy campaign by Thorpe's sons and daughters and many supporters, the International Committee agreed to restore Thorpe's status and return replicas of the medals.

Thorpe is considered the greatest American male athlete in history. He was named "The Legend" on the all-time NFL team; his statue graces the lobby of the Pro Football Hall of Fame in Canton, Ohio, and his portrait hangs in the Oklahoma State Capitol. The NFL's annual most valuable player award is called the Jim Thorpe Trophy. In 1996, the Atlanta Committee for the Olympic Games honored his memory by routing the Olympic torch relay through his birthplace of Prague, Oklahoma. In 1999, the U.S. House and Senate passed resolutions designating Thorpe America's Athlete of the Century.

SELECTED WRITINGS BY THORPE:

(With Thomas F. Collison) *Jim Thorpe's History of the Olympics,* Wetzel Publishing, 1932.

FURTHER INFORMATION

Books

Bernotas, Bob. *Jim Thorpe: Sac and Fox Athlete.* New York: Chelsea House, 1992.

Brown, Ralph Adams. "James Francis Thorpe." *Dictionary of American Biography, Supplement 5: 1951-1955.* American Council of Learned Societies, 1977. Reproduced in *Biography Resource Center.* Detroit: Gale Group, 2002.

Dictionary of American Biography, Supplement 5: 1951-1955. "Glenn Scobey Warner." American Council of Learned Societies, 1977. Reproduced in *Biography Resource Center.* Detroit: Gale Group, 2002.

Wheeler, Robert W. *Jim Thorpe: World's Greatest Athlete.* Norman: University of Oklahoma Press, 1979.

Periodicals

Gould, Stephen Jay. "The Athlete of the Century." *American Heritage* (October 1998): 14.

Hannigan, Dave. "Thorpe Restored to Land of Giants." *Sunday Times* (London) (September 19, 1999).

Kindred, Dave. "Jim Thorpe Wins Again." *Sporting News* (January 8, 1996): 6.

Kindred, Dave. "The Flame Burns Forever in Prague." *Sporting News* (May 27, 1996): 7.

Other

American Indians in Football. http://members.tripod. com/~johnny rogers/ (October 15, 2002).

Baseball-Reference.com. http://www.baseball-reference.com/ (October 18, 2002). "Jim Thorpe."

Canning, Whit. "Profile: Jim Thorpe, 1888-1953." *Fort Worth Star-Telegram*. National Environmental Coalition of Native Americans. http://oraibi.alphacdc.com/necona/jim_thorpe_news.html (October 15, 2002).

CMG Worldwide. http://www.cmgww.com/sports/thorpe/ (October 14, 2002).

DISCovering Biography. "Jim Thorpe." Detroit: Gale Group, 1997.

Internet Movie Database. http://us.imdb.com/ (October 14, 2002), "Jim Thorpe."

Jim Thorpe Association. http://www.jimthorpeassoc. org/ (October 15, 2002). "Biography of Jim Thorpe."

National Environmental Coalition of Native Americans. http://oraibi.alphacdc.com/necona/jim_thorpe_news. html (October 15, 2002). "Congress Designates Jim Thorpe as Athlete of the Century."

Professional Football Researchers Association. http:// www.footballresearch.com/ (October 15, 2002). "Thorpe Arrives: 1915."

Pro Football Hall of Fame. http://www.profootballhof. com/ (October 18, 2002). "Jim Thorpe."

Sketch by Ann H. Shurgin

Bill Tilden
1893-1953

American tennis player

Bill Tilden has been called the greatest men's single players of all time, a player's player whose cannon of a serve, psychological know-how, paralyzing drop shot, and canny backcourt play transformed the game of tennis. Tilden's dazzling eighteen-year career as an amateur took him to three Wimbledon titles and seven U.S. singles championships. Dominating the game from 1920

Bill Tilden

to 1926 and capturing 13 successive Davis Cup singles matches against the top players in the world, Tilden became the first celebrity tennis player, every bit as well-known as baseball's **Babe Ruth** or boxing's **Jack Dempsey**. Unlike modern players who are past their prime by their late 20s, Tilden had a career that spanned decades. After retiring from amateur tennis in 1930, he went on to participate in the fledgling professional tour, helping to establish the legitimacy of for-pay tennis. He played into his fifties, winning his last title—the Pro doubles—in 1945. In addition to his performance on the court, Tilden also penned over a dozen books, both fiction and nonfiction, on tennis, and was an aspiring actor. However, the success he found in his professional life was not duplicated in his private life. A homosexual in a time when such an orientation was kept firmly in the closet, Tilden was twice convicted of having sex with minors and died at the age of 60, penniless and alone, scrounging money from friends to buy racquets and balls to give lessons or to drive to the next professional exhibition match.

Born Into Privilege

William Tatem Tilden, Jr., was born on February 10, 1893, at the family mansion, Overleigh, in the wealthy Germantown section of Philadelphia, Pennsylvania. The home, a Tudor-like structure on McKean Street, was symbolic in two regards: it demonstrated the Tilden wealth and lineage, and its location, less than three football fields distant from the gates of the local tennis club, the Germantown Cricket Club, presaged baby William Jr.'s future field of endeavor. Bill Tilden was born into a family with deep Anglo-Saxon roots. His father's family came from Kent, England, of a long and distinguished British line whose ancestors included, among others, in-laws to the family of William the Conqueror and a Tilden who helped finance the *Mayflower*. The first Tilden came to the colonies in 1634, accompanied by seven servants. From that beginning on the American continent, the Tildens spread north to Canada, where subsequent generations established that country's largest rental car company, to New York, where one of the offspring, Samuel Tilden, lost the presidential election in 1876, and to Delaware and Maryland. Bill Tilden's father was a result of this southern line of the Tilden clan. He moved to Philadelphia in 1855 where he found work with the woolen firm of David Hey, married the boss's daughter, Selina Hey, and set about becoming partner in the wool business and a wealthy man.

Before Bill Tilden's birth in 1893, William Sr. and his wife Selina had three children in rapid succession. The family prospered and became members of the best social and athletic clubs. However, in 1884, tragedy struck. The diphtheria epidemic of that year did not distinguish between the poor and the wealthy. Within two weeks in late November and early December all three children had died of the disease, and that sad event changed Selina forever. When more children came, she would dote on them and try to protect them from every germ and danger in the world. "Bill Tilden was not to be born for another nine years," wrote Frank Deford, in a *Sports Illustrated* profile of the great tennis player. "But for these sad events of 1884, he almost surely would not have been born at all. And because of them, he was greatly affected. It is not an exaggeration to say that much of the way Bill Tilden was to be was determined years before his birth." A brother was born six years before Bill Tilden, but with the birth of this fifth child, the mother decided she would shelter him from the world. He thus was schooled at home in a mansion that included eight apartments and a large domestic staff, and was vastly spoiled. Named after his father, he bore the Jr. on his name and was called Junior or June, a name he grew to resent and ultimately changed. The father left the rearing of this last child to the mother, who decided early on that Tilden was a sickly child and had to be kept safe. He grew up at his mother's side, learning to love music as he sat by her at the piano, and learning to speak "proper" English from her, one that contained few American slang expressions.

Tilden, however, found another early outlet for his self-expression. At the age of five, while summering at the family vacation home at the Onteora Club in the Catskills, he first picked up a tennis racquet and began hitting balls against the back of the house. Tennis professionals who taught the game were a rarity at this time, but his older brother also played, and Tilden styled much of his game after him. At the age of eight he won his first singles trophy, defeating all comers at the 15-

Chronology

1893	Born February 10, in Philadelphia, Pennsylvania, to William Tatem Sr. and Selina Hey Tilden
1898	First picks up a tennis racquet, copying serve and volley style of his brother
1901	Wins first singles title in 15-and-under tournament
1908	Upon illness of his mother, is sent to live with his aunt
1910	Graduates from Germantown Academy in Philadelphia and enters the University of Pennsylvania
1911	Mother dies
1913	Coaches Germantown Academy tennis team and begins serious study of lawn tennis
1913	Wins first U.S. mixed doubles title, with Mary Kendall Browne
1915	Both father and brother die and Tilden leaves college to work as a reporter and build a tennis career
1916	Loses first U.S. singles championship
1917	Enlists in U.S. Army, serving in Pennsylvania
1918	Discharged from the army, he wins 11 of 15 singles tournaments and maintains a number two ranking
1919	Spends almost a year developing a driving backhand
1921	Publishes book of instruction, *The Art of Lawn Tennis*
1922	Top joint of right middle finger is amputated
1924	Challenges U.S. Lawn Tennis Association ban on amateur players writing about tennis
1925	Publishes *Match Play and the Spin of the Ball*, considered a classic in tennis technique
1926	Knee injury leads to his first loss in a match in six years
1928	USLTA suspends Tilden for his tennis writing
1930	Ends amateur career
1930	Signs movie contract with MGM
1930	Publishes novel, *Glory's Net,*
1931	Enters professional playing career with Tilden Tennis Tour
1934	Tours with tennis great Ellsworth Vines
1937	Tours with Fred Perry
1939	Moves from Philadelphia and his aunt's house to Los Angeles, California
1941-45	Plays benefit tournaments to support the war effort
1946	Arrested for contributing to the delinquency of a minor for sexually molesting a 14-year-old boy and sentenced to a year in prison
1948	Again convicted of contributing to the delinquency of a minor and sentenced to a second prison term
1950	Publishes *How to Play Better Tennis*, the distillation of his tennis wisdom
1950	Named greatest player of 1900-1950 by Associated Press poll
1953	Dies of a heart attack in Los Angeles
1959	Inducted posthumously into the Tennis Hall of Fame
1969	Voted greatest male player of all time by panel of international tennis journalists

and-under Boys championships at the Onteora Club. He continued his tennis playing at the Germantown Cricket Club—scene of some of his most memorable matches in later years—just steps from his home in Philadelphia. In 1908 Tilden's life was turned upside down when his mother was taken ill with a kidney disease and he was sent to live with an aunt and cousin on his mother's side in a more modest dwelling nearby. He would maintain this room for the entire time he lived in Philadelphia. Away from Overleigh, he was enrolled in the prestigious Germantown Academy, graduating in 1910.

Despite his early tennis trophy, there was little about Tilden's game as a youngster to suggest that he would be the greatest player of the century. He played on the

Awards and Accomplishments

1913	U.S. mixed doubles
1914	U.S. mixed doubles
1918	U.S. doubles; U.S. Clay Court Singles
1919	U.S. Indoor doubles
1920	Wimbledon singles; U.S. singles; U.S. Indoor singles; U.S. doubles; U.S. Indoor doubles
1921	Wimbledon singles; U.S. singles; U.S. doubles; U.S. Indoor mixed doubles
1922	U.S. singles; U.S. doubles; U.S. mixed doubles; U.S. Clay Court singles; U.S. Indoor mixed doubles
1923	U.S. singles; U.S. doubles; U.S. mixed doubles; U.S. Clay Court singles
1924	U.S. singles; U.S. Indoor mixed doubles; U.S. Clay Court singles
1925	U.S. singles; U.S. Clay Court singles
1926	U.S. Indoor doubles; U.S. Clay Court Singles
1927	Wimbledon doubles; U.S. doubles; U.S. Clay Court singles
1929	U.S. singles; U.S. Indoor doubles
1930	Wimbledon singles; French mixed doubles
1931	Pro singles
1932	Pro singles; Pro doubles
1933	Pro singles
1934	Pro singles
1935	Pro singles
1945	Pro doubles

Davis Cup: (as player) 1920-30, won 25 singles and 9 doubles.

Tilden retired as an amateur in 1930 with a career record of 907 wins, 62 losses, winning 138 of 192 tournaments.

Academy team as well as on the University of Pennsylvania team when he entered that institution in 1910, but was a star on neither. Then in 1911 his mother died and Tilden, losing this anchor, foundered for a time. He stayed in college, but was never a brilliant student in the best of times. He also continued to play tennis, winning the U.S. mixed doubles in 1913 and 1914. When his father and then his brother died in quick succession in 1915, Tilden's life utterly changed. He left the university, took a reporting job for the Philadelphia *Evening Ledger,* and determined to devote his life to his one enduring passion: tennis.

A Self-Taught Genius

Tilden, at over six feet tall, trim with long legs and wide shoulders, had the perfect tennis build. He moved quickly and gracefully, had a powerful forehand, a strong serve, and a slicing backhand. Tilden was also able to mix it up on the court, slicing and dicing, and adapting his play to that of his opponents. He was ranked for the first time in 1915, in the top 70. By the summer of 1916 he had begun playing major tournaments, accepted at Forest Hills for the U.S. singles, but losing in straight sets in his first round. He began to concentrate on the game of tennis not only on the court, but off, as well, examining the game from the standpoint of geometry and physics, figuring out angles and lines of direction. He also became a student of the psychological aspects of the game, determining that it must be part of

his strategy to get into the head of his opponent and disrupt that person's own game plan. Such studies were in part due to an unpaid position he took as tennis coach to his former alma mater, the Germantown Academy. Tilden's ranking in the amateur standings steadily rose, elevated to the top twenty by the end of 1916.

With the advent of U.S. involvement in the First World War in 1917, Tilden joined the Army Medical Corps, but was stationed in Pittsburgh, where his commanding officer, a tennis enthusiast, decreed that the young man should continue to play as many tournaments as possible. His time in the military actually saw a boost in his game as a result of this time spent playing. In 1918, out of the Army, Tilden won his first major singles title, the U.S. Clay Court, and his first major doubles at the National Doubles, but lost in the finals at Forest Hills. The following year Tilden again lost in the finals of the U.S. singles at Forest Hills, this time to Bill Johnston, who became his Davis Cup teammate and rival for much of the next decade. He decided that something radical had to be done with his game or else he would remain forever a talented player who could just not break through to number one.

In 1919 Tilden, at age 26, decided to overhaul his game, in particular his backhand. He knew that he needed more than a defensive slice, and he spent the greater part of the fall and winter of 1919 and 1920 developing a backhand drive, a flat, powerful shot that could equal his forehand. In the era before California and Florida tennis camps, he needed to find an available playing surface for the winter months, and thus took a job for an insurance company in Providence, Rhode Island, where part of his duties were tutoring the son of the local manager, thus gaining the use of that man's indoor court. He worked daily on his stroke production until he felt confident with his new backhand. By the late spring of 1920 he was ready. Chosen for the Davis Cup team as a replacement player, he sailed for England, where first he would play the tournament at Wimbledon. To the surprise of everyone there, Tilden won Wimbledon and even won over the British crowds with his showmanship on court. He was the first American to win this title in several decades and his victory in England thrust him into the first rank of Davis Cup players. He and Johnston were chosen to play both singles and doubles, beating the English and the French teams later that summer without losing a match.

Back in America, Tilden faced Johnston again in the finals at Forest Hills, a match that is generally considered to be one of the greatest in the history of that tournament. After splitting the first two sets 6-1 each, Tilden took the third at 7-5 and then Johnston stormed back to take the fourth 7-5. Tilden pulled out all the stops with his new backhand, mixing it up with both defensive slices and driving flat shots from both sides. He also confused Johnston with his serve, hitting not only his trademark cannonball, but also high kicking serves and sliders, serving up 20 aces overall. With the match even, the drama was heightened even more by the crash of an airplane just outside the grounds. The players continued the game, and Tilden won the final set 6-3, securing for him the number one position in the world, a ranking he would maintain for the next six years. He and Johnston were then chosen to lead the Davis Cup team to New Zealand where they were victorious, bringing the cup back to America for the next seven years. The Tilden era in tennis had begun.

The Tilden Age

Tilden continued his dominance in world tennis in 1921, successfully defending his Wimbledon and U.S. singles titles. At Wimbledon that year he beat a South African newcomer, Brian "Babe" Norton, in what many viewers have termed the strangest match in Wimbledon history. Exhausted from previous play and suffering from boils, Tilden had to get out of his sickbed for the Norton match. During the course of play, Tilden employed his drop shot, a stroke he had not invented but had perfected and was the first to use in major competitions. The British crowd started booing him, finding the shot unsportsmanlike. Tilden's opponent, Norton, infatuated with the great Tilden, became as angry with the crowd as Tilden did. Down two sets, it looked as though Tilden would not regain his title. But suddenly he came back, or as some observers mention, Norton began to throw points his way. Later that summer, in the U.S. singles championship, Tilden won the U.S. singles title on his home turf, at the Germantown Cricket Club where he had played as a youngster, as a new stadium was being built at Forest Hills. Tilden attracted record crowds of 12,000 people to see him demolish his opponents. In 1922, Tilden again faced Johnston in the finals of the U.S. singles. As each had won the title twice by this time, this match determined who would be able to keep the trophy permanently. Played again at Germantown in front of overflow crowds, the match became a trademark Tilden affair. Down two sets, Tilden came roaring back to with the match in the final three sets. He then took the trophy to his Auntie Hey's house on nearby Hansbury Street where he placed it in a prominent position in the living room. Shortly thereafter, Tilden was playing an exhibition match in New Jersey when he scratched the middle finger of his right hand on some chicken wire that was part of the backstop. Gangrene set in and he almost lost the entire finger. Finally amputated above the second joint, the finger was a setback for Tilden, but he adjusted his grip and in time was able to compensate for it, playing better than ever.

Tilden maintained his number one position throughout the first half of the 1920s, winning the U.S. singles titles six years in a row and leading his Davis Cup teams in an unprecedented run against worldwide challengers. It was not only his stroke production that made Tilden

Related Biography: Tennis Player Bill Johnston

Known as "Big Bill" and "Little Bill," Tilden and Johnston were the two greatest stars in American men's tennis during the 1920s. Together the terror twins were able to successively defeat the French, Australians, British, and Japanese in Davis Cup matches from 1920 to 1926, creating a seven-year stretch of American dominance in those competitions. But the two were also rivals. It has been said that it was Bill Johnston's bad luck that he was playing during the reign of Tilden, or else he would have accumulated more national championships. As it was, he was able to win the U.S. singles title twice, in 1915 and again in 1919. It was Tilden's defeat in that 1919 match that convinced "Big Bill" that he needed more firepower on his backhand side. Johnston was runner-up to the title six times; in five of those competitions he lost to Tilden—five inches taller than him—in the final.

Johnston was born in San Francisco, California, on November 2, 1894. Unlike Tilden, he developed his tennis skills and techniques on the public courts of that city. He was an aggressive player, with a gritty competitive attitude. Johnston developed an angled overhead smash that was the despair of many opponents. He was also known for his western grip and the resulting topspin forehand drive, turning such a shot into one of the most effective in tennis history. He would take the ball shoulder height and was one of the first to leap off the ground on his follow-through.

Johnston was ranked in the World Top Ten for eight straight years from 1919 until his health began to fail in 1927. In the U.S. he was in the top ten 12 times from 1913. In addition to his two U.S. singles titles, he also won Wimbledon in 1923, and won 11 of 14 Davis Cup matches in seven challenge rounds. He retired from tennis after the 1927 season, as he had never regained his health from the time he served in the Navy in World War I. Johnston died on May 1, 1946, and was inducted into the Tennis Hall of Fame in 1958.

such a strong competitor, but also his psychological read on the game. As early as 1920, while sitting in his London hotel room in preparation for that year's Wimbledon, he began putting his thoughts on technique down on paper in the book *The Art of Lawn Tennis*. Another classic title from Tilden is *Match Play and the Spin of the Ball* in which he not only describes his amazing ball spin technique, but also informs readers of the importance of impressing one's personality on the opponent. Tilden was always the first to throw his racquet down before the match to decide who would begin serving, and always the first to call out to see if the opponent was ready to begin play. With such tactics he subtly put himself in charge of play even before it had begun. A gentleman on the court, Tilden was also a master of gamesmanship.

As Tilden's reputation grew, more and more fans were attracted to the unlikely sport of lawn tennis in America, formerly thought of as a "sissy" sport. Ironically, it was Tilden, an admitted but also very private homosexual, who popularized the sport in this country. As his fame grew, his other aspirations came to the fore. Always a frustrated actor, he began to spend his family fortune on Broadway plays featuring him in the lead, one time even playing Dracula. Such shows were generally failures and a drain on his resources and time. He lived high, spending money easily, and continued to write books and articles. Such activities got him in trouble with the United States Lawn Tennis Association in 1924. His threatened resignation from the Davis Cup team in protest forced the USLTA to reconsider its new

Our Greatest Athlete

Tilden was sixty when he died and it is only about a year since he played in the professional championship, where he defeated Wayne Sabin and played a close match with Frank Kovacs. This represents a period of thirty-five years of continuous championship play in a game as strenuous as any. And at fifty-nine Tilden still was the world's finest tennis player over the short span of one set. . . .

The usual thing is to say that Tilden belonged to the so-called Golden Age of sport, the age of Bobby Jones, Jack Dempsey, Red Grange, the Four Horsemen and Babe Ruth, that he was one of the great ones. Well, there above is the evidence to support the contention that Tilden was our greatest athlete in any sport....

Great as he was as a player, it is impossible to consider Tilden outside the rich soil of his nature. He was arrogant, quarrelsome, unreasonable; very hard to get along with and all his life an unhappy man. It is not generally known that Tilden was a wealthy man and that he ran through at least two substantial family fortunes to die with ten dollars in his pocket. And he probably made more money out of tennis than even the modern plutocrats of the professional exhibition racket. Throughout his life he lived on a scale befitting an Indian Prince. Through the wonderful era of the 1920s he spent with a lavish hand....

Tilden longed beyond all else to be a great actor, and he dropped a small fortune producing plays with him as the star, plays that failed miserably. For Tilden, who was indisputably a great actor on the tennis court—who ever can forget those majestic entrances and exits at Forest Hills and Wimbledon?—was a tragic figure behind the footlights....

Tilden, unquestionably, was one of the great personalities of our time. He died alone, in poverty. But even those who defeated him on the courts could never hope to be his equal. Probably we shall never see his like again.

Source: Al Laney, *The Fireside Book of Tennis*, edited by Allison Danzig and Peter Schwed, New York: Simon & Schuster, 1972.

rules banning players from writing about the sport. More arguments ensued between Tilden and the USLTA in 1928 when he was suspended from play for his writing. The intercession of powerful political friends in the United States and in France allowed him to play Davis Cup that year, but he was barred from the Forest Hills championships.

End of an Era

Tilden continued his string of victories until the fateful year of 1926 when, in a match with the Frenchman Rene Lacoste, part of the famed French Musketeers, he injured the cartilage in his knee and lost his first Davis Cup match. Later that summer he was defeated in the quarterfinals at Forest Hills by Henri Cochet, another member of the French Musketeers who had been gunning for him for years. The following year he was determined to become number one again, but lost a heartbreaking match at the French Championships at St. Cloud to Lacoste 11-9 in the fifth set, and again lost to Cochet in a world-famous semifinal at Wimbledon after being up two sets and 5-1 in the third. The power balance had shifted to the French, and though Tilden continued to play world class tennis, he would not win another major until his 1929 victory at Forest Hills and his final 1930 win at Wimbledon. He was 37 when he

took the Wimbledon title for the third time, the second oldest man to win that title.

Tilden retired from amateur tennis in 1930, and immediately went on the new professional circuit, touring around the country with other tennis stars such as Karel Kozeluh, Vinnie Richards, Ellsworth Vines, and Fred Perry. In 1939 he finally moved from Philadelphia to Los Angeles, where he made friends with movie folk including Charlie Chaplin and Joseph Cotton, both of whom allowed Tilden to use their courts to teach. By this time he was already experiencing money problems, and was forced to give lessons and continue the relentless tour schedule just to make ends meet. During World War II he played exhibition matches to raise money for the war effort, and following the war, he was instrumental in forming the Professional Tennis Players Association.

In addition to his money problems, Tilden was increasingly losing control over his proclivity for young boys. During his pro career such an orientation had been well hidden, even though many of the players knew that he would travel with a favorite ball boy. In 1946 he was arrested on a morals charge for engaging in sexual activities with a 14-year-old, and served eight months at a minimum security prison north of Los Angeles. Out of prison, most of his friends had abandoned him. In 1948 he was again arrested, and served another ten months in prison. Thereafter, he barely scraped by, living on what he could make on his occasional lessons or on a professional tour. On June 5, 1953, preparing to leave for a tournament in Cleveland, Ohio, Bill Tilden died of a heart attack in his small Hollywood apartment.

Tilden's Legacy

Bill Tilden changed the sport of tennis forever. Not only did he revolutionize the game with his emphasis on variety of stroke production, but also with his reliance on a sort of inner tennis, in which psychology was an acknowledged on-court partner. "No man ever bestrode sports as Tilden did during [1920 to 1930]," wrote Deford in *Sports Illustrated*. "It was not just that he could not be beaten, it was as if he had invented the game." And as Bud Collins noted in *Bud Collins' Modern Encyclopedia of Tennis*, "If a player's value is measured by the dominance and influence he exercises over a sport, then William Tatem 'Big Bill' Tilden II could be considered the greatest player in the history of tennis."

If his off-court behavior was questionable, it was also pitiable. But his contributions to the game of tennis can not be discounted because of such personal indiscretions. Almost single-handedly he transformed the game of tennis from one that was considered an effete pastime, to a national obsession that filled stadiums and brought to the game an entire new generation not only of spectators, but also of players anxious to best Tilden and his records. Instrumental in transforming the elitist amateur game of tennis into the modern professional, open-era game, Tilden will be long remembered as one of the greats of the sport. As tennis writer Allison Danzig wrote in *The Fireside Book of Tennis,* Tilden "was the master of his time and for all time."

SELECTED WRITINGS BY TILDEN:

The Art of Lawn Tennis, Doran Company, 1921.
It's All in the Game, and Other Tennis Tales, Doubleday, Page and Company, 1922.
Better Tennis for the Club Player, American Sports Publishing Company, 1923.
Singles and Doubles, Doran Company, 1923.
The Common Sense of Tennis, Simon & Schuster, 1924.
The Phantom Drive, 1924.
The Pinch Quitter, 1924.
The Expert, American Sports Publishing Company, 1925.
Match Play and the Spin of the Ball, American Lawn Tennis, 1925.
Tennis for the Junior Player, the Club Player, the Expert, American Sports Publishing Company, 1926.
Me—The Handicap, 1929.
Glory's Net, Methuen, 1930.
Aces, Places and Faults, Hale, 1938.
My Story, a Champion's Memoirs, Hellman, Williams, 1948.
How to Play Better Tennis, Simon & Schuster, 1950.

FURTHER INFORMATION

Books

Baltzell, E. Digby. *Sporting Gentlemen: Men's Tennis from the Age of Honor to the Cult of the Superstar.* New York: Free Press, 1995.
Bartlett, Michael and Bob Gillen, editors. *The Tennis Book.* New York: Arbor House, 1981.
Christopher, Andre. *Top Ten Men's Tennis Players.* Hillside, NJ: Enslow, 1998.
Collins, Bud and Zander Hollander, editors. *Bud Collins' Modern Encyclopedia of Tennis.* Detroit: Gale, 1994.
Cummings, Parke. *American Tennis: The Story of a Game and Its People.* Boston: Little, Brown, 1957.
Danzig, Allison and Peter Schwed, editors. *The Fireside Book of Tennis.* New York: Simon & Schuster, 1972.
Deford, Frank. *Big Bill Tilden: The Triumph and the Tragedies.* New York: Simon & Schuster, 1976.
Flink, Steve. *The Greatest Tennis Matches of the Twentieth Century.* Danbury, CT: Rutledge Books, 1999.
Garraty, John A. and Mark C. Carnes. *American National Biography.* New York: Oxford University Press, 1999.
Phillips, Caryl, editor. *The Right Set: A Tennis Anthology.* New York: Vintage Books, 1999.
Vecchione, Joseph J. *The New York Times Book of Sports Legends.* New York: Times Books, 1991.

Periodicals

Deford, Frank. "Hero with a Tragic Flaw." *Sports Illustrated* (January 13, 1975): 51.
Deford, Frank, "Hero with a Tragic Flaw: Part 2." *Sports Illustrated* (January 20, 1975): 31.
Heldman, Julius D. "Styles of the Great, Bill Tilden." *World Tennis* (April, 1980): 12-14.
Obituary. *New York Times* (June 6, 1953).
Parrish, K. "The Champ and the Tramp." *World Tennis* (February, 1990): 96.

Other

"Bill Johnston, Class of 1958." International Tennis Hall of Fame. http://www.tennisfame.org/ (September 22, 2002).
"Bill Tilden, Class of 1959." International Tennis Hall of Fame. http://www.tennisfame.org/ (September 17, 2002).

Sketch by J. Sydney Jones

Alberto Tomba
1966-

Italian skier

For thirteen years, Alberto Tomba was the face of skiing. He was known as much for his off-the-slopes carousing and womanizing and for his outrageous comments as he was for his skiing, but his on-the-slopes prowess alone would have been enough to win him a place in skiing history. Over the course of his career he won fifty World Cup skiing events, thirty-five in slalom and fifteen in giant slalom. He also became the first skier ever to successfully defend an Olympic title, winning gold medals in slalom in two successive Winter Games, and the first to medal in three successive Olympic games. A taller, heavier, and more powerful slalomer than those who came before, Tomba revolutionized the style of slalom skiing. Instead of letting his skis come apart in the "skating step" between turns, Tomba kept them tight together, creating smoother turns. This style of slaloming has since been adopted by many current champions.

"I am the new messiah of skiing!"

Tomba blasted onto the skiing scene, going from virtual unknown to Olympic champion in only a few months. He won his first World Cup event, at Sestriere, Italy, in November of 1987, and went on to win the next four races straight. He lost his sixth race of the season, a giant slalom, after spending two days raucously celebrat-

Alberto Tomba

ing his twenty-first birthday, but after continuing the celebration for a third night he came back to win the slalom.

From the beginning, Tomba was known for his eccentricity. At the world skiing championships in 1987, where Tomba won a bronze medal in the giant slalom, he earned extra money by washing cars between races—despite the fact that his family was extremely wealthy. That eccentricity blossomed into flamboyance as Tomba began winning in the 1987-88 season. He shouted "Sono una bestia!" ("I am a beast!") as he crossed the finish line in Sestriere. In Madonna di Campiglio, where he achieved his fourth victory of the 1987-88 season, his cry was "I am the new messiah of skiing!" At the end of one race, he cheerfully autographed several female fans' bottoms. (They were wearing ski pants at the time.) "I'm considered the clown of my team because I cannot be serious for two minutes," Tomba told Bruce Newman of *Sports Illustrated* shortly before the 1988 Winter Olympics. "I'm afraid if I become more serious I will stop winning. Maybe I will learn not to say bad words in the future, but that is the best to be hoped for." Certainly, it was too much to be hoped for that Tomba might be well-behaved at the Olympic training camp in the Canadian Rockies, where he slipped ice cubes down people's shirts and launched spitballs at meals.

Tomba's reputation, for skiing prowess and for outrageous behavior, only grew at the 1988 Calgary, Alberta Olympics. Early on, he predicted that he would win the slalom and giant slalom races. He did indeed win both

of them — the giant slalom by the unheard of margin of over one second, in a sport where victory is usually decided by tenths or even hundredths of a second. In the slalom, Tomba came from behind in the second run to win, in dramatic fashion, by a mere six-hundredths of a second. In between races, Tomba flirted shamelessly with all of the female athletes, even promising German figure skater **Katerina Witt** one of his gold medals. (She passed up his offer and won one of her own.)

Tomba's 1988-89 season was not as strong as the preceding one, although he maintained his rock-star status among his Italian fans. When he returned to Madonna di Campiglio, a tiny hamlet with a year-round population of just 1,000 people, for a World Cup event in December 1988, 20,000 people came to watch him compete, creating a traffic jam that lasted for a full 24 hours. Tomba won the slalom at Madonna di Campiglio, but it was his only victory that season.

Even though he was adored by the fans, Tomba's relationship with his Italian teammates was often rocky. Starting during the run-up to the 1992 Olympics, Tomba trained separately from the rest of the Italian team, which led to some jealousy and hard feelings. While most skiers share coaches and trainers with a whole team, at one point Tomba had his own coach, physical therapist, and sports psychologist, as well as assorted other trainers and assistants. Sometimes, when various national teams were all assigned their own practice slots before a competition, the "nation" of Tomba even got its own training slot.

Slump and Comeback

After suffering a broken collarbone in 1989 and having weak seasons in 1988-89 and 1989-90, Tomba lost the 1991 World Cup in part as a result of a bizarre scandal at Lake Louise, Canada. Tomba was in Lake Louise preparing for a World Cup Super G race, when the manager of the Lake Louise ski area accused him of bad behavior, including knocking a female skier over while cutting into a lift line, and not showing proper respect to officers of the Royal Canadian Mounted Police. Tomba would not be permitted to compete in that Super G unless he publicly apologized. He refused, saying that he had already apologized to the woman whom he had bumped into, that he had done nothing else to apologize

Awards and Accomplishments

1988	Olympic gold medals in slalom and giant slalom
1988, 1992, 1994-95	World Cup champion, slalom
1988, 1991-92, 1995	World Cup champion, giant slalom
1992	Olympic gold medal in giant slalom
1995	World Cup champion, overall
1996	World Championships gold medals in slalom and giant slalom

Retired in 1998 with fifty World Cup wins (thirty-five in slalom and fifteen in giant slalom)

Where Is He Now?

Although he is now retired, Tomba has not disappeared from the spotlight. In 2000 he fulfilled a long-time aspiration of becoming an actor, starring in an Italian made-for-TV action movie called *Alex l'ariete* ("Alex the Ram"). He participates in ski events to benefit various local youth skiing programs and is an active sponsor of the United Nations Children's Fund (UNICEF). In 1996, Tomba signed a multi-year deal to be the major promoter for the Vail ski area and built a home near Vail, in Avon, Colorado. Tomba is also involved in business ventures that include selling his own fragrance, *Indecente,* and promoting a fairy-tale book written by his younger sister, Alessia.

for, and blaming the misunderstanding on language differences. The race went on without Tomba (and without an another Italian skier who refused to race in protest of the Tomba decision), and Tomba finished the season just a few points short of the World Cup title. However, a cameraman for the Tele Monte Carlo station later wrote a letter to the International Skiing Federation saying that he had witnessed the incident at Lake Louise and that Tomba really had done nothing wrong. The skiing federation then declared that Lake Louise would no longer be allowed to host World Cup events, but for Tomba, the damage was already done.

Tomba was back in full form by the time the 1992 Albertville, France Olympics rolled around. Or the Albertoville Olympics, as Tomba soon dubbed them. His most often-repeated comment came at those games, when he told reporters that he had changed his training routine in light of the fact that he was getting older: now, instead of sleeping with three women until five A.M., he would sleep with five women until three A.M. (He was kidding.) He also set a new record, becoming the first Alpine skier ever to win back-to-back Olympic gold medals in the same event when he won the giant slalom. Tomba only narrowly missed winning a second gold in slalom as well: he placed second, twenty-eight-hundredths of a second behind the Norwegian Finn Christian Jagge.

Family Ties

Tomba's relationship with his well-to-do family has always been a part of his mystique. He amazed many by calling home to Italy—collect—between giant slalom runs in the 1988 Olympics, just to chat with his father and his eleven-year-old sister, Alessia. His father, a textile magnate from Bologna, promised him a Ferrari if he won a gold medal that year, and as he celebrated his first gold at the bottom of the slope, Tomba told his father and everyone else who was watching on television that he wanted the car to be red.

This and other incidents prompted some, in the early years of Tomba's career, to wonder if Tomba was skiing because he enjoyed it or because it was what his father wanted him to do. Certainly Tomba's father, Franco, did

encourage his two sons, Tomba and his older brother Marco, to ski. Although the family lived near Bologna, in a flat part of the country, Franco would drive Marco and Alberto from their sixteenth century villa an hour up into the Apennine Mountains to watch skiing races in the winter. Then the elder Tomba would turn around, go to work for the day, and come back and pick the boys up at night. On their holidays, the whole family would head for the mountains and hit the slopes. Tomba first strapped on skis at age three, and he started racing at seven. At first, it looked as if Marco would be a better skier than Tomba, but this only motivated Tomba to try harder to prove to his father that he could be a champion, too. Alberto succeeded, and today, Marco is preparing to take over the family's clothing business.

In some ways Tomba's love for his family may have held him back. At an early age, he promised his mother that he would avoid the more dangerous downhill races. He kept this promise, even though it probably cost him the World Cup in some years: it is extremely difficult to accumulate enough points to win the World Cup when one is not skiing in all of the events. Tomba did ski in the Super G for a time, but he avoided that event, too, after breaking his collarbone when he fell in a Super G race in France in 1989.

Still Going Strong

After a disappointing performance in the 1994 Lillehammer Olympics—no golds, and only one silver—Tomba had another phenomenal season in 1994-95. For over a year, starting on January 16, 1994, he was undefeated in slalom events. As in his early years, some of his victories were so lopsided as to be almost comical. He won one slalom race, early in 1995, by nearly two full seconds. There was more distance between Tomba and the runner-up than there was between the runner-up and the thirteenth-place finisher. In another race, on December 22, 1994, Tomba slid to a halt midway down the course, realigned himself, finished the course, and still won. This season, for the first time in his career, Tomba won the overall World Cup title, as well as the slalom and giant slalom titles.

Some in the media noted a mellowing of Tomba, at least in his personal life, in the 1994-95 season. At the

Alberto Tomba

bottom of the hill in Kranjska Gora, Slovenia, in January of 1995, instead of making an outrageous self-congratulatory remark of the type he was known for when he was twenty-one, Tomba instead dedicated his win in the giant slalom that day to the victims of the war going on in Bosnia, a few hundred miles to the southeast. Reportedly, he became less of a womanizer as well, and started looking more seriously for someone to settle down with. He was engaged to a former Miss Italy for a time, although they broke up after a semi-nude photograph of her was run in a magazine.

To Retire or Not to Retire?

In the spring of 1996, Tomba announced that he was taking a three-month break from skiing and considering retiring permanently. After winning the overall World Cup title in 1995 and two gold medals at the World Championships in February of 1996 (Tomba's first golds at that event), there was nothing left for him to win. However, the biggest incentive to retire was the pressure that Tomba felt from constantly being in the media spotlight. "It's not enough just to race," Tomba said in 1996, according to *Outdoor Online*. "Alberto must win every day. If I come in second, they say Alberto lost. In Italy they want to know about me every minute. . . . If I kiss a friend on the cheek, the papers

say, 'Alberto's new girlfriend.' Then she has to hide. And her family, too. In Italy, they love me too much. They want to kill me. Now Alberto is tired. More than tired." Tomba was occasionally accused of assaulting photographers who violated his privacy, including throwing a trophy at one photographer, who had sold nude photographs of him. The photographer sued, claiming that he suffered a hand injury in the incident, and Tomba paid a fine to settle the suit. In 1996, Tomba was accused of karate-kicking another photographer, who was trying to photograph him outside of a party in Florence.

Not all of Tomba's run-ins with the law stemmed from the paparazzi. In 1998 he and his father were indicted for allegedly failing to pay taxes on 23 billion lire (about $12 million) that Tomba earned from sponsorships between 1990 and 1996. Tomba was eventually cleared, but in 2002 his father was convicted and sentenced to sixteen months in prison. Over the years, Tomba was also accused of abusing the police badge and flashing lights that came with his (mostly ceremonial) position with the Italian national police force, the Carabinieri.

Tomba did decide to come back to skiing. He had a weak 1997 season, but seemed poised to make a comeback in 1998. Unfortunately, the 1998 Nagano Olympics were not good to Tomba. He injured his back and groin in a fall during the giant slalom, and two days later, after coming in seventeenth place in the first run of the slalom, he withdrew from the event and did not make a second run. Speculation was rampant that this was the end for Tomba, but he came back at the end of the 1998 World Cup season, achieving his fiftieth career victory in the last race of the World Cup finals that year. In October of 1998 he announced his retirement with a simple one-line statement: "I reflected a lot before deciding, but I leave skiing with much affection for all of those who in these many years followed me and incited me to victory."

Skiing after Tomba

"The ultimate anomaly in a sport filled with sinewy, dour hermits from Switzerland, Austria and Scandinavia who grew up tending cows and learning to ski out of necessity, Tomba was a lowlander, a rich kid and an urban dude—in truth, the first big-city guy ever to win Olympic skiing gold," Curry Kirkpatrick wrote in *Sports Illustrated* in 1992. With his rock-star status, he brought scores of people who might not otherwise have been skiing fans to the sport, and with his flamboyant lifestyle and his dominance in the slalom and giant slalom, Tomba is sure to be remembered for years to come.

FURTHER INFORMATION

Periodicals

Brennan, Christine. "Tomba True to Word: Gets Gold in Giant Slalom." *Washington Post* (February 26, 1988): G1.

Bronikowski, Lynn. "Playboy's Tour of Duty: Promote Vail." *Rocky Mountain News* (Denver, CO) (May 12, 1996): 2B.

"Bronze Medal Helps to Salvage Tomba's Pride." *Times* (London, England) (February 17, 1997): 24.

Cassert, Raf. "Muted Farewell for La Bomba." *Independent Sunday* (London, England) (February 22, 1998): 16.

Chadband, Ian. "La Bomba Goes for Last Descent." *Sunday Times* (London, England) (December 15, 1996): 15.

Clarey, Christopher. "For a Struggling Tomba, an Uncertain Bronze." *International Herald Tribune* (February 17, 1997): 20.

Clarey, Christopher. "Irrepressible Tomba, Having Won It All, Hangs Up His Skis." *International Herald Tribune* (October 5, 1998): 24.

"Coy Tomba Spins a Web of Intrigue." *Buffalo News* (Buffalo, NY) (February 18, 1998): C4.

Dufresne, Chris. "Quake Makes Presence Known on Slopes; Tomba Doesn't." *Los Angeles Times* (February 21, 1998).

Dufresne, Chris. "Tomba, Old Man of the Mountain, Is Ready to Take on the Youngsters." *Los Angeles Times* (February 17, 1998): 1.

Farber, Michael. "Back in Style." *Sports Illustrated* (January 16, 1995): 34-37.

Grudowski, Mike, and Kvinta, Paul. "Alberto: A Life." *Outside Magazine* (December, 1998).

Holford, Nicky. "Bomba Proof: Italy Will Always Come First for Alberto 'la Bomba' Tomba." *Guardian* (London, England) (December 4, 1999): 13.

"Italian Ski Lift." *Financial Times* (March 22, 1996): 19.

Johnson, William Oscar. "The Alberto-ville Games." *Sports Illustrated* (March 2, 1992): 22-25.

Johnson, William Oscar. "It Turned out Schuss Fine." *Sports Illustrated* (February 1, 1988): 16-19.

Johnson, William Oscar. "Master of the Mountain." *Sports Illustrated* (March 7, 1988): 46-49.

"Kaelin Gets Even with Tomba." *Star-Ledger* (Newark, NJ) (March 10, 1996): 22.

Kirkpatrick, Curry. "La Bomba." *Sports Illustrated* (February 3, 1992): 52-60.

Kiszla, Mark. "Sated Tomba Seeks New Hills to Conquer." *Denver Post* (March 14, 1997): C-02.

Loverro, Thom. "Make Way for Italy's Minister of Fun." *Washington Times* (February 13, 1998): 8.

Meyer, John. "Vail Puts Tomba in the Saddle: Skiing Star Signs Deal to Promote Resorts." *Rocky Mountain News* (Denver, CO) (February 22, 1996): 1B.

Newman, Bruce. "La Bomba's a Real Blast." *Sports Illustrated* (January 25, 1988): 30-33.

O'Hagan, Simon. "Weaver of a Golden Legend: Close-Up: Alberto Tomba." *Independent Sunday* (London, England) (February 25, 1996): 22.

Paige, Woody. "Tomba and I, Just Out Being Playboys." *Denver Post* (February 13, 1998): D-06.

Skow, John. "Champagne Runs." *Time* (March 7, 1988): 67-68.

Starcevic. "Amiez Edges Past Tomba for World Cup Slalom Title." *Rocky Mountain News* (Denver, CO) (March 11, 1996): 15B.

Thomas, Pete. "Entertainment Mogul: Retirement Has Hardly Slowed Alberto Tomba, the Flamboyant Fun-Loving Former Olympic and World Skiing Champion." *Los Angeles Times* (January 26, 2001): D-10.

"Tomba Accused of Assault." *Independent* (London, England) (March 20, 1996): 23.

"Tomba Cleared." *Times* (London, England) (February 1, 2002): 6.

"Tomba Flashes His Olympic Form." *Rocky Mountain News* (Denver, CO) (January 9, 1998): 16C.

"Tomba Is Gracious in Losing Slalom Crown." *Seattle Times* (March 11, 1996): C8.

"Tomba Is Indicted." *International Herald Tribune* (November 27, 1998): 22.

"Tomba Joins Rush to Laud Maier's Show." *Independent* (London, England) (February 20, 1998): 27.

"Tomba May Go Out a Winner After All." *Rocky Mountain News* (Denver, CO) (March 16, 1998): 18C.

"Tomba Out of Slalom." *Tampa Tribune* (February 21, 1998): 10.

"Tomba Straps on His Racing Skis for One Final Slalom Exhibition." *Seattle Post-Intelligencer* (December 31, 1998): E6.

"Tomba Swoops on Second Title." *Independent* (London, England) (February 26, 1996): S16.

"Vail Gets Lift from Tomba: Italian Racer to Help Colo. Resort Lure Foreign Skiers." *Denver Post* (February 22, 1996): C-01.

"Vail Lands Tomba as Ski Ambassador." *Seattle Times* (February 25, 1996): D2.

Wade, Stephen. "Blazing Second Run Takes Tomba to His Second Alpine Gold Medal." *Rocky Mountain News* (Denver, CO) (February 26, 1996): 16B.

Zgoda, Jerry. "Tomba Still Draws a Crowd." *Star Tribune* (Minneapolis, MN) (February 6, 2001): 13C.

Other

"Alberto Tomba." Laureus World Sports Awards. http://www.worldsport.com/academy/members/tomba.php (October 11, 2002).

"Alberto Tomba." Ski World Cup. http://www.skiworldcup.org/load/champions/men/tomba/01.html (October 11, 2002).

Alberto Tomba Official Web site. www.albertotomba.it (October 22, 2002).

"Alberto Tomba Profile." CNN/SI. http://sportsillustrated.cnn.com/skiing/news/1998/10/03/tomba_profile/ (October 11, 2002).

"Athlete of the Day: Alberto Tomba." CNN/SI. http://sportsillustrated.cnn.com/olympics/events/1998/nagano/athlete_of_day/tomba.html (October 11, 2002).

Hornblower, Margot. "Viva la Bomba!." Time.com. http://www.time.com/time/daily/newsfiles/olympics/winter92/tomba.html (October 11, 2002).

"Man of the Week: Alberto Tomba." AskMen.com. http://www.askmen.com/men/sports/31_alberto_tomba.html (October 11, 2002).

"Olympian Skier Alberto Tomba—Community & Chat." CBS Sportsline. http://cbs.sportsline.com/u/chat/1999/CBSsports/tomba030599.htm (October 11, 2002).

"Olympic Athlete Bios: Skier Alberto Tomba." The Mountain Zone. http://classic.mountainzone.com/olympics/nagano/tomba.html (October 11, 2002).

"That's Enough: Alpine Skiing Legend Tomba Calls It Quits." CNN/SI. http://sportsillustrated.cnn.com/skiing/news/1998/10/03/tomba_retires/ (October 3, 1998).

"Tomba la Bomba!." International Olympic Committee. http://www.olympic.org/uk/passion/museum/events/past/event_tomba_uk.asp (October 11, 2002).

"Tomba's Troubles: Skiing Legend Indicted on Tax Charges." CNN/SI. http://sportsillustrated.cnn.com/skiing/news/1998/11/26/tomba_taxcharges/ (November 26, 1998).

Sketch by Julia Bauder

Joe Torre
1940-

American baseball manager

Best known today as the manager of the New York Yankees, Joe Torre began his career in major league baseball as a player. Torre was 20 years old when he was signed with the Milwaukee Braves in 1960, and he remained a professional baseball player until 1977. In 1977, Torre began a new career as a manager of baseball teams, starting out as manager of the New York Mets, moving on to the Atlanta Braves, and then the St. Louis Cardinals, and finally to the New York Yankees. Torre's numerous honors include playing on All-Star teams in 1963-1967, and again in 1970-1973. In 1971, he led the National League in runs batted in (RBIs) and in batting average. Also in 1971, he was named Most Valuable Player. He has received recognition as an outstanding manager as well, in 1982 and 1998 earning distinction as Manager of the Year.

Following in His Brothers' Footsteps

Joe Torre was born in Brooklyn, NY on July 18, 1940. He was the youngest of two girls and three boys born to a New York City police department detective and his wife Margaret. Torre's older brothers, Rocco and Frank became professional baseball players before Torre did, although Rocco's baseball career was cut short when he joined the Navy. Frank Torre became a major league baseball player in 1956. Torre himself began his pro baseball career at the age of 20 as a player for the Milwaukee Braves in 1960. For this one season, Torre and his older brother Frank played on the same team.

Torre's career got off to a great start; on his very first time at bat, he hit a single. The following season, he was named the number two rookie of the year, second only to Billy Williams. By 1963, Torre was playing as both catcher and at first base, and that year was named to the All-Star Team—a distinction that would be repeated for the next four seasons. In 1964, Torre was the leading fielder among National League catchers, and in 1965, he won the catchers Golden Glove award. Also, in that year's All-Star Game, he hit a two-run homer that assured the National League's victory over the American League in a score of 6-5.

In 1966, Torre went with the Braves when they moved to Atlanta. That year was one of his best; he hit 36 home runs, a feat he would never repeat. His batting average that year was .315, and he batted in 101 runs. Torre's pace was slowed in 1968 when he broke a broken cheekbone. He moved to the St. Louis Cardinals in 1969 when he was traded for Orlando Cepeda. His first position with the Cardinals was at first base, and he again became a catcher in 1970, but moved to third base

Joe Torre

that same season. He again hit his stride in 1971. In that year, he led the National League in batting and was named the league's Most Valuable Player.

From Player to Manager

Torre was traded to the team that was to be the last of his playing career in 1974, the New York Mets. He welcomed this chance to play for his hometown, New York City. He traded his career as player for a managing career in 1977. That year he retired as a player and became the Mets' manager, replacing outgoing manager Joe Frazier. Torre managed the Mets until 1984. In his final year as manager of the Mets, his team lost about as many games as they won, and this led to Torre's dismissal. He stayed in the game, however, becoming a television broadcaster for the California Angels, a position he held for close to six seasons.

In 1990, Torre returned to managing, this time working for another of his old teams, the St. Louis Cardinals. The Cardinals performed well under Torre, in 1991 becoming the second-ranked team in the National League. The year 1994, however was not as good a year for the Cardinals, and Torre was replaced as manager by Mike Jorgensen.

Leading the Yankees to Victory

The American League's New York Yankees hired Torre the following year to manage their club, and his first year there saw the Yankees' triumph over the At-

lanta Braves for their first World Series win since 1978. Torre never lost his touch with the Yankees, in 1998 leading his team to an American League record number of wins, 114. Also in 1998, Torre was named American League Manager of the Year.

Torre's success with the Yankees during this time was tempered by the death of his brother Rocco, who died of a heart attack in June 1996. Torre himself had a scare when, in March 1999, he was found in a routine exam to have prostate cancer. He left the team to undergo treatment, which included surgery. Treatment was successful, and he returned to managing the Yankees in May 1999. By 2001, the Yankees had won five World Series under Torre—in 1996 (the first since 1978), 1998, 1999, 2000, and 2001.

Many observers credit Torre's rock-steady demeanor in part for the Yankees' phenomenal success with Torre as manager. As catcher Joe Girardi told the *Denver Post*'s John Henderson, of Torre, "He has a calming effect.... He never panics. You can see it on the bench. He never panics when we're going through rough times. And he never gets too high."

Torre gives his players more credit than himself for their success. His job, as he sees it, is largely to stay out of their way and let them do their jobs. As he told Henderson in the *Denver Post,* "I know as a player, I wanted the manager to give me the benefit of the doubt that I

Career Statistics

Yr	Team	AVG	GP	AB	R	H	HR	RBI	BB	SO	SB
1960	MIL	.500	2	2	0	1	0	0	0	1	0
1961	MIL	.278	113	406	40	113	10	42	28	60	3
1962	MIL	.282	80	220	3	62	5	26	24	24	1
1963	MIL	.293	142	501	57	147	14	71	42	79	1
1964	MIL	.321	154	601	87	193	20	109	36	67	2
1965	MIL	.291	148	523	68	152	27	80	61	79	0
1966	ATL	.315	148	546	83	172	36	101	60	61	0
1967	ATL	.277	135	477	67	132	20	68	49	75	2
1968	ATL	.271	115	424	45	115	10	55	34	72	1
1969	STL	.289	159	602	72	174	18	101	66	85	0
1970	STL	.325	161	624	89	203	21	100	70	91	2
1971	STL	.363	161	634	97	230	24	137	63	70	4
1972	STL	.289	149	544	71	157	11	81	54	64	3
1973	STL	.287	141	519	67	149	13	69	65	78	2
1974	STL	.282	147	529	59	149	11	70	69	88	1
1975	NYM	.247	114	361	33	89	6	35	35	55	0
1976	NYM	.306	114	310	36	95	5	31	21	35	1
1977	NYM	.176	26	51	2	9	1	9	2	10	0

ATL: Atlanta Braves; MIL: Milwaukee Braves; NYM: New York Mets; STL: St. Louis Cardinals.

knew how to play the game." And, "What I try to do…is insulate them from distractions and have them concentrate on playing the game."

To the title of manager, Torre has added the title of motivational speaker; in the off-season, he coaches executives on how to successfully manage their teams of employees. As a speaker, he commands fees of $50,000 to $75,000 per appearance.

SELECTED WRITINGS BY TORRE:

Chasing the Dream: My Lifelong Journey to the World Series. New York: Bantam, 1997.

Joe Torre's Ground Rules for Winners: 12 Keys to Managing Team Players, Tough Bosses, Setbacks, and Success. New York: Hyperion, 1999.

FURTHER INFORMATION

Periodicals

Henderson, John. "Serenity Now Joe Torre Doesn't Have to Burn with Fire to Manage the Most Fiery Franchise in Baseball." *Denver Post* (May 29, 1998): D1.

Kennedy, Randy. "Torre Far From Sandlot but Close to Home." *New York Times* (October 19, 1996): 1.

Other

"Frank Torre." BaseballLibrary.com. http://www.pubdim.net/baseballlibrary/ballplayers/T/Torre_Frank.stm (November 22, 2002).

"Frank Torre: 'I Didn't Pull a Pettitte." CANOE. http://www.canoe.ca/96WorldSeries/oct28_front.html (November 25, 2002).

"Frank Torre Statistics." Baseball-Reference.com. http://www.baseball-reference.com/t/torrefr01.shtml (November 25, 2002).

"Joe Torre." BaseballLibrary.com. http://www.pubdim.net/baseballlibrary/ballplayers/T/Torre_Joe.stm (November 13, 2002).

"Joe Torre." Leading Authorities. http://www.leadingauthorities.com/search/biography.htm?s=4203. (November 13, 2002).

"Joe Torre." RLR Associates Ltd. http://www.rlrassociates.net/clients/torre.html (November 13, 2002).

" Joe Torre Statistics." *Baseball Almanac*. http://www.baseball-almanac.com/players/player.php?p=torrejo01 (November 13, 2002).

"Joe Torre Statistics." Baseball-reference.com. http://www.baseball-reference.com/t/torrejo01.shtml (November 13, 2002).

Sketch by Michael Belfiore

Gwen Torrence
1965-

American track and field athlete

In 1995, sprinter Gwen Torrence was ranked No. 1 in the 100 meters and the 200 meters by *Track and Field*

Gwen Torrence

Chronology

1965	Born in Atlanta, Georgia
1980-83	State champion in 100 meters and High School All-American
1983-87	Attends University of Georgia
1984	Qualifies for Olympic trials, but decides not to compete
1988	Competes in Seoul Olympics
1992	Competes in Barcelona Olympics
1995-96	Widely considered the fastest woman in the world
1996	Competes in Atlanta Olympics
1997	Retires from competition to become a hair stylist and raise her children

News; the magazine also named her the top American athlete overall. She has won numerous championships, and at the 1992 Olympics, won gold medals in the 200 meters and 4 x 100 meter relay, as well as a silver medal in the 4 x 100 meter relay. At the 1996 Olympics, she won bronze in the 100 meters and gold in the 4 x 100 meter relay.

"Shoooosh, She Was Gone"

Torrence was the youngest of five children in a working-class family; because she was seven years younger than the next-oldest sibling, she received a lot of attention from her older brothers and sisters. Torrence's mother, Dorothy, told Rick Reilly in *Sports Illustrated* that Torrence was born with her umbilical cord wrapped around her neck, and that at birth, "she had a strange look in her eye that I never saw in any of my children." Torrence was walking at eight months, and began running when she was three years old. "You'd set her down," her mother told Reilly, "and shoooosh, she was gone."

When Torrence was an infant, her family lived in a housing project in Atlanta; the project was so filled with crime, drugs, and danger that locals called it "Vietnam." By the time Torrance began school, however, they had moved to a better neighborhood in the Atlanta suburb of Decatur, where Torrence attended Columbia High School. A tough child, she was known for beating up anyone who challenged her or hassled her. Paradoxical-

ly, she was also known for her sense of fashion, and was voted best dressed girl in the school by her peers.

Torrence's running ability and hot temper combined one day when a fellow student, Fred Lane, teased her by taking her purse and running off with it. Torrence, who was wearing pumps, tight jeans, and a short jacket, took off after him and caught him after a 70-yard spring, snatching her purse out of his hands. Lane later went on to become a football player at Georgia.

Physical education teacher and coach Ray Bonner saw the chase and was astounded that a girl could run down an athlete like Lane. Bonner told Reilly, "We thought Fred Lane was the fastest thing since sliced bread, and she walked him down!" However, he had to convince her to give running a try. She planned to become a hairdresser and had no interest in sports. And she did not want to wear running shoes or athletic shorts, because she felt too conspicuous and ugly in them; she was embarrassed because she thought her legs were too thin.

Bonner let her wear whatever she wanted to wear as long as she ran, and during one gym class in tenth grade, Torrance set an unofficial record in the 200-yard dash. She was wearing patent-leather pumps. After this, Bonner insisted that she wear the proper clothes and shoes to run in; according to *Great Women in Sports,* he told her that God would be angry with her if she wasted her natural talent.

Torrence went on to become a high school All-American and three-time state champion in the 100 meters and 200 meters. At the 1983 TAC Junior Olympics during her senior year, she won gold medals in both these events. Torrence received an athletic scholarship to the University of Georgia and began her studies there in 1983. She began by taking remedial classes. After four quarters in that program, she moved into the mainstream curriculum, and eventually made the dean's list.

In 1984, Torrence qualified for the U.S. Olympic trials, but she did not believe she was good enough to make the team, so she did not go to the trials at all. In 1986, Torrence beat 1984 Olympic gold medalist **Evelyn Ashford** in the 55-meter dash at the Millrose Games. She won with a time of 6.57 seconds, a Millrose Games

Awards and Accomplishments

1986	Gold medal, 55-meter dash, Millrose Games
1987	Gold medals, 55, 100, and 200 meters, NCAA Championships
1987	Gold medals, 100 and 200 meters, World University Games
1991	Silver medals, 100 and 200 meters, World Championships
1992	Gold medals, 200 meters and 4 x 100 meter relay; silver medal, 4 x 400 meter relay, Olympic Games
1995	Gold medal, 100 and 200 meters, U.S. Outdoor Championships; gold medal, 100 meters, World Championships
1995	Top Athlete Overall
1996	Gold medal, 4 x 100 meter relay, and bronze medal, 100 meters, Olympic Games
2002	Inducted into Track and Field Hall of Fame

Where Is She Now?

Torrence quit competing after the 1997 season. She now lives in Lithonia, Georgia, where she is finally living her long-held dream of working as a hair stylist and raising her two children, Manley Jr. and E'mon.

record. In 1987, she won NCAA championships in the 55 meters, 100 meters, and 200 meters, and won gold medals in the 100 meters and 200 meters at the World University Games in Zagreb, Yugoslavia.

Competes in Olympics

In 1988, Torrence went to the Olympic Games is Seoul, Korea. She came in fifth in the 100-meter finals and sixth in the 200-meter finals. In 1989, Torrence became pregnant; the pregnancy was difficult, and she was confined to bed for three months. Because of this enforced rest, she lost a great deal of her strength and conditioning. Her son, Manley Waller, Jr., was born late in 1989, and she realized that she had to regain her ability to run.

In 1990, Torrence did not win races, but she kept training, and in 1991, she came in second in the 100 meters and the 200 meters at the world championships. The first-place winner, German runner Katrin Krabbe tested positive for an illegal performance-enhancing drug, but because of a technicality, her medals were not given to Torrence.

Torrence went to the 1992 Olympics, and came in fourth in the 100-meter sprint final. According to *Great Women in Sports,* Torrence said that she believed some of the other runners had taken performance-enhancing drugs. She didn't accuse anyone by name, but other runners were offended, and in the press, some writers commented that Torrence was simply suffering from a case of "sour grapes" because others had beaten her. Torrence eventually had to make a public apology. Perhaps fueled by anger over this incident, Torrence then won the gold medal in the 200 meters, won another gold in the 4 x 100 relay, and won silver in the 4 x 400 relay.

In 1995, Torrence injured her right hamstring and knee, but continued to train, and won gold medals in the 100 meter and 200 meter at the U.S. outdoor championships. She also won gold in the 100 meters at the world championships. Although she also came in first in the 200 meters, she was disqualified because she stepped on a lane marker.

Fastest Woman in the World

By 1996, Torrence was considered the fastest woman in the world, but she was resistant to the fame that came along with the title. She told Reilly, "I don't want to be the person society wants me to be. I don't want to be a celebrity, I know that. I don't want to be a star, walking on eggshells, afraid to do this, afraid to do that, with people who don't even know me automatically making me a role model for their kids. I don't want the pressure of being a perfect person." In truth, Torrence would rather have spent her time shopping, eating fast food at the mall, watching daytime television, and raising her son.

Over the course of her career, Torrence had become known for her outspokenness; she was not a people-pleaser, and admitted to Karen Springer in *Newsweek* that she was often "frosty" to other athletes, fans, or even her husband. Although she occasionally wished she had the same gracious personality as famed track athlete **Jackie Joyner-Kersee**, "I don't," she told Springer. And her husband, Manley Waller, added, "She don't put on no phony act."

Torrence looked forward to the 1996 Olympics, held in her hometown of Atlanta. According to *Great Women in Sports,* she told a *Track and Field* reporter that the Games being held in Atlanta was "a gift from God. He didn't like what happened to me in '92, so he's trying to make up for that by bringing the Games here." At the 1996 Olympics, Torrence won a gold medal as a member of the 4 x 100 meter relay, and won a bronze medal in the 100 meters. In 2002, Torrence was inducted into the Track and Field Hall of Fame.

"Track is OK, But It's Not My Life"

Torrence told Springer that after the Games she was looking forward to simply raising her son, eating fast food, and relaxing. She had never been fully committed to her track career, and ran simply because she had the talent and the ability to do so; she was never as driven or as consumed by her sport as some other athletes. She told Springer, "Track is OK, but it's not my life. Many days I think, 'What am I doing, a 30-year-old woman out here?'"

FURTHER INFORMATION

Books

"Gwen Torrence," *Great Women in Sports,* Visible Ink Press, 1996.

Periodicals

Bloom, Marc, "The World's Fastest Mom," *Runner's World,* (May, 1996): 42.

Reilly, Rick, "She Stands Alone," *Sports Illustrated,* (June 10, 1996): 92.

Springer, Karen, "She Can Run with the Wolves. And Bite, Too," *Newsweek,* (June 10, 1996): 76.

Other

USA Track and Field Hall of Fame, www.usatf.org/ (January 27, 2003).

Sketch by Kelly Winters

Jayne Torvill and Christopher Dean

British ice dancers

Jayne Torvill and Christopher Dean

For followers of sport, the insinuating rhythm of Maurice Ravel's instrumental composition "Bolero" may forever evoke images of the swirling figures of the ice-dancing pair who electrified the 1984 Olympic winter games in Sarajevo, in the former Yugoslavia. Great Britain's Jayne Torvill and Christopher Dean are perhaps best remembered as the "Bolero"-skating gold medalists, but in fact the pair have numerous amateur and professional championships to their credit. Following their Olympic gold (and subsequent, controversial 1994 bronze), the two have kept busy in their sport, both as performers and as choreographers.

Sport Or Art?

Ice dancing is a complex endeavor. "Less gymnastic and acrobatic than pairs skating, ice dancing, which bears more than a passing resemblance to ballroom dancing, works its wonders within a smaller compass," explained *Time* writer Gerald Clarke. The discipline allows moves that emulate traditional dance, precluding such crowd-pleasing stunts as fast spins, high tosses, and extended lifts. Nor was ice dancing's place on the Olympic podium always assured. "For years," Bob Ottum of *Sports Illustrated* noted, "certain members of the International Olympic Committee opposed accepting dance as an Olympic sport because, they huffed, it was art and not sport." Eventaully, ice dancing was invited to the games as an exhibition event. In 1976 ice dancing was accepted as an official medals event.

The discipline was refined as early as the 1960s with such pairs as Britain's Diane Towler and Bernard Ford, and was dominated in the 1970s by pairs representing the Soviet Union. But it could be argued that ice dancing reached a new peak of maturity with the ascendency of Torvill and Dean. Not only superior stylists, they were innovators in the sport. Indeed, skating authority **Dick Button** told Clarke in 1986, "all new skaters will in some way look like Torvill and Dean. They are wonderfully creative. Much of what they do is unique to them."

Jayne Torvill and Christopher Dean both grew up in Nottingham, England. Both began skating at age ten; at fourteen, Torville, with then-partner Michael Hutchinson, became British National Pairs champion. At the same age, Dean was named British Junior Dance champion. Torvill and Dean first teamed up in 1975. By that time, each skater held a "day job," Torvill's in clerking, Dean's as a police recruit. "For a time," remarked Bob Ottum in *Sports Illustrated*, the duo "tried to combine both worlds—working out while their occupational colleagues slept. At one point they had regular training sessions from 4 to 6 a.m." The grueling schedule paid off when Torvill and Dean gained their first national title in 1978.

Bound for Sarajevo

Recognizing that they had the potential to rise to the top of the international standings, Torvill and Dean committed themselves to full-time training in 1980. (The Nottingham City Council staked the two to a

Chronology

1975	First teamed as ice dancers
1976	First international win, St. Gervais
1984	Represented Great Britain at the Olympic winter games, Sarajevo, Yugoslavia
1984	Begin touring as professionals
1987	Dean begins as choreographer for other skaters
1990	Torvill marries Philip Christensen
1991	Dean marries Isabelle Duchesnay (divorced, 1993)
1994	Dean marries Jill Trenary
1994	Represented Great Britain at Olympic winter games, Lillehamer, Norway
1994	"Face the Music" farewell tour
1998	"Stars on Ice" tour
1999	Torvill begins work as choreographer for other skaters

Awards and Accomplishments

1976	First international win, St. Gervais
1978	First of seven British national championships
1981	First of four European championships
1981	First of four world championships
1981	Named Members of the British Empire (MBE)
1983	Win Gold Star Ice Dance test
1984	Gold medal, Olympic winter games
1984	BBC Sports Personalities of the Year
1984	First of five World Professional Ice Dance championships
1989	Inducted into World Figure Skating Hall of Fame
1993	Honorary Master of Arts, Nottingham Trent University
1994	Bronze medal, Olympic winter games
1995	Honored by German Federation for contribution to sport
2000	Named to Order of the British Empire (OBE)

$21,000 grant, freeing them to pursue their craft.) In 1981 the team took the European ice dancing championship, which had been dominated by Soviet skaters for the previous decade. By 1982 Torvill and Dean were the pair to beat, ranking first in the world and netting perfect "6.0" scores.

Skating fans soon noticed a difference in the presentation of the two dancers. They elevated their routines to display a physical and emotional intimacy that led many to believe that the partners were romantically involved off the ice. But the two were quick to refute that belief. "This is constant, unglamorous work," Dean told Ottum. Torvill and Dean eventually married, but not each other.

In 1983, Torvill and Dean scored an unprecedented nine perfect "sixes" in artistic impression at the world championship. Setting their sights on Sarajevo, the ice dancers decided to push the artistic envelope by choosing "Bolero" for their accompaniment. "Bolero" was seen as a contentious piece of music for ice dancing, as it featured a single repetitive tempo instead of changes of rhythm. But as they entered the arena in Zetra, Yugoslavia, Torvill and Dean prepared to show the world a new form of ice dance.

The music began. "Not since the great Soviet pair of the '60s, Ludmila and Oleg Protopopov," wrote B. J. Phillips of *Time,* "has anyone in skating so melded music, blades and bodies into a unified whole. Torvill and Dean performed an extended pas de deux in which difficult athletic feats are made to appear effortless, though the beat is so slow that the skaters can never build momentum. Like the music, the movements are eerily erotic and mesmerizing." *Life* writer Robert Sullivan saw the performance as groundbreaking: "There were no tempo shifts but rather sustained elegance, cohesion, narrative, drama. This was dancing: a Swan Lake to everyone else's prom night." When the scores were posted, again history was made: the skaters not only scored across-the-board sixes in artistic impression, but also in technical merit.

Torvill and Dean took home the gold medal and left behind a new standard for ice dancing. From then on, many pairs sought to recreate the sensuality of the two Britons. For years, "team after team of T&D wannabes spilled onto the ice in Grand Guignol costuming," wrote Sullivan. "Nostrils perpetually aflare, the new generation of ice dancers—too many of them artless and only modestly talented—acted out their wildest passions and torments, climaxing in death swoon after death swoon."

A Challenge in Lillehamer

As for the originators, Torvill and Dean had to follow their own considerable act. Turning pro, they toured the ice-show circuit for a decade. "They got rich," said Sullivan. "Eventually they got bored." When they heard of a rules change that allowed professional skaters to compete in the Olympics, the pair convinced each other to prepare for the 1994 winter games. When they arrived in Lillehamer, Norway, the now-senior members of ice-dancing's elite had to share the rink with a new generation of ice dancers. It was a "rude awakening," according to Diane Pucin, in a 1994 *Knight-Ridder/Tribune News Service* wire story. "For the first time in their international careers, Torvill and Dean didn't lead after the compulsories." They were tied for second after enduring a humiliating 5.2 from one judge on the required *pasa doble* movement. But for the two-minute dance, the partners returned to form, performing a lively rumba that earned them two perfect sixes. They had moved back into first place in time for the free-dance finale, which counted for fifty percent of the total score.

But this time, gold eluded Torvill and Dean. They performed a technically challenging Fred Astaire-and-Ginger-Rogers-type routine with characteristic innovation—including backflips, splits, and the woman lifting the man—and the audience responded with a sustained standing ovation. But the cheers changed to boos when Torvill and Dean's technical merit scores—averaging around 5.7—were posted. The Britons finished third to two Russian dance pairs, Oksana Grichtchuk and Yevgeny Platov (gold), and Maya Usova and Aleskandr Zhulin (silver). Not coincidentally, three of the judges who placed the Russians higher represented Russia, Belarus and Ukraine.

A Judging Flap

Did dishonest judging take place? Some thought so. "The result did nothing to improve the reputation of ice dancing, which is ridiculed by other skaters for its lack of jumps and rigged scoring," declared Linda Robertson in a *Knight-Ridder/Tribune News Service* article. "Ripped off" was sports columnist Ann Killion's opinion. Writing for *Knight-Ridder/Tribune News Service,* Killion labeled the judges "Corrupt. Blind. Or both." As for the skaters, "we were a little surprised," Dean said to Robertson, before he amended his comment: "A lot." Torvill told Killion, "I'm glad we came back to perform."

Torvill and Dean's farewell tour, "Face the Music" traveled the world in the mid-1990s. They have appeared in several videos, including a comic turn by Torvill skating with actor Rowan Atkinson's bumbling "Mr. Bean" character in a Comic Relief presentation. She also appeared as a contestant on the British game show *They Think It's All Over* in June 2001

Between their Olympic appearances, Torville and Dean continued to represent their sport. Dean, in particular, made his mark as a choreographer, mapping out the routine of France's 1992 Olympians Isabelle and Paul Duchesnay (Dean was married to Isabelle from 1991-93). Dean later married 1990 World Champion skater Jill Trenary. The couple and their two sons live in Colorado Springs, Colorado, where they work as skating coaches. Torville married Philip Christensen, who manages her appearances. Torvill and Dean were honored by their country by being named Members of the British Empire (MBE) in 1981, and to the Order of the British Empire (OBE) in 2000. One more unique honor came their way: the Torvill and Dean, a flower of orange, white, and pink hues, was named for them.

CONTACT INFORMATION

Address: c/o Sue Young, P.O. Box 32, Heathfield, East Sussex, TN21 0BW, England.

SELECTED WRITINGS BY TORVILL AND DEAN:

(With Neil Wilson) *Torvill and Dean: Fire on Ice.* Weidenfeld & Nicolson, 1994.

FURTHER INFORMATION

Books

Hennessey, John. *Torvill and Dean.* David and Charles, 1993.

Hilton, Christopher. *Torvill and Dean: The True Story.* Oxford Illustrated Press, 1994.

Shuker-Haines, Franny. *Torvill & Dean: Ice Dancing's Perfect Pair.* Blackbirch Press, 1995.

Torvill, Jane, with Christopher Dean and Neil Wilson. *Torvill and Dean: Fire on Ice.* Weidenfeld & Nicolson, 1994.

Periodicals

Caple, Jim. "Torvill and Dean Placed 3rd in Controversial Ice Dancing Judging." *Knight-Ridder/Tribune News Service.* (February 21, 1994).

Clarke, Gerald. "Sensuality and Ice Magic." *Time.* (November 24, 1986).

Killion, Ann. "Torvill and Dean Were Ripped Off." *Knight-Ridder/Tribune News Service.* (February 21, 1994).

Ottum, Bob. "Just the Perfect Couple." *Sports Illustrated.* (November 7, 1983).

Phillips, B. J. "A Little Touch of Heaven." *Time.* (February 27, 1984).

Pucin, Diane. "Torvill and Dean Back with a Vengeance." *Knight-Ridder/Tribune News Service.* (January 20, 1994).

Pucin, Diane. "Torvill and Dean Dance to the Top." *Knight-Ridder/Tribune News Service.* (February 20, 1994).

Robertson, Linda. "Crowd Prefers Torvill and Dean, But Judges Prefer Russians." *Knight-Ridder/Tribune News Service.* (February 21, 1994).

Sullivan, Robert. "Torvill and Dean." *Life.* (February, 1994).

Other

Ice-Dance.com. http://www.ice-dance.com/profiles/torvill.htm (January 6, 2003).

Six Zero. http://www.jhalle.demon.co.uk/ (January 6, 2003).

Torvill and Dean Web Site. http://members.aol.com/tanddfanp/ (January 6, 2003).

Sketch by Susan Salter

Vladislav Tretiak
1952-

Russian hockey player

Often called the greatest goaltender of all time, Vladislav Tretiak continues to impact the world of hockey with his words of wisdom and his vast experi-

Vladislav Tretiak

ence. He made his mark in hockey at the tender age of 20 in the 1972 Summit Series, where the Soviets played against the Canadians. He continually crafted his game and became feared in the hockey arena. He had one dark spot on his record, the 1980 Olympic games. It is a memory that haunts and angers him to this day. However, he did not let his anger consume him. He went on to win a gold medal at the 1984 Olympics, retiring afterward. He continues to inspire up and coming goalies through various partnerships with hockey schools in Russia and the United States, as well as the National Hockey League (NHL). With a career punctuated by over ninety medals, a testament to his hockey prowess, Tretiak is perhaps equally well remembered for his character.

Talented Youth

Tretiak once said "talent without diligence is nothing." It is this attitude that was ever-present when he began his long journey into the world of hockey and the history books. Tretiak grew up with a father who was an airline pilot and a mother who was a physical education teacher for the Central Army Sports Club. Young Tretiak wanted to grow up to be a pilot like his father, but fate had a different plan for his life.

Tretiak began the steps towards his career in hockey when his mother first began to teach him to skate at a very young age. A few years later, at the age of 11, he began playing hockey as a forward for the Red Army Hockey School in Moscow. Later, he chose the position of goalie because he wanted a uniform and that was the only uniform left. It was this incident that changed Tretiak's life forever and brought him to a position where he truly shined.

Tretiak was very diligent in everything he did. He was quoted as saying, "I like to do my job best whatever I do," in an interview for the *Sporting News*. Because he felt he was not getting enough practice, as the Red Army played only two games a week, he began playing in any game he could find. He truly wanted to refine his game and knew the only way that was possible was through a great deal of practice. Those many hours of practice playing with other teams paid off, as at the age of twenty he was feared and revered by those in the world of hockey.

A Secret No Longer

His reputation as a first class goaltender was no longer limited to Russia, but spread throughout the

Awards and Accomplishments

1970	Becomes starting goalie for Soviet National Team
1971-84	Elected first team All-star
1972	Wins victory in Montreal with a final of 7-3 in the first game of the Summit Series
1972	Wins 5-3 in Vancouver, game four of the Summit Series
1972	Wins 5-4 in Moscow, game five of the Summit Series
1972	Wins Olympic Ice Hockey Gold Medal
1974, 1979, 1981-83	Named best goaltender at World and European Championships
1974-76, 1981, 1983	Awarded Player of the year
1976	Wins Olympic Ice Hockey Gold Medal
1978	Awarded the Order on Lenin for his service to the USSR
1980	Wins Olympic Ice Hockey Silver Medal
1981	Named tournament most valuable player, Canada Cup
1983	Drafted by Canadiens
1984	Wins Olympic Ice Hockey Gold Medal
1989	First player born in the Soviet Union to be Inducted into the Hockey Hall of Fame
1990	Receives Canadian Society of New York Achievement Award for his contribution to the 1972 Canada-Russia Series
1995	Voted number four All-Time Goaltender, Recreation Sport Hockey Goaltender Survey #2
1995	Voted number 6 All-Time Goaltender, Recreation Sport Hockey Goaltender Survey #3
1996	His Jersey, #20, was retired and raised to the rafters of the Moscow Ice Palace
1998	Wins Olympic Silver Medal as coach
2001	Attends the 45th annual London Sports Celebrity Dinner and Auction
2002	Named eighth greatest Winter Olympian by filmmaker Bud Greenspan

Decorated with The Order of the Red Banner of Labor—USSR

Decorated with The Order of Friendship of Peoples—USSR

Decorated with The Badge of Honor—USSR

Where Is He Now?

Although Tretiak never fulfilled his dream of playing in the National Hockey League, in 1989 he was elected to the Canadian Hockey Hall of Fame. Tretiak stated, "To be elected was like a present." Since Tretiak's retirement in 1984, he has split his time between Russia and the United States, providing training for goalies from young children all the way up to the NHL. In 1990 he was offered a contract with the Chicago Blackhawks. In his work with the Blackhawks he met Ed Belfour, who is one of the notable students of his tutelage. Tretiak stated on the Web site for his goaltending school, "My knowledge and experience are passed on to these goaltenders with the hope of making them not only better goaltenders but also better people." Belfour said of Tretiak in an interview with the *Dallas Morning News*, "He helped my work ethic and practice habits. He is a great leader who has won so many championships." Tretiak coached the Russians during the 2002 Winter Olympics and now has largely focused his consulting on Canada and the United States while continuing to coach for the Blackhawks. He was honored recently as the 8th greatest Olympian of all-time.

world when he participated in the Summit Series against Canada in 1972. Just weeks prior to the series, Canadian hockey scouts had witnessed him allowing eight goals during an intra-squad contest. They went back to tell the Canadian coaches of Tretiak's poor goaltending, leading the Canadian Hockey Team to believe they had an easy win ahead of them. In the Web site dedicated to the Summit Series, the writer stated, "The scouting reports were wrong about Tretiak-not only could he stop the puck, but time would prove he was one of the all time greats." They had no idea that he had been out late the night before celebrating for his wedding the following day. This mistake would cost the Canadians dearly in the first game of the Summit Series.

In the first two minutes of the first period Tretiak allowed two goals. However, from then on he only allowed one more goal to the Canadian Hockey Team, resulting in a 7-3 Soviet victory. The Canadians were stunned, but now knew with whom they were dealing. The Canadians did go on to win the series, but not without a fight. With several wins and a tie, the Soviets gave the Canadians a run for their money. In fact,

Tretiak was one save short of a victory for his team in the final game of the series. He referred to that last goal as the "most maddening of all goals scored on me in hockey," as stated on the Summit Series Web site. He was getting no support from his fellow defensemen and Paul Henderson, after falling down behind the net, shot the winning goal. Despite the loss, Tretiak made a name for himself beyond the Eastern Block. The writer for the Summit Series Web site stated, "while Tretiak's save percentage of .884 isn't spectacular by today's standards, his play was spectacular by any era's standards."

He continued to awe the hockey world by leading the Soviet Union to a Gold Medal at the 1972 Winter Olympics. The accomplishment surprised no one, and the Soviets were proud of the team they had assembled, particularly of their star goalie. Tretiak had endeared himself not only to his Soviet National Team, but also to fans of hockey everywhere. The writer for the Summit Series stated, "no Russian player has the respect of Canadians more so than Tretiak." They admired his "intuitive perception of hockey," according to Anatoly Tarasov in his book *The Father of Russian Hockey: Tarasov*. This prowess was apparent in a notable game on New Years Eve in 1975. The Central Red Army Squad skated to a 3-3 tie with the Montreal Canadiens. What makes the accomplishment noteworthy is that the Soviets only managed 13 shots to the Canadiens' 38.

From Disappointment to Diligence

A dark hour was coming in Tretiak's career. In the 1980 Olympics held in New York's Lake Placid, Tretiak was denied an opportunity to continue the Russian legacy of Olympic Gold. Three days prior to the historic "Miracle on Ice," the Soviets beat the United States in a warm up game by a landslide 10-3. Tretiak believes it is this incident that led to overconfidence for the Soviets. In the first period of the semi-final game, the Americans were very aggressive and scored two goals. The Soviet National Team coach, Viktor Tikhonov, felt uneasy

Vladislav Tretiak

Career Statistics

Yr	Team	GP	MIN	GAA	TGA
1968-69	CSKA	3	180	0.67	2
1969-70	CSKA	34	2040	2.24	76
1970-71	CSKA	40	2400	2.03	81
1971-72	CSKA	30	1800	2.60	78
1972-73	CSKA	30	1800	2.67	80
1973-74	CSKA	27	1620	3.48	94
1974-75	CSKA	35	2100	2.97	104
1975-76	CSKA	33	1980	3.03	100
1976-77	CSKA	35	2100	2.80	98
1977-78	CSKA	29	1740	2.48	72
1978-79	CSKA	40	2400	2.78	111
1979-80	CSKA	36	2160	2.36	85
1980-81	CSKA	18	1080	1.78	32
1981-82	CSKA	41	2460	1.59	65
1982-83	CSKA	29	1740	1.38	40
1983-84	CSKA	22	1320	1.82	40
TOTAL		482	28920	2.40	1158

CSKA: Central Red Army Team (Moscow).

about the goals Tretiak allowed and pulled him after the first period in favor of Tretiak's back up, Vladimir Myshkin. Myshkin allowed two more goals and the United States won the game 4-3, going on to capture the gold. Tretiak stated in an interview for the *Sporting News,* "I didn't want to go home. I was very, very angry." He had never been benched before, and was so shocked and incensed he considered giving up his career in hockey. However, after spending time away from the hockey arena, he decided not to let his anger get the best of him. He wanted to prove to everyone that the choice that was made was wrong.

With a strong passion within, Tretiak reaffirmed his great skill, winning the Canada Cup in 1981. It was this game that proved that his competitive nature was still alive. The final result was an 8-1 Soviet victory. It was nothing new for Tretiak, who by now was considered not only the Soviet Union's best goalie, but also the world's best goalie. Following the victory, the Montreal Canadiens grew more and more interested in this Russian hockey player. When asked by a reporter, after receiving a four-minute standing ovation at the Canada Cup, if he would like to play for Montreal, he answered with an unequivocal yes. He was photographed holding up **Ken Dryden**'s jersey, which then appeared on the cover of a Montreal newspaper. This was scandalous in the eyes of the Soviet Union. Not only did it make them look bad because it appeared Tretiak no longer wanted to play for the Red Army

Team, it was a slap in the face to the Central Committee of Young Communist League, which Tretiak belonged to. Feeling the pressure from the Soviet authorities, Tretiak renounced his statements, saying the press had misrepresented him.

NHL Pipe Dreams

It truly was Tretiak's greatest dream to play for the National Hockey League (NHL). He mentioned his desire to play for the NHL to the great **Wayne Gretzky**, and asked Gretzky if he would be able to earn as much as the Islander's all-star defenseman Denis Potvin. Gretzky believed Tretiak could without a doubt. It was this discussion, as well as Tretiak's continued performance, that led to him being drafted by the Montreal Canadiens. He petitioned the Soviet Federals to allow him to leave the country to play for the Canadiens, but his request was denied. They could not let their prize goalie leave the country.

Vladislav Tretiak, Man of Character

Tretiak went on to earn several more awards, and finally vindicated himself in the 1984 Olympics, reclaiming the Gold. He was the first Soviet hockey player to appear in four Winter Olympics. Tretiak had proven his point, that he was the better goalie. He was satisfied with his career and his accomplishments, so he decided to retire. He still was in great shape and his performance was never better. But he had made his mark and wanted to go gracefully. He also wanted to share his experience with others. Looking at Tretiak's career, it is quite clear he was not only a phenomenal goalie, he was an exceptional human being with great character. Jeff Hackett of the Blackhawks stated, "I feel like I am a better goalie just by working with him," in an interview for the *Sporting News.* Although he endured a major disappointment with the 1980 Olympic games, he retired walking tall, knowing he was the best person he could be and considered the best goalie in the world.

SELECTED WRITINGS BY TRETIAK:

The Hockey I Love, Lawrence Hill & Co, 1983.
Tretiak:The Legend, Plains Publishing, 1987.
The Art of Goaltending, Plains Publishing, 1989.

FURTHER INFORMATION

Books

Tretiak, Vladislav. *The Art of Goaltending.* Plains Publishing, 1989.

Tretiak, Vladislav. *The Hockey I Love.* Lawrence Hill & Co, 1983.

Tretiak, Vladislav. *Tretiak:The Legend.* Plains Publishing, 1987.

Periodicals

Allen, Kevin. "Series that changed a nation." *USA Today* (September 17, 2002): 03C.

Fraley, Garry. "Belfour credits style to legendary Soviet." *Dallas Morning News* (June 20, 1999): 25B.

Langford, David. "Tretiak attending London sports dinner." *London Free Press* (November 18, 2000): B3.

MacGregor, Scott and Larry Wigge. "A safety nyet." *The Sporting News* (December 30, 1996): 37.

McClain, John. "Fetisov, Tretiak return to restore Russia's place in hockey." *Houston Chronicle* (February 16, 2002).

"Morrison on hockey." *Toronto Sun* (October 22, 2000): SP15.

O'Connor, Ian. "Tretiak still haunted by benching." *Journal News* (February 16, 2002).

St. James, Helene. "Now Ducks depend on Russian One." *Detroit Free Press* (May 7, 1997).

Stevenson, Chris. "'Bulin Wall' just too tall/Talk from Tretiak an inspiration for Khabibulin in beating Hasek." *Edmonton Sun* (February 21, 2002): OS9.

Swift, E.M. "An army man to the core." *Sports Illustrated* (November 14, 1983): 38(6).

Other

"A September to remember." http://www.1972 summitseries.com/tretiak.html (October 18, 2002).

"Biography." http://www.goaltending.net/biography/biography.htm (October 17, 2002).

Cazenueve, Brian. "Olympic Highlights: Gold medal goalie in 1972, '76, '84." *Sports Illustrated.* http:// sportsillustrated.cnn.com/olympics/2002/daily_guide/news/2002/02/14day7_where/ (October 23, 2002).

"Goaltending coach of the Chicago Blackhawks! 1998 Olympic Silver-Medalist Coach." Vladislav Tretiak Elite School of Goaltending. http://www.goaltending.net/about/about.htm (October 18, 2002).

"Media alert:Vladislav Tretiak to be honored as one of the greatest Olympians of all-time." Media Online. http://media.gm.com/division/chevrolet/news/releases/020213_tretiak.html (October 18, 2002).

"The Miracle of Lake Placid." http://www.thequickandthedead.com/Sports/Centruy/Games/Miracle.htm (October 26, 2002).

Sedov, Artur. "Vladislav Tretiak." The Hockey Nation. http://soviethockey.hypermart.net/tretiak.html (October 17, 2002).

"The Legends: Biography—Vladislav Tretiak." Hockey Hall of Fame and Museum, The Learning Edge Corporation. http://www.legendsofhockey.net:8080/LegendsOfHockey.htm (October 17, 2002).

"Vladislav Tretiak." University of Colorado. http://ucsu.colorado.edu/~norrisdt/bio/tretiak.html (October 18, 2002).

"Vladislav Tretiak-Russian Hockey Legend." http://www.hockeysandwich.com/tretiak.html (October 17, 2002).

"Vladislav Tretiak North American Hockey Academy." Capital Computer Consultants. http://tretiakhockeyacademy.com/ (October 16, 2002).

Sketch by Barbara J Smerz

Lee Trevino
1939-

American golfer

Completely self-taught, Lee Trevino's unorthodox swing has made golf pros shudder throughout his career. With a wide stance and a closed club face, he drives through the ball with a flat baseball-type swing. By the standards of traditional golf, he does everything wrong, which somehow turns out right. Trevino, who has long shunned golf instructors, once told the *San Antonio Express-News,* "I'll hire [an instructor] when I find one who can beat me." Over his career, which has spanned more than three decades, Trevino has found little need for any advice. Known as the Merry Mex for his nonstop chatting around the course, Trevino is an exceptional golfer as well as a favorite of galleries wherever he plays.

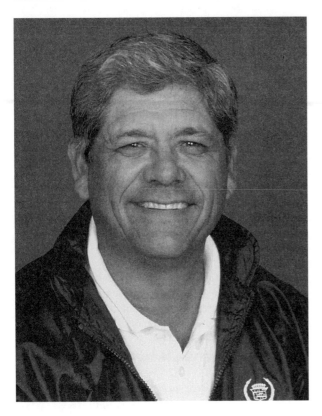

Lee Trevino

Caddie Shack Golfer

Lee Trevino was born on December 1, 1939 in Dallas, Texas. His father, Joseph, was not a part of his life, and he was raised by his mother, Juanita, a domestic, and his maternal grandfather, Joe Trevino, a Mexican immigrant who worked as a grave digger. The family lived in a four-room house with no electricity or plumbing that was about 100 yards off the seventh fairway of Glen Lakes Country Club. As a child, Trevino watched the golfers out on the fairway, and, after finding an old club, began to practice hitting balls around his yard. At the age of eight he began working as a caddie, and played golf on three short holes behind the caddie shack.

Trevino quit school after the seventh grade and took a job at Glen Lakes as an assistant groundskeeper. On the side he would work as a caddie and play a few holes at the end of the day. Lying about his age, Trevino joined the U.S. Marines when he was seventeen and served two two-year stints in Asia and played for the Third Marine Division golf squad. By the time he was discharged in 1961, he was a good golfer, with a four-handicap, but wanted to get better. He took a job at Hardy's Driving Range and played on the rough flat terrain of the Tenison Golf Course, a municipal course in Greenville, Texas, where he worked on developing his unusual swing to perfection.

To supplement his income, Trevino began hustling golf bets. At first, he d simply wager that he'd come out

Chronology	
1939	Born in Dallas, Texas
1956-60	Serves in the U.S. Marines
1960-65	Head professional at Hardy's Driving Range in Dallas
1966	Joins the Professional Golf Association (PGA) Tour; becomes chairman of the board of Lee Trevino Enterprises, Inc.
1966-67	Assistant professional as Horizon Hills Country Club, El Paso, Texas
1983-89	Golf commentator for the National Broadcasting Network (NBC)
1984	Retires from the PGA Tour
1989	Joins the Champions Tour

ahead in a round of golf. But when his winning ways scared off most of his competition, he began taking bets that he could win using a 26-ounce Dr. Pepper bottle wrapped in adhesive tape for a club. He later boasted that he never lost with that bottle. His early experience of wagering more money than he had to lose helped Trevino develop his competitive edge and his coolness under extreme pressure later in his career. Early in his professional career, Trevino would often place off-course bets on his performance, sometimes winning as much on his wagers as he did in prize money.

Turns Professional

Eventually Trevino found someone willing to subsidize his expenses for a few tournaments that didn't require Professional Golf Association (PGA) membership. During 1965 he played in three events, finishing first at the Texas State Open, second at the Mexico City Open, and fifth at the Panama Open. His performance was good enough to garner the support of Martin Lettunich, a wealthy cotton farmer from El Paso, who secured a job for Trevino at El Paso's Horizon Hills Country Club.

In 1965 Lettunich and his buddies invited Raymond Floyd, a rising star on the PGA, to challenge a local player. As *Sports Illustrated* retold the now-legendary anecdote, "Floyd pulled into Horizon Hills in a white Cadillac, where he was met by a young Hispanic club-house boy, who retrieved Floyd's clubs from the trunk, escorted him to the locker room, and shined his shoes. 'Who am I playing today?' Floyd asked. 'You're talking to him,' Trevino replied." The two played three rounds, and with one hole left, Trevino was up by a stroke. Floyd saved himself from the embarrassment of losing by eagling the final hole to win by one. Packing up his clubs, Floyd told Trevino, "Adios. I've got easier games than this on the Tour." The two would meet again many times on the PGA and Champions Tours.

Joining the PGA in 1966, Trevino played in the U.S. Open at the Olympic Country Club in San Francisco. Tying for fifty-fourth place, he returned home with $600 and severe doubts about his future in golf. The following year, Trevino's wife sent off the twenty dollar registration fee for the 1967 U.S. Open trials despite her hus-

Awards and Accomplishments

1966	Named Rookie of the Year by the Professional Golf Association (PGA)
1968	Wins U.S. Open
1970	Named Texas Professional Athlete of the Year by the Texas Sports Association
1970-74, 1980	Awarded the Vardon Trophy from the PGA five times for lowest average strokes per round by a professional golfer
1971	Wins U.S. Open; wins British Open; receives Hickok Belt for professional athlete of the year; received Gold Tee Award; named Player of the Year by PGA and *Golf*; named Sportsman of the Year by *Sports Illustrated*; named International Sports Personality of the Year by the British Broadcasting Association; named Male Athlete of the Year by the Associated Press; named Top Performer in Golf by *Sport*; named Sports Man of the Year by *The Sporting News*.
1972	Wins British Open
1974	Wins PGA Championship; wins World Series of Golf
1978	Inducted into the Texas Golf Hall of Fame
1979	Inducted into the American Golf Hall of Fame
1981	Inducted into the World Golf Hall of Fame
1984	Wins PGA Championship
1990	Wins U.S. Senior Open
1992, 1994	Wins PGA Seniors Championship

Related Biography: Golfer Hale Irwin

Hale Irwin was a two-sport athlete at the University of Colorado, winning the 1967 National Collegiate Athletic Association golf championship as well as being a two-time All-Big-8 football defensive back. His first PGA Tour victory came in 1971 when he won the Sea Pines Heritage Classic, and he had 20 tournament wins by 1994, including three majors (the U.S. Open title in 1974, 1979, and 1990).

Irwin joined the Champions Tour in 1995, finishing first in two events his rookie year and two in his sophomore year, one being the PGA Seniors Championship. By 1997 Irwin had begun his domination of the senior tour in earnest. He won an incredible nine tournaments, including his second PGA Seniors Championship, which he won for the third consecutive year in 1998. He continued to finish on top of the leader board, including wins at the 1999 Ford Senior Players Championship and at the 2000 U.S. Senior Open.

In 2001 Irwin surpassed Trevino as the winningest player on the senior tour by taking his thirtieth win. By the end of the 2002 season, he had 36 Champion Tour victories. He also set a new record for earnings, surpassing his previous record of $2.86 million with a total of $3.3 million in 2002, becoming the oldest player to win the money title.

band's misgivings. At the qualifying event, Trevino shot under 70 in both rounds, posting the best score of all qualifiers. He then shocked everyone, including himself, by finishing fifth in the U.S. Open. With new confidence, Trevino played a dozen more tournaments in 1966, finishing out of the money only twice and was named Rookie of the Year.

Trevino's first tournament, and first major, win came in 1968 when he took the U.S. Open, shooting a record four rounds under 70 (69, 68, 69, 69). Later in the year he won the Hawaiian Open. Although he only won total of three tournaments in 1969 and 1970 (the Tucson Open twice and the National Airlines Open Invitational), he managed to place in the money often enough to place him among the tour's top money winners.

A Year and a Career to Remember

Coming off a 13-month winless stretch, Trevino's breakthrough came between April and July 1971, during which time he won six tournaments. He won the U.S. Open, Canadian Open, and British Open championships in sucession within a 23-day period. In a thrilling finish that remains one of the highlights of his career, Trevino won his second U.S. Open championship in four years by beating legendary golfer **Jack Nicklaus** by three strokes in a playoff round. Although an acute case of appendicitis requiring emergency surgery slowed Trevino during the second half of the 1971 season, he received numerous awards, including *Golf*'s PGA Player of the Year, *Sports Illustrated*'s Sportsman of the Year, and the Associated Press Male Athlete of the Year.

By the time he retired from the PGA Tour in 1984, Trevino had won 29 PGA tournaments along with an array of international and special events. His six major titles included his two U.S. Open titles in 1968 and 1971, the British Open title in 1971 and 1972, and the PGA Championship in 1974 and 1984. Suffering from chronic back problems, brought on by being struck by lightening in 1975, Trevino retired from the PGA Tour in 1984 and spent some time in the broadcasting booth for NBC Sports.

Joins the Seniors

In 1989 Trevino turned fifty and became eligible for the Champions Tour (previously known as the PGA Senior Tour) and joined the tour for the last event of the season. If he was a star on the PGA Tour, Trevino quickly became a superstar on the senior tour. In 1990 he was the leading money winner in all of golf, with over $1 million in single-season earnings. He won seven titles during the year, including once again beating Nicklaus, this time at the U.S. Senior Open by shooting a 67 on his final round. He was named both Rookie of the Year and Player of the Year.

Trevino won three tournaments in 1991 and in 1992 had five victories before injuring his thumb in June, which required surgery. Despite his shortened season, he was once again named Player of the Year and once again took home more than $1 million in winnings. Still recovering from his thumb injury, Trevino managed just three wins in 1993, but stormed back in 1994 with six victories and a career-high $1.2 million in earnings. He was named the Champion's Tour Player of the Year for the third time. The following year he became the tour's all-time winningest player after notching his twenty-five victory, a position he held until overtaken by Hale Irwin, six years his junior, who had a total of 36 Champions Tour titles by 2002.

Although he continued to win an occasional tournament during the latter part of the 1990s, Trevino's presence in the top spot of the leader board became less frequent. He captured his first victory in two years when he won the Cadillac NFL Golf Classic in 2000. He is one of only two golfers (the other is Gary Player) who has won a tournament in each of three decades. "I wouldn't still be playing if I didn't think I could still win," Trevino told *Golf World* after his twenty-ninth senior tour win. "If I don't think I can win, then I'll just quit. It may even happen in the middle of a round." In 2002 his best finish was a tie for ninth at the Napa Valley Championship. Despite his slide down the points and win list, Trevino remains one of the game's most popular players.

The Merry Mex

A gifted if unorthodox player, Trevino, known as the Merry Mex, is gregarious and talkative, usually chatting nonstop around the course. He is a fan favorite, who adds a sense of showmanship and fun to a sport that often emphasizes reserve and rectitude. Known for his easy laugh and sometimes sharp wit, he has an uncanny ability to focus, relax, and refocus his way around a golf course that can unnerve his competitors who don't possess the same gift. Married for the third time, Trevino has two children with his wife, Claudia, and four children from his previous marriages. Trevino summed up his simple golfing philosophy that has carried him through his 35-year career with a characteristically caustic bit of wisdom: "The two things that don't last," he told *Sports Illustrated,* "are pros putting for bogey and dogs chasin' cars."

CONTACT INFORMATION

Address: Assured Management Company, 1901 W. 47th Place, Ste. 200, Westwood, Kansas 66205.

SELECTED WRITINGS BY TREVINO:

(With Oscar Fraley) *I Can Help Your Game.* Greenwich, CT: Fawcett Publications, 1971.
(With Dick Aultman) *Groove Your Golf Swing My Way.* New York: Atheneum, 1976.
(With Sam Blair) *They Call Me Super Mex.* New York: Random House, 1982.
(With Sam Blair) *The Snake in the Sandtrap (And Other Misadventures on the Golf Tour).* New York: Holt, Rinehart, and Winston, 1985.

FURTHER INFORMATION

Books

The Complete Marquis Who's Who. New York: Marquis Who's Who, 2001.
Dictionary of Hispanic Biography. Detroit: Gale Research, 1996.

St. James Encyclopedia of Popular Culture. 5 vols. Detroit: St. James Press, 2000.

Periodicals

Anderson, Kelli. "Lee Trevino." *Sports Illustrated* (June 7, 1993): 52-3.
Fields, Bill. "Solitary Man." *Golf World* (January 19, 2001): 23.
Garrity, John. "Lee Trevino." *Sports Illustrated* (April 25, 1994): 46-7.
Looney, Douglas S. "Artistry Revisited." *Sports Illustrated* (July 9, 1990): 20-1.
McDermott, Barry. "It's an Old Man's Game After All." *Sports Illustrated* (August 27, 1984): 28-30.
Moore, Kenny. "It's Nifty Being 50." *Sports Illustrated* (December 18, 1989): 34-7.
"Trevino Ends Drought." *Golf World* (June 30, 2000): 34.
Yocom, Guy. "My Shot." *Golf Digest* (May 2002): 124.

Other

Contemporary Authors Online. Gale, 2003. Reproduced in *Biography Resource Center.* Detroit: The Gale Group, 2003. http://www.galenet. com/servlet/BioR (January 8, 2003).
"Lee Trevino." *American Decades CD-ROM.* Detroit: Gale Research, 1998. Reproduced in *Biography Resource Center.* Farmington Hills, Mich.: The Gale Group, 2003. http://www. galenet.com/servlet/BioR (January 8, 2003).
"Lee Trevino." Golf Europe. http://www.golfeurope. com/almanac/players/trevino.htm (January 8, 2003).
"Lee Trevino." Professional Golf Association. http:// www.pgatour.com (January 8, 2003).

Sketch by Kari Bethel

Felix Trinidad
1973-

American boxer

Throughout most of the 1990s Felix Trinidad was perhaps the most underrated professional boxer in the world. In a sport where the heavyweights get most of the publicity, recognition of Trinidad was hampered further by the more glamorous of the smaller champions. By the end of the decade, however, Trinidad proved he was a fighter to be reckoned with.

Felix "Tito" Trinidad Jr. was born January 10, 1973, in Cupey Alto, Puerto Rico. His father, who was the younger Trinidad's manager and trainer, was Puerto

Felix Trinidad

Chronology

1973	Born January 10 in Cupey Alto, Puerto Rico
1985	Begins boxing
1990	Turns professional
1993	Wins IBF welterweight title with 2nd-round knockout of Maurice Blocker
1994	Unanimous decision over Hector "Macho" Camacho
1999	Defeats Pernell "Sweat Pea" Whitaker
1999	Decision over Oscar De La Hoya captures WBA welterweight title
2000	Defeats David Reid to capture WBA super welterweight title
2000	TKO of Fernando Vargas, wins IBF super welterweight title
2001	Knocks out WBA middleweight champion William Joppy
2001	Loses to Bernard Hopkins by a TKO in fight to determine undisputed middleweight champion
2002	Wins by TKO over Hasine Cherifi in 4th round
2002	Announces his retirement in July

Rican featherweight champion in the 1970s. Trinidad's boxing career began not too many years after his father's ended. He was twelve years old when he first started fighting and over the next five years he captured five Puerto Rican National Championships in five different weight classes: 100, 112, 119, 126, and 132 pounds). His overall amateur record was fifty-one wins against six losses. However Trinidad never fought in the Olympics and this may have been a contributing factor for his low profile among boxing fans.

A Power Puncher

Trinidad's first professional bout came on March 10, 1990, in San Juan, Puerto Rico. He defeated Angel Romero by a technical knockout (TKO) in the second round. It was a harbinger of a new style in which Trinidad, known for his speed, would now become a power puncher as well. Of the fifty-one victories in his amateur career, only twelve had come by knockout; nine of his first ten professional victories would come that route. During this time Trinidad stayed close to home, venturing outside Puerto Rico only twice—to Italy and to Miami—winning both fights by TKO. In fact, Trinidad fought fourteen of his first twenty fights in his native Puerto Rico, another factor that contributed to his being overlooked by the public in his early years. However, on the island Trinidad was a hero.

Trinidad's twentieth fight, on June 19, 1993, against Maurice Blocker in San Diego, California, proved to be a

milestone in his career. He knocked out Blocker in the second round and won the International Boxing Federation (IBF) welterweight title. It was Trinidad's twentieth consecutive victory as a professional, eighteen by knockouts. Trinidad returned to Puerto Rico a champion and seven weeks later made his first title defense; he knocked out Luis Garcia in the first round in a bout on Bayamon, Puerto Rico. Trinidad had a tougher time against his next opponent, Anthony Stephens, but still managed to score a knockout in the tenth round of a fight staged in Ft. Lauderdale, Florida on October 23, 1993. Soon after, Trinidad began preparing for the man who, up to that time, would be his toughest opponent, former lightweight champion Hector "Macho" Camacho.

Welterweight Champion

Trinidad fought Camacho, who had moved up in weight class, on January 29, 1994, in Las Vegas, Nevada. The bout went the distance, twelve rounds, ending Trinidad's streak of nine consecutive knockouts, but in the end he triumphed with a unanimous decision. In September 1994 began his next knockout streak with a fourth-round TKO over Luis Ramon Campas in Las Vegas. Over the next five years Trinidad would run his knockout string to ten in a row.

On February 20, 1999, Trinidad took on Pernell "Sweat Pea" Whitaker in New York City. Whitaker was also one of the most dominating boxers of the 1990s, first winning the World Boxing Council (WBC) lightweight crown in 1989. He unified the title in 1990 and held it until 1992 when he moved up in weight class to the welterweight division. He was WBC welterweight champion from 1993 to 1997. Now against Trinidad, Whitaker was attempting a comeback, of sorts, and hoping to capture the IBF welterweight title. But once again Trinidad was not to be denied. The fight lasted the full twelve rounds, with Trinidad winning by a unanimous decision. After a May tuneup bout against Hugo Pineda,

Awards and Accomplishments	
1993	IBF welterweight title
1999	WBA welterweight title
2000	WBA super welterweight title
2000	IBF super welterweight title
2001	WBA middleweight title

Trinidad signed to fight boxing's "Golden Boy" of the 1990s—**Oscar De La Hoya**.

De La Hoya was another dominating boxer in the 1990s. A 1992 Olympic gold medallist, De La Hoya had defeated Whitaker for the WBC welterweight title in 1997; at the time of his fight with Trinidad, De La Hoya was undefeated in thirty-one bouts. The fight's victor would take the other's crown.

It was a classic fight between a power puncher (Trinidad) and a boxer (De La Hoya) when the two met on September 19, 1999 in Las Vegas. The fight was scheduled for twelve rounds. De La Hoya won most of the early rounds as he seemingly befuddled Trinidad. But Trinidad never lost heart. He won the final three rounds on stamina and power and took a majority decision—two judges voted for Tinidad and the third scored the fight even—to claim De La Hoya's WBC title as well as retain his own IBF title.

In his next victory, on March 3, 2000, against David Reid in Las Vegas, Trinidad won the WBA super welterweight title. By the end of the year Trinidad had unified the super welterweight title with a TKO in the twelfth round over Fernando Vargas.

Don King's Middleweight Tournament

In 2001, fight promoter **Don King** put together a tournament that would unify the middleweight division. He invited the three champions at that time—Bernard Hopkins (IBF), Keith Holmes (WBC), and William Joppy (WBA)—as well as Trinidad (who had moved up to the higher weight class) to participate. The winner would not only be the undisputed middleweight champion but the first recipient of the **Sugar Ray Robinson** trophy, named for the great boxer of the 1940s and 1950s. Trinidad and Joppy fought in New York City's famed Madison Square Garden (known as the Mecca of boxing) on May 12, 2001, with Trinidad winning by a fifth-round knockout. Technically he was now WBA middleweight champion but that was merely a step for the final prize.

On September 29, 2001 he fought Hopkins (who had beaten Holmes) in Madison Square Garden. Hopkins knocked down Trinidad in the twelfth (and final) round, and the fight was stopped midway through the round. Trinidad not only lost the middleweight crown, he had suffered his first defeat.

Trinidad's next fight was against former WBC middleweight champ Hasine Cherifi on May 11, 2002 in San Juan. He scored a TKO over Cherifi in the fourth round. But the loss to Hopkins had seemingly taken the desire to box out of Trinidad. He announced his retirement through his lawyer on July 2, 2002. In September, 2002 there was speculation that Trinidad might come out of retirement to fight the winner of the bout between two of his old foes—De La Hoya and Vargas (which De La Hoya won). But Trinidad reiterated his plans to remain retired.

Felix Trinidad had a professional record of forty-one wins and one loss. Of those forty-one victories, thirty-four came by knockout. Combined with his amateur record he fought ninety-nine times between 1990 and 2002, winning ninety-two and losing seven. As a professional, Trinidad held the IBF and WBA welterweight titles, the IBF and WBA super welterweight titles, and the WBA middleweight title. His record in championship bouts was twenty-one wins and one loss.

FURTHER INFORMATION

Periodicals

Agence Presse France (February 21, 1999).
Agence Presse France (July 3, 2002).
Independent (London, England) (September 25, 2001).
New York Times (February 13, 1999).
New York Times (September 19, 1999).
Sports Illustrated (May 14, 2001).

Other

"Cyber Boxing Champion: Pernell Whitaker." The Cyber Boxing Zone. http://www.cyberboxingzone.com/boxing/whitaker.htm (January 22, 2003).
"Felix 'Tito' Trinidad's Biography." Latino Legends of Sports. http://www.latinosportslegends.com/Trinidad_Felix_bio.htm (January 16, 2003).
"Felix 'Tito' Trinidad's Career Pro Boxing Record." Latino Legends of Sports. http://www.latinosportslegends.com/stats/boxing/Trinidad's_career_boxing_record.htm (January 16, 2003).
"Pernell Whitaker." Infoplease.com. http://print.infoplease.com/ipsa/A0109744.html (January 22, 2003).

Sketch by F. Caso

Bryan Trottier
1956-

Canadian hockey player

Bryan Trottier

Chronology

1956	Born in Val Marie, Saskatchewan, Canada, on July 17
1974	Selected 22nd overall in the NHL Amateur Draft by the New York Islanders
1975-76	Makes professional debut as center for New York Islanders
1990	Traded to Pittsburgh Penguins by Islanders
1994-97	Serves as assistant coach with Penguins
1997-98	Serves as head coach with Portland Pirates of the American Hockey League
1998-2002	Serves as assistant coach with Colorado Avalanche
2002	Hired as head coach of the New York Rangers on June 5

O ne of the greatest two-way centers ever to play professional hockey, Bryan Trottier is finding success these days on the sidelines as a coach. Trottier was an assistant coach with the Colorado Avalanche in 2001 when the Denver-based team won the Stanley Cup. During his 18 seasons on the ice, Trottier played on six Stanley Cup-winning teams-including four consecutive wins with the New York Islanders (1980, 1981, 1982, and 1983) and two back-to-back wins with the Pittsburgh Penguins (1991 and 1992). In early June of 2002, Trottier, who ranks 12th on the National Hockey League's all-time scoring list and sixth on the NHL's all-time playoff scoring list, was hired as the head coach of the New York Rangers. Interestingly, the Rangers are the archrivals of the Islanders, the team for which Trottier played the bulk of his career.

Born in Val Marie, Saskatchewan

Trottier was born in Val Marie, Saskatchewan, on July 17, 1956. Like thousands of young Canadians, he spent much of his free time playing hockey, showing a real aptitude for the game early on. Years before he began playing professional hockey, Trottier often found himself playing the role of teacher, passing along his expertise in the game to his younger brothers and other would-be hockey players in the neighborhood. One of his pupils—younger brother Rocky—eventually made it to the NHL as a forward for the New Jersey Devils. For the older Trottier, mentoring others in the game was a talent that would come in handy later in his career.

Trottier began his hockey career playing for the Swift Current Broncos of the Western Canada Junior Hockey League during the seasons of 1972-1973 and 1973-1974. In the latter season, Trottier scored 41 goals and 71 assists for a total of 112 points in 68 games. In 1974, the NHL, feeling pressure from the rival World Hockey Association (WHA), held a semi-secret draft focusing on younger players, mostly 17- and 18-year-olds. Trottier was drafted by the New York Islanders in the second round of the draft and 22nd overall. The Islanders agreed to pay the young forward all the salary and bonuses he would have received in the NHL while playing in the junior league for yet another year. Trottier spent the 1974-1975 season playing for the Lethbridge Broncos, scoring 46 goals and 98 assists for a total of 144 points in 67 games.

Shines in NHL Debut

Trottier was brilliant in his debut with the NHL, finishing the season with league records for a rookie in assists (63) and points (95), making him a natural choice for the NHL's Calder Trophy, awarded annually to the most outstanding newcomer. Trottier's record in 1976-1977 was not quite as lustrous as in his rookie season, but it was solid nevertheless. He ended the year with 30 goals and 42 assists for a total of 72 points. He really bounced back in 1977-1978, helping to power the Islanders to a dominant position in the league. Playing in 77 games that season, Trottier compiled an enviable record of 46 goals and 77 assists for a total of 123 points.

The Islanders' winning combination had Trottier playing most of the time with **Mike Bossy** on the right wing and Clark Gillies on the left. The Islanders troika of Bossy, Trottier, and Gillies was by far the most dominant in the NHL since **Phil Esposito** had teamed Ken Hodge and Wayne Cashman for the Bruins earlier in the 1970s. During the season of 1978-1979, Trottier enjoyed what was to be his best year ever, scoring 47 goals and 87 assists for a total of 134 points, making him the league's top scorer and earning him the Hart Trophy as the NHL's most valuable player. Trottier's power scoring

Awards and Accomplishments

1974	Named World Junior Championship MVP as member of Team Canada
1976	Wins Calder Trophy as NHL Rookie of the Year
1976, 1978, 1982-83, 1985-86, 1992	Selected to play in NHL All-Star Game
1979	Wins Art Ross Trophy as NHL's leading scorer
1979	Wins Hart Trophy as NHL's most valuable player
1980	Wins Conn Smythe Trophy as most valuable player in playoffs
1980-83	Leads New York Islanders to Stanley Cup four years in a row
1984	Leads Team Canada to Canada Cup
1989	Receives King Clancy Memorial Award for humanitarian contributions
1991-92	Leads Pittsburgh Penguins to back-to-back Stanley cup victories
1997	Inducted into the Hockey Hall of Fame
2001	Helps coach the Colorado Avalanche to Stanley Cup victory

Career Statistics

Yr	Team	GP	G	A	PTS	PIM
1975-76	Islanders	80	32	63	95	21
1976-77	Islanders	76	30	42	72	34
1977-78	Islanders	77	46	77	123	46
1978-79	Islanders	76	47	87	134	50
1979-80	Islanders	78	42	62	104	68
1980-81	Islanders	73	31	72	103	74
1981-82	Islanders	80	50	79	129	88
1982-83	Islanders	80	34	55	89	68
1983-84	Islanders	68	40	71	111	59
1984-85	Islanders	68	28	31	59	47
1985-86	Islanders	78	37	59	96	72
1986-87	Islanders	80	23	64	87	50
1987-88	Islanders	77	30	52	82	48
1988-89	Islanders	73	17	28	45	44
1989-90	Islanders	59	13	11	24	29
1990-91	Penguins	52	9	19	28	24
1991-92	Penguins	63	11	18	29	54
1993-94	Penguins	41	4	11	15	36

Islanders: New York Islanders; Penguins: Pittsburgh Penguins.

helped fuel the Islanders' drive to a Stanley Cup victory at the end of the 1979-1980 season. With a total of 29 points, Trottier was far and away the leading scorer in the playoffs. He won the Conn Smythe Trophy as the most outstanding performer in NHL post-season play.

Causes Stir with Canada Cup Decision

The 1980 Stanley Cup victory was to be only the first of four consecutive wins for the Islanders in the early 1980s. In 1981 Trottier played in the Canada Cup. During the 1981-1982 regular season, he tallied a career-high 50 goals, and in the playoffs, he collected a total of 29 points to lead the league in post-season scoring. In 1984 Trottier stunned the hockey world—particularly its sizeable Canadian contingent—with the announcement that he would play for the United States rather than Canada in the Canada Cup competition. He was booed mercilessly by Canadian fans during Canada Cup play.

Although his numbers progressively fell for the remainder of the 1980s, Trottier stayed with the Islanders until 1990 when he was signed by the Pittsburgh Penguins. The Penguins hoped the addition of Trottier to their lineup would bolster their playoff chances, and their hunch proved correct. Joining other Penguin stars such as **Mario Lemieux** and **Jaromir Jagr**, Trottier helped power Pittsburgh to two consecutive Stanley Cup victories. After the Penguins' second Stanley Cup win in 1992, Trottier retired as a player and took a desk job in the front office of the Islanders. After sitting out the 1992-1993 season, Trottier decided he'd had enough of the front office and returned to the Penguins as a player for the 1993-1994 season. He played 41 games with the team while also acting as assistant coach. At the end of the season, he finally hung up his skates for good but continued as assistant coach until 1997. He worked as head coach for the Portland Pirates of the AHL for the 1997-1998 season, after which he moved to the Col-

orado Avalanche as assistant coach until 2002. The Avalanche won the Stanley Cup in 2001.

Inducted into the Hockey Hall of Fame in 1997, Trottier was one of the top candidates for the head coaching job with the New York Rangers. In announcing that the job would go to Trottier, Rangers' general manager Glen Sather said: "Since joining the coaching ranks in 1994, Bryan Trottier has demonstrated the same type of passion, determination, and knowledge of the game that he displayed during his Hall of Fame playing career. I am confident that he is the ideal leader for the New York Rangers." In taking the Rangers' job, Trottier became the fifth member of the Islanders' dynasty to become an NHL head coach, joining Lorne Henning, Butch Goring, Greg Gilbert, and Duane Sutter.

CONTACT INFORMATION

Address: Bryan Trottier, c/o New York Rangers, 2 Pennsylvania Plaza, New York, NY 10121.

FURTHER INFORMATION

Periodicals

Gulitti, Tom. "Trottier Paid His Dues." *Record* (Bergen County, NJ) (June 9, 2002): S2.
Podell, Ira. "Trottier Hired as New Rangers Coach." *AP Online* (June 6, 2002).

Other

"Bryan Trottier—Career Highlights." New York Rangers. http://www.newyorkrangers.com/team/highlights_trottier.asp (November 2, 2002).

"Bryan Trottier, 'Trots.' " Joy of Hockey. http://www. joyofhockey.com/xRet1BryanTrottier.html (November 2, 2002).

"The Legends: Players: Bryan Trottier." Legends of Hockey. http://www.legendsofhockey.net:8080/ LegendsOfHockey/jsp/LegendsMember.jsp?mem= p199702&type=Player&page=bio&list=#photo (November 8, 2002).

"Management/Coaching/Training Staff: Bryan Trottier Head Coach." New York Rangers. http://www. newyorkrangers.com/team/coach.asp?coachid=113 (November 2, 2002).

"NHL Player Search: Rocky Trottier." Legends of Hockey. http://www.legendsofhockey.net:8080/ LegendsOfHockey/jsp/SearchPlayer.jsp?player= 14576 (November 8, 2002).

Sketch by Don Amerman

Alex Tudor

Alex Tudor
1977-

British cricket player

An up-and-coming right-handed fast bowler, Alex Tudor was a powerful young British cricket player who showed plenty of promise as a bowler and a batter, but injuries and inconsistency plagued his early career.

Great Promise

Born in the Kensington district of London, Alex Tudor came from a family with origins in Barbados and a cricket background. His father was a bus driver who became a gateman at the Oval, the famous cricket stadium, and his older brother was on the playing staff there.

Tudor excelled in cricket at any early age, playing for London Schools from the age of eight. A right-hand fast bowler and batsman, he was selected to England's U15 team that played in South Africa in 1992-93 and for the U17 team that squared off against India in 1994. In 1996-97, Tudor played on the U19 squad that toured Pakistan. In 1995, he made his first-class debut, playing for Surrey at the age of 19. Tudor was impressive but suffered an injury in his fifth game that ended his season prematurely.

Britain hadn't seen such a strong, speedy bowler in some time. Touted by Wisden, the foremost cricket authority, as "an out-and-out speed merchant who can also bat a bit," Tudor used his size (6 foot 5, 195 pounds) and muscular power to execute powerful bowls and tough bounces that left opposing batsmen befuddled. He had a dignified bearing and an excellent attitude, and was eager to learn and progress. Tudor was hailed as a blazing fast bowler with a naturally smooth delivery.

Injuries and problems with his bowling form plagued Tudor in 1996, and he did not make the Surrey squad. But he earned a call-up to practice with the England team before the First Ashes Test at Edgbaston in 1997. Back at Surrey, Tudor again lost his form and was ineffective, and had another disappointing season in 1998. Still, he was selected for the Ashes tour so that he could work with national bowling coach Bob Cottam.

Cottam awas impressed with Tudor's eagerness and no-nonsense approach. His test debut was in the second Test in November 1998 against Australia, and he impressed observers. But Tudor was cut from the squad for the next test, then recalled for the fourth, but could not play because of a hip injury. In the fifth Test, he was healthy and again impressive.

In his first home series, against New Zealand at Edgbaston, Tudor bowled competently but made headlines with the bat, hitting an unbeaten 99. He was named Man of the Match and the Cricket Writers' Club named him Young Cricketer of the Year. "I've always enjoyed my batting," Tudor explained to CricInfo. "When I was younger, I was an all-rounder but I lost it a bit after concentrating on my bowling. I'd love to go as high in the order as possible." His future seemed assured, but a knee injury kept him out of the next Test.

Chronology	
1995	Makes first-class debut for Surrey
1998	Selected to England squad for Ashes tour
1998	Makes test debut
2002	Returns to England team after rash of injuries

Awards and Accomplishments	
1992	England U15 team
1994	England U17 team
1996	England U19 team
1999	Man of the Match in home Test debut
1999	Young Cricketer of the Year, Cricket Writers Club
2002	Man of the Match, Third Test

Tudor did not make the Test squad in 2000 but was a late replacement on a tour of Pakistan late in the year. Then, on the A Tour of the West Indies, he took five wickets in his debut in the Busta International Shield in Grenada, the beginning of a good tour. Tudor started the 2001 season with a career-high 116 against Essex, and he made five wickets for the first time in Test cricket in a match at Test Bridge, but overall he had an up-and-down season and was left out of England's winter touring squads.

After a good start for Surrey in 2002, Tudor was back on the England team. In the Third test, he was Man of the Match after taking seven wickets. After making his one-day international debut in the NatWest series, playing in three matches, he got shin splints and was unimpressive for the rest of the season.

Battling Back

Tudor's career hadn't yet fulfilled its promise. "It has been frustrating," he admitted to CricInfo. "…these injuries come along and you have to accept it." But Tudor exuded optimism, saying: "I'm a more confident cricketer now, and I'm fitter too." Off the field, Tudor was active promoting youth cricket, helping to launch an innovative after-school cricket program in the London borough of Southwark early in 2002.

Despite his injuries and inconsistencies, Tudor remained one of England's most promising bowlers. He also developed into a reliable fielder and strong batsman, and many experts still believed he could become one of England's best cricket players.

FURTHER INFORMATION

Other

"Alex Jeremy Tudor." _ECB.co.uk_. http://www.cricket.org/link_to_database/PLAYERS/ENG/T/TUDOR_AJ_01007003/(February 3, 2003).

"Alex Tudor Launches Southwark Youth Cricket Scheme at the Elephant." _londonse1_. http://www.london-se1.co.uk/news/view.php?ArtID=410(February 2, 2003).

The Ashes Tour: Squad Profiles. _BBC Sport_. http://news.bbc.co.uk/sport1/shared/spl/hi/cricket/02/ashes/squads/html/tudor.stm (February 2, 2003).

Cricket Writers Club Young Cricketer of the Year Award. _ECB.co.uk_. http://www.cricket.org/link_to_

database/ARCHIVE/CRICKET_NEWS/2000/JUL/044303_ENG_28JUL2000.html (February 2, 2003).

Martin-Jenkins, Christopher. "Test of Young Lion as Tudor Squares Up to his Rival." _Electronic Telegraph_. http://www.cricket.org/link_to_database/ARCHIVE/CRICKET_NEWS/1998/DEC/CMJ_PREVIEW_26DEC1998.html (February 2, 2003).

Martin-Jenkins, Christopher. "Tudor Learns Fast How to Make Best Use of His Pace." _Electronic Telegraph_. http://www.cricket.org/link_to_database/ARCHIVE/CRICKET_NEWS/1998/NOV/CMJ_ON_TUDOR_07NOV1998.html (February 2, 2003).

"Practice Makes Perfect for the Unlikely Batting Hero." _CricInfo News_. http://www.cricket.org/link_to_database/ARCHIVE/CRICKET_NEWS/1999/JUL/TUDOR_BATTING_HERO_04JUL1999.html (February 2, 2003).

"Tudor Celebrates but England Rue Their Ill-Fortune." _CricInfo.com_. http://www.cricket.org/link_to_database/ARCHIVE/CRICKET_NEWS/2001/AUG/264470_ASHES2001-04AUG2001.html (February 2, 2003).

"Tudor Determined to Break Into Test Team." _ecb.co.uk_. http://www.cricket.org/link_to_database/ARCHIVE/CRICKET_NEWS/2000/OCT/056698_ENG_19OCT2000.html (February 2, 2003).

"Tudor's Five Takes England to Victory." _CricInfo.com_. http://www.cricket.org/link_to_database/ARCHIVE/CRICKET_NEWS/2001/JAN/-070038_CI_08JAN2001.html (February 2, 2003).

Sketch by Michael Betzold

Gene Tunney
1897-1978

American boxer

Considered one of the giants of sports in the 1920s, Gene Tunney became heavyweight boxing champion of the world when he defeated **Jack Dempsey** in 1926. In a rematch with Dempsey in 1927, Tunney held on to his title in the hotly debated "battle of the long count,"

Gene Tunney

in which Tunney got the benefit of an extra long count when the referee, following standard boxing rules, refused to start the count until Dempsey returned to his corner. Known for his dispassionate, "scientific" boxing style, which involved a careful study of his opponents before he encountered them, Tunney suffered only one defeat in his career as a professional boxer. He was also the first heavyweight champion to retire as champion and not risk a comeback.

A Boxing New Yorker

Gene Tunney was born James Joseph Tunney to a working class Irish Catholic family in New York City. His father worked as a longshoreman, loading and unloading freighter cargo at New York harbor, and was a fan of boxing. An amateur boxer, Tunney's father fought in matches at Owney Geaghan's boxing club on the Bowery. The young Tunney got into fights in the streets of his Greenwich Village neighborhood as a boy, and his father gave him a pair of boxing gloves for his tenth birthday in the hopes that he would learn to properly defend himself.

At fifteen years of age, Tunney dropped out of school and got a job as an office boy at the Ocean Steamship Company, earning five dollars a week. He moved up to mail clerk, more than doubling his pay to eleven dollars a week, and from there was promoted to freight classifier, bringing in seventeen dollars a week. During breaks, Tunney sparred with any of his office mates who were willing, shoving desks and filing cabinets aside to form

a makeshift ring. In the evenings, Tunney further honed his boxing skills at the Greenwich Village Athletic Club.

In 1915, fresh out of his teens, Tunney became a professional boxer. This was when he fought his first professional match, against an accomplished young boxer named Bobby Dawson. Tunney's seven-round knockout of Dawson earned him eighteen dollars—more than his weekly pay at the steamship company, and it left him with a taste for more.

First North America, then the World

After the United States entered World War I in 1917, Tunney joined the Marines and was stationed in France. While there, he fought in the American Expeditionary Force light heavyweight championship and won. He continued his civilian boxing career on his return from Europe, moving up the ranks to defeat successively more powerful opponents. Finally, in 1922, Tunney defeated Battling Levinsky in twelve rounds to take the title of light heavyweight boxing champion of North America.

Tunney's success was short lived. Only months later, he was forced to defend his title against Harry Greb, a highly aggressive boxer who was known for intimidating his opponents with unusually savage attacks. Greb gave no quarter to Tunney in their match, pounding away at the champion for fifteen rounds, and using a number of tactics that were on the borderline of legality. Tunney put up a heroic defense, managing to stay on his feet with a broken nose Greb gave him by head-butting him, and with his eyes swollen almost shut, until the fight was ended with Greb the winner by decision.

But Tunney made a comeback the following year, 1923, challenging Greb to a rematch. This fight also went a full fifteen rounds before being called in a decision. This time, however, it was Tunney who got the upper hand. He had taken the advice of a boxing tactician, Benny Leonard, who had advised him to keep

---

Awards and Accomplishments

1919	American Expeditionary Force light heavyweight champion
1922	Light heavyweight champion of North America
1923	Light heavyweight champion of North America (regains title)
1926-28	Heavyweight champion of the world
1990	Inducted into the International Boxing Hall of Fame

Tunney was defeated only once in is professional boxing career, retiring with a record of seventy-six wins to his one loss. He was the first heavyweight champion to retire without losing his title.

Two Flaws in Tunney's Public Life; Gene Tunney: A Man in Search of Oblivion

Gene Tunney should have been the living portrait of the certified American hero. He was the young handsome stalwart fighting Marine of World War I, square-jawed and fearless....

But complete admiration escaped Tunney. The flaws were two. He was the man who beat a popular idol when he twice destroyed Dempsey. And ... he lacked the common touch, choosing to hang out with scholars.

Source: Povich, Shirley. *Washington Post.* (November 10, 1978): C1

Greb off balance with as many punches to the body as he could manage. The strategy paid off, and Tunney took back his North American light heavyweight title.

Tunney now had his ultimate goal in sight: the title of heavyweight boxing champion of the world. This title was held by Jack Dempsey, and the two squared off on September 23, 1926. The match was held at Philadelphia's Sesquicentennial Stadium. This site had been chosen because Dempsey had been banned from fighting in New York because he had refused to accept a challenge from African-American boxer Harry Wills.

Tunney had trained hard for his fight against Dempsey, watching films of the champion in action over and over again, probing for weaknesses. He also enlisted the aid of boxers who had fought Dempsey, both opponents and former sparring partners. Brought to Tunney's training camp, these fighters gave Tunney access to a pool of expert knowledge on Dempsey's fighting strengths and weaknesses from which to draw in the formation of his own strategies. He also drew on his own experience gained during his then-seventy-seven professional bouts, only one of which he had lost.

On the day of the fight, the stadium was jammed with more than 120,000 spectators who shelled out a combined two million dollars to see the championship bout. Tunney's meticulous study of his adversary paid off. He came on strong in the first round, rocking Dempsey with a hard right to the face and then keeping him off balance for the remainder of the bout, until the fight was called in Tunney's favor after ten rounds. It was the first time that anyone had won a heavyweight championship in a decision rather than a knockout.

The "Battle of the Long Count"

A year later, almost to the day, on September 22, 1927, Tunney and Dempsey met in a rematch. This time the venue was Soldier Field in Chicago, Illinois. Once again, more than 100,000 fans mobbed the grounds, paying a record $2.6 million to see the match (some sources say the box office take was more than $4.6 million). This fight was also the first to be covered by a professional radio announcer. Tunney and Dempsey slugged it out for the first six rounds, with neither boxer gaining a serious advantage, although Tunney managed to stay ahead in points.

Then, in the seventh round, Dempsey dealt Tunney a staggering right to the temple and quickly pressed the attack with a fury of blows. Tunney went down. Dempsey, caught up in the heat of the moment, failed to promptly retire to his corner of the ring so that the count could start. The referee pleaded with Dempsey to stop hovering over Tunney so that he could start the count, and finally Dempsey yielded.

Getting Dempsey to move took all of four or five seconds, but those extra few moments were all Tunney needed to recover. As one of the spectators, sports writer Shirley Povich wrote fifty-one years later in the *Washington Post,* "I was positive then, as now, that Tunney would not have been up at a proper count of ten, but those precious seconds were heaven-sent for him, and at nine he made a gutsy rise to his feet." The fight was allowed to continue. Tunney managed to avoid Dempsey for the remainder of the round, buying himself even more time to recover. Maintaining his point lead for the remainder of the bout, Tunney won the match by decision in the 10th round.

Many fans felt that an injustice had been done, that Dempsey should have won the fight in that fateful seventh round. Povich recalled that there were "more cheers for Dempsey in that one round than for Tunney in the eight he won in the 10-round fight." The fight came to be known in boxing lore as the "battle of the long count."

Undefeated to the End

Tunney defended his title once more before hanging up his gloves for good. This was in a match with Tom Heeney in New York City on July 26, 1928. Tunney won that match after ten rounds in a technical knockout, allowing him to retire undefeated, the first heavyweight champion to do so.

Tunney led a full and active life following his retirement from boxing. He married Mary Josephine ("Polly") Lauder, niece of a steel baron Andrew Carnegie on October 3, 1928, and then started what was to be a lucrative career in business. After the United States entered World War II in 1942, Tunney served in the U. S. Navy. On his return from the war, he returned to his business career, seeking to remain out of the public eye for much of the remainder of his life. In 1945, he contributed an entry on boxing for the *Encyclopedia Britannica,* and in the 1950s and 1960s, he joined forces with his friend Jack Dempsey to argue before congress for the creation of a national commission that would oversee boxing.

Known for his intellect and appreciation for literature, Tunney befriended noted author and sportsman Ernest Hemingway as well as renown playwright and boxing fan George Bernard Shaw. He himself penned three books, *Boxing and Training, A Man Must Fight,* and *Arms for Living.* Tunney had four children, one of whom, John Varick Tunney, went on to become a member of the United States Senate representing California. Tunney died in 1978 at the age of eighty.

SELECTED WRITINGS BY TUNNEY:

Boxing and Training, A. G. Spaulding & Bros., 1928.
A Man Must Fight, Houghton Mifflin, 1932.
Arms for Living, W. Funk, Inc., 1941.

FURTHER INFORMATION

Books

Dictionary of American Biography, Supplement 10: 1976-1980. Detroit: Charles Scribner's Sons, 1995.
Merriam-Webster's Biographical Dictionary. Springfield, MA: Merriam-Webster Inc., 1995.

Periodicals

"Gene Tunney." *Washington Post.* (November 12, 1978): B6.
Povich, Shirley. "Two Flaws in Tunney's Public Life; Gene Tunney: A Man in Search of Oblivion." *Washington Post* (November 10, 1978): C1.

Other

"Gene Tunney." Cyber Boxing Zone. http://www.cyber boxingzone.com/boxing/tunney-g.htm (October 15, 2002).
"Gene Tunney." International Boxing Hall of Fame. http:www.ibhof.com/tunney.htm (October 15, 2002).

Sketch by Michael Belfiore

Cathy Turner
1962-

American speed skater

Cathy Turner

At the 1994 Olympics, speedskater Cathy Turner was being just like the Cathy Turner everyone knew; tough, competitive and controversial. She took a tight corner in the 500 meter short-track race, shoulder to shoulder with her competition. A speedskater's hands glide over the surface of the ice to keep balance, but in this case, some said she used her hands as a weapon. One of them seemed to grab hold of the ankle of China's Zhang Yanmei, knocking her out of contention for the gold. Most other athletes would have had the benefit of the doubt. But this was Cathy Turner and she had spent years in the sport developing a bad reputation for "dirty skating." The incident didn't quite match the furor that **Tonya Harding** was facing at the same time but it challenged Turner's love of the sport. Even though she's spent many years trying to clean up her image, ultimately her performance that night would end up being what many people remember about her otherwise impressive career.

An Outsider Sport

Turner was born in Rochester, New York on April 10th, 1962. She was a strong skater from an early age, displaying a strength that tended to push her out in front of the pack early in a race. Because of this her trainer decided to focus her on short-track speedskating, the skating equivalent of track's 100-yard dash.

Turner showed a lot of promise as an amateur skater, displaying explosive speed and climbing the amateur circuit, quickly garnering the U.S. championship. But there was one big problem that all of her determination couldn't overcome; the Winter Olympics, a goal so many young athletes aspire to, did not include short-track speedskating in its lineup. Disillusioned with the sport, she left it for another love, music. Under the name Nikki Newland, she performed as a lounge singer around the United States. But after a few years passed, speedskating was again beckoning to her. The decision to compete again got a lot easier when the Olympic committee finally saw fit to include short-track speedskating in the winter Olympics of 1992. Even though Turner had found some success in her singing career she decided to get back into competitive skating at twenty-six years old.

There were many people who had serious doubts about Turner's ability to stage a comeback at her age. But she decisively overcame the skepticism by quickly qualifying to compete in the 1992 Winter Olympics in Albertville, France. After dreaming of the Olympics throughout her childhood, she didn't want to miss the debut of her sport as an international competition. Her performance was almost perfect. She won the gold in the 500 meter race by 4/100th of a second and helped the U.S. team win the silver in the 3000 meter relay, showing off her incredible short sprints of speed to the world.

A Horse Race on Ice

Turner developed a reputation as a tough competitor over the course of her interesting career, some would say a little too tough. Turner's own perception of her sport sums it up best. "I describe it as a horse race on ice with a lot of passing and position changes," she told Sara Walker of *Sports Illustrated for Kids*. "There are tight, fast turns and lots of spills." Indeed, speedskating on an Olympic level can see the athlete hitting thirty-five miles per hour on the ice, the kind of speed that usually requires a seat-

belt. The sport can get very physical, with skaters jostling for position with cunning and, many times, elbows. Some skaters would argue that part of the sport is getting away with whatever device you can to grab the lead and Turner always embraced that philosophy.

The infamous example of this reputation was in the Lillehammer Olympic Games in 1994 when, among other things, Turner crossed skates on the course with favorite and champion, Nathalie Lambert. Lambert was knocked out of contention as a result. Later in the games, after settling for the silver behind Turner in the 500 meter sprint, China's Zhang Yanmei stormed off the ice and threw her bouquet on the track, frustrated and upset by what she thought was an illegal shove by Turner during the competition. It was reported in *Macleans*, that when Zhang was asked in a news conference if Turner was the sport's dirtiest skater she was quick to answer, "Yes. Absolutely." Turner was hurt by this but defended herself by saying she was simply very competitive and that the others were upset because their performances had been so dismal. "It's nothing new. It's an ongoing thing," she told Leigh Montville of *Sports Illustrated*. "They say I'm too aggressive. They're not used to someone fighting for the turns the way I do."

Later in the competition Turner went up against Zhang one last time in the 1000-meter race. She needed to place second to qualify for the finals, but after what appeared to be a brilliant victory on her part, she was disqualified for cross tracking. Cross tracking is a difficult call for a referee to make since it means one competitor illegally prevented another competitor from passing; a subjective call that is always open for debate. Many believe this was just a way for the Olympic officials to punish Turner for what she was accused of a couple of nights prior. Turner, at age thirty-one, had planned to leave the sport for the last time in the world championships in England. But after her experience at the 1994 Lillehammer Olympics she decided it was time to go home. "I have a husband and a life," she told Montville. "I don't want to be around these people. The Olympics were fine, but this day was not fun."

As if to prove her talent she went on to race pro hockey player Al Lafrate of the Washington Capitals in a post-Olympics exhibition race. Lafrate was one of the fastest skaters in the league at the time, but Turner beat him easily.

But, like many "retiring" athletes, she sensed one last opportunity to compete and returned to her sport to be in the 1998 Winter Olympics in Nagano, Japan. This time, though, her appearance was without incident and yielded no medals.

Active Retirement

Turner started her own fitness club in upstate New York after leaving competitive sports. She shot a number of fitness videos as well, which were nationally distributed. She's made a good business out of traveling around the country giving motivational speeches to corporate audiences as well as mental health charities and young athlete organizations. She's been the National Spokesperson for the Special Olympics World Games and the American Heart Association. Turner also put her singing talents to the test by singing the National Anthem at a Buffalo Bills home game and for President Clinton at the Xerox 100 Golden Olympians Gala.

Cathy "Burner" Turner's record as a short-track speedskater is impressive by any standard. Her victories in the 1992 and 1994 Olympics cemented her name, and nickname 'Turner Burner', in the annals of her sport. She stands as one of the most adorned female athletes in Winter Olympic history—with four medals total.

CONTACT INFORMATION

Address: Cathy Turner, Cathy Turner's Empire Fitness, 83 South Avenue, Hilton, NY 14468.

FURTHER INFORMATION

Periodicals

Deacon, James. "Wild and Wooly." *Maclean's* (March 7, 1994): 56.
Hunter, Sarah, and Adam Hunter. "Winter Wonderland" *Sports Illustrated for Kids* (May, 1994): 26.
Montville, Leigh. "Fire on Ice." *Sports Illustrated* (March 7, 1994): 34.

Sketch by Ben Zackheim

Ted Turner
1938-

American baseball executive

World-class sailor. Sports impresario. Stadium developer. Philanthropist. Media maverick and ty-

Ted Turner

coon. These are just some of the many roles played by Robert Edward Turner III, better known as Ted Turner.

"He has set ocean racing records that will never been equaled. (With the launch in 1980 of Cable News Network) he has revolutionized the broadcast industry and made Marshall McLuhan's 'global village' real by tying the world together in one television network," Porter Bibb says in *It Ain't as Easy as It Looks,* a seminal Turner biography published in 1993. "He is complicated and contradictory, but utterly compelling," Bibb writes.

Where to begin with this multifaceted man who grew up in a privileged, but somewhat dysfunctional household? How about at Brown University where Turner, after serving a six-month suspension during his freshman year in 1956, returned to win nine intercollegiate sailing races. Later Turner, who held his own against some of the nation's best collegiate sailors, was elected Brown team captain, as well as commodore of the Brown Yacht Club.

Sailing became an outlet for Turner, who started his business career working for his father's billboard company in 1960. Their relationship was strained, at best. "Nothing could have suited his temperament or his talent better. Alone against the elements, his fate in his

Chronology

1938	Born November 19 in Cincinnati, Ohio
1976	Starts TV "SuperStation" concept, transmitting by satellite from WTBS in Atlanta to cable systems nationwide.
1977	Wins America's Cup match, world's top sailboat competition.
1980	Founded Cable News Network, the first 24-hour, all-news network, through his company, Turner Broadcasting System.
1985	Makes unsuccessful $5 billion bid for CBS
1986	Buys MGM's prized film library from Kirk Kerkorian for about $1.5 billion, providing raw material for Superstation TBS.
1986	Stages Goodwill Games, Olympic-style competition between communist and capitalist countries, that continue in 1990, 1994 and 1998 in New York
1991	Purchases Hanna-Barbera cartoon library, which consists of 8,500 espisodes of such cartoon classics as the Flintstones and Yogi Bear, providing basis for 24-hour cartoon network
1991	Marries actress and fitness guru Jane Fonda on December 21; his third marriage
1996	Sells TBS to Time Warner Inc. for $7.6 billion and becomes vice chairman and a company director of the media conglomerate.
2000	Contributes $34 million to United states to help reduce U.S. dues to international body.
2000	Turner and Fonda announce separation; divorce becomes final in 2001
2002	Instrumental in ouster of CEO Steve Case as chairman of AOL Time Warner
2003	Announces resignation as AOL Time Warner Inc. vice chairman, effective May 2003

Awards and Accomplishments

1970	U.S. Sailing Yachtsman of the Year
1973	U.S. Sailing Yachtsman of the Year
1977	U.S. Sailing Yachtsman of the Year
1979	Outstanding Entreprenuer of the Year, Sales Marketing and Management Magazine
1979	U.S. Sailing Yachtsman of the Year
1984	Lifetime Achievement Award, N.Y. International Film and TV Festival
1988	Citizen Diplomat Award, Center for Soviet-American Dialogue

own hands ... he could sail away from the banalities of the business world, the petty demands of ordinary existence," Bibb writes.

By the late 1960s, Turner was sailing virtually full-time because of the success of the family billboard company. But Turner, the consummate sailor and businessman, was not complacent in either endeavor. Troubled by spending money to maintain unrented billboards, Turner turned them into a vehicle to promote local radio stations he just had purchased. Essentially, Turner was validating what would become a keystone of his business strategy: cross fertilization among the disparate parts of the far-flung media empire that Time Warner ultimately swallowed in 1996.

Brash and Abrasive

Turner refused to modify his occasionally abrasive style, even when navigating the somewhat staid sailing ranks. Because of his brashness he was awarded the moniker "Mouth of the South." His outspokenness, however, did not affect his sailing prowess. A string of successes culminated in Turner being named Yachtsman of the Year in 1970. In fact, he bested Bill Ficker who, as Intrepid captain earlier that year, engineered an America's Cup victory over Australia's Gretel II. Turner won the same award again in 1973, 1977 and 1979.

Meanwhile, Turner continued to build a media empire. In January 1970, Turner Communications Corp.'s merger with Rice Broadcasting brought it WJRJ, the weaker of two UHF (Ultra High Frequency) indepen-dent stations in the Atlanta market. To fill what seemed like endless programming hours, Turner broadcast popular, low-cost 1960s fare such as "Leave it to Beaver" and reruns of "I Love Lucy." Moreover, he won a bidding contest in 1973 with a competing Atlanta television station for rights to 60 baseball games played by the then-struggling Atlanta Braves, three times the number previously televised.

Looked to Expand

With this plethora of programming at hand, Turner sought a wider outlet. He found it in late 1974 when he decided to send television signals to an orbiting communications satellite that, in turn, would relay them to dish-shaped receivers owned by the cable television stations across the country. Thus on December 17, 1976, Turner's "Superstation" was born. The signal was seen from Honolulu to the Virgin Islands and throughout all of North America. "Ted's strategic thinking was sound and foresighted. He essentially was doing an end run around the networks—ABC, CBS, and NBC—and their huge investment in landlines," says Jeremy Byman in his short biography, "Ted Turner, Cable Television Tycoon."

To ensure that the Braves would remain a TBS regular, Turner bought the money-losing team in 1976. Because the Braves provided guaranteed programming, Turner said he could afford to lose $5 million a year on team operations and still come out ahead.

But such subsidies did not sit well with Turner. To bolster the sagging team's fortunes and endear himself and the team to a nonplussed Atlanta, Turner became its prime cheerleader and marketing guru. Seemingly nothing was off limits when building Braves mania. Promotions included Easter egg hunts, ostrich races, free halter-top giveaways and belly dancer performances.

His work paid off when the Braves captured the first professional sports championship for Atlanta after they beat the Cleveland Indians, four games to two, in the 1995 World Series. Through the 2002 season, the team won 11 straight division titles.

Clashed with Baseball Hierarchy

However, prior to registering such unprecedented success, some of Turner's antics did not sit well with the baseball establishment. Turner even managed the Braves for one game, in May 11, 1977, before Commissioner Bowie Kuhn ordered him out of the dugout. Charged with tampering in the signing of outfielder Gary Matthews, Kuhn suspended Turner for the balance of the 1977 season.

That gave Turner the opportunity to focus elsewhere. In late December 1976, Turner also added the struggling Atlanta Hawks basketball team to his growing professional sports stable. Making the deal sweeter was the low price tag: $400,000, plus assumption of a $1 million note.

Freed at least for a year from his pressing baseball obligations, Turner threw himself into his other passion, sailing. He underwrote construction of the innovatively designed, aluminum-hulled *Courageous,* a boat selected to defend the America's Cup against challenger Australia. Turner piloted his craft to a sweep over the challenger from Down Under.

Clashed with Baseball Hierarchy

However, Turner's bid to defend the Cup three years later fell short, with his loss to Dennis Connor. The result: Turner renounced competitive sailing and sold his boats, *Courageous* and *Tenacious*. In fact, most of Turner's subsequent racing has been with an 18-foot catamaran crew, with son, Rhett, on the crew.

Turner in 1986 launched the quadrennial Goodwill Games, an alternative international sports competition, that were played through 1998. The motivations were twofold: to provide an alternative athletic forum following Washington's decision to boycott the 1980 Winter Olympics in Moscow (the Soviet Union boycotted the Los Angeles Summer Olympics in 1984) and, of course, provide a source of ready programming for TBS during the slack periods.

Turner also expanded his sports franchise when he founded the Atlanta Thrashers, a National Hockey League expansion team that began play in 1999. It plays at the $213 million Philips Arena, a new face on the Atlanta sports skyline that complements the $235 million Turner Field, named after the owner of the Atlanta Braves, the primary tenant. It opened in March, 1997.

Turner's Impact

As sportsman, Turner was a sailing champion. As a sports entrepreneur in the 1970s, Turner represented a new breed of owner. He epitomized corporate ownership while remaining a hands-on maverick. He blurred the distinction between business and sports, and remains highly influential today in both, despite his departure from AOL Time Warner early in 2003 amid a management shakeup. Turner, at the time of his announcement, remained the largest individual shareholder of AOL Time Warner.

SELECTED WRITINGS BY TURNER:

(With Gary Jobson) *The Racing Edge*. New York: Simon and Schuster, 1979.

Captain Planet and the Planeteers (original idea by Ted Turner). Atlanta: Turner Publications, 1992.

(With Janet Lowe) *Ted Turner Speaks: Insights from the World's Greatest Maverick*. New York: Wiley, 1999.

FURTHER INFORMATION

Books

Bibb, Porter. *It Ain't As Easy As It Looks*. New York: Crown, 1993.

Byman, Jeremy. *Ted Turner: Cable Television Tycoon*. Greensboro, NC: Morgan Reynolds, 1998.

Periodicals

Peers, Martin and Ken Brown. "AOL's Winners and Losers." *Wall Street Journal* (January 14, 2003): B1.

Other

"Future Muddy for Braves, Hawks, Thrashers." *Atlanta Journal-Constitution*. http://www.accessatlanta.com/ajc/sports/0103/30turner.html (January 29, 2003).

"Ted Turner Bio Information." *Austin American-Statesman*. http://www.austin360.com/aas/business/ap/ap_story.html/Financial/AP.V7172.AP-Turner-Bio-B ox.html (January 29, 2003)

Sketch by Paul Burton

Mike Tyson
1966-

American boxer

He was one of the best, and he blew it. The youngest heavyweight champion in history, the most inspiring champ since **Muhammad Ali**, Mike Tyson became the most notorious modern boxer when he went to jail for rape, and then, in his comeback tour, for biting off a piece of **Evander Holyfield**'s ear. Even before that, Tyson was the man who bragged about wanting to kill his opponents, to punch a man so hard his nose would go through his skull. It is tempting to see Tyson's story as a classic Greek tragedy, the same primal brutality that carried him to the top destroying him in the end. But Tyson was not a plaything for the gods and the Furies. At each step he had opportunities, chances not often given to

Mike Tyson

ghetto kids. And despite appearances, he was not stupid. He had a choice. And he blew it.

Mike Finds a Mentor

Michael Gerard Tyson was born in Brooklyn, New York, on June 30, 1966, to Lorna Tyson and Jimmy Kirkpatrick. His father ran off before he was two years old, and Mike grew up with all the temptations of ghetto life. By the age of twelve, he was in a street gang and had been in and out of juvenile court. Finally, after an armed robbery conviction, in 1978, he was sent to the Tryon School for Boys, a reformatory, where the physical education instructor, Bobby Stewart, spotted his potential as boxer. In 1981, Stewart introduced the 14-year-old Tyson to his friend, the legendary Cus D'Amato, and D'Amato introduced him to the "sweet science" of boxing.

Cus D'Amato took Tyson in, and when Tyson's mother died a couple of years later, D'Amato became Tyson's legal guardian. Slowly, he and Camille brought Tyson out of his shell, nurturing his aspirations and overcoming his self-doubts. As he explained it to reporter William Plummer, "people, especially if they come up in a rough area, have to go through a number of experiences in life that are intimidating and embarrassing. These experiences form layer upon layer over their capabilities and talents. So your job as teacher is to peel off those layers." As D'Amato peeled layers, he discovered a young man who'd grown up wild, and who was deeply ashamed that he couldn't even read. D'Amato soon corrected that, providing a tutor and introducing Tyson to books on **Joe Louis** and **Jack Dempsey**, and other "heavyweights" like Napoleon and Alexander the Great. These were life lessons that would reshape the young fighter, and for a time it seemed the "priestly" D'Amato had redeemed the soul of Mike Tyson.

Iron Mike

When Tyson first stepped into the ring for a professional boxing match, on March 4, 1985, there was no fanfare or boasts before the cameras. Tyson didn't even have a robe to cast off dramatically before the match. But he did have something. He had a menacing glare that would intimidate many fighters in the years ahead, sometimes defeating them before they even stepped in the ring. If that did not work, a single, stunning blow usually did the trick. And he had a thorough grounding in the methods of great fighters of the past, and perhaps most importantly, a sense of his own strength. Tyson would go 15-0 in his first year, but in November he lost his only real father figure, Cus D'Amato, who died at age 77.

It was a bitter blow, but far from a knockout punch. Tyson still had his co-manager, Jimmy Jacobs, D'Amato's old friend and a legendary trainer in his own right. He had a good team around him, he had that glare, a strong neck that let him take a fair amount of punishment, and fists that seemed unstoppable. Before long they were calling him "Iron Mike," and not long after that, they were calling him champ.

On November 22, 1986, he took out Trevor Berbick in two rounds, winning the World Boxing Council (WBC) heavyweight title. Tyson destroyed Berbick. As one of the judges, District Attorney Lane, told *Sports Illustrated,* "If I had let the fight continue, if I let him get hit with more of those terrible punches, it would have been criminal." A year after D'Amato's death, Tyson had fulfilled his dream and become the youngest heavyweight champion in history. It was a sweet moment, but the confused state of modern boxing meant his title was incomplete. In addition to the WBC, there was also a WBA (World Boxing Association) and IBF (International Boxing Federation) champion.

The following year, Tyson did the necessary consolidation. On March 7, 1987, Tyson went up against WBA placeholder James "Bonecrusher" Smith in Las Vegas. Smith fought not so much to crush Tyson's bones as to preserve his own, and after 12 dull rounds Tyson was declared the winner. On August 1, 1987, Tyson went up against IBF champion Tony Tucker to reunite the triple crown of boxing. Tucker did manage to land a blow in the first round, and ultimately he did go the distance, but it was clearly Tyson's fight throughout. "Aw, he stopped fighting after the fifth round," Tyson told *Sports Illustrated.* "After that he was just in there to survive." Tucker survived, but his championship did not. When it was over, Mike Tyson was the undisputed World Heavyweight Championship (complete with crown and chinchilla robe, provided, inevitably, by the showman who always managed to climb into the ring with a champ, **Don King**). An embarrassed Mike Tyson sat in brooding silence during this "coronation."

The Troubled Champ

By the end of 1987, Tyson was being hailed as the most exciting champ since Muhammad Ali, an example for ghetto kids, and indeed all kids, to aspire toward. Interestingly, he was surrounded by white men, including his co-managers Jim Jacobs and Bill Cayton, and so he seemed to embody racial harmony and a "we can all get along" spirit that only added to the allure of the "reformed" delinquent. In 1988, it all began to go wrong.

As if sleep-walking in a film noir, Tyson soon found his femme fatale, Robin Givens. The beautiful star of ABC's "Head of the Class," Givens represented class and sophistication to the newly crowned champ. To Givens, or at least to her mother, Ruth Roper, Tyson represented money—a lot of money. Tyson had earned millions of dollars in fight purses and television contracts, including a $26 million deal with HBO for a series of seven fights, signed in 1987. More unusually for a prizefighter, he had honest management that had allowed him to keep the lion's share of that money. After a whirlwind courtship, Tyson married Givens on February 7, 1988. Soon, she and her mother began to do a little house-

---

Related Biography: Trainer Cus D'Amato

Cus D'Amato was more than a boxing trainer with a good eye for talent. D'Amato was a legend, hailed as the man who had successfully fought mobster Frank Carbo's boxing monopoly and made Floyd Patterson "king of the sport," in the words of *People* reporter William Plummer. Norman Mailer had called him a Zen master. He was more of a teacher than a trainer, a teacher in the old, all-encompassing sense. While he taught his fighters the moves, he also drew them out, discovering their hidden talents and fears. "Fear is like a fire," he'd tell them. "If you control it, as we do when we heat our houses, it is a friend. When you don't it consumes you and everything around you."

By the time Mike Tyson met him, D'Amato had largely retired from the sport, but he maintained a training camp at an old Victorian house in the Catskills, courtesy of his mistress, Camille Ewald. Usually there were five or six aspiring fighters in residence. Fight-film entrepreneur Jimmy Jacobs provided the equipment. (D'Amato had helped others to riches, but his own money always seemed to slip through his fingers, often lent to friends unable to pay him back.) When he saw Tyson, he saw the kind of champion he'd almost forgotten, one who could reach the top, and actually deserve the honor.

---

cleaning, banishing many of Tyson's friends and closely questioning others about the state of his finances.

A month later, Tyson's co-manager, Jim Jacobs, died. While Tyson was at the funeral, his wife Robin was at the bank, demanding to know the whereabouts of "her money." Shortly thereafter, they confronted Tyson's surviving manager, Bill Cayton, demanding a full accounting and ultimately reducing his share of the champ's earnings from one-third to 20 percent. Tyson's behavior became increasingly erratic, ramming cars into trees, getting into a street brawl with boxer Mitch Green and, on a disastrous trip to Russia, chasing Robin and her mother through the hotel corridors in a drunken rage. In a nationally televised interview with Barbara Walters, Givens told America of her "life of horror" with a manic-depressive Mike Tyson, while the heavyweight champ sat meekly at her side, looking to some observers like a tranquilized pit bull. Shortly after the interview Tyson smashed up furniture, glassware, and windows at their mansion in Bernardsville, N.J., and Givens fled to Los Angeles, where she filed for divorce. At the time, she was generally seen as the villain. Her image was splashed across the tabloids with the simple caption: Most Hated Woman in America.

Out of the Frying Pan ...

Almost as soon as Givens left Tyson's life, Don King entered. King had waited a long time. For years, Tyson had been making mincemeat of King's stable of heavyweight champions, and it frustrated the promoter deeply that he had no piece of the champ. King's first opening came at Jim Jacob's funeral, which he attended uninvited, loudly condemning Tyson's managers for such indignities as not having a limo ready for the champ. He had also worked strenuously to bring to light the suspicions of Givens and her mother toward Bill Cayton. And now, with Givens out of the picture, he pounced, offering Tyson the use of his farm in Ohio to recuperate from

Awards and Accomplishments

1986	Takes WBC heavyweight championship, November 22 (youngest heavyweight champ in history)
1987	Takes WBA heavyweight title, March 7
1987	Takes IBF heavyweight championship, August 1 (becomes undisputed World Heavyweight Champion)
1989	Defeats former champ Michael Spinks, by a knockout in 90 seconds

his disastrous marriage. King also proved useful, moving swiftly to close Tyson's joint accounts with Givens, just in time to prevent her from transferring over $600,000 into her own account.

At the same time, King began to plant doubts in Tyson's mind about all the "white men" around him, particularly his manager. Perhaps drained from his recent experiences, Tyson began to listen, and before long he was firmly in King's corner, even giving him a limited power of attorney. "I think Don has sold black to Tyson," former heavyweight champ and King client Larry Holmes told *Sports Illustrated*. Cayton could only add, "I feel very sad that Mike appears to have gone from a manipulative situation … to another, far more manipulative situation."

Tyson, however, wasn't worried. He still had his millions, he still had his undefeated pro career, and he still had his title. In April, 1989, he successfully defended the latter two against England's Frank Bruno, easily overpowering him in the fifth round. Then, on June 27 in Atlantic City, in what may have been his greatest night in the ring, he floored former champ **Michael Spinks** in all of 90 seconds. Then, on February 10, 1990, the unthinkable happened in Tokyo. James "Buster" Douglas, a 42-1 underdog who couldn't even get a photographer to come to his weigh-in, came back from an eighth round knockdown to fell the champ in the tenth. It was impossible, and at first, Don King wouldn't let it happen. He got representatives from the WBC, the WBA, and even the Japan Boxing Commission to declare that Douglas should have been counted out in the eighth round, awarding the fight to Tyson. But King too suffered a rare defeat, and in the face of enormous public outrage, the fight and the title were soon awarded to Buster Douglas.

And into Hot Water

For Tyson, it was the beginning of the end. Not that it was obvious in the ring. Shortly after the Douglas fiasco he began his comeback, knocking out former Olympian Henry Tillman in the first round on June 16, and defeating Donovan "Razor" Ruddick twice in 1991. He was all set to take on the new heavyweight champ, Evander Holyfield, in November, 1991. The fight never happened.

While attending the Miss Black America Pageant in July, Tyson had earned a bizarre new title when a pageant

organizer called him a "serial buttocks fondler," accusing him of assaulting 11 of the 23 contestants. It was easy fodder for late-night comedians. But nobody was laughing when one of those contestants, Desiree Washington, brought a much more serious charge. According to her, Tyson had lured her to a hotel room during the contest and then raped her. He was tried and convicted, and in March 1992, he was sentenced to six years in prison.

It was a stunning turnaround for the champ who once seemed so unbeatable, so exciting, and of course it brought an immediate backlash. In the popular mind, Tyson was now a brutal thug who could not control his impulses, and had landed where he should have been all along. Before long Tyson was in trouble, accused of assaulting a guard, and placed in solitary confinement. Before long, odd stories began to leak out, that Tyson was reading up on communism. Perhaps this was a response to rumors that Don King was squandering his fortune, that Tyson might be a penniless proletarian by the end of his jail term. There were stories that he had converted to Islam. People wondered if Tyson was a changed man. At any rate, he emerged from prison on March 25, 1995, having served only three of his six years.

On the Comeback Trail—Again

Mike Tyson's first stop after being released was a mosque, where he prayed with Muhammad Ali. Some speculated that it was a sign that things were changing. But one aspect remained the same. On the day he was released Don King negotiated a deal with Showtime on behalf of "his" champ. Tyson's first post-prison bout was with Peter McNeely, who looked good on paper with a 36-1 record. But the 36 victories were against habitual losers, and the loss was to McNeely's only opponent with a winning record. McNeely's manager threw in the towel 85 seconds into his match with Tyson. A broken thumb postponed his next match, but on December 16, Tyson knocked out Buster Mathis in the third round. In March of 1996, he likewise dispatched Frank Bruno in the third. After three easy victories, and not incidentally, $65 million richer, Tyson was feeling on top again. On September 7, 1996, he met Bruce Seldon, who was on the mat in 109 seconds. Some fans said they did not actually see a punch, and wondered if the fight was fixed. Seldon's manager speculated that his client had actually suffered a nervous breakdown in the face of Tyson—and, in fact, Seldon has not fought another boxing match since then.

Finally, boxing fans could look forward to a long-delayed match-up, when Evander Holyfield agreed to fight Tyson in November of 1996 for the heavyweight championship. Against all odds the 34-year-old Holyfield ended what *Sports Illustrated's* Richard Hoffer called Tyson's "machinery of menace," when he won a technical knockout in the eleventh round. It was a huge upset, defying all expectations. In fact, pay-per-view channels had offered a per-round price, so customers would not blame them when Tyson felled Holyfield in the first round. Boxing officials had forced Holyfield to undergo a battery of tests, fearing he might actually lose his life. It was a stunning result, but nothing could prepare the boxing world for the shock they were about to get.

The Holyfield-Tyson rematch, held was one of the most anticipated in history. The MGM Grand sold out on the first day, all 16,000 tickets. Millions tuned in on pay-per-view, anticipating a spectacle. They got one. The fight was brutal from the start, with Holyfield at one point head butting Tyson in the second round. Then in the third, Tyson chomped down on Holyfield's left ear. The referee deducted two points from Tyson, but then let the fight go on. Again the fighters met in the center, and again Tyson spat out his mouthpiece and chomped down, on Holyfield's right ear. And this time he bit a piece off, spitting it out. This time the referee called the fight, disqualifying Tyson.

It was bizarre. It was savage. And for many it was the last straw. Tyson had nearly proved himself too brutal for boxing—not an easy feat. The Nevada State Commission withheld his paycheck and suspended his license. Outrage poured in from all sides, with even the White House weighing in. Tyson became constant fodder for late night comedy, and the Hollywood Wax Museum moved his image from sports to the Chamber of Horrors. But in the end, Tyson escaped. He was banned for a year, and fined $3 million, but ultimately, boxing decided to let Tyson keep doing the only thing he was really good at: hitting people until they fell down.

The Unrepentant

And Tyson wasn't finished, with boxing or with outrages. On October 19, 1998, the Nevada State Boxing Commission restored Tyson's boxing license. In December of 1998, he pled no contest to a road rage incident and spent a short time in jail the following March. That year he also initiated a $100 million lawsuit against Don King after discovering that his $200 million career winnings had dwindled away, and that in fact he owed $13 million in back taxes. In the summer of 2000, after knocking down an opponent, Lou Savarese, he continued to pound the fighter and even lashed out at the referee. Incredibly, in the post-fight press conference, Tyson revived his cannibal image in remarks addressed to heavyweight champ **Lennox Lewis**, whom Tyson hoped to meet in the ring some day. "I want your heart. I want to eat your children," Tyson declared, adding, "I will rip out his heart and feed it to him."

Then, in the runup to the actual Tyson-Lewis match, Mike Tyson seemed to blow his chances. While the Nevada State Athletic Commission was considering whether to give Tyson a license to box there, Tyson charged at Lewis during a pre-fight press conference. Lewis' bodyguard intervened, and a brawl ensued. Nevada turned him down for a license, but Washington, D.C.,

Mike Tyson

allowed the fight to take place there. When the fight finally took place in June of 2002, Lennox knocked Tyson out in the eighth round. It was almost anti-climactic that the unbeatable Iron Mike had been felled again.

Tyson had come a long way from the days when Cus D'Amato had dreamed of making him a legend. He had almost fulfilled those dreams, winning a world championship at the age of 19 and consolidating all of boxing's dubious crowns into one that nobody could dispute. For awhile he seemed like the champ everyone had been waiting for. But in the end, he seemed to willfully throw it all away. Tyson continues to fight, in the face of public outrage, and maybe he will win back fans and reclaim his titles—but with every year and every comment and every altercation, it seems like that goal, if it is his goal, slips further away.

CONTACT INFORMATION

Address: Office: 10100 Santa Monica Blvd. #1300, Los Angeles, CA 90067.

FURTHER INFORMATION

Periodicals

Boyle, Robert. "The final bell rings for Cus D'Amato." *Sports Illustrated* (November 18, 1985): 20.

Callahan, Tom. "Boxing's allure." *Time* 49 (June 27, 1988): 66.

Gross, Ken. "People Weekly." *Life* (October 17, 1998): 60.

Hoffer, Richard. "All the rage." *Sports Illustrated* (May 20, 2002): 34.

Hoffer, Richard. "Buster Douglas was floored by Mike Tyson in the eighth round,but then he got up ..." *Sports Illustrated* (February 19, 1990): 12.

Hoffer, Richard. "Destined to fall." *Sports Illustrated* (February 17, 1992): 24.

Hoffer, Richard. "Out of the darkness." *Sports Illustrated* (April 3, 1995): 44.

Kram, Mark. "The tiger king." *Esquire* (April 1996): 74.

Loverro, Thom. "Tyson apologizes for his 'worst night.'" *The Washington Times* (July 1, 1997): 74.

"Main Event: Tyson-King." *Sports Illustrated* (March 16, 1998): 16.

"Mike Tyson vs. Robin Givens: the champ's biggest fight." *Ebony* (January 1989): 116.

Plummer, William. "Cus D'Amato." *People* (July 15, 1985): 77.

"Professional boxing: It was a very good year." *Sports Network* (December 31, 2002): 16.

Putnam, Pat. "All the king's man." *Sports Illustrated* (November 7, 1988): 20.

Putnam, Pat. "Getting a belt out of life." *Sports Illustrated* (December 1, 1986): 18.

Putnam, Pat. "Only one number 1." *Sports Illustrated* (August 10, 1987): 20.

Shulan, Michael. "Heavyweights." *Nation* (July 30, 1988): 102.

"Tyson's win is boxing's loss." *Business Week Online* (March 14, 2002).

Sketch by Robert Winters

Wyomia Tyus
1945-

American track and field athlete

She became a world champion barely out of high school. She broke records in almost all the track events in which she competed. She was the first person, man or woman, to win consecutive Olympic gold medals for the 100-meter race. Yet, despite three Olympic gold medals and one silver medal, her accomplishments seemed to slip by with barely a commentary from the world around her. Whether it was racism, sexism, or the political climate, Wyomia Tyus stood up to the challenges of her time and proved herself a world-class athlete.

Wyomia Tyus

Early Training

Tyus was born in Griffin, Georgia, on August 29, 1945. She was the youngest child of Willie and Marie Tyus. She was also the only girl. With three older brothers to keep up with, Tyus learned early how to hold her own. Her father insisted that Wyomia not be left out by her brothers, no matter what they played. She had an early education in backyard football and basketball and other neighborhood games, playing equally with the boys.

She also had an early education in the inequities caused by racism and sexism. Tyus had to spend an hour on the bus to school each day because the school she could walk to was for white children only. In spite of these difficulties she believed in herself and in working hard to achieve her goals. Tyus explained to Lyn Votava of *Ethnic NewsWatch,* "Now in my day, this wasn't something women were encouraged to do." Through the love and encouragement of her father and her coach, Tyus was able to focus on her athletic abilities, letting them guide her to a better place.

In high school, she was originally drawn to basketball. In 1960, she was invited to a summer clinic at Tennessee State University (TSU) by the track coach Ed Temple. Tyus discovered her own talent for running through Temple's clinic and became serious about track. That same year, her father died, leaving her without his guidance. Temple would take on an impor-

Chronology

1945	Born August 29 in Griffin, Georgia
1960	Attends Coach Ed Temple's summer track program at Tennessee State University; father dies
1963	Graduates from high school
1964	Competes in the Olympic Games in Tokyo, Japan
1967	Graduates from Tennessee State University
1968	Competes in the Olympic Games in Mexico City, Mexico
1974	Co-founds Women's Sports Foundation
1984	Participates in opening ceremonies at Olympic Games in Los Angeles, California
1997	Spokesperson for Active and Ageless exercise program
2000	Leads United States Olympic Committee's Project Gold 2000

Awards and Accomplishments

1964	First place in Amateur Athletic Union (AAU) 100-meter race; gold medal in 100-meter race and silver medal in 4 x 100-meter relay at Olympic Games in Tokyo, Japan
1965	First place in AAU 100-yard and 60-yard race; set world record for 60-yard race
1966	First place in AAU 100-yard, 220-yard, and 60-yard races; sets world record for 60-yard race
1967	Gold medal for 200-meter dash at Pan American Games
1968	Gold medals for 100-meter race and 4 x 100-meter relay at Olympic Games in Mexico City, Mexico; sets world record for 100-meter race at 11.08 seconds
1969	Governor of Georgia names January 25, 1969 Wyomia Tyus Day
1974	Set world indoor record for 70-meter race
1980	Inducted into National Track and Field Hall of Fame
1981	Inducted into International Women's Sports Hall of Fame
1984	Inducted into "Avenue of Athletes" by Echo Park Chamber of Commerce, Los Angeles, California
1985	Inducted into United States Olympic Hall of Fame
2001	Voted one of Georgia's top athletes by Georgia Sports Hall of Fame

tant role in Tyus's life, stepping in where her father once stood.

While still in high school Tyus competed in the Amateur Athletics Union (AAU) Girls' National Championships. She won first place in the 50-yard, 75-yard, and the 100-yard races. She ended up attending TSU in Nashville, Tennessee, based upon Temple's invitation and the fact that it was one of the only universities that offered women athletic scholarships. The women's scholarships were unlike those given to men. While men could focus exclusively on their sports, women were required to work two hours a day for their scholarships.

Olympic Success

In college, Tyus continued to win races. Her win at the National AAU women's outdoor meet in the 100-meter race earned her a spot on the 1964 Olympic track team. Her TSU teammate Edith McGuire was also on the Olympic team that year. The games were played in Tokyo, and McGuire was favored to win. Tyus sped past McGuire in the final heat to win the gold medal. She was proud of her accomplishment, but that pride was tempered by the certain knowledge that she was expected to be a woman first. She explained to Votava, "Coach Temple always told us that we could break world records and win gold medals, but we probably still wouldn't be recognized because we were women and we were Black."

Those words became truer in 1968 during the Olympic games held in Mexico City, Mexico. Tyus, who had been encouraged by her family to quit before then, was again competing for the United States track team. She was determined to defend her 100-meter race championship despite suggestions that at twenty-three she was too old to be competing. She was also troubled by her choice to compete as a representative of the United States during a time of extreme racial turmoil. Many black athletes from the U.S. had boycotted the games. Tyus chose to go, but protested silently by always wearing black during awards ceremonies.

At the games, Tyus set the world record with her time in the 100-meter race at 11.08 seconds and secured a record-breaking gold medal in the same race. She also contributed to the 4 x 100-meter relay team that won the gold medal. Her time in the 100-meter race would not be topped by another American athlete until 1984. In addition, she became the first person to defend the 100-meter race title in successive Olympics. That record would not be broken until **Carl Lewis** won his second Olympic gold for the race in 1988.

In the climate of protest that existed during the 1968 Olympics, Tyus's accomplishments passed by unnoticed. Wanting to register protest against the expulsion of **Tommie Smith** and John Carlos, U.S. track runners who had raised their arms in a Black Power salute during an awards ceremony, Tyus gave her medals to Smith and Carlos. Years later she described her admiration to *People,* "What I did … was win a track event. What they did lasted a lifetime, and life is bigger than sport." Tyus continued competing on the amateur circuit until 1973 when she started competing professionally. In 1974, she set the world indoor track record for the 70-meter race at 8.3 seconds.

A Coach's Influence

A consistent presence in Tyus's life from high school through college and for the 1964 Olympics was Ed Temple. Tyus told Mary Reese Boykin of the *Los Angeles Times,* "Coach Ed Temple came into my life after my father died. A man of integrity, Coach Temple had many sayings to encourage us during the rough times." He expected a lot from his team. He taught Tyus the value of an education and expected her and each of his athletes to graduate from college. He also knew that the public did not readily accept women athletes and encouraged Tyus and her teammates to always be "ladies first." Speaking almost twenty years after Tyus's Olympic win, Temple said to Bert Rosenthal of the Associated Press, comment-

Where Is She Now?

Wyomia Tyus currently lives in Los Angeles with her second husband, Duane Tillman. She has two grown children: a daughter, Simone, and a son, Tyus. She made no money from her amateur track career through endorsements and other similar contracts that support today's world-class athletes. She did use the advantages of her Olympic status to continue in a positive direction for herself and for others. As history has caught up with the importance of her contributions to track, Tyus has proved the value of her experience through leadership roles in a number of important areas.

In 1974 Tyus, along with tennis star Billie Jean King and Olympic swimmer Donna de Varona and other female athletes, founded the nonprofit Women's Sports Foundation. The Foundation was created to help girls coming up in sports find guidance through education, advocacy, recognition, and opportunity. By 1994, the Women's Sports Foundation was handing out grants that totaled over $800,000 to programs that supported girls in sports and to individuals who needed funding to achieve their athletic goals.

Tyus has been a tireless speaker on behalf of female participation in sports as well as other areas of athletics and physical fitness. In 1982, she traveled to sixty cities on a tour that promoted women's athletics. In 1985, she participated in a clinic at Pepperdine University that enlightened high school students of all abilities to the variety of careers available in sports. In 1997, she was spokesperson for the Active and Ageless program that encouraged people over 50 to exercise. In 2000, she served in a leadership role on the United States Olympic Committee's (USOC) Project Gold 2000.

During most of this time, Tyus has been an outdoor education specialist for the Los Angeles Unified School District. It's a job that she finds very satisfying, one in which she considers the Angelus National Forest her office. She told *People,* "I get to hike every day and leave the smog behind."

ing on the women he coached, "The most famous one was **Wilma [Rudolph]**…. But maybe the best was Tyus."

Wyomia Tyus's reign as one of the world's fastest female runners may have had a different outcome if she'd come along twenty years later. She competed during a time when the public had difficulty accepting the athleticism of female athletes. She overcame the impediments of a college sports program that favored men. She even proved that twenty-three was not too old to compete successfully in world-class events.

There is no doubt that she set a high standard for herself and overcame many obstacles. That's not uncommon for Olympic-level athletes. What is exceptional about Tyus is that despite being overlooked by history and despite never having made any money from her track career, she made the most of what track had to offer. Most extraordinary of all she did it with a smile and with humble recognition of her own talents. She explained to Boykin, "I wasn't paid a dime for my track career. But participating in the Olympics gave me the opportunity to learn about different cultures; it made me a better person. I wouldn't trade the time I competed for anything." She is able to look back on her career and recognize the gifts of the people around her that helped her succeed. When she spoke to a group of high school students, Tyus told them, as reported by Ann

Japenga of the *Los Angeles Times,* "You can be the best in the world and not be recognized…. A lot of it has to do with breaks. If a coach at Tennessee State hadn't given me a break at 14, I never would have been in the Olympic Games."

CONTACT INFORMATION

Address: Wyomia Tyus, 1102 Keniston Avenue, Los Angeles, CA 90019. Phone: (323) 934-6559.

SELECTED WRITINGS BY TYUS:

Inside Jogging for Women, Contemporary Books, 1978.

FURTHER INFORMATION

Books

Johnson, Anne Janette. *Great Women in Sports.* Detroit: Visible Ink Press, 1996.

Periodicals

Boykin, Mary Reese. "Voices / A Forum for Community Issues; Community Interviews; Go for the Gold Throughout Life." *Los Angeles Times* (September 16, 2000): B9.

"A Child of Jim Crow, She Refused to Run Second to Anyone." *People* (July 15, 1996): 109.

Crouse, Karen. "Wyomia Tyus: Jones Minus Hype." *Daily News* (Los Angeles, CA) (July 13, 2000): S1.

"For Your Information." PR Newswire (June 6, 1984).

Japenga, Ann. "Workouts, Words on Right Track to Career in Sports." *Los Angeles Times* (June 28, 1985): P5.18.

Lawrence, James. "Wyomia Tyus Speaks Up for Female Athletes." United Press International (August 28, 1982).

New York Times (February 24, 1974): S5.3.

Rosenthal, Bert. Associated Press (November 28, 1989).

"Three-time Olympic gold medal sprinter headlines USOC diversity project." Associated Press (March 24, 2000).

Votava, Lyn. "They Raced for Their Lives." *Ethnic NewsWatch* (March 31, 1994): 62.

Other

"Wyomia Tyus." Women's Sports Foundation. http://www.womenssportsfoundation.org/cgi-bin/iowa/sports/ggg/ind.html?record=305 (January 6, 2003).

Sketch by Eve M. B. Hermann

Johnny Unitas
1933-2002

American football player

Ignored and overlooked in his early years, Johnny Unitas went on to become one of the greatest quarterbacks in football history. Unitas, whose passing ability earned him the nickname "the Golden Arm," led the winning team in what is widely regarded as the greatest game in the annals of professional football. His was in some ways a Horatio Alger story, but his heroism never stopped him from being human, and thus his career served as a reminder that even the greatest of gridiron giants is still just a man. On the day he died, September 11, 2002, America was busy commemorating the terrorist attacks that had occurred exactly a year earlier, and thus Unitas, always known for his stoicism, passed quietly from the scene. Yet football had been changed forever because of him.

Humble Beginnings

The third of Leon and Helen Unitas's fourth children was born John Constantine Unitas, in Pittsburgh, Pennsylvania, on May 7, 1933. The family was of Lithuanian descent, and strongly Catholic. Leon, who operated a small coal-delivery business, died when his son was just five years old. Helen took over the business, and with that and odd jobs, she supported the family.

Unitas decided he wanted to become a professional football player when he was just 12 years old. As quarterback for St. Justin's High School, a position he won after the original quarterback broke his ankle, he made enough of a name for himself that as a senior he earned a spot on Pittsburgh's All-Catholic High School team. This was to be his greatest success for half a decade.

Laboring in Obscurity

As a high-school senior, Unitas already sported the crewcut that would be his trademark. He stood six feet tall, but weighed only 138 pounds, making him light even by the standards of a high-school player in 1951. He dreamed of playing for Notre Dame, but the Fighting Irish rejected him because he did not appear likely to gain any weight. The University of Pittsburgh offered

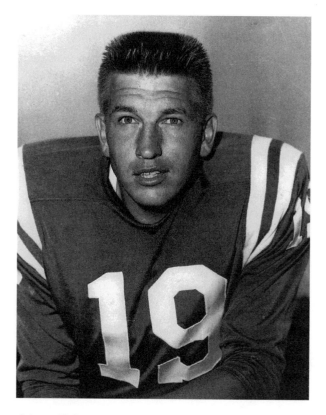

Johnny Unitas

Unitas a scholarship, yet he failed the entrance exam, and this left only the University of Louisville, which gave him a scholarship. In his years at Louisville (1951-55), he remained in the shadows, but he did manage to gain 56 pounds and grow two inches.

In 1954, at the beginning of his senior year, Unitas married long-time girlfriend Dorothy Jean Hoelle, with whom he would eventually have five children. After graduation, his hometown Steelers picked him on the ninth round of the college draft, only to drop him before he even played in an exhibition game.

Disappointed but far from ready to give up, Unitas moved his family to Bloomfield, New Jersey, where he worked on a construction crew and played quarterback for the Bloomfield Rams. The Rams played on fields that were often strewn with litter, and for his troubles, Unitas earned just six dollars per game. Still, his efforts

Chronology	
1933	Born in Pittsburgh, Pennsylvania, on May 7
1951	Graduates from St. Justin's High School, for which he played quarterback and earned a spot on Pittsburgh's All-Catholic High School team
1951	After being rejected by Notre Dame, takes scholarship at the University of Louisville
1954	Marries long-time girlfriend Dorothy Jean Hoelle, with whom he eventually has five children
1955	Graduates from University of Louisville, chosen by Pittsburgh Steelers on ninth round, but dropped before playing a single game
1956	After a year spent working construction and playing semiprofessional ball, is signed by Baltimore Colts as backup to quarterback George Shaw; later becomes Baltimore's lead quarterback after Shaw breaks his leg
1957	Leads the league in touchdown passes and passing yardage
1958	On December 28, leads the Colts to overtime victory against the New York Giants in the NFL Championship Game. This, the first nationally televised game and the first to make use of the new overtime rule, is often considered the greatest single game in the history of football
1959	Completes the season at head of league in passing yardage and completions, and again leads the Colts to victory over the Giants in the NFL Championship
1964	Colts lose to Cleveland Browns in NFL Championship Game
1966	Breaks season records for passes thrown for touchdowns, and for yards gained
1968	After tearing a muscle in his right arm, has to sit out most of the season, including the Colts' victory in NFL Championship
1969	Despite his heroic showing in Superbowl III against the New York Jets, the Colts lose this historic game
1971	Begins to develop long-term arm problems, and tears Achilles tendon
1974	After being traded to the San Diego Chargers, plays one season as backup quarterback before retiring
2002	Dies of a heart attack in Baltimore on September 11

Awards and Accomplishments	
1957	Jim Thorpe Trophy; NFL Most Valuable Player Award; All-Pro Quarterback
1958	NFL Championship Game Most Valuable Player Award
1959	Bert Bell Award; NFL Most Valuable Player Award; NFL Championship Game Most Valuable Player Award; All-Pro Quarterback
1964	Bell Trophy; NFL Most Valuable Player Award; All-Pro Quarterback
1967	Jim Thorpe Trophy; Bell Trophy; NFL Most Valuable Player Award; All-Pro Quarterback
1969	Named Greatest Quarterback in History at NFL 50th Anniversary
1970	NFL Man of the Year Award
1979	Inducted into Pro Football Hall of Fame
1994	Named to NFL 75th Anniversary Team

At the time of his retirement, Unitas held the following records: greatest number of yards gained for passes thrown in a career (40,239); most seasons passing for more than 3,000 yards (3); most games passing for 300 yards or more (27); most touchdowns thrown (290); highest post-season pass completion percentage (62.9%); and most yards gained passing during championship play (1,177).

were not in vain: an admiring fan noticed his talents, and mentioned him to a scout for the Baltimore Colts.

First Years with the Colts

The Colts gave Unitas a tryout, and were impressed enough to sign him as a backup to quarterback George Shaw. Then, in a virtual repeat of the circumstances that had put him in the quarterback position for his high-school team, Shaw broke his leg in the fourth game of the 1956-57 season, and suddenly Unitas was moved front and center.

Even then, it was not immediately apparent that one of the most legendary careers in the history of the NFL (National Football League) had just been launched: Unitas's first pass as Baltimore quarterback was intercepted. However, he managed to finish the season with an impressive pass completion percentage of 55.6. In 1957, he led the NFL in touchdown passes and passing yardage, and by 1958, Baltimore's No. 19 was recognized as the best quarterback in the NFL.

A History-Making Game

On December 28, 1958, the Colts faced the New York Giants in the NFL championship game at Yankee Stadium. This was the first football game in history to go into overtime, and—of perhaps even greater importance—the first football game broadcast to a national audience. The mythical quality of that event can be glimpsed in the fact that on the field that day were 12 future NFL Hall of Fame players, including Unitas and **Frank Gifford**, with three more Hall of Famers on the sidelines coaching.

Though suffering from three broken ribs, Unitas took to the field to lead his team. Near the end of the fourth quarter, the Giants were leading 17-14, with five of their points scored by another figure destined for national prominence, Pat Summerall. Then Unitas did something almost inconceivable: in the space of less than 90 seconds, he managed to complete seven passes, moving the Colts forward and setting up Steve Myhra for a game-tying field goal with just seven seconds remaining.

According to old league rules, the game would have ended with a tie, but as the fans discovered on that day in 1958, overtime—with its promise of a single victor, no longer how much struggle it took—added a great deal more excitement to the game. In the course of 13 plays, Unitas led his team forward by 80 yards, putting Alan Ameche in place for the touchdown that won the game 23-17. Not surprisingly, Unitas was named the championship's most valuable player (MVP).

A national audience estimated as high as 50 million watched this thrilling game, and thereafter the marriage of television and football was sealed. It is easy to see the importance of the game in retrospect, but at least one person recognized it on that day: bursting out of his box at the sidelines, football commissioner **Bert Bell** shouted, "This is the greatest day in the history of professional football!"

An Unlikely Hero

By then, Unitas's reputation as "the Golden Arm" was sealed, and along the way he gained other epithets, including "Mr. Quarterback" and "Johnny U." Still, he seemed an unlikely hero. Teammate Alex Hawkins, who many years later recalled his first encounter with the new quarterback, described him thus in *Sports Ilustrated*: "Here was a total mystery. [Unitas] was from Pennsylvania, but he looked so much like a Mississippi farmhand that I looked around for a mule. He had stooped shoulders, a chicken breast, thin bowed legs, and long dangling arms with crooked, mangled fingers." And though today the name Johnny Unitas could not sound more perfect for a star quarterback, at the time it seemed embarrassingly ethnic in a sport that had theretofore been dominated by western Europeans.

True to his hardworking immigrant heritage, Unitas developed a reputation for his ability to withstand pain, as exemplified by the injured quarterback's performance in the 1958 championship game. Speaking to *Sports Illustrated*, **Merlin Olsen** later said of Unitas, against whom he played for the Los Angeles Rams, "I often heard that sometimes he'd hold the ball one count longer than he had to just so he could take the hit and laugh in your face." When Unitas retired, he wore the crooked index finger on his passing hand as a badge of honor.

Soldiering on Through the Pain

During the 1958-59 season, Unitas led the NFL in passing yardage and completions and won the Bert Bell Award. His team again trounced the Giants in the championship game, this time by a larger margin of 31-16, and Unitas once again became the championship MVP. During the next few years, the team's performance slumped, but Unitas' did not, and he continued to lead the league in yardage and completions.

The Colts returned to the championships to face the Cleveland Browns in 1964 and lost, but Unitas remained as strong a performer as ever. During the 1965-66 season, he broke season records for passes thrown for touchdowns and yards gained, but in 1967-68 he tore a muscle in his right elbow. This time, even "the Golden Arm" could not simply swallow the pain and soldier on, and he had to sit out for most of the season.

Another Historic Game

The Colts won the 1968 NFL Championship without Unitas, but he returned in the following season, and helped lead the team into Superbowl III against **Joe Namath** and the New York Jets. Torn ligaments in his throwing arm kept Unitas out of the game until the fourth quarter, and though the injured veteran performed heroically, with 11 of 24 passes completed for 110 yards, this was not enough to save the Colts from a 16-7 loss to the Jets.

Marking the emergence of the American Football League (AFL) as a rival of the NFL, Superbowl III was a

---

Related Biography: Football Player George Shaw

Though Johnny Unitas went on to become a legend, and George Shaw is hardly remembered today, things looked very different in 1955. From the University of Oregon, Shaw was that year's number-one NFL draft pick. Unitas, on the other hand, came in on the ninth round, and became 102nd overall when the Steelers finally picked him up.

The Steelers dropped Unitas before his first exhibition game, claiming that he was not intelligent enough to be a quarterback. Shaw, on the other hand, was a golden boy, and even had a good Anglo-Saxon name. Chosen by the Colts on January 27, 1955, he seemed destined for immortality even as Unitas was destined for obscurity.

Even when the Colts signed Unitas in 1956, it was only as a backup to Shaw. Then, just four games into the 1956-57 season, Shaw broke his leg, and Unitas came in to replace him. Thereafter, the course was set, with Unitas bound for superstardom, and Shaw for the status of a footnote to football history.

After his recovery, Shaw went back to the Colts, only now *he* was the backup quarterback, and with Unitas' stoicism in the face of injury, he had few opportunities to play. He stayed with the Colts until 1958, when they traded him to the New York Giants. By this point, Shaw's career was already half over, and after two years with the Giants, he spent a year apiece with the Minnesota Vikings and the Detroit Lions before leaving the NFL in 1962. In his eight-year career, he gained 5,829 passing yards—just over a fifth of Unitas's record for 18 years.

---

match of almost as great historic importance as the championship game 11 years earlier, and indeed, many fans called this "the greatest game ever." Later, Unitas—never known to mince words when it came to talking about coaches—said that the blame for that loss fell on Baltimore coach **Don Shula**. According to *Sports Illustrated*, it was Unitas' contention that Shula should have sent him in during the second quarter instead of the fourth.

In any case, it was Unitas and not Namath who gained recognition as the Greatest Quarterback in History at the NFL's 50th Anniversary in 1969. A quarter century later, he would be among just four quarterbacks (the others were **Otto Graham**, **Sammy Baugh**, and **Joe Montana**) on the NFL 75th Anniversary Team.

Declining Years

Though he would continue to play until 1973, Unitas had his last great season in 1969-70. During that time, he completed 166 of 221 pass attempts, gaining 2,213 yards and 14 touchdowns, and he finished out the season by earning the NFL Man of the Year Award. The Colts even went to Super Bowl V against the Dallas Cowboys, but a bruised rib in the middle of the second quarter took Unitas out of the game.

The early 1970s were not a good time for Unitas. Long-term arm problems appeared in 1971, the same year in which he tore his Achilles tendon. In 1973, he divorced Dorothy after nearly two decades of marriage, and within a scandalously short time, he married Sandra Lemon. (He would remain with Sandra, by whom he fathered a child, until his death in 2002.) In 1973 he also saw the end of another long-term relationship, when the Colts traded him to the San Diego Chargers. Unitas

Johnny Unitas, throwing pass

spent a year as backup quarterback for San Diego before retiring.

The Entrepreneur

With his thrifty, hardworking, immigrant background, Unitas had long had an interest in business, and after retirement, he launched a second career as an entrepreneur. First he opened a Baltimore restaurant called the Golden Arm, then he became involved in Florida real estate. He served as spokesman for several companies, including manufacturers, a trucker, and a mortgage firm called First Fidelity Financial Services. This last involvement would prove troublesome to Unitas in the mid-1980s, when the company's founder was convicted of fraud, and Unitas himself became the target of a lawsuit for his endorsement of the company.

Though retired from the NFL, Unitas remained active in the world of football. Beginning in 1974, he spent five seasons in the CBS broadcast booth as a commentator, during which time he gained a reputation—as he had long before

on the field—for candor and plainspokenness. In 1979, Unitas was inducted into the Pro Football Hall of Fame.

In the last decade of his life, Unitas was chairman of Unitas Management Corporation, a sports management firm, and worked as vice president of sales for National Circuits, a computer electronics firm. He was also heavily involved in providing opportunities for promising young talents through his Johnny Unitas Golden Arm Educational Foundation. Just 69 years old, Unitas died on a heart attack in Baltimore on September 11, 2002.

Calling His Own Plays

The sheer numbers Unitas achieved in his career are impressive, and in some cases even staggering. His lifetime completion percentage of over 55%, while extremely good, is not the greatest ever, but in light of the vast number of passes this represents—5,186, with 2,830 completions—this in itself is a stunning statistic. So, too, is the number of yards these passes gained for the Colts: 40,239, an NFL record at the time.

Career Statistics

Yr	Team	Passing					Rushing			
		ATT	COM	YDS	COM%	TD	INT	ATT	YDS	TD
1956	BAL	198	110	1498	55.6	9	10	28	155	1
1957	BAL	301	172	2550	57.1	24	17	42	171	1
1958	BAL	263	136	2007	51.7	19	7	33	139	3
1959	BAL	367	193	2899	52.6	32	14	29	145	2
1960	BAL	378	190	3099	50.3	25	24	36	195	0
1961	BAL	420	229	2990	54.5	16	24	54	190	2
1962	BAL	389	222	2967	57.1	23	23	50	137	0
1963	BAL	410	237	3481	57.8	20	12	57	224	0
1964	BAL	305	158	2824	51.8	19	6	37	162	2
1965	BAL	282	164	2530	58.2	23	12	17	68	1
1966	BAL	348	195	2748	56.0	22	24	20	44	1
1967	BAL	436	255	3428	58.5	20	16	22	89	0
1968	BAL	32	11	139	34.4	2	4	3	0	0
1969	BAL	327	178	2342	54.4	12	20	11	23	0
1970	BAL	321	166	2213	51.7	14	18	9	16	0
1971	BAL	176	92	942	52.3	3	9	9	5	0
1972	BAL	157	88	1111	56.1	4	6	3	15	0
1973	SDG	76	34	471	44.7	3	7	0	0	0
TOTAL		5186	2830	40239	54.6	290	253	450	1777	13

BAL: Baltimore Colts; SDG: San Diego Chargers.

Unitas also achieved a number of other distinctions that were NFL records at the time of his retirement: most seasons passing for more than 3,000 yards (3); most games passing for 300 yards or more (27); most touchdowns thrown (290); highest post-season pass completion percentage (62.9%); and most yards gained passing during championship play (1,177).

Among the greatest of modern football's founding fathers, Unitas's career marked a high point between that of such early pioneers as **Red Grange** and the advent of the "hot shot," exemplified by Namath. In a world that has come to be characterized, all too often, by prima donnas, Unitas was as no-nonsense as his hairstyle, and he excelled at calling his own plays, something modern quarterbacks cannot do. The game has become too complicated today for any one quarterback to call all his own plays, and ironically, Unitas, by helping to inaugurate the modern era with that historic game in 1958, paved the way for the more complex game that came into being.

SELECTED WRITINGS BY UNITAS:

(With Ed Fitzgerald) *Pro Quarterback, My Own Story,* Simon and Schuster, 1965.

(With Harold Rosenthal) *Playing Pro Football to Win,* Doubleday, 1968.

FURTHER INFORMATION

Books

Gildea, William. *When the Colts Belonged to Baltimore: A Father and a Son, a Team and a Time.* Baltimore: Johns Hopkins, 1996.

King, Peter. *Greatest Quarterbacks.* Des Moines, IA: Nelson, 1961.

Shapiro, Milton J. *The Pro Quarterbacks.* New York: J. Messner, 1971.

Unitas, Johnny and Ed Fitzgerald. *Pro Quarterback, My Own Story.* New York: Simon and Schuster, 1965.

Unitas, Johnny and Harold Rosenthal. *Playing Pro Football to Win.* New York: Doubleday, 1968.

Periodicals

Deford, Frank. "The Best There Ever Was: For the Author—a Baltimore Native and Future Sportswriter—the Colts' Quarterback Was More Than a Boyhood Hero. He Was an Inspiration for the Entire City." *Sports Illustrated* 97 (September 23, 2002): 58.

King, Peter. "Field General: Mass Substitutions, Sophisticated Defenses and the Pressure to Win Add up to One Conclusion—We'll Never See Another Johnny U." *Sports Illustrated* 97 (September 23, 2002): 71.

Zimmerman, Paul. "Revolutionaries." *Sports Illustrated* 89 (August 17, 1998): 78-85.

Zimmerman, Paul. "Talking Football: In an Interview More Than Two Decades After His Last Game, the Old Pro Showed the Passion of an All-Pro Still in His Prime." *Sports Illustrated* 97 (September 23, 2002): 66.

Other

"Al's NFL Football Videos." http://www.nfl-football-videos.com/1958_nfl_championship.htm (November 20, 2002).

Johnny Unitas.com. http://www.johnnyunitas.com (November 20, 2002).

The Johnny Unitas Web Site. http://www.cmgww.com/football/unitas/index.html (November 20, 2002).

Levinson, Barry. "Baltimore Always Raven Mad for Pro Football." ESPN. http://espn.go.com/page2/s/levinson/010122.html (November 20, 2002).

Sketch by Judson Knight

Al Unser, Sr.
1939-

American race car driver

Al Unser, Sr.

Al Unser Sr., a legend in the world of auto racing, is one of only three drivers to have won the Indianapolis 500 four times. Unser, a member of the second of three generations of Unsers to race cars, also shares the distinction of having won races on paved ovals, road courses, and dirt tracks in a single season with only two other Indy drivers. In fact, Unser managed that latter feat three years in a row—1968, 1969, and 1970. Retired since 1994 to his native New Mexico, Unser in recent years has been working to build an automobile museum on family land in Albuquerque. For this most recent venture, Unser has partnered with son, Al Jr., a racing star in his own right and sometime competitor with his father, to create a museum that will appeal to both adults and children. Before retiring, Unser Sr. compiled an enviable record on the Indy car circuit of thirty-nine wins, accumulating more than $6 million in winnings. Collectively, the Unsers are the winningest family at Indianapolis, having collected a total of nine checkered flags, or more than 10 percent of the races run at Indy.

Born in Albuquerque, New Mexico

He was born Alfred Unser in Albuquerque, New Mexico, on May 29, 1939. The youngest son of Jerry H. and Mary (Craven) Unser, he was born into a racing family. His paternal uncle, Louie Unser, had attempted to qualify at the Indianapolis 500 in 1940, and Al's older brother, Jerry, was national stock car champion in the mid-1950s but died of injuries suffered on a practice lap at Indianapolis in May 1959. Jerry's death left Al and older brothers **Bobby Unser** and Louie Unser—Jerry's twin—to carry on the racing tradition of the Unser family. Only a few years after Jerry's death at Indianapolis, Louie was stricken with multiple sclerosis. He has struggled against the disease, however, and in 1965 served as Al's mechanic at his first Indy 500. Al freely admits that a major motivation throughout his racing career was sibling rivalry. "I wanted to outrun Bobby," Unser told an interviewer for Indy500.com. "Bobby always was the oldest, and he set the pace, and I wanted to outrun him."

Unser said that growing up as a member of a racing family, it was difficult not to want to be a race driver. He said as far back as he could remember he never had any doubt about what he would do in life. "My Lord, when I went to school I told my teachers you can't teach me what I want to do in life. They asked me what I wanted to do, and I said I wanted to be a race driver."

Unser wasted little time getting into racing. By the age of eighteen, he was driving modified roadsters in competitions in and around Albuquerque. He later progressed to midgets, sprints, stock cars, sports cars, Formula 5000, championship dirt cars, and Indy cars. He took time off from racing in 1958 to marry Wanda Jesperson, with whom he had three children, Alfred Jr., Mary Linda, and Debra Ann (deceased). In 1960, he competed in the Pike's Peak Hillclimb for the first time, finishing second to brother Bobby. Four years later, Unser made his Indy car debut at Milwaukee and later that year won the Pikes Peak race, putting an end to Bobby's six-year winning streak. In 1965 he repeated his win at the Pikes Peak Hillclimb and raced for the first time in the Indy 500.

Helping Unser to break into competition at Indianapolis was **A.J. Foyt**, one of the two other racers to have won four times at Indy. It looked as though Unser would have to race the Indy in a substandard car until Foyt came to the rescue and offered to let the rookie use his back-up car. In an interview with Indy500.com, Unser recalled Foyt's generosity. "Still today, I say, why did A.J. do that? Bignotti [George, chief mechanic for Foyt] was against it.

```
┌─────────────────────────────────────────────────────────┐
│ Chronology                                                │
│                                                           │
│ 1939   Born in Albuquerque, New Mexico, on May 29         │
│ 1957   Begins driving modified roadsters in competition   │
│        around Albuquerque                                  │
│ 1958   Marries Wanda Jesperson on April 22 (divorced in   │
│        1971)                                               │
│ 1959   Older brother Jerry dies as a result of injuries   │
│        suffered in practice run at Indianapolis Motor     │
│        Speedway on May 2                                   │
│ 1977   Marries Karen Barnes on November 22                │
│ 1979   Breaks ankle in a motorcycle accident, forcing him │
│        to miss Indy 500                                    │
│ 1983   Joins Penske Racing                                │
│ 1994   Retires from auto racing                           │
│ 2002   Invests $1.5 million, with son Al Jr, to build an  │
│        auto museum in Albuquerque                         │
└─────────────────────────────────────────────────────────┘
```

He threw a fit. He was with Foyt and didn't want that car to run. I took it over. Louie, my brother, came over [as a mechanic]." Foyt's faith in the rookie proved to be well-placed, for Unser finished his first race at Indy in ninth place, well ahead of Foyt, who came in 15th.

Finishes Second in Indy 500 of 1967

In 1967 Unser finished second to A.J. Foyt at the Indy 500. He also claimed his first pole at Langhorne. In addition to his Indy car racing, he also raced U.S. Auto Club (USAC) stock cars and was named Rookie of the Year in 1967. The following year, he really established himself, winning five races in a row and grabbing five poles.

Unser's big breakthrough at Indianapolis came in 1970 when he won, beating brother Bobby. For the year as a whole, he won ten races and a total of eight poles, including the pole at the Indy 500. For his impressive performance in 1970, which included wins on ovals, road courses, and dirt tracks, Unser was named Driver of the Year. He made it back-to-back wins at the Indy 500 when he took the checkered flag once again in 1971. After the glory days of the early 1970s, Unser went through a dry spell of about four years, during which time his only win was at Texas in 1973. He came back with a vengeance, however, in the late 1970s. In 1977, Unser won at Pocono, Milwaukee, and Phoenix, moving him to second place in Indy-car points and moving him into eighth place in the International Race of Champions (IROC) competition. That same year, Unser married Karen Barnes, his second wife. The following year he swept the Indy car events of Pocono, Ontario, and the Indy 500, his third win at the Brickyard, to become the first driver in history to win an "Indy Car Triple Crown." He also won the IROC championship for 1978.

Throughout the early years of his racing career, finding a free-spending sponsor was one of the major challenges faced by Unser. He told Indy500.com that it was critical to find an owner who was willing to spend money because in a "nickel-and-dime" operation, some small part was almost certain to break. Particularly ironic is the alliance Unser built in the early 1970s with me-

```
┌─────────────────────────────────────────────────────────┐
│ Related Biography: Racecar Driver Jerry Unser            │
│                                                           │
│    More than any other family in auto racing history,     │
│ the Unsers have dominated the Indianapolis 500. Unsers    │
│ have competed in the Indy 500 about 70 times, and         │
│ family members have won the race a total of nine          │
│ times—four wins by Al Unser Sr., three wins by his        │
│ older brother, Bobby, and two by his son, Al Jr. The      │
│ first Unser to launch an assault on the legendary         │
│ Brickyard in Indianapolis was Jerry Unser, older          │
│ brother of both Bobby and Al Sr., and twin brother of     │
│ Louie, who suffers from multiple sclerosis but works as   │
│ an auto mechanic.                                         │
│                                                           │
│    Jerry Unser was born on November 15, 1932, in          │
│ Colorado Springs, Colorado. Although Jerry was the first  │
│ Unser to seek glory at the Indy, he never managed to      │
│ complete a full lap. In his 1958 debut at the Brickyard,  │
│ Jerry became extricated in a massive accident and was     │
│ catapulted over the wall on his very first lap. The       │
│ following year he returned but was severely injured in a  │
│ practice run on May 2. Fifteen days later, Jerry          │
│ succumbed to injuries sustained in that accident.         │
│                                                           │
│    Before deciding to race at Indy, Jerry raced stock     │
│ cars for a few years and in 1956 he was the national      │
│ stock car champion. He and wife Jeanie had two sons,      │
│ Jerry, who was born June 10, 1957, and Johnny, born       │
│ October 22, 1958.                                         │
└─────────────────────────────────────────────────────────┘
```

chanic George Bignotti, with whom he had clashed in 1965 over the use of Foyt's back-up car. Forgetting their earlier differences, Bignotti and Unser forged one of auto racing's toughest teams ever. Unser, Bignotti, and the Johnny Lightning Special were the terrors of the Indy 500 in both 1970 and 1971. Unser won the race both years and in 1971 set a speed record of 157.735 miles per hour. In 1970 Unser won from the pole; in 1971 he won from fifth position.

Joins Penske Racing in 1983

In 1983, Unser joined Penske Racing. That year he posted ten finishes in the top five and claimed his second PPG championship. Two years later, he was pitted in a razor-thin race against his son, Al Jr., for the PPG Cup. In the end, father edged son by a single point, 151-150, to win the 1985 PPG Cup, earning for Al Sr. his second title in three years. Unser Sr. had only one victory and one pole, but his consistency saw him through, as it had in 1983. In his other thirteen starts, he placed in the top five nine times. However, he still needed a strong final run to take the cup. He closed the season with a runner-up finish at Laguna Seca, a victory from the pole at Phoenix, and a fourth-place showing at Phoenix. In the same three races, Al Jr. finished third, second, and third, respectively.

In 1987, at the age of 47, Unser won his fourth and final Indy 500 in a race he only got into at the last minute when Danny Ongais crashed during a practice run and wasn't healthy enough to race. He raced to victory 4.496 seconds ahead of runner-up Roberto Guerrero with an average speed of 162.175 miles per hour. Son Al Jr., who finished fourth, told ESPN: "It means everything to Dad. They called him retired and washed up and all that. He's far from that. I've got goose bumps. I'm ecstatic for Dad."

Unser retired to Albuquerque in 1994 but has not strayed far from racing. Unser, along with Johnny

Awards and Accomplishments

1960	Finished second to brother Bobby at Pike's Peak Hillclimb
1964	Made Indy car debut at Milwaukee and won Pikes Peak Hillclimb
1965	Finished ninth in first Indy 500 and won Pikes Peak Hillclimb
1967	Finished second at Indy 500 and named USAC Rookie of the Year
1968	Won five races in a row and grabbed five poles
1970	Won first Indy 500 and nine other races; named Driver of the Year
1971	Indy 500 win
1977	Won Indy car races at Pocono, Milwaukee, and Phoenix
1978	Took "Indy Car Triple Crown" with wins at Indy 500, Pocono, and Ontario; named Driver of the Year
1987	Fourth Indy 500 win
1991	Inducted into the Motorsports Hall of Fame of America
1998	Inducted into International Motorsports Hall of Fame

Rutherford, who also retired in 1994, offers his expertise to aspiring race car drivers as a staff member of the Indy Racing League as coach and consultant. Some of the new drivers see him as a dinosaur who couldn't possibly help them, Unser told Hank Kurz Jr. of the Associated Press. But "I tell them in 1992 and 1993, I was still running 230 miles an hour around the speedway. That wakes them up." Another passion of Unser's is shared with son, Al Jr. The two have committed $1.5 million of their own money to building an auto museum on family land in Albuquerque. Father and son have set up a nonprofit foundation to raise more money for the planned 50,000-square-foot center on a twelve-acre site.

One of the greatest auto racers of all time, Unser stands as an inspiration for aspiring racers everywhere and especially for other members of the Unser clan who remain active in racing. This latter group includes his son, Al Jr., and nephews, Johnny and Robby Unser. Only Unser Sr., Foyt, and **Rick Mears** have managed to take four checkered flags at Indy, an incredible feat for a racer of any age, but made all the remarkable for Unser, who posted his final win at the Brickyard at the age of 47. Unser, who was active in racing across four decades, has been enshrined in both the Motorsports Hall of Fame of America (1991) and the International Motorsports Hall of Fame (1998) in honor of his unique contributions to the sport.

CONTACT INFORMATION

Address: Al Unser Sr., c/o Indy Racing League, 4567 W. 16th St., Indianapolis, IN 46222-2513.

FURTHER INFORMATION

Books

"Al Unser." *St. James Encyclopedia of Popular Culture,* five volumes. Detroit: St. James Press, 2000.

Bentley, Karen. *The Unsers.* Broomall, PA: Chelsea House, 1996.
Dregni, Michael. *The Indianapolis 500.* Minneapolis: Capstone Press, 1994.

Periodicals

Kurz, Hank, Jr. "Unser Sr., Rutherford Use Status to Teach." *Associated Press* (July 3, 2002).
Latta, Dennis. "Unsers Rev Up Plans for Car Museum." *Albuquerque Journal* (March 14, 2002).

Other

"Al Unser Sr." International Motorsports Hall of Fame. http://www.motorsportshalloffame.com/halloffame/1998/Al_Unser_Sr_main.htm (October 23, 2002).
"Al Unser Sr. Is Oldest Indy 500 Winner." ESPN Classic. http://espn.go.com/classic/s/add_unser_al.html (October 23, 2002).
"Champion Details: Al Unser." CART: Championship Auto Racing Teams. http://www.cart.com/Fan Resources/Champion.asp?ID=7 (October 23, 2002).
"Sibling Rivalry Pushed Al Unser to Indy Greatness." Indy500. com. http://www.indy500.com/press/1998/champions/aunser.html (October 23, 2002).
"Unser Brothers Find Success on Different Life Paths." Indy500. com. http://www.indy500.com/press/1999/unser-051999.html (October 23, 2002).

Sketch by Don Amerman

Bobby Unser
1934-

American race car driver

Bobby Unser came from a family of racecar drivers. He made a name for himself as a driver who pushed himself and his cars to the limit. He drove fast and hard all of the time, and has won numerous racing championships throughout his career, including three Indianapolis 500 titles. Unser has been the center of controversy because of his sharp opinions about what is fair and just, both on and off the track.

Born to Race

Robert William Unser was born on February 20, 1934 in Colorado Springs, Colorado to a family destined to race. His grandfather, Louis Unser, was a mechanic whose three sons were the first to ride up Pike's Peak, a 14,110 foot high mountain on the edge of the Great Plains, in the 1920s. This was the first race of what

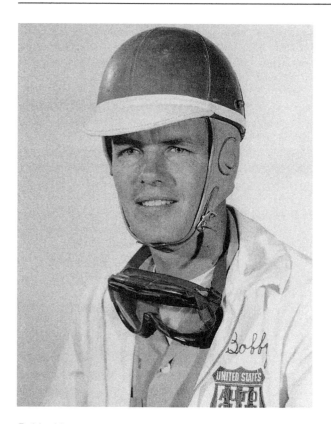

Bobby Unser

would become an annual tradition. Of the 40 competitors, only the Unser boys made it to the top. The Unsers dominated both Pike's Peak and the racing profession in the years to come.

One of the Pike's Peak pioneers, Jerry Unser, married schoolteacher Mary Craven and had four sons—fraternal twins Jerry, Jr. and Louie, Robert (known as Bobby), and **Al Unser, Sr.** In 1956 Jerry Unser moved his family to Albuquerque, New Mexico where he opened a garage and gas station called Jerry Unser Motors on Route 66. His four boys helped him in the garage. The boys bought an old Model A Ford from their father, fixed it up, and began driving. When the boys were teenagers they began driving racecars on the short tracks in New Mexico, Colorado, and Arizona.

Jerry, Jr., Bobby Unser's older brother, became the first Unser racecar champion, winning the 1957 United States Auto Club (USAC) stock car championship. Tragically he died in 1959 from a crash during a practice run for the Indianapolis 500. Louie Unser, Bobby's other older brother, started a racing career but was later diagnosed with multiple sclerosis and was unable to continue racing. This left racing open to the two younger Unser boys. At age 16, Bobby Unser won his first race at the Southwest Modified Stock Car Championship, which he won again the following year.

In 1953 Unser enlisted in the United States Air Force, a decision he later regretted because he had wanted to spend more time racing. He trained at Warren Air Force Base in Cheyenne, Wyoming where he studied automotives. He continued racing during his free time and his brother Louie served as his manager. After basic training Unser pulled some strings to get stationed in Albuquerque so that he could pursue his racing career. In 1954 he married his first wife, Barbara Schumaker, and the couple had two children together. Unser finished his military service in 1955 and then focused solely on racing.

Became a Racing Champion

In 1955 Bobby Unser debuted at Pike's Peak, dubbed "Unser's Peak" because of his family's history of success at the hill climb. He finished fifth that year, behind his two brothers. A year later he won his first of a record 13 championships at Pike's Peak. He won six straight titles from 1958 to 1963. His streak ended in 1964 when his younger brother Al won the race. However, his sweetest victory at

Awards and Accomplishments

1950-51	Southwest Modified Stock Car Championship
1956, 1958-63, 1965-66, 1968-69, 1974, 1986	Pike's Peak Hill Climb Winner
1968, 1975	Indianapolis 500 winner
1969, 1974	United States Auto Club National Champion
1974	Martini and Rossi Driver of the Year
1974, 1976, 1979-81	California 500 Champion
1975	International Race of Champions title
1979	Six Championship Auto Racing Teams wins
1980	Pocono 500 Champion
1990	Inducted into Auto Racing Hall of Fame
1993	Fastmasters Champion
1994	Inducted into International Motorsports Hall of Fame
2000	Inducted into Colorado Springs Sports Hall of Fame

"Unser's Peak" came ten years later when he tied his uncle's record of nine wins. "The Unser brothers raced at Pike's Peak to beat each other and most of all to beat Uncle Louis," Unser told Karen Bentley in *The Unsers*.

Unser's professional racing career took off in 1963 when he raced in his first Indianapolis 500. He crashed early and placed thirty-third. His first Indy-car win came in 1967 at Mosport, Ontario. A year later he not only won his first Indianapolis 500, but also set the record as the first driver to race over 170 miles per hour at Indianapolis. In 1969 Unser won his first USAC National Driving Championship.

Bobby Unser earned a reputation as a driver who not only liked to drive fast, but who also pushed himself and his cars to the limit. On the contrary, younger brother Al Unser was a much more patient driver with a more laid-back personality than Bobby. Al Unser kept the competition tight within the family. Two years after Bobby's first Indianapolis 500 win, Al won the prestigious race and followed up with a second consecutive win in 1971. "It would get tense between me and Al about who would win," Bobby Unser told Karen Bentley, "but it never stayed. We were able to separate business and family — we never really got in a fight."

However, Bobby Unser was not going to let his little brother have all of the glory. In 1972 Unser set another Indianapolis 500 record for the fastest qualifying time at 195.94 miles per hour. In 1974 he won his second USAC National Driving Championship and a year later he won his second Indianapolis 500. In the late 1970s Unser also won several races for Championship Auto Racing Teams (CART). In 1980 he became the first driver to win the California 500 four times.

Indy Controversy Led to Retirement

Unser's biggest and most controversial win came at the 1981 Indianapolis 500. Unser had started the race in the pole position. Three and a half hours later he won the race, beating **Mario Andretti** by only 5.3 seconds. This was Unser's third Indianapolis 500 win and at the age of 47 he was the oldest driver to win the race. However, when the race was over, Andretti complained that Unser had passed illegally during the race. On lap 149 Unser was coming out of the pits during a yellow flag and had passed seven cars, even though passing is not allowed during a yellow flag. Upon reviewing the videotapes, race officials decided that Unser should be penalized one lap for this infraction, which meant that Andretti was the new winner of the race. This was the first time in Indy history that a winner had been stripped of a victory. Unser and car owner **Roger Penske** were furious and they filed protests. "We weren't cheating," *Sports Illustrated* quoted Unser from a press conference following the incident, "We had the fast car, no matter what the decision." Eventually a USAC appeals panel overruled the decision. Unser was reinstated as the 1981 champion, but he was fined $40,000 for the passing infraction. Despite the victory, Unser was bitter about the whole experience and no longer desired to race Indy cars.

In 1982 Unser decided to retire from Indy racing. "For the first time I realized that I had been thinking only of Bobby Unser, and perhaps it was time to think about my family," the *New York Times* quoted Unser. By this time Unser had been married three times. He had two children, Bobby Jr. and Cindy, with his first wife Barbara Schumaker. He also had two children, Robby and Jeri, with his second wife Norma Davis.

Being a professional racecar driver meant that Unser was not home most of the time. "Successful as my racing has been, my family life, in a lot of ways, has been a failure," wrote Unser in *The Bobby Unser Story*. "You're not successful unless you spend part of every day with your kids." By the time Unser decided to retire, his son Bobby, Jr. and his nephew Al, Jr. had already begun their racing careers and his younger son Robby was also showing an interest in the sport. Unser wanted to be available to help the next generation of Unser drivers.

More Controversy Off the Tracks

Although Unser retired from Indy cars, he did not stop racing altogether. In 1983 Unser was the owner and manager of the car that won Pike's Peak, driven by his nephew, Al, Jr. Three years later Unser himself won the race, setting a record 13 wins at "Unser Peak." In 1991 Unser participated in the 24 Hours of Daytona Race with his brother Al, his nephew Al Jr., and his son Robby. In 1993 he set a new land speed record of 223.709 miles per hour racing a gas-modified roadster. The same year he also won the Fastmasters Championship for drivers over 50 years old.

Unser also did not leave the public spotlight when he retired. In 1987 he began working as a commentator for ABC Sports Television. Unser's commentary was very

---

Related Biography: Racecar Driver Bobby Unser, Jr.

Bobby Unser, Jr. was the first son of Bobby Unser and Barbara Schumaker. Although he grew up in a racing family, Bobby, Jr. was not immediately interested in the sport. As a teenager he was more interested in drums than cars. He enjoyed racing motorcycles and snowmobiles and then eventually started racing go-karts. In 1976 Bobby, Jr. made his debut at the Pike's Peak Hill Climb with his father coaching him. Bobby, Jr. did not have the same kind of success as his father at Pike's Peak and in 1978 he even ran off the road. While Unser was supportive of his son, it was difficult for him to watch someone other than an Unser win that particular race.

Bobby Unser, Jr. was very conscious of his family's history at Pike's Peak and on the racing world in general. "I used to have these weird complexes that I had to do well because of the name," Bobby, Jr. wrote in *The Bobby Unser Story*. "My dad and uncle have won so much it makes it hard on me. It's a good name for a race driver to have but by the same token I don't want to ride on it." Bobby, Jr. won the Western World Sprint Car Championship in Arizona and also won the Toyota Father Son Championship twice with his father. However, Bobby, Jr. did not make a career of racing. In 1989 he started a stunt driving company called Unser Driving. He has also worked in real estate development and has done some commentating for ESPN. Bobby, Jr. resides in Albuquerque, New Mexico with his wife, two daughters, and son, Bobby Unser, III.

---

blunt and he did not always agree with his coworkers on the air. Unser later found another media outlet for his expertise; in 2001 he began writing a column about off-road vehicles for *Sports Afield* magazine.

This was not the only public attention Unser received after his retirement. In 1994 Unser made national news for assaulting a police officer at the Albuquerque International Airport. He was stopped by the police officer for speeding, began arguing with the officer, and then pushed her. He was charged with misdemeanor assault, resisting arrest, and careless driving.

Two years later Unser had another encounter with the law. In December of 1996 he and a friend, Robert Gayton, were snowmobiling in the mountains near Unser's ranch in Chama, New Mexico. Both snowmobiles broke down and the pair spent two days trying to find their way home on foot. They had no food or water and they had to endure temperatures as low as minus 20 degrees Celsius, as well as 70 mile per hour winds. Luckily Unser and his friend survived the experience without injury. However, it was later discovered that Unser had been driving in the San Juan Wilderness of the Rio Grande National Forest near the Colorado and New Mexico border. Unser had violated the Wilderness Act of 1964 by riding his snowmobile in a federally protected area. Unser was convicted of the misdemeanor on June 12, 1997. The maximum penalty was $5,000 and six months in jail, but Unser was only fined $75 because of his harrowing ordeal in the mountains. Despite the small fine, Unser was outraged by the conviction and as a matter of principle he filed an appeal. The conviction was upheld by the Tenth United States Circuit Court of Appeals on January 5, 1999.

Whether on or off the track Unser was never afraid to speak his mind, particularly when he felt he had been treated unjustly. Bobby Unser has helped build the lega-cy of the Unser family in racing through his own prestigious career as well as by mentoring the next generation of Unser racers.

CONTACT INFORMATION

Address: 7700 Central Ave. SW, Albuquerque, NM 87105. Phone: (505) 831-1500.

SELECTED WRITINGS BY UNSER:

(With Joe Scalzo) *The Bobby Unser Story*. Doubleday, 1979.

FURTHER INFORMATION

Books

Almanac of Famous People. Detroit: Gale, 1998.

Bentley, Karen. *The Unsers*. New York: Chelsea House Publishers, 1996.

Scalzo, Joe, and Bobby Unser. *The Bobby Unser Story*. New York: Doubleday, 1979.

St. James Encyclopedia of Popular Culture. Detroit: St. James Press, 2000.

World Almanac and Book of Facts. Primedia Reference, 2000.

Periodicals

Anderson, Dave. "Sports of the Times: Con Is In and Conscience Is Out." *New York Times* (May 28, 1981).

Andrews, Edmund L. "Patents: A Device to Foil Radar." *New York Times* (January 27, 1990): 37.

Axthelm, Pete, and Jon Lowell. "Indy Downshifts Unser." *Newsweek* (June 8, 1981): 107.

"A Bitter Bobby Unser." *New York Times* (September 4, 1981).

"Bobby Unser and Friend Are Alive and Well." *Calgary Herald* (December 23, 1996).

"Bobby Unser Grabs Pole for the Indy 500." *New York Times* (May 17, 1981).

"Bobby Unser Jr. Arrested After Flunking Sobriety Test." *Associated Press* (March 11, 1997).

"Bobby Unser Seeks Trial; Son Is Arrested." *Washington Post* (March 12, 1997): C02.

"Bobby Unser, Son in Legal Wrangles." *USA Today* (March 12, 1997).

"Bobby Unser to Enter Racing Hall of Fame." *United Press International* (April 27, 1990).

"Bobby Unser Win Didn't Come Easily." *Dayton Daily News* (May 11, 1997).

"Bobby Unser's Conviction of Snowmobiling in Wilderness Upheld." *Associated Press* (January 5, 1999).

"Bobby Unser's Son Wins at Pikes Peak." *Charleston Daily Mail* (July 5, 1994).

Carey, Jack. "Bobby Unser Accused." *USA Today* (May 19, 1994).

Dorsey, Chris. "Unser Drives You Wild." *Sports Afield* (March 2001): 10.

El-Bashir, Tarik. "Another Indy 500 Brings Another Unser to the Track." *New York Times* (May 20, 1998).

Jones, Robert F. "A Fierce and Fiery 500." *Sports Illustrated* (June 1, 1981): 22-27.

Kindred, Dave. "Mears Victor at Indianapolis Second Try: Mears Backs Off, Wins as Bobby Unser Falters." *Washington Post* (May 28, 1979).

Kirshenbaum, Jerry. "Attention, Auto-Racing Fans, There's Been Another Lead Change at Indy." *Sports Illustrated* (October 19, 1981): 35.

Kohler, Judith. "Bobby Unser Convicted of Violating Federal Wilderness Act." *Associated Press* (June 12, 1997).

Kohler, Judith. "Race Car Champ Bobby Unser Convicted of Violating Federal Wilderness Act." *Associated Press* (June 13, 1997).

Korte, Tim. "Bobby Unser Says He Will Appeal Judge's Ruling." *Associated Press* (June 23, 1997).

Lefevre, Lori. "Spinning His Wheels." *Mediaweek* (February 26, 2001): 46.

Long, Gary. "Bobby Unser Behind Wheel Once Again." *Toronto Star* (January 14, 1991).

Mabin, Connie. "Federal Trial Begins for Race Car Champ Bobby Unser." *Associated Press* (June 11, 1997).

Massey, Barry. "Bobby Unser Takes 1994 Case to State's Highest Court." *Associated Press* (November 12, 1997).

May, Tim. "Bobby Unser: Without Stars, Indy a Shadow of Former Self." *Columbus Dispatch* (May 12, 1998).

Moran, Malcolm. "Bobby Unser Wins Indy 500 Marred by Crashes, Fires." *New York Times* (May 25, 1981).

Moran, Malcolm. "Reluctantly, Unser Bows Out." *New York Times* (December 23, 1982).

Moses, Sam. "I Will Go Fast Until the Day I Die." *Sports Illustrated* (January 11, 1982): 66-79.

"New Mexico Supreme Court Won't Rule in Bobby Unser Appeal." *Associated Press* (November 17, 1997).

"Race Driver Bobby Unser Reported Missing." *Record* (December 22, 1996).

Tuschak, Beth. "Bobby Unser Survives Two Days in Mountains." *USA Today* (December 23, 1996).

Other

"2000 Colorado Springs Sports Hall of Fame Class of Inductees." Colorado Springs Sports Corporation. http://www.thesportscorp.org/events/09200hof_unser.htm (November 7, 2002).

About Bobby Unser Jr. http://unser.hypermart.net/AboutUs.html (November 7, 2002).

"Bobby Unser." CART World-Drivers. http://www.cartworld.free-online.co.uk/drivers/bunser (November 7, 2002).

"Bobby Unser Stays Busy In Life After Racing." Indianapolis 500. http://www.indy500.com/press/1998/bunser.html (November 7, 2002).

Indianapolis 500. http://www.indy500.com (November 7, 2002).

Statement of Bobby Unser on Wilderness. http://www.wildwilderness.org/wi/unser.htm (November 7, 2002).

Sketch by Janet P. Stamatel

1980 U.S. Men's Olympic Hockey Team

American hockey team

History is replete with examples of epic struggles where ordinary people face overwhelming odds to achieve monumental victories. David, a simple shepherd boy, bore the weight of a nation and armed with only a sling slew the most feared and seasoned warrior Goliath. Local militias comprised of farmers, artisans, and volunteers defeated the professional armies of the British Empire in securing independence during the American Revolution. In U.S. Olympic history, perhaps there is no greater example than when a group of college kids came together in February 1980 to strike gold and ignite a long dormant flame of national pride and patriotism.

On November 4, 1979, militant Iranian students stormed the U.S. Embassy in Tehran taking several American citizens hostage. One month later military forces from the Soviet Union invaded neighboring Afghanistan lowering the temperature of an already frigid Cold War. In the United States inflation and unemployment rates were on the rise and lines for gasoline were growing longer. In February of 1980, as the Winter Olympics approached, world events had served to foster a growing sense of national pessimism and hopelessness.

Low Expectations

Overall, international amateur ice hockey was thoroughly dominated by the Soviet Union. The Soviets had captured gold in five consecutive Olympics prior to Lake Placid and with **Vladislav Tretiak** in net, widely regarded as the best goaltender of all time, they were expected to tally a sixth. Although technically amateurs, the men of the Soviet hockey team were officially members of the Red Army whose only responsibility was to eat, sleep, and breathe ice hockey. Despite growing rumblings within the international community over a boy-

1980 U.S. Men's Olympic Hockey Team

cott of the upcoming 1980 Summer Olympics in Moscow in protest of the Afghanistan invasion, the Soviet government was determined to send a team to Lake Placid to not only compete but win on American soil.

Expectations were low for the U.S. Hockey team going into the 1980 winter games. Since 1960, American presence on the world hockey stage had been dwindling. To counter this trend, the U.S. turned to the gruff hard-edged coach from the University of Minnesota, **Herb Brooks**. During the 1970's, Brooks was the most successful college hockey coach in the nation. He led the University of Minnesota to three NCAA ice hockey championships. Coach Brooks' first responsibility was to recruit a team that would be able to compete on the world stage. In doing so he relied heavily on his successful Minnesota squad. More than half his roster was comprised of Minnesota players such as Mike Ramsey, Neal Broten, and David Christian. In order to avoid the appearance of favoritism, Brooks rounded out his team with players from several mid-western schools such as Wisconsin, Bowling Green, and the University of Minnesota at Duluth. Other notable additions to the team were supplied by long time Minnesota rival Boston University, namely goaltender Jim Craig and team captain Mike Eruzione.

Divide and Defeat, Unite and Conquer

The next problem that befell Coach Brooks was how to eliminate the regional rivalries amongst the team and unite them into a single American squad. To accomplish this Herb Brooks created an adversarial environment pitting him against the team. He went so far as to bring in new tryouts only weeks prior to the start of the Olympics threatening to replace the current team. The move forced his players to threaten to quit thus galvanizing them into a solid, single unit. Although abrasive and confrontational, the style worked well.

In preparation for Lake Placid, the U.S. team engaged in several pre-Olympic matches against World Class opponents in both Europe and North America. The American squad performed extremely well posting a 42-15-3 record. During a Christmas tournament in 1979, held in Lake Placid, the U.S. defeated the Soviet National B team to claim a gold medal. The success of the Americans began to raise questions as to whether or not the team had the potential to seriously compete for a medal. Any bourgeoning hopes were soon to be dashed.

On February 9, 1980, just three days prior to the opening ceremonies in Lake Placid, an exhibition game was held in Madison Square Garden in New York City between the streaking U.S. squad and the Soviet national team. Given the deep freeze of the "Cold War," further aggravated by the Soviet invasion of Afghanistan and boycott talks, the crowd was rather hostile towards the visiting Russians. The men of the Red Army completely dominated the youthful Americans. The final score was eleven to three and left no doubt in the minds of U.S. hockey fans as well as the rest of the world as to just who would win gold in Lake Placid. The Americans were left wondering how they could compete.

Let the Games Begin

Opening ceremonies for thirteenth Winter Olympic Games were held February 12, 1980. In the ice hockey competition there were twelve teams competing, organized into two pools of six. The U.S. team was seeded seventh and there were some who believed the Americans would be able to compete for the Bronze. It was widely believed the Soviet Union had all but claimed the Gold and that Czechoslovakia and Sweden would be the main contenders for the Silver.

During the first round of pool competition, the Soviet hockey machine rolled to a perfect 5-0 record outscoring

1980 U.S. Men's Olympic Hockey Team Roster

Pos	Name	Age	Hometown	College
D	Bill Baker	22	Grand Rapids, Minn.	Minnesota
F	Neal Broten	19	Roseau, Minn.	Minnesota
D	Dave Christian	20	Warroad, Minn.	North Dakota
F	Steve Christoff	21	Richfield, Minn.	Boston Univ.
G	Jim Craig	22	North Eaton, Mass.	Boston Univ.
F	Mike Eruzione	25	Winthrop, Mass.	Boston Univ.
F	John Harrington	22	Virginia, Minn.	Minn.-Duluth
G	Steve Janaszak	22	White Bear Lake., Minn.	Minnesota
F	Mark Johnson	21	Madison, Wis.	Wisconsin
F	Rob McClanahan	21	St. Paul, Minn.	Minnesota
D	Ken Morrow	22	Flint, Mich.	Bowling Green
D	Jack O'Callahan	21	Charlestown, Mass.	Boston Univ.
F	Mark Pavelich	21	Eveleth, Minn.	Minn.-Duluth
D	Mike Ramsay	18	Minneapolis, Minn.	Minnesota
F	Buzz Schneider	24	Babbitt, Minn.	Minnesota
F	Dave Silk	21	Scituate, Mass.	Boston Univ.
F	Eric Strobel	21	Rochester, Minn.	Minnesota
D	Bob Suter	22	Madison, Wis.	Wisconsin
F	Phil Verchota	22	Duluth, Minn.	Minnesota
F	Mark Wells	21	St. Clair Shores, Mich.	Bowling Green

Where Are They Now?

Ironically, less than half of the "Miracle On Ice" 1980 U.S. Olympic hockey team pursued careers in hockey. Goaltender Jim Craig became an advertising salesman. Defensemen Bill Baker is an oral surgeon. Mike Eruzione works for his alma mater in the alumni office of Boston University. Several players now work as investment bankers and stockbrokers, while a handful are coaching hockey at either the professional or high school level. David Christian, Mike Ramsey, and Neal Broten have played hockey professionally. Finally, Herb Brooks, the coach of the 1980 team, owns a manufacturing agency in Minnesota and returned to the Olympics to coach the 2002 Olympic hockey team to a Silver medal.

their first two opponents, Japan and The Netherlands, 33-4. The U.S. did not have as easy a time.

The U.S. faced Sweden as their first opponent in the first round. The Swedish team was heavily favored and took a 2-1 lead late into the third period. With only 41 seconds remaining in the game, Herb Books pulled goaltender Jim Craig from the net and added an extra forward. With just seconds remaining, forward Bill Baker put a shot passed the Swedish goaltender. The U.S. held on and skated off with a 2-2 tie.

The next opponent in the first round for the young American squad was Czechoslovakia. The Czechs were widely regarded as the only team with any real chance of beating the Soviet juggernaut. Relishing their role as the underdog, the U.S. thoroughly dominated the Czech team by posting a commanding 7-3 victory.

The Americans went on to easily defeat Norway and Romania and struggled slightly to pull out a come from behind win against Germany. The U.S. captured Pool A with a 4-0-1 record and advanced to the medal rounds and a date with destiny.

Battle Against the Red Army

Friday, February 22, 1980, the United States met the Soviet Union on the ice in Lake Placid during the medal round of the Winter Olympics ice hockey competition. Just fifteen days prior the Soviets devastated the U.S. team in an exhibition game, winning 11-3. On this date, bolstered by their own remarkable accomplishments in the first round and an inspirational speech from coach Herb Brooks, the American boys were ready to leave the memory of Madison Square Garden behind and take on the Red Army.

During the opening minutes of the game, the Soviets were met by a significantly different team than they were expecting. The Americans were playing with strength and emotion previously unseen. However, the Russians adapted and put the first point on the board at just over nine minutes into the first period. At the fourteen minute mark, Buzz Schneider took the puck up the left side and entered the Soviet zone, releasing a soft shot which surprisingly beat Vladslav Tretiak. The goal rejuvenated the U.S. team and fired up the home crowd. The goal did not affect the Soviets and they responded quickly with a go ahead goal to make the score 2-1. With seconds remaining in the first period Mark Johnson took advantage of a rebound and tied the game at two apiece.

During the first intermission, Soviet coach Viktor Tikinov was so disappointed with the play of his team that he made the decision to bench the greatest goaltender in the world. Vladislav Tretiak would shoulder the responsibility of his team's first period performance and remain out of the game. Perhaps inspired, perhaps threatened by the removal of their star net minder, the Soviet team commanded the second period. They took an early 3-2 lead and dominated shots on goal by a 12-2 margin. If not for the magnificent play of Jim Craig in the American goal, the game would have been lost.

The U.S. was not disheartened by being down a goal going into the start of the third period. They had been down to Sweden and Germany and were able to come back, so they felt comfortable with the position they were in. At about eight and a half minutes into the third period, Mark Johnson once again scored the game equalizer. Eighty-one seconds later a deflected pass found its way to the stick of American team captain Mike Eruzione. He skated to the center of the Soviet zone and snapped a wrist shot beating Soviet goalie Myshkin to his right. The team, the crowd, and the entire country erupted into celebration as for the first time ever this group of college kids took the lead in a game against the Soviet Union. With nearly ten minutes remaining in the game the U.S. team relied entirely on the skills of Jim Craig to protect the lead. The Soviets poured everything into an effort to score.

The moment finally arrived and the country joined those in the arena in Lake Placid counting down the seconds until victory. The final seconds were punctuated by

1980 U.S. Men's Olympic Hockey Team

ABC commentator Al Michaels as he shouted the gleeful question "Do you believe in miracles? Yes!" The victory, as well as those famous words, have now become an unforgettable part of sports history.

On To Victory

The task for the U.S. team was not complete however. Two days later, on Sunday February 24th, the Americans faced Finland for the Gold medal. Once again the Americans fell behind in the game. After two periods they were trailing 2-1. Returning to the ice for the third period the U.S. team found themselves with a familiar goal deficit. Inspired by their victory over the Soviets, and the emotion and support of the home crowd and the prospect of claiming gold, the U.S. squad exploded. They scored three unanswered goals in that final period and completed the incredible feat of securing Olympic Gold.

Perhaps the most indelible images of the "Miracle On Ice" were provided by the medal ceremony. Team captain Mike Eruzione stood alone atop the medal stand while his teammates were aligned behind him. The "Star Spangled Banner" played and the flag of the United States was raised prominently above those of the Soviet Union and Finland, the Silver and Bronze medal finalists respectively. All the players stood with their hands over their hearts singing enthusiastically. Upon completion of the anthem, an exuberant Eruzione turned to his team and beckoned them to the stand. All twenty players squeezed onto the platform embracing and holding their fingers aloft in the classic "number one" sign.

Miracles Do Happen with Team Work

The accomplishment of the 1980 U.S. Men's Olympic hockey team served to boost the nation's spirit, patriotism, and hope during a darker period of the country's history. Their victory did not drive down gas prices or inflation, it did not free the U.S. hostages in Iran, and it did not drive the Soviet Army out of Afghanistan. It did however serve to inspire the nation. It showed that adversity could be overcome and gave the nation hope in a time of hopelessness.

FURTHER INFORMATION

Periodicals

"1980 U.S. hockey team lights Olympic flame." *Newstribune* (February 9, 2002): 6C.

"'80 Olympians set for ice breaker." *Capital Times* (September 18, 1997): 1B.

BeDan, Michael. "Frozen in time the 1980 U.S. Olympic hockey team overcame a near revolt and great odds to secure its gold." *Denver Rocky Mountain News* (August 22, 1999): 8C.

Cronin, Don. "Hockey Honors." *USA Today* (December 24, 1998): 1C.

"Gold medalists from Lake Placid to raise funds for victims of September 11 attacks." Associated Press Worldstream (November 12, 2002).

Jeansonne, John. "Nagano Winter Olympics/Opportunity Lost/Coach has no regrets about missing '80." *Newsday* (February 4, 1998): A67.

"Men's Hockey." *Minneapolis Star Tribune* (February 16, 2002): 6S.

Pennington, Bill. "Ghosts of '80 Haunt U.S. Hockey." *Record* (January 30, 1994): S01.

Starkey, Joe. "Miracle on Ice Reunites." *Pittsburgh Tribune* (February 3, 2002).

Swift, E. M. "The golden goal." *Sports Illustrated* (March 3, 1980).

Swift, E. M. "A reminder of what we can be." *Sports Illustrated* (February 21, 1994).

Weiner, Jay. "Miracle on Ice." *Minneapolis Star Tribune* (February 22, 2000): 6C.

"Where are U.S. hockey heroes now?" *Wisconsin State Journal* (April 15, 1995): 1C.

Other

Huber, Jim. "A golden moment." CNNSI.com. http://sportsillustrated.cnn.com/thenetwork/news/2000/02/21/cnnsicomprofile_miracleonice/ (November 6, 2002).

"Ice Hockey." Infoplease.com. http://www.infoplease.com/ipsa/A0301105.html (December 4, 2002).

Swift, E.M. "Brooks to head 2002 men's Olympic hockey team." CNNSI.com. http://cnnsi.co.il/more/news/2000/11/01/us_hockey_ coach_ap/ (November 6, 2002).

Sketch by Barbra J. Smerz

Amy Van Dyken
1973-

American swimmer

Champion swimmer Amy Van Dyken began swimming at age six to help in her battle against asthma. She could not swim the full length of an Olympic-size pool until age twelve, but by college she was highly decorated for her speed and ability. At the 1996 Olympic Games in Atlanta, Georgia, she and her teams placed first in the 50-meter freestyle, 100-meter butterfly, 400-meter freestyle relay, and 400-meter medley relay. These victories made her the first American woman to win four gold medals in one Olympic Games. In spite of two shoulder surgeries, Van Dyken returned to the Olympics in 2000 to win two more gold medals in relays, for a total of six. Since retiring from swimming after the Sydney, Australia, games, Van Dyken has taken up a new sport, the triathlon.

Swimming to Control Asthma

Amy Deloris Van Dyken was born February 15, 1973, in Englewood, Colorado, the daughter of Don Van Dyken, president of a computer software company, and Becky Van Dyken. She has a brother and a sister. From the age of ten months, Amy suffered from asthma and allergies that prevented her from joining other children in activities such as school field trips and overnight stays with friends. When she was six, her doctor prescribed swimming for the beneficial moisture in the air and because it requires control of breathing. Although she could not swim the full length of an Olympic-size pool without stopping until she was twelve, Amy kept swimming and fell in love with the sport.

By the time she entered Cherry Creek High School, Van Dyken was six feet tall and a self-described "nerd," who was shunned by other swimmers on the high school team. They called her too slow, threw her clothes in the pool, and spit at her. But Van Dyken, with her strong competitive drive, overcame the insults and worked harder. By her junior year, she was the star of Cherry Creek's swim team, earning six All-American honors, setting three state records, and breaking five school

Amy Van Dyken

records. She was named Colorado Swimmer of the Year and was sought by colleges throughout the West.

Success in College

Beginning her career at the University of Arizona, Tucson, in 1991, Van Dyken barely missed making the 1992 U.S. Olympic team as a freshman, when she finished fourth in the 50-meter freestyle swim. However, she went on to win silver medals at the 1992 U.S. Swimming Championships and took a second and a third place at the 1993 National Collegiate Athletic Association (NCAA) Swimming Championships. She earned All-American honors fourteen times while at Arizona but was not happy with her progress there and trans-

Chronology

1973	Born February 15 in Englewood, Colorado
1979	Takes up swimming on doctor's advice, to help with asthma
1990-91	Becomes star of Cherry Creek High School swim team
1991-93	Attends University of Arizona at Tucson; earns All-American honors fourteen times; in 1992 just misses a place on the U.S. Olympic swim team; suffers from mononucleosis in 1993 and says she will give up swimming but comes back
1994	Transfers to Colorado State University, where she sets seven school and Western Athletic Conference (WAC) records as a junior; wins three medals at World Swimming Championships in Rome, Italy
1995	Wins three gold medals and one silver medal at Pan American Games; accepts invitation to join U.S. Resident National Team to train for Olympics but has to give up last season at Colorado State; marries Alan McDaniel in October—the couple will later divorce
1996	Qualifies for U.S. Olympic team; wins 50-meter and 100-meter freestyle races and finishes second in 100-meter butterfly at Olympic Trials; places fourth in 100-meter freestyle at Summer Olympics in Atlanta, Georgia, but goes on to win four Olympic gold medals and becomes an international celebrity
1997	Resumes training, for World Swimming Championships
1998	Wins two gold medals at World Swimming Championships in Perth, Australia; has shoulder surgery in June to repair a tear
2000	In January, has another shoulder surgery to repair rotator cuff, remove scar tissue, and shave bone spurs; surgeons say she will never race again; qualifies for U.S. Olympic team and competes in 2000 Olympics in Sydney, Australia, placing fourth in 50-meter and winning two more gold medals in women's relays
2001	Marries Tom Rouen, punter for the Denver Broncos football team; finishes sixth place in her first triathlon on February 24 in Colorado Springs; finishes second triathlon in July 2001; begins working part-time as sports reporter for a Denver television station
2002	Continues to train as triathlete, setting her sights on 2003 Hawaiian Ironman Championships

Awards and Accomplishments

1990-91	Earned six high school All-American honors, set three state records, and broke five school marks in swimming; earned Colorado Swimmer of the Year honors
1991	Named Colorado Swimmer of the Year
1992	Silver medals in 50-meter and 50-yard freestyle races at U.S. Swimming Championships
1993	Finished second in 50-meter freestyle and third in 100-meter butterfly at National Collegiate Athletic Association (NCAA) Swimming Championships
1994	Set seven school and Western Athletic Conference (WAC) records at Colorado State University; named Colorado State's 1994 Female Athlete of the Year; given Joe Kearney Award by WAC as best females athlete of the year; set new American record at NCAA Swimming Championships, winning women's 50-meter freestyle in 21.77 seconds, becoming only the second woman in the world to break the 22-second barrier in this event; named NCAA Swimmer of the Year; earned All-American honors in 100-meter freestyle, 200-meter freestyle relay, and 200-meter medley relay; named Collegiate Swimming Coaches Athletic Association National Swimmer of the Year; inducted into Sportswomen of Colorado Hall of Fame; won silver medals in 400-meter freestyle and 400-meter medley relays and a bronze medal in 50-yard freestyle at World Championships
1995	Won three gold medals and one silver at Pan American Games; named Swimmer of the Year by *Swimming World* magazine
1996	Won four gold medals in the 1996 Olympic Games in Atlanta, Georgia, in 50-meter freestyle, 100-meter butterfly, 400-meter freestyle relay, and 400-meter medley relay, making her the first American woman to win four gold medals in one Olympic Games; named Sportswoman of the Year by the Women's Sports Foundation; voted Swimmer of the Year by U.S.A. Swimming; voted Sportswoman of the Year by the Associated Press and by the U.S. Olympic Committee
1998	Won two gold medals at World Swimming Championships in Perth, Australia, in 50-meter freestyle and 4 x 100-meter relay
2000	At Olympic Games in Sydney, Australia, won gold medal in women's 400-meter freestyle relay, as part of U.S. team that broke the record for this event, with a time of 3:36.61; won gold medal for swimming preliminaries of the 400-meter medley relay; finished fourth in 50-meter freestyle
2001	Inducted into Colorado Sports Hall of Fame

ferred to Colorado State University for her junior year. There she earned numerous awards. Her coach, John Mattos, called her "the type of athlete most coaches only dream about having in their program."

Van Dyken set a new American record at the NCAA Championships in 1994, winning the women's 50-meter freestyle at 21.77 seconds. She earned more All-American honors, was named National Swimmer of the Year, and won a bronze and two silver medals at the World Swimming Championships in Rome, Italy. In 1995 she won three gold medals and one silver at the Pan American Games.

Van Dyken's college success led to the offer of a place on the U.S. Resident National Team, where she would train for the Olympics. Although she did not want to leave Colorado State, she accepted the invitation, as her chance to go for Olympic gold.

1996 Olympic Superstar

In the 1996 Olympic Trials, Van Dyken finished in first place in the 50-meter and 100-meter freestyle races and second in the 100-meter butterfly race. In addition

to these three events, she would also swim in the women's relays at the Olympics in Atlanta.

In her first event, the 100-meter freestyle, Van Dyken was extremely nervous and finished in fourth place, lying at the side of the pool suffering from leg and neck cramps. But she bounced back after this disappointment and won a gold medal as part of the women's 400-meter freestyle relay team, swimming the second fastest relay leg ever, at 53.91 seconds. She then won the 100-meter butterfly—which she had qualified for but had not practiced—with a time of 59.13 seconds, beating world champion Liu Limin of China by one one-hundredth of a second. Van Dyken's third gold medal came as part of the 400-meter medley relay team, and her fourth in the 50-meter relay. Just before that final race, she later told how she gave world champion Le Jingyi of China a nasty look, clapped her hands at her, and spat pool water in her lane. Van Dyken beat Jingyi with a time of 24.87 seconds-three one-hundredths of a second ahead of the champion, and set a new American record. The win earned Van Dyken the title of world's fastest female swimmer. She told the press, "This victory is for all the nerds out there. For all the kids who are struggling, I hope I'm an inspiration for them to keep plugging away."

Van Dyken's four Olympic gold medals made her an overnight superstar. She was named Sportswoman of the Year by both the Associated Press and the U.S. Olympic Committee. She received a visit from U.S. President Bill Clinton and made numerous television appearances. Her gold medal wins put her in the category of Olympic greats **Janet Evans**, **Florence Griffith-Joyner**, and Melissa Belote, each of whom won three gold medals in an Olympics.

Road to a Second Olympics

After Atlanta, Van Dyken took some time off for a honeymoon with then husband Alan McDaniel and earned money from product endorsements. But she soon resumed training and won two gold medals at the World Swimming Championships in Perth, Australia, early in 1998. That June, however, she had the first of two shoulder surgeries to repair injuries and a bone spur. After the second surgery in January 2000, doctors told her she would never swim competitively again. She proved them wrong.

Van Dyken qualified for the 2000 Olympics in Sydney, Australia, and there won two more gold medals-one as part of the women's 400-meter freestyle relay and the other for her performance in swimming preliminaries of the 400-meter medley relay. On her team in the 400 freestyle were Americans **Jenny Thompson**, Dara Torres, and Courtney Shealy. The team broke the world record for the event, with a time of 3:36.61 (the former record, 3:37.91, was set by a Chinese team in 1994). Van Dyken placed fourth in the 50-meter freestyle race, which she had won in 1996.

After bringing home her sixth Olympic gold medal, in the fall of 2000, Van Dyken announced her retirement from swimming. By the following year, however, she had turned her attention to a new sport, the triathlon, which combines swimming, biking, and running in what can be the most grueling of sports. She competed in triathlons beginning in June 2001, with the possible goal of competing in the Hawaiian Ironman-a 2.4-mile ocean swim, 112-mile bike ride, and 26.2-mile run-in 2003.

Amy Van Dyken has proved that athletic ability and a drive to succeed can help overcome many physical obstacles. In 2000 she participated in an asthma education campaign, the Asthma All-Stars, cosponsored by five medical and respiratory organizations. An outcast in her own early high school years, she has also been active in helping the survivors of the 1999 Columbine (Colorado) High School shootings, participating in school events and talking one-on-one with students. Her four gold medals and record-breaking 50-meter race in the 1996

Van Dyken Is Toughing It Out

[Amy] Van Dyken, who hopes to make it back from major shoulder injuries ..., has raised the pre-race psyche-job to an art form. She will do just about anything she can think of within legal limits—or nearly so—to distract and demoralize foes just before the start of races. The imposing 6-footer will grunt, spit into the opponents' lane, stick out her tongue at them, clap her hands or simply lock on with a cold, Mike Tyson-style stare.

Source: Harris, Stephen. *Boston Herald* (May 28, 2000): B2.

Olympics put Van Dyken into the Olympic history books. Her spunk and competitive drive have won many fans and supporters along the way, and they continue to cheer her on in her quest for victory in the triathlon.

CONTACT INFORMATION

Address: c/o U.S. Swimming, Inc., 1 Olympic Plaza, Bldg. 2A, Colorado Springs, CO 80909-5770.

FURTHER INFORMATION

Books

Great Women in Sports. "Amy Van Dyken." Detroit: Visible Ink Press, 1996.
Newsmakers 1997. Issue 4. "Amy Van Dyken." Detroit: Gale Group, 1997.
Sports Stars. Series 1-4. "Amy Van Dyken." Detroit: U•X•L, 1994-98.

Periodicals

"Amy Van Dyken: Winner of 4 Gold Medals in Swimming in the Olympics Enjoys Post-Olympics Fame." *People* (December 30, 1996): 152.
Harris, Stephen. "Van Dyken Is Toughing It Out: U.S. Swimming Star Shows Nose for Winning—and a Heart for Healing—As She Makes Comeback." *Boston Herald* (May 28, 2000): B2.
"Olympic Notebook: Van Dyken Says This Is Last Games; Swimmer: Body Starting to Wear Down." *Seattle Times* (September 1, 2000): D12.

Other

"Amy Van Dyken Returns to the Water." USA Swimming. http://cgi.swimmersworld.com/news/ (July 10, 2001).
"'Asthma All-Stars' Jackie Joyner-Kersee, Amy Van Dyken and Jerome Bettis to Appear in New Asthma Education Campaign." PR Newswire. http://galenet.galegroup.com/ (June 28, 2000).
"Olympic Wrap Up." Compiled from usswim.org. The Victor.com. http://www.thevictor.com (January 21, 2003).

Parrish, Paula (Scripps Howard News Service). "Olympic Gold-Medal Swimmer Amy Van Dyken Plunges into Triathlon." Active.com. http://www.active.com/ (January 8, 2003).

Rainsberger, Lisa, and *Tri Digest*. "Van Dyken Completes First Triathlon." Triathlete Online. http://www.winningmag.com/news/ (January 14, 2003).

"U.S. Men, Women Set World Records in Relays: Olympics 2000." SportsLine.com Wire Reports. http://cbs.sportsline.com/ (September 23, 2000).

Zinser, Lynn. "Amy Van Dyken to Take Home Matched Set of Four Gold Medals." Knight Ridder/Tribune News Service. http://galenet.galegroup.com/ (July 27, 1996).

Sketch by Ann H. Shurgin

Mo Vaughn

Mo Vaughn
1967-

American baseball player

K nown as much for his athletic prowess as for his good-guy persona, baseball player Mo Vaughn is one of the most popular sports figures of the 1990s and early 2000s. During his heyday with the Boston Red Sox in the mid-90s, the hefty slugger built a reputation as one of the most powerful hitters in the game. Vaughn was also widely regarded as the clubhouse leader who roused the Sox to a 1995 playoff. That year, the two-time All-Star was voted American League Most Valuable Player. In one of the most lucrative deals in baseball, $80 million for six years, Vaughn signed as a free agent with the Anaheim Angels in 1998; however, a series of injuries hampered his playing time and performance. Vaughn's talents seemed on the decline when he played with the New York Mets in 2002, but the charismatic player showed no signs of retiring.

Born on December 15, 1967, in Norwalk, Connecticut, Maurice Samuel Vaughn is the son of Leroy, a former high school principal, and Shirley, a former elementary school teacher. He grew up in Norwalk with his two older sisters, Catherine and Donna. When young Vaughn was two years old, his mother taught him how to hit a baseball in the family's yard. Although her son was right-handed, she taught him her left-handed stance, which he never altered.

As a ten-year-old in Little League, Vaughn had become such a powerful slugger that opposing teams' pitchers were often told to walk him intentionally. A roly-poly child, he shed his baby fat playing baseball and football, and honed his skills by playing with older athletes. As a hefty, muscular prep school student at Trinity-Pawling in Pawling, New York, Vaughn practiced baseball devotedly with his father. Upon graduation he was offered a football scholarship from Miami State University, but he turned it down on his father's insistence. Instead, Vaughn played baseball for Seton Hall University in South Orange, New Jersey.

Known as Maurice throughout his childhood, Vaughn was dubbed "Mo" by a Seton Hall athletic director. When he was only a freshman, he broke the university's career home run record, slugging twenty-eight home runs. During the three years that he attended Seton Hall, he held a .417 batting average and was named to the All-America team every year. Known as Hit Dog among his friends, the college star was named Big East Conference Player of the Decade. During summers he played baseball in the Cape Cod League.

Honed Batting Skills

In the 1989 major-league baseball draft, Vaughn was selected 23rd overall by the Boston Red Sox. His three years in the Sox's minor-league farm system was perhaps the most trying period in the young athlete's career. Not an overnight success in pro baseball, Vaughn suffered through batting slumps that damaged his confidence. After starting off the Red Sox's 1992 season with a poor .189 average, he was shuttled back temporarily to the minor leagues—a move that hurt the rookie player, but that ultimately made him more determined.

Chronology

1967	Born on December 15 in Norwalk, CT
1989	Graduates from Seton Hall University
1989	Drafted by Boston Red Sox
1993	Plays first full major-league season
1995	Voted league's Most Valuable Player
1998	Signs free-agent contract with Anaheim Angels
2001	Signs with New York Mets

Related Biography: Hitting Coach Mike Easler

Born on November 29, 1950, in Cleveland, Ohio, Michael Anthony Easler was drafted by the Houston Astros in the early 1970s. A skillful and powerful hitter, Easler was less adept in the outfield. For nearly a decade he languished in the minor leagues before joining the Pittsburgh Pirates in 1980 and batting a strong .338 in his first full season. Traded to the Boston Red Sox in 1984, Easler briefly played first base, but was ultimately moved to designated hitter. In 1986 he joined the New York Yankees, but despite batting an impressive average he was released within a year. Easler then took up work as a hitting coach for various teams, including the Boston Red Sox (1993-96). The "Hit Man" is perhaps best known for working his magic on Boston's Mo Vaughn, transforming the slugger into one of the game's most formidable hitters. In 1996 Vaughn hired Easler as his personal hitting coach. The two remain close friends and collaborators.

Fortunately, the Red Sox employed a gifted batting coach, Mike Easler, known as the Hit Man. Easler worked with Vaughn on his batting stance, preparation, and swing, giving the young player the skills he needed to succeed. "The Hit Man taught me to take all my anger—and after I was sent back to the minors there was a lot of anger—and channel it into the barrel of the bat," Vaughn told Gerry Callahan of *Sports Illustrated*. Under Easler's tutelage Vaughn developed into a powerhouse hitter the likes of which pro baseball had rarely seen before. Throughout his career Vaughn would express gratitude toward Easler, whom he credited with saving his career.

During his first two full seasons with the Red Sox, 1993-94, Vaughn established himself as a force to be reckoned with. The heaviest player on his team, he used his 6-foot-1, 140-pound frame to his advantage when he stepped up to the plate, socking twenty-nine home runs his first year, and ending the 1994 season with a .310 batting average. But it was during his third year on the team that the 27-year-old first-baseman really shined. After leading the Sox to a division title in September 1995, he emerged onto the field amid chants of "Mo, Mo, Mo" from an adoring crowd at Boston's Fenway Park.

Recognized as the heart and soul of his team, Vaughn was voted the league's Most Valuable Player in 1995. Two other players, **Albert Belle** and Edgar Martinez, had outdone Vaughn with higher numbers; Belle had fifty home runs, while Vaughn had thirty-nine. But it was not only statistics that determined this award. Players recognized that Vaughn was a leader who infused the Sox with a determination and a belief in themselves to win. "Mo has been carrying this team consistently, day in and day out, and that to me is what makes an MVP," Boston player, **Jose Canseco** told Callahan of *Sports Illustrated*. "It's his presence," said third-baseman Tim Naehring. "He brings a confidence and an attitude to this team that is hard to explain."

Vaughn's contributions extended beyond the baseball diamond and into the greater Boston community. In 1994 he established the Mo Vaughn Youth Development Program, a counseling facility for inner-city kids in Dorchester. The Red Sox star also participated in an adopt-a-school program that involved his regular visits to an elementary school in urban Mattapan. Eager to help children, especially those in need, Vaughn had an unusual ability to connect with kids and to influence them as a role model and idol. The slugger captured media attention in 1993 when, before a game, he told an eleven-year-old cancer patient that he would try to hit a home run for him. The home run came in his third at-bat.

Vaughn's performance was stronger than ever in his remaining three years with the Red Sox. In 1996 he knocked forty-four home runs and batted .326; two years later he hit for a career high .337 average. But an ongoing feud between Vaughn and the Sox's general manager, Dan Duquette, prompted the All-Star player to test the free-agent market after the 1998 season. Duquette had told the media that he was concerned about the player's alcohol use after Vaughn flipped his truck while driving home from a strip club the previous winter. Vaughn, acquitted of drunken-driving charges in the incident, complained that Duquette was trying to wage a smear campaign against him. In August 1998, Boston's powerhouse hitter announced that he was leaving. He had been courted by the Anaheim Angels with one of the most lucrative deals in baseball: a six-year, $80 million contract.

Plagued by Injuries

After he left the Sox, Vaughn's luck took a turn for the worse. On opening day with the Angels, he fell down the stairs of the visitor's dugout while chasing a foul pop-up. (The incident prompted many major-league clubs to put fences in front of dugouts to prevent future accidents.) Injuries kept Vaughn on the sidelines briefly and affected his swing for the remainder of the season. His batting average dropped below .300 for the first time in six years, but he hit a respectable thirty-three home runs and 108 RBIs. Injuries again sidelined Vaughn in 2001, when he discovered that he had been playing with a ruptured tendon in his left arm. Surgery kept him out of the game for the entire 2001 season.

Returning to baseball, Vaughn signed with the New York Mets in December 2001. But the player's comeback was marred by yet another injury—a fractured right hand, sustained in April 2002. When he returned to the game, Vaughn seemed to struggle with his confidence. Time away from baseball had resulted in significant weight gain, and the once powerful hitter's bat

Career Statistics

Yr	Team	Avg	GP	AB	R	H	HR	RBI	BB	SO	SB
1991	BOS	.260	74	219	21	57	4	32	26	43	2
1992	BOS	.234	113	355	42	83	13	57	42	67	3
1993	BOS	.297	152	539	86	160	29	101	79	130	4
1994	BOS	.310	111	394	65	122	26	82	57	112	4
1995	BOS	.300	140	550	98	165	39	126	68	150	11
1996	BOS	.326	161	635	118	207	44	143	95	154	2
1997	BOS	.315	141	527	91	166	35	96	86	154	2
1998	BOS	.337	154	609	107	205	40	115	61	144	0
1999	ANA	.281	139	524	63	147	33	108	54	127	0
2000	ANA	.272	161	614	93	167	36	117	79	181	2
2002	NYM	.259	139	487	67	126	26	72	59	145	0
TOTAL		.294	1485	5453	851	1605	325	1049	711	1407	30

ANA: Anaheim Angels; BOS: Boston Red Sox; NYM: New York Mets.

Awards and Accomplishments

1987–89	All-America Team
1989	Big East Conference Player of the Decade
1995	American League Most Valuable Player
1995	All-Star
1998	All-Star

speed had slowed. Vaughn scoffed at any suggestions that he would retire at age thirty-four. Meanwhile, the Mets threatened to terminate his contract if the slugger did not lose weight and get into shape before the start of the 2003 season. "I'm not going out like this," a determined Vaughn told Pete Caldera of the *Record* (Bergen County, New Jersey). "I want to be the dude that I was. I think I can play this game five more years."

Whether or not Vaughn will make his promised comeback remains to be seen. When he does retire, Vaughn will be remembered for his batting prowess, charisma, large-heartedness, and leadership abilities. It is with this combination of talents and qualities that Vaughn has made his own personal, and very significant, contribution to modern baseball.

FURTHER INFORMATION

Periodicals

Caldera, Pete. "Slugger Promises Less Mo." *Record* (Bergen County, NJ) (September 17, 2002): S5.

Callahan, Gerry. "Clashing Sox." *Sports Illustrated* (August 10, 1998): 88.

Callahan, Gerry. "Sox Appeal." *Sports Illustrated* (October 2, 1995): 42.

Cavanaugh, Jack. "Mo Vaughn: Still Smiling after All These Years." *New York Times* (July 9, 1995): 8-1.

"Mets Owner Tells Mo to Get in Shape." Associated Press (November 2, 2002).

Ryan, Bob. "It's a Nice Tribute to This Nice Guy." *Boston Globe* (November 17, 1995): 88.

Other

"Mike Easler." BaseballLibrary.com. httphttp://www. pubdim.net/baseballlibrary/ballplayers/E/Easler_Mike.stm (December 10, 2002).

"Mike Easler Statistics." Baseball-Reference.com. http://www.baseball-reference.com/e/easlemi01. shtml (December 10, 2002).

"Mo Vaughn." BaseballLibrary.com. http://www. pubdim.net/baseballlibrary/ballplayers/V/Vaughn_Mo.stm (December 10, 2002).

"Mo Vaughn Statistics." Baseball-Reference.com. http://www.baseball-reference.com/v/vaughmo01. shtml (December 11, 2002).

Sketch by Wendy Kagan

Jesse Ventura
1951-

American wrestler

Known as Jesse "The Body" Ventura as a wrestler with the American Wresting Federation, and later with the World Wrestling Federation (WWF), Jesse Ventura appealed in 1998 to Minnesota voters who wanted a change in the governor's mansion. Change they got when Ventura became governor Ventura. A master of self-reinvention, Ventura has reached the top of four professions: in the Navy as a member of the elite cadre of commandos known as SEALs, as one of the most popular pro wrestlers in the United States, as a Hollywood movie actor, and finally as a politician.

Jesse Ventura

Minnesota Native

Ventura was born James George Janos in 1951 and grew up in Minneapolis. His father, George Janos, was a World War II veteran who grew up in the Swede Town section of Minneapolis. Ventura's father was a maintenance worker for the city of Minneapolis while Ventura was growing up. His mother, Bernice, started as a nurse in the U.S. Army, and later worked as a civilian nurse.

Ventura and his older brother, Jan, spent a lot of time around the Mississippi River as youths, fishing for carp under a bridge that spanned the river between the cities of Minneapolis and St. Paul. They often cooked their catches over bonfires along the river banks. The brothers both became captains of their Roosevelt High School swim teams—Jan in 1966, and Ventura his senior year, 1969. Ventura knew by then he wanted a professional wrestling career.

Dinner conversations at the Janos family table may have sparked Ventura's interest in politics; his father would complain bitterly about establishment politics, calling then-presidential candidate Richard Nixon a tail-less rat, according to Jan, who spoke with reporters about Ventura's political origins.

In the Navy

Again following his brother, Ventura entered the U.S. Navy soon after graduating from high school. In the

Navy, he joined the SEALs, an elite corps of servicemen. While with the SEALs, he spent time in the brig at least once for brawling in bars. Starting in 1971 until the end of 1973, he served in an Underwater Demotion Team-SEALs unit that was posted at various points in Southeast Asia.

While Ventura has told reporters that he served in combat areas a SEAL in the Vietnam War, he has always kept the details to himself, saying only, according to Pat Doyle and Mike Kaszuba of the Minneapolis *Star Tribune,* "What I did there is between me and the man upstairs." However, a former SEAL comrade of Ventura's, Mike Gotchey has said that his and Ventura's unit saw very little action, since the war was winding down by then.

Ventura spent part of his Navy time at a base in Subic Bay in the Philippines. There, he later recounted, he had the time of his life, partying at several of the 350 bars near the base every night, and meeting lots of women. He also began to develop the reputation that he would cultivate in later years as something of a rough neck, "a little bit scuzzy looking," according to one of his superiors, who later spoke to the *Star Tribune.*

Motorcycle Gang Member

After his discharge from the Navy, in the early 1970s, Ventura joined a motorcycle gang based in San Diego, known as the Mongols. In the mid-1970s, Ventura left the gang and headed back to the Minneapolis area, where motorcycles were still very much a part of his lifestyle. During this time, he favored a German Army-style helmet when he rode his bike.

In 1974, Ventura enrolled at the North Hennepin Community College, where a different side of him emerged. Tom Bloom, Ventura's English teacher at the college, told the *Star Tribune,* "This action-adventure character—I don't think that's him at all. This lug of a guy—that's a put-on. My sense is, he's emotionally sensitive."

Ventura consistently earned As on his papers in the class, slipping only once to a B. He wrote about James Joyce, D.H. Lawrence, and other authors. By night, he worked as a bouncer at a biker bar called the Rusty Nail in a Minneapolis suburb; there he met his future wife, recent high school graduate Teresa Masters.

After playing the part of Hercules in the ancient Greek comedy *The Birds* by Aristophanes, Ventura dropped out of college in 1975. He had found a new career.

Jesse "The Body" Ventura

From the beginning, Ventura took on the role of the bad guy in the theatrical world of pro wrestling. Also at the start of his wrestling career, Ventura took the name of Jesse Ventura, dying his long hair blond, and bulking up to look the part. He worked out at the 7th Street Gym

Chronology

1951	Born in Minneapolis, MN
1969	Graduates from Roosevelt High School in Minneapolis
1969	Joins U.S. Navy as a SEAL
1973	Leaves the Navy after tours in Southeast Asia
1975	Becomes a pro wrestler
1975	Marries Terry Masters
1984	Retires as a wrestler, becomes wrestling commentator
1987	Appears with Arnold Schwarzenegger in *Predator*
1987	Appears in the major motion picture *Running Man*
1991	Becomes mayor of Brooklyn Park, Minnesota
1995	Finishes term as mayor of Brooklyn Park
1997	Appears in the major motion picture *Batman and Robin*
1999	Becomes governor of Minnesota
1999	Publishes autobiography *I Ain't Got Time to Bleed*
2003	Finishes term of office as Minnesota governor
2003	Becomes a talk show host on the MSNBC television network

Predator

Jesse Ventura's role alongside action star Arnold Schwarzenegger in the 1987 science-fiction blockbuster, *Predator,* cemented Ventura's career as a Hollywood film actor. The film features Ventura as Blain, a member of Schwarzenegger's commando unit sent to a Central American jungle to take out a gun-running gang. When the commandos are picked off one by one by the extraterrestrial predator of the film's title, Blain and his remaining comrades are drawn into the fight of their lives, their original mission forgotten. Roger Ebert, writing on the *Chicago Sun-Times* Web site, called the film "a slick, high-energy action picture."

in downtown Minneapolis, where he met the man who became his mentor—famous wrestling villain Super Star Billy Graham. Ventura studied Graham carefully, learning his banter and watching all of his matches.

Ventura made his pro debut in the minor leagues in Kansas City, where he substituted for a wrestler who didn't show up. As the bad guy in the scripted match, Ventura got himself disqualified by throwing his opponent out of the ring.

At the beginning of his wrestling career, Ventura worked on a match-to-match basis, typically earning $35 to $65 a performance, traveling around the Midwest. Commentators would bill him as coming from Hollywood, and began introducing him as Jesse "The Body" Ventura.

Ventura married Teresa Masters when she was 19 years old, he 24. By then, Ventura's hard work at the gym, and, he later admitted, steroids, which were legal at the time, had made him an imposing figure. A diet that included 12 raw eggs a day and 30 different vitamins also helped him to add muscle mass.

End and a Beginning

The newlyweds went to Portland, Oregon, where Ventura found more and better wrestling opportunities. His popularity among fans grew, and he made his best earnings to date there—$100 for a single match. More traveling followed, as he drove from match to match, once performing 63 consecutive nights.

By the early 1980s, Ventura had graduated to the major leagues, working in the American Wrestling Federation, which he left for the World Wresting Federation following a disagreement over payment and working conditions. In a prelude to his political career, Ventura tried unsuccessfully to organize his fellow WWF performers into a union.

In 1984, now the most popular villain in pro wrestling, Ventura was preparing to perform in a match with Hulk Hogan, the wrestling world's most popular good guy, when he was stricken with a pulmonary embolism, a dangerous condition caused by blood clots in the lungs. The condition ended his wrestling career while he was at the top of his game. "I mean," he later told the *Star Tribune,* "one minute I'm preparing to meet [Hogan] in the Los Angeles Coliseum, and the next minute I'm lying flat on my back fighting for my very existence."

After recovering, Ventura parlayed his fame into a successful career as a wrestling announcer. Fast talking, rather than athleticism, was more his attribute as a wrestler. Announcing seemed a better fit, and he quickly won favor with fans.

In 1990, Ventura and WWF owner Vince McMahon differed over the use of Ventura as a video-game character. Ventura had been offered $40,000 for this use of his image, but the WWF felt this would create competition for its own products. Ventura not only left the WWF over the dispute, but also sued it, seeking royalties for the use of his wrestling commentaries on videotapes. To the astonishment of the WWF and outside observers, Ventura won the suit, winning more than $750,000 in a judgment, despite Ventura having signed a contract waiving the right to collect royalties. A federal court ruled his signature had been obtained fraudulently.

Moving on the from the WWF, Ventura landed a 2-year contract to announce events for World Championship Wrestling (WCW). His contract, worth close to a million dollars, made him the highest paid figure in wrestling. But WCW bought out his contract before it was completed, charging that Ventura cared more about promoting himself than the events he was supposed to be covering.

Of his fallings out with wrestling executives, Ventura remained bitter even years later, telling reporters, according to Doyle and Kaszuba, "The question was whether I would fall under their thumb—whether they could control my talent. They're not even talented enough to hold my jock."

Nevertheless, Ventura left the wrestling business a wealthy man. In 1994, Ventura and his wife, with son, Tyrel, and daughter, Jade, moved into a luxurious custom

---

Awards and Accomplishments	
1987	Appears with Arnold Schwarzenegger in *Predator*
1987	Appears in the major motion picture *Running Man*
1990	Elected mayor of Brooklyn Park, Minnesota
1997	Appears in the major motion picture *Batman and Robin*
1998	Elected governor of Minnesota
1999	Publishes autobiography *I Ain't Got Time to Bleed*

Where Is He Now?

At the end of January, 2003, the cable network MSNBC announced that Ventura would host would host his own talk show. At the time, MSNBC was struggling, and network officials hoped Ventura would lift the network's ratings. "I'm going to educate 'em, entertain 'em and tell people the truth," Ventura said on "The Tonight Show with Jay Leno" on February 5. "I don't know if they're ready for me," he growled to Leno. "If there's one person that can get MSNBC off the air, you're looking at it."

home in the Maple Grove suburb of Minneapolis, and bought luxury automobiles. Ventura was modest about his new wealth, telling reporters he was happy just being able to walk into a restaurant and order anything he wanted.

An Actor in Hollywood

Meanwhile, Ventura had been developing a career as an actor, landing his first role in 1985 on the NBC television series *Hunter,* a police drama starring former pro football defensive lineman Fred Dryer. The role earned him $850, and gave him a leg up into feature films. He shot his first feature in 1986, appearing alongside superstar Arnold Schwarzenegger in the 1987 film *Predator.* This role netted him $5,000 a week, and within the year, he was earning $20,000 a week acting in films.

In 1989 and 1990, Ventura worked as a commentator on Tampa Bay Buccaneers football games. But this job ended after he attended only half the games during his second season, because of his acting commitments. He lasted only one year working Minnesota Vikings games.

Career in Politics

Ventura reinvented himself yet again in 1990, when he ran for mayor of the Minneapolis suburb of Brooklyn Park. He had waged a fight against that city over the placement of a storm sewer and a housing complex he believed would harm the wetlands near his home. He took his fight straight to the top by running against 18-year incumbent James Krautkremer, and winning easily. Voter turnout was high, at 71 percent.

Ventura used his charisma to push through several initiatives in which he believed strongly, including a new highway. When necessary, he went on lobbying trips to Washington, D.C.

Ventura's career in Hollywood continued to occupy his time, and he missed a fifth of Brooklyn Park's City Council meetings. He had also landed his own talk show on the St. Paul radio station KSTP, further distracting from his mayoral duties. In 1994, Ventura said he would not seek re-election.

Governor Ventura

In January, 1998, Ventura became the Reform Party candidate for Minnesota governor. Ventura presented himself as a sane alternative to the mainstream Republicans and Democrats, whom he said were mired in establishment politics at the expense of running the state. "Let's put Minnesotans first," he said. "There's more of us than there are Democrats and Republicans."

Commentators refused to take Ventura seriously at first, noting that no third-party candidate had won a statewide election in more than 50 years. They favored his opponents, Republican Norm Coleman, then mayor of St. Paul and Democrat Hubert H. Humphrey III, the state's attorney general and son of the former U.S. vice president and 1968 presidential candidate. Undaunted, Ventura charmed voters with his colorful style and his refusal to mince words. Asked at press conferences about issues he knew little about, he had no problem saying that he didn't know enough to provide a good answer— something many voters found extremely refreshing.

Ventura became the governor of Minnesota in 1999 by appealing to Minnesota voters disaffected with ordinary politics—people much like Ventura himself, who, according to *USA Today,* rarely bothered to vote in previous elections.

Among Ventura's first goals as governor were to cut taxes, reduce class size in public schools, and to enjoy himself. "What's the first thing I'm going to do after I'm inaugurated?" he said to *USA Today*'s Debbie Howlett. "I'm going to put my feet up on the desk and light me a stogie in a nonsmoking building. And who can stop me? I'll be governor."

During his term as governor, Ventura furthered his reputation for outspokenness, for being blunt, and for refusing to compromise. On leaving the governor's office, he regretted only that the state legislature refused to pass some of his recommendations, among them reducing the legislature from the current two-house system to one. That measure, he said, would have alleviated the budget deficit.

Ventura's gubernatorial term ended at the start of 2003. He made plans to host a talk show on the cable network MSNBC. He did say that he had no plans to run for public office, and that he would remain in the public eye as a critic of the media "because no one does that, and I think someone should."

As Ventura left office, a seven-month old story about his hospitalization for a blood clot in his lung mistakenly

Jesse Ventura, center

appeared on the news wires, "causing some frantic moments for Ventura's staff and embarrassment to a few news organizations," Kavita Kumar wrote in the *Star Tribune*.

The Associated Press (AP) transmitted the story February 10 through its New York headquarters, referring to Ventura's condition in July. A Twin Cities television reporter saw the story and contacted the AP's Minneapolis office. Although the AP sent advisories to subscribing media outlets to disregard the story, CNN and the online Drudge Report reported the illness, though they recanted after the advisories.

"The unfortunate thing is that this will only contribute to the [former] governor's mistrust of the media and be fodder to further his cause against the media, which I guess is amusing," said John Wodele, Ventura's former spokesman and adviser on the MSNBC talk show.

SELECTED WRITINGS BY VENTURA:

The Wit and Wisdom of Jesse "the Body—the Mind" Ventura. New York: Quill, 1999.

I Ain't Got Time to Bleed: Reworking the Body Politic from the Bottom Up. New York: Signet, 2000.

(With Julie Mooney) *Do I Stand Alone?: Going to the Mat against Political Pawns and Media Jackals*. New York: Pocket Books, 2000.

(With Myron Rupp) *Quotations of Chairman Jesse*. St. Paul, MN: Ruminator, 2000.

(With Heron Marquez) *Jesse Ventura Tells It Like It Is: America's Most Outspoken Governor Speaks Out About Government*. Minneapolis, MN: Lerner, 2002.

FURTHER INFORMATION

Books

Davis, Leslie. *Always Cheat: The Philosophy of Jesse Ventura*. Minneapolis, MN: Tell The Truth Books, 2002.

Hauser, Tom. *Inside the Ropes with Jesse Ventura*. Minneapolis, MN: University of Minnesota Press, 2002.

Lentz, Jacob. *Electing Jesse Ventura: A Third-party Success Story*. Boulder, CO: Rienner, 2002.

Tapper, Jake. *Body Slam: The Jesse Ventura Story*. New York: St. Martin's Paperbacks, 1999.

Periodicals

deFiebre, Conrad. "Ventura Wraps Things Up His Way." *Star Tribune* (January 4, 2003): 1A.

Doyle, Pat and Kaszuba, Mike. "Rebellious Road; Jesse Ventura's Life Is Riddled by Confrontation and Theatrics." *Star Tribune* (January 10, 1999): 1A.

Howlett, Debbie. "Some in Minnesota Irked By Tamer Ventura: Governor Elect Sounds More and More Like a Politician." *USA Today* (December 23, 1998): 1A.

Jeter, Jon and Jim Mone. "In Minnesota, the 'Body' Goes Public—and Wins." *Chicago Sun-Times* (November 5, 1998): 2.

Smith, Dane. "Ventura Joins the Fray in Race to Follow Carlson; the Reform Party Gets a Colorful Candidate to Take on the DFL and GOP." *Star Tribune* (January 27, 1998): 1A.

Other

Ebert, Roger. "Predator." Chicago Sun-Times. http://www.suntimes.com/ebert/ebert_reviews/1987/06/237873.html. (January 24, 2003).

"Jesse Ventura." Internet Movie Database. http://us.imdb.com/Name?Ventura+Jesse. (January 24, 2003).

Kumar, Kavita. "Old News about Ventura Travels Fast." Star Tribune. http://www.startribune.com/stories/ (February 11, 2003).

"Predator (1987)—Movie Info." Yahoo! Movies. http://movies.yahoo.com/shop?d=hv&id=1800107656&cf=info&intl=us. (January 24, 2003).

Sketch by Michael Belfiore

Georges Vezina
1887-1926

Canadian hockey player

Because of a trophy given out by the National Hockey League (NHL) to the best goalie in the league in his honor, the name of Georges Vezina remains alive to this day. Many consider Vezina—who played for 15 seasons (1910-25) all for the Montreal Canadiens—the NHL's first great goaltender. Playing in 328 straight games, Vezina was an innovative goalie who mastered and defined the early stand-up style of play. Nicknamed the "Chicoutimi Cucumber" for his hometown and calm coolness during games, Vezina's career was cut short by several seasons when he developed tuberculosis. Though he played for at least two seasons while in the early stages of the disease—holding the league's lowest goals against average and backstopping the Canadiens to one of the two Stanley Cups they would win with him in goal—Vezina played his last game at the beginning of the 1925-26 season, dying several months later. As Stan Fischler wrote in *The All-New Hockey's 100: A Personal Ranking of the Best Players in Hockey History,* "Georges Vezina … was a nonpareil athlete whose ability was matched only by his infinite sportsmanship."

Georges Vezina

Early Years

Vezina was born on January 21, 1887 in Chicoutimi, Quebec, Canada, a small town located on the Saguenay River. He was the son of Jacques Vezina and his wife, who were both employed as bakers. Vezina played hockey from his youth when the game was still in its infancy. He might have played on his town's first hockey team ever. The game probably had been brought to Chicoutimi by some employees of Price Bros. who had attended McGill University in Montreal. Price Bros. was a local company who built a rink in town, which Vezina's father later bought.

While playing the goalie position for amateur teams in his youth, Vezina wore boots instead of skates, a common practice of goalies in this time period. When Vezina was 18 years old, he learned to skate and wore skates while playing after that. By 1909, he was the goalie for the Chicoutimi Sagueneens, an amateur team that

Chronology

1887	Born January 21 in Chicoutimi, Quebec, Canada
c. 1905	Learns to skate after playing goalie position in boots since his youth
1910	Signed by the Montreal Canadiens after playing well in an exhibition game against the professional team
c. 1910	Marries wife with whom he would have 22 children (only two would survive to adulthood)
1910	Makes debut with the Montreal Canadiens, December 31
1910-12	Vezina's goals against average leads the NHA
1912-13	Backstops his way to first shutout of his career
1917-18	Becomes first goalie to post shutout in NHL
1923-25	Leads NHL in goals against average
1925	Plays in last game on November 25, collapsing on the ice
1926	Dies of tuberculosis on March 24
2000	Pair of his goalie pads (perhaps the only ones in existence) are cut up and attached to certain collectable trading cards, outraging hockey historians

played in the Montreal Senior League. Vezina was only 5'6" and weighed, at most, 185 lbs., and was described as thin and frail-looking for much of his career, but his focused demeanor in goal was about to take him to professional ranks.

In 1910, Vezina played in two exhibition games in Chicoutimi which would lead to his professional career. In preparation for upcoming Allan Cup play, the Sagueneens played against a touring Grand'Mère Senior club early in the year. Vezina garnered recognition because he got a shutout. He had the same result a short time later when he and the Chicoutimi team played against the newly formed Montreal Canadiens, a professional team of the first year National Hockey Association, in a barnstorming game in February 1910. Vezina backstopped his team to a 2-0 win. At this time, shutouts were very uncommon in part because goalies were forced to stand in goal for the whole game and were not allowed to drop to their knees to block shots. Vezina's stick-handling skills were already in evidence and his play impressed the opposition.

After the game, the goalie for the Montreal team, Joseph Cattarinich, recommended Vezina to the team's owner, George Kennedy. Vezina agreed to play for the Canadiens beginning in the 1910-11 season for $800. He actually never signed a contract, but had a handshake agreement with the Canadiens manager. Vezina was known for such indiscriminate ways involving his money. He often loaned money to friends, which was never repaid. After agreeing to play with the Canadiens, he maintained a tannery business in his hometown. Vezina was also married in this time period.

Joined the Montreal Canadiens

Vezina joined the Montreal Canadiens in the fall of 1910, and he would spend his entire professional career with the team. The Canadiens were part of the National Hockey Association (NHA) until 1917, when the league folded. They then joined the NHL in 1917. Before the 1926-27 season, the Stanley Cup was played for by the team that won the NHA/NHL, against whichever team won the Pacific Coast Hockey Association (PCHA) and/or the Western Canada Hockey League (WCHL). After Vezina made his debut with the Canadiens on December 31, 1910, he played in 328 straight games, plus an additional 39 playoffs, for 15 seasons until he was forced to leave the game because of illness. During the course of his career, the Canadiens won two NHA league championships, three NHL league championships, and two Stanley Cups.

Vezina's debut with the Canadiens was inauspicious: he lost his first game. Though the Canadiens were not a great team for his first few seasons, in the 1910-11 season, Vezina's goals against average led the five-team NHA. He repeated the feat in the 1911-12 season, when there were only four teams in the league, and Montreal was at the bottom of the standings. Vezina scored his first shutout during the 1912-13 season.

By this time, Vezina had acquired his nickname, "Chicoutimi Cucumber." On the ice, he was known for his gentlemanly play, and his steadiness in goal. Though Vezina did not get excited, he was still very competitive. Because goalies were forced to stand in goal until at least 1919—when the rules were changed because of Clint Benedict, who began dropping to his knees and sitting on the ice to make saves—Vezina's accomplishments in terms of low goals against average even more remarkable. Some believed Vezina was better with his stick than his glove. This was emphasized by his ability to clear the puck, which resulted in few rebounds. Off the ice, Vezina also had an even reputation, not indulging in smoke or drink. He also did not speak much English.

Won First Stanley Cup

It was not until the 1915-16 season that the Montreal Canadiens became a really competitive team, with good offensive players on board like Newsy Lalonde, to match the defensive prowess given by Vezina. This led to Montreal's playing for its first Stanley Cup, after winning the NHA championship, against the Portland Rosebuds of the PCHA. The series went to a decisive fifth game in Portland, which Montreal won 2-1. Vezina held off a number of Portland rushes until the Canadiens scored the game winner. In honor of winning the Stanley Cup, Vezina named his newborn son Marcil Stanley. This son was one of two children of Vezina and his wife's that survived to adulthood of the 22 born to them.

The following season, Vezina and the Montreal Canadiens again won the NHA championship, but lost to the Seattle Metropolitans of the PCHA in the Stanley Cup series. By the time the first season of the NHL's existence, 1917-18, Vezina was known as one of the best goalies in the new league, and he had the privilege of being the first goalie to earn a shutout in the league.

In 1919, Vezina again backstopped the Canadiens to victory in the NHL championships, but did not get a chance to finish playing for the Stanley Cup. Because of the on-going influenza epidemic in the city of Seattle, the last game in the series against the Seattle Metropolitans was cancelled. A number of men on both teams were ill, and a few, including Vezina's teammate Joe Hall, later died. Montreal lost the first game 7-0, but tied series before it was called. Within a few years Vezina was making a career-high salary of $7200 per season.

Played Through Injury, Illness

By the early 1920s, Vezina showed how tough of a player he really was when he played after suffering a serious injury, then a deadly disease. During one game in Hamilton, Ontario in the 1922-23 season, Vezina's head was cut open and he suffered a broken nose when an opponent slammed into him. Vezina continued to play in every game, and played well. He won a game against Ottawa a short time later, stopping 79 of 80 shots. By this time, Vezina already had the beginnings of tuberculosis, yet he played for several more seasons and led the league in goals against average during both the 1923-24 and 1924-25 campaigns.

During the 1923-24 season, Vezina only allowed 48 goals in 24 regular season games for a goals against average of 2.00. Montreal placed second to Ottawa and defeated them in the 1924 playoffs with victories of 1-0 and 4-2 to win the league championship. The Canadiens went on to compete for the Stanley Cup by playing against both the WCHL and PCHA teams, Calgary and Vancouver. Vezina led the team to victory against both teams, winning four total games and allowing only four goals.

In the 1924-25 season, as tuberculosis continued to grow stronger in Vezina, he still posted the NHL's best goals against average of 1.90. The Canadiens finished third to Hamilton and Toronto, but Montreal made the playoffs to compete for the Stanley Cup by winning the first round against Toronto (with Vezina allowing only two goals in two playoff games), the team lost to Vancouver by losing three of four games.

By the time of training camp before the 1925-26 season, tuberculosis was catching up to Vezina. He had problems such as fatigue during the camp. Still, he remained the starting goalie on opening night, as he had for 13 previous seasons. Vezina was expected to be a draw for the new American teams in the NHL (Boston, New York, and Pittsburgh) as his reputation in goal preceded him. However, he only made it to opening night.

Career Statistics

Yr	Team	GP	W	L	T	GAA	SHO
1910-11	Montreal	16	8	8	0	3.80	0
1911-12	Montreal	18	8	10	0	3.57	0
1912-13	Montreal	20	11	9	0	3.99	1
1913-14	Montreal	20	13	7	0	3.14	1
1914-15	Montreal	20	6	14	0	3.86	0
1915-16	Montreal	24	16	7	1	3.08	0
1916-17	Montreal	20	10	10	0	3.94	0
1917-18	Montreal	22	13	10	0	3.82	1
1918-19	Montreal	18	10	8	0	4.33	1
1919-20	Montreal	24	13	11	0	4.71	0
1920-21	Montreal	24	13	11	0	4.13	0
1921-22	Montreal	24	13	11	1	3.92	0
1922-23	Montreal	24	13	9	2	2.54	2
1923-24	Montreal	24	13	11	0	2.00	3
1924-25	Montreal	30	17	11	2	1.87	5
1925-26	Montreal	1	0	0	0	0.00	0

Montreal: Montreal Canadiens.

Career, Life End Because of Tuberculosis

During the season opener against Pittsburgh in his home ice, Mt. Royal Arena, on November 28, 1925, he played in the first period despite a 102-105 degree temperature, fatigue, and serious chest pains. Vezina did not allow one goal. During the intermission, Vezina had an arterial hemorrhage, bled from the mouth, and lost consciousness. The goalie insisted on playing the second period, but collapsed on the ice, bleeding from the mouth, and was carried off. He never played in goal again.

As per his request, Vezina was taken to his home in Chicoutimi, where he was diagnosed with advanced tuberculosis. While he was dying, the Canadiens did not do well. They were removed from playoff contention a week before his death. Vezina managed to visit his team one last time, shortly before his death. He came to dressing room at the time he would normally come for games. His skates and pads were set out for him, but Vezina only took the sweater (jersey) he wore in the last playoffs, and went home.

On March 24, 1926, when he was only 39 years old, Vezina died of tuberculosis. A huge funeral was given for him in Chicoutimi. A year after his death, the Canadiens bought a trophy for the fledgling NHL to be awarded to goaltenders in Vezina's honor. Hockey historians believe that if he had not developed this disease, Vezina could have played for several more seasons. Instead, his legacy as one of the innovators of the goalie position and one of the original stars of the National Hockey League rests on his 15 seasons with Montreal in which he won two Stanley Cups and other league championships. He led the league in goals against average several times, even while ill with tuberculosis. Vezina allowed only 1267 goals in his combined 328 regular season and 39 play off games. As Dan Diamond and Joseph

Awards and Accomplishments	
1916	Led the Montreal Canadians to their first Stanley Cup; also won the NHA championship
1917	With the Canadiens, won the NHA championship; lost the Stanley Cup to the Seattle Metropolitans
1919	With the Canadiens, won the NHL championship
1924	Led the Montreal Canadians to his second and last Stanley Cup; also won the NHL championship
1925	Won the NHL championship with the Canadiens
1945	Named to the Hockey Hall of Fame as one of its 12 charter members

The Vezina Trophy

The Vezina Trophy was named in honor of Georges Vezina. After his tragic death from tuberculosis, the owners of the Montreal Canadians (Leo Dandurand, Louis Letourneau, and Joe Cattarinich) donated a trophy to the National Hockey League during the 1926-27 season. The Vezina was originally given to the goaltender who played the most games for his team and allowed the fewest number of goals during the regular season. The first goalie to win it was George Hainsworth, who succeeded Vezina between the pipes for the Canadians. Beginning in the 1964-65 season until the 1981-82 season, the Vezina was given to all the active goalies on the team with the lowest goals against average, as many teams used two goalies after the NHL expanded. After the 1981-82 season, the trophy was given to the best goalie in the league. Jacques Plante won the most Vezinas with seven, followed by Bill Durnan and Dominik Hasek with six each. The modern day winner also received $10,000, with the runners up receiving $6000 and $4000.

Romain wrote in *Hockey Hall of Fame: The Official History of the Game and Its Greatest Stars,* "Vezina was the nearest thing to the perfect athlete … . He was a strong competitor on the ice, and always [a] gentleman."

FURTHER INFORMATION

Books

Diamond, Dan, and Joseph Romain. *Hockey Hall of Fame: The Official History of the Game and Its Greatest Stars.* New York: Doubleday, 1988.

Fischler, Stan. *The All-New Hockey's 100: A Personal Ranking of the Best Players in Hockey History.* Toronto: McGraw-Hill Ryerson Limited, 1988.

Fischler, Stan. *Golden Ice.* New York: Wynwood Books, 1990.

Fischler, Stan, and Shirley Fischler. *Fischlers' Hockey Encyclopedia.* New York: Thomas Y. Crowell Company.

Fischler, Stan and Shirley Walton Fischler. *The Hockey Encyclopedia: The Complete Record of Professional Ice Hockey.* New York: MacMillan Publishing Company, 1983.

Hickok, Ralph. *The Encyclopedia of North American Sports History.* New York: Facts on File, 1992.

Hickok, Ralph. *A Who's Who of Sports Champions: Their Stories and Records.* Boston: Houghton Mifflin Company.

Hunter, Douglas. *A Breed Apart: An Illustrated History of Goaltending.* New York: Penguin Books, 1995.

Kariher, Harry C. *Who's Who in Hockey.* New Rochelle: Arlington House, 1973.

Vernoff, Edward, and Rima Shore. *The Penguin International Dictionary of Contemporary Biography from 1900 to the Present.* New York: Penguin Reference, 1987.

Periodicals

Allen, Kevin. "Historians can't save Vezina's pads." *USA Today* (August 3, 2000): 2C.

Bailey, Arnold. "Collectors Corner-Companies, fans trade arguments in historic debate." *Providence Journal-Bulletin* (July 9, 2000): 20D.

Frayne, Trent. "New ways to frustrate the guy with the puck." *Maclean's* (January 8, 1996): 49.

"Goalie's pads fall victim to bottom line." *Seattle Times* (August 9, 2000): D2.

Goldberg Goff, Karen. "Unfinished business: Epidemic ended '19 Stanley finals." *Washington Times* (May 10, 1999): 1.

Other

Canadian Press Newswire, August 3, 2000.

"Georges 'Chicoutimi Cucumber' Vezina." http://ucsu. colorado.edu/~norrisdt/bio/vezina.html (September 26, 2002).

"Georges Vezina." http://www.southcoastal.com/history/ vezina.htm (September 26, 2002).

"Georges Vezina: 'Chicoutimi Cucumber.'" Joy of Hockey. http://www.joyofhockey.com/xRet1 GeorgesVezina.html (September 26, 2002).

"Legends of Hockey-NHL Trophies-Vezina Trophy." Legends of Hockey. http://www.legendsofhockey. net/html/silver_splashvezina.htm (September 26, 2002).

"Moments to Remember." CBS SportsLine. http://cbs. sportsline.com/u/ce/feature/0,1518,17772028_ 60,000.html (September 26, 2002).

Sketch by A. Petruso

Dick Vitale
1939-

American sportscaster

ESPN's "mouth that roars," Dick Vitale, is more than a college basketball announcer. He is a cult figure, showman, power broker, author, columnist,

Dick Vitale

cameo actor, motivational speaker and frequent lightning rod for controversy. Players, coaches, fans and media respect his wisdom and influence; some mimic his "V-Speak," his self-styled vocabulary; others cringe at his shtick. Vitale and ESPN have ridden each other's coattails since the all-sports cable network's launch in 1979.

Some critics say Vitale's appearance on ESPN's telecasts of high school games involving prized recruit LeBron James of Akron, Ohio, reflects a maddening overhype of scholastic sports. Others say Vitale spares coaches, some of whom are his closest friends, when he addresses the ills of college basketball. And still others say Vitale and the network encourage carnival barking to the detriment of the game.

Coaches At All Levels

Vitale, raised in New Jersey, graduated from Seton Hall University and received a master's degree from William Patterson College. After coaching Garfield High School one year, he took over at his alma mater, East Rutherford High, and won two New Jersey state championships and four sectional championships.

After serving as Rutgers University assistant for two years, Vitale took the head job at the University of Detroit. In four seasons under Vitale, the Titans went 78-30, a .722 winning percentage. They won 21 straight in 1976-77, defeated eventual national champion Mar-

quette and played in the NCAA Tournament. After one year as Detroit athletic director, the National Basketball Association's Detroit Pistons named Vitale head coach. He lasted but one year in the NBA, however; the Pistons went 30-52 and missed the playoffs.

Soars with Cable Network

Vitale joined ESPN for the 1979-80 season, shortly after the Bristol, Connecticut-based network went on air. He worked its first college basketball telecast, DePaul's 90-77 victory over Wisconsin in Chicago. His stock rose as the network's did. ESPN in the early-to-mid 1980s carried the early rounds of the NCAA tournament, thus widening Vitale's exposure. (CBS got exclusive rights to the tournament in the late 1980s.) "The cable network, the home of early-round tournament games since 1980, developed a cult following of sorts and many believe the increased exposure given Cinderella teams helped revolutionize recruiting, making it easier for coaches at lesser-known schools to lure high school prospects," Mike Duchant wrote in *CBS SportsLine*. Vitale now also calls games for ABC, which shares an ownership with ESPN.

In addition to its game telecasts, ESPN introduced SportsCenter, its one-hour nightly sports newscast. SportsCenter freed TV sports news from ESPN Senior Vice President John Walsh once called "the five minute ghetto" on the local 11 p.m. news.

Vitale maintains his "V-Speak" glossary on the Internet. "While his knowledge, preparation and enthusiasm are unparalleled, his 'Vitale-isms' have unwittingly taken on a life of their own," ESPN wrote on its Web site. A Vitale arrival for a telecast is often a happening in itself. Mike Krzyzewski, coach of powerhouse Duke and

---

Awards and Accomplishments

1964-70	Coaches East Rutherford High School (N.J.) to four state sectional championships, two state championships and 35-game win streak over seven years
1976	Honorary alumnus, University of Detroit
1977	Coaches University of Detroit to 21-game win streak, upset of eventual national champion Marquette and berth in NCAA tournament
1977	Man of the Year Award, Detroit Athletic Club
1983	Named one of Five Most Influential Personalities by Basketball Times
1989	American Sportscasters Association "Sportscaster of the Year."
1994-95	Wins Cable ACE Awards
1997	Honorary degree, Notre Dame University
1998	Curt Gowdy Media Award, Basketball Hall of Fame
2001	Sarasota Boys and Girls Club inducts Vitale into Hall of Fame, names new fitness center in his honor
2002	Named one of area's most influential citizens by Sarasota Magazine

a good friend of Vitale's, good-naturedly needled the announcer on air for not coming to a game at Cameron Indoor Stadium until January of the 2002-03 season.

Vitale, though, is unabashed in his admiration for Duke's program-and building. "Oh, man. I think everyone out there is trying to emulate what goes on at Cameron Indoor Stadium," he wrote in an e-mail response to a fan at his "Dickie V" Web site. "You certainly have to say that at any school with a big program, you have super, super fans. The (Maryland) Terp fans at Comcast Center … the Cameron Crazies down at Duke … Rock, Chalk, Jayhawk out at Kansas … the fans in Lexington (Kentucky) at Rupp Arena. When programs are winning, it breeds that special environment. The Pittsburgh fans at the new Peterson Events Center are into it because the team is faring so well. There are so many special places in college basketball today."

In another fan response, Vitale railed at trash talking in sports. "The sports scene plays a pivotal role in developing youngsters in a positive way," he said. "I think it has lots of good potential for developing the kinds of attitudes needed in a competitive world. I was recently with several leading executives who were former athletes, and they said sports played an important part in their growth."

LeBron James Controversy

Skeptics, however, say Vitale's act serves to encourage the very showboating he says he disdains. And, his over-the-top style clearly does not appeal to everyone. "Over the last 20 years, Vitale has established himself as a leading expert in college basketball. His knowledge of the game rivals that of Peter Gammons in baseball. He has quick facts and stats at his fingertips, and is as credible an announcer as there can be," said Boston writer Bob George on his web site. "But the guy is an absolute horror to listen to. Annoying? At least. Aggravating? Definitely."

A media firestorm erupted during the winter of 2002-03 when ESPN assigned Vitale to cover high school games. LeBron James, a star at St. Vincent-St. Mary in Akron, was the 2002 *Parade* All-America High School Boys Basketball Player of the Year, and had appeared on the covers of *Sports Illustrated.* and *ESPN The Magazine.* ESPN assigned another marquee announcer, former NBA star **Bill Walton**, to join Vitale. What resulted,

critics said, was a carnival atmosphere when St. Vincent-St. Mary played (and defeated) what Minneapolis writer Steve Aschburner called "a traveling troop of NBA wannabes from a hoops factory in Virginia (Oak Hill Academy)." "Oh, every so often, the two hired shills (Vitale and Walton) would verbally wring their hands about the hype and how this might be too much pressure for the young man. Then Vitale would crank himself up again and rave about the money ("Millions, ba-by!") that one lucky sneaker company will lavish upon him," Aschburner wrote in the *Star Tribune.*

Vitale defended himself after Billy Packer of CBS joined the criticism. "ESPN is not hyping LeBron James," he said. "(He) is just the latest teenage phenom to capture the public's attention."

Vitale, who is signed with ESPN through 2006, has written six books and received countless awards from basketball and civic organizations. He has a merchandise Web site and regularly contributes to ESPN The Magazine, USA Today and other periodicals. He has also played his own character in various television shows. He and his wife, Lorraine, have two daughters, Terri and Sherri, each of whom attended Notre Dame University on tennis scholarships and have earned master's degrees.

Vitale's Impact

Some critics say Vitale represents over-the-top showmanship in broadcasting. "I'm taking up a collection to bribe Dicky V into doing one entire game without raving about some stupid dunk," wrote Bob Ryan, longtime *Boston Globe* basketball columnist. "The man is a sweetheart human being, but he has no idea how much harm he causes by encouraging on-court nonsense."

But Vitale's knowledge of college basketball, and influence within it, are without question. And ratings attest to his recognition factor. "Dick Vitale has been synonymous with college basketball," said Rudy Martzke, media critic for *USA Today*. "He brings an insider's perspective to each broadcast, and his lifelong relationships provide him a wealth of knowledge few can equal."

SELECTED WRITINGS BY VITALE:

(With Curry Kirkpatrick) *Vitale: Just Your Average Bald, One-eyed Basketball Wacko Who Beat the Ziggy and Became a PTP'er.* New York: Simon and Schuster, 1988.

(With Dick Weiss) *Time Out, Baby!* New York: Putnam, 1991.

(With Mike Douchant) *Tourney Time—It's Awesome, Baby* Indianapolis: Masters Press, 1993.

(With Charlie Parker and Jim Angresano) *Dickie V's Top 40 All-Everything Teams.* Indianapolis: Masters Press, 1994.

(With Dick Weiss) *Holding Court: Reflections on the Game I Love.* Indianapolis: Masters Press, 1995.

(With Dick Weiss) *Campus Chaos: Why the Game I Love Is Breaking My Heart.* Indianapolis: TimeOut Publishing, 1999.

FURTHER INFORMATION

Other

Ashburner, Steve. "NBA Insider: Sad Case of LeBron James." Star Tribune, http://www.startribune.com, (December 15, 2002).

"Dick Vitale Bio." ESPN.com, http://www.espn.go.com/dickvitale/vfile/index.html (January 17, 2003).

Douchant, Mike. "A Look at How All the Madness Has Evolved." CBS SportsLine, http://live.sportsline.com/u/page/covers/basketball/mar98/ncaaprev3198.htm, (March 1, 1998).

George, Bob. "Final Four Becomes Final Bore." Bob George's BOSSports, http://www.bossports.net/celtics/cb040200.html, (April 4, 2000).

Lincicome, Bernie. "Media Hype Keeps Driving LeBronmania." Rocky Mountain News, http://www.rockymountainnews.com, (January 15, 2003).

Ryan, Bob. "Running a Few Thoughts Up the Opinion Pole." Boston Globe, http://www.boston.com/dailyglobe2/363/sports, (December 29, 2002).

Shapiro, Leonard. "Highs, Lows of Television Sports in '02." Salt Lake Tribune, http://www.sltrib.com, (January 2, 2003).

Telander, Rick. "A Bunch of Hypocrites." Chicago Sun-Times, http://www.suntimes.com/index/telander.html, (December 15, 2002).

"V Speak: Glossary of Terms and Teams." ESPN.com, http://espn.com/dickvitale/vspeak/index/html, (January 17, 2003).

Wendorff, Hermann. "Devils Dump Hoyas." Fayetteville Observer, http://www.fayettevillenc.com, (January 15, 2003).

Sketch by Paul Burton

Honus Wagner
1874-1955

American baseball player

Considered by many baseball experts the greatest shortstop of all time, Honus Wagner was one of the National Baseball Hall of Fame's five original inductees in 1936. Among his fellow inductees were **Ty Cobb** and **Babe Ruth**. At first glance, Wagner looked somewhat ungainly and awkward. Stocky, barrel-chested, and bow-legged, he nevertheless exhibited great speed, which, in tandem with his heritage, earned him the nickname of "The Flying Dutchman." Wagner compiled a lifetime batting average of .326 and managed to top .300 for an incredible fifteen consecutive seasons. John McGraw, the legendary manager of the New York Giants for more than thirty seasons, said of Wagner: "While Wagner was the greatest shortstop, I believe he could have been the number one player at any position he might have selected. That's why I vote him baseball's foremost all-time player."

Born in Western Pennsylvania

Wagner was born in Mansfield, Pennsylvania, on February 24, 1874, one of nine children born to Peter and Katheryn (Wolf) Wagner, who had immigrated to western Pennsylvania from Germany's Bavaria in 1866. Big, clumsy, and bowlegged from birth, Wagner was called Honus (a German term often applied to awkward children) by his family. He also acquired the nickname "Dutch," a corruption of "Deutsch," the German word for German, and fairly common in this heavily German-settled region of Pennsylvania. Wagner was raised in Chartiers, Pennsylvania, not far from Mansfield. The two towns, close to Pittsburgh, were eventually merged and renamed Carnegie. His father worked in the mines, where twelve-year-old Honus joined him in 1886.

Young Wagner labored in the mines during the day, but most evenings and Sunday afternoons found him playing sandlot baseball with his brothers and neighbors. By the time he entered the mines, Wagner had already acquired star status on his neighborhood team, the Oregons. His older brother, Albert, was thought by many in the area to be the better ballplayer, but Al never

Honus Wagner

really took the game seriously. He did, however, recognize Honus's potential and encouraged his younger brother to learn every playing position. In time, the brothers graduated from sandlot play to positions on area church and company teams, often earning up to five dollars a week in pay and tips.

Honus and brother Al began playing semiprofessional baseball in 1894 for Mansfield, a member of the Allegheny League. The following year the Wagner brothers jumped to the Carnegie Athletic Club and in 1895 joined the Steubenville, Ohio, team, part of the newly formed Inter-State League. In his first game for Steubenville, Honus hit a home run. Not long thereafter, Honus Wagner was signed by manager Ed Barrow to play for Paterson (New Jersey) in the Atlantic League. Older brother Al meanwhile went north of the border to play for a team in Toronto. So impressive was the younger Wagner's per-

Chronology

1874	Born in Mansfield, Pennsylvania, on February 24
1886	Begins work in the coal mines at the age of 12
1894	Plays with older brother Al for Mansfield in the semipro Allegheny League
1895	Breaks into professional baseball, playing for Steubenville (OH) in Inter-State League
1896	Signs to play first base for Paterson (NJ) in the Atlantic League
1897	Makes major league debut playing center field for Louisville on July 19
1900	Joins Pittsburgh Pirates after Louisville folds
1901	Begins playing shortstop, position for which he would become famous
1909	Leads Pirates to victory over the Detroit Tigers and Ty Cobb in the World Series
1916	Marries Bessie Baine Smith
1928	Loses electoral race for Allegheny County Sheriff
1933	Becomes a coach for the Pittsburgh Pirates
1942	Appointed deputy country sheriff
1955	Dies in Carnegie, Pennsylvania, on December 6

Awards and Accomplishments

1896	Batted .348 for Paterson (NJ) in Atlantic League
1897	Compiled batting average of .338 during his first season in the major leagues
1898	First of eight National League batting championships with .381 average
1901	Led National League in doubles and runs batted in
1903	Led Pirates to National League championship with .355 batting average
1904-11	Acclaimed best player in the National League
1907	Batting average of .350 tops league average by 107 points
1909	Pirates win World Series over the Detroit Tigers
1917	Retired from Pirates with all-time records for games, at-bats, hits, runs, stolen bases, and total bases
1936	Inducted into the National Baseball Hall of Fame

formance for Paterson that he soon became the object of a bidding war between a number of major league baseball clubs. Louisville eventually took the prize, paying Paterson $2,100 for the rights to sign Wagner.

Breaks Into Major Leagues

On July 19, 1897, Wagner made his major league debut for the Louisville Nationals, playing center field, and occasionally filling in at second base. In the sixty-one games he played for Louisville in 1897, Wagner compiled a batting average of .338. His batting average slipped a bit in 1898, falling to .299, but Wagner proved his versatility, playing first, second, and third base. His batting average bounced back in 1899, when he hit .336. However, at the end of the season the Louisville team disbanded, and Wagner, along with his close friend Fred Clarke, signed with the Pittsburgh Pirates. Clarke played left field for the Pirates and also managed. In 1900, Wagner won the first of eight batting championships with an impressive batting average of .381. Happy to be playing near his hometown, Wagner resisted tempting offers from American League teams to lure him away from Pittsburgh.

Wagner in 1901 began playing shortstop, the position for which he became best known. He also led the National League in doubles and runs batted in with an average of .353 and won the first of five stolen-base titles. His ungainly appearance was deceptive, for as awkward as he looked, Wagner could turn on the speed when it was needed. He established a career record of 722 stolen bases, a record that stood until it was eventually broken by Ty Cobb. The Pittsburgh Pirates, thanks in large part to Wagner's superlative batting, was the strongest club in the early days of the National League, finishing first in 1901, 1902, 1903, and 1909. In the very first World Series, a best-of-nine series in 1903, Pittsburgh faced off against Boston of the American League. It was not Wagner's finest moment, however, and he batted only .222 during the series. Boston took the series, five games to three.

Despite his less-than-stellar performance in the first World Series, Wagner led the National League as its best player for the next eight seasons, his batting average never dipping below .320. He acquired a reputation as one of the game's best bad-ball hitters, and this in an era when the rules allowed pitchers to hurl spitballs and battered, muddy balls usually stayed in the game for lack of replacements. In the World Series of 1909, the thirty-five-year-old Wagner and the Pirates faced off against the Detroit Tigers and their twenty-two-year-old wunderkind, Ty Cobb. The Pirates took the series, and Wagner outbatted Cobb .333 to .231.

Retires from the Pirates in 1917

Wagner played for the Pirates until 1917, when he was forty-three years old. In the latter years of his baseball career, he struggled against the effects of aging and multiple injuries but still managed to perform impressively. He last compiled a batting average of .300 or better during the 1913 season, although his average never dropped lower than .252 in his remaining years of play. In 1916, Wagner married Bessie Baine Smith, the daughter of another professional baseball player. The couple had two daughters, Betty and Virginia. After his retirement from the Pirates, Wagner continued to play semiprofessional ball in the Pittsburgh area until he was well past fifty. His one run for political office—the sheriff of Allegheny County—in 1928 ended in failure, but in 1942 he was appointed deputy county sheriff. In between, he served briefly as sergeant-at-arms in the Pennsylvania legislature. He also returned to professional baseball in 1933, this time as a coach for the Pirates.

In 1936, Wagner, along with Ty Cobb, Walter Johnson, **Christy Mathewson**, and Babe Ruth, were the first players to be inducted into the newly opened National Baseball Hall of Fame. In 1955 Wagner, by then eighty-one years

Career Statistics

Yr	Team	Avg	GP	AB	R	H	HR	RBI	BB	SO	SB	E
1897	LOU	.338	61	237	37	80	2	39	15	NA	19	16
1898	LOU	.299	151	588	80	176	10	105	31	NA	27	43
1899	LOU	.336	147	571	98	192	7	113	40	NA	37	28
1900	PIT	.381	135	527	107	201	4	100	41	NA	38	13
1901	PIT	.353	140	549	101	194	6	126	53	NA	49	48
1902	PIT	.330	136	534	105	176	3	91	43	NA	42	32
1903	PIT	.355	129	512	97	182	5	101	44	NA	46	52
1904	PIT	.349	132	490	97	171	4	75	59	NA	53	51
1905	PIT	.363	147	548	114	199	6	101	54	NA	57	60
1906	PIT	.339	142	516	103	175	2	71	58	NA	53	52
1907	PIT	.350	142	515	98	180	6	82	46	NA	61	49
1908	PIT	.354	151	568	100	201	10	109	54	NA	53	50
1909	PIT	.339	137	495	92	168	5	100	66	NA	35	49
1910	PIT	.320	150	556	90	178	4	81	59	47	24	52
1911	PIT	.334	130	473	87	158	9	89	67	34	20	47
1912	PIT	.324	145	558	91	181	7	102	59	38	26	32
1913	PIT	.300	114	413	51	124	3	56	26	40	21	24
1914	PIT	.252	150	552	60	139	1	50	51	51	23	43
1915	PIT	.274	156	566	68	155	6	78	39	64	22	38
1916	PIT	.287	123	432	45	124	1	39	34	36	11	35
1917	PIT	.265	74	230	15	61	0	24	24	17	5	10
TOTAL		.326	2792	10430	1736	3415	101	1732	963	327	722	824

LOU: Louisville Nationals; PIT: Pittsburgh Pirates.

old, attended the unveiling of a statue in his honor at the Pirates' Forbes Field. (The statue was later relocated to Three Rivers Stadium.) Later that year, on December 6, he died at his home in Carnegie, Pennsylvania.

One of the most dynamic forces in baseball, Wagner was active in professional ball for nearly forty years, more than thirty-five of which were spent with the Pittsburgh Pirates, first as a player and later as a coach and manager. One of his greatest admirers throughout his baseball career was John J. McGraw, the longtime manager of the New York Giants. According to McGraw, Wagner had a "sixth sense of baseball" when it came to defense, knowing just where to play certain batters on certain pitches. In perhaps his highest tribute to Wagner, McGraw once observed: "Wagner is a whole team in himself."

FURTHER INFORMATION

Books

American Decades CD-ROM. Detroit: Gale Group, 1998.

Dictionary of American Biography, Supplement 5: 1951-1955. American Council of Learned Societies, 1977.

Encyclopedia of World Biography Supplement. Volume 20. Detroit: Gale Group, 2000.

Hageman, William. *Honus: The Life and Times of a Baseball Hero.* Champaign, IL: Sagamore Publishing, 1996.

Hittner, Arthur D. *Honus Wagner: The Life of Baseball's "Flying Dutchman."* Jefferson, NC: McFarland & Co., 1996.

Periodicals

Neff, Craig. "Scorecard: Honus or Bogus." *Sports Illustrated* (June 4, 1990): 15.

"Saga." *Bulletin Index* (September 7, 1939).

Weir, Tom. "Top Shortstops Brought More Than Glove to Work: Honus Wagner Established Standard with Success at Plate, on Basepaths." *USA Today* (August 27, 1999): 6C.

Other

"Clarke, Fred C." HickockSports.com. http://www. hickocksports.com/biograph/clarkefr.shtml (October 15, 2002).

"Fred Clarke." National Baseball Hall of Fame. http:// www.baseballhalloffame.org/hofers_and_honorees/ hofer_bios/Clarke_Fred.htm (October 15, 2002).

"Honus Wagner." Baseball Almanac. http://www. baseball-almanac.com/players/p_wagner0.shtml (October 15, 2002).

"Honus Wagner: Career Batting Statistics." CNN/Sports Illustrated. http://sportsillustrated.cnn.com/baseball/ mlb/stats/alltime/player/batting/12792.html (October 14, 2002).

"Honus Wagner." http://members.aol.com/stealth792/ wagner/wagner.html (October 14, 2002).

"Honus Wagner." National Baseball Hall of Fame. http://www.baseballhalloffame.org/hofers_and_ honorees/hofer_bios/wagner_honus.htm (October 14, 2002).

"Player Pages: Honus Wagner." The Baseball Page. com. http://www.thebaseballpage.com/past/pp/ wagnershonus/default.htm (October 15, 2002).

Sketch by Don Amerman

Grete Waitz
1953-

Norwegian marathon runner

Grete Waitz

Distance runner Grete Waitz has set world records in the 3,000 meter, 8 kilometer, 10 kilometer, 15 kilometer, 10 mile, and the marathon. She was the first woman to run a marathon in under 2 hours and 30 minutes, and the first female world champion in the marathon. She has won the New York City Marathon nine times.

A Norwegian Tradition

Born Grete Andersen in Oslo, Norway in 1953, Waitz grew up with the Norwegian tradition of exercise and outdoor activity. Norwegians customarily hike during the summer and cross-country ski in the winter, as well as engaging in other sports; she told Michael Sandrock in *Running with the Legends* that Norway is "a sports heaven."

Waitz loved to run, and her two older brothers, Jan and Arild, encouraged her and included her in their games with other boys. Waitz's mother thought their games were too rough for her and bought her a piano, but she preferred running to playing it. When she went on errands to the grocery store, she timed herself to see how fast she could get there and back, and on the way she raced cars and buses. When she played cops and robbers with other children, none of them could catch her.

By the time she was 12, she had participated in handball, gymnastics, and track, but she loved running most of all. She joined the Vidar Sports Club in Oslo, at the encouragement of her neighbor, Terje Pedersen, who was a world record holder. At the club, she participated in the high jump, long jump, and shot put, winning her first prize, a silver spoon, in a ball-throwing contest. Although she did not do well in short races of 60 or 80 meters, she did better at distances of 300 meters or longer, and began training for the 400 and 800 meters. She also began making longer runs of 6 miles, keeping up with the boys.

Waitz often got up before dawn to run, a practice she continued throughout her running life. In 1969, when she was 16, she won the Norwegian junior champi-

onships in the 400 and 800 meters. In 1971, she won the Norwegian open 800 and 1,500 meters, and set a European junior record of 4:17.0 in the 1,500. Although Waitz also ran at the Helsinki European Championships in 1971, she did not qualify for the 1,500. According to Sandrock, she later said, "I was disappointed, perplexed, angry, and only 17 years old.... My bitterness fed my desire to excel. Just as with my parents, this denial of support strengthened my determination."

In 1972, when Waitz was 18, she experienced a tragedy—her boyfriend and coach became ill and died. Waitz stopped eating and running, but her teammates from the track club helped her through the difficult time and encouraged her to use her running and training to help heal her grief.

Competes in 1972 Olympics

In *First Marathons,* Waitz commented, "My two older brothers set a wonderful example for me and since we were always in friendly sibling competition with one another and I tended to follow their training habits, other girls found me tough to bear. That's probably one of the reasons I made the 1972 Olympic team at 18 years old."

Waitz competed in the 1,500 meters in the 1972 Munich Olympics. Although she did not expect to win a medal, she enjoyed the experience and had fun with her friends on the team. She ran a personal best of 4:16 in the 1,500 meters, but the competition was so talented

Cool Controlled Grace

"I knew I was out of my league and hadn't trained properly. Finally, exhausted and hurting, I crossed the finish line. Immediately, I was swarmed by the media, pushing microphones and cameras in my face. I didn't understand what they were saying and tried to run away from them.... I had no idea that I had set a course and world record."

Source: Waitz, Greta, *First Marathons,* edited by Gail Waesche Kislevitz, Breakaway Books, 1999.

that she did not make it into the final competition. However, she realized that she could eventually become a great runner if she continued to train.

In that same year, Waitz began studying at a teacher's college in Oslo, fitting her training into the early hours before school. In 1974, she won a bronze medal in the 1,500 meters at the European Championships, and was named Norwegian Athlete of the Year.

As Waitz matured, she began running longer distances, and in 1975, set a world record in the 3,000 meters. It was only the second time she had raced that distance. In that same year, she was ranked No. 1 in the world in the 1,500 meters and 3,000 meters.

Competes in 1976 Olympics

In 1976, Waitz returned to the Olympics, but this time she knew what to expect and trained more seriously. In fact, she had not missed a day of training for more than two years, and she was expected to win a medal. However, there was no women's 3,000-meter race, and she had to enter the 1,500 meters, the farthest distance women were allowed to run in the Olympics at the time. Although she made it to the semifinals, she placed eighth—not good enough to make it to the finals, even though she had set a personal best and Scandinavian record in the 1,500.

Waitz was attacked in the Norwegian press, and she became angry: she had trained twice a day for two years, despite having a full-time job as a teacher and spending two hours each day commuting to her work. According to Sandrock, she said, "I became a victim of the Norwegian expression, 'A silver medal is a defeat'— if you don't win, you lose." In 1977, Waitz decided in the future to run without the support of the Norwegian Federation scholarship.

Waitz won world cross-country titles in 1978, 1979, 1981, and 1983. During this time, she worked as a schoolteacher, training during her time off. In the winter, she switched to cross-country skiing, which kept her in shape while giving her legs a break from running. At one point, according to Sandrock, she was running during the winter but could find only a quarter-mile of plowed road to run on. Resolutely, she ran back and forth on it for eight miles.

Wins New York City Marathon

In 1978, Waitz was considering retiring, but her husband convinced her to try running a marathon. Waitz was reluctant at first, but eventually called the New York City Road Runners Club to get an invitation to run the event. She was turned down. Although she was a champion, she had never run the 26.2-mile distance. Waitz was disappointed, mainly because she and her husband, Jack Waitz, were hoping to have a vacation in New York but could not afford to go unless they were sponsored by the club.

However, soon after this, Fred Lebow, president of the club, called with an offer. He suggested that she run as a "rabbit," setting a fast pace for the elite women, She would not be expected to run fast for the entire distance, but only for a portion of the course.

Up to that point, the farthest Waitz had ever run was 12 miles, less than half the marathon distance. She had no idea what to expect, so when the race began, she went out fast. By the 19th mile, she began to tire, and she had lost track of how much farther she had to run because she was used to reading distances in kilometers, not miles. Nevertheless, she continued to run. Like everyone who runs the New York City marathon, she looked desperately for any sign that she was close to Central Park, where the finish line was. Each patch of trees in the distance gave her hope, then despair when it turned out not to be the park.

Finally, she reached the finish line. She had registered so late that her bib number was not listed in the official guide to the runners, and no one knew who she was. When Fred Lebow asked who had won, all anyone could tell him was "Some blond girl," according to Peter Gambaccini in *Runner's World.* Mobbed by reporters, she had no idea that she had won. In addition, she had set a new women's world record for the distance with a time of 2:32.30, two minutes faster than the old record.

Back home in Norway, Waitz returned to her teaching job, but her students had trouble comprehending how far she had run because they were not used to distances expressed in miles. When she told them it was 42 kilometers, they still did not understand. Finally, accord-

Grete Waitz

Awards and Accomplishments

1975	World record, 3000 meters, 8:46.6
1976	World record, 3000 meters, 8:45.4
1978	Winner, New York City Marathon
1978	World record, marathon, 2:32.30
1978	World cross-country champion
1979	World record, 10 miles, 53:05
1979	Winner, New York City Marathon
1979	World record, marathon, 2:27.33
1980	World record, 10K, 31:00
1980	Winner, New York City Marathon
1980	World record, marathon, 2:25.41
1981	World cross-country champion
1982	Winner, New York City Marathon
1983	Winner, New York City Marathon
1983	World record, marathon, 2:25.29
1983	Winner, world marathon championships
1983	World cross-country champion
1984	Winner, New York City Marathon
1984	World record, 15K, 47:53
1984	Silver medal, marathon, Los Angeles Olympics
1985	Winner, New York City Marathon
1986	Winner, New York City Marathon
1986	World record, 8K, 25:03
1988	Winner, New York City Marathon
2000	Inducted into Distance Running Hall of Fame

Wins Silver in Los Angeles Olympics

In 1984, Waitz went to the Los Angeles Olympics. That year was the first that women were allowed to compete in the marathon. Previously many observers believed the event was too grueling for women to complete, but in the preceding 15 years women, including Waitz, had proved this prejudice wrong by performing strongly in non-Olympic marathons. Waitz was expected to win, but came in second to **Joan Benoit Samuelson**, winning a silver medal. Waitz did not make excuses for coming in second, but praised Benoit for her excellent race. She was relieved to have finally won an Olympic medal: now the pressure for her to win one for Norway was gone.

Waitz ran in the 1988 Olympic Marathon in Seoul, Korea but did not finish the race, hampered by knee surgery she had undergone before the race. Later that year, however, she made a comeback, winning the New York City Marathon for the ninth time. "Everything feels good," she said before the race, according to Marc Bloom in *Runner's World*. American runner Joan Benoit Samuelson, who came in third, told Bloom, "Losing to Grete is an honor. She owns New York." In 1990, Waitz retired from competition to devote her time to serving as a spokesperson for women's sports.

Since retiring from competition, Waitz has used her ability to help others who have difficulty in running. In 1992, Waitz ran the New York City Marathon with Fred Lebow, who was suffering from brain cancer. Because of his illness, he could only run very slowly, and the two took 5 hours, 32 minutes and 34 seconds to complete the

ing to Sandrock, she told them it was the distance between Oslo and a town that was 26 miles away. They were shocked.

In 1979, now a running star, Waitz quit teaching in order to run full-time. She knew that, if she could set a world record in the marathon despite being totally unprepared for the distance, she could do even better if she trained for it. She went on to win the New York City marathon eight more times; she won 13 of 19 marathons that she entered between 1978 and 1988. In 1979, 1980, and 1983 she set new world records in the event. She won the World Marathon Championships in 1983, beating the second-place runner by three minutes. In that same year, Waitz founded the 5-km Grete Waitz Run in Oslo, Norway; 3,000 runners participated.

Where Is She Now?

Waitz and her husband divide their time between their homes in Oslo, Norway, and Gainesville, Florida. Waitz still runs the New York City marathon every year, but does it for the enjoyment, not as a competitor. She often signs autographs and talks to runners at an expo held before the race. Although she enjoys encouraging other runners to stay fit and do their best, she has said, according to Sandrock, "I have no more interest in competing." She is a spokesperson for Avon Running-Global Women's Circuit and for Adidas.

---

course; when they finished, Waitz cried, knowing that Lebow's condition was terminal and it was the last time she would run with him. In 1993, Waitz waited at the finish line for runner Zoe Koplowitz, who had multiple sclerosis, to finish the course. Koplowitz took 24 hours to complete the marathon distance. Waitz wrote in *First Marathons,* "No one had a medal for her, so I rushed back to my hotel to get my husband's medal for her." In 1991, Waitz was named Female Runner of the Quarter Century by *Runner's World* magazine.

In *First Marathons,* Waitz wrote, "I prefer to train in the dark, cold winter months when it takes a stern attitude to get out of bed before dawn and head out the door to below-freezing weather conditions. Anyone can run on a nice, warm, brisk day."

Legacy of a Trailblazer

Michael Sandrock wrote in *Running With the Legends,* "Waitz has no rival in terms of depth and breadth of career. Her place as the pioneer of women's marathoning is secure, and it is not farfetched to say that women's marathoning entered the modern era when Waitz entered New York in 1978." Sandrock pointed out that when Waitz began running, there are no women's 3,000-meter, 10,000-meter, or marathon races in the Olympics, no women-only races, no prize money for women, and very little regard from the running press for women runners. For example, when Waitz entered an Oslo 3,000-meter event, one journalist wrote "Oh, save us from these women running seven laps around the track," according to Sandrock.

By the time she ran her tenth New York City Marathon in 1990, the status of women's running was nearly equal to that of men's. Waitz, like other champions of her time, was a trailblazer throughout this change.

CONTACT INFORMATION

Address: 3448 NW 104th Way, Gainesville, FL 32606.

FURTHER INFORMATION

Books

"Grete Waitz," *Great Women in Sports,* Visible Ink Press, 1996.

"Grete Waitz: Queen of the Marathon," in *Running with the Legends,* edited by Michael Sandrock, Human Kinetics, 1996.

Waitz, Greta, "Cool Controlled Grace," in *First Marathons,* edited by Gail Waesche Kislevitz, Breakaway Books, 1999.

Periodicals

Bloom, Marc, "Grete Waitz," *Runner's World,* (December, 1991): 52.

Bloom, Marc, "Revival of the Fittest," *Runner's World,* (January, 1989): 30.

Gambaccini, Peter, "The Queen," *Runner's World,* (November, 1994): 64.

Other

"Grete Waitz," Distance Running Hall of Fame, http://www.distancerunning.com/ (January 27, 2003).

Sketch by Kelly Winters

Jersey Joe Walcott
1914-1994

American boxer

One of the most persistent boxers of the 20th century, Jersey Joe Walcott refused to give up his dream of winning the world heavyweight title. Long after most boxers would have abandoned all hope, Walcott battled on. On July 18, 1951, he became, at the age of thirty-seven, the oldest boxer ever to become the heavyweight champ, knocking out Ezzard Charles in the seventh round to finally take the title he had so long pursued. For more than four decades, he held the distinction of being the oldest boxer to win the heavyweight title, until 45-year-old **George Foreman** won the crown in 1994. After retiring from the ring, Walcott remained active in boxing as a referee and later became chairman of the New Jersey State Boxing Commission. Sadly, his tenure in the latter position was marred by charges that he had taken bribes. Despite this stain on his reputation, Walcott will forever stand as an inspiration to dreamers everywhere that perseverance can pay off.

Born in Merchantville, New Jersey

He was born Raymond Arnold Cream in Merchantville, New Jersey, on January 31, 1914. When he was only thirteen years old, his father, an immigrant from Barbados, died. Young Walcott quit school and began looking for any kind of work he could find to help

Jersey Joe Walcott

support his family. Not long thereafter, he stopped in one day at Battling Mac's Gym in Camden, New Jersey, where he soon became a regular, sparring with some of the fighters who called the gym home. He was just a skinny kid and nothing particularly remarkable as a boxer in those early years, but he stayed with it and began fighting on the club circuit of southern New Jersey and nearby Philadelphia.

Walcott made his professional boxing debut in 1930 at the age of sixteen, knocking out Cowboy Wallace in the first round of a match in Vineland, New Jersey. He won his next five matches before losing, on November 16, 1933, in a rematch with Henry Taylor in Philadelphia. Early in his professional career, the young New Jersey boxer decided his last name of Cream seemed wholly inappropriate for a fighter who hoped some day to be a champion. He decided to borrow the name of his father's favorite boxer from the islands, Joe Walcott, a former welterweight champion who was also known as the "Barbados Demon." To personalize his new name, he added "Jersey," to signify the state of his birth.

Blackburn Takes Over as Trainer

Over the next several years, Walcott fought in dozens of matches, winning most of them but losing occasionally. However, boxing failed to provide a dependable source of income. After he married and started a family, Walcott was forced more and more to take jobs outside

the ring to make ends meet. His ring career took a positive turn after the unschooled Walcott began to work with trainer Jack Blackburn, who helped to teach him more about the art of boxing. His association with Blackburn ended abruptly when the trainer received an offer from a couple of gamblers to come to Chicago to train an amateur champion named **Joe Louis**. As a condition for accepting the job, Blackburn wangled an invitation for Walcott to accompany him and join the gamblers' Chicago stable of fighters, but Walcott came down with typhoid and was unable to make the trip.

Without Blackburn's guidance, Walcott's boxing career once again seemed to lose direction. He continued to box when he could but was forced increasingly to work at low-paying jobs outside the ring to support his family. Walcott began to lose hope. Then came a call from Blackburn, telling him that Joe Louis, training for a fight with **Max Schmeling**, was looking for sparring partners. Walcott eagerly headed for the Louis training camp, but on his very first day on the job, he dropped Louis with a left hook, abruptly ending his stint as sparring partner.

Loses to Four Top-Ranked Fighters

The situation grew even gloomier for Walcott in the latter half of the 1930s. Four times during that period, he squared off against one of the ten top-ranked fighters—Al Ettore in 1936, Tiger Jack Fox in 1937 and 1938, and Abe Simon in 1940—in his weight class, only to lose every match. By the early 1940s, Walcott was working in the Camden shipyards, and his boxing career seemed all but over. He fought only five matches from 1940 through 1944, one of which was his loss to Simon. Salvation came in the form of Felix Bocchicchio, a Camden area sports club owner and gambler. Bocchicchio offered to manage Walcott, who at first refused, saying, "Fighting never got me nothin' before, and all I want now is a steady job, so my wife and kids can eat regular. I'm over 30 and just plain tired of it all."

Fortunately for Walcott, Bocchicchio was not so easily dissuaded. He bought food and coal for Walcott's family, got the boxer's license renewed, and finally persuaded Walcott to give it a try. Jersey Joe returned to boxing with a vengeance, winning eight of

Related Biography: Boxer Ezzard Charles

Ezzard Charles won the National Boxing Association heavyweight crown in a fifteen-round decision over Jersey Joe Walcott on June 22, 1949. But two years later, on July 18, 1951, Walcott turned the tables on Charles, knocking him out to take the heavyweight title for himself. The following year, Charles failed in an attempt to recapture the title from Walcott, who lost it barely three months later to Rocky Marciano.

He was born Ezzard Mack Charles on July 7, 1921, in Lawrenceville, Georgia. After a brilliant amateur boxing career, Charles turned pro in 1940 and went on to win twenty consecutive fights in the first eighteen months of the decade. He temporarily left boxing in 1943 to enlist in the U.S. Army. Charles eventually moved up in weight class and became the heavyweight champion from 1949 until 1951. His attempts to recapture the title, first from Walcott and later from Marciano, all ended in failure.

Charles retired from boxing in the late 1950s. In 1966 he was stricken with Lou Gehrig's disease that before long confined him to a wheelchair. Charles died on May 28, 1975.

his nine bouts in 1945, three of them against top ten fighters Joe Baski, Lee Murray, and Curtis Sheppard. The following year he beat top ten contender Jimmy Bivins, following which Bocchicchio lined up a fight for Walcott with another leading contender, Lee Oma, in Madison Square Garden. Walcott took the match in a ten-round decision. Later that year he experienced something of a setback, losing to Joey Maxim and Elmer Ray in back-to-back bouts. But Walcott bounced back in 1947, beating Maxim in January, Ray in April, and Maxim again in June.

Walcott Almost Upsets Joe Louis

Prominent boxing promoter Mike ("Uncle Mike") Jacobs in late 1947 set up what was supposed to be a ten-round charity exhibition match between World Heavyweight Champion Joe Louis and Walcott. It turned into a title match after the New York State Athletic Commission ruled that any match of more than six rounds with Louis had to be for the title. Odds makers gave Walcott little chance against the Brown Bomber.

Before a sold-out crowd of 18,000, Walcott suckered Louis with a right-hand lead and then dropped him with a left hook in the very first round. Spectators were incredulous, applauding wildly for the plucky Walcott. Walcott wasn't through. In the fourth round, Louis, confused by the "Walcott Shuffle," which involved shifting the feet around so that first the left and then the right were the lead, and pivoting the body to match, was dropped again by the challenger.

Perhaps sensing that he was comfortably ahead on points, Walcott took it easy on Louis in the final rounds of the fight. Nevertheless, boxing fans, as well as Louis, were all convinced Walcott had cinched the fight. Referee Ruby Goldstein agreed, observing, "Walcott punched his ears off." But the two judges—Frank Forbes and Marty Monroe—gave the fight to Louis.

Years later, Walcott recalled: "After the fight, Joe put his arm around me and whispered in my ear, 'I'm sorry.' I looked across the ring, and I could tell that Louis thought he had lost the fight. In fact, he wanted to leave the ring, but his handlers held him back."

The following year, on June 25, Louis and Walcott met once again, although this time Louis was clearly the dominant force, knocking out Walcott in the 11th round. Shortly after winning his rematch with Walcott, Louis announced his retirement from the ring. The retirement of Joe Louis after just over eleven years as heavyweight champ set the stage for a match between Walcott and Ezzard Charles for the now-vacant World Boxing Association heavyweight title. The two faced off on June 22, 1949. Walcott lost a 15-round decision to Charles and promptly announced his retirement. Manager Bocchicchio had other ideas for Walcott, who was now 35. The two took a short vacation together, after which they issued a press release announcing that Walcott had changed his mind and would continue his boxing career. Walcott won a match in Sweden against Ollie Tandberg and once again hinted at retirement. Again, Bocchicchio persuaded him to continue boxing.

Wins First Four Matches of 1950

In 1950 Walcott won his first four matches of the year, only to lose to Rex Layne on November 24. He also lost his first rematch with Charles on March 7, 1951. But on July 18, 1951, Walcott made boxing history when he knocked out Charles in the seventh round to become the oldest boxer ever to win the world heavyweight title. In 1952, Walcott fought a series of exhibition bouts with Jackie Burke before squaring off against Charles once again on June 5. Walcott successfully defended his title, winning a fifteen-round decision over Charles. Just over three months later, however, **Rocky Marciano** knocked out Walcott in the 13th round to take the heavyweight title. In a rematch with Marciano on May 15, 1953, Walcott was knocked out in the first round. Just after his second defeat by Marciano, Walcott announced his retirement from boxing.

Walcott continued to live in the Camden area after leaving boxing. Shortly after retiring from the ring, he took a job as a parole officer for juvenile offenders. He later had a brief stint as a boxing referee, officiating at the second match between Cassius Clay (before changing his name to **Muhammad Ali**) and **Sonny Liston**. He was widely criticized for his handling of the match. In the early 1980s, Walcott was appointed chairman of the New Jersey State Athletic Commission. During the course of his time on the commission, charges surfaced that Walcott had accepted bribes from undercover agents.

Walcott died at the age of 80 on February 25, 1994, in Camden, N.J. In one of his last public appearances, Walcott traveled across the Delaware River to Philadelphia in 1992 to attend the first outdoor professional boxing show since the 1950s. Speaking haltingly to the assembled crowd, Walcott said, "I tried to be a champion for everybody. I did my best. I tried to make a way for our young people." The deafening applause was proof that in the minds of the spectators anyway Walcott had succeeded.

FURTHER INFORMATION

Books

"Ezzard Mark Charles." *Dictionary of American Biography: Supplement 9: 1971-1975*. New York: Scribner, 1994.

"Joe Walcott." *Almanac of Famous People,* 6th edition. Detroit: Gale Group, 1998.

Periodicals

Davis, Samuel. "Jersey Joe Walcott Is Remembered." *Philadelphia Tribune* (March 4, 1994).

Jefferies, Eddie. "Ex-Heavyweight Champ's Calling Card Was Perseverance: Walcott Dead at 80." *New Pittsburgh Gazette* (March 2, 1994).

Matthews, Wallace. "No Champion Out of Ring." *Newsday* (February 27, 1994): 18.

Mee, Bob. "Obituary: Jersey Joe Walcott." *Independent* (February 28, 1994).

Other

"Enshrinees: Jersey Joe Walcott." International Boxing Hall of Fame. http://www.ibhof.com/walcott.htm (October 25, 2002).

"Jersey Joe Walcott." New Jersey Boxing Hall of Fame. http://www.njboxinghof.org/cgi-bin/henryseehof.pl? 286 (October 25, 2002).

"Jersey Joe Walcott: 1914-1994." Kelta's Kavern. http://www.cyberenet.net/~kelta/jerseyjoe.html (October 25, 2002).

"Jersey Joe Walcott: The Improbable Champion." The History of the Sweet Science. http://www.game masteronline.com/Archive/SweetScience/Jersey JoeWalcott.shtml (October 26, 2002).

"Time Tunnel: Jersey Joe Walcott; The Long, Long Journey." East Side Boxing. http://www.eastside boxing.com/news/Jersey-Joe-Walcott.php (October 26, 2002).

Sketch by Don Amerman

Jan Ove Waldner
1965-

Swedish table tennis player

Jan Ove Waldner has been called the "Mozart of table tennis" because of his ability to play many different compositions on the table. If not Mozart, Waldner is certainly the **Michael Jordan** of his sport. His domination and nearly mythical status among the sport's players and fans is unprecedented in the history of the game. Although table tennis doesn't enjoy the respect reserved for the world's more recognized sports, Waldner, in countries that take the sport seriously, is widely recognized as the best player of all time. He is one of two players in the sport's history to win all three major titles—at the World Championships, the Olympics and the World Cup. He is also known for possessing the finest serve technique in the European game.

Born October 3, 1965 in Stockholm, Sweden, Waldner quickly became interested in the sport to which he would ultimately devote his life. At the age of six, he asked his parents if he and his brother could participate in a small local tournament. With the encouragement of his parents, Waldner would go on from there to become the Swedish champion for his age group by the time he was nine years old. He turned professional at the age of fifteen and won his first tournament, and a Porsche, at the age of sixteen.

Pride and Prejudice

While Waldner enjoys a faithful fan base in Sweden, table tennis hasn't been given the respect its players and fans believe it deserves. In China, the sport's other powerhouse, the sport is played by the masses. The Chinese play in clubs and schools and even on cement slabs in the park. In the United States, however, the game is largely recreational and usually called Ping-Pong, a name given to the game when Parker Brothers first manufactured a set of equipment more than fifty years ago. Although in some corners of the world the game is wildly popular and highly competitive, it has never risen above its recreational reputation in much of the Western world.

Jan Ove Waldner

It was in this environment that Waldner began his domination of the sport. Coming up in the liberal Stockholm of the 1970s, he quickly gained a reputation for a punishing serve and outstanding offensive and defensive technique. He began to climb the ranks on both the Swedish and European tour. He won his first Swedish title, one which he would go on to win seven times in his career, in 1983. He has also won the European Top-12 Championship seven times. His reputation was solidified, however, in 1989 when he won his first ever World Singles title and was ranked number one in the world. It was his second appearance in a world singles final but the first time he'd left victorious.

Guerrilla Foreman

Waldner was given the nickname "Guerrilla Foreman" by his Chinese counterparts because of his domination and growing reputation. Going into the 1992 Olympic Games, Waldner had already achieved an astonishing amount at a very young age but was about to compete on a much more visible stage. Every year at the Olympics, fans of table tennis hope that their adopted sport will catch on with a larger audience and ultimately lead to the universal respect they crave. Waldner's appearance at the 1992 games did nothing to change the sport's international standing but it did earn him his first Olympic Gold medal in the men's single competition. It was the only table tennis gold the Chinese didn't win that year.

Following his Olympic performance, Waldner continued playing at a high level, even winning a European Championship in 1996. Despite a disappointing appearance in the 1996 Olympic games, Waldner surprised the experts in 1997 by taking his second World Men's Singles title at the age of thirty-one, eight years after his first. It was his fourth appearance in a world singles final. "I think the first time you win a big tournament is the best feeling," he said, following his win. "But it is eight years since I won and that is a long time. Today I remembered how good it can feel to win."

One Last Time

Waldner returned again to the Olympic stage in 2000. After announcing that it would be his last Olympic appearance, he faced an emotional battle in the semi-finals with the gold medallist from the 1996 Olympics. Waldner, at the age of thirty-four, outlasted the reigning champion, China's Liu Guoliang, but eventually succumbed to top seeded Kong Linghui in the finals. "I lost because Kong played a bit better," Waldner said after the match. Kong, who had studied the game briefly in Sweden, paid respect to his opponent by saying he had watched and idolized Waldner while growing up in China.

Waldner's career has slowed considerably since 2000. He has been hampered by injuries but vows to

Chronology

1967	Born on April 6 in Crane, Texas
mid-1980s	Plays high school football; receives football scholarship from University of Nebraska
late 1980s	Named Big Eight Conference Defensive Player of the Year
1991	Selected by Denver Broncos in eighth round of NFL draft
1993	Released by Broncos
1994	Signs with Calgary Stampeders
1995	Plays last season with Stampeders
late 1990s	Becomes football coach at Iowa School for the Deaf
1999	Publishes autobiography, *Roar of Silence: The Kenny Walker Story*

make another comeback. Regardless of his current status, Waldner has already left a lasting impact on the sport he loves. His mythological reputation will continue to influence and inspire newcomers to the game while he continues to serve as an ambassador for a sport that desperately needs the support of its stars.

FURTHER INFORMATION

Periodicals

Berlin, Peter. "Kong Holds Off Swedish Rival As Chinese Sweep Gold Medals." *International Herald Tribune* (September 26, 2000): 26.

Corwin, Michael. "A 'Racquet' Heard 'Round The World." *Parks & Recreation* (September 2000):31.

Ford, Bob. "Table Tennis Players Want Their Sport To Come Out Of The Basement." *Philadelphia Inquirer* (July 17, 1996).

Syed, Matthew. "Chinese Domination Complete With Defeat of Old Maestro." *Times* (August 9, 1999): 31.

"Table Tennis: Waldner Regains the World Crown." *Independent* (May 7, 1997): 23.

"Table Tennis: Waldner Shines Amid The Chaos." *Independent* (May 7, 1997): 28.

Other

"The Lightening of Jan-Ove Waldner." Fenerbahce. http://www.geocities.com/fb_table_tennis/english/roportaj3.htm (January 14, 2003).

"Waldner Reaches Final in Last Olympics." *Sports Illustrated* http://sportsillustrated.cnn.com/olympics/newswire/2000/09/24/268268093547_afp/ (January 24, 2003).

Sketch by Aric Karpinski

Kenny Walker
1967-

American football player

When football player Kenny Walker made his professional debut in the early 1990s, he became the first deaf player in the National Football League (NFL) in nearly twenty years. A defensive lineman with the Denver Broncos in 1991 and 1992, Walker became a hero among the hearing-impaired with his against-the-odds success story. The 6-foot-4-inch, 260-pound player picked up his defensive calls by reading other players' lips, and distinguished himself on the playing field with a strong performance. After two years with the Broncos, Walker joined the Calgary Stampeders, becoming the first deaf player in the history of the Canadian Football League (CFL).

Born on April 6, 1967, in Crane, Texas, Kenny Walker was the youngest of six children born to a cafeteria-worker mother and an oil-field worker father. He was two years old when he contracted spinal meningitis, which left him deprived of his ability to hear. While his family helped him with his disability, his two older brothers, Darren and Gus, made sure their little brother did not fall prey to self-pity. "If I was pouting, or wanting sympathy, they'd deck me," Walker told Tom Keyser of the *Calgary Herald*.

After young Walker's parents separated, his mother relocated with her children to Denver, Colorado. Here Walker attended a deaf program at the University of Denver. A natural athlete, he played street sports with friends, and made the football team as a starter in the tenth grade. As a defensive end and split end, he was a fast, capable player who excelled on the field. Upon graduation from high school he was offered a football scholarship from the University of Nebraska.

Named Defensive Player of the Year

Playing a defensive end for Nebraska's Cornhuskers, Walker gained a reputation as one of the fastest linesman in the state. "He's pretty much unstoppable," teammate Brian Boerboom told Ken Hambleton of the *Sporting News*. "He's so quick and so strong, it's hard to get in his way. You can be doing a good job on him and not look very good when the play is over." The press marveled at the way Walker's deafness did not hold him

---

Awards and Accomplishments

late 1980s	All-American team
1990	Big Eight Conference defensive player of the year
1991	NFL's first deaf player in nearly 20 years
1994	CFL's first deaf player in history

Career Statistics

Yr	Team	GP	Sack	Int	TD
1991	DEN	16	3.0	0	0
1992	DEN	15	1.5	0	0
TOTAL		31	4.5	0	0

DEN: Denver Broncos.

---

back as a player. However, there were limitations to what positions he could play. Although his speed and relatively small size made suited him to play inside linebacker, his inability to pick up changes in defense made the position inappropriate for him. Instead he played defensive tackle—a position usually reserved for the biggest, heaviest players on the team.

Nicknamed "Mumbles" for his reticence during meetings, Walker gained confidence as he adjusted to the world of college football. As a player, he stole the hearts of Cornhuskers fans. When he ran onto the field for his final game at Nebraska, a crowd of some 76,000 raised their hands and wiggled their fingers in the international sign for applause. He responded with "I love you" in sign language. An All-American player, Walker was named Big Eight Conference defensive player of the year in 1990.

As the first deaf student to attend the university, Walker was initially shy about speaking and using sign language in public. But as he adjusted to campus life he became more comfortable in public and more involved in campus activities. Walker, who draws children's cartoons in his spare time, majored in art and held a 3.1 grade point average. When he was not studying or playing football, he indulged in one of his favorite pastimes, catfishing, and often volunteered working with deaf children in the Lincoln, Nebraska, area.

Joined Denver Broncos

Selected by the Denver Broncos in the eighth round of the 1991 NFL draft, Walker became professional American football's first deaf player since Bonnie Sloan, who had played for the St. Louis Cardinals for one season in 1973. While many teams had overlooked Walker because of his handicap, Broncos' coach Dan Reeves was willing to take a chance on Nebraska's star player. As a defensive linebacker for the Broncos, Walker distinguished himself with his superior vision, strength, and speed. For assistance at meetings, practice, and chalkboard talks, Walker hired an interpreter. He read quarterback Karl Mecklenberg's lips in the huddle, and received defensive calls via signals from fellow linebackers.

Within a few months Coach Reeves was touting Walker as one of the best late-round draft choices the team had made in years. Said Reeves to Tom Farley of the *Seattle Times*: "Whether it's in the near future or next year, I don't think there is any question [Walker]

will end up being a starting defensive end for us." However, Reeves did not follow through on this promise. After playing with the Broncos for two seasons, Walker—who had been named the NFL's Most Inspirational player—was cut from the team in August 1993.

Although the Broncos had suggested that Walker's deafness was a liability, the Canadian Football League was willing to give the talented player a chance. He joined the Calgary Stampeders as a starting linebacker in July 1994, becoming the CFL's first deaf player in history. As a starting linebacker, Walker proved his mettle and once earned the distinction of "defensive player of the week." "[Walker] really wanted to play football, and mentally he had a sense of relief because [Calgary] didn't want him to carry a lot of weight like the Denver Broncos did," Walker's wife, Marti, told Brian Lahm of the *Omaha World Herald*. Although he enjoyed playing for the Stampeders, Walker told the press that he would take advantage of any future opportunities to come back to the NFL and play in his home country. Such an opportunity did not present itself, however. Walker played with the Stampeders for two seasons, leaving in 1995.

The same year, the Associated Press reported that Walker had sued the Denver Broncos for misrepresenting his disability to other NFL teams. The suit also claimed that the Broncos had violated the Americans with Disabilities Act. "Despite proving beyond question that a deaf person could play professional football in the NFL," stated the lawsuit, "the Broncos falsely represented to other NFL teams that Walker's handicap ... created an undue hardship." The Broncos' general manager, John Beake, told the Associated Press that the team was prepared to counter the case in court. The press did not follow up on the outcome of the case, however.

Retired from football, Walker pursued another dream: teaching and coaching deaf children. Returning to the United States to be with his family, he took a job coaching football at the Iowa School for the Deaf in Council Bluffs, Iowa. In 1999 he published his autobiography, *Roar of Silence: The Kenny Walker Story*, cowritten with Bob Schaller. Valued for his contribution to football history, Walker remains a hero and role model among the hearing-impaired and at large.

FURTHER INFORMATION

Books

Moore, Matthew S., and Robert F. Panara. *Great Deaf Americans,* 2nd edition. Rochester, NY: MSM Productions, 1996.

Periodicals

Associated Press (June 6, 1995).

Farrey, Tom. "Deafness No Barrier for Denver Lineman." *Seattle Times* (September 13, 1991): B1.

Hambleton, Ken. "Walker's Hits Do the Talking." *Sporting News* (May 14, 1990): 41.

Keyser, Tom. "Proud Gridiron Warrior." *Calgary Herald* (September 30, 1994): C4.

Lahm, Brian. "Kenny Walker Finds Niche in Calgary Stampeders." *Omaha World Herald* (December 14, 1994): 27SF.

Other

"Atlanta Falcons Coaching Staff." NFL.com. http://www.nfl.com/teams/coaching/ATL (December 12, 2002).

"Kenny Walker." About.com. http://deafness.about.com/library/weekly/aa042401.htm (December 10, 2002).

Sketch by Wendy Kagan

Bill Walton

Bill Walton
1952-

American basketball player

The professional basketball career of Bill Walton, though plagued by injury, had flashes of brilliance that prompted sportscasters to compare him with the greatest centers in the history of the National Basketball Association (NBA). In a pro ball career spanning thirteen years, Walton played for three teams—the Portland Trailblazers, the San Diego (later Los Angeles) Clippers, and the Boston Celtics—helping to lead two of them to national championships. Elected to the Naismith Memorial Basketball Hall of Fame in 1993, he was named one of the fifty greatest players in NBA history in 1996. Since 1990, Walton has worked as a sportscaster covering basketball.

Hooked on Basketball Early

He was born William Theodore Walton III in La Mesa, California, not far from San Diego, the son of a father who worked as a music teacher and a mother who was a librarian. Although neither of his parents had any particular interest in athletics, preferring art, literature, and music, Walton followed in the footsteps of his older brother, Bruce, and gravitated toward sports. Another major influence was Frank "Rocky" Graciano, a volunteer coach at the Catholic elementary school Walton attended. Young Walton's first coach "made it [basketball] fun and really emphasized the joy of playing the team game," Walton told ESPN. The game proved a haven for Walton, who told ESPN, "I was a skinny, scrawny guy. I stuttered horrendously, couldn't speak at all. I was a very shy, reserved player and a very shy, reserved person. I found a safe place in life in basketball." He also found time to keep his parents happy by taking music lessons.

After an early growth spurt, Walton had reached a height of more than six feet by the time he entered Helix High School in La Mesa. During Walton's junior and senior years in high school, the Helix basketball team, coached by Gordon Nash, won forty-nine consecutive games to win the California Interscholastic Federal High School title two years in a row. For his part, Walton, who towered nearly seven feet tall as a senior, was ranked as the best high school basketball player in the state. Among Walton's honors during his last two years in high school were being named All-State and All-Conference in both 1969 and 1970 and All-American and Helix Athlete of the Year in 1970.

Throughout his years in elementary and high school, Walton had avidly followed the exploits of UCLA's bas-

Chronology

1952	Born in La Mesa, California, on November 5
1969-70	Leads Helix High School team to California Interscholastic Federal High School title two years in a row
1970	Enrolls at University of California, Los Angeles (UCLA)
1971	Plays on UCLA's freshman basketball team
1972-74	Plays center on UCLA varsity team coached by John Wooden
1973	Arrested while participating in a protest demonstration against the Vietnam War
1974	Drafted by Portland Trailblazers as number one overall pick in NBA draft
1974-78	Plays with Trailblazers, leading team to NBA championship in 1977
1979-85	Plays with San Diego (later Los Angeles) Clippers
1985-87	Plays with Boston Celtics, winning NBA championship in 1986
1987	Retires from professional basketball
1990	Undergoes surgery to fuse bones in left foot and ankle
1990	Joins Prime Ticket Network as analyst
1991-2001	Works as basketball commentator for major network and cable networks, including CBS, NBC, MNBC, and Turner Sports
2002	Hired by ESPN/ABC as lead analyst for NBA coverage

Awards and Accomplishments

1969-70	Named All-State and All-Conference as a high school junior and senior
1970	Named All-American and Helix (H.S.) Athlete of the Year as a senior
1972-73	National Collegiate Athletic Association (NCAA) championship at UCLA; Most Valuable Player in the NCAA tournament both of those years
1972-74	Led UCLA to 86-4 record during his three years of varsity play
1972-74	Sporting News College Player of the Year and winner of Naismith Award
1977	Led Portland Trailblazers to NBA Championship; named NBA Finals Most Valuable Player
1978	NBA's Most Valuable Player
1986	Helped Celtics win NBA Championship and received NBA Sixth Man Award
1992-93, 1995-96, 1998-2000	Named Best Television Analyst/Commentator by the Southern California Sports Broadcasters Association
1993	Inducted into Basketball Hall of Fame
1994	Voted into the Verizon Academic All-American Hall of Fame
1997	Named as one of NBA's 50 best basketball players of all time
1997	Became first male basketball player from the state of California to be inducted into the National High School Sports Hall of Fame
1999	Received NCAA's Silver Anniversary Award for his extensive civic and professional contributions
2001	Became inaugural inductee into the Grateful Dead Hall of Fame
2001	Emmy Award for best live sports television broadcast

ketball team on the radio, silently promising himself that someday he would play ball for the team. His outstanding record as a high school player made him a hot property for college basketball recruiters, but the one offer he was most interested in came from UCLA. Walton quickly accepted the university's invitation to enroll there and play basketball for the Bruins under legendary coach **John Wooden**, a man who was to have a major impact on his life. Of Wooden, Walton writes on his Web site: "The joy and happiness in John Wooden's life comes today, as it always has, from the success of others. He regularly tells us that what he learned from his two favorite teachers, Abraham Lincoln and Mother Theresa, is that a life not lived for others is not a life."

Leads UCLA to Two NCAA Championships

In his first year at UCLA, Walton played on the freshman basketball team, after which he played the next three years on the varsity team, coached by Wooden. During that period, the Bruins basketball team won eighty-six games and lost only four, winning the National Collegiate Athletic Association (NCAA) championship in both 1972 and 1973. Walton was named Most Valuable Player in the NCAA tournament both of those years. By the time Walton graduated from UCLA, he was widely recognized as the best college basketball player in the country, having scored 1,767 points and 1,370 rebounds in his eighty-seven college games. During his college years, Walton earned a reputation as something of a rebel with his support for left-leaning causes, long hair, and commitment to vegetarianism. He was also an outspoken critic of President Richard Nixon and the Federal Bureau of Investigation. During his junior year at UCLA, Walton was arrested while participating in a protest demonstration against the Vietnam War.

In the NBA draft of 1974, Walton was the number one overall pick, tapped by the Portland Trailblazers. Walton had shown himself to be unusually prone to injury during his years of playing basketball in high school and college, and this vulnerability seemed to grow during his early years with the Trailblazers. During his first two seasons of NBA play, injuries sidelined Walton for about half of the team's scheduled games. He seemed to come into his own during the season of 1976-1977, averaging nearly nineteen points per game and leading the league in rebounding and blocked shots. In the post-season, the Trailblazers faced off against Philadelphia in the NBA Championships. Portland lost the first two games but, led by Walton, came back to win the next four to take the championship. Walton was named Most Valuable Player of the championship, having set single-game records for defensive rebounds and blocked shots.

Walton began the 1977-1978 season with an even more impressive performance, leading the Trailblazers to victory in fifty of their first sixty games. However, injury sidelined Walton for the final twenty-four games of the regular season. He returned to play during the NBA playoffs but was forced to drop out again when it was discovered that he had broken a bone in his left foot. Without Walton, Portland fell to the Seattle Supersonics in the playoffs. Injury forced Walton to sit out all of the 1978-1979 season. Despite his history of injury, Walton in 1979 was signed to a five-year contract with the San Diego Clippers, a franchise that in 1984 moved to Los

Career Statistics

Yr	Team	GP	PTS	FG%	FT%	RPG	APG	TO
1974	POR	35	448	.513	.686	12.6	4.8	0
1975	POR	51	823	.471	.583	13.4	4.3	0
1976	POR	65	1210	.528	.697	14.4	3.8	0
1977	POR	58	1097	.522	.720	13.2	5.0	206
1979	SDC	14	194	.503	.593	9.0	2.4	37
1982	SDC	33	465	.528	.556	9.8	3.6	105
1983	SDC	55	668	.556	.597	8.7	3.3	177
1984	LAC	67	676	.521	.680	9.0	2.3	174
1985	BOS	80	606	.562	.713	6.8	2.1	151
1986	BOS	10	28	.385	.533	3.1	0.9	15
TOTAL		468	6215	.521	.660	10.5	3.4	865

BOS: Boston Celtics; LAC: Los Angeles Clippers; POR: Portland Trailblazers; SDC: San Diego Clippers.

Angeles. Injury kept Walton out of play for most of his first two seasons with the Clippers, drawing widespread criticism from San Diego fans and his teammates. During the Clippers' 1983-1984 and 1984-1985 seasons, Walton bounced back, once again playing impressively, but the Clippers never experienced the success of the Trailblazers in NBA play.

Ends Basketball Career with Celtics

In 1985 Walton was traded by the Clippers to the Boston Celtics. In a last flash of brilliance, he rose above his injuries to play in eighty games for the Celtics during the 1985-1986 season, averaging 7.6 points per game. With Walton's help, the Celtics advanced to the playoffs and eventually won the NBA championship. The following season, Walton played only ten games before his recurring injury forced him to retire from professional basketball. For the whole of his career, Walton played in a total of 468 games, averaging 13.3 points per game, with 6,215 points, 4,923 rebounds, and 1,034 blocked shots.

By the time of his retirement, Walton's chronic injury had grown so severe that it limited his ability to get around. In 1990 he underwent surgery to fuse some of the bones in his left foot and ankle. However, the surgery forever ended any hopes of playing basketball again, making it impossible for Walton to bend or flex his left foot. To keep busy, Walton got involved in charity work and coached a handful of individual promising college players, including **Shaquille O'Neal** at Lousiana State University. In time, Walton decided to see if he could find a job as a sportscaster or color analyst. Making the transition proved one of the toughest hurdles in his life, Walton told ESPN. "When I started in this business . . . , I couldn't get a job. They'd look at me and say, 'No way, Walton. Don't call us back and don't come around here any more."

But Walton was not to be so easily discouraged. His persistence eventually paid off, and he landed a job in 1990 as analyst for cable's Prime Ticket Network. Not

long after that he joined CBS Sports to cover the NCAA Final Four. He next jumped to NBC, where he provided commentary for NBA games and also the 1996 Atlanta and 2000 Sydney Summer Olympics Games. In between jobs for NBC, he found time to fulfill assignments for a number of broadcast and cable networks, including Fox, KCAL in Los Angeles, Turner Sports, MSNBC, and the NBA itself. Although it wasn't easy for him to break into broadcasting, Walton over time proved a natural. The Southern California Sports Broadcasters Association honored him with its Best Television Analyst/Commentator Award seven times between 1992 and 2000. He's also been nominated for a number of Emmy awards and in 2001 won an Emmy for best live sports television broadcast.

Inducted into Basketball Hall of Fame

The 1990s also brought Walton some well-deserved recognition for his contributions to basketball. He was inducted into the Basketball Hall of Fame in Springfield, Massachusetts, in 1993. The following year he was voted into the Verizon Academic All-American Hall of Fame. In 1997 Walton was named one of the NBA's fifty best players of all time, and that same year Walton became the first male basketball player from the state of California to be inducted into the National High School Sports Hall of Fame. For his extensive civic and professional contributions over the twenty-five years since graduating from UCLA, Walton in 1999 received the NCAA's Silver Anniversary Award. A longtime fan of the Grateful Dead, in June 2001 Walton became the inaugural inductee into the Grateful Dead Hall of Fame, a non-profit charitable organization founded by members of the band and their friends.

Interviewed by ESPN in 2002, Walton was asked who he thought was his toughest opponent on the basketball court during his years of college and professional play. He replied: "Without question, no hesitation, **Kareem Abdul-Jabbar** was the best player I ever played against. Not just the best center, he was the best player, period. He was better than **Magic (Johnson)**, better than **Larry (Bird)**, better than **Michael (Jordan)**. He was my source of motivation. Everything I did was to try to beat this guy. I lived to play against him, and I played my best ball against him. No matter what I threw at him, though, it seemed like he'd score fifty against me. His left leg belongs in the Smithsonian. And it wasn't just offense. He was a great defender and rebounder, a great passer, a wonderful leader. He was phenomenal."

Walton has been married twice. With his first wife, Susan, whom he married in the 1970s, he had four sons, all of whom play basketball. All of Walton's sons are tall, at least 6 feet 7 inches, but none is as tall as their father, who stands 6 feet 11 inches. Susan and Walton were divorced in the 1990s, and Walton lives today in San Diego with his second wife, Lori. He is close to his sons and follows their basketball exploits closely. His eldest son, Adam, played ball at Louisiana State and now helps coach a high school junior varsity team in San Diego. Next in line is Nate, who played at Princeton. Luke is a standout player at the University of Arizona, while younger brother, Chris, plays for San Diego State. When asked by the *Washington Post* if he was disappointed that none of his sons went to UCLA, he said: "I've had nothing to do with where they go to school. Both Chris and Luke were offered scholarships by UCLA and turned down UCLA. I've always told the kids, it's your life, you have to make this decision. I'm more than happy to talk to you about it, more than happy to expose you to all the factors that go into your decision. But you're not living your life for me."

For more than four decades, Walton's life has revolved around basketball, first as a player and now for more than a decade as a broadcaster. Although chronic injury wrenched him from the basketball court prematurely, Walton has found a way to remain close to the game he loves. And, to the surprise of almost everyone, including Walton himself, he's proved as much a champion in his second career behind the microphone as he was during his days of playing college and professional ball. Jack Ramsay, his coach on the Trailblazers, told the *Los Angeles Times*, "if he could have stayed healthy, he probably would have been the greatest center of all time." But Walton is not one to dwell on what might have been. He lives very much in the present and of his present career as a sportscaster, Walton told ESPN, "I love my job."

CONTACT INFORMATION

Address: Bill Walton, c/o ABC Sports, 47 W. 66th St., New York, NY 10023. Phone: (212) 456-7777. Online: http://www.billwalton.com.

SELECTED WRITINGS BY WALTON:

(With Gene Wojciechowski) *Nothing But Net: Just Give Me the Ball and Get Out of the Way,* Hyperion, 1994.

(With Bryan Burwell) *At the Buzzer! Havlicek Steals, Erving Soars, Magic Deals, Michael Scores,* Doubleday, 2001.

FURTHER INFORMATION

Books

Almanac of Famous People, 6th ed. Detroit: Gale Group, 1998.

St. James Encyclopedia of Popular Culture. five volumes. Detroit: St. James Press, 2000.

Walton, Bill, and Bryan Burwell. *At the Buzzer! Havlicek Steals, Erving Soars, Magic Deals, Michael Scores.* New York: Doubleday, 2001.

Walton, Bill, and Gene Wojciechowski. *Nothing But Net: Just Give Me the Ball and Get Out of the Way.* New York: Hyperion, 1994.

Periodicals

"Fox Sports Radio Network Signs Stellar Talent." *PRNewswire* (January 30, 2001).

Gildea, William. "For the Waltons, Life Is a Ball; Four Sons Inherited a Gift for the Game from Dad." *Washington Post* (March 5, 2000): D1.

Rushin, Steve. "Just Chill, Says Bill: Hot about the Glacial Pace of the NBA Playoffs? A Wise Old Deadhead Advises You to Cool It." *Sports Illustrated* (May 6, 2002): 19.

Other

"Bill Walton." Basketball Hall of Fame. http://www. hoophall.com/halloffamers/Walton.htm (October 5, 2002).

"Bill Walton: Biography." Bill Walton Web site. http://www.www.billwalton.com/bio.html (October 5, 2002).

Biography Resource Center Online. http://www.galenet.galegroup.com (October 5, 2002).

"Jack Ramsay." Basketball Hall of Fame. http://www.hoophall.com/halloffamers/Ramsay.htm (October 9, 2002).

"Page 2: 10 Burning Questions for Bill Walton." ESPN.com. http://espn.go.com/page2/s/questions/billwalton.html (October 8, 2002).

Sketch by Don Amerman

Shane Warne
1969-

Australian cricket player

Shane Warne

One of the greatest leg-break bowlers in the history of cricket, Australian Shane Warne almost singlehandedly revived the audacious style of leg spinning, combining devastating deliveries with pinpoint control. A favorite to break the world record for wicket-taking in Tests, the outspoken and controversial Warne was selected as one of the five top cricket players of the twentieth century.

Revives Leg Spinning

From his earliest days in cricket, Warne had a reputation as a carouser. He attended Australia's prestigious Cricket Academy but was expelled for "indiscipline." Reportedly Warne spent too much time drinking and partying.

Warne made his Test debut for Australia versus India on January 2, 1992. Immediately he began a national sensation. He revived the nearly dying bowler's craft of leg-spinning, and eventually some experts claimed he was the best leg-break bowler ever. Leg spinning requires incredible control, and Warne combined it with wrist spinning—bowling out of the back of the hand with a cocked wrist. His style was one of the most difficult to master. Most wrist spinners have to sacrifice control to get their bowls to break, but Warne combined exceptional control with pronounced and devastating spins. He could fire the ball at the batsmen's legs and still get it to curl back and hit a stump.

Warne also mastered the difficult "flipper," a delivery which starts with a long, lazy hop before diving fast and low past the batter. He also could bowl a "googly," a ball delivered to look like a leg break but which turns the other direction at the last moment. Varying his pace and flight, Warne was a master of deception and a sensational bowler who delighted crowds by making opposing batsmen look foolish. He was also a competent right-handed batsman who could hit the ball hard, and he often pinch-hit during one-day games.

"Hollywood"

Warne represented a new generation of bowler, even though his style harkened back to the classic days of the sport. He invaded the conservative sport with his poster-boy looks, dyed blonde hair, and an ear stud. Warne often wore zinc-colored face paint to protect his cheeks from the sun. Lots of young Australian boys imitated his look and tried to mimic his unorthodox bowling style. Warne remained a sex symbol in Australia even as his paunchy stomach grew bigger and even after he and his wife, Simone, had three children, Brooke, Jackson, and Summer. Something of a showoff, Warne was a larger-than-life presence on the pitch and was nicknamed "Hollywood." Fans either loved or hated him, and he became one of the game's most popular draws.

He also rewrote the cricket record book. In 1992 Warne became Australia's top wicket taker and remained so for many seasons. In 1998 he underwent shoulder surgery. But the following year he led Australia to victory in the World Cup. He was named Man of the Match twice in the World Cup, in the semifinal against Australia and in the final against Pakistan.

Chronology

1990	Joins Australian Cricket Academy
1992	Makes Test debut for Australia against New Zealand
1998	Admits selling match information to bookie
1999	Leads Australia to World Cup victory
2003	Announces retirement from one-day cricket

Awards and Accomplishments

1994	Wisden Cricketer of the Year
1999	Man of the Match, World Cup semifinal and final
2000	One of five Wisden Cricketers of the Century

In 2000 Warne was named one of Wisden's five top cricketers of the twentieth century. That year, he became the highest wicket taker in Australian cricket history, surpassing Dennis Lillee's 355 wickets, and he went over 400 in 2001. By the end of 2002, he was closing in on Courtney Walsh's world record of 519 wickets in Tests.

Warne's career was blemished by revelations about his association with bookies. In 1994 the Pakistans allegedly tried to bribe him to bowl badly in a crucial test. In 1998 he and fellow Australian Mark Waugh were fined after admitting they gave a bookkeeper in India critical information about the weather and the pitch in exchange for money in Sri Lanka in 1994.

Nothing to Prove

As one of the most marketable players in cricket, Warne earned extra money with endorsement deals. During the 2000 season, he wrote an exclusive cricket column for the *Times* of London. In 2001 Warne signed a promotional contract with British Channel 5 to paint his face with that network's logo to promote the soap opera series *Home and Away*. That same year, he signed an endorsement contract to plug cricket boots for British sporting goods manufacturer Mitre, ending a seven-year deal with Nike.

In December 2002, with 488 wickets recorded in his career in Tests, Warne discloated his shoulder in a match against England in Melbourne. A month later, he pronounced himself ready for the 2003 World Cup. "I don't think I have to prove anything to anybody about what I can do on the field on the big occasion," Warne explained to CricInfo News.

In January 2003, Warne announced he was retiring from one-day cricket after the World Cup to concentrate exclusively on Tests. With 288 wickets in one-day internationals, he ranked six in such contests. "I love playing cricket for Australia," he told CricInfo News, "but the No. 1 priority for me is to play Test cricket for as long as I can… This could prolong my Test career by five or six years, who knows?"

FURTHER INFORMATION

Periodicals

"Australian Stars Admit Giving Tips." *New York Times,* (December 10, 1998): D7.

"The Belly of the Beast." *Sports Illustrated,* 88 (April 6, 1998): 30.

Hall, Emma. "Shane Warne Fronts Times Push." *Campaign,* (June 16, 2000): 4.

"In Brief." *Sports Marketing,* (June 2001): 2.

"No Spin Required." *Sports Marketing,*(August 2001): 2.

"Warne Meets Lara."*The Economist,*334 (March 4, 1995): 88.

Other

Buckle, Greg. "I am Almost Back to My Best, Warne says." *CricInfo News*.http://www.cricket.org/link_to_database/ARCHIVE/CRICKET_NEWS/2003/JAN/127379_REUTERS_26JAN2003.html (February 2, 2003).

Hoult, Nick. "Warne Calls Time on His One-Day Life." *CricInfo News*.http://www.cricket.org/link_to_database/ARCHIVE/CRICKET_NEWS/2003/JAN/125954_ET_23JAN2003.html (February 2, 2003).

McConnell, Lynn. "Warne Closing in on 500 … and Beyond." *CricInfo News*.http://www.cricket.org/link_to_database/ARCHIVE/CRICKET_NEWS/2002/OCT/072592_NZ_08OCT2002.htm l(February 2, 2003).

"Shane Keith Warne." *baggy green.* http://www.cricket.org/link_to_database/PLAYERS/AUS/W/WARNE_SK_02002000/ (February 2, 2003).

Warne, Shane Keith (Victoria). *thatscricket.com.* http://servlet.indiainfo.com/indiainfo/cricket.PlayerProfile?countryId=11&playId=156 (February 2, 2003).

Sketch by Michael Betzold

Kurt Warner
1971-

American football player

Kurt Warner went from $5.50-an-hour grocery clerk to National Football League (NFL) and Super Bowl Most Valuable Player. He has won the league MVP twice and competed in two Super Bowls since taking over as St.

Kurt Warner

Louis Rams' quarterback in 1999 following a teammate's injury. Ironically, Warner himself struggled during an injury-riddled and controversial 2002 season that left him with his own job in question—his coach, Mike Martz, said the first-string job may be up for grabs in 2003.

Iowa Roots

Warner, born in Burlington, Iowa, lettered in football, basketball, and baseball at Cedar Rapids Regis High School. He was a *Des Moines Register* all-state selection as a senior. At the University of Northern Iowa, where he graduated with a degree in communications, Warner didn't start until his senior season, 1993, when he was Gateway Conference offensive player of the year and led the conference in total offense and passing efficiency.

Green Bay drafted Warner in 1994, but cut him during training camp. Warner then made a living at a Hy-Vee supermarket in Cedar Rapids, stocking shelves. He and his wife, Brenda, needed food stamps. Tragedy also struck when a tornado killed Brenda's parents at their home in Arkansas in 1996. "There were times I remembered praying that no matter what I had to do, just praying that the Lord would give me a job that I could take care of my family," Warner said years later. "I didn't care if I had to work till I was 90."

"We loved each other and he loved the kids, so our dates really involved him playing with the kids," Brenda Warner said. "So it was a cheap date."

Chronology

1971	Born June 22 in Burlington, Iowa
1989-93	Quarterback at University of Northern Iowa
1994	Cut by Green Bay Packers of National Football League; works as grocery clerk at Hy-Vee store in Cedar Falls, Iowa.
1995-97	Plays for Iowa Barnstormers of Arena Football League; leads Iowa to two straight Arena Bowl appearances
1998	Plays for Amsterdam Admirals of NFL Europe.
1998	Makes NFL debut for St. Louis Rams against San Francisco 49ers.
2002	Quarterbacks Rams during 20-17 loss to New England Patriots in Super Bowl XXXVI (2001 season)
2002	Misses part of the season with broken hand; Rams miss playoffs amid quarterback controversy.
2002	Announces partnership with Back Home Studios to create the Kurt Warner's Good Sports Gang children's home video programs.

Warner, meanwhile, persevered in football. He played for the Iowa Barnstormers for the Arena Football League from 1995 to 1997, twice leading the team to the championship game, the Arena Bowl, and passing for 10,164 yards and 183 touchdowns in three seasons. (Arena football is an indoor version of the game played on a shorter field). The Rams signed Warner in December 1997 and optioned him to the Amsterdam Admirals of NFL Europe. In the spring/summer 1998 season, Warner started all ten Admirals games and led the league in passing yards, completions and touchdowns.

Warner, after the NFL Europe season ended in summer 1998, was the Rams' inactive third quarterback for fourteen of their first sixteen games that fall. He finally saw action in the team's final game, against the San Francisco 49ers, completing four of eleven passes for thirty-nine yards.

Warner, Rams Rise

In August 1999, St. Louis starting quarterback Trent Green tore his left medial collateral ligament in an exhibition game against the San Diego Chargers, and was out for the season. Things looked dark for the Rams, who had lost twelve of sixteen games the year before. But Coach Dick Vermeil immediately embraced Warner, a 28-year-old second year player. "We will rally around Kurt Warner and we will play good football," Vermeil said.

"I always felt that I had the talent," Warner told the *Des Moines Register*. "I just felt that I had to get in the right situation and organization to utilize my talent. That is what has happened here with the Rams." Warner started the team's final exhibition that summer and never looked back. The Rams opened the regular season with six straight victories and finished atop the NFC West with a 13-3 record. Warner, en route to winning the league's Most Valuable Player, led the NFL in touchdown passes and completion percentage, and was second in the league in passing yards. He threw more

---

Kurt Warner

He is a family man and a man of God, an out-of-nowhere sensation whose story has been called too schmaltzy even for Hollywood.... With Super Bowl XXXIV slipping out of the grasp of the St. Louis Rams, Warner took over in a way that must have impressed even the game's legendary signal-callers.... Warner dropped five steps in the pocket and, an instant before absorbing a hellacious hit from defensive end Jevon Kearse, launched the 73-yard touchdown pass to wideout Isaac Bruce that gave the Rams a 23-16 victory in the greatest Super Bowl ever. All across the land spines straightened and eyes moistened, and anyone who has ever been doubted felt a surge of satisfaction.

Source: Silver, Michael. *cnnsi.com*, February 7, 2000.

touchdown passes in his first four starts (14) than any NFL player.

In the NFC playoffs, Warner completed twenty-seven of thirty-three passes for 391 yards and five touchdowns in a 49-37 victory over the Minnesota Vikings, then threw the winning 30-yard touchdown pass to wide receiver Ricky Proehl with 4:44 remaining to give Rams 11-6 win over the Tampa Bay Buccaneers in the NFC Championship game.

In Super Bowl XXIV in Atlanta, against the American Football Conference champion Tennessee Titans, Warner passed for a record 414 yards and threw the winning 73-yard touchdown pass to a leaping Isaac Bruce with 1:54 remaining. The Rams stopped Tennessee on the 1-yard line on the game's final play and St. Louis emerged a 23-16 winner. It was the first championship since 1951 for the franchise, which began in Cleveland in 1937, moved to Los Angeles in 1946 and then to St. Louis in 1995.

"It is not a fairy tale, it is real life," Vermeil said of Warner, who wears number 13 largely to show his disdain for superstition. "He is a great example of persistence and believing in himself and a deep faith. He is a movie; he is a book, this guy."

After the season, the Rams signed Warner to a seven-year, $46.5 million deal that included a $11.5 million signing bonus. "We just laughed," Brenda Warner said. "Our first two kids were born in poverty and our next two years are born with, you know, riches. It's kind of a different world." The Warners established charities with some of their money. Hy-Vee stores throughout Iowa, meanwhile, began stocking shelves with Warner's new frosted flake cereal, Warner's Crunch Time.

Returns to Super Bowl

Warner missed five games in 2000 with a broken right little finger and the Rams exited in the first round of the playoffs. St. Louis stormed back the following season, and Warner, despite difficulties with his hand, earned MVP honors for the second time in three seasons, edging teammate and running back **Marshall Faulk** by one vote. Warner led the NFL in passing yards with 4,830, second most in league history, and touchdown passes.

In three postseason games, Warner completed sixty-eight of 107 passes for 793 yards with four touchdowns.

The Rams, under Martz, who succeeded the retired Vermeil in 2000, beat Green Bay 45-17 and Philadelphia 29-24 to capture another NFC title, and were 14-point favorites to beat the New England Patriots in Super Bowl XXXVI in New Orleans.

New England, however, won 20-17 on Adam Vinatieri's 48-yard field goal as time expired. The Patriots forced Warner to throw two interceptions, one of which defensive back Ty Law returned for a 47-yard touchdown. Warner completed twenty-eight of forty-six passes and rallied St. Louis from a 17-3 fourth-quarter deficit to tie the game right before Vinatieri's winning kick. Warner ran for a two-yard touchdown and threw a twenty-six-yard pass to Ricky Proehl.

Turbulent 2002

The Rams, picked by many to return to the Super Bowl, stumbled badly in the 2002 season, dropping their first five games. In the fourth loss, Warner broke the same right pinkie. In stepped rookie Marc Bulger, as Warner had for Green in 1999; the Rams won five straight under Bulger to pull to 5-5 and within a shot of a playoff berth.

But Bulger sprained his right index finger and Warner returned, insisting his hand was fine; St. Louis, though, dropped three straight to fall out of playoff contention. Warner reinjured his hand, this time a hairline fracture at the knuckle of his little finger. Although Martz during the season accused Warner's critics of being part of an "amnesia crowd," controversy erupted in early December when Brenda Warner called a radio talk show to complain that she, not Martz, insisted her husband have his hand X-rayed. "Martz had nothing to do with it," she said. "All week long I said, 'Kurt, I'm a nurse, you should go get it X-rayed.' The doctors never once said he should get an X-ray. They said, 'No, it's only bruised.'"

"Once he let his wife take the lead in fighting his football battles, then he lost sight of what it takes to play this game," Michael Kinney wrote in the *Sedalia Democrat*. The Rams in mid-December put Warner on the injured reserve list, thus ending his season. One day before doing so, Martz said that if Bulger picked up

Career Statistics

Yr	Team	Att	Com	Yds	Com%	TD	Int	SK	RAT
1998	STL	11	4	39	36.4	0	0	0	47.2
1999	STL	499	325	4353	65.1	41	13	29	109.2
2000	STL	347	235	3429	67.7	21	18	20	98.3
2001	STL	546	375	4830	68.7	36	22	38	101.4
2002	STL	178	124	1213	69.7	3	9	-	73.1
TOTAL		1581	1063	13864	67.2	101	62	-	99.6

STL: St. Louis Rams.

where he left off, the quarterback job in St. Louis would be wide open in 2003.

Future in Question

Warner seized the opportunity in 1999 when he stepped in for an injured teammate; three years later, his season ended with backup Bulger more than eager to fill Warner's shoes. Whether Warner starts or not in 2003, some of the luster, for sure, is off.

"More than Kurt Warner's hand has taken a beating this football season," Les Winkeler wrote in the *Southern Illinoian.* "His reputation as the perfect quarterback, the perfect man and the perfect teammate has been shredded. Warner's actions this season have been nothing short of selfish. Warner insisted he was healthy. (But) even the casual observer knew that couldn't be true. It has become clear that Warner has put himself above the team. Despite the public bravado, he apparently is worried about losing his job. That doesn't make him a bad person—only human."

SELECTED WRITINGS BY WARNER:

(With Greg Brown) *Keep Your Head Up,* Taylor, 2000.
(With Michael Silver) *All Things Possible: My Story of Faith, Football, and the Miracle Season,* HarperSanFrancisco, 2000.

FURTHER INFORMATION

Other

AFL Roundhouse. Kurt Warner Profile. http://www.aflroundhouse.com, (December 6, 2002).
"The Greatest: Kurt Warner Was His Usual Stellar Self as the Rams Hung On to Beat the Titans in the Best Super Bowl Ever." cnnsi.com, http://www.cnnsi.com/football/nfl/features/superbowl/archive/2000 (February 7, 2000).
NFL.com. Kurt Warner profile. http://www.nfl.com/players/playerpage (December 12, 2002).
St. Louis Rams Official Web Site. Kurt Warner Profile. http://www.stlouisrams.com (December 12, 2002).
"Selfish Warner Just May Be Tarnishing His Perfect Image." *Southern Illinoian* http://www.thesouthern.com/rednews/2002/12/12/build/sports/SPO004.html (December 11, 2002).
"Warner Cereal Benefits Kids." *Des Moines Register.* http://www.DesMoinesRegister.com (December 21, 1999).
"Warner 'Ready' for NFL Break." *Des Moines Register.* http://www.DesMoinesRegister.com (August 31, 1999).
"Warner's Wife Stirs Controversy." *San Jose Mercury News.* http://www.bayarea.com (December 5, 2002).
"Who's Really Running the Rams?" *Sedalia Democrat.* http://www.sedaliademocrat.com/Sports (December 5, 2002).

Sketch by Paul Burton

Ora Washington
1898-1971

American tennis and basketball player

Before **Serena Williams** and **Venus Williams**, before the Women's National Basketball Association, and before civil rights created equity on the tennis and basketball courts across the United States, there was Ora Washington. Washington was a talented athlete who flourished in her chosen sports of tennis and basketball. She was the reigning champion of the American Tennis Association (ATA) from 1929 to 1935. She was the star player for the Philadelphia Tribunes and Germantown Hornets women's basketball teams. By the time she retired from play, she had played twelve years of undefeated tennis and earned 201 trophies for both tennis and basketball. Her accomplishments have placed her among the top female athletes of the twentieth century.

Ora Washington

Chronology

1899	Born January 16 in Philadelphia, Pennsylvania
1924	Begins playing tennis
1925	Beats Dorothy Radcliffe in her first national African American tournament
1931	Joins Philadelphia Tribune women's basketball team
1934	Philadelphia Tribune wins against Greensboro, North Carolina's Bennett College women's basketball team in a three-game series that is heavily attended
1936	Loses ATA singles title to Lulu Ballard due to sunstroke
1938	Tours the South with Philadelphia Tribune
1940	Philadelphia Tribune team disbanded
1971	Dies in May in Philadelphia, Pennsylvania

Born on January 16, 1899, Washington grew up in Philadelphia, Pennsylvania. As a girl she attended the Young Women's Christian Association (YWCA) in Germantown. It was here that she would get her start in tennis. In 1924, an instructor counseled Washington to take up some kind of sport to help her overcome the grief she felt over the death of one of her sisters. Washington picked up the tennis racket and within a year she entered her first national tournament for black players. She played against Dorothy Radcliffe at Druid Hill Park in Baltimore, Maryland, and won. Malcolm Poindexter related to A. S. Young in *Negro Firsts in Sports,* "From the moment she tried tennis, Ora found a deep and sincere interest in the game.... Her blossoming years showed victory after victory in New England, New York, Indiana, Virginia, and Pennsylvania—and all of them over name players."

Within four years of this first victory, Washington established herself as the ATA's women's singles champion. In 1929, she beat the preceding year's champion, Lulu Ballard, and for the next six years held onto that title. In 1936, she faced off against Ballard in a match that broke Washington's winning streak. In that game, which was played in Wilberforce, Ohio, Washington suffered a case of sunstroke. The weakness she experienced because of the sunstroke made it impossible for her to defend her title. Not ready to hand over the title permanently, she came back the next year and reestablished her championship status when she beat Catherine Jones in a match in Springfield, Massachusetts.

In addition to being the ATA's singles champion, Washington also proved her mettle on the court by being on the winning women's doubles team from 1928 to 1936. For the majority of those years, her partner was Ballard, her consistent rival for the singles title. Poindexter related to young Washington's extraordinary tennis career, "During her lengthy reign, Miss Washington bested many of the American Tennis Association's top-seeded starts. Women like Emma Leonard, Frances Giddens and Lillian Hines were no match for the blazing pace that became a trademark of Ora's." Poindexter further described Washington's style of play, "She had the strategy and was dynamic to watch ... and her overhead game was terrific. She played an entirely different style—using mostly forehand, backhand drive, and slice.... Ora had a dependable service."

Eventually, Washington decided to retire from tennis. She ended up retiring twice. The first time she retired, she was pressured back into play by a challenge from then singles champion Flora Lomax. Lomax had been disappointed that she could not prove herself against the long-reigning champion. Washington came out of retirement and easily beat Lomax. She stayed in the game for a while longer until pressure from within the tennis community convinced her to retire permanently. A tennis official complained that younger players were afraid to meet the challenge of playing against Washington and were avoiding the sport.

One of Washington's biggest goals was never met. As the women's singles champion in the African American tennis circuit, she had wanted to prove herself against the United States Lawn Tennis Association's champion, **Helen Wills** Moody. Segregation and Moody's unwillingness to take the challenge kept Washington from proving that she was the best women's singles tennis player in the United States. Upon her retirement, Washington's consecutive championships in the ATA's singles and doubles categories alone established her as one of the best female tennis players in the United States. Her accomplishments on the court set the stage for later players such as the ground-breaking **Althea Gibson** and the inspiring Williams sisters.

Awards and Accomplishments

1928-29, 1932, 1934-36	American Tennis Association (ATA) women's doubles champion with Lula Ballard
1929-35, 1937	ATA women's singles champion
1930-31	ATA women's doubles champion with Blanche Winston
1933	ATA women's doubles champion with Anita Grant

American Tennis Association

On November 30, 1916, the American Tennis Association (ATA) was founded in Washington, D.C. The intent of the ATA was to provide opportunities for African Americans to compete on a national level. The ATA was founded out of necessity because African Americans were excluded from participation in the United States National Lawn Tennis Association (USLTA), which was not integrated until the 1950s when Althea Gibson became the first African American to play in the USLTA. From August 19 to 26, 1922, one of the first ATA National Championship tournaments was held at the Germantown YWCA in Philadelphia, Pennsylvania.

The ATA has been influential in establishing the early careers of several outstanding African American tennis stars. Althea Gibson, who broke the color barrier in the United States and abroad, was first successful within the ATA. Arthur Ashe also got his start winning ATA junior championship tournaments. The ATA is the oldest African American sports organization in the United States and continues to hold true to its mission, "To promote the sport of tennis among men and women of all races through sportsmanship, unity and goodwill."

In 1931, in the midst of her highly successful tennis career, Washington began playing basketball on a traveling team. She played center for the Philadelphia Tribune, a highly successful team sponsored by the popular African-American newspaper of the same name. Washington was considered one of the most valuable players for the team. As the center, she was often their top scorer. For several years she acted as coach. During most of the 1930s, black papers named the Philadelphia Tribune the women's basketball national champions. According to **Arthur Ashe** in *A Hard Road to Glory,* "The Philadelphia Tribune was black America's first premier female sports team." Their record was proof. The Tribune only lost six times in games played during the 1930s.

Women's basketball at the time was primarily played with three players on offense and three on defense. Ashe described the style, "The Tribune squad ... played the typical six-players-per-team style which had separate threesomes for offense and defense at opposite ends of the court. This was done so as to minimize the 'strain' on the players. It was still fervently, but erroneously, believed that women had innately delicate natures and too much exercise would damage their equilibrium." Not all games were played by women's rules though. Washington's team often played by men's rules, without any noticeable strain. In fact, her team was successful playing by either set of rules.

As a traveling team, the Philadelphia Tribune played games throughout the East, Midwest, and South. They played teams like their own, which were sponsored by businesses or newspapers; they played white and black teams; and they played against high school and college teams. Wherever they played they would also sponsor clinics to help other women and girls learn about basketball. In total, Washington played basketball for eighteen years for the Tribune and another Philadelphia team called the Germantown Hornets.

One of their better attended games was in 1934 when they played against the women of Bennett College, an elite black college in Greensboro, North Carolina. The Tribune faced off against Bennett in a three-game series that attracted attention even from the white press. Their initial game was so well attended that it was played at the Greensboro Sportsarena, a venue in which blacks did not usually play. Rita Liberti quoted a contemporary *Greensboro News* report in her article in the *Journal of Sport History,* "The Tribune girls, led by the indomitable, internally famed and stellar performer, Ora Washington, national women's singles champ in tennis, comes with enviable reputation." Not only was Washington the top scorer and team captain, she dominated the court in a manner that is often found in the modern game. Liberti noted Bennett player Lucille Townsend's response to Washington's court manner, "I told the referee she's [Ora] hittin' me in the stomach every time I jump." Despite the roughness, Washington's team prevailed in the series, winning all three games.

Many historians consider Washington one of the premiere athletes in women's sports. Young compared Washington with Gibson, "The difference in eras—consequently in the styles of play—comprises the major point of conjecture as to who was the greater of women players, Althea Gibson or the earlier Ora Washington of Philadelphia.... Washington ... might well have been 'the first Althea Gibson' had she been the beneficiary of the all-out sponsorship Miss Gibson received." Washington's continuity and endurance were hallmarks of long and distinguished careers in both basketball and tennis. Even after her career ended, Washington continued to help younger generations learn to play tennis in her hometown of Germantown. Her historical anonymity in the face of her accomplishments can be blamed on the existence of racial segregation, bias, and lost opportunities. In 1975, Washington was inducted into the Black Athletes Hall of Fame. The organization was unaware that she had died four years earlier in 1971.

FURTHER INFORMATION

Books

Ashe, Arthur. *A Hard Road to Glory.* New York: Amistad Press, Inc., 1993.

Lumpkin, Angela. *Women's Tennis: A Historical Documentary of the Players and Their Game.* New York: Whitston Publishing Company, 1981.

Notable Black American Women, Book II. Detroit: Gale Group, 1996.

Young, A. S. *Negro Firsts in Sports.* Chicago: Johnson Publishing Company, Inc., 1963.

Periodicals

Liberti, Rita. "'We Were Ladies, We Just Played Basketball Like Boys': African American Womanhood and Competitive Basketball at Bennett College, 1928-1942." *Journal of Sport History* (Fall, 1999): 567.

Sketch by Eve M. B. Hermann

Tom Watson

Tom Watson
1949-

American golfer

Tom Watson won eight major golf tournaments, including five British Opens, and challenged Jack Nicklaus for golf supremacy in the late 1970s. Regarded as a failure under pressure in his early years, Watson silenced critics by winning all major tournaments but the PGA at least once. He was twice a Masters champion and took the U.S. Open once.

"Beginning in 1977, Watson won six PGA Tour Player of the Year awards, and he led the money list five times," *Web Golf Village* wrote. "Yet it was his head-to-head victories against Nicklaus, ten years his senior, that cemented him as a player for the ages." After joining the Senior PGA Tour, Watson atoned in part for his one Grand Slam void, the PGA, by winning the Seniors' version in 2001.

Quiet But Determined

Watson, nicknamed "Huckleberry Dillinger" while growing up in Kansas City, was a capable all-around athlete. His sporadic success at Stanford University hardly foreshadowed a Hall of Fame career. His peers, however, admired Watson's work ethic when he turned pro. Part of Watson's growth progress included painful defeats, such as the 1974 U.S. Open at Winged Foot Golf Club in Mamaroneck, New York. Watson led by a stroke entering the final round, but shot 79 and fell to fifth. The following year, at Medinah, Illinois, Watson led the U.S. Open after two rounds, but fizzled again. Legend Byron Nelson advised Watson and later became his coach.

In 1975, Watson achieved his watershed victory, a British Open playoff triumph that quelled doubts and paved the way for five British titles. (Watson is one of the few Americans to have received honorary membership to the Royal & Ancient Golf Club of St. Andrews, a frequent British Open site.) Watson made birdie on the last hole with a 20-foot putt that pulled him even with Jack Newton, then defeated Newton by one stroke in an 18-hole playoff the following day.

"Young Tom Watson finally became a champion, a new person and one hellacious player," Dan Jenkins wrote in *Sports Illustrated.* "After a lot of slightly baroque things had happened on the becalmed, deroughed and tranquilized beast of Carnoustie, it all came down to a Sunday match between the 25-year-old Watson, who admits he possibly thinks too much, and an equally young Australian, Jack Newton, who admits he drinks too much."

"Holding together was not something Watson had done so well in the past," Jenkins wrote. Watson's litmus test was on No, 17, but this time he held his own, making a necessary five-foot putt for par. "Tom rammed it home as if it were a gimme. That would have been the perfect spot for Watson to do what he had so often done in the past—to miss, and start blowing another one."

Nicklaus, and "The Shot"

Despite that British Open victory, Watson's reputation for hitting the wrong shot at the wrong time resurfaced. "I choked plenty before I finally won," Watson

Chronology

1949	Born September 4 in Kansas City, Missouri
1971	Graduates from Stanford University with degree in psychology
1971	Turns professional
1990	Resigns from Kansas City Country Club over admission policies, forcing rift with his father
1993	Criticizes comedian Bill Murray for behavior at pro-am tournament
1994	Writes letter of complaint to CBS about golf broadcaster Gary McCord
1999	Final year as PGA Tour regular

Awards and Accomplishments

1974	Wins Western Open for first pro championship
1975	British Open champion
1977	Masters and British Open champion
1977-79	Wins Vardon Trophy for lowest stroke average on PGA Tour for three straight years
1977-80	Leading PGA Tour money winner four straight years
1980	British Open champion
1981	Masters champion
1982	U.S. Open and British Open champion
1983	British Open champion
1984	Leading PGA Tour money winner
1988	Inducted into World Hall of Fame
1989	Member of winning Ryder Cup team
1993	Member of winning Ryder Cup team
1999	Joins Senior PGA Tour September 6 and wins Bank One Championship two weeks later
1999	Named honorary member of the Royal & Ancient Golf Club of St. Andrews
2001	Wins Senior PGA Championship
2001	Inducted into Bay Area Sports Hall of Fame

said in a March, 2001 interview with *Golf Digest*. "And some since." But at the 1977 Masters, Watson nailed four birdies on the final six holes to beat Nicklaus by two at Augusta National. Cautious play that day was not an option. "I knew I had to make some birdies to win," Watson said. "I couldn't make pars to beat Jack."

Among Watson's challenges was an approach shot on No. 12 with a bug resting on his ball. "I asked a USGA (United States Golf Association) official could I lift it and he said, 'Of course you can't,'" Watson recalled. "Nicklaus makes birdie and this little bug was on the back of my ball." But Watson made par on 12. The two dueled again a few months later, at the British Open in Turnberry. Watson prevailed by a stroke, shooting 65s each of the last two rounds.

Then came "The Shot" in 1982. "No matter how many victories have may still have left in him, Watson will always be remembered for The Shot," said Florida-based golf writer Edward Kiersh on the *Cigar Aficiando* web site. Locked against Nicklaus again, this time at the U.S. Open at Pebble Beach, California, Watson found himself in jeopardy on the 17th hole, "a ticklish par-3 hugging the coastline," Kiersh wrote.

Watson's tee shot landed in a grass thicket with a brutal downslope. A bogey loomed. "Then came what many golf aficionados call The Miracle," Kiersh wrote. "Standing ankle-deep in the rough, with the winds buffeting his slight torso, Watson hit a very high chip shot that seemed to have enough momentum to roll six to eight feet past the cup. Yet the ball broke right, straight into the cup." The crowd screamed in delight, and Watson birdied No. 18 to secure the trophy.

Took Strong Stands

Watson's stridency emerged frequently in the 1990s, first by resigning from the Kansas City Country Club because it denied membership to Jewish friend Henry Bloch, the founder of tax preparation company H&R Block. His move triggered a rift with his father that took years to settle. When the club adjusted its membership criteria, Watson rejoined. He also took aim at comedian Bill Murray and CBS commentator Gary McCord when

he felt they carried their irreverence too far. He also refused to autograph a menu for European team member Sam Torrance while captain of the competing U.S. Ryder Cup team. "That humorless, moral absolutism has made him an anachronism in this era of over-indulged **Latrell Sprewell**s," Kiersh wrote, referring to a pro basketball player who once tried to choke his coach.

Watson's game tailed off through the 1990s, largely because his putting game took a turn for the worse. He blew a final round lead in the 1994 British Open (putting also cost him at the 1987 U.S. Open, which he lost by a stroke), and several three-putts that year cost him a victory at Pebble Beach. He joined the Senior Tour in 1999, and in May, 2001, his Senior PGA Championship provided some consolation for the one mainstream Grand Slam event he never won. He painfully recalled blowing a five-stroke lead on the final day in 1978 and losing a playoff to John Mahaffey.

Watson finished in the top 31 on the 2002 Champions Tour money list. Twice in three years he won the season-ending Senior Tour Championship. He still competes in the Grand Slam events, and at the PGA Championship in Chaska, Minnesota, made the cut and on the final day, tied **Tiger Woods** for low round of the day, at 67.

In late January, 2003, Watson acknowledged that Bruce Edwards, his caddie of more than three decades, has been diagnosed with amyotrophic lateral sclerosis, commonly known as **Lou Gehrig**'s disease. Watson said he would stick by his caddie and longtime friend.

Watson's Legacy

Watson is active with many charities and other community-based endeavors, particularly around his native

Kansas City. He has designed golf courses and has worked to make golf more accessible to children.

FURTHER INFORMATION

Books

Corcoran, Mike. *Duel in the Sun: Tom Watson and Jack Nicklaus in the Battle of Turnberry.* New York: Simon & Schuster, 2002.

Other

"An Interview with Tom Watson." ASAP Sports, http://www.asapsports.com/golf/2001pgasench/052701TW.html, (May 27, 2001).

Eubanks, Robert. "Watson Outguns Nicklaus for Masters Championship." *Sports Illustrated,* http://sports illustrated.com/augusta/history/ac/1977, (January 15, 2003).

Giannone, John. "Senior Citizen: Tom Watson Ready to Challenge Senior Tour." *CNN-Sports Illustrated,* http://sportsillustrated.com/thenetwork/news/1999/09/09/one_on_one_watson/, (April 23,2000).

Jenkins, Dan. "The Beast Brought Out His Best." *Sports Illustrated,* http://sportsillustrated.cnn.com/golf/1999/british_open/news/1999/07/12/britishflash75/, (January 15, 2003).

Kiersh, Edward. "Watson in Winter." *Cigar Aficiando,* http://www.cigaraficiando.com/Cigar/Aficiando/people/fd1098.html, (September/October, 1998).

PGA.com, Tom Watson Biographical Information. http://www.golfweb.com/players/00/22/56/bio.html, (January 15, 2003).

Seitz, Nick. "Tom Terrific." *Golf Digest,* http://www.golfdigest.com/features/index.ssf?/features/tom_terr_5681fxic.html, (March, 2001).

Voepel, Mechelle. "Bruce Edwards, caddie and friend to Tom Watson, diagnosed with ALS." *Kansas City Star,* http://www.kansascity.com/mld/kansascity/sports/5008974.htm, (January 23, 2003).

Westin, David. "Watson's Farewell Tour Grinds On." *CNN-Sports Illustrated,* http://www.cnnsi.com/augusta/stories/040499/oth_124-8021.shtml, (April 3, 1999).

Westin, David. "Who's Won What? Even the Major Golfers Aren't Sure." *CNN-Sports Illustrated,* http://sportsillustrated.cnn.com/augusta/stories/040998/oth_majors.shtml, (April 9, 1998).

World Golf Village, Tom Watson Profile. http://www.wgv.com/hof/members/twatson.html, (January 15, 2003).

Sketch by Paul Burton

Ricky Watters
1969-

American football player

Running back Ricky Watters scored five touchdowns in a National Football League playoff game and three in a Super Bowl. He also helped Notre Dame win a national collegiate championship from a different position, wide receiver. So it was no surprise that as the 2002 playoffs beckoned, the Tampa Bay Buccaneers and other NFL teams tried to coax Watters out of retirement. No one, however, could come to terms with Watters and his agent.

Watters in 10 seasons rushed for 10,643 yards while helping the San Francisco 49ers, Philadelphia Eagles, and Seattle Seahawks make the playoffs. He became the first NFL running back to rush for more than 1,000 yards for three different teams and qualified five times for the Pro Bowl, the NFL's all-star game.

Helped Irish Win Title

Watters, born and raised in Harrisburg, Pennsylvania, was twice an all-state running back at Bishop McDevitt High School, where he also lettered in basketball and track. At Notre Dame, Coach Lou Holtz switched Watters to wide receiver and Watters helped lead the Irish to a national championship with 15 receptions for 286 yards and two touchdowns. In the decisive Fiesta Bowl against West Virginia, Watters caught a 54-yard pass that set up Notre Dame's final touchdown in a 34-21 victory. While at Notre Dame, Watters also returned a 97 yard punt for a touchdown, one of three punt-returns touchdowns he had for the Irish.

Drafted by 49ers

San Francisco took Watters in the second round of the 1991 draft, but he missed the entire season when he

Ricky Watters

Chronology

1969	Born in Harrisburg, Pennsylvania
1987	Graduated from Bishop McDevitt High School in Harrisburg; enrolled at University of Notre Dame
1991	Graduated from Notre Dame with B.A. in design; second-round pick by San Francisco 49ers in NFL draft, but missed entire season with broken left foot suffered in first week of training camp.
1992	Selected to first of five straight Pro Bowl squads after rushing for 1,013 yards, most ever by a 49er rookie
1995	Signed with Philadelphia Eagles as transition player when 49ers did not match offer sheet.
1998	Signed as free agent with Seattle Seahawks
2001	Retired after playing only five games for Seahawks that season; missed his first start after 116 games due to shoulder injury

Awards and Accomplishments

1988	Converted from running back to wide receiver and helped Notre Dame win national championship
1989	Returned punt for 97-yard touchdown, a Notre Dame record, against Southern Methodist
1993	Scored NFL-record five touchdowns in playoff game against New York Giants
1994	American Cancer Society's Man of the Year
1995	Scored three touchdowns as San Francisco 49ers routed San Diego Chargers 49-26 in Super Bowl XXIX
1998	Became first NFL rusher to gain 1,000 yards with three different teams

broke his left foot in the first week of training camp. He made up for his disappointment the following season, rushing for 1,013 yards, the most ever by a first-year 49er. He was selected to the NFL squad in the Pro Bowl, and he also led the team with nine rushing touchdowns. A year later, Watters rushed for an NFL-record five touchdowns in an NFC divisional playoff game in San Francisco, which the 49ers won 44-3. But San Francisco, as it did the previous year, lost the NFC title game to the Dallas Cowboys and ended their season one victory short of the Super Bowl.

Super Bowl Champs

In 1994, the 49ers scored 505 points, a 31.6 points-per-game average, during the season while sporting a 13-3 mark. They set a record 131 points in three postseason games, averaging almost 44 points. And, they finally emerged from the Cowboys' shadows, defeating Dallas 38-28 in the NFC championship game in San Francisco.

Super Bowl XXIX was played in Miami, and San Francisco lived up to its billing as a heavy favorite, scoring four first-half touchdowns in a 49-26 rout that was even more lopsided than the score indicated (it was 49-10 late in the fourth quarter). Watters scored on touchdown passes of 51 and eight yards, and rushed for a nine-yard score in the second half; he rushed 15 times for 47 yards. "After you work so hard and finally attain it, it is just a beautiful thing," said Watters, who performed

rap impersonations at the interview podium. "It's a dream come true, and it seems like I'm going to wake up and realize we haven't played yet. And I don't want that to happen." He added: "I hope we rank up there with the best of them. I think we put ourselves in a position to be ranked up there. But I'll leave that to those fat guys on ESPN who sit around and talk about it."

Helps Eagles, Seahawks

Unfortunately Watters and the 49ers parted amid acrimony. He criticized the front office and offensive coordinator for lack of respect; the team said he was selfish. Watters was a transition free agent, and the Eagles signed him to an offer sheet that San Francisco chose not to match. He helped lead the Eagles into the NFC playoffs for two consecutive years. In 1995 and 1996, Watters rushed for 1,273 and 1,411 yards, respectively, in the regular season and a combined 24 touchdowns. Some media and fans, however, criticized him for his attitude.

In 1998, Watters became a free-agent and signed with the Seattle Seahawks. He gained more than 1,200 yards in both 1998 and 1999, and in his second year with the team, **Mike Holmgren**, who had been his offensive coordinator in San Francisco, became the Seahawks' head coach. Seattle surprisingly won the AFC West title that season. Beset by injuries, Watters played but five games in 2001.

Career Statistics

Yr	Team	Rushing				Receiving				Fumbles	
		ATT	YDS	AVG	TD	REC	YDS	AVG	TD	FUM	LST
1992	SF	206	1013	4.9	9	43	405	9.4	2	2	0
1993	SF	208	950	4.6	10	31	326	10.5	1	5	0
1994	SF	239	877	3.7	6	66	719	10.9	5	8	3
1995	PHI	337	1273	3.8	11	62	434	7.0	1	6	3
1996	PHI	353	1411	4.0	13	51	444	8.7	0	5	5
1997	PHI	285	1110	3.9	7	48	440	9.2	0	3	2
1998	SEA	319	1239	3.9	9	52	373	7.2	0	4	2
1999	SEA	325	1210	3.7	5	40	387	9.7	2	4	4
2000	SEA	278	1242	4.5	7	63	613	9.7	2	5	2
2001	SEA	72	318	4.4	1	11	107	9.7	0	1	0
TOTAL		2622	10643	4.1	78	467	4248	9.1	13	43	21

PHI: Philadelphia Eagles; SEA: Seattle Seahawks; SF: San Francisco 49ers.

Watters sat out the entire 2002 season, rejecting offers from several teams because he wanted more money. He often emphasized that he would retire rather than play for the minimum base salary. "People might think he's bluffing but, believe me, he isn't," agent Ralph Cindrich said in August, 2002. "He feels he has a value beyond the minimum. If that's all teams are going to offer him, then he's going to sit, and that will be it. Ricky will be retired and he is at peace with that." In early 2003, his future in football remained unclear.

Worthy of Enshrinement?

Michael Lev, senior editor of ProFootballWeekly, wrote in 2000: "Ricky Watters deserves to go to the Hall of Fame. And he shouldn't have to pay to get in. Watters' teams win games. Funny how the 49ers, Eagles and Seahawks made the playoffs despite having a supposed locker-room cancer dragging them down. Watters' reputation for selfishness and immaturity precedes him. No one can forget his alligator-arms maneuver with the Eagles, when he failed to reach for a slightly overthrown pass for fear of getting clocked and basically said afterward, 'Why should I?' But how bad of an influence could Watters have been (especially early in his career) if the teams he played for kept winning?"

FURTHER INFORMATION

Other

Lev, Michael. "Watters Works: Ricky's Résumé is Worthy of Future Hall of Fame Debate." ProFootball-Weekly. http:/archive.profootballweekly.com/content/archives/features_2000/lev_071000.asp, (July 10, 2000).

NFL.com, Ricky Watters Profile, http://nfl.com, (January 2, 2003).

Pasquarelli, Len. "Watters Sitting and Waiting." ESPN.com, http://espn.go.com/nfl/columns/pasquarelli_len/1421908.html, (August 23, 2002).

"Watters Puts on Show during and after the Game." Nando Times, http://cgi.nando.net, (January 2, 2003).

Sketch by Paul Burton

Karrie Webb
1974-

Australian golfer

Australian golf star Karrie (pronounced "kahr-rie," rhymes with "starry") Webb has been fighting **Annika Sorenstam** for the title of the best female golfer in the world since Webb joined the Ladies Professional Golf Association (LPGA) Tour in 1995. Webb, who was only 20 when she joined the tour, has been compared repeatedly to **Tiger Woods**, since both are young phenoms—with excellent records of wins—who regularly outplay most of the veterans on their respective tours.

Good Teachers

Webb was drawn to the sport of golf at a very young age. Her parents and maternal grandparents were golfers, and by age four Webb, with her toy club, was following them on the links around their hometown of Ayr, Australia. "They were about the only two people in the world who were patient enough to go out with a four-year-old and play golf on a Sunday morning," Webb later said of her grandparents.

Webb's parents bought her a real set of golf clubs for her eighth birthday, and soon after she started taking golf lessons from her neighbor, Kelvin Haller, a self-taught local golf player and greenkeeper at the Ayr course. Haller

Karrie Webb

Chronology

1974	Born December 21 in Ayr, Queensland, Australia, the first of Robert and Evelyn Webb's three daughters
1990	Her golf teacher, Kelvin Haller, becomes a quadriplegic
1992-94	Represents Australia in amateur international competitions
1994	Turns professional in October
1995	Joins LPGA Tour in October
1996	Breaks up with fiancé
1999	Achieves first victory in a major tournament

lived next door to a drive-in movie theater, and during the day he would have his students practice their drives by hitting balls into the theater's empty parking lot. By the age of 12 Webb had decided that she wanted to be a professional golfer, and by her mid-teens she was well on her way, competing in amateur events and becoming one of the best golfers in the area. She and Haller's nephews, Ryan and Todd Haller, often played together, and Karrie and Todd eventually became engaged. He served as her caddie early in her career, but the two broke up in 1996.

Kelvin Haller has remained Webb's only coach since those first lessons, even though he suffered a stroke in 1990, at the age of 36, that left him almost completely paralyzed. He still helps Webb to improve her swing when she returns to Ayr during the off-season, and Webb says that having his coaching fresh in her mind is why she usually performs so well in the early events of the tour each year. The two have also developed a unique long-distance coaching relationship that they use during the season: Webb's caddie uses specialized, fixed cameras to record digital videos of Webb's swing from the same two angles each time, and then e-mails the videos, along with such data as the distance and location of each shot, to Haller. Haller then analyzes Webb's swing and gives her advice over the phone.

LPGA Career

Webb turned professional two months before her twentieth birthday and then spent a year playing professional golf in Europe and on the Futures Tour in the United States. In 1995 she won the Weetabix Women's British Open while still on the Women Professional Golfers' European Tour. That year Webb qualified for the LPGA Tour, on her first try, by finishing second at the LPGA qualifying tournament despite playing with a broken wrist.

The next year Webb took the golf world by storm. She won the HealthSouth Inaugural, only the second tournament she competed in as a member of the LPGA Tour, and then went on to win three other events that season. She set an earnings record by becoming the first female player ever to win more than $1 million in a season, and she was also the only rookie, male or female, to make over $1 million in his or her first season.

Not long after Webb joined the LPGA Tour, a rivalry of sorts developed between her and the then-current champion, Sorenstam. It is not a particularly acrimonious rivalry, but the two young women find themselves battling each other for wins and for first place in the statistics more often than they find themselves battling any other single golfer. Not since 1994 has a golfer not named Webb or Sorenstam won the Vare Trophy for lowest scoring average, for example, and when Webb won an astounding seven tournaments in 2000, Sorenstam came roaring back to win eight in 2001.

In 1999 Webb got her first victory in a major tournament, the du Maurier Classic, and set an LPGA scoring average record with 69.43. Then, in 2000, Webb won the first four tournaments she entered. She added only three more wins in the rest of the season (partially because she took some time off to return to Australia and run with the Olympic torch before the Sydney Olympics), but two of those wins were at majors: the Nabisco Championship and the U.S. Women's Open. That year Webb also won her second consecutive player of the year award and Vare Trophy. Throughout the year, comparisons between Webb and Professional Golfers' Association star Tiger Woods were ubiquitous. Fans of women's golf saw sexism in the fact that Woods's achievements received so much more attention from the media than Webb's did, and several even suggested that the two compete head-to-head to prove that Webb was just as good a golfer as Woods.

Awards and Accomplishments

1994	Australian Stroke Play champion
1995	Named Rookie of the Year on the Women Professional Golfers' European Tour
1995, 1997, 2002	Wins Weetabix Women's British Open
1996	Becomes the first player in LPGA history to earn more than $1 million in a single season
1996	Named Rookie of the Year on the LPGA Tour
1996	Receives ESPY Award from ESPN for Female Golfer of the Year
1997, 1999-2000	Wins Vare Trophy for lowest scoring average
1999	Wins du Maurier Classic
1999-2000	Named Rolex Player of the Year
2000	Wins Nabisco Championship
2000	Earns enough points to qualify for LPGA Hall of Fame (but must still meet ten-year membership requirement)
2000	Recipient of Crowne Plaza Achievement Award
2000-01	Wins U.S. Women's Open
2001	Wins McDonald's LPGA Championship
2001	Becomes youngest woman ever to achieve career Grand Slam

Total of 28 official LPGA and 2 unofficial victories.

Webb Feat

In victory Webb showed her subtle wit and indomitable competitiveness, too. Late on Sunday afternoon somebody reminded her that Woods needed six attempts to win the U.S. Open and that Webb had needed only five. She smiled, licked her right index finger, and made a notch mark in the air. That's how she does her best public speaking: with actions.

Source: Bamberger, Michael. *Sports Illustrated* (July 31, 2000): G5+.

Early in the 2001 season, Sorenstam seemed to be emerging as the dominant player and Webb seemed to be fading. Webb was still playing excellent golf—for the second consecutive year she made every single cut, and she usually finished in the top—but she just could not seem to win. Then, in June, Webb ran away from the rest of the field at the U.S. Women's Open to win by eight strokes. Not since 1980 had someone won that event by that large of a margin.

A Victory and a Loss on the Same Day

A month later, Webb became only the fifth woman in history to win the career Grand Slam when she won the McDonald's LPGA Championship at the DuPont Country Club in Wilmington, Delaware. At 26, she was also the youngest woman to achieve this feat. The achievement, however, was bittersweet for her: her maternal grandfather, Mick Collinson, had suffered a stroke back in Australia, and Webb revealed after her last round that she had considered withdrawing from the tournament and flying home to be with him. Her parents, who had flown in from Australia for the event, booked seats on a flight home early Sunday afternoon after they heard about Collinson's condition, and Webb went so far as to reserve a seat for herself as well. But her parents convinced her that, golf lover that he was, Collinson would have wanted her to stay and play her last round. She did, fighting back tears, but she could not really appreciate her achievement at the time. As Bill Fields of *Golf World* reported: "It will sink in eventually, and I know it will be really special," she said after the final round. "The only thing I wanted to do was win for my granddad, and that's all I kept thinking about."

Webb did not have as strong of a year in 2002 as she did in 2000 and 2001. She won only two tournaments, although one of them, the Women's British Open, was a major. It was her sixth win in the last 19 Grand Slam events. Some golf aficionados thought that Webb should be credited with a Super Career Grand Slam for this win, since with it she had won five out of four major championships: When Webb won the du Maurier in 1999 it was a major, but in 2001 the Women's British Open replaced it.

Potential Ambassador for the Sport

Throughout much of her early career, Webb was reticent to speak openly to reporters or to create much of a public personality at all, particularly after the press wrote some speculative articles about her personal life after her breakup with Todd Haller. She is notorious for rarely removing her sunglasses, for example. Yet Webb and her friends have always insisted that she is a warm person in private, that she is simply shy. Indeed, after her first few seasons she did become more open and humorous on and off the course. Her masterful remarks at the gala party that the LPGA held at the beginning of the 2000 season to mark the association's fiftieth anniversary, for example, did a great deal to erase her former reputation for shyness. They also did much to endear her to the powers that be in the LPGA, which is searching for a charismatic and successful player to sell professional women's golf to potential fans.

Between Webb and Sorenstam, fans of women's professional golf have been enjoying an unusual treat: A record-breaking level of golf excellence and a degree of competition that has been absent from the Tiger Woods-dominated men's scene. As Webb entered her eighth full year of touring with the LPGA in 2003 at a still-young 28, her fans would have many more years of phenomenal golf to look forward to.

FURTHER INFORMATION
Books

Happell, Charles. *Karrie Webb*. Melbourne, Australia: Legend Books, 2002.

Tresidder, Phil. *Karrie Webb: The Making of Golf's Tigress*. Sydney: Pan Macmillan Australia, 2000.

Periodicals

Bamberger, Michael. "Webb Feat." *Sports Illustrated* (July 31, 2000): G5+.

Callahan, Tom. "Webbmaster: Karrie and Kel." *Golf Digest* (January 2001): 92.

Diaz, Jaime. "Karrie Webb's Final Frontier." *Golf World* (July 6, 2001): 48.

———. "Unharried Karrie." *Sports Illustrated* (August 9, 1999): G6.

Fields, Bill. "Mixed Emotions." *Golf World* (June 29, 2001): 16.

———. "Walking the Walk." *Golf World* (June 8, 2001): 20.

Garrity, John. "Peer Group." *Sports Illustrated* (May 12, 1997): 68-71.

———. "Sixth Sense: Despite a So-so Year, Karrie Webb Had a Feeling She'd Make History at the Final Major of 2002." *Sports Illustrated* (August 19, 2002): G4+.

———. "Somber Slam: Karrie Webb's Concern over a Loved One Took the Joy Out of a Historic Victory." *Sports Illustrated* (July 2, 2001): 1.

Huggan, John. "Webb Gem." *Golf World* (August 16, 2002): 14.

Johnson, Sal. "The Week." *Sports Illustrated* (March 4, 2002): G25+.

"Landing in the Green." *People Weekly* (April 28, 1997): 68.

Mickey, Lisa D. "Leaving Well Enough Alone." *Golf World* (September 15, 2000): 9.

Moriarty, Jim. "History for the Taking." *Golf World* (June 28, 2002): 22.

Rosaforte, Tim. "Sitting Pretty." *Golf World* (March 10, 2000): 16.

Shipnuck, Alan. "Ayr Power." *Sports Illustrated* (March 13, 2000): 46+.

Yen, Yi-Wyn. "Trumped." *Sports Illustrated* (November 26, 2001): G17+.

Other

"Karrie Webb." LPGA.com. http://www.lpga.com/players/playerpage.cfm?player_id=53 (January 17, 2003).

"LPGA Player Bio: Karrie Webb." GolfWeb. http://services.golfweb.com/ga/bios/lpga/webb_karrie.html (January 16, 2003).

Sketch by Julia Bauder

Spud Webb
1963-

American basketball player

Spud Webb

Standing only five feet, seven inches tall, Spud Webb was one of the shortest players in National Basketball Association (NBA) history. Despite his diminutive size, Webb enjoyed superstardom as a small man in a big man's game. In what was perhaps the crowning achievement of his twelve-year career in professional basketball, Webb won the NBA Slam Dunk Championship in 1986. Looking back on this win, Webb recalled, "No one expected or imagined that a person of my size could win the slam dunk contest. It was the highlight of my career and everybody recognizes me from the slam dunk contest. But I played twelve years in the NBA and performed every year, that's what you really want to be recognized for. There's no way to dodge the stigma that's put on you for winning the slam dunk contest at my size."

Born in Dallas, Texas

He was born Anthony Jerome Webb in Dallas, Texas, on July 13, 1963. Living with his parents and five siblings in a small, three-bedroom home, he began playing basketball while still quite young, overcoming the limitations of his small stature with his uncanny ability to jump higher than the bigger kids in the neighborhood. Early in his teens, Webb, standing only four feet, 11 inches tall, found that he could dunk the basketball by hurling his small frame high into the air to bring himself closer to the basket. He would rush at the basket, push himself into the air, clearing the ground by more than four feet, and slam the basketball through the hoop.

<table>
<tr><td colspan="2">Chronology</td></tr>
<tr><td>1963</td><td>Born July 13 in Dallas, Texas</td></tr>
<tr><td>1981</td><td>Graduates from Wilmer-Hutchins High School</td></tr>
<tr><td>1981-83</td><td>Attends Midland Junior College in Midland, Texas</td></tr>
<tr><td>1983-85</td><td>Attends North Carolina State University</td></tr>
<tr><td>1985</td><td>Drafted by Detroit Pistons but later cut from the team</td></tr>
<tr><td>1985-91</td><td>Plays for Atlanta Hawks</td></tr>
<tr><td>1991-95</td><td>Traded by Hawks to Sacramento Kings</td></tr>
<tr><td>1995</td><td>Traded by Kings to Hawks</td></tr>
<tr><td>1996</td><td>Traded by Hawks to Minnesota Timberwolves</td></tr>
<tr><td>1998</td><td>Signed to 10-day contract by Orlando Magic</td></tr>
</table>

Although Webb made it onto his junior high school basketball team, he found himself spending almost all of his time on the bench, once again hampered by his small size. When he finally convinced the coach to let him play, Webb scored twenty points in his first game. At Wilmer-Hutchins High School, Webb was rejected by the varsity team and told to play junior varsity ball because of his size. So discouraged that he almost abandoned basketball altogether, he decided instead to devote all his energies to improving his game. When he eventually made it onto the varsity team, he averaged twenty-six points a game and as a senior was named Player of the Year. He also was one of ten Texas high school players to be named to the All-State team.

Enrolls at Midland Junior College

Despite his impressive high school record, colleges showed little interest in Webb. Unwilling to give up on his dream of college, he enrolled at Midland Junior College and in 1982 led Midland's basketball team to the national junior college championship. After seeing Webb play for Midland, Tom Abatemarco, assistant basketball coach at North Carolina State University, suggested to his boss—the late Jim Valvano—that they invite the diminutive player to visit N.C. State. Despite his initial misgivings, based on Webb's small stature, Valvano was impressed enough by the Texan to offer him a scholarship. It proved to be a wise decision, for Webb in 1985 led N.C. State's Wolfpack to the Sweet 16 in the NCAA Tournament.

Passed over in the NBA draft because of his size, a disappointed Webb played briefly for the United States Basketball League. Finally, in the fourth round of the 1985 NBA draft, he was selected by the Detroit Pistons, only to be cut by the team before the season began. Given an opportunity to try out for the Atlanta Hawks, Webb impressed the team's coaching staff with his incredible jumping ability and was signed to a contract. For the next six years, he teamed with Doc Rivers to average over ten points and five assists a game. In 1986, Webb blew away the competition—including high-flying teammate **Dominique Wilkins**—to win the NBA Slam Dunk Championship.

<table>
<tr><td colspan="2">Awards and Accomplishments</td></tr>
<tr><td>1981</td><td>Named Player of the Year at Wilmer-Hutchins High School</td></tr>
<tr><td>1981</td><td>Named to the Texas All-State High School Team</td></tr>
<tr><td>1982</td><td>Led Midland Junior College team to national junior college title</td></tr>
<tr><td>1985</td><td>Led N.C. State to Sweet 16 in NCAA Tournament</td></tr>
<tr><td>1986</td><td>Wins NBA Slam Dunk Contest</td></tr>
</table>

Spends Hours Training

Although Webb somehow made it all look easy, he made it clear that his performance was the result of years of hard work and practice. "Most people believe that I can dunk and play in the NBA because of my God-given talent," he said. "This is only half true. I also spent countless hours training to improve my jumping ability. I must have tried dunking over 1,000 times before I actually did it. I never gave up on my goal no matter how impossible it seemed, and neither should you."

After six seasons with the Hawks, Webb was traded from Atlanta to the Sacramento Kings, where he played from 1991 until 1995, when he was traded back to the Hawks by the Kings. His second stint with the Hawks was short-lived. In February 1996 he and Hawks center Andrew Lang were traded to the Minnesota Timberwolves in exchange for forward Christian Laettner and center Sean Rooks. After playing out the remainder of the 1995-1996 season with the Timberwolves, Webb left the NBA to play briefly in Italy. In 1998 he returned to American basketball after signing a ten-day contract with the Orlando Magic. When the Magic waived Webb, he announced his retirement from professional basketball.

Since leaving basketball Webb has kept busy by making the rounds on the professional speaking circuit. As founder and president of Spud Webb Enterprises, headquartered in central Florida, Webb speaks extensively around the country, focusing on his personal experiences in overcoming insurmountable obstacles and achieving the seemingly unachievable. As he tells audiences, "I never let my size keep me from excelling in a sport in which the odds of making it to the professional level are nearly impossible." At home near Dallas, Webb today spends most of his free time trying to perfect his golf game. In an interview with Tony Haynes, a contributing editor for N.C. State's GOPACK.com, Webb said: "I get up and go play golf just about every day. I live on the golf course. I've been bitten by the bug and am addicted to the game. It wasn't tough to leave the game of basketball because no one ever expected me to be able to play. I still have a passion for watching the game, but the only thing I miss about it is the competition and hanging out with the fellows. The competitiveness is still there to go out and take on any golf course."

Career Statistics

Yr	Team	GP	Pts	FG%	3P%	FT%	RPG	APG	SPG	BPG
1985-86	ATL	79	7.8	48.3	18.2	78.5	1.6	4.3	1.0	0.1
1986-87	ATL	33	6.8	43.8	16.7	76.2	1.8	5.1	1.0	0.1
1987-88	ATL	82	6.0	47.5	5.3	81.7	1.8	4.1	0.8	0.1
1988-89	ATL	81	3.9	45.9	4.5	86.7	1.5	3.5	0.9	0.1
1989-90	ATL	82	9.2	47.7	5.3	87.1	2.5	5.8	1.3	0.1
1990-91	ATL	75	13.4	44.7	32.1	86.8	2.3	5.6	1.6	0.1
1991-92	SAC	77	16.0	44.5	36.7	85.9	2.9	7.1	1.6	0.3
1992-93	SAC	69	14.5	43.3	27.4	85.1	2.8	7.0	1.5	0.1
1993-94	SAC	79	12.7	46.0	33.5	81.3	2.8	6.7	1.2	0.3
1994-95	SAC	78	11.6	43.8	33.1	93.4	2.3	6.2	1.0	0.1
1995-96	ATL	51	5.9	46.8	31.6	85.1	1.2	2.7	0.5	0.0
1995-96	MIN	26	9.4	39.4	40.3	87.9	1.5	5.9	1.0	0.2
1997-98	ORL	4	3.0	41.7	0.0	100.0	0.8	1.3	0.3	0.0
TOTAL		814	9.9	45.2	31.4	84.8	2.1	5.3	1.1	0.1

ATL: Atlanta Hawks; MIN: Minnesota Timber Wolves; ORL: Orlando Magic; SAC: Sacramento Kings.

CONTACT INFORMATION

Address: Spud Webb, c/o Spud Webb Enterprises, Orlando, FL . Phone: (407) 445-7180. Email: spud@spudwebb.net. Online: http://www.spudwebb.net.

SELECTED WRITINGS BY WEBB:

Flying High, HarperCollins, 1988.

FURTHER INFORMATION

Books

"Jim Valvano." *Almanac of Famous People,* 6th ed. Detroit: Gale Group, 1998.

"Spud Webb." *Almanac of Famous People,* 6th ed. Detroit: Gale Group, 1998.

"Spud Webb." *Who's Who Among African Americans,* 14th ed. Detroit: Gale Group, 2001.

Periodicals

Cornwell, Susan. "T-Wolves Trade Laettner to Hawks on Trade Deadline Day." Reuters (February 22, 1996).

McCallum, Jack. "Inside the NBA." *Sports Illustrated* (March 18, 1991).

McKay, Matt. "Webb Stays with Basketball, But His New Passion Is Golf." *Dallas Morning News* (May 1, 1998): 17B.

Other

"Anthony 'Spud' Webb." NBA Stars in Europe. http://www.geocities.com/tzovas/nbastars/webb_spud.html (December 27, 2002).

"Behind the Scenes with Tony Haynes: Spud Webb Is Still Looking Up." GoPack.com. http://gopack.ocsn.com/genrel/011702aaa.html (December 27, 2002).

"NBA Great Spud Webb Joins the Pro-Speaking Circuit!" Spud Webb Enterprises. http://www.nopasports.com/spudwebb/main.htm (December 27, 2002).

Sketch by Don Amerman

Chris Webber
1973-

American basketball player

Chris Webber, known as C-Webb, is an athletic and dynamic forward who, at six-feet-ten-inches, can get the crowd on its feet with spectacular dunks and nearly poetic play up and down the floor. In the media limelight since high school, Webber has become one of the shining stars of the National Basketball Association (NBA) during his ten-year career. As a member of the Sacramento Kings since 1999 he is a team leader and a fan favorite. However, the path for this member of the University of Michigan's acclaimed "Fab Five" had several tough years in the NBA before putting it all together.

Growing up in Detroit

Mayce Edward Christopher Webber III was born on March 1, 1973, in Detroit, Michigan, the oldest of five children. His father, Mayce, was a plant foreman for General Motors, often working double shifts, and his mother, Doris, taught special needs children in the Detroit school system. Although reared in a tough lower-middle-class Detroit neighborhood with few positive economic and social opportunities, Webber benefited

Chris Webber

Chronology

1973	Born March 1 in Detroit, Michigan
1987-91	Stars in basketball at Country Day High in Birmingham, Michigan
1991-93	Stars as a member of the University of Michigan's "Fab Five"
1993	Begins career in National Basketball Association (NBA) with the Golden State Warriors
1994	Traded to the Washington Bullets (now known as the Wizards)
1998	Stopped for speeding, arrested for marijuana possession, assault, and resisting arrest; traded to the Sacramento Kings
2001	Leads Kings to first postseason victory in 20 years

from a close-knit family with supportive parents who kept a close eye on their son.

Webber did not play much basketball until the summer before entering the sixth grade. His father encouraged him to take up the sport because his son was already exceptionally tall for his age. Joining a summer basketball program, with little idea how to play, Webber almost quit because the other kids teased him for his awkwardness. Encouraged by his father to tough it out, Webber was helped by a local coach who recognized his potential and spent hours working with him to improve his play, which paid huge dividends for Webber. Despite Webber's protests, his parents enrolled him as a freshman at Detroit Country Day High, located in an upper-middle-class suburb of Birmingham. During his time at Country Day, Webber led the school to three state basketball championships and averaged twenty-eight points and thirteen rebounds per game during his senior year. In 1991 he was named Michigan's Mr. Basketball and National High School Player of the Year.

The "Fab Five"

After the final game of the 1991 state championship, Webber announced to a group of reporters that he would play for the University of Michigan Wolverines. There, under the leadership of Coach Steve Fisher, Webber joined four other highly recruited freshmen: Ray Jackson, Juwan Howard, Jim King, and Jalen Rose. When Fisher put all five freshmen in the starting line in February of 1992, the team was dubbed the Fab Five. Known

for their cocky, self-assured play, on-court trash talk, and knee-length shorts that soon became the national trend in uniforms, the Fab Five earned a bid to the 1992 National Collegiate Athletic Association (NCAA) tournament as a sixth seed. Webber and his teammates reached the finals, but were soundly beaten by the Duke Blue Devils, 71-51. Webber was named the Big Ten Freshman of the Year, averaging 15.5 points per game and leading the conference in rebounding.

With all the Fab Five returning as sophomores, great things were expected of the Wolverines. Webber did not disappoint: he led his team in points per game (19.2) rebounds per game (10.1), blocks per game (2.1), and field goal percentage (.619). In March of 1993, the Wolverines were back in the final game of the NCAA tournament, this time favored to beat their opponent, the University of North Carolina Tar Heels. Webber poured in twenty-three points and grabbed eleven rebounds; however, in a fateful play, down by two points with eleven seconds left on the clock, he got caught in a trap in the corner near the Michigan bench. To avoid a turnover, he signaled for a timeout. But, because the Wolverines had no remaining timeouts, Webber was called for a technical foul. The Tar Heels made both free throws and ultimately won the championship 77-71.

Rookie of the Year

Webber was devastated by his mistake and at first vowed to return for his junior year to atone for his fatal error. However, with the NBA knocking at his door with promises of large salaries and future superstardom, Webber soon announced that he would forego his remaining years of college eligibility to enter the 1993 NBA draft. He was selected as the first overall pick by the Orlando Magic, who moments later traded him to the Golden State Warriors for **Penny Hardaway** and three draft choices. Webber signed a 15-year contract with the Warriors worth $74 million.

During his first season in the NBA, Webber posted extraordinary numbers, becoming the first NBA rookie to attain 1,000 points, 500 rebounds, 250 assists, 150 blocks, and 75 steals. However, even after earning Rookie of the Year honors and leading his team to a re-

Career Statistics

Yr	Team	GP	Pts	P/G	FG%	3P%	FT%	RPG	APG	SPG	BPG	TO
1994	GS	76	1333	17.5	.552	.000	.532	9.1	3.6	1.2	2.2	206
1995	WASH	54	1085	20.1	.495	.276	.502	9.6	4.7	1.5	1.6	167
1996	WASH	15	356	23.7	.543	.441	.594	7.6	5.0	1.8	.06	49
1997	WASH	72	1445	20.1	.518	.397	.565	10.3	4.6	1.7	1.9	230
1998	WASH	71	1555	21.9	.482	.317	.589	9.5	3.8	1.6	1.7	185
1999	SAC	42	839	20.0	.486	.118	.454	13.0	4.1	1.4	2.1	148
2000	SAC	75	1834	24.5	.483	.284	.751	10.5	4.6	1.6	1.7	218
2001	SAC	70	1898	27.1	.481	.071	.703	11.1	4.2	1.3	1.7	195
2002	SAC	54	1322	24.5	.495	.263	.749	10.1	4.8	1.7	1.4	158
TOTAL		529	11667	22.1	.498	.301	.627	10.2	4.3	1.5	1.8	1556

GS: Golden State Warriors; SAC: Sacramento Kings; WASH: Washington Wizards.

spectable record of 50-32, Webber let it be known that he was unhappy at Golden State. In the media frenzy that ensued to discover the source of Webber's discontentment, the young Warrior found himself in the midst of an ugly and well-publicized feud with Coach Don Nelson. The controversy tarnished Webber's image, causing him to be labeled as an overpaid prima donna. One month into his second NBA season Webber was traded to the Washington Bullets (now known as the Wizards), signing a one-year contract for $2.08 million.

Reunited with former Wolverine teammate Juwan Howard, Webber worked to regroup personally and professionally after arriving in Washington, D.C. An injured shoulder that eventually required surgery shortened Webber's 1994-95 to fifty-four games and the 1995-96 season to just fifteen games. Returning healthy in 1996, Webber posted excellent numbers, leading the Bullets in scoring (20.1 points per game), rebounding (9.6 per game), steals (1.5 per game), and minutes played (38.3 per game), earning his first invitation to the NBA All-Star Game.

Off the court, Webber once again ran into problems. In January of 1998 he was stopped for speeding on the way to practice. He was charged with numerous traffic violations as well as possession of marijuana. Assault and resisting arrest were also added after he became involved in an altercation with the arresting officer. Webber failed to clear his image and lost his contract with Fila after custom officials found marijuana in his gym bag while he was on a promotional tour for the footwear company.

Sacramento: A New Beginning

Despite his basketball abilities, the Wizards decided to rid themselves of the headaches caused by Webber's off-court antics and traded him to the Sacramento Kings in 1998. Webber, who responded bitterly to the trade, felt that the Wizards' organization was acting punitively and unfairly. Yet unexpectedly Sacramento became

Webber's chance to begin afresh. He later told *Sport,* "I thought it was the end of the world coming here, but it was a new beginning."

As a member of the Kings, Webber has cleaned up his image and consistently proves himself on the court. After a rough first five years in the NBA, he once again enjoys the game of basketball. Despite an opportunity to exercise his rights as a free agent in 2001, Webber chose to remain in Sacramento, a place he once considered the Siberia of professional basketball. In 2001 the Kings won its first postseason series in twenty years. During his tenure with the Kings, Webber has averaged over twenty-four points and eleven rebounds per game. With ongoing success on the floor and a new maturity, he continues to push himself to become an NBA superstar of the highest degree.

CONTACT INFORMATION

Address: Sacramento Kings, One Sports Parkway, Sacramento, California 95834. Phone: (916) 928-6900.

FURTHER INFORMATION

Books

Henderson, Ashyia, ed. *Contemporary Black Biography,* Volume 30. Detroit: Gale Group, 2001.

Newsmakers 1994, Issue 4. Detroit: Gale Research, 1994.

Sports Stars. Series 1-4. Detroit: U•X•L, 1994-98.

Who's Who Among African Americans, 14th ed. Detroit: Gale Group, 2001.

Periodicals

Adande, J. A. "The Quick Turn Around." *Sporting News* (November 22, 1999): 50.

Ballantini, Brett. "King for (Just) a Day?" *Basketball Digest* (April 2001): 24.

Dick Weber

Deveney, Sean. "A 'Desperate' Man." *Sporting News* (March 11, 2002): 20+.

Deveney, Sean. "Now is No Time for Webber to Leave Kings." *Sporting News* (July 9, 2001): 50.

"NBA Star Chris Webber Arrested." *Jet* (February 9, 1998): 51-52.

Ribowsky, Mark. "King Leery." *Sport* (February 2000): 28.

Sabino, David. "A Whole New Rap." *Sports Illustrated* (April 12, 1999): 42.

Schoenfeld, Bruce. "Getting a Read on Chris Webber." *Sporting News* (January 24, 1994): 36.

Taylor, Phil. "Beating the Blues." *Sports Illustrated* (April 19, 1993): 54.

Taylor, Phil. "Capital Gain." *Sports Illustrated* (November 28, 1994): 16.

Other

"Chris Webber." National Basketball Association. http://www.nba.com/ (December 11, 2002)

"Chris Webber." Sports Stats.com. http://www.sportsstats.com/bball/national/players/1990/Chris_Webber/ (December 11, 2002)

Sketch by Kari Bethel

Dick Weber
1929-

American bowler

Legendary professional bowler Dick Weber made bowling history in 2002 when he became the first bowler ever to win at least one Professional Bowlers Association (PBA) title in six consecutive decades. Weber, who won his first PBA title in 1959, grabbed his first title of the new millennium by winning the PBA Senior Regional Championship at New North Lanes in Taylorville, Illinois, on January 20, 2002. For his contributions to the world of pro bowling, Weber was inducted into the American Bowling Congress (ABC) Hall of Fame in 1970 and the PBA Hall of Fame in 1975. Weber ranks sixth on the PBA's all-time win list with twenty-six PBA Tour titles, and he's still going strong. Strong enough, in fact, to challenge his son, Pete Weber, a PBA Hall of Famer in his own right. With the younger Weber's induction into the PBA Hall of Fame in 1998, Dick and Pete Weber became the only father-and-son inductees. The Webers also became the only father-and-son inductees in the ABC Hall of Fame when Pete was inducted in 2002.

Born in Indianapolis

He was born Richard Anthony Weber in Indianapolis, Indiana, on December 23, 1929. The son of Carl John and Marjorie Amelia (Dunn) Weber, he began bowling while still a boy. After finishing school, Weber took a job as a postal clerk in Indianapolis but bowled whenever he could. He entered his first American Bowling Congress (ABC) tournament in 1948. Of that first tournament, Weber years later told the *St. Louis Post-Dispatch* that "the ABC I remember the most is my first one in Detroit in 1948. I had never been there before, and walking out to the lanes was a thrill." That same year he married

Chronology

1929	Born in Indianapolis, Indiana, on December 23
1948	Marries Juanita Delk on December 23
1948	Bowls in first ABC tournament
1955	Joins Budweiser bowling team
1958	Helps establish PBA as one of 33 charter members
1969-70	Serves as PBA president
1981	Joins PBA Senior Tour
1995	Announces plan to cut back on tournament play
2002	Bowls in 55th ABC tournament

Awards and Accomplishments

1959	First PBA tournament win
1961, 1963, 1965	Named Bowler of the Year by the Bowling Writers Association of America (BWAA)
1965	PBA Player of the Year Award
1970	Inducted into ABC Hall of Fame
1975	Inducted into PBA Hall of Fame
2001	Hired to do color commentary for TV coverage of AMF Bowling World Cup
2002	Named one of 20 best bowlers of the 20th century by *Bowling Magazine*
2002	Won PBA Senior Tour tournament to become first bowler to win a PBA title in six different decades

Juanita Delk on December 23, his birthday. The couple has four children, Richard Jr., Paula Kae, Carl John, and Peter David.

In the mid-1950s, Weber left his postal job and Indianapolis behind when he received an offer to join the famed Budweiser bowling team of St. Louis. Also playing for the St. Louis bowling team were future Hall of Famers **Don Carter**, Ray Bluth, Pat Patterson, Tom Hennessey, and Bill Lillard. "I had a beat-up car and not much more, but it was a great opportunity," Weber told Chuck Pezzano of the Bergen *Record.*

One of the biggest factors in propelling professional bowling into the spotlight in the second half of the 20th century was the formation in 1958 of the Professional Bowlers Association, in which Weber played a key role. However, the unlikely central figure in the establishment of the PBA was a lawyer/television personality named Eddie Elias. In the 1950s, while working his way through law school, Elias hosted a television talk show at WAKR.

Bowlers' Low Pay Outrages Elias

It was an interview with Dick Weber and some other leading bowlers of the day that planted the seed that eventually grew into the PBA. During the course of the interview, Weber years later told the *St. Louis Post-Dispatch,* the conversation got around to compensation. "Eddie wondered how much we got paid. We told him, and he was outraged and said we should be getting more. He asked us what we would think about a professional bowling association."

Not long thereafter, thirty-three of the leading bowlers of the 1950s met with Elias to discuss the idea at a motel in Mountainside, New Jersey, after the American Bowling Congress Masters Tournament. "He said he needed 50 bucks from each of us before we started talking," Weber recalled. "He told us he would make money first and we would make money second. He started getting tournament sponsorships and the purses went from $2,000 to $2,500 and from there it blossomed to what we have today. Everything he said, he did, and it worked." And thus the PBA was born. Elias served as the fledgling organization's legal counsel and

worked diligently to promote the sport during the PBA's early years. With the help of television coverage and larger purses, Elias managed to bring bowling into the mainstream. In 1959, the nineteen-year-old Weber, one of the PBA's thirty-three charter members, won the last two of the three tournaments on the inaugural PBA Tour. He went on to win eight of the PBA's first twenty-one tournaments.

Helps Popularize Bowling

Weber is perhaps as well known for his efforts to popularize bowling as for his bowling expertise itself. Weber used television to tell millions of Americans about the joys of bowling and to legitimize bowling as a sport. He was there when ABC-TV first began televising the PBA Tour in the early 1960s and has outlived that relationship to become a frequent guest on David Letterman's late-night talk show. Over the years Weber has helped to promote bowling as an owner of a bowling center, a charter member and president of the PBA, TV announcer and analyst, and inventor and salesman for dozens of bowling products. Further cementing Weber's reputation as one of bowling's best ambassadors have been his frequent tours around the United States and abroad to conduct bowling clinics and exhibitions. In the mid-1990s he conducted such a tour of South Korea.

With the advent of nationwide televised coverage of professional bowling, Weber's fame as a bowler grew rapidly. He dominated the bowling scene in the first half of the 1960s and was named Bowler of the Year by the Bowling Writers' Association of America (BWAA) in 1961, 1963, and 1965. Because Weber's best years on the PBA Tour came relatively early in the history of professional bowling, his career earnings of just under $1 million on the PBA Tour are dwarfed by the leading bowlers of the late 20th and early 21st centuries. But Weber was among the best of his era, and he still hasn't lost his touch, as he proved in January 2002 when he won another tournament on the PBA Senior Tour. For his career as a whole, Weber has won four All-Star titles, eleven All-American Team honors, twenty-six PBA tournaments, and six PBA Senior titles.

Inducted into ABC Hall of Fame

Weber's brilliance as a bowler was recognized in 1970 by the American Bowling Congress, which inducted him that year into its Hall of Fame. In accepting the honor, Weber was moved to tears, according to Chuck Pezzano, bowling columnist for the *Record* (Bergen County, NJ). The bowling great walked to the podium and said: "I had so much to say when I was in the dressing room, but I find the words coming hard now," as the tears began to roll down his cheeks. Looking back on his emotional reaction, Weber later told Pezzano: "My mind just went blank. I got a feeling the whole world was looking down on me. I was surprised because basically I'm a ham. I like the spotlight. I never thought I'd see the day when I was speechless."

In February 2000 *Bowling Magazine,* the official publication of the ABC, conducted a poll to identify the twenty best bowlers of the 20th century. Weber topped the list, followed by **Earl Anthony**, Don Carter, Walter Ray Williams Jr., Mark Roth, Mike Auby, Hank Marino, Don Johnson, Ned Day, Joe Norris, Peter Weber (Weber's youngest son), Andy Varipapa, Billy Hardwick, Junie McMahon, Marshall Holman, Nelson Burton Jr., Bill Lillard, Carmen Salvino, Harry Smith, and Dick Ritger.

Seeks to Make Bowling Better

Generally an easy-going man, Weber sometimes gets fired up when he's fighting for the future of bowling. As keynote speaker at the 1999 convention of the East Coast Bowling Centers, Weber said: "Bowling is not just fun and recreation; it's a legitimate sport. But we must clear up the confusion between amateur and pro bowlers. It bewilders those who aren't into bowling. They can't figure out how amateurs can earn more money than pros, and how league bowlers can outscore pros because of easier lane conditions. There should be better ways to judge the elite bowlers."

Weber's still playing the game he loves, but there's no question his pace has slowed. Although he still competes on the PBA Senior Tour, he spends more and more of his time these days watching—with pride—the bowling exploits of his son, Pete Weber. When Pete was inducted into the PBA Hall of Fame in 1998, his father was fairly bursting with joy. "I'm the most honored that a dad can be," he told the *St. Louis Post-Dispatch.* "This is a very elated honor."

CONTACT INFORMATION

Address: 1305 Arlington Drive, Florissant, MO 63033-2201. Phone: (314) 837-0412.

SELECTED WRITINGS BY WEBER:

Champion's Guide to Bowling, Simon & Schuster, 1979.
Weber on Bowling: The Complete Guide to Getting Your Game Together, Prentice Hall, 1980.

FURTHER INFORMATION

Books

"Dick Weber." *Almanac of Famous People,* 6th edition. Detroit: Gale Group, 1998.

Periodicals

Clark, Tom. "Weber Has PBA on Edge." *USA Today* (March 1, 2002): 3C.
Clark, Tom. "Weber Rolls Out the Fun." *USA Today* (February 15, 2002): 12C.
Friedman, Jack. "Jocks: Young, Gifted and Reckless, Bowler Pete Weber Tries to Keep His Life Out of the Gutter." *People* (February 22, 1988): 69.
Pezzano, Chuck. "Legendary Weber the First to Win Titles in Five Decades." *Record* (Bergen County, NJ) (August 16, 1992): S16.
Pezzano, Chuck. "One More Honor for Dick Weber." *Record* (Bergen County, NJ) (October 15, 1995): S23.
Pezzano, Chuck. "Weber Remains the Sport's Best Ambassador." *Record* (Bergen County, NJ) (November 7, 1999): S16.
Pezzano, Chuck. "20th Century's Top 20 to be Honored by ABC." *Record* (Bergen County, NJ) (February 6, 2000): S15.
Reed, Don. "No Matter the Time of Day, Weber Strikes Up Interest at His 50th ABC." *St. Louis Post-Dispatch* (March 11, 1997): 2C.
Schildroth, Keith. "Bowlers Hope Sale of League Saves PBA; Dick Weber Says the Proposed Sale Is the Start of a New Era." *St. Louis Post-Dispatch* (January 23, 2000): F11.
Schildroth, Keith. "PBA Founder Elias Used Television to Carry Bowling Into Mainstream." *St. Louis Post-Dispatch* (November 27, 1998): D2.
Schildroth, Keith. "Weber Joins His Dad in PBA Hall of Fame." *St. Louis Post-Dispatch* (November 16, 1998): B3.

Other

"Dick Weber." PBA.com. http://www.pba.com/players/playerbio.asp?ID=33 (October 24, 2002).
"Dick Weber." St. Louis Hall of Fame. http://www.stlouiswalkoffame.org/inductees/dick-weber.html (October 24, 2002).
"Dick Weber to Do Color Commentary for 2001 Bowling World Cup." AMF. http://www.amf.com/wc01/pr100801a.html (October 24, 2002).

"Dick Weber Wins PBA Titles in Six Consecutive Decades." AMF. http://www.amf.com/pr/pr022502.html (October 24, 2002).

"Hall of Famer Dick Weber Always Thrilled to Bowl at ABC Championship." BowlingFans.com. http://www.bowlingfans.com/tour411/tour03122002.shtml (October 24, 2002).

"Obituary for Eddie Elias." CafeArabica.com. http://www.cafearabica.com/people/people13/peoelias13.html (October 25, 2002).

"Pete Weber." PBA.com. http://www.pba.com/players/playerbio.asp?ID=12 (October 24, 2002).

Sketch by Don Amerman

Ulrich Wehling

Ulrich Wehling
1952-

German skier

E ast German skier Ulrich Wehling is one of six competitors who have won three consecutive Olympic gold medals in the same event—the Nordic Combined. After retiring from skiing, he moved to Switzerland, and is a member of the National Olympic Committee in Germany. In 2002, he was named to **Bud Greenspan**'s list of 25 Greatest Winter Olympians.

Olympic Competition

At the age of 19, Wehling participated in the 1972 Olympic Games in Sapporo, Japan, in the Nordic Combined event, which consists of two ski jumps and a 15km race. A self-proclaimed "nobody," he went on to win the gold medal in the Nordic Combined with a total point score of 413.340. Wehling was said to have "stolen" the gold medal from the Finnish star Rauno Miettinen, who had nearly secured his place as best in the Nordic Combined. Two years later in 1974, Wehling won the Nordic Combined world championship title.

At the 1976 Winter Olympics in Innsbruck, Austria, he again won the gold in the Nordic Combined with points totaling 423.39, a sizable margin from his closest competitor. His performance in the event was dominated by the jumping competition. Wehling was not known for being the fastest skier in the 15km race at the Olympics. To assure his victory, he needed to build a tremendous lead during the ski-jumping portion of the combined.

In 1980 at the Winter Olympics in Lake Placid, New York, Wehling defeated his countryman Uwe Dotzauer to earn the gold medal in the Nordic Combined with 432.200 points. Said to perform his best under stress, he accomplished this feat despite surgery on his shoulder and hamstring. Wehling became the first male competitor, who was not a figure skater, to win three consecutive gold medals in the same individual Winter Olympic event.

Move to Switzerland

Wehling retired from competition immediately following his third Olympic victory in Lake Placid. He became a member of the skiing association in East Germany in Berlin, a member of the National Olympic Committee in Germany, and held the post of president of the GDR ski federation.

Although he had been working in Berlin, he moved to Seftigen, Switzerland where, for the past ten years, he has been racing director of the International Skiing Federation (FIS), responsible for the Nordic Combined event. He said he does not plan to return to Berlin, and annually renews his permit to live in Switzerland.

In 2002, Ulrich Wehling was named to Bud Greenspan's list of the 25 Greatest Winter Olympians. Wehling is married and has two daughters.

In a 2002 interview to commemorate Wehling's 50th birthday, Ulrich Wehling spoke with Peter Stracke about his achievements in sport. On his 1972 visit to the Winter Olympics in Sapporo, Japan, Wehling said he was a

Chronology

1952	Born July 8, in East Germany
1961	Becomes a member of SC Traktor Oberwiesenthal
1972	Participates in Winter Games in Sapporo, Japan, wins Nordic Combined gold medal
1974	Wins Nordic Combined world championship
1976	Participates in Winter Olympics in Innsbruck, Austria, wins Nordic Combined gold medal
1980	Participates in Winter Olympics in Lake Placid, New York, wins Nordic Combined gold medal

Awards and Accomplishments

1972	Nordic Combined gold medal, Winter Olympics, Sapporo, Japan
1974	Nordic Combined world championship
1976	Nordic Combined gold medal, Winter Olympics, Innsbruck, Austria
1980	Nordic Combined gold medal, Winter Olympics, Lake Placid, New York

"nobody. I just was the last one who luckily qualified for the Olympic team, and nobody was expecting anything from me." He admitted, "I wasn't very good in training, but I always was a fighter. You can lose despite fighting. And you can lose because you resign. For me, success in sport always was a question of attitude."

Wehling noted that today, media interest and attendance for Nordic Combined events are growing, and world cup events have been popular. He plans to continue extending his permit to live in Switzerland, and does not plan to return home to Berlin, where he had a successful career as an operative of the skiing association in the German Democratic Republic.

Although his career was short, Ulrich Wehling earned his place in the history books as the first Winter Olympian to win three successive gold medals in the Nordic Combined skiing event.

FURTHER INFORMATION

Books

Chronicle of the Olympics. New York: DK Publishing, 1998.

Other

Fact Monster. http://www.factmonster.com/ipka/A0758118.html (November 15, 2002).
Nordic Combined Web Site. http://www.nordic-combined.net/information/Meldungen/wehling.shtml (November 15, 2002).

Sketch by Lorraine Savage

Erik Weihenmayer
1969-

American mountain climber

Ninety percent of climbers who attempt Mount Everest—at 29,035 feet, the world's highest mountain—do not make it to the summit. In 2001, Erik Weihenmayer managed to accomplish the grueling and dangerous trek to the "top of the world," making history in the process. Weihenmayer, who suffers from a retina disease, is completely blind. An accomplished mountaineer, Weihenmayer has reached the top of each of the Seven Summits—the highest mountains on each of the seven continents. "I like doing things that are new and thrilling. Blindness," Weihenmayer told *People,* "is just a nuisance." In climbing, "you just have to find a different way of doing it."

Weihenmayer was born in 1969 and grew up in Hong Kong and then Weston, Connecticut with his parents, Ed and Ellen Suzanne Baker Weihenmayer, and two brothers. A slight irregularity in his eyes when he was an infant alerted his parents to seek medical attention. He was diagnosed with a rare retina disease and, by the time he was three, it was clear that he would be blind before he was a teenager. He wore thick glasses and learned to read, but was legally blind. His parents made sure their son grew up as normal as possible and taught him to be self-sufficient. He played football, one-on-one basketball, and loved to ride bikes, under the careful watch of his father. He was completely blind by the time he was 13.

At first, Weihenmayer refused to use a cane or learn Braille, insisting he could live as he had. Incapable of playing ball anymore, he learned to wrestle, and as a senior in high school went all the way to the National Junior Freestyle Wrestling Championship in Iowa. He soon found that his guide dog was a good lure for women, and began dating at age seventeen. He graduated Boston College as an English major, and became a middle-school teacher and wrestling coach. He married his wife, Ellie Reeve, on Mount Kilimanjaro in Tanzania in 1997. The two have a daughter, Emma, and live in Golden, Colorado. Weihenmayer now works as a motivational speaker.

Weihenmayer first hiked with his father, and fell in love with rock climbing at age sixteen at a camp for the blind, where they called him Monkey Boy. After his mother was killed in a car crash, his father took him and his brothers trekking in Peru, Spain, Pakistan, and Papua New Guinea to bond. He began mountaineering in his early 20s. For the blind, environmental patterns are the key to making one's way through the world; city blocks are roughly the same length, curbs are the same height, and household furniture remains in the same place. In climbing, there are no patterns. The natural landscape of mountain, ice, and rock is entirely patternless.

Erik Weihenmayer

"Watching Erik scramble up a rock face is a little like watching a spider make its way up a wall," according to *Time.* "His hands are like antennae, gathering information as they flick outward, surveying the rock for cracks, grooves, bowls, nubbins, knobs, edges and ledges, converting all of it into a road map etched into his mind." An accomplished climber, Weihenmayer is rated 5.10, with 5.14 being the highest. "It's like instead of wrestling with a person, I am moving and working with a rock," he told *Time.* "It's a beautiful process of solving a puzzle." He climbed Alaska's Denali (Mount McKinley) in 1995, California's El Capitan in 1996, Kilimanjaro in 1997, Argentina's Aconcagua in 1999, Canada's Polar Circus in 2000, and Antarctica's Mount Vinson. He follows the shouts of the climbers in front of him, who call out hazards and wear a bell and a rope attached to Weihenmayer. He is an exceptional leader under conditions that challenge the most talented mountaineers—in the dark. Weihenmayer also enjoys skydiving. Strangely, he is mildly afraid of flying.

In 1999, almost as soon as Weihenmayer met Pasquale Scaturro, a geophysicist and mountaineer who had led seven Everest expeditions, the two began setting up an expedition. They put together a nineteen-person team of experienced climbers and friends of Weihenmayer's. The National Federation of the Blind (N.F.B.), pledged $250,000 to sponsor the climb. Aventis Pharmaceuticals, which manufactures the allergy medication Allegra, sponsored a documentary of the climb; Weihen-

mayer suffers from allergies. All of his existing gear and clothing manufacturers backed the climb. Confident of his mountaineering experience, Weihenmayer felt sure that if he failed, it would be because of his heart, lungs, or brain—not his eyes.

The N.F.B. team arrived in Lukla, Nepal, in March 2001 to begin the trek. At the start of the climb, Weihenmayer was so sure on his feet that some Nepalese Sherpas believed he was lying about his sight. He convinced everyone when he removed one of his glass eyes, and offered to remove the other. Climbing Everest is physically, mentally, and emotionally grueling for the best climbers, under the best conditions, and many considered Weihenmayer foolhardy. By the time they ascended from Base Camp, the lowest camp on the mountain, to Camp One, Weihenmayer looked awful—he was suffering from the altitude and was bloody from getting hit in the face with a trekking pole. But it looked worse than it was and Weihenmayer and the team continued up to Camps Two, Three, and Four, the final stop.

At Camp Four, preparing to head for the summit, a storm came in that almost dashed their hopes. After a break in the weather, they continued to push on to the South Summit, with a 10,000-foot vertical fall into Tibet on one side, and a 7,000-foot fall into Nepal on the other. South Summit is often where climbers turn back. Hillary Step, a 39-foot rock face, is the last obstacle before reaching the true summit of Everest. Because of an approaching storm, Weihenmayer only had a few minutes at the top to soak it all in. After returning home, Weihenmayer added a chapter, titled "Everest," to his autobiography, *To Touch the Top of the World,* which was originally published before his climb.

On June 13, 2002 Weihenmayer reached the top of Russia's Mount Elbrus, number six on his list. On September 5, 2002, Weihenmayer reached the top of his seventh, Australia's Mount Kosciusko. Because there is some debate whether Australia or Australiasia is the seventh continent, some climbers argue that he must still summit Indonesia's Carstensz Pyramid to join the Seven Summits, which he plans to attempt in 2003. "What Erik achieved is hard for a sighted person to comprehend," according to *Time*. "Perhaps the point is really that there is no way to put what Erik has done in perspective because no one has ever done anything like it. It is a unique achievement, one that in the truest sense pushes the limits of what man is capable of."

SELECTED WRITINGS BY WEIHENMAYER:

Touch the Top of the World: A Blind Man's Journey to Climb Farther Than the Eye Can See, Dutton, 2001.

FURTHER INFORMATION

Periodicals

Beech, Mark and Anderson, Kelli. "Inside Out: News and news and notes from the world of adventure sports." *Sports Illustrated* (September 23, 2002): 18.

"Blind to Failure: Mountaineers scoffed at the notion that Erik Weihenmayer, sightless since he was 13, could climb Everest. But a killer peak is no obstacle for a man who can conquer adversity." *Time* (June 18, 2002): 52.

Carlin, Peter. "World at his fingertips: guided by touch, not sight, a blind climber takes on El Capitan." *People* (August 12, 1996): 48.

Gray, Taylor. "The other guy on top of the world." *Time* (June 11, 2002).

"Livin' it: Blind mountaineer Erick Weihenmayer summits Mount Elbrus - and leads the way in a dramatic descent." *Sports Illustrated* (July 1, 2002): 30.

Other

"Eric Weihenmayer." Eric Weihenmayer Home Page. http://www.touchthetop.com (January 15, 2003).

Pegg, Dave. "Super Blind." *Climbing.* http://www.climbing.com/pages/feature_stories/feature 213.html (January 15, 2003).

Swift, E.M. "Blind Ambition." *Sports Illustrated.* http://sportsillustrated.cnn.com/features/siadventures/2001/blind_ambition (January 15, 2003).

Weihenmayer, Eric. "Tenacious E." *Outside.* http://outside.away.com/outside/adventure/200112/200112 tenacious_e.adp (January 15, 2003).

Sketch by Brenna Sanchez

Paula Weishoff
1962-

American volleyball player

Paula Weishoff is a two-time Olympic medalist in volleyball, and is one of the top volleyball players of her generation. She was inducted into the U.S. Volleyball Hall of Fame in 1998. She currently acts as assistant coach for the top-rated women's volleyball team at the University of Southern California (USC).

Paula Weishoff was born in 1962 in Los Angeles, California. She began playing organized volleyball while in the eighth grade. Weishoff first distinguished herself as an outstanding volleyball player on her school team at West Torrance High in California. A well-rounded athlete in high school, Weishoff lettered in not only volleyball, but also in track, soccer, and softball.

Weishoff's introduction to volleyball came at about the time that the U.S. national women's volleyball team was founded. But it was not the national team that inspired Weishoff to begin to dream that she could make volleyball her living; it was watching a local team playing in exhibition games in Los Angeles that inspired her to attend a sports festival in Colorado Springs, Colorado as a volleyball player.

Still in high school, Weishoff attended the Colorado Springs festival, and successfully competed with young women from all over the country for the chance to play in the Pacific Rim Tournament in Hawaii. Traveling to Colorado Springs to play volleyball opened her eyes to the broader world of volleyball beyond California. She made lifelong friends at the event, and it was there that she first began to dream of playing for the U.S. national team. The Pacific Rim Tournament became Weishoff's first international volleyball competition, and there she dared to set her sights even higher.

After winning a silver medal in volleyball at the U.S. Olympic Festival in 1979 and earning Most Valuable Player (MVP) honors at the 1980 U.S. Junior Olympics, Weishoff enrolled in college at the University of Southern California (USC) in 1980. At USC, Weishoff played for the school's women's volleyball team, the USC Trojans. During her first year on the Trojans, Weishoff led her team to victory at the Association of Intercollegiate Athletics for Women (AIAW) Championships.

While she was in school, Weishoff tried hard to balance the demands of an academic life with her volleyball schedule, and found that she had difficulty doing justice to both. Finally, after a year at USC, she decided to devote herself full-time to volleyball. Weishoff left college in 1981, after a achieving her dream of signing with the U.S. national women's volleyball team.

Paula Weishoff

In her first season with the U.S. national team, Weishoff and her teammates took home the gold medal at the North and Central America and Caribe (NORCECA) Championships. Her team continued to win awards at tournaments through the early 1980s, including the bronze medal at the World Championship games in 1982, and the silver medal at the Pan American Games.

In 1984 the summer Olympics were held in Weishoff's home state of California, and she was named to the U.S. women's volleyball team. The U.S. women took home the silver medal at the Olympics, and Weishoff was named Team USA's MVP.

After the Olympics, Weishoff played for no less then five Italian First (A1) Division teams into the 1990s. She also continued to play for the U.S. national team, which continued to win awards into the 1990s, including the bronze medal at the Goodwill Games in 1986 and the silver medal at the NORCECA Championships in 1991.

In 1992, Weishoff, then 30 years old, again played on the U.S. women's volleyball team at the Olympics. The team lost its chance for a gold metal after losing to the Cuban team, but took home the bronze metal after overcoming Brazil. Weishoff herself was named Most Valuable Player of the entire Olympics. She was delighted with the honor and with having won her second Olympic medal. As she was later quoted by Bill Dwyre in the *Houston Chronicle* as saying, "In 1984, it was a great feeling winning the silver. And it was great to be able to come back and compete in the Olympics. I guess I'm lucky to have two chances and have two medals. I may not have a gold medal, but I have a heart of gold."

Weishoff continued to play for the U.S. women's national team after the 1992 Olympics. The team won bronze at the Fédération Internationale de Volleyball (FIVB) Super Four in 1992 and the gold medal at the World Grand Prix in 1995. Also in 1995, Weishoff went to play for the Japanese team Daiei, leading it to the Japanese professional league title, and earning herself MVP honors.

Weishoff went to the Olympics with Team U.S.A. one last time in 1996. The team did not medal this time, and the following year, Weishoff retired from competition to return to USC to complete her undergraduate studies. The year 1997 was a big one for Weishoff. Not only did she retire from playing volleyball competitively and return to school, but she also started a new career as assistant coach for her old team, the UCS Trojans. Also that year, she married her husband, Karl Hanold.

Weishoff was inducted into the U.S. Volleyball Hall of Fame in 1998. She graduated from USC in 2000 with a B.A. in humanities with a minor in business. By 2003, she had become head assistant coach for the USC Trojans, and had helped to make it the top-rated college women's volleyball team in the country.

Weishoff is proud of what the USC women have accomplished. "This team could win two or three national championships," she told Phil Collin in the *Daily Breeze* in December of 2002. "I think this team could establish itself as the dynasty that USC used to be. That was kind

Awards and Accomplishments

1979	Wins silver medal at U.S. Olympic Festival
1980	Named Most Valuable Player at U.S. Junior Olympics
1980	Leads her college volleyball team, the USC Trojans to victory at the AIAW championships
1982	Wins bronze medal on U.S. national team at World Championships
1983	Wins silver medal on U.S. national team at Pan American Games
1984	Wins silver medal on U.S. women's volleyball team at the Olympics
1984	Named U.S. women's volleyball MVP of the Olympics
1984	Named USOC Female Volleyball Athlete of the Year
1986	Wins bronze medal on U.S. national team at Goodwill Games
1992	Wins bronze medal on U.S. women's volleyball team at the Olympics
1992	Voted MVP of the Olympic Games
1995	Named Japanese pro league's MVP
1996	Plays on U.S. women's volleyball team at the Olympics
1998	Inducted into the U.S. Volleyball Hall of Fame
2001	As assistant coach, leads USC women's volleyball team to NCAA Championship Semifinal
2001	Leads USC women's volleyball team to NCAA Regional Finals

of their goal when they were recruited. . . to create a team as good as the legendary ones of the past." Weishoff also serves as the international player representative for USA Volleyball, the national governing body for the sport of volleyball in the United States, and has served as assistant coach for USA Volleyball's High Performance programs and the Youth National team.

When asked if she had any advice for young athletes considering a career in sports, Weisoff offered this: "I would just say to follow your heart.... Don't let people talk you out of it or convince you to do other things if this is where your heart is." Most of all, she said, have fun playing.

FURTHER INFORMATION

Periodicals

Collin, Phil. "All the Pieces Together for a USC Dynasty." *Daily Breeze,* (December 19, 2002).

Dwyre, Bill. "Barcelona '92; U.S. Women Regroup for Bronze." *Houston Chronicle,* (August 8, 1992): Sports, 13.

Powers, John. "Women Grab the Bronze; Summer Olympics '92." *Boston Globe,* (August 8, 1992): Sports, 62.

Other

Additional information was obtained from an interview with Paula Weishoff on January 29, 2003.

"Paula Weishoff Profile." USC Trojans. http://usctrojans.ocsn.com/sports/w-volley/mtt/weishoff_paula00.html (January 27, 2003).

Sketch by Michael Belfiore

Johnny Weissmuller
1904-1984

American swimmer

One of the most outstanding swimmers of all time, Johnny Weissmuller won five Olympic gold medals and set dozens of national and world records. His stellar performance as a competitive swimmer helped to focus the attention of Americans on the health benefits of the sport. However, he is perhaps best remembered by most Americans for his portrayals of author Edgar Rice Burroughs' Tarzan of the Apes and Jungle Jim on the screen from the early 1930s through the mid-1950s. After his retirement from work in motion pictures and television, Weissmuller lent his name to a swimming pool company and became a spokesman for the product.

Born in Austria-Hungary

Not until after his death in 1984 did the full truth about Weissmuller's origins emerge. Throughout his lifetime, he claimed to have been born Peter John Weissmuller, the son of recent immigrants from Eastern Europe, on July 2, 1904, in the small Pennsylvania mining town of Windber, near Johnstown. Olympic historian David Wallechinsky uncovered credible evidence in the 1980s that Weissmuller had in fact been born in Freidorf, Austria-Hungary, now a part of Romania, and was brought to the United States shortly after his birth. Wallechinsky further contended that Weissmuller's parents later switched his identity with that of his American-born brother, Peter, to qualify their older son to compete on the U.S. Olympic swimming team.

The Weissmullers did not linger long in Windber, where Johnny's father toiled in the coal mines to scratch out an existence for his family. By 1908 they had relocated to Chicago, where Weissmuller's father owned and operated a neighborhood tavern while his mother cooked in the city's famous Turn-Verein restaurant. Johnny was enrolled in St. Michael's Parochial School. He later attended Chicago's Menier Public School but quit after completing the eighth grade when his father died of tuberculosis, probably contracted during his years as a coal miner in Pennsylvania.

To help support his family, Weissmuller worked as a bellhop and elevator operator at Chicago's Plaza Hotel. In his spare time, he and younger brother Peter, both avid swimmers, joined the Stanton Park pool, where Johnny won all the junior swim meets in which he competed. At the age of twelve, he lied about his age to win a berth on the local YMCA swim team. During the summer, he spent every spare moment at Chicago's Oak Street Beach, where he and Peter pulled twenty people from the waters of Lake Michigan after a boating accident. Only eleven of those they rescued survived the

Johnny Weissmuller

mishap. The incident impressed upon Weissmuller the importance of learning to swim at an early age.

Trains under "Big Bill"

Not long after the death of his father, Weissmuller came under the influence of a new father figure when he began to train at the Illinois Athletic Club under the guidance of William "Big Bill" Bachrach, already famous as the trainer of several Olympic swimming champions. According to Ralph Hickok, author of *A Who's Who of Sports Champions,* the red-mustachioed Bachrach, an imposing figure at 340 pounds, was a tough taskmaster. When Weissmuller asked Bachrach to train him, "Big Bill" laid out his conditions for doing so: "Swear that you'll work a year with me without question, and I'll take you on. You won't swim against anybody. You'll just be a slave, and you'll hate my guts, but in the end you just might break every record there is."

Bachrach's promise seemed strangely prophetic. In Weissmuller's first major competition, the 1921 Amateur Athletic Union (AAU) outdoor championship, he handily won his very first race, the 50-yard freestyle swim. But that was just the beginning. Over the next three years, he won every race he entered. In the run-up to the 1924 Olympic Games in Paris, twenty-year-old Weissmuller looked unbeatable. He was already the world record-holder for the 100-meter freestyle. In Paris he would compete with the defending Olympic champi-

on, **Duke Kahanamoku**, who also represented the United States, and his younger brother, Sam. According to biographer David Fury, before the 100-meter event, Duke turned to Weissmuller and said: "Johnny, good luck. The most important thing in this race is to get the American flag up there three times. Let's do it!" And do it, they did. Weissmuller won the race, finishing in 59 seconds flat, winning the gold medal, followed closely by Duke and Sam Kahanamoku, who took the silver and bronze medals, respectively.

Two days before the 100-meter freestyle event in Paris, Weissmuller had taken gold in the 400-meter freestyle race. Later in the day of his 100-meter win, he swam as part of the winning U.S. team in the 800-meter relay. Weissmuller left Paris with three gold medals around his neck. Four years later at the summer games in Amsterdam, he carried the American flag at the opening ceremonies and went on to repeat his wins in the 100-meter freestyle and the 800-meter relay for a total of five gold medals at the two Olympics. Throughout the 1920s, Weissmuller was invincible in amateur competition, winning thirty-six national individual AAU championships and sixty-seven world championships. In 1924 he set a world record in the 100-meter freestyle, finishing in 57.4 seconds, and became the first swimmer to break the one-minute mark. His record in this event lasted for a decade. He was named American Swimmer of the Year in 1922, won the Helms Trophy in 1923, and was elected to the Helms Swimming Hall of Fame in 1949.

Turns Pro

Not long after the Amsterdam Olympics, Weissmuller turned professional. He toured Florida resort hotels, putting on exhibition swims in return for enough compensation to cover the costs of his travel expenses. He also signed a lucrative contract (paying $500 weekly) with B.V.D. to promote the company's swimwear. In 1929 he appeared in his first film, making a cameo appearance as himself in *Glorifying the American Girl*. The following year he teamed with writer Clarence Bush to produce his first book, *Swimming the American Crawl* and also wrote two articles for the *Saturday Evening Post*. In 1931, Weissmuller married Bobbe Arnst, the first of his five wives. They were divorced in 1932. The following year, Weismuller wed Latin actress Lupe Velez, whom he divorced in 1938. He married Beryel Scott, his third wife, in 1939. The couple had three children but were divorced in 1948, the same year that Weissmuller married Allene Gates, his fourth wife. He and Gates divorced in 1962. Weissmuller married his fifth and final wife, German-born Maria Bauman, in 1963.

The early 1930s brought a second career for Weissmuller, who in 1932 made his debut as Edgar Rice Burroughs' Tarzan in the film version of *Tarzan the Ape Man,* opposite Maureen O'Sullivan, who played Jane. For Weissmuller, it was just the first of twelve Tarzan films he starred in over the next decade and a half. Of all of the Tarzan films with or without Weissmuller in the leading role, the swimming champion's second outing, *Tarzan and His Mate,* is widely considered the best. A compelling romance, the 1934 film, directed by Cedric Gibbons and Jack Conway, costarred Maureen O'Sullivan as Jane. Although the story line at first glance might seem a trifle hokey, the on-screen chemistry between Weissmuller and O'Sullivan is by far the most effective of all their screen pairings. The sudden appearance of Jane's old flame and his hunting chum threatens the idyllic love match between Tarzan and Jane. The two Englishmen try their best to persuade Jane to forsake the jungle and return with them to the delights of London's Mayfair. In the end, Jane's love for Tarzan prevails, and she sends her ivory-hunting former love packing. The performances of both Weissmuller and O'Sullivan in this film are by far the best of all the Tarzan movies they made together. Of the film, the late critic Pauline Kael wrote: "It's cheerful and outrageously preposterous. You are right in the heart of the craziest Africa ever contrived for your entertainment; no wild beast ever misses a cue."

When Weissmuller had grown too old to don Tarzan's trademark loincloth, he took on the screen persona of Jungle Jim for another twelve films, running from the late 1940s through 1953. Although he appeared in a handful of films after the last of the Jungle Jim movies, his career in motion pictures was effectively over by the mid-1950s.

Leaving Hollywood behind, Weissmuller returned to Chicago where he launched his own swimming pool company and lent his name to assorted other business ventures, including health food stores and cocktail lounges. Hardly the world's sharpest businessman, he got himself into some unfortunate business deals, largely because of his in-

Awards and Accomplishments	
1921	Won 50-yard freestyle in amateur debut at Amateur Athletic Union (AAU) championship
1922	Named American Swimmer of the Year
1922	World records in 150-yard backstroke and 300-meter freestyle
1923	Set new world record in 150-yard backstroke, 6.8 seconds faster than previous record
1923	Helms Trophy as North American Athlete of the Year
1924	Three gold medals at Paris Olympics, in the 100- and 400-meter freestyle events and as a member of U.S. team in 800-meter relay
1924	World record in 100-meter freestyle with time of 57.4 seconds
1928	Two gold medals at Amsterdam Olympics in 100-meter freestyle and 800-meter relay
1949	Elected to Helms Swimming Hall of Fame
1951	Voted Best Swimmer of the Half-Century by a panel of sportswriters
1972	Awarded honorary sixth gold medal at Munich Olympics
1974	Named King of Swimming Undefeated by International Palace of Sports

herent naivete. Weissmuller's choices in the business arena cost him dearly, draining away much of his earnings.

In the mid-1960s, Weissmuller moved to Florida to manage the International Swimming Hall of Fame in Fort Lauderdale. In 1973, he headed west to Las Vegas and worked for a time as a greeter at the MGM Grand Hotel. Beginning in the mid-1970s, Weissmuller's health began to deteriorate significantly. After suffering a series of strokes, he and his wife moved to Acapulco, Mexico, where he died of pulmonary edema on January 20, 1984.

For more than a decade, Weissmuller dominated the international competitive swimming scene, quickly accumulating an impressive array of American and world records. Sportswriters in the 1920s vied with one another to come up with the most creative nickname for the rugged American swimming champion, conjuring up such colorful entries as "Flying Fish," "King of Swimmers," "America's Greatest Waterman," and "Prince of the Waves." Although his fame as a swimmer was eventually overshadowed by his popularity as the star of a dozen Tarzan movies, Weissmuller will forever be remembered as one of the greatest swimmers of all time.

SELECTED WRITINGS BY WEISSMULLER:

(With Clarence A. Bush) *Swimming the American Crawl.* Grosset & Dunlap, 1930.
(With Narda Onyx) *Water, World, and Weissmuller.* Vion Publishing, 1964.

FURTHER INFORMATION

Books

Encyclopedia of World Biography Supplement. Volume 21. Detroit: Gale Group, 2001.

Fury, David A. *Johnny Weissmuller: "Twice the Hero."*
Thorndike, ME: Thorndike Press, 2001.
International Dictionary of Films and Filmmakers, Volume 3: Actors and Actresses. Detroit: St. James
Press, 1996.
St. James Encyclopedia of Popular Culture. five volumes. Detroit: St. James Press, 2000.
Weissmuller, Jr., Johnny, et al. *Tarzan, My Father.*
Toronto, Ontario: ECW Press, 2002.

Periodicals

Fury, David. "Johnny Weissmuller . . . the Two Career
Star." *Burroughs Bulletin* (April 1993).
"Tarzan, The Ape Man." *Magill's Survey of Cinema*
(June 15, 1995).

Other

Contemporary Authors Online. Detroit: Gale Group,
2000.
"Johnny Weissmuller Pools: The Legend of Excellence." Delair Group. http://www.delairgroup.com/
pools/jw/history.html (October 4, 2002).
"Tarzan and His Mate." Tarzan en Jane. http://users.
skynet.be/sky40152/tarzan6.htm (October 5, 2002).
"Tarzan and His Mate (1934)." At-A-Glance Film Reviews. http://rinkworks.com/movies/m/tarzan.and.
his.mate.1934.shtml (October 5, 2002).
"Tarzan and His Mate (1934)." Reel.com. http://www.
reel.com/movie.asp?MID=6705 (July 7, 2002).

Sketch by Don Amerman

Hanni Wenzel
1956-

Liechensteinian skier

Hanni Wendel is the first person from the tiny European country of Liechtenstein to win an Olympic
gold medal. She won not just one, but two gold medals
for skiing at the 1980 Winter Olympic Games held in
Lake Placid, New York. She very nearly swept all three
of the women's Alpine skiing events, earning, in addition to her two golds, a silver medal as well. Her brother, Andreas, too, took home a silver medal at the 1980
Olympics, for the men's downhill event. Together, the
brother-and-sister team won fully a third of the 12 total
metals for alpine skiing at the 1980 Winter Olympics.

Born in Saubirnen, Germany in 1956, Hanni Wenzel
moved to the smallest country in Europe, the nation of
Liechtenstein (just 60 square miles), when she was one

Hanni Wenzel

year old. She entered international skiing competition in
1974 at the age of 18, winning a gold and a silver medal
at the World Championships. When Wenzel was 20
years old, in 1976, she took home the bronze medal for
the slalom in the Winter Olympic Games, held in Innsbruck, Austria. After the 1976 Olympics, Wenzel competed once more at the World Championships, bringing
home a silver medal.

At the age of 23, Wenzel competed in the next Winter
Olympics, which were held in Lake Placid, New York in
1980. In the 1980 Olympics, she competed in each of
the three women's Alpine skiing events. She earned the
silver medal in the downhill event and the gold medals
in the giant slalom and the slalom. It was the first time
anyone from her nation had won a gold medal at the
Olympics.

Wenzel's brother Andreas and her sister Petra were
also on the Liechtenstein Olympic skiing team. Although Petra did not win a metal, Andreas took home
the silver medal for the men's downhill event. The
brother-and-sister metal-winning performance was a
first for Alpine skiing at the Olympic Games.

The Wenzel's combined four medals at the Olympics
made them national heroes in their tiny homeland of
Liechtenstein (population of 25,000). As Wenzel began
her gold medal-winning run on the giant slalom, the
bars of Vaduz, Liechtenstein's capital city, were packed
with citizens watching the event on television. As soon

<table>
<tr><td colspan="2">Chronology</td></tr>
<tr><td>1956</td><td>Born in Staubirnen, Germany</td></tr>
<tr><td>1957</td><td>Moves to Liechtenstein</td></tr>
<tr><td>1974</td><td>Wins a gold and a silver medal at World Championships</td></tr>
<tr><td>1976</td><td>Wins bronze medal for slalom at Winter Olympics</td></tr>
<tr><td>1980</td><td>Becomes first athlete from Liechtenstein to win an Olympic gold medal</td></tr>
<tr><td>1980</td><td>Becomes first athlete from Liechtenstein to be named UPI Sportswoman of the Year</td></tr>
<tr><td>1985</td><td>Co-founds Liechtenstein-based agency for sporting events</td></tr>
</table>

<table>
<tr><td colspan="2">Awards and Accomplishments</td></tr>
<tr><td>1974</td><td>Wins gold and silver medals at World Championships</td></tr>
<tr><td>1976</td><td>Wins bronze medal for slalom at Olympics</td></tr>
<tr><td>1980</td><td>Wins silver medal in downhill event at Olympics</td></tr>
<tr><td>1980</td><td>Wins gold medal for giant slalom at Olympics</td></tr>
<tr><td>1980</td><td>Wins gold medal for slalom at Olympics</td></tr>
<tr><td>1980</td><td>Voted UPI Sportswoman of the year</td></tr>
</table>

as Wenzel completed the second run of the giant slalom and it was clear that she had won Liechtenstein's first Olympic gold medal, the streets of Vaduz erupted in raucous celebration. Red and blue flags were draped from windows, and people poured out into the streets to hug and kiss each other.

The owner of the best restaurant in Vaduz had promised Wenzel's mother that he would invite her to dinner if Wenzel won the gold medal, and he kept his promise. Crown Prince Hans-Adam, son of Franz Joseph II, the ruler of Liechtenstein, and Hans-Adam's wife joined Wenzel's mother for the dinner.

Among the celebrants were a group of Vaduz business owners who had promised that if Wenzel won the gold medal, they would immediately fly to Lake Placid to congratulate Wenzel personally. And so they did, arriving not long after Franz Joseph II's congratulatory telegram

Also in 1980, Wenzel was voted by European sports writers UPI Sportswoman of the Year. It was another first for Liechtenstein—no other athlete from that nation had ever won this honor.

Wenzel retired from competitive skiing in the early 1980s. In 1985, Wenzel and her husband, Harti Weirather, who won the men's downhill skiing event at the World Cup in 1981, founded a company called Weirather, Wenzel and Partner. Based in Liechtenstein, the company acts as an agency for sporting events organizers who wish to find corporate sponsors for their events. The agency has proven successful, making possible such events as the Hahnenkamm downhill event in Kitzbühel, Austria. Liechtenstein's first Olympic gold medal winner has found a way to stay in the game, and she and her company are still going strong into the 21st century.

FURTHER INFORMATION

Periodicals

Atkin, Ross. "Remembered Highlights of the Winter Games." *Christian Science Monitor,* (February 26, 1980): Sports, 15.

"'Golden Hanni' Cheered at Home." *Associated Press,* (February 22, 1980): International News.

"Heiden and Wenzel Win UPI Poll." *UPI* (November 19, 1980): Sports News.

Shapiro, Leonard. "World Cup; Bank on It; Big Money Makes the Circuit, Too." *Washington Post,* (February 5, 1984): Magazine, 70.

Other

"Liechenstein's Olympic Champion." International Olympic Committee. http://www.olympic.org/uk/athletes/heroes/bio_uk.asp?PAR_I_ID=74381 (January 27, 2003).

"Where Are They Now?" CNNSI.com. http://sports illustrated.cnn.com/olympics/2002/daily_guide/news/2002/02/21/day14_where/ (January 27, 2003).

Sketch by Michael Belfiore

Jerry West
1938-

American basketball player

One of the best shooting guards in professional basketball history, Jerry West went on to lead the Los Angeles Lakers to basketball dominance during the last quarter of the twentieth century as first a coach and later general manager and executive vice president. After nearly four decades with the Lakers organization, West stepped down in 2000, but it did not take him long to decide that retirement was not for him. In October 2002, West hired on as president of the Memphis Grizzlies, a young team that had not yet made it into the playoffs. Nicknamed "Mr. Clutch" for his reputation for saving the game with last-minute heroics, West is the model for the silhouetted figure who is the focal point of the National Basketball Association (NBA) logo. As a player from 1960 through 1974, West became only the third player in NBA history to reach the 25,000-point plateau. He still holds the NBA record for the most free throws (840 in 1965-66) made in a single season. Only five years after leaving the game as a player, West was inducted into the NBA Hall of Fame in 1979. As his biography on the NBA's Web site states, West brought to the

Jerry West

Chronology

1938	Born in Cheylan, West Virginia, on May 28
1956-60	Attends West Virginia University
1960	Picked by Minneapolis Lakers in first round of NBA draft
1974	Steps down as a player
1976	Rejoins Lakers as head coach
1979-82	Serves as special consultant to the Lakers
1982	Named general manager of the Lakers
1995	Named executive vice president of the Lakers
2000	Retires as executive with the Lakers
2002	Hired as president of the Memphis Grizzlies

game "a deadly jump shot, tenacious defense, obsessive perfectionism, unabashed confidence, and an uncompromising will to win."

Born in Cheylan, West Virginia

He was born Jerome Alan West in Cheylan, West Virginia, on May 28, 1938. One of six children of Howard Stewart (a coal mine electrician) and Cecil Sue West (a homemaker), he was kept out of sports as a boy because of his small stature. He spent much of his free time shooting basketballs at a hoop nailed to a neighbor's storage shed, gradually perfecting his shooting style. So preoccupied was the young West with his home-based basketball practice that he often forgot to eat. He dropped so much weight that he eventually was forced to take vitamin injections to preserve his health. Although he finally managed to win a spot on East Bank High School's varsity basketball team, he spent most of his junior year on the bench. The summer between his junior and senior years in high school, West experienced a much welcomed growth spurt, shooting up six inches. During his senior year, West became the first high school player in West Virginia history to score 900 points in a single season. He also led his high school team to a state championship, prompting a thankful East Bank High School to rename itself West Bank High School (for one week) in his honor.

Recruited by a number of colleges, West decided upon West Virginia University in Morgantown. The tran-

sition from a small high school to a large college full of strangers was a difficult one for West. He had drawn inward six years earlier after learning of the death of his older brother, David, in the Korean War. Although he found it difficult to handle his academic workload, he seemed to have no such difficulty on the basketball court. During his years as a West Virginia Mountaineer, West twice was named an All-American, and in 1959 he led his team to the championship game of the National Collegiate Athletic Association (NCAA) tournament. Although the Mountaineers lost the NCAA championship to the University of California, West was named the tournament's most valuable player. The following summer, he joined with another dynamic guard, **Oscar Robertson**, to lead the U.S. Olympic basketball team to gold at the 1960 Olympic Games in Rome.

Picked by Lakers in NBA Draft

The late-blooming West was the number one pick in the first round of the 1960 NBA draft, tapped by the Minneapolis Lakers on the eve of their move to Los Angeles. Although he helped the Lakers to improve their record from a dismal 25-50 in 1959-60 to 36-43 in 1960-61, his rookie season, West years later admitted that he did not yet feel truly comfortable in the NBA. "I was like a fish out of water," he told an interviewer for NBA.com. West's comfort level must have improved significantly his second year with the Lakers, as he nearly doubled his points per game from 17.6 in his rookie season to 30.8 during the 1961-62 season. He also averaged 7.9 rebounds and 5.4 assists per game. Largely on the strength of play by West and **Elgin Baylor**, dubbed the "dynamic duo," the Lakers made it to the NBA finals but lost to the Celtics.

West began to acquire a reputation as a perfectionist. Looking back on a game in which he hit 16 of 17 shots from the field, sank all 12 free-throw attempts, and notched 12 rebounds, 12 assists, and 10 blocked shots, West told the *National Sports Daily:* "Defensively, from a team standpoint, I didn't feel I played very well. Very rarely was I satisfied with how I played." He also showed a remarkable ability to withstand physical pain. According to his biography on the NBA's official Web site, West was "not blessed with great size, strength, or dribbling

Career Statistics

	GP	PTS	P/G	FG%	FT%	REB	AST	STL	BLK
NBA Regular Season	932	25192	27.0	.474	.814	4449	6238	81	23
NBA Playoffs	153	4457	29.1	.469	.805	855	970	—	—
NBA All-Star Games	12	160	13.3	.453	.720	47	55	—	—

ability," but "made up for these deficiencies with pure hustle and an apparent lack of regard for his body. He broke his nose at least nine times. On more than one occasion West had to be helped to the court before games in which he ultimately scored 30 or 40 points."

Shines in Playoffs

As good as he was as a player overall, West really shone in the playoffs. In the Lakers' 1965 finals against the Celtics, he averaged 46.3 points per game, the highest points-per-game average for any playoff series. When the Lakers again faced off against the Celtics in the 1969 finals, West was named most valuable player, the first and only time such honors have gone to a member of the losing team. In an interview West did with NBA.com on the occasion of the NBA's 50th anniversary, West recalled: "I thought we should have won in '69—I felt we had the better team. Those are the ones that leave emotional scars." Despite West's brilliance on the basketball court, the record of the Lakers through 1970 was a study in frustration. In the nine seasons from 1962 through 1970, the Lakers made it into the finals six times but lost all six times—five times to the Celtics and once to the New York Knicks. Half of the finals in which the Lakers played went to seven games, and in two of them against the Celtics, Boston won the seventh and deciding game by a single basket.

In the 1970 finals against the Knicks, West launched his famous bomb, dazzling not only the opponents but his own teammates as well. Walt Frazier of the Knicks recalled thinking: "The man's crazy. He looks determined. He thinks it's really going in!" Much to the amazement of Frazier and others, it did, sending Game 3 of the finals into overtime. In the end, however, the Lakers again came up dry, with the Knicks taking not only Game 3 but the series as well to win the NBA championship.

Briefly Considers Retirement

As much as West wanted to win an NBA championship, the toll taken by numerous injuries had forced him to seriously consider retirement prior to the 1971-72 season. In the end, he returned to the Lakers and helped the Los Angeles team to write a new chapter in NBA history. With Baylor largely sidelined by injury, the Lakers looked to West, **Wilt Chamberlain**, and Gail Goodrich to carry them through. And carry them

through, they did. The trio helped power the Lakers to a 33-game winning streak under new coach Bill Sharman, a former star of the Celtics. At the middle of the season, the Lakers had an unprecedented record of 39-3. The team ended the season with a record of 69-13, the best single-season record in NBA history. Throughout the regular season, West, though increasingly hampered by injuries, managed to average 25.8 points per game while leading the NBA in assists with 9.7 per game.

It began to look as though the Lakers were finally on track to win the NBA championship that they had sought for so long. In the playoffs, the Lakers demolished the Chicago Bulls in four games and took the Milwaukee Bucks in six. Facing off against the Knicks in the finals, the Lakers lost the first game to New York but came back to win the next four games in a row, all by relatively large margins, taking the team's combined record for the regular season and playoffs to a remarkable 81-16. Not only had West finally won an NBA championship, but he had done it with a team enjoying one of the greatest seasons in NBA history. Thus revitalized, West went on to play another two seasons for the Lakers. In the 1972-73 season, the Lakers again made it into the NBA finals but lost the championship to the Knicks. A pulled groin injury during the 1973-74 season kept West out of all but 31 games during the regular season and a single game in the playoffs. At season's end, West announced his retirement, telling the *Los Angeles Herald-Examiner:* "I'm not willing to sacrifice my standards. Perhaps I expect too much." Always high-strung, West was increasingly bothered in his later years as a player by a nervous condition.

Steps Down as Player in 1974

West left professional basketball in 1974 as the third highest career scorer in NBA history, with a total of 25,192 points in 932 games. Only Chamberlain and Robertson had better records at that time, although in the years to come five other NBA players would surpass him. His career average of 27 points per game is the fourth highest ever, behind **Michael Jordan**, Chamberlain, and Baylor. West still retains the record for the highest average points per game for a player over the age of 30, for 31.2 points per game during the 1969-70 season, when he was 31.

West's absence from basketball was relatively brief. He returned as the Lakers coach for the 1976-77 season

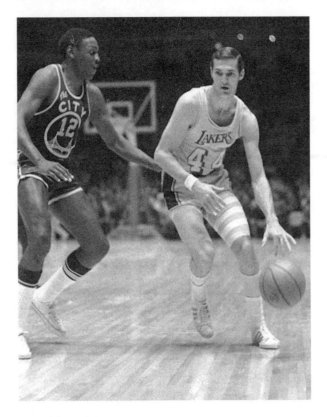

Jerry West, right

Whipping the hapless Grizzlies into a world-class basketball team will pose a major challenge for West, but if anybody can pull it off, he can. Shortly after moving into his new post in Memphis, West told *USA Today:* "I'm excited about going forward with this team in terms of trying to have a team here that would be a play-off team. In many ways, that would be something that maybe would bring as much joy as I had when I worked in Los Angeles as a player and as an executive."

CONTACT INFORMATION

Address: c/o Memphis Grizzlies, 175 Toyota Pl., Ste. 150, Memphis, TN 38103. Fax: (901) 205-1235. Phone: (901) 888-4667.

SELECTED WRITINGS BY WEST:

(With Bill Libby) *Mr. Clutch: The Jerry West Story.* New York: Prentice Hall, 1969.

FURTHER INFORMATION

Books

"Jerry West." *Encyclopedia of World Biography Supplement,* Volume 21. Detroit: Gale Group, 2001.
"Jerry West." *St. James Encyclopedia of Popular Culture,* 5 volumes. Detroit: St. James Press, 2000.

Periodicals

Ballard, Chris. "Memphis Grizzlies: The Franchise Player Here Is New Boss Jerry West, Who Is Trying to Recreate the Magic (and Kareem) He Possessed with the Lakers." *Sports Illustrated* (October 28, 2002): 156.
Boeck, Greg. "Jerry West Enjoying New Challenge." *USA Today* (October 28, 2002).

Other

"Bill Sharman." Basketball Hall of Fame. http://www.hoophall.com/halloffamers/Sharman.htm (December 8, 2002).

and over the next three years coached Los Angeles to a 145-101 record and the team's first return to the playoffs since he had left the team as a player. After three years as coach, West worked for another three years as a special consultant and scout for the Lakers and in 1982 signed on as the team's general manager. In that post he played a pivotal role in building the Lakers dynasty of the 1980s. West found that even off the court he was unable to shake the nervous condition that had troubled him in his years as a player. But he found that it was an essential part of who he was and how he operated as an executive. In a 1990 interview with the *Orange County Register,* West observed: "If I'm not nervous, if I don't have at least a little bit of the same self-doubt and anxious feelings I had when I started playing, then it will be time for me to go on. I must have that tension."

Named Executive Vice President

In 1995 West was named executive vice president of the Lakers. During his years as an executive with the Lakers organization, the team made it into the playoffs eight times and won the NBA championship four times (1985, 1987, 1988, and 2000). In 1995 West was named the NBA Executive of the Year. Increasingly troubled by an irregular heartbeat caused by nervous tension, West retired from basketball in the summer of 2000. After two years of relaxation away from the game, he returned to basketball again, signing on as president of the Memphis Grizzlies in October 2002.

"Jerry West's Career Highlights." CBS SportsLine.com. http://cbs.sportsline.com/u/ce/feature/0,1518, 2644466_54,00.html (December 6, 2002).

"NBA Legends: Jerry West." NBA. http://www.nba.com/ history/west_bio.html (December 6, 2002).

Sketch by Don Amerman

Reggie White

Reggie White
1961-

American football player

Defensive end Reggie White, known as the "Minister of Defense," was named the NFL Defensive Player of the Year in 1987 and 1988. He was a Pro Bowl player 13 consecutive seasons from 1986 to 1998 and he is football's career sacks leader with 68½. In 1997 and 1998, he helped take the Green Bay Packers to the Super Bowl, coming away with a victory in Super Bowl XXXI. A devoutly religious man, White has been as controversial off the field as he was tremendous in the huddle.

A Football Player and a Minister

White grew up in the housing projects of Chattanooga, Tennessee, and was raised by his mother; he barely knew his father, but his mother remarried and White's stepfather helped raise him. When he was 12, White told his mother that he wanted to be a football player and a minister. He attended a Baptist church and began preaching at age 17. He combined his religious fervor with a drive to compete and a gift of athletic talent; he was an All-American player in his senior season at the University of Tennessee, and then spent two years playing with the Memphis Showboats of the United States Football League (USFL). In 1985, he joined the Philadelphia Eagles. In 1992, White was ordained as a nondenominational minister.

White played with the Philadelphia Eagles for eight seasons. In every one of those seasons he recorded double-digit sack numbers, with a high of 21 in 1987. He became one of the most feared players in the NFL and a nightmare to quarterbacks, averaging 15.5 sacks per season. White and his wife, Sara, were also deeply involved in a ministry in the housing projects of north Philadelphia. White, Sara, and some of White's Eagles teammates often spent Friday nights in the projects, and on weekdays, White often went back to lead Bible studies, to volunteer at church councils, and to assist at fundraising events.

In 1993, White was eligible to be a free-agent. Many NFL teams joined in the bidding for the superstar defensive lineman. When Norman Braman, owner of the Eagles, refused to pay White the salary he wanted in order to prevent him from leaving as a free agent, thousands of fans rallied to try and convince Braman to pay. He wouldn't, and at a farewell luncheon, White cried as over 300 fans gave him a lengthy standing ovation. Fi-

Chronology

1961	Born in Chattanooga, Tennessee
1979-83	Plays for University of Tennessee
1983-84	Plays with Memphis Showboats of USFL
1985	Signs with Philadelphia Eagles
1993	Leaves Eagles; signed by Green Bay Packers
1996	Inner City Church in Knoxville, Tennessee, where White was assistant pastor, is burned to the ground as a result of arson
1997	Helps Packers win Super Bowl XXXI
1998	Loses potential job at CBS Sports after making remarks about homosexuality and race
1999	Retires from play; Packers retire his number, 92
2000	Comes back to play for Carolina Panthers

Awards and Accomplishments

1986-98	Pro Bowl player
1997	Green Bay Packers win Super Bowl
1997-98	Named top defensive player in NFL
1998	Associated Press Player of the Year
1999	Green Bay Packers retire his number, 92

nally, he said tearfully, "I didn't give up on the Eagles. It seems as though the Eagles gave up on me," according to Johnette Howard in *Sports Illustrated.*

After leaving the Eagles, White set out on a seven-city tour, lasting 37 days, looking for a position. He wanted to go to a contending team, but it had to be a team where he could continue his inner-city ministry. However, when the Green Bay Packers—then a mediocre team, and a team based in the smallest city in the league—offered him a four-year, $17-millon contract, White accepted. Braman, hearing of this, scoffed at White's decision, saying, according to Howard, that it "wasn't made by a ghetto or by God. It was going to be made for the reason most human beings make decisions today, money." The comment troubled White, who did not like his integrity to be questioned. He told Howard, "How dare he speak for what was in my heart? He doesn't know me."

Packers fans, however, were delighted to have White on the team. Almost 2,000 of them attended his first day of training camp. The year before, the Packers had had a 9-7 season, but White was hopeful about great days for the team in the future.

In 1993, the Packers were 9-7 again, but won a playoff game. The team's defense, which had ranked 23rd the year before, finished second in the league. Coach **Mike Holmgren** told Howard that White was the reason: "Reggie has changed everything—the way we play, the other team's offensive scheme."

In 1995, the Packers advanced all the way to the NFC Championship Game, which they lost to the Dallas Cowboys, 38-27. On the plane home, Howard reported, White told Holmgren, "Coach, I've never been this far. I just want to thank you."

In the locker room, White, nicknamed "the Minister of Defense," was known for giving advice to younger players, as well as for his habit of calling player meetings; safety LeRoy Butler told Howard, "He calls more meetings than Congress." Butler also noted that during their shared rides to practice, White would only listen to gospel music. Another teammate, tight end Keith Jackson, commented on White's tendency to see every event

as a divine message, saying, "The walk with God that Reggie has is almost, you know, scary." His choice to join the Packers came after a night of prayer, asking for guidance. "And the Lord spoke to me," he told Howard. One factor in his decision might have been the fact that Holmgren called and left a message on his machine, saying, "Reggie, this is God. Go to Green Bay," according to Paul Attner in the *Sporting News.*

When White sustained an elbow injury in 1994, a thigh bruise in 1995, and a hamstring injury in 1995, he believed God had healed him. He almost missed the 1995 playoffs because of the hamstring injury, but it healed in time for him to play. On the field, he often ruthlessly knocked over opponents during play, but once a play was over, he helped them up, saying "Jesus loves you."

A Church Burning

In addition to playing football, White became an associate pastor at an evangelical church in an inner-city area of Knoxville, Tennessee. With a congregation of about 450, the church focused on community development; members rebuilt condemned houses for resale to low-income people, and also built homes that low-income people could afford. The church also ran an AM radio station with religious programming, and planned to create a daycare center. White donated $1 million to the project, and in 1994 the church opened an investment bank, which makes loans to people who couldn't qualify for traditional bank loans. The bank also run seminars in job skills and financial planning, and provides credit to small-business owners. White told Howard that the church's goal was to "get people off welfare and help them become tax-paying citizens." White and his wife also opened a home for unwed mothers on their own property, near their home.

On January 8, 1996, White's church was burned to the ground; someone had placed kerosene, gunpowder, and several Molotov cocktails in the church, lit them, and fled, leaving racist graffiti behind. The burning angered White, and aroused him to speak on television, radio, and in print about the event, as well as several other church-burnings that had occurred. He and his family subsequently received racist letters and a bomb threat that later turned out to be a hoax. White told Howard, "[I'm] willing to die for the things I believe in." White, who often refers to civil rights history, insists that the African-American struggle against slavery and racism should be remembered. "If you remember it. . ." he told Howard,

Career Statistics

Yr	Team	Tackles				Fumbles		Interceptions	
		Tot	Solo	Ast	Sack	FF	BK	Int	TD
1985	PHI	100	62	38	13.0	0	0	0	0
1986	PHI	98	83	15	18.0	1	0	0	0
1987	PHI	76	62	14	21.0	4	0	0	0
1988	PHI	133	96	37	18.0	1	0	0	0
1989	PHI	123	82	41	11.0	3	0	0	0
1990	PHI	83	59	24	14.0	4	0	1	0
1991	PHI	100	72	28	15.0	2	0	1	0
1992	PHI	81	54	27	14.0	3	0	0	0
1993	GB	79	48	31	13.0	3	0	0	0
1994	GB	49	40	9	8.0	2	0	0	0
1995	GB	42	32	10	12.0	2	0	0	0
1996	GB	39	30	9	8.5	3	1	1	0
1997	GB	46	36	10	11.0	0	0	0	0
1998	GB	47	36	11	16.0	4	0	0	0
2000	CAR	16	15	1	5.5	1	0	0	0
TOTAL		1111	793	318	198.0	33	0	3	0

CAR: Carolina Panthers; GB: Green Bay Packers; PHI: Philadelphia Eagles.

"then you begin to say, 'This can't happen anymore.'" And, he commented, "Then you'll begin to understand why I hurt like I hurt. And why I get so mad." After the burning, White's church moved to a nearby high school auditorium; by June of 1996, more than $250,000 had been donated to help the church rebuild.

In 1997, White finally realized his one last NFL feat. The Packers defeated the New England Patriots 35-21 in Super Bowl XXXI. White was a terror on defense, recording three sacks and hurrying Patriots quarterback into four interceptions. Green Bay repeated as NFC champions the next season, but lost in Super Bowl XXXII to the Denver Broncos.

In 1998, White lost a chance to work as a commentator at CBS Sports when he made remarks about homosexuality and race that many people found offensive. According to an article in *Jet,* CBS Sports spokesperson said, "CBS has a hard and fast policy against bias at all times." When asked about the event later, White said, "Forget about me. I don't need your money."

Retired from Play

In 1997 and 1998, White was named the top defensive player in the NFL. In 1998, he had led the NFL in sacks, with 16, and was also voted Associated Press Defensive Player of the Year. After that season he told a reporter from *Jet* that he was retiring from play due to several nagging injuries. In November of 1999, White was honored when the Packers retired his number, 92, from play. In 2000, White returned to play when he signed a contract with the Carolina Panthers; he played with the team for one year.

In an interview in *Sports Illustrated for Kids,* White advised, "Sometimes, being a leader means that you have to become independent of everybody. That's not easy. But you have to stand up for what you believe in, even if you're standing alone."

CONTACT INFORMATION

Address: 325 N. Roosevelt Street, Green Bay, WI 54301. Fax: 920-448-6460 ext. 298. Online: www.urbanhopegb.org.

SELECTED WRITINGS BY WHITE:

(With Larry Reid) *The Reggie White Touch Football Playbook: Winning Plays, Rule, and Safety Tips,* Warrenton Press, 1991.

(With Terry Hill) *Reggie White: Minister of Defense,* Word Publishing, 1991.

(With Jim Denney) *In the Trenches: The Autobiography,* Thomas Nelson, 1997.

(With Steve Hubbard) *God's Playbook: The Bible's Game Plan for Life,* Thomas Nelson, 1998.

(With Andrew Peyton Thomas) *Fighting the Good Fight: America's "Minister of Defense" Stands Firm on What It Takes to Win God's Way,* Thomas Nelson, 1999.

FURTHER INFORMATION

Periodicals

Attner, Paul. "As for Me and My House, We Will Serve the Lord." *Sporting News,* July 8, 1996: 40.

Attner, Paul. "Confronting the Lombardi Legend." *Sporting News,* January 27, 1997: 12.

Howard, Johnette. "Up From the Ashes." *Sports Illustrated,* September 2, 1996: 140.

"Reggie White Rejects Criticism for His Remarks about Homosexuality and Race." *Jet,* April 13, 1998: 55.

"Sackman!" *Sports Illustrated for Kids,* January, 1997: 24.

"Terrell Davis, Reggie White Named Top Offensive and Defensive Players in NFL." *Jet,* January 25, 1999: 48.

Other

"Heads, Carolina." CNNSI.com, http://www.sports illustrated.cnn.com/ (July 21, 2000).

"Reggie White." ESPN.org. http://football.espn.go.com/ (January 5, 2003).

Urban Hope. http://www.urbanhopegb.org/ (January 5, 2003).

Sketch by Carol Brennan

Kathy Whitworth

Kathy Whitworth
1939-

American golfer

Kathy Whitworth's professional golfing career spanned 32 years. From 1959 to 1991, she was a consistent figure in the Ladies Professional Golf Association (LPGA). She started out with the LPGA when it was just beginning to take hold and participated in bringing it into its own. During that time she broke ground that set high standards for the women who follow in her footsteps. She was the first woman to earn a million dollars in LPGA tournament play. She holds the record for the most wins in tournament play for both the men's and women's professional associations. She was also the captain for the first American team to play in the Solheim Cup—a tournament that pits the top European women golfers against the top American women golfers. Her only disappointment in the midst of many achievements is never having won a U. S. Open tournament. In spite of that, she continues to maintain a proud yet humble opinion of her career, while having earned the respect of peers and fans.

Early Signs of Potential

Kathrynne Ann Whitworth was born on September 27, 1939, in Monahans, Texas. She is the youngest child of Morris and Dama Robinson Whitworth. Whitworth's father worked for a lumber company in Monahans, but eventually moved the family to Jal, New Mexico where their extended family lived. The small town of Jal had originally been a ranching community but by the 1950s the oil industry had built up around it. Whitworth's parents owned and operated a hardware store there until 1981.

Whitworth was a talented athlete who adapted to sports easily. She claims that most of her competitive spirit and athletic ability are due to her mother. In high school, Whitworth played tennis since it was the only organized sport available to women at the time. When she was 15 some friends from the tennis team convinced her to join them in a round of golf. It was Whitworth's first experience with golf and she was amazed when she couldn't play the game well. Sensing a challenge and wanting to prove that she could play the game, Whitworth spent the next year playing alone until she felt she was good enough to play in public.

Impressed by Whitworth's dedication to the sport, Morris and Dama joined the Jal Country Club so that Whitworth could play whenever she wanted. Around that time she started taking lessons from the professional at the country club who felt she had potential. Hardy

Chronology

1939	Born September 27 in Monahans, Texas
1954	Begins playing golf
1957	Begins attending Odessa Junior College in Odessa, Texas; wins first of two New Mexico State Amateur titles
1958	Drops out of college to turn professional; finishes almost last in Titleholders Championship in Augusta, Georgia
1961	Attends 6-week golf clinic held by Patty Berg, co-founder of LPGA
1962	Wins first LPGA tournament
1967	Becomes president of the LPGA for first time; other years as president are 1968, 1971 and 1989
1985	Wins last LPGA tournament
1986	Loses entire retirement fund of $388,000 when Technical Equities Corporation declares bankruptcy
1988	Mother diagnosed with cancer, goes into remission by 1991; serves as vice president of LPGA
1989	Serves as president of LPGA for final time
1990	Acts as captain for first U.S. team to play the Solheim Cup
1991	Retires from professional golf
1995	Finishes tied for 35th in the Chrysler-Plymouth Tournament of Champions
1996	Competes in the Chrysler-Plymouth Tournament of Champions and the Nabisco Dinah Shore
2001	Finishes tied for 13th at Hy-Vee Classic in Des Moines, Iowa; competes in the Great Lakes Classic in Green Bay, Wisconsin

Awards and Accomplishments

1965, 1967	Named Associate Press Athlete of the Year
1965-67, 1969-72	Awarded the Vare Trophy for best scoring average
1966-69, 1971-73	Named LPGA Player of the Year
1966-69, 1971-73	Named Rolex Player of the Year
1968-77	Named "Golfer of the Decade," by *GOLF Magazine*
1970	Wins Orange Blossom Classic third year in row; second in LPGA history to win same event three times in a row
1975	Inducted into LPGA Hall of Fame
1981	Becomes first LPGA player to surpass $1 million in career earnings
1982	Inducted into Texas Sports Hall of Fame
1984	Breaks record for number of tournament titles with 85th win; inducted into International Women's Sports Hall of Fame
1985	Sets record for number of tournament titles with 88th win; awarded William Richardson Award for consistent outstanding contribution to golf, Golf Writers Association of America; with Mickey Wright, first woman to play in the Legends of Golf tournament
1986	First recipient of the William and Mousie Powell Award
1987	Presented with the Patty Berg Award
2000	Named one of the LPGA's top 50 players and teachers
2001	Presented with the Leadership Award, Executive Women's Golf Association
2002	Inducted into the Sun Country Hall of Fame, New Mexico Golf Academy, Albuquerque

Loudermilk was Whitworth's first tutor, but he felt his skills were limited. When he thought she was ready Loudermilk contacted one of golf's legendary teachers and asked him if he would work with her. Harvey Penick, a renowned tutor at the Austin Country Club, agreed to meet with Whitworth.

Whitworth began making periodic trips to Austin, a 400-mile trek, for three- and four-day lessons. She would make the drive with her mother who would take notes of Penick's suggestions. Penick would contact Loudermilk with information about Whitworth's progress and what she needed to practice. Whitworth explained to Dave Anderson of the *New York Times,* "Harvey changed the whole game for me.... He gave me a knowledge of the game and the swing." Armed with this knowledge, Whitworth began making the rounds of amateur tournaments in the Southwest.

Dedication and Focus

In 1957, Whitworth's tireless practicing and the dedication of her mentors and family helped her win the New Mexico State Women's Championship. Her prize was a turquoise necklace that she turned down, instead asking that the awarding committee give her a trophy. The committee obliged. In 1958, Whitworth won the state championship again. This second win bolstered her confidence and she began to meet the professionals of women's golf. With financial backing from her father and several Jal businessmen, Whitworth decided to turn professional.

Whitworth's first season of professional golf was in 1959. She had dropped out of Odessa Junior College to pursue her career and was learning the realities of tournament play. Although she was thrilled to be playing professionally, she did not play well and made no money. Increasingly discouraged, Whitworth went home to discuss plans of leaving the tour. She credits a pep talk from her parents with inspiring her to return to the tour. The next week she tied for last place and won $33. That win was enough to keep her going.

Whitworth became determined to make golf her career. In 1961 she attended a six-week golf clinic held by LPGA co-founder Patter Berg. Through Berg's clinic, Whitworth learned many different styles of shots, which she relentlessly practiced. The practice paid off. She started placing in the top ten. In 1962, at the Kelly Girls Open in Elicott City, Maryland, Whitworth won her first match. After that she routinely placed in the top two spots along with women's golf legend **Mickey Wright**.

From 1965 to 1974, Whitworth claimed at least two of the following three titles each year: player of the year, lowest scoring average, or leading earner. She earned all three titles five different years. For 17 years in a row, she won at least one tournament; a record matched only by male players **Arnold Palmer** and **Jack Nicklaus**.

The extreme competitiveness of professional golf eventually took a toll on Whitworth's nerves. By 1973, she was beginning to feel its effects and she began to back off from the idea of winning. Her game deteriorated significantly through the 1970s, hitting an all-time low in 1979 and 1980 when she recorded no wins. In

Related Biography: Golf Professional Harvey Penick

Harvey Penick might have remained one of the most obscure yet most important figures in professional golf had it not been for the 1992 publication of his book, *Harvey Penick's Little Red Book: Lessons and Teachings from a Lifetime of Golf.* The book sold more than one million copies and spent weeks on the *New York Times* best-seller list.

Penick started as a caddie at the Austin (Texas) Country Club (ACC) in 1913. During the 1920s he played the Texas PGA tours, and served as its president. In 1922, he was hired as the ACC's golf professional. He held that position until he retired in 1971. In 1931 he started coaching for the University of Texas golf team, retiring in 1963.

For 60 years, Penick collected his thoughts and observations about golf in a small red notebook. Penick mentioned the book to author Bud Shrake, and together they created one of the best-selling books about the sport to ever be published. Their collaboration also created two other notable books on golf.

Penick died on April 4, 1995, after suffering for many years from poor health. In 2002, he was named to the World Golf Hall of Fame in the lifetime achievement category.

1981, Whitworth recollected herself. She began focusing on her practicing again, and met with her former coach Penick to pick up a few refreshing pointers.

Returning to basics did the trick for Whitworth's game. In May of 1981, Whitworth broke her losing streak with a win at the Coca-Cola Classic in Paramus, New Jersey. The win set her on track to break several more records. She became one of four women close to topping the one million dollar mark. She also started encroaching on Mickey Wright's record number of wins for a woman golfer. By August, Whitworth placed third at the U.S. Open held in La Grange, Illinois, putting her earnings over the one million mark. In 1982, she topped Wright's wins with her 82nd win at the Lady Michelob Classic.

Quietly Making Her Mark

Pete Axthelm of *Newsweek* wrote of Whitworth, "She is one of the quiet, gracious ladies of sport." In many ways, Whitworth was the epitome of the long, tall Texan. She dressed conservatively and sported a hairstyle that relied heavily on hairspray. She never wanted to draw attention to herself as a celebrity or a star. She explained to Barry McDermott of *Sports Illustrated,* "It's not necessary for people to know you.... The record itself speaks."

Whitworth made many sacrifices for a professional career in golf, including giving up the chance of having a family of her own. She explained to McDermott, "I wanted to be a golfer, the best I could be, and marriage and golf didn't mix." She further commented in her book, *Golf for Women,* "I didn't give up a family, I decided I didn't want one. I freely made the decision to dedicate myself to professional golf. No one held a gun to my head; the hours that I spent on the practice tee were hours I wanted to spend on the practice tee."

Whitworth's dedication put her in the history books. In 1984, she surpassed golfing great Sam Snead's record for professional wins when she won her 85th tournament. By 1988, she added three more tournament wins to that number and placed herself firmly at the top as the winningest professional golf player, man or woman.

Surviving Hard Times

Despite continuing wins, those were not easy years for Whitworth personally. In 1986, the entirety of Whitworth's retirement fund disappeared when the company she had invested in, Technical Equities Corporation, went bankrupt. Whitworth described the effect of losing her retirement fund to Sonja Steptoe of *Sports Illustrated,* "It definitely took something out of me.... I felt like I'd worked so hard. I didn't know if I had the energy to start over." Two years later her mother was diagnosed with cancer. Her mother's cancer eventually went into remission, but Whitworth told Steptoe, "There was lots of heartbreak and lots of tears."

In 1991, Whitworth announced her retirement. Instead of focusing on competition she began holding golf clinics and participating in exhibitions and eventually joined the Senior LPGA tour. As of 2002, she teaches the Kathy Whitworth Women's School at the Grand Cypress Academy of Golf in Orlando, Florida. She regularly contributes articles to *Golf for Women Magazine,* and has written a book titled *Golf for Women.*

Throughout her career, Whitworth has exhibited the finer traits of professional competition: control, concentration, humility, and persistence. With 32 years of play in the LPGA under her belt, she witnessed and participated in the growth of women's professional golf. Shelley Hamlin, former president of the LPGA described Whitworth's career to Axthelm, "She didn't fall into greatness.... She grew into it. It's been an inspiration for all of us to watch her keep reaching for perfection."

CONTACT INFORMATION

Address: Kathy Whitworth, 1735 Mistletoe Drive, Flower Mound, TX 75022.

SELECTED WRITINGS BY WHITWORTH:

(With Rhonda Glenn) *Golf for Women,* St. Martin's Press, 1990.
"Kathy Says," *Golf for Women Magazine,* 2002-.

FURTHER INFORMATION

Books

Whitworth, Kathy and Rhonda Glenn. *Golf for Women.* New York: St. Martin's Press, 1990.

Periodicals

Anderson, Dave. "The Lady Is a Champ." *New York Times* (May 11, 1981): C3.

Axthelm, Pete. "The Million-Dollar Lady." *Newsweek* (August 10, 1981): 62.

Cartwright, Gary. "The Old Man and the Tee." *Texas Monthly* (December 2000): S20.

Eskenazi, Gerald. "Harvey Penick, 90, Golf's Top Author, Dies." *New York Times* (April 4, 1995): D25.

McDermott, Barry. "Wrong Image But the Right Touch." *Sports Illustrated* (July 25, 1983): 38.

Nichols, Bill. "Crenshaw and Penick: Inseperable Even Now As They Head To Hall." Knight Ridder/Tribune News Service (November, 13, 2002).

Steptoe, Sonja. "Playing Out of Deep Rough" *Sports Illustrated* (September 30, 1991): 6.

"Sun Country Will Have Its Own Hall of Fame." *Albuquerque Journal* (June 15, 2002): D1.

Other

"LPGA-Players." http://www.lpga.com/players/index.cfm?cont_type_id=1681&player_id=31544#Persona (December 30, 2002).

Sketch by Eve M. B. Hermann

Hayley Wickenheiser
1978-

Canadian hockey player

Canadian hockey star Hayley Wickenheiser stands likely to become the first female position player in professional men's hockey (three other women have played in goal). In 2002, a few teams in the National Hockey League (NHL) minors realm were expressing tentative interest signing this Olympic gold medallist and her formidable skills as a forward. *Maclean's* called her "arguably the best player in women's hockey today."

Backyard Rink

Wickenheiser was born in 1978 and grew up in Shaunavon, in the province of Saskatchewan. The oldest of three, she first learned to skate at the age of six when her parents created a backyard ice rink with the help of a garden hose and some two-by-fours. She played her first hockey games on it, and was soon devoted to the sport; her father once woke in the middle of night to find her out in the backyard taking shots. As a youngster, she joined a local team as its sole female participant, at a time when organized hockey for female players was almost nonexis-

Chronology	
1978	Born August 12 in Shaunavon, Saskatchewan, Canada
1990	Joins Calgary, Alberta, junior girls' team
1993	Wins spot on Canadian women's national team
1994, 1997, **1999-2000**	Member of winning team at Women's World Hockey Championships
1998	Attends Philadelphia Flyers prospects camp
1998	Silver medal, women's hockey, 1998 Winter Olympics
1999	Attends Philadelphia Flyers prospects camp
2002	Gold medal, women's hockey, 2002 Winter Olympics

tent. Often there was no available dressing room for her to use, and she was forced to don her gear in boiler rooms or other areas of the rink. Her mother battled to have her enrolled in a hockey school in Swift Current, Saskatchewan, and again, she tested her mettle as the only player of her gender there. When she was in middle school, the Wickenheiser family relocated to Calgary, Alberta, so that she could play on an all-girls' team in the city.

At fifteen, Wickenheiser made the Canadian women's national team, and joined players who were, in some cases, twenty years her senior; they nicknamed her "High-Chair Hayley" because of her youth. With Team Canada she went on to play in winning World Championship contests in both 1994 and 1997. She had also become an outstanding softball player, and made the Canadian junior women's team in 1995. Women's ice hockey became an Olympic medal sport for the first time at the 1998 Nagano Winter Olympics in Japan, and though Wickenheiser and her Canadian team were heavily favored, they suffered an upset to the United States and went home with the silver medal instead. Her on-ice performance impressed Bobby Clarke, the Philadelphia Flyers president who served as general manager of the men's Olympic hockey team, and he invited her to the Flyers prospects' camp that summer. Wickenheiser realized that her chances for a contract were slim, but she relished the chance to compete against other Olympic-caliber players. "I'm basically just seeing it as a chance to improve my game," she told *Maclean's*

Made Olympic History

Wickenheiser balanced her hockey career with studies at the University of Calgary, where she enrolled in its pre-med program. In 2000, she and Team Canada won another World Championship—the fourth for her—and later that year she qualified for a spot on the Canadian women's softball team and traveled to the 2000 Summer Olympics in Sydney, Australia. After Sue Holloway, a cross-country skier at the 1976 Winter Games and 1984 medalist in two kayak events, Wickenheiser was the second Canadian woman ever to compete in both Winter and Summer Olympics. She returned to hockey once again at the 2002 Winter Games in Salt Lake City, and emerged as her team's leading scorer. This time, they

Awards and Accomplishments

1991	Member of gold medal team, Canada Winter Games
1991	Most Valuable Player in gold medal game, Canada Winter Games
1994, 1997, 1999-2000	Member of gold medal World Championship team
1996, 2001	Member of gold medal team at Four Nations Cup
1997	National champion with the Edmonton Chimos
1998	National champion with the Calgary Oval X-Treme Team
1998	Member of silver medal team at the Winter Olympics in Nagano, 1998
2002	Member of gold medal team at the Winter Olympics in Salt Lake City, Utah, 2002

Career Statistics

Yr	Event	G	A	PIM
1994	World Championships	0	1	4
1995	Pacific Rim	3	6	8
1996	Pacific Rim	5	4	12
1997	World Championships	4	5	12
1997	Three Nations Cup	3	5	12
1998	Olympic Games	2	6	4
2002	Pre-Olympic Tour	12	11	16

avenged the loss four years earlier and beat Team USA for the gold medal. Wickenheiser scored the second goal of the final contest.

A member of the Edmonton Chimos team in the National Women's Hockey League of Canada, Wickenheiser sought a berth on the Merano Eagles, an Italian team, but just before the contract was inked in the fall of 2002, the Italian Ice Hockey Federation declared her ineligible. She signed a letter of intent to play with the Port Huron Beacons, a minors team in the United Hockey League, but soon reports surfaced that she was poised to join another minor league, the East Coast Hockey League (ECHL). Once known for a rough style of play dramatized in the 1977 Paul Newman film *Slap Shot,* the ECHL was home to teams like the Cincinnati Cyclones and Richmond Renegades, both of whom expressed interest in making her the first woman skater in the minors. **Phil Esposito**, co-owner of the Cyclones, had used **Manon Rheaume** as goalie in 1992 NHL preseason game with Tampa Bay Lightning when he served as the latter team's general manager, and told a reporter for the *St. Petersburg Times* that Wickenheiser's gender was irrelevant to him. "For me, I don't care if they're black, white, pink, blue, giraffe, hippopotamus," Esposito said in an interview with Damian Cristodero. "If they can skate and can play, I want them."

Ready to Rumble?

Some wondered if Wickenheiser, at five feet, nine inches in height and 170 pounds, could withstand the likely assaults from male players who dwarfed her. Richmond Renegades coach Gord Dineen theorized that Wickenheiser would be happy to prove herself. "I don't think guys would really hold back," he told Eric Duhatschek of the *Cincinnati Post*. "They're playing for their jobs, too. Plus, being a competitor and knowing what she's done for women's hockey, I don't think she'd want guys holding back either." Even Canada's top female player confessed her doubts about playing in co-ed hockey at the pre-NHL level. She knew the ECHL was a rough arena, and had played against some of its members in the occasional pick-up game. Characterizing it as "a

desperate league, full of guys trying to make it," she told the *Detroit Free Press* the ECHL was "a North American style of hockey and I don't know if it's a style I'm capable of playing." She preferred the European leagues, and her agent was still attempting to find her a spot for her on a German, Austrian, Swiss, or Italian team as a forward. The agent, Wade Arnott, told David Naylor in a report that appeared in the *Cincinnati Post* that "Europe is still priority No. 1 for Hayley. We believe Europe is the right place for her because it—especially the Italian League—has the right emphasis on skating and skill for her. . . . [But] we haven't ruled anything out."

Even if Wickenheiser never made it to the NHL, she worked to ensure that a younger generation of female players would have the chance. She promotes hockey for women of all ages, and has even founded her own traveling hockey clinic for girls, the "Wick One-on-One Tour."

CONTACT INFORMATION

Address: c/o Edmonton Chimos Hockey Club, #205, 8908-99 St., Edmonton, Alberta T6E 3V4, Canada. Phone: (780) 44-CHIMO. Online: http://www.edmonton chimos.com.

FURTHER INFORMATION

Periodicals

"A hockey heroine goes to boys camp." *Maclean's* (June 8, 1998): 37.

"Canada Beats United States." *Cincinnati Post* (November 11, 2002): C7.

"Canada Captures Four Nations Cup." *Seattle Post-Intelligencer* (November 11, 2002): D13.

"Canada Defeats U.S. In Four Nations Cup." *New York Times* (November 11, 2002): D11.

"Canada rallies, finishes Finns." *Detroit News* (February 20, 2002): 8.

"Canada's Wickenheiser Is a Cousin of Ex-Blues Star." *St Louis Post-Dispatch* (February 21, 2002): D1.

Chere, Rich. "Role player is now an international star." *Star-Ledger* (Newark, NJ) (February 8, 1998): 11.

Chere, Rich. "Team USA relieved to say bye to Sweden." *Star-Ledger* (Newark, NJ) (February 10, 1998): 56.

Cristodero, Damian. "Espo's at it again." *St. Petersburg Times* (St. Petersburg, FL) (November 3, 2002): 5C.

Duhatschek, Eric. "ECHL Tough Place for a Lady." *Cincinnati Post* (October 31, 2002): C1.

Frei, Terry. "Women's gold-medal game: Canada 3, United States 2." *Denver Post* (February 22, 2002): C1.

"Hayley Wickenheiser: Ready for Men's League?" *Detroit Free Press* (November 7, 2002).

"Japanese no match for Canadian women's team." *Tampa Tribune* (February 9, 1998): 10.

Jollimore, Mary. "Double Play: The best female hockey player in the world plays softball too." *Time International* (September 11, 2000): 50.

Naylor, David. "Cyclones invite woman to try out." *Cincinnati Post* (October 31, 2002).

Paul, Tony. "Beacons show interest in female player." *Times Herald* (Port Huron, MI) (October 31, 2002): 1C.

Sketch by Carol Brennan

Deena Wigger

Deena Wigger
1967-

American rifle shooter

Deena Wigger is a one-time world record holder in women's air rifle, and was a member of the 1988 U.S. Olympic rifle team. In 1983 she won the gold medal at her very first international competition, the Pan American Games, which she competed in when she was just 16 years old. Wigger has also won medals at the rifle shooting world championships.

Born in Montana in 1967, Deena Wigger grew up at Fort Benning, Georgia. It was no accident that she became a world-class sharpshooter. Her father is Lones Wigger, an Olympic gold medal-winning marksman. He won his medals at the 1964 and the 1972 Olympics, and he taught his daughter to shoot before she was a teenager.

Wigger seemed born to the sport of shooting. The first time her father handed her a rifle and pointed out the target for her to shoot, she very carefully set up her shot before pulling the trigger. She fired the rifle five times, and "When we got the target back," her father later told Vicki Michaelis in the *Denver Post*, "the five-shot group looked like one hole. That was a pretty good indication that she was going to do well."

Since it doesn't require extraordinary physical strength or endurance like other sports, the sport of rifle shooting presents an even playing field for all participants. Men and women of all ages compete against each other. What is required is a sharp focus and a steady hand—attributes of a prepared mind more than a fit body.

Wigger decided early on to shoot competitively, just as her father had before her. At first the elder Wigger acted as her coach, but as she got older, her father turned her training over to others. As he explained later it, teaching one's daughter to shoot was similar to teaching one's wife to drive a car. "I stay away from that," he revealed to Vicki Michaelis in the *Denver Post*.

In 1983, when she was 16 years old, Wigger competed in her first international competition as a member of the U.S. national shooting team. The event was the Pan American Games, and she took home the gold medal in prone shooting. Wigger went on to college at Murray State University in Kentucky, where she played on the school's rifle team. The highlight of her time at Murray State came when she helped her team to win the NCAA shooting championship. Wigger competed in the World Championships for shooting in 1986, and took home a bronze medal.

In 1988, when Wigger was 21 years old, she competed at the Olympic Games on the U.S. rifle team. Her father acted as the team's manager. Wigger's 9th place performance disappointed her, and she considered giv-

Chronology

1967	Born in Montana
1979	Learns to shoot a rifle at the age of 12
1983	Competes in her first international rifle competition, the Pan American Games, and wins gold medal
1986	Wins bronze medal at World Championships
1988	Competes on U.S. rifle team at Olympic Games
1988	Breaks women's air rifle record
1990	Wins silver medal at World Championships
1990	Named U.S. Olympic Committee female shooter of the year
1995	Joins U.S. Air Force

Awards and Accomplishments

1983	Wins gold metal at Pan American Games
1986	Wins bronze medal at world rifle championships
1988	Competes on U.S. Olympic rifle team
1989	Breaks women's world air rifle record with 389 points out of 400 possible
1990	Wins silver medal at world championships; named U.S. Olympic Committee female shooter of the year
1994	Wins gold medal at Olympic Festival

ing up the sport. It didn't help that she had big shoes to fill—she questioned whether she would ever be as good as her father.

Olympic rifle competition involves three phases of competition—air rifle, three-position rifle, and free rifle prone. Each phase presents its own challenges. Air rifle involves shooting a .177 caliber gun at a target that is 10 meters away. The bull's eye in this phase of the competition measures just half a millimeter. Three-position rifle has competitors shooting .22 smallbore rifles from their stomachs, from kneeling positions, and while standing at targets 50 meters away. Free rifle prone also involves shooting at targets that are 50 meters away, with rifles that can be specially modified for individual shooters. In both of these last phases of competition, the bull's eyes on the targets are less than the size of a dime.

Because Olympic rifle competition involves shooting small caliber rifles at extremely small targets, the slightest movement on the part of a shooter can spoil the shooters aim. In fact, the competition requires such accuracy that even the shooter's heartbeat can cause a missed shot, and so competitors wear insulated clothing to dampen the vibrations caused by their heartbeats.

Wigger overcame her disappointment over not medaling at the Olympics. She got back on her feet, again shooting in competitions. Wigger's persistence paid off, and in 1989, she broke the women's world air rifle record, with 389 points out of a possible 400 (another shooter broke her record within a year). Wigger went on to won a silver medal at the World Championships in 1990.

Although she was one of the best female shooters in the world, Wigger put enormous pressure on herself to perform better. "The better you get," she explained to Karen Rosen in the *Atlanta Journal and Constitution* in 1994, "the more pressure you feel." That pressure led her to relocate to the Olympic Training Center in Colorado Springs, Colorado in 1991. In retrospect Wigger considered this move a mistake. In Colorado Springs, she practiced shooting seven hours a day, often firing 400 rounds in a single session. The intense training schedule pushed her toward burnout, and worse yet, she did not qualify for the 1992 Olympic U.S. shooting team.

After reconsidering her priorities, Wigger joined the Wyoming Air National Guard and also took a job as an administrative assistant with the U.S. shooting team. Working and earning money proved to be just what she needed to take some of the pressure off to make shooting her life, and she took home the gold medal for the three-position at the 1994 Olympic Festival.

In 1995, Wigger joined the U.S. Air Force, where she became a medical technician. She also became the assistant rifle coach at the Air Force Academy, and continued to shoot competitively, notably for the U.S. Air Force International Rifle Team. Wigger tried out for the 1996 Olympic Games, but again failed to qualify. Undaunted, she stayed in the Air Force. Wigger continued to train for shooting with the United States Army Marksmanship Unit (USAMU), and to shoot in competitions such as the World Military Shooting Championships.

FURTHER INFORMATION

Periodicals

Michaelis, Vicki. "Mind Games Key to Pulling the Trigger." *Denver Post* (July 11, 1995): D1.

"Nominees for SportsMan, SportsWoman of the Year." *USA Today* (January 4, 1991): 9C.

Rosen, Karen. "Olympics: Her Confidence Is in Sight Again: Wigger Is Back for '96." *Atlanta Journal and Constitution* (April 22, 1994): D12.

Other

Barela, Tech. Sgt. Timothy P. "Wigger at the Trigger: Airman Shoots for Olympic Glory." Airman. http://www.af.mil/news/airman/0696/oly4.htm (January 27, 2003).

"CISM Shooting Team Leaves for Turkey." ArmyLINK News. http://www.dtic.mil/armylink/news/Jul2000/a20000718cism-promo.html (January 31, 2003).

Clark, Capt. Douglas. "Rifle Team Members Selected for Olympic Tryouts." Air Force News. http://www.af.mil/news/Feb1996/n19960215_960160.html (January 27, 2003).

Sketch by Michael Belfiore

Lenny Wilkens
1937-

American basketball coach

With 1,268 victories in his first twenty-nine seasons as an National Basketball Association (NBA) coach, Lenny Wilkens is clearly the winningest coach in professional basketball history. Wilkens began his coaching career more than three decades ago in Seattle where he served as player-coach for the SuperSonics from 1969 until 1972. He pulled the same double duty with the Portland Trail Blazers during the 1974-1975 season but hung up his uniform at season's end and stuck to coaching the following season with Portland. In the years since, he has served as head coach for the Supersonics (1977-1985), Cleveland Cavaliers (1986-1993), Atlanta Hawks (1993-2000), and Toronto Raptors (2000—). During his years as player and coach in the NBA, Wilkens has collected one Coach of the Year Award, an NBA championship ring, two Olympic gold medals, and been named one of the fifty top players and ten top coaches in NBA history.

Born in Brooklyn

He was born Leonard Randolph Wilkens Jr. in Brooklyn, New York, on October 28, 1937, son of an African American father and white mother. His father, Leonard Sr., worked as a chauffeur, while his mother, Henrietta (Cross) Wilkens, worked in a candy factory. His father died suddenly when Wilkens was still a preschooler, and he suddenly found himself "the man of the house" at the tender age of five. Making life even more difficult for the young Wilkens were the taunts of schoolmates about his interracial origins. Ignoring the taunts as best he could, Wilkens worked hard in school and stayed out of trouble. He took his first after-school job—delivering groceries—at the age of seven. Of the pressures he felt as a child, he later told *Sports Illustrated*: "I couldn't have sympathy. I couldn't trust. I couldn't get involved with people because then I'd have to feel. What scared me so much was seeing no one going out of their way to help my mother and my family after my father died. Seeing people look down their noses at us. You realize that no one really cares. So how do you get through? You start building the wall. You never let anyone know what's inside. It sounds awful now to say I'd never cry."

In his spare time, Wilkens began playing basketball with local youth leagues and found he had a real talent for the game. He was encouraged by a priest named Tom Mannion to play basketball for Boys High School as a senior and made so positive an impression that he was offered an athletic scholarship to Providence College, a catholic school in Rhode Island. In his senior year at Providence, the school's basketball team made it

Lenny Wilkens

into the finals of the National Invitational Tournament (NIT), where Wilkens was named Most Valuable Player of the NIT. Although he received offers to play professionally for a number of basketball leagues, he chose to enter the NBA draft in 1960. There he was picked sixth in the first round by the St. Louis Hawks, whose general manager, Marty Blake, had first spotted Wilkens at the NIT finals. Wilkens wasted no time in firmly establishing himself as an invaluable team player. In the ten years between 1963 and 1973, he was voted to nine All-Star teams. In 1968 he finished second to **Wilt Chamberlain** in voting for the NBA's MVP Award.

Player-Coach

In July 1962, two years into his stint with the Hawks, Wilkens married Marilyn J. Reed. The couple has three children: Leesha, Randy, and Jamee. When the Hawks moved to Atlanta in 1968, Wilkens was unable to negotiate an acceptable contract with the new owners, so he was traded to the Seattle SuperSonics. It turned out to be the start of a whole new career for Wilkens, who was asked to be player-coach of the struggling team at the beginning of the 1969-1970 season. Although he had never coach basketball before, Wilkens drew on the same fundamentals that had served him so well as a player. These fundamentals emphasized defense, passing, and the proper execution of all assignments. In 1971-1972, Wilkens coached the SuperSonics to a record of 47-35, their first winning season ever. During

Chronology

1937	Born October 28 in Brooklyn, New York
1960	Receives bachelor's degree in economics from Providence College
1960	Joins St. Louis Hawks as player
1962	Marries Marilyn J. Reed on July 28
1969	Joins Seattle SuperSonics as player-coach
1972	Joins Portland Trail Blazers as player-coach
1977	Returns to Supersonics as head coach
1986	Joins Cleveland Cavaliers as head coach
1993	Joins Atlanta Hawks as head coach
1994	Named NBA Coach of the Year by IBM
1996	Coaches gold-medal winning U.S. team in Atlanta Olympics
2000	Joins Toronto Raptors as head coach

Related Biography: NBA Scout Marty Blake

Marty Blake, director of scouting for the National Basketball Association (NBA), is the man most often credited with discovering Lenny Wilkens. Blake, general manager of the NBA's Hawks in both St. Louis and Atlanta for seventeen years, first saw Wilkens perform at the National Invitational Tournament (NIT) in 1960. He was impressed by the point guard from Brooklyn, although he admitted a few years ago he had no idea how far Wilkens would go in professional basketball. Blake was interviewed by Jeffrey Hawk of the *Atlanta Constitution* shortly after Wilkens was inducted into the Naismith Memorial Basketball Hall of Fame as a coach in October 1998 (he'd previously been inducted as a player in 1989). Blake told the *Constitution*: "But you couldn't know all this was going to happen. You knew he was going to be a great player. You knew he was a coach on the floor at Providence. I mean, he ran the show. There was no question who was in charge. You had a sense watching him that Lenny could someday become a coach, but all this? That was impossible to forecast."

Involved in basketball for more than half a century, Blake helped found the Continental Basketball Association in 1946. During his seventeen years with the Hawks, the team won eight division titles and in 1957-1958 beat the Boston Celtics to cinch the NBA championship. Earlier Blake had served as president of the Pittsburgh Condors of the American Basketball Association (ABA), which was later merged into the NBA.

the 1972-1973 season Wilkens left coaching behind to concentrate on playing for the Cleveland Cavaliers, but he again pulled double duty as player and coach for the Portland Trail Blazers, beginning in 1974.

Released by Portland in 1977, Wilkens briefly considered leaving basketball altogether but instead returned to the SuperSonics as head coach midway through the 1977-1978 season. When Wilkens returned to Seattle, he took over a team with a dismal record of 5-17, but by season's end he had coached the team to a 42-18 record and into the NBA finals. The following season, the SuperSonics took the championship, defeating the Washington Bullets in five games. In his eight seasons with the SuperSonics, from 1977 until 1985, Wilkens compiled a record of 357-277 for a winning percentage of 56.3 percent. At the end of the 1984-1985 season, Wilkens stepped down as coach of the SuperSonics and became the team's general manager for a year.

Signs on as Head Coach of Cavaliers

In June of 1986 Wilkens signed on as head coach of the Cleveland Cavaliers, a team that had won only twenty-nine games during the 1985-1986 season. Wilkens engineered an almost miraculous turnaround for the Cavaliers, compiling a record of 316-273, for a winning percentage of 53.7, during his seven seasons with the team. In 1993, Wilkens, then in his late 50s, decided to retire from basketball. However, not long thereafter he received an offer from the Atlanta Hawks that was just too attractive to refuse. The Hawks signed Wilkens to a five-year contract, worth $6.5 million. As he had done before, he quickly turned things around in Atlanta, coaching the Hawks to a 1994-1995 record of 57-25 and the Central Division championship. At season's end, Wilkens was named NBA Coach of the Year.

Wilkens became the winningest coach in NBA history on January 6, 1995, when a Hawks 112-90 victory over the New Jersey Nets gave him his 939th win, topping the marks set by such legendary NBA coaches as **Arnold 'Red' Auerbach**, Dick Motta, and Jack Ramsay. Wilkens told New York's *Amsterdam News* that he dedi-

cated his landmark win to Auerbach, the man he replaced as number one. "It was a testament to him. I still look upon him as do most of the other coaches in this league as 'The Coach.'"

Honored as One of NBA's Top Players and Coaches

When the NBA celebrated its 50th anniversary in 1996, Wilkens was the only man to be named both one of the fifty greatest players and one of the top ten coaches in league history. He's also one of only two men (**John Wooden** is the other) to be inducted into the Naismith Memorial Basketball Hall of Fame as both player and coach. Wilkens was inducted into the Naismith Hall of Fame as a player on May 9, 1989, and as a coach on October 2, 1998.

In 1996, Wilkens coached the USA Basketball Dream Team to a gold medal victory of 95-69 over Yugoslavia in the Olympic Summer Games held in Atlanta. Four years earlier, Wilkens had served as an assistant coach on the 1992 original USA Basketball Dream Team that captured gold in Barcelona, Spain. Shortly after his first Olympics coaching experience, he had a brush with life-threatening illness. During a pickup basketball game in Barcelona, Wilkens tore an Achilles tendon. As he recovered from the injury, blood clots from his leg traveled into his lungs, forcing hospitalization and jeopardizing his life. He later told the *Akron Beacon Journal*: "I think that was the first time I realized my own mortality. I was always healthy. Now I see how fragile it is. I felt vulnerable."

Coaches Hawks to Eastern Conference Semifinals

During the 1996-1997 season, Wilkens, with the help of newly signed center **Dikembe Mutombo**, molded the

Awards and Accomplishments

1956-57	Led Providence College freshman team to 23-0 record
1960	Led Providence to NIT Finals
1960	Named MVP of NIT
1963-71	Named NBA All-Star
1969-70	Led NBA in assists
1973	Named NBA All-Star
1978-79	Coached SuperSonics to world championship
1989	Inducted into Naismith Hall of Fame as player
1994	Named NBA Coach of the Year
1995	Becomes NBA's winningest coach with 939th victory on January 6
1996	Coaches USA Dream Team to Olympic gold
1996	Named one of top 50 players and top 10 coaches in NBA history
1998	Inducted into Naismith Hall of Fame as coach

Lenny Wilkens

Atlanta Hawks into one of the most effective defensive machines in the NBA. He coached the Hawks to an impressive 56-26 record and another berth in the Eastern Conference semifinals. The Hawks handily stood off the Detroit Pistons in the fifth game of their first round match but fell to the Chicago Bulls in the fifth game of the second round. The Bulls went on to win the NBA championship. During the season of 1997-1998, Wilkens further distinguished himself by reaching a pair of milestones in his coaching career: On February 10, 1998, the longtime coach won his 1,100th career game at Milwaukee and eight days later coached his 2,000th regular season NBA game against the New Jersey Nets. The Hawks ended the regular season with a creditable record of 50-32 but lost to the Charlotte Hornets in the fourth game of the first round of the playoffs.

The Hawks ended the lockout-shortened 1998-1999 season with their seventh consecutive winning record (31-19) and battled their way into the second round of the playoffs, where they fell to the New York Knicks in four games. After a disappointing 1999-2000 season in which the Hawks compiled its most dismal record (28-54) since moving to Atlanta, Wilkens stepped down as head coach.

Agrees to Coach Toronto Raptors

Wilkens didn't stay idle for long. Less than two months after quitting as head coach of the Hawks, he joined the Toronto Raptors as head coach. Interviewed by the *Toronto Star* shortly after the announcement of his appointment, Wilkens said he welcomed the opportunity to coach a team on the rise. "I like the competition of the games; I like the last two minutes of the game when you're up one or you're down one. I'm a competitor; I like to compete." He dismissed concerns about his final season with Atlanta, calling it an "aberration." He elaborated: "It's over, it's behind me, and it's time to move on. I'm a guy who wakes up and says 'Good morning, God.' Not 'Good God, it's morning.'"

In their first season under Wilkens' direction, the Raptors compiled a record of 47-35, the best in franchise history. In the first round of the playoffs, Toronto faced off against the New York Knicks in a rematch from the previous year, when the Knicks overpowered the Raptors. This time around, the results were different, with the Raptors triumphing over New York in five games. Advancing to the conference semifinals, Toronto met the Philadelphia 76ers, led by **Allen Iverson**, the league's MVP. Raptors star **Vince Carter** and Iverson engaged in a classic scoring duel with each recording games of fifty points or more, but in the end Philadelphia triumphed in its seventh games against Toronto.

Raptors Falter Without Carter

The Raptors were less impressive in their 2001-2002 season, barely eking out a winning record of 42-40. The season started on an extremely optimistic note, and the team had put together an impressive record of 29-21 during the first half of the season. But in the final game before the All-Star break, Raptors star Carter aggravated an existing injury to his knee and was unable to rejoin the team as it began the second half of the season. The loss of Carter clearly hurt the Raptors, whose record for the remainder of the season was a dismal 13-19. In the first round of the playoffs, Toronto faced off against the Pistons. The two teams split the first four games, but Detroit triumphed in the fifth game to take the match.

In the early months of the 2002-2003 season, Wilkens came under heavy criticism as the Raptors plodded to a disappointing record of 8-25 by the opening days of January 2003. But Wilkens showed few signs that the pressure was getting to him. He didn't become the NBA's winningest coach by shrinking from adversity. Interviewed by Doug Smith of the *Toronto Star,* Wilkens said: "Every year as a coach, I'm going to take stock of what I'm doing and we'll reevaluate how we do things and ask if there's a better way." And if there is a better way, Wilkens almost certainly will find it.

CONTACT INFORMATION

Address: Lenny Wilkens, c/o Toronto Raptors, 40 Bay St Ste 300, Toronto, ON, Canada, M5J 2X2.

SELECTED WRITINGS BY WILKENS:

The Lenny Wilkens Story, Kampmann & Co., 1974.
(With Terry Pluto) *Unguarded: My 40 Years Surviving in the NBA,* Simon & Schuster, 2000.

FURTHER INFORMATION

Books

"Lenny Wilkins." *Almanac of Famous People,* 6th ed. Detroit: Gale Group, 1998.
"Lenny Wilkins." *Newsmakers 1995,* Issue 4. Detroit: Gale Group, 1995.

Periodicals

Denberg, Jeffrey. "Lenny Wilkens: Already in Hall as Player, He Will Be Inducted as Coach." *Atlanta Constitution* (October 2, 1998): D1.
Evans, Howie. "Brooklyn's Lenny Wilkens Has Reached a Coaching Milestone." *New York Amsterdam News* (January 14, 1995).
"Players Vote Robinson as MVP; Wilkins Gets Nod as Best Coach." *Jet* (May 16, 1994): 53.
Smith, Doug. "After 30 Years, Lenny's Not About to Lose His Cool." *Toronto Star* (October 30, 2002).
Smith, Doug. "Wilkens Signed, Sealed." *Toronto Star* (June 22, 2000).

Other

"About Marty Blake." MartyBlake.com. http://www. martyblake.com/about_marty.htm (January 4, 2003).
"Coach Bio: Lenny Wilkens." NBA.com. http://www. nba.com/coachfile/lenny_wilkens/?nav=page (January 2, 2003).
"Leonard 'Lenny' Wilkens." Basketball Hall of Fame. http://www.hoophall.com/halloffamers/Wilkens.htm (January 4, 2003).

Sketch by Don Amerman

Dominique Wilkins
1960-

American basketball player

One of the most outstanding basketball players in National Basketball Association (NBA) history, Dominique Wilkins retired as a player after the 1998-99 season. At the time of his retirement, Wilkins ranked eighth on the all-time NBA scoring list with 26,668 points and 10th in career scoring average with 24.8 points per game. Wilkins did not stay away from the game for long, joining the administrative staff of the Atlanta Hawks in October 2000 as special assistant to the executive vice president. In October 2002 he was given additional responsibilities with the Hawks' basketball staff as an assistant in the area of player development. Wilkins not only played 15 seasons in the NBA but also spent a couple of seasons playing in Europe, leading Panathinaikos Athens of the Greek League to the European Championship for Men's Clubs in 1996 and playing for Italy's Teamsystem of Bologna during the 1997-98 season.

Born in Paris, France

He was born Jacques Dominique Wilkins in Paris, France, on January 12, 1960. The son of an officer in the U.S. Air Force, Wilkins lived in a total of 10 cities in three different countries by the time he was 15. From his father, Wilkins and his siblings learned the value of self-confidence, perseverance, and self-discipline. His mother taught her children the importance of family, spiritual values, and old-fashioned good manners. Back in the United States in his early teens, Wilkins attended high school in Washington, North Carolina, where he excelled in both basketball and track and was named to seven All-America teams in both sports. After high school he enrolled at the University of Georgia, where he was named an All-Southeastern Conference player three years in a row. In 1982 he was named to the All-America first team by *Basketball Times, Basketball Weekly,* and the NBA coaches, and to the All-America second team by the Associated Press.

Ending his college basketball career after his junior year as Georgia's leading scorer of all time-averaging 21.6 points and 7.5 rebounds per game, Wilkins put himself into the 1982 NBA draft. He was picked by the Utah Jazz in the first round and third pick overall, but Wilkins refused to sign with the Jazz. In September 1982, Wilkins was traded by the Jazz to the Atlanta Hawks for John Drew, Freeman Williams, and cash. He enjoyed an outstanding rookie season with the Hawks, averaging 17.5 points per game. During the 1983-84 season, his scoring average improved to 21.6 points per game. Wilkins's 1984-85 season with the Hawks was

Dominique Wilkins

Chronology

1960	Born in Paris, France, on January 12
1978	Graduates from high school in Washington, North Carolina
1982	Enters NBA draft after junior year at University of Georgia and is drafted by Utah Jazz
1982	Refuses to sign with the Jazz and is traded to Atlanta Hawks
1992	Marries Nicole Berry on September 26
1994	Traded by Hawks to Los Angeles Clippers
1994-95	Plays for Boston Celtics
1995-96	Plays for Panathinaikos Athens of Greek League
1996-97	Plays for San Antonio Spurs
1997-98	Plays for Teamsystem of Bologna, Italy
1999	Retires from pro basketball after season with the Orlando Magic
2000	Hired as special assistant to executive vice president of Atlanta Hawks

even more impressive, but the team's performance overall was lackluster. Although Wilkins finished sixth in the league in scoring with 27.4 points per game, the Hawks ended the year with a disappointing record of 34-48. Wilkins also won his first slam dunk contest.

Leads the NBA in Scoring

During the 1985-86 season, Wilkins led the NBA in scoring with an average of 30.3 points per game. During the Hawks' playoff series against Detroit, he set records with an amazing 50 points, 19 field goals, and 15 free throws. He also made his first appearance in the NBA All-Star Game. The following season, Wilkins was named NBA Player of the Week after he scored his 10,000th point in the league. He finished second in scoring in the NBA for the 1986-87 season with an average of 29 points per game. He also returned to the All-Star Game for the second year in a row. With strong scoring from Wilkins, the Hawks recorded 50 wins or more for four straight seasons-from 1985-86 to 1988-89. In 1988 he turned in a dazzling performance during his third All-Star Game, scoring 29 points in 30 minutes of action. He went on to score an average of 31.2 points per game in the postseason. One of Wilkins's most memorable moments as an athlete came in the Eastern Conference semifinals, when he and **Larry Bird** of the Boston Celtics engaged in a point-for-point, basket-for-basket duel in the seventh game of the series. Sadly for the Hawks, the

Celtics prevailed, crushing Atlanta's hopes of making it into the Eastern Conference finals.

Wilkins was again selected to play in the NBA All-Star Game during the 1988-89 season. For the season as a whole, he ranked seventh in NBA scoring, averaging 26.2 points and 6.9 rebounds per game. Twice during the season, he scored 41 points during a single game. During the 1989-90 season, Wilkins was selected to play in his fifth All-Star Game and also won his second slam dunk contest. He ranked fifth in NBA scoring with an average of 26.7 points per game and led the Hawks in steals with a total of 126.

Named NBA All-Star for Sixth Time

For the sixth time in his career, Wilkins was selected to play in the NBA All-Star Game during the 1990-91 season. Averaging 25.9 points and 9 assists per game for the season as a whole, he was honored by being named NBA Player of the Week during January 1991 and Player of the Month for February. Wilkins led the Hawks in scoring for the eighth consecutive season. Injury brought an early end to Wilkins's 1991-92 season but not before he was named an NBA All-Star for the seventh time in his career. During a game against Philadelphia in late January 1992, he ruptured his Achilles tendon, forcing him to miss the All-Star Game and the last 40 games of the season. Prior to his injury, Wilkins was averaging 28.1 points per game.

Wilkins bounced back from his injury in 1992-93 to score his 20,000th point in the Hawks' season opener against the New York Knicks. He also set an NBA record by sinking 23 free throws in a row without missing and set career and team highs with a total of 120 three-pointers for the season. For the season as a whole, he averaged 29.9 points and 6.8 rebounds per game. Although Wilkins enjoyed another strong season in 1993-94, he was traded in February 1994 to the Los Angeles Clippers. For the season as a whole, he averaged 26 points and 6.5 rebounds per game. After finishing up the

Career Statistics

Yr	Team	GP	PTS	FG%	3P%	FT%	RPG	APG	SPG	BPG
1982-83	ATL	82	17.5	49.3	18.2	68.2	5.8	1.6	1.0	0.8
1983-84	ATL	81	21.6	47.9	0.0	77.0	7.2	1.6	1.4	1.1
1984-85	ATL	81	27.4	45.1	30.9	80.6	6.9	2.5	1.7	0.7
1985-86	ATL	78	30.3	46.8	18.6	81.8	7.9	2.6	1.8	0.6
1986-87	ATL	79	29.0	46.3	29.2	81.8	6.3	3.3	1.5	0.6
1987-88	ATL	78	30.7	46.4	29.5	82.6	6.4	2.9	1.3	0.6
1988-89	ATL	80	26.2	46.4	27.6	84.4	6.9	2.6	1.5	0.7
1989-90	ATL	80	26.7	48.4	32.2	80.7	6.5	2.5	1.6	0.6
1990-91	ATL	81	25.9	47.0	34.1	82.9	9.0	3.3	1.5	0.8
1991-92	ATL	42	28.1	46.4	28.9	83.5	7.0	3.8	1.2	0.6
1992-93	ATL	71	29.9	46.8	38.0	82.8	6.8	3.2	1.0	0.4
1993-94	ATL	49	24.4	43.2	30.8	85.4	6.2	2.3	1.3	0.4
	LAC	25	29.1	45.3	24.7	83.5	7.0	2.2	1.2	0.3
1994-95	BOS	77	17.8	42.4	38.8	78.2	5.2	2.2	0.8	0.2
1996-97	SA	63	18.2	41.7	29.3	80.3	6.4	1.9	0.6	0.5
1998-99	ORL	27	5.0	37.9	26.3	69.0	2.6	0.6	0.1	0.0
TOTAL		1074	24.8	46.1	31.9	81.1	6.7	2.5	1.3	0.6

ATL: Atlanta Hawks; BOS: Boston Celtics; LAC: Los Angeles Clippers; ORL: Orlando Magic; SA: San Antonio Spurs.

Awards and Accomplishments

1981	Named most valuable player at Southeastern Conference tournament
1983	Named to NBA's All-Rookie Team
1985-86	Wins NBA scoring title
1985,1990	Wins NBA slam dunk title
1986	Named NBA Player of the Month for January
1986	Named to All-NBA first team
1986-94	Picked to play in NBA All-Star Game
1987-88, 1991,1993	Named to All-NBA second team
1989,1994	Named to All-NBA third team
2001	#21 jersey retired by Atlanta Hawks

1993-94 season in Los Angeles, Wilkins returned to the East Coast, signing on with the Boston Celtics for the 1994-95 season, but he still did not feel at home. The following season he played for Panathinaikos Athens of the Greek League, leading the team to the European Championship. He returned to the United States for the 1996-97 season, playing for the San Antonio Spurs, but his scoring average, while still quite respectable, had dropped sharply to 18.2 points per game.

Plays for Italy's Teamsystem Bologna

After his year with the Spurs, Wilkins returned to Europe for the 1997-98 season, playing this time with Italy's Teamsystem Bologna. He returned to the United States in 1999, signing to play with the Orlando Magic, for which his younger brother, Gerald, also played. By season's end, however, both Wilkins brothers had been released by Orlando. For Dominique, it was the end of the road as a player. When he left the game, he ranked eighth on the NBA's all-time scoring list with 26,668 points and 10th in career scoring with an average of 24.8 points per game.

For Wilkins, Atlanta was home. For 12 seasons, he had played for the Hawks, and it was to the Hawks that he returned after a brief interval away from basketball altogether. In October 2000, he was hired as assistant to the executive vice president of the Hawks. In October 2002 his responsibilities increased when he was made a special assistant in the area of player development. In announcing that Wilkins was rejoining the Hawks organization, the club's president, Stan Kasten, who was general manager when the team acquired Wilkins's rights from the Jazz in 1982, said: "There were times when I was mad at him and there were times when I was frustrated with him, but I always loved him. He's the kind of guy for whom you will always feel great affection."

CONTACT INFORMATION

Address: c/o Atlanta Hawks, One CNN Center, Atlanta, GA 30303. Fax: (404) 827-3880. Phone: (404) 827-3800.

FURTHER INFORMATION

Books

"Dominique Wilkins." *Who's Who among African Americans,* 14th ed. Detroit: Gale Group, 2001.
"Gerald Bernard Wilkins." *Who's Who Among African Americans,* 14th edition. Detroit: Gale Group, 2001.

Periodicals

Denberg, Jeff. "Wilkins' Retirement Officially Ends an Era." *Atlanta Constitution* (October 19, 2000): F4.

Laura Wilkinson

Pearlman, Jeff. "The Brothers' Magic Act: For the First Time in Their Long Careers, the Wilkinses Suit Up on the Same Team." *Sports Illustrated* (March 8, 1999): R4.

Other

"Dominique Wilkins Bio." NBA History. http://www. nba.com/history/players/wilkins_bio.html (December 9, 2002).

"Dominique Wilkins: Bio." Dominique Wilkins Official Website. http://www.humanhighlight.com/bio.php (December 9, 2002).

"Dominique Wilkins: Career Averages." ESPN. http:// espn.go.com/nba/profiles/stats/avg/0366.html (December 9, 2002).

Sketch by Don Amerman

Laura Wilkinson
1977-

American diver

Laura Wilkinson's inspiring story captured many hearts at the 2000 Olympics in Sydney, Australia. Wilkinson, a champion diver from the University of Texas, broke her foot only months before the Olympics but fought through the pain to defeat the heavily favored Chinese divers for the gold medal. It was the first time that an American woman had won a gold medal in platform diving since 1964.

Early Years

Wilkinson did not start diving competitively until she was 16, but she had some background in aerial acrobatics already: she had been a competitive gymnast until she was 13. (In the intervening years she stayed active, playing tennis, softball, and track and field.) She first made the U.S. national diving team in 1995, while still in high school, and that year she also won her first national competition, in synchronized platform diving.

In 1996 Wilkinson began attending the University of Texas and diving for their team. She became one of the strongest divers in the United States, winning more championships in synchronized platform and in her specialty, solo platform diving, as well as in the 3-meter springboard.

Olympic Hopes in Question

Wilkinson's dream of competing in the 2000 Olympics almost came to an end months before the Olympics began. In March 2000 she hit her right foot against a wooden board that she was jumping off of to practice her dives on dry land. She fractured three metatarsal bones and would require surgery.

The next day her coach, Ken Armstrong, knocked on her door at six o'clock in the morning and told her that he did not care if her foot had been amputated, she was going to the Olympics. There was no way that Wilkinson could have the surgery and still be ready to compete

Chronology

1977	Born November 17 in Houston, Texas
1993	Begins diving in May
1995	Makes U.S. national diving team
1996	Begins attending the University of Texas
2000	Breaks her right foot in three places in a training accident March 8
2000	Has surgery to repair broken foot November 14
2001	Graduates from the University of Texas in Austin in December
2002	Last year on U.S. national diving team
2002	Marries Eriek Hulseman September 7

Awards and Accomplishments

1995	HTH Classic, synchronized platform (with Patty Armstrong)
1995	U.S. National Outdoor Championships, synchronized platform (with Patty Armstrong)
1996	U.S. National Indoor Championships, synchronized platform (with Patty Armstrong)
1996	U.S. National Outdoor Championships, synchronized platform and synchronized 3-meter springboard (with Patty Armstrong)
1997	U.S. National Outdoor Championships, platform and 3-meter springboard
1997	World Championship Team Trials, platform
1997-98	Big XII Conference Championships, platform
1997, 1999	National Collegiate Athletic Association Championships, platform
1998	U.S. National Indoor Championships, platform
1998	Goodwill Games, platform
1999	Big XII Conference Championships, platform and 3-meter springboard
1999, 2002	U.S. National Outdoor Championships, platform
2000	All American-Austin Cup, 3-meter springboard
2000	U.S. Olympic Team Trials, platform
2000	Communidad de Madrid, platform and synchronized platform (with Jenny Keim)
2000	U.S. National Outdoor Championships, platform and synchronized platform (with Jenny Keim)
2000	Olympic gold medal, platform
2000	Named U.S. Diving Athlete of the Year
2000-01	Named Female Diver of the Year by the U.S. Olympic Committee

in time for the Olympics, so a cast was put on and the bones were allowed to fuse and heal just as they were. This resulted in a knot of bone on the bottom of her foot that felt, she said, like walking on a rock. The cast stayed on until just weeks before the Olympic trials, but Wilkinson used visualization and other dry-land practices to stay in the best shape that she could.

Low Expectations

Despite Wilkinson's impressive record, she was not a favorite going into the 2000 Olympics even before she broke her foot. The Chinese team had dominated the event in the previous years, winning the gold in the platform event in every Olympics since 1984. The two Chinese competitors this year, 15-year-old Sang Xue and 16-year-old Li Na, were already international champions and were heavily favored to win in Sydney as well.

Indeed, after the first round of the platform competition Li was first and Sang was second in the standings. Wilkinson was eighth, which was quite an accomplishment considering her handicaps. To climb the 40 steps to the top of the diving tower in Sydney, Wilkinson had to wear a kayaker's boot to protect her right foot. She was limited in her selection of dives, since the lump of bone on the bottom of her foot was extremely painful to run on, which ruled out dives that required running starts.

"Do It for Hilary"

The final round of the platform diving event included five dives by each of the qualifying athletes. Wilkinson gave solid performances in her first two dives, but she still trailed several other competitors. She then performed a near-perfect third dive, a reverse two-and-a-half somersault tuck, which earned a score of 9.5 from most of the judges. It would be the highest-scoring dive of the night, and it moved her into the lead. The Chinese divers could have come back to take the lead, but both of them faltered: Li garnered average scores, fives and sixes, while Sang did a belly flop and scored as low as 3.5. This was the opening that Wilkinson needed.

But Wilkinson's fourth dive was an inward two-and-a-half somersault in the pike position, the dive that she

had broken her foot practicing in March. It had made her nervous ever since, and just that morning she had done a poor job with it in the preliminary round. It was also painful, since to take off she had to stand on her tiptoes with much of her weight on the lump of fused bone under her right foot. She would have substituted another dive, but the rest of her dives required running starts.

As Wilkinson began climbing to the top of the platform, Armstrong told her, "Do it for Hilary." Hilary Grivich was a former member of the University of Texas diving team who had been killed in an automobile accident three years earlier. "I'm thinking, 'What is he trying to do to me?' Then, everything clicked," Wilkinson recalled to Linda Robertson of the *Knight Ridder/Tribune News Service*. "I thought of all the kids on the team who had written me good luck cards. The whole meet wasn't about winning anymore. It was about the journey." Wilkinson got to the top of the tower, recited her favorite Bible verse—"I can do all things through Christ, who strengthens me"—as she does before every dive, and then did her inward two-and-a-half somersault pike near perfectly, earning scores between 8.5 and 9.5. Li recovered from her poor third dive to close to within two points of Wilkinson, but in the end Li could not overtake her. Wilkinson won the gold.

After the Olympics

Wilkinson thought about retiring after the 2000 Olympics, but she found that she missed the water and the competition. After having surgery to rebreak and reset the fused bones in her right foot on November 14, 2000, she returned to competitive diving at the national outdoor championships in August 2001. She placed fifth in the platform event at the 2001 outdoor championships, but by July 2002, when that year's national championships were held, Wilkinson had reclaimed her spot as America's best platform diver. Barring any more injuries, Wilkinson should be a strong contender to win another medal at the Athens Olympics in 2004.

CONTACT INFORMATION

Address: 14606 Falling Creek, Houston, TX 77068. Email: diver@laurawilkinson.com. Online: www.laurawilkinson-usa.com.

FURTHER INFORMATION

Periodicals

Barron, David. "American Medal Hopes Take a Dive in All Events." *Houston Chronicle* (September 28, 2000): 4.

———. "For Potter, Hometown Hero Shines." *Houston Chronicle* (September 25, 2000): 2.

———. "Splash of Gold." *Houston Chronicle* (September 25, 2000): 1.

———. "Wheaties Box Cover to Feature Wilkinson." *Houston Chronicle* (October 2, 2000): 3.

Campbell, Bill. "Diver Overcomes Fear to Win Gold for U.S." *Knight Ridder/Tribune News Service* (September 24, 2000): K3246.

Collison, Cathy. "U.S. Diver Wins Gold in 10-Meter Platform." *Knight Ridder/Tribune News Service* (September 24, 2000): K3236.

Farber, Michael. "Bent on Winning." *Sports Illustrated* (October 2, 2000): 76+.

———. "High Marks." *Sports Illustrated* (October 18, 2000): 64+.

Frawley, Lara. "Texas Rose Grabs Glory." *Advertiser* (Adelaide, Australia; September 25, 2000): L20.

Greer, Jim. "Diving Champ Takes Business Plunge." *Houston Business Journal* (January 26, 2001): 3.

Kaufman, Michelle. "Wilkinson's Gold an Aberration for U.S. Divers." *Knight Ridder/Tribune News Service* (September 24, 2000): K3221.

Lopez, John P. "Comeback Kid." *Houston Chronicle* (September 25, 2000): 1.

Robertson, Linda. "Gold Medal Diver Hits Foot on Platform but Will Compete This Week at Championships." *Knight Ridder/Tribune News Service* (August 7, 2001): K2944.

Steele, David. "Golden Surprise: U.S. Diver Laura Wilkinson Beats Pain, Heralded Opponents." *San Francisco Chronicle* (September 25, 2000): A1.

Zinser, Lynn. "Surprise! American Diver Wins Gold." *Knight Ridder/Tribune News Service* (September 24, 2000): K3238.

Other

"Athlete Bios: Laura Wilkinson." U.S. Olympic Committee. http://www.olympic-usa.org/cfdocs/athlete_bios/bio_template.cfm?ID=361&Sport=Diving (January 3, 2003).

"From the Athlete: Laura Wilkinson." Copernicus Education Gateway. http://www.edgate.com/summer games/ inactive/from_the_athlete/laura_wilkinson. html (January 3, 2003).

Halperin, Andy. "10 Questions for . . . Gold Medalist Laura Wilkinson on Diving, the Olympics and Her Worst Accident." U.S. Olympic Committee. http:// www.olympic-usa.org/10_questions/041902swim. html (January 3, 2003).

Sketch by Julia Bauder

Esther Williams
1922-

American swimmer

Esther Williams is best known for her starring roles in MGM's aquatic musical films of the 1940s and 1950s—films which are often credited with introducing synchronized swimming to the world—but she was a pioneer in many other ways as well. Williams was one of the best competitive female swimmers of her day, and after becoming a movie star she became the first celebrity to have a product endorsement. She was also a pioneer in the design of women's swimsuits, creating designs which allowed women freedom of movement in the water.

Learning to Swim

Williams was born in a tiny house in southwestern Los Angeles, California, on August 8, 1922. She was the youngest of Louis Stanton Williams and Bula Myrtle Gilpin Williams's five children, and the only one of the bunch to have been born in California. The family had moved there after their oldest child, Stanton, became an actor at the age of six. The boy used to sneak into the theater in Salt Lake City, where the family lived, to watch rehearsals, and one day Broadway actress Marjorie Rambeau spotted him and recruited him. When Stanton died suddenly at the age of sixteen, the family was devastated, especially the eight-year-old Williams, who had been particularly close to him. In her autobiography, *Million Dollar Mermaid*, Williams recalls decid-

Esther Williams

Chronology

1922	Born August 8 in Los Angeles, California, the youngest of Lou and Bula Williams's five children
1937	Begins swimming for the Los Angeles Athletic Club
1939	Wins gold in three events at the U.S. National Championships
1940	Stars in the Aquacade show at the San Francisco World's Fair
1940	Marries Leonard Kovner, June 27
1941	Signs a contract with Metro-Goldwyn-Mayer (MGM)
1942	Appears in her first movie, *Andy Hardy's Double Life*
1944	Divorces Leonard Kovnar
1944	Stars in *Bathing Beauty,* the first movie ever made that featured synchronized swimming
1945	Marries Ben Gage, November 25
1948	Becomes the first star to endorse a product, a line of swimsuits made by Cole of California
1949	Benjamin Stanton Gage born August 6
1950	Kimball Austin Gage born October 30
1952	Breaks three vertebrae filming *Million Dollar Mermaid*
1953	Susan Tenney Gage born October 1
1957	Divorces Ben Gage
1958	Begins a business selling backyard swimming pools
1961	Appears in her final starring role, in *The Magic Fountain*
1969	Marries Fernando Lamas, December 31
1982	Fernando Lamas dies of cancer October 8
1984	Becomes a sports commentator for synchronized swimming
1988	Launches her own line of swimsuits, The Esther Williams Collection
1999	Publishes her autobiography, *The Million Dollar Mermaid*

ing at this time that she had to take Stanton's place as the family's hopes for being successful in those difficult Depression years.

It was only a few months later that Williams learned to swim. When her mother found out that the city was planning to build a park near their home, she convinced them to add a pool to the design. Her mother volunteered Williams to inaugurate the pool, even though Williams didn't know how to swim at the time. Williams's older sister Maureen took her to the beach and taught her. Even though Williams just barely completed her thirty-yard swim across the pool, she was greeted by cheers from the crowd that had come for the inauguration. Williams, already in love with the water and the accolades, was now hooked on swimming. She took a job at the pool so she could afford to swim there, and over her lunch breaks, the lifeguards taught her how to swim fast and well, with proper racing strokes, including men-only strokes like the butterfly.

In 1937, Williams was recruited to swim for the Los Angeles Athletic Club. This was a breeding ground for champions, and swimming on their teams was an honor for a young athlete. With the LAAC, Williams won two medals, in the 100 meter freestyle and the 400 meter relay, on her first day of competition at the 1939 national championships. On the second day, she was the first swimmer on the LAAC's 300 meter medley relay team. Most girls swam the breast stroke as their opening, but swimming the much more challenging butterfly was also allowed: so few people could do the stroke at that time that it was not worthwhile to make it a separate event. Williams beat the national record for that lap by an unheard of nine seconds.

A Career Change

Williams's three gold medals should have guaranteed her a place at the 1940 Pan American games in Buenos Aires, Argentina, but she waited for her invitation in vain. A few weeks after the games, at the 1940 U.S. National championships, Williams learned from another athlete that she had indeed been invited. A stunned Williams confronted the LAAC coach, Aileen Allen, and discovered that Allen had received her invitation but had kept it hidden, fearing that Williams would spend her time in Buenos Aires partying and meeting boys and not training. Furious, Williams quit the LAAC team, forfeiting her chance to defend her titles.

Williams still had a chance to make the 1940 Olympic team, but the outbreak of World War II forced the cancellation of those games. Williams even lost her chance to compete in swimming at the collegiate level when she got a D in her high school algebra class, which made her lose her swimming scholarship to the University of Southern California. Although Williams made up the class at Los Angeles City College, her career in the water had been indefinitely postponed, and she took a job as a stock girl at the upscale I. Magnin department store.

Awards and Accomplishments

1939	U.S. Nationals 100 meter freestyle, 400 meter relay, 300 meter medley
1953	Received Golden Globe award for *Million Dollar Mermaid*
1966	Inducted into the International Swimming Hall of Fame
1993	Received Femme Award from the Dallas Fashion Awards for contributions to the swimsuit industry
1997	Received Lifetime achievement award from the Academy of Motion Picture Arts and Sciences, the Academy Foundation, and the Museum of Modern Art

---

A month after Williams took that job, she received a call from the Aquacade, a swimming and diving show put on by producer Billy Rose at the New York World's Fair. The San Francisco World's Fair had now asked Rose to organize a similar show there. Olympic swimming champion **Johnny Weismuller**, who had starred in the New York version of the show, would be coming to San Francisco, but Rose needed to find a new female lead to swim opposite him. Rose, who had seen Williams in *Life* magazine, was in California auditioning swimmers, and he wanted Williams to be the lead. On her lunch break that day, in a swimsuit given to her as a gift from her supervisor at I. Magnin, Williams auditioned for Billy Rose. The next day, Williams left Los Angeles for San Francisco. She was now, before she had even turned eighteen, a professional swimmer.

Williams swam with the Aquacade the entire summer of 1940. She faced sexual harassment from many of the men, old and young, who were involved with the show—not an uncommon fate for female stars at that time, especially single ones. She was also cheated out of much of her salary by her agent. Frustrated at her powerlessness to remedy either situation, Williams agreed to marry a young medical student, Leonard Kovner, whom she had met while attending Los Angeles City College. The two were married between shows on June 27, 1940, shortly before Williams turned 18. Kovner returned to school, and when the Aquacade closed on September 29, 1940, Williams returned to Los Angeles to join him.

The Metro-Goldwyn-Mayer (MGM) studio had sent representatives to the Aquacade to try to recruit her, but Williams turned them down. She went back to her job at I. Magnin and settled into her new life as a wife and soon, she hoped, a mother. However, MGM was not accustomed to people refusing them, and additionally, Williams's marriage to Kovner soon turned rocky. Nearly a year after the end of the Aquacade, Williams finally agreed to meet with the head of MGM, Louis B. Mayer. Kovner and Williams separated over her decision to sign a contract with MGM, but by October of 1941, Williams was ensconced in her own dressing room, earning $350 a week and learning to be an actress.

Related Biography: Swimmer Annette Kellerman

If Esther Williams was the mother of synchronized swimming, Annette Kellerman was its grandmother. Williams was aware of this, and she had great respect for Kellerman, even titling her autobiography *Million Dollar Mermaid* after the movie she made about Kellerman's life.

Kellerman's career paralleled Williams's in many ways. Like Williams, Kellerman began as a swimmer, became a star of live water shows, and later became an actress.

Annette Marie Sarah Kellerman was born July 6, 1887 (some sources say 1888), in Sydney, Australia. As a child, she suffered from polio, which left her with weak, bowed legs, and she took up swimming to try to strengthen them. She was soon walking without leg braces, and by age ten she was a champion swimmer.

Kellerman excelled in distance swimming. After her family moved to England when she was fourteen, she swam the twenty-six mile length of the Thames River, from Putney to Blackwall, amid much media fanfare. It was unprecedented for anyone, let alone a teenage girl, to complete such a feat. Kellerman received many lucrative sponsorships for her long-distance swims, including her two failed attempts to become the first woman to swim the English Channel. Later, Kellerman parlayed this fame into a career in vaudeville, and she also made appearances at the London Hippodrome.

In 1907, Kellerman came to the United States, where she toured the country with a swimming and high-diving show. That summer, while performing in Boston, Kellerman achieved international notoriety by being arrested for indecent exposure. Her crime? She appeared on the city's Revere Beach wearing a unitard swimsuit which left her neck, all of her arms and much of her legs exposed. At that time, proper women "swam" as best they could in full, loose skirts and long-sleeve blouses.

Kellerman appeared in several silent films, starting in 1909 with three films in one year: *The Bride of Lammermoor, Jepthah's Daughter: A Biblical Tragedy,* and *The Gift of Youth.* She caused another moral scandal with the skinny-dipping scenes in her next film, *Neptune's Daughter* (1914), but she went on to star in several more movies, including *Daughter of the Gods* (1916), *Queen of the Sea* (1918) *The Art of Diving* and *What Women Love,* both 1920, and her final film, *Venus of the South Seas,* in 1924. After she married and retired from film, Kellerman opened a health food store in the Pacific Palisades.

Becomes a Movie Star

Williams's first screen role was in *Andy Hardy's Double Life.* The Andy Hardy movies were lighthearted fare about a teenage boy and his family. The series, although formulaic, had already proved to be a major success for MGM, and the studio often used roles in these films as tests for up-and-coming starlets. Williams passed with flying colors. Audiences loves the scene where she kissed Andy Hardy underwater, and the two-piece swimsuit that she wore in the movie became a fashion must-have.

Williams was soon cast in another romantic film. She played a swimming instructor at a girls' college, where Red Skelton's character tried to enroll to be able to woo her. The film was originally titled *Mr. Coed,* but after preview audiences raved over the aquatic finale, the title was changed to *Bathing Beauty.*

The finale of *Bathing Beauty* is often credited with inventing synchronized swimming as we know it today. In a brand new, ninety by ninety foot pool with $250,000 worth of special-effects rigging, scores of swimmers practiced for ten weeks to create elaborate patterns, lines,

Where Is She Now?

Esther Williams lives in Beverly Hills, California, where she swims every day in her own pool. She and her husband, Edward Bell, collaborate in running her two successful businesses, designing and manufacturing swimsuits and selling backyard swimming pools. In 2003, Williams will be co-producer, choreographer and costume designer for a $30 million aquatic show in Las Vegas, Nevada, which tells the story of the Greek goddess Persephone through swimming, snowboarding, and ice skating. She is also working on a film version of her autobiography, *Million Dollar Mermaid*.

and pinwheels as they swam and dove in unison. Williams claimed in her autobiography that, due in large part to this finale, *Bathing Beauty* grossed more than any other film of the time except *Gone With the Wind*.

Many people immediately embraced synchronized swimming as it was demonstrated in *Bathing Beauty*. The first synchronized swimming competition in the United States was held in Chicago about a year after the film's release. Over the years, early fans of the sport contacted Williams and asked for her advice in starting their own synchronized swimming team. With the help of her mother, Williams put together instructional packets to send to them. In only eleven years, the sport gained enough international recognition to become an event at the Pan American games, and the next year, 1956, synchronized swimming became an Olympic demonstration sport.

Williams was in the water in her next film, *Thrill of a Romance*, in which she plays a neighborhood swimming teacher who is torn between her absent husband and a young hero who is recovering from his war wounds. *Thrill of a Romance* was also a hit, but Williams's third movie, *The Hoodlum Saint*, flopped. This was a serious film, done in black and white, and Williams did not swim in it. MGM did not make those mistakes again soon. For her next several films, Williams was in the water, in lighthearted musical romances, in Technicolor.

Box Office Hits

In her next few movies, Williams played roles as varied as a rich young lady suing a newspaper for libel (*Easy to Wed*), a woman who breaks into bullfighting by pretending to be her brother (*Fiesta*), a movie star (*On an Island with You*), and a swimsuit designer (*Neptune's Daughter*), but all of them were variations on the same romantic theme. The films were not all critical successes, but by this time Williams's reputation was firm enough that the occasional uneven film did not hurt it: she was one of the top ten box office stars in the nation. Her personal life was looking up as well. Williams had married another show business figure, Ben Gage, in 1945. Although she had a traumatic miscarriage in 1946, by 1949 she had finally achieved her long-time wish to be a mother: Benjamin Stanton Gage was born on August 6 of that year.

Less than a year later, while shooting the film *Pagan Love Song* in Hawaii, Williams discovered that she was pregnant again. At that time, on the island of Kauai, calling the mainland was very difficult, but Williams needed to let someone back at MGM headquarters know her situation. Gage had met a ham radio operator while playing golf, and he convinced the man to let Williams use his radio to contact California. However, no one told Williams that anyone could be listening in on that conversation, so news of her pregnancy was broadcast to the entire West Coast.

In 1952, Williams made what is probably her best-known movie, *Million Dollar Mermaid*, for which she won a Golden Globe award. This film is a biography of Australian swimming pioneer Annette Kellerman, and like most of Williams's films, it contains plenty of aquatic extravaganzas. One scene called for Williams, dressed in a gold bodysuit covered in gold sequins, a turban, and a crown, to do a swan dive from 50 feet above the water. The crown, made of aluminum, caused Williams's head to snap back when she hit the water, fracturing three vertebrae in her neck. She was in a cast from her neck to her knees for six months, but she made a nearly full recovery. The only lasting effect was that the three vertebrae fused as they healed, which sometimes causes Williams to get headaches.

Personal Problems

This was not the first disaster or near-disaster Williams had undergone while working on a movie. While filming *Pagan Love Song*, she had almost been dashed to pieces against some coral while filming a scene on an outrigger canoe, and she filmed the second half of *On an Island with You* on crutches after she sprained her ankle falling into a hole. The script called for her to fall in, but the set designers had forgotten to put any padding at the bottom. Her closest call, before *Million Dollar Mermaid*, may have been in *Texas Carnival*. Again, it was the fault of the set designers' carelessness. One sequence called for Williams to swim around her leading man's bed as he dreamed of her. The set designers built a replica of the room, painted in black for the best contrast with Williams's white negligee, in the pool. They even put a ceiling on it, which was where the danger lay: Williams entered the room through a trapdoor, but when she needed to come up for air, she couldn't find the trapdoor from the inside. Luckily, a prop man noticed her distress and pulled her out before she drowned.

Williams's career did not go well after *Million Dollar Mermaid*. She had been blamed when the 1954 film *Jupiter's Darling* flopped, even though the film had many faults, and in 1955, when MGM tried to assign her another film with a weak script, Williams packed up her things and walked out on her contract, forfeiting millions of dollars in deferred pay. She acted in four more films for other studios after that, but none were very well received. She also coordinated and participated in

Esther Williams

some live shows, which had some success; one live show, in London, was sold out during its entire run.

Williams was also having problems in her personal life. Gage had mismanaged the couple's money, losing most of it and getting them into deep trouble with the Internal Revenue Service. The two eventually divorced in 1957. Williams later married the movie star Fernando Lamas, who had starred opposite her in the 1953 film *Dangerous When Wet.* The two met again in 1960, while Williams was producing the television special *Esther Williams at Cypress Gardens,* in which Lamas also swam. This special, which aired on Williams's birthday, was a huge hit: fifty-two percent of the televisions in the United States that were in use were tuned into it that night. Williams appeared in two more films in the early 1960s, but by the end of the decade she had settled down to be Fernando Lamas's wife and had disappeared from the public eye.

Williams the Swimsuit Designer

At the time that Williams first became a star, women's swimsuit design was still in its infancy. Lycra and other stretchable materials had not yet been invented, and wool was still a common swimsuit component. The costume designers at MGM had had little practice in designing swimwear for films, and their results, al-

though creative, were often highly impractical, with sometimes disastrous results. Williams's seventh film, *This Time for Keeps,* was set on Mackinac Island in northern Michigan, and in keeping with the woodsy theme, Williams's costumer created a swimming suit out of plaid flannel. Flannel, being made of cotton, absorbs tremendous amounts of water, and the saturated swimsuit nearly dragged Williams to the bottom of the pool. In desperation she unzipped the suit and let it fall. Her costume designer, who luckily was poolside, had to cut a hole in the middle of a towel and drape it over Williams's head so she could get out of the pool without exposing herself to the crowds of tourists who had come to watch the filming. After that debacle, Williams participated much more actively in the design process.

In 1948, Williams was asked by designer Cole of California to endorse one of their swimsuits. This suit, one of the first ever to be made with latex, was revolutionary: the stretchable material meant that a zipper was no longer necessary. It also meant that the suit fit better and was more suitable for maneuvering in the water. Cole approached Williams independently of MGM and asked her to endorse the suit. At that time, celebrity endorsements were unheard of: while celebrity images were often used in advertisements, such uses were strictly controlled by the studio, and all profits went to the studio as well. After Williams won her fight with MGM to be allowed to make the deal, she made as much money per year from the endorsement as she did from her contract with MGM. Her success opened the door to the multi-million dollar endorsement deals from which today's athletes now profit.

Williams was also a star saleswoman for the Cole's suit. In 1952, MGM created a patriotic movie titled *Skirts Ahoy!*, about three young women in the Navy's "Women Accepted for Volunteer Emergency Service" program. MGM worked closely with the Navy on the film, and the Navy asked them to dress their stars—Williams, Joan Evans, and Vivian Blaine—in regulation Navy dress. Williams was appalled when she saw the Navy's regulation women's swimsuit: it was made of a thin, shapeless, see-through cotton which was unflattering and uncomfortable, especially for well-endowed women who needed a suit which would support their bust. Williams managed to get an appointment with the Secretary of the Navy, where she modeled the regulation suit for him. One glimpse of the suit on her was enough to convince him of its faults, and by the end of their conversation, Williams had convinced him to make the Cole's suit the new regulation swimsuit and to order 50,000 of them on the spot.

After her acting career was over, Williams put these design and sales skills to use running her own swimwear company. Now worth $3 million, the Esther Williams Swimsuit Collection produces fashionable, practical suits for women who are not shaped like fashion models. "I have something for [women who do not have perfect bodies], to which I've given a great deal of thought because I'm all for wonderful-looking women." Williams told Marcy Medina of *WWD*. "I don't undress women at the beach, I dress them so they have a good time. She can throw a volleyball and the whole front of her suit won't fall down."

Godmother to a Sport

Although people had been competing in synchronized swimming since not long after the release of *Bathing Beauty*, and although it had been a demonstration sport at the Olympics since 1956, it did not become a medal event until 1984. The head of the International Olympic Committee during many of those years, Avery Brundage, did not consider something so pretty to be a real sport, and it was not until after his death that the Committee decided to make synchronized swimming a medal event. Williams returned to the public eye for the first time in twenty years around the time of the 1984 Los Angeles Summer Games, acting as a television commentator for synchronized swimming events and being an honored guest at many of the special events celebrating the occasion.

CONTACT INFORMATION

Email: ew@esther-williams.com. Online: www.esther-williams.com.

SELECTED WRITINGS BY WILLIAMS:

(With Digby Diegh) *The Million Dollar Mermaid,* New York: Simon & Schuster, 1999.

FURTHER INFORMATION

Books

Bawden, Liz-Ann, editor. *The Oxford Companion to Film.* New York: Oxford University Press, 1976.

Contemporary Authors, Detroit: Gale, 2000.

Halliwell, Leslie. *Halliwell's Filmgoer's Companion, Ninth Edition.* New York: Charles Scribner's Sons, 1988.

Williams, Esther, and Digby Diehl. *Million Dollar Mermaid.* New York: Simon & Schuster, 1999.

Periodicals

Agins, Teri. "Can Esther Williams Coax Older Women Back into the Pool?" *Wall Street Journal* (April 19, 1989): A1.

"Army Archerd." *Daily Variety* (April 18, 2002): 2.

Conn, Earl. "Different Strokes." *Saturday Evening Post* (November, 2000): 72.

Feitelberg, Rosemary. "Esther's Bold Strokes." *WWD* (February 6, 1997): 8-9.

Gottlieb, Robert. "Liquid Asset: A Memoir by Esther Williams, whose All-American Good Looks and Talent in the Water Turned Her Into a Hollywood Star." *New York Times Book Review.* (October 3, 1999): 11.

Haber, Holly. "Star Quality: Esther Williams Put Splashy Swimwear in the Spotlight." *WWD* (July 27, 1993): D7.

Holston, Kim R. Review of *Million Dollar Mermaid. Library Journal* (September 1, 1999): 196.

Lacher, Irene. "Esther Williams Swims Again at Film Festival." *Los Angeles Times* (January 14, 1995): F1.

Medina, Marcy. "Swim Goddess: For More Than Half a Century, Esther Williams Has Been a Glamorous and Influential Figure on the Swimwear Circuit." *WWD* (July 11, 2002): 36S.

Mehren, Elizabeth. "This Isn't Like Being in the Movies: Synchronized Swim Definitely a Sport, Says Esther Williams." *Los Angeles Times* (August 13, 1984): 4.

Michaelson, Judith. "Esther Williams Back at Poolside." *Los Angeles Times* (June 13, 1984): 1.

Murray, Jim. "Mermaid Who Started a New Olympic Sport." *Los Angeles Times* (August 2, 1984): 1.

Perry, Pat. "Esther Williams: Still in the Swim." *Saturday Evening Post* (January-February, 1998): 36-39.

Purdum, Todd. "Swimming Upstream." *New York Times* (September 2, 1999): D7.

Review of *Million Dollar Mermaid. Entertainment Weekly* (September 24, 1999): 141.

Review of *Million Dollar Mermaid. People* (September 20, 1999): 57.

Review of *Million Dollar Mermaid. Publishers Weekly* (August 23, 1999): 34.

Sachs, Andrea. "Eddie & Esther: Two Much Married Former Stars Cast a Look Backward." *Time* (September 27, 1999): 107.

Shapiro, Laura. "Telling Tales Out of Pool: Esther Williams Makes a Splash with a Fab Memoir." *Newsweek* (September 13, 1999): 69.

Thompson, David. "The Original Splash" (interview with Williams). *Interview* (February, 1998): 40-41.

Tribby, Mike. Review of *Million Dollar Mermaid. Booklist* (August, 1999): 1983.

Wedlan, Candace A. "Water Power." *Los Angeles Times* (July 9, 1997): E2.

Other

CNN.com. http://www.cnn.com/ (September 29, 2002).

Internet Movie Database. http://www.imdb.com/ (September 29, 2002).

Sketch by Julia Bauder

Serena Williams

Serena Williams
1981-

American tennis player

Together with her older sister, **Venus Williams**, Serena Williams has taken the tennis world by storm, soaring to the top of a game traditionally dominated by white players. For Serena, 2002 was particularly sweet. The year didn't get off to a particularly auspicious start. A sprained ankle forced Williams to miss the Australian Open in January 2002, but things brightened up considerably for the remainder of the year. She won seven of her next 12 events, winning three of the four 2002 Grand Slam tournaments—the French Open, Wimbledon, and the U.S. Open—and snatching from sister Venus the number one world women's ranking. In recognition of her impressive performance in 2002, Williams, along with Australian Lleyton Hewitt, was named International Tennis Federation world champion in December. As 2003 dawned, Williams became only the fifth woman in tennis history to hold all four Grand Slam titles, beating Venus in the finals of the Australian Open. Of Williams' brilliance on the tennis court, tennis great **Chris Evert**, told *People*: "Serena really is too good. I'd like to see some players get close to athleticism, and I don't see it yet on the horizon."

Born in Saginaw, Michigan

Williams was born in Saginaw, Michigan, on September 26, 1981, 15 months after older sister Venus. The youngest of the five daughters of Richard and Oracene (nicknamed Brandi) Williams grew up in the gritty Los Angeles suburb of Compton, where her father ran a private security firm. Richard Williams, long a fan of televised tennis competition, resolved that he would teach all of his daughters to play the game. The three oldest Williams girls showed only minimal interest in and little aptitude for tennis, but both Serena and Venus showed promised from the very start. Of her younger sisters' enthusiasm for the game, older sister Lyndrea told *Sport* magazine: "Venus and Serena took to tennis as soon as rackets were put in their hands." Their father taught his daughters on the public tennis courts of Compton. Both girls' skills developed rapidly, and by the age of four-and-a-half Serena entered her first tournament. Over the next five years, according to her father, she won 46 of the 49 tournaments she entered and succeeded Venus as the number one player in Southern California's competitive age-12-and-under rankings. It was not long before both girls began winning national attention in the form of favorable coverage in both broadcast and print media, invitations to prestigious tennis camps, and offers of lucrative product endorsement deals.

In 1991 Richard Williams, who has served as both coach and manager to his youngest daughters from the

Chronology

1981	Born in Saginaw, Michigan, on September 26
1991-95	Studies tennis at Ric Macci's academy in Delray Beach, Florida
1995	Makes professional debut at Bell Challenge in Vanier, Quebec, Canada
1998	Enters Australian Open, her first Grand Slam tournament
1999	Graduates from Driftwood Academy of Lake Park, Florida, in August

start, pulled Serena and Venus out of the junior tournament circuit, preferring to shelter them from the competitive pressures of the tour. Instead he opted to send his girls to teaching pro Ric Macci's tennis academy in Delray Beach, Florida. From 1991 until 1995 the Williams girls studied with Macci, who had also worked with **Jennifer Capriati** and **Mary Pierce**. While studying tennis with Macci, the sisters were home-schooled by family members. After a few years, they were enrolled at Driftwood Academy, a private, 30-student high school in Lake Park, Florida. In 1993 the Williams family moved from Compton to a new home in Palm Beach Gardens, Florida. Serena graduated from Driftwood in August 1999 with a B-plus average.

Father Takes Charge of Career

After the Williams sisters left Macci's tennis academy in 1995, their father, with the help of his wife, once again took over the responsibility of coaching the girls. Even more importantly, he devoted a great deal of his time and energy to promoting his daughters, publishing a newsletter about the girls' background and training. He also used the newsletter to blow his own horn, claiming that he had come to be known as "'King Richard' ... Master and Lord of the ghettos in Compton, CA." Of Williams' blatant self-promotion, Julia Reed wrote in *Vogue* that he "has a reputation for being a bit pompous and not just a little bit irritating. But he is also wickedly funny."

Serena turned professional in October 1995, making her debut at the Bell Challenge in Vanier, Quebec, an event not sanctioned by the Women's Tennis Association (WTA). She lost quickly to her opponent, a virtual unknown. For the next few years, she lived in the shadow of Venus, who shot up into the top 10 in women's tennis, while Serena as of the end of 1996 had been unable to break into the top 500. In 1997, however, things began to look up for the youngest Williams, who began the year ranked at number 453 and before long rose to number 307. Later in the year she jumped to number 100 among women players in the space of a single week. At the Ameritech Cup tournament in Chicago late in 1997, she upset number four **Monica Seles** and number seven Mary Pierce before losing to third-ranked **Lindsay Davenport**. Williams' wins over Seles and Pierce made her the lowest ranked player ever to defeat two top-ten players in a single tournament. An injury forced Serena to pull out of the doubles competition with sister Venus.

Related Biography: Father/Coach Richard Williams

The biggest booster of Serena and Venus Williams is their father, who has also served as their coach and manager from the very beginning of their tennis careers. In fact, it's doubtful either Williams sister would be playing tennis at all were it not for Richard Williams' fervent belief that he could raise his daughters to be champions on the court. Working with the three older sisters of Venus and Serena, Williams had had little success, but his two youngest girls took to the game from the start.

Despite his undeniable success in coaxing and coaching Venus and Serena to positions of dominance in the sport, Williams continues to come under fire for some of his unorthodox techniques but mostly for what he has to say about his perceptions of racism and the stuffiness of the people who run the game. He also shows no lack of confidence in his ability to guide his daughters to tennis stardom. He admitted however, to Kevin Chappell of *Ebony* that sometimes the criticism hurts. "When people criticize you, I don't care how much you say it doesn't bother you, it does. It bothers you when people criticize you, especially when you're doing the best that you can do. Because once you are doing the best you can do, you realize there is nothing else you can do. They are criticizing you, and you can't fight back, you can't make a noise. It's almost like someone has beaten you dead. It's somewhat disturbing."

When Serena, his younger daughter with former wife Oracene, was still quite young, Williams moved his family from Saginaw, Michigan, to the dicey neighborhoods of Compton, California, a suburb of Los Angeles. He taught his girls the game on the public tennis courts of Compton, an area so riddled with gang violence that the girls had to be schooled in how to dodge errant bullets. In 1991, he sent Serena and Venus off to Florida to train at the tennis academy of Ric Macci in Delray Beach. Both girls turned professional by the age of 14 and have been guided by their father through every step of their careers.

Enters First Grand Slam Tourney

At the age of 16, in January of 1998, Williams entered her first Grand Slam tournament—the Australian Open—after winning a qualifying match. Facing off against second-seeded Davenport, who had defeated her at the Ameritech Cup in late 1997, she turned the tables, handily winning the match. Venus shocked top-ranked **Martina Hingis**. When the two sisters met on the court in the second round of the finals, Venus carried the day, taking the match 7-6, 6-1. Just to show there were no hard feelings, a smiling Serena and Venus posed for photographers after the match.

After losing her match with Venus at the Australian Open in January 1998, Serena trailed her sister in the rankings, but she was the first of the two to win a Grand Slam title. Still only 16 years old, she teamed with Max Mirnyi of Belarus to win the mixed doubles tournament at Wimbledon in July of 1998. Although the spotlight was still trained on Venus, more and more observers of the game began to predict that Serena, with her power, eventually would overshadow her older sister. By August of 1998, Serena's ranking had improved to number 21. Whatever the fans or critics were saying, nothing seemed to have any effect on the close relationship between the sisters. That relationship—seemingly strengthened by their occasional face-to-face meetings on the court—captured the interest of the media, which ran numerous features about the sisters. Away from tennis, the two loved to gossip about boys and shop, the latter pastime easily

Serena Williams

financed by the sisters' lucrative product endorsement deals. In 1998 Serena signed a $12 million deal with Puma, helping her to keep pace with Venus, who had an equally impressive deal with Reebok.

Beats Mauresmo to Win First WTA Title

Williams won the first WTA title of her career early in 1999, overpowering Amelie Mauresmo of France 6-2, 3-6, 7-6 in the Open Gaz de France tournament in Paris. In besting Mauresmo, Serena became the first American ever to win that tournament. Making the victory even sweeter for the Williams family was an almost simultaneous win by Venus in the IGA SuperThrift Tennis Classic in Oklahoma City. Serena followed her Open Gaz victory with a win over **Steffi Graf** at the Evert Cup tournament in Indian Wells, California, the very next week, grabbing her second WTA title in a row. During a three-week period ending with her defeat of Graf in California, Serena won 11 consecutive matches. In an interview with Michael Silver of *Sports Illustrated*, Williams made it clear who she saw as her main competitor. "Whatever my potential is, I want to reach it now," she told Silver. "And if I do, I see Venus as my biggest competition."

The head-to-head sibling rivalry of which Serena spoke was not long in coming. On March 28, 1999, Venus beat her younger sister 6-1, 4-6, 6-4 at the Lipton Cham-

pionships in Key Biscayne, Florida. The Williams face-off marked the first time in more than a century that two sisters met each other in a tennis tournament finals match. The previous match between sisters had come in 1884 when 19-year-old Maud Watson beat older sister Lillian, 26, at the first women's Wimbledon. Serena's loss to Venus at Key Biscayne was not really the first time she'd fallen to her older sister but actually her third consecutive loss to Venus, the others coming at the Australian Open and Italian Open in 1998. Despite these defeats, Serena was moving up impressively in the world tennis rankings, finding herself at number 10 by mid-April 1999.

Wins First Singles Title

Later in 1999 the Williams sisters teamed up to win the doubles title at the French Open. The sweetest victory came for seventh-ranked Serena at the U.S. Open in 1999 when she became the lowest seed to win the women's title since 1968. In taking her first Grand Slam singles title, Williams became only the second African-American woman to do so. The win boosted Serena's world ranking to number four, the highest ranking of her career. Although she'd started out way back in the rankings, Serena now found herself running neck and neck with Venus. On the heels of Serena's singles victory at the U.S. Open, the sisters teamed up again to win the doubles title at the U.S.

Awards and Accomplishments

1997	Becomes lowest ranked player (no. 304) to defeat two top 10 players (Mary Pierce and Monica Seles) in a single tournament
1999	Wins first WTA title by beating Amelie Mauresmo in Open Gaz de France
1999	Wins first Grand Slam singles title at U.S. Open; teams with Venus to win U.S. Open doubles title
2000	Advances to semi-finals at Wimbledon but falls to sister Venus
2002	Defeats Venus to win singles title at French Open
2002	Wins Italian Open with defeat of Justine Henin
2002	Wins Wimbledon singles title
2002	Wins U.S. Open singles title
2003	Wins Australian Open singles title.

Open, making them the first African American team to do so in the history of the tournament.

In July 2000, Venus defeated Serena in the semi-finals at Wimbledon. Crushed by the loss to her older sister, Williams left the court in tears, as Venus attempted to comfort her. Serena bounced back to join her older sister to take the women's doubles title at Wimbledon, marking the first time the event had been won by a sister team. In 2000 singles competition, Serena took her first singles title of the year by defeating Denisa Chladkova of Czechoslovakia at the Faber Grand Prix. Perhaps the high point of the year for both Serena and Venus came at the 2000 Summer Olympics in Sydney. Team Williams defeated the Dutch team of Miriam Oremans and Kristie Boogert, 6-1, 6-1, to take the gold medal in women's doubles.

Williams won her first singles title of 2001 at Indian Wells, California, with a victory over Kim Clijsters, 4-6, 6-4, 6-2. At the Australian Open that year, she advanced to the quarter-finals, where she fell to Martina Hingis, who later defeated Venus as well. In doubles competition, the Williams sisters once again triumphed. Later that year Serena was stopped by Jennifer Capriati in the quarter-finals of both the French Open and Wimbledon. At the U.S. Open, Serena and Venus faced off against each other in the women's finals, where Venus carried the day, winning the match 6-2, 6-4.

What was to be the brightest season yet of Serena's tennis career started off on a decidedly unpromising note. Williams was forced to sit out the Australian Open in January 2002 because of a sprained ankle. But the injury was not to keep her down for long. Serena won seven of her next 12 events, replacing Venus as the number one-ranked woman in tennis. In an interview with *People*, she said: "I'm physically strong but mentally stronger. I think if you have the attitude that you can do anything, you really can." Williams proved conclusively that she had the right attitude by taking three of the big four Grand Slam titles—the French Open, Wimbledon, and the U.S. Open—in 2002. The following year got off to a promising start, as a healthy Serena nailed the last of the four Grand Slam tournaments for the season, beating sister Venus in the finals of the Australian Open.

Still in her very early 20s, Serena Williams has made an indelible impression on the world of tennis, quickly moving up through the ranks of the game to draw even with older sister Venus and then to moving into the number one ranking. Only time will tell what lies ahead for Williams, but of one thing she is certain: "Family comes first, no matter how many times we play each other," she told *Sports Illustrated*. "Nothing will come between me and my sister."

CONTACT INFORMATION

Address: c/o Women's Tennis Association, 133 First St. NE, St. Petersburg, FL 33701.

FURTHER INFORMATION

Books

"Serena Williams." *Complete Marquis Who's Who*. Marquis Who's Who, 2001.

"Serena Williams." *Contemporary Black Biography*, Volume 20. Gale Group, 1998.

"Serena Williams." *Newsmakers 1999*, Issue 4. Gale Group, 1999.

"Serena Williams." *Who's Who Among African Americans*, 14th ed. Gale Group, 2001.

Periodicals

Chappell, Kevin. "Richard Williams: Venus and Serena's Father Whips the Pros and Makes His Family No. 1 in Tennis." *Ebony*, (June 2000).

Fendrich, Howard. "Little Sister Gets Her 'Serena Slam.'" *AP Online*, (September 8, 2000): 128.

Harris, Beth. "Serena Williams Advances to Final in WTA Championships; Venus Williams Injured." *AP Worldstream*, (November 11, 2002).

"Hewitt, Serena Williams Named 2002 World Champions." *AP Worldstream*, (December 3, 2002).

O'Connor, Ian. "Richard Williams Getting the Last Laugh." *USA Today*, (September 6, 2002).

Price, S.L. "A Grand Occasion: While Serena Williams Blitzed the Women's Field, Pete Sampras Won His Fifth U.S. Open and Left No Doubt That He's the Greatest Men's Player Ever." *Sports Illustrated*, (September 16, 2002): 52.

"Serena Williams: Queen of the Court." *People*, (December 30, 2002): 99.

Other

"Players: Serena Williams." WTA Tour. http://www.wtatour.com/index.cfm?section=players&contid=playerid=237237&rosterid=12 (January 21, 2003).

"Serena Williams: Biography." Tennisrulz.com. http://www.tennisrulz.com/players/swilliams/biography.htm (January 19, 2003).

"Serena Williams Biography—Part I." William Hill Wimbledon 2002. http://wimbledon.willhill.com/serena_williams_1.htm (January 19, 2003).

"Serena Williams: Career Highlights." ESPN.com. http://espn.go.com/tennis/s/wta/profiles/swilliams.html (January 19, 2003).

Sketch by Don Amerman

Ted Williams
1918-2002

American baseball player

Ted Williams

Baseball player Ted Williams—nicknamed the Splendid Splinter, Thumper, and Teddy Ballgame—has been called one of the two greatest hitters of all time, along with **Babe Ruth**. Over his nineteen seasons with the Boston Red Sox, Williams had a .344 batting average, even though he lost nearly five seasons in his prime to service as a combat pilot in World War II and the Korean War. Williams, a left-handed batter, was known for his perfect swing and 20/10 eyesight. He would not swing at bad balls and therefore was often walked by pitchers. This talent contributed to his yet-unbroken record of bases on balls, at .482. Williams was also outspoken and hot-tempered and did not cater to fans and sports writers. Yet, he was a staunch supporter of children's charities. He was inducted into the Baseball Hall of Fame in 1966. Williams made news of a different kind after his death in July 2002, when his son reportedly shipped Williams's body to Arizona to be cryogenically preserved in order to harvest the great player's DNA.

Young Ball Player

Theodore Samuel Williams was born August 30, 1918, in San Diego, California, the son of Samuel Steward Williams, who ran a passport photography shop, and May Venzer Williams, a woman of some Mexican heritage who worked for the Salvation Army. Young Ted played baseball after school until dark and even took his bat to school to practice. In junior high, the tall, lanky youth played American Legion baseball and played on the Herbert Hoover High School team. He developed a talent for judging good and bad pitches as a teen and did not hesitate to walk if the balls were not worth striking at. He later said, "Getting on base is how you score runs. Runs win ball games."

Williams played his first professional games with the minor league San Diego Padres, in 1936. The following season the Padres sold him to the Boston Red Sox, where he spent the rest of his career. As a young player, he was extremely cocky and had a violent temper, often smashing things when he got angry. He was a perfectionist at hitting, and he practiced constantly, even in hotel rooms, where he smashed a bed and a mirror with his powerful swing. A contemporary of the great **Joe DiMaggio** of the New York Yankees, Williams was batting .400 in 1941, at age 23, his third season in the major leagues. When his manager offered him a chance to sit out a doubleheader on the last day of the season and preserve his batting average, Williams declined. He played the games, getting six hits and finishing with a .406 average, leading the Red Sox to a second-place finish behind the Yankees. DiMaggio was voted the American League's Most Valuable Player (MVP) that year, but Williams won the first of six American League batting championships. He also won the first of his four home run titles.

In 1942, Williams won his first American League Triple Crown, when he finished the season with a .356 batting average, thirty-six home runs, and 137 runs batted in (RBIs). However, the peak of his career would soon be interrupted by war.

Military Service and Continuing Career

At the end of the 1942 season, Williams became a fighter pilot and flight instructor in the U.S. Marine Corps, during World War II. He served through 1945

Chronology

1918	Born on August 30 in San Diego, California
1936	Begins career with San Diego Padres
1937	Is traded to the Boston Red Sox
1939	Plays first season in major leagues
1941	With Boston Red Sox, finishes season hitting .406; wins first of six American League batting championships
1942	After baseball season, joins Marines as fighter pilot and flight instructor; serves three years in World War II
1946	Returns from military service and rejoins Red Sox; hits only .200 in his only World Series
1947	Leads American League in batting average, home runs, and runs batted in
1950	Injures elbow after crashing into a fence in outfield during All-Star game
1952-53	Serves in military during Korean War
1957	Hits .388 and becomes oldest player to ever win a batting championship
1960	Retires at end of baseball season, at age 42
1966	Inducted into the Baseball Hall of Fame
1969-72	Manages Washington Senators (which became Texas Rangers in 1972)
1994	Establishes Ted Williams Museum and Hitters Hall of Fame in Hernando, Florida; establishes Greatest Hitters Award
1995	City of Boston names tunnel under Boston Harbor for Williams
2000	Receives pacemaker for heart problems
2001	Has open-heart surgery
2002	Dies July 5 of cardiac arrest at Citrus Memorial Hospital in Inverness, Florida; son John Henry has his body cryogenically preserved at Scottsdale, Arizona

Awards and Accomplishments

1939	Led American League in RBI
1940-42, 1946-51, 1954-60	All-Star Team
1941	Led American League in batting and home runs
1941-42	Named *Sporting News* Player of the Year
1942, 1947	Won American League Triple Crown
1946, 1949	American League Most Valuable Player Award
1947, 1949, 1957	Named *Sporting News* Player of the Year
1948	Led American League in batting
1949	Led American League in home runs and RBIs
1957-58	Led American League in batting
1966	Elected to Baseball Hall of Fame
1969	Named American League Manager of the Year
1995	Boston named tunnel under Boston Harbor for Williams
1999	Was honored at the All-Star Game with a pregame ceremony at Fenway Park, Boston

Triple Crown is given to player who leads league in batting, home runs, and runs batted in.

and returned to the Red Sox in 1946, helping the team win the American League pennant and taking home the MVP award. Although the Red Sox lost the World Series (the only one Williams played in) to the St. Louis Cardinals that year, Williams's reputation as an outstanding hitter grew. He became known as the Splendid Splinter and the Thumper, for his 6'3" rail-thin frame and his power behind the bat.

In 1947, Williams won his second Triple Crown but lost the MVP title to DiMaggio by only one vote, a slight by the sportswriters that Williams never forgot. In 1949, he was voted American League MVP for the second time. In 1950, while having a great season, Williams fractured his elbow during the All-Star Game at Comiskey Park in Chicago; he smashed into the wall while catching a fly ball. He finished that game, but the injury cost him more than sixty games, although he played well during the games he did play. He hit .318 in 1951 but then went back into the military service in 1952 and 1953, during the Korean War. After a crash landing of his fighter plane and a bout with pneumonia, he was sent back to the states. He announced his retirement from baseball in 1954 but then changed his mind and stayed on with the Red Sox, because he would have been ineligible for Hall of Fame election on the first ballot if he quit too soon. He suffered a series of injuries in the mid-1950s, but in 1957, at almost forty years old, he hit .388 and became the oldest player to ever win a batting championship. He hit .453 during the second half of the season. Williams was more

popular than ever before and finished second only to **Mickey Mantle** in MVP balloting. The following year, Williams batted .328, still high enough to lead the league in batting. During this part of his career he won the nickname Teddy Ballgame, although his favorite nickname for himself was always "The Kid."

"Terrible Ted"

Williams was known for his indifference, even hostility, toward the press and sometimes the fans, earning him another nickname, Terrible Ted. Constantly chasing the perfect hit, Williams was often gruff and critical. S. L. Price, of *Sports Illustrated,* once wrote that Williams's speech was a "uniquely cadenced blend of jock, fishing and military lingo, marked by constant profanity." Price also called him "savagely independent." Williams called hitting a baseball "the hardest single feat in sports," and at age nineteen he said his goal was "to have people say, 'There goes Ted Williams, the greatest hitter who ever lived.'"

He might have been the greatest hitter, but Williams would not smile for the camera, and he once spat toward the stands after being booed for dropping a fly ball. He was fined by Red Sox owner Tom Yawkey for spitting at the pressbox during a home run, and he once flipped his bat into the stands after a strikeout, hitting a woman on the head. Boston fans booed him, but Hall of Famer Eddie Collins said, "If he'd just tip his cap once, he could be elected mayor of Boston in five minutes."

At the height of his career, Williams was the highest paid player in the major leagues, earning $125,000 a year. His theory was that if he was being paid so much money "the very least I could do was hit .400." He made every trip to the plate an information-gathering session and said in his autobiography, *My Turn at Bat,* "I honestly believe I can recall everything there was to know

Ted Williams, swinging bat

about my first 300 home runs—who the pitcher was, the count, the pitch itself, where the ball landed." His eyesight was legendary—it was said he could read the label on a spinning record and distinguish between a fastball and a curve ball as the ball approached the plate.

Retirement and Hall of Fame

Williams retired at the end of the 1960 season, at age 42, batting .316 that year and finishing his career with a home run. He was inducted into the Baseball Hall of Fame in 1966, along with famed baseball manager **Casey Stengel**. Williams showed his refreshing humanity when he read a speech he had written in a motel room the night before. He said being elected to the Hall of Fame was "the greatest thrill of [his] life." He also said, "Ballplayers are not born great. . . . No one has come up with a substitute for hard work. I've never met a great player who didn't have to work harder at learning to play ball than anything else he ever did. To me it was the greatest fun I ever had, which probably explains why today I feel both humility and pride, because God let me play the game and learn to be good at it."

Manager and Fisherman

Williams took over as manager of the Washington Senators in 1969 and was named American League

Manager of the Year. He stayed with them when they became the Texas Rangers in 1972. He then retired to the Florida Keys and pursued his love of fishing, specializing in tarpon. He served as a sporting goods consultant to Sears department stores, designing fishing equipment.

After suffering three strokes in his seventies that left him partially blind, he remained active in sports, campaigning to get **Shoeless Joe Jackson** inducted into the Hall of Fame. Williams was cheated out of approximately $2 million by a partner dealing in sports memorabilia during the 1980s; his signature was forged on bats and other souvenirs. Williams's son, John Henry, ferreted out the forgeries and started a business selling authentic Ted Williams memorabilia. In 1994, Williams opened his own baseball museum in Hernando, Florida, adding the Hitters Hall of Fame in 1995, complete with his own annual Greatest Hitters Award. The museum is known as "the Cooperstown of the South."

Figure of Honor

As Williams aged, he became a revered figure in Boston. The city named a tunnel for him, and in 1999 he was saluted at the All-Star Game with a special ceremony in which the star players from both leagues gathered around him on the pitcher's mound at Boston's Fenway Park. Among those honoring him were **Cal Ripken, Jr.**, **Tony Gwynn**, **Mark McGwire**, and **Ken Griffey, Jr.**

Career Statistics

Yr	Team	AVG	GP	AB	R	H	HR	RBI	BB	SO	SB
1939	BOS	.327	149	565	131	185	31	145	107	64	2
1940	BOS	.344	144	561	134	193	23	113	96	54	4
1941	BOS	.406	143	456	135	185	37	120	147	27	2
1942	BOS	.356	150	522	141	186	36	137	145	51	3
1946	BOS	.342	150	514	142	176	38	123	156	44	0
1947	BOS	.343	156	528	125	181	32	114	162	47	0
1948	BOS	.369	137	509	124	188	25	127	126	41	4
1949	BOS	.343	155	566	150	194	43	159	162	48	1
1950	BOS	.317	89	334	82	106	28	97	82	21	3
1951	BOS	.318	148	531	109	169	30	126	144	45	1
1952	BOS	.400	6	10	2	4	1	3	2	2	0
1953	BOS	.407	37	91	17	37	13	34	19	10	0
1954	BOS	.345	117	386	93	133	29	89	136	32	0
1955	BOS	.356	98	320	77	114	28	83	91	24	2
1956	BOS	.345	136	400	71	138	24	82	102	39	0
1957	BOS	.388	132	420	96	163	38	87	119	43	0
1958	BOS	.328	129	411	81	135	26	85	98	49	1
1959	BOS	.254	103	272	32	69	10	43	52	27	0
1960	BOS	.316	113	310	56	98	29	72	75	41	1
TOTAL		.344	2292	7706	1798	2654	521	1839	2021	709	24

BOS: Boston Red Sox.

Suffering from heart problems, Williams received a pacemaker in 2000. He spent many of his last days watching baseball on television, saying, "I'll always be a die-hard Red Sox fan." He died on July 5, 2002, at age 83, of cardiac arrest at Citrus Memorial Hospital in Inverness, Florida.

On the evening of his death, in preparation for the ballgame at Fenway Park, a giant number 9, Williams's jersey number, was mowed into the grass at left field, his longtime position. Thousands of people lined the streets outside the park to mourn the city's favorite son, and the game between the Detroit Tigers and the Red Sox went on, after a solemn playing of taps and singing of the national anthem. An empty red chair marked the spot where Williams once hit a 502-foot home run into the right-field bleachers, the longest ball ever hit at Fenway Park.

Shortly after Williams's funeral, his son, John Henry, shipped his father's body in ice to a cryogenic laboratory in Arizona, to be preserved. His daughter, Barbara Joyce Williams Ferrell (Williams had three children from two marriages—the third was another daughter, Claudia), claimed that her father had wanted to be cremated and have his ashes scattered over the Florida Keys. The disagreement between the children made headlines, and many scientists and ethicists, as well as fans and players, were shocked at the notion that Williams's body might be used to harvest his DNA.

Ted Williams was indeed one of the greatest baseball players who ever lived. His batting record remains a standard by which many players measure achievement. Six players finished their careers with higher batting averages than Williams, but only Babe Ruth was in his class as an all-around hitter. Sports historians have speculated as to the heights Williams might have reached had he not given up five of his best years to serve his country in the military. Yet, he was much more than simply a great athlete. Williams worked for years, often anonymously, for the Jimmy Fund, a children's charity supporting the Dana Farber Cancer Institute in Boston. He also worked for the Shrine Hospitals and other charities. Williams was an outspoken supporter of minorities in baseball and worked to see that the great Negro leagues players were recognized in the Baseball Hall of Fame and that players of all ethnicities were made welcome in the sport.

SELECTED WRITINGS BY WILLIAMS:

(With John Underwood) *The Science of Hitting*. New York: Simon & Schuster, 1971.

(With John Underwood) *Ted Williams Fishing the "Big Three" : Tarpon, Bonefish, and Atlantic Salmon*. New York: Simon & Schuster, 1982.

(With John Underwood) *My Turn at Bat: The Story of My Life*. New York: Simon & Schuster, 1988.

(With Jim Prime) *Ted Williams' Hit List*. Indianapolis, IN: Masters Press, 1996.

(With David Pietrusza) *Ted Williams: My Life in Pictures*. Kingston, NY: Total/Sports Illustrated, 2001.

FURTHER INFORMATION

Books

Encyclopedia of World Biography Supplement, Volume 19. "Ted Williams." Detroit: Gale Group, 1999.

Rounding Third

In 1941 Williams hit .406 for the Red Sox. In the 55 years since then, few players have come close to hitting .400, and the legend of The Kid's eyesight has only grown: He could follow the seams on a baseball as it rotated toward him at 95 mph. He could read the label on a record as it spun on a turntable. He stood at home plate one day and noticed that the angle to first base was slightly off; measuring proved him right, naturally, by two whole inches. In the '60s [Frank] Brothers—the son of Williams's friend Jack Brothers, a famous Florida Keys fishing guide—would show up on Williams's porch in Islamorada every Saturday morning to spend the day helping Williams pole his skiff through the shallows. Each time, Williams would bet Brothers one hour's poling that he could cast his line and guess, within six inches, how far the lure had flown. "I lost every time," Brothers says. "He'd cast 112 feet and say, 'A hundred eleven feet, 10 inches.' No marks on the line."

Source: Price, S.L. *Sports Illustrated,* November 25, 1996, p. 92.

Periodicals

"Bizarre Family Feud." *Maclean's* (July 22, 2002): 11.

Corliss, Richard. "A Little Respect for the Splendid Splinter: Ted Williams, 1918-2002." *Time* (July 15, 2002): 72.

"Red Sox Pride: Tributes—and a Family Feud—Follow Ted Williams's Death." *People* (July 22, 2002): 92.

Stout, Glenn. "The Case of the 1947 MVP Ballot." *Sporting News* (December 20, 1993): 7.

Thomsen, Ian. "Boston Mourns Its Hero: The Fenway Fans Paid Their Respects to Ted Williams, a Towering Figure Who Fought the Good Fight." *Sports Illustrated* (July 17, 2002): 70.

Underwood, John. "Gone Fishing: His Baseball Days behind Him, the Kid Took to the Waters off the Keys with a Boatload of Yarns, a Few Friends and One Mission: Bring in the Big Ones." *Sports Illustrated* (July 17, 2002): 46.

Verducci, Tom. "Splendor at the Plate: Over Two Brilliant Decades, Ted Williams Proved He Was What He Always Wanted to Be: The Best Hitter Who Ever Lived." *Sports Illustrated* (July 17, 2002): 10.

Williams, Ted. " 'Humility and Pride'." (Speech on induction into the Baseball Hall of Fame). *Sports Illustrated* (July 17, 2002): 84.

Other

Baseball-Reference.com "Ted Williams." http://www.baseball-reference.com/ (November 26, 2002).

Bergen, Phil, and Mike Shatzkin. "Ted Williams." BaseballLibrary.com. http://www.pubdim.net/baseball library.com/ (November 27, 2002).

Pope, Edwin. "Finally, a Time to Celebrate Baseball as Wing Opens at Ted Williams Museum." *Knight Ridder/Tribune News Service* (February 9, 1995).

Sketch by Ann H. Shurgin

Venus Williams
1980-

American tennis player

Venus Williams' route to superstardom in professional tennis was quite unlike that of most of her fellow players, the majority of whom learned the game from pros at country clubs or expensive tennis academies. Venus and younger sister **Serena Williams** practiced their tennis basics in a city torn by gang warfare, Compton, California, playing the game on municipal courts. Coached by their father, Richard, the girls showed a natural aptitude for the game and quickly advanced to amateur competition. When Venus made her professional debut in October 1994, Robin Flinn of the *New York Times* called her "the most unorthodox tennis prodigy her sport has ever seen." Venus, older than sister Serena by about 15 months, was the first to soar to the top of the world women's rankings, and she has stayed firmly entrenched at the top of the game ever since. In the opening years of the new millennium, the sisters were trading the number one ranking back and forth. It became almost a given that the sisters would face off against each other in the finals of the major tournaments on the women's tour. Surprisingly, despite the increased competition between the sisters, Venus and Serena remained as close as ever, the winner comforting her losing sibling after every major tournament in which they played against each other. A striking figure, standing more than 6 feet tall, Venus remains in firm control of her game. Despite a flurry of rumors that she was considering pulling out of the game, she continues to play and play well, handily defeating most comers, except little sister Serena, who has been on the winning side more often than Venus.

Compton Childhood

Williams was born in Lynwood, California, a suburb of Los Angeles, on June 17, 1980, the fourth of five daughters born to Richard and Oracene (nicknamed Brandi) Williams. Sister Serena, the last of the five Williams sisters, was born in September 1981. Her father ran a private security firm in Compton and was a dedicated fan of tennis, who became hooked on the game by watching televised coverage of professional tournaments, told his wife that he wanted to make tennis stars out of his daughters. He had little luck with his older girls—Isha, Lyndrea, and Yetunde—none of whom showed any particular aptitude for the game. His efforts proved far more successful with Venus and Serena, both of whom turned out to be naturals on the court. The girls learned the game on nearby Compton municipal courts, frequently having to take cover to avoid being hit by stray gunfire from the gang violence that gripped the city. As Richard Williams schooled Venus and Serena in the finer points of the game, their mother,

Venus Williams

a devout Jehovah's Witness, home-schooled her daughters, all of whom adopted her faith and became active members of the church.

Venus began playing tennis when she was only 4 years old. By the time she was 7, she had come to the attention of tennis great **John McEnroe** and **Pete Sampras**, both of whom encouraged her to continue to pursue the game. At the tender age of 10, Venus was ranked the number one player in the keenly competitive under-12 division of Southern California, a ranking inherited not long thereafter by younger sister Serena. So strong was Venus's game as a pre-teen that she won 63 consecutive matches without a single loss. Word of her talent reached the media, and in the summer of 1991 both *Sports Illustrated* and *Tennis* ran stories about the amazing tennis prodigy from the mean streets of Compton. All the publicity was accompanied by growing criticism of Richard Williams' single-minded focus on making Venus into a tennis star with little regard for giving her any semblance of a normal childhood. The criticism hit home with Venus's father, who told *Sports Illustrated*: "I'd like for the racket to stay out of her hand for a while. Venus is still young. We want her to be a little girl while she is a little girl. I'm not going to let Venus pass up her childhood. Long after tennis is over, I want her to know who she is." In 1991 Williams pulled both Venus and Serena out of junior tennis competition and moved the family to Palm Beach Gardens, Florida.

Attends Ric Macci's Academy

Although she was temporarily out of tennis competition, Venus continued to work on her game. Her father enrolled Venus and Serena in Ric Macci's tennis academy. Venus continued to be schooled at home and spent about six hours a day, six days a week practicing tennis. Even though she had officially withdrawn from competition, sports-related manufacturers still expressed an interest in signing her to product endorsement deals if she decided to turn pro. In October 1994, at the age of 14, Venus made her professional debut at the Bank of the West Classic in Oakland, California. The unranked teen handily defeated Shaun Stafford, a player ranked number 59 in the world. She went on to play the world's second-ranked woman player, **Arantxa Sanchez Vicario**, giving the Spaniard a good game before losing. In an interview with Robin Finn of the *New York Times,* Stafford said of Venus: "She's going to be great for women's tennis." In joining the pro tour before the end of 1994, Williams dodged a new rule of the Women's Tennis Council of the World Tennis Association that, beginning in 1995, would bar women under the age of 18 from competition.

Because Venus entered into professional competition before the new rules took effect, she maintained a limited schedule at first, continuing her schooling at home. She next took to the courts professionally in August 1995, 10 months after her debut. On this outing she didn't fare nearly as well as she had in her debut, losing in the first round. Her loss prompted some tennis analysts to suggest that Venus's game lacked the competitive edge she might have developed had she continued to compete in junior tournaments. To rectify this and energize his daughter's game, Richard Williams sometimes cheered for her opponent in public matches. "Every time she loses, I pay her $50," Williams told Pat Jordan, a writer for *New York Times Magazine*. Like a lot of other "tennis dads," men who took an active role in their daughters' careers on the court, Richard Williams came in for a fair share of negative publicity. But giving Williams his due, *New York Times* writer Finn concluded that Venus's father and coach Macci together had "produced a player who appears to possess wit and wisdom beyond her years—with a serve, volley, and vocabulary to match."

Makes Her Debut at French Open

Venus managed to stay out of the limelight for most of 1996 but in May 1997 made her debut at the French Open, winning her first match against Naoko Sawamatsu in three sets. However, she fell in the second round of the tournament to Natalie Tauziat of France. Equally uninspired was Venus's debut the following month at Wimbledon, where she lost in the first round to Poland's Magdalena Grzybowska. On the basis of her disappointing performances at the French Open and Wimbledon, most tennis observers expected little from Venus at the U.S. Open in 1997. Surprising everyone but herself,

Williams advanced to the semi-finals, facing off against Irina Spirlea of Romania. In doing so, Venus became only the second female ever to reach the semi-finals in her first appearance at the U.S. Open. She defeated Spirlea 7-6, 4-6, 7-6, becoming the first unseeded woman and only the second African-American female player ever to reach the tournament's final (**Althea Gibson** was the first). Of Gibson's contribution to the game, Venus said she "paved the way for us to play, because other than that, we would still be fighting to play on the tour. To live up to what she did would be great. It's important for me to know my history."

In the finals of the U.S. Open, Williams faced number one-rated **Martina Hingis**, who handily dispatched Venus, 6-0, 6-4. Despite the loss, she felt that she had proved herself a force to be reckoned with in tennis. She told a reporter, "In the past I really didn't worry about what other people thought because it was important what I thought, what my family thought. There's a lot of myths floating around. I knew one day people would see. It would just be a little bit of time; I hadn't played that much. So, I guess this is a great tournament for me. Maybe a fraction of the talk will stop."

Turns Tables on Hingis

Early in 1998, Williams turned the tables on Hingis at the Australian Open, advancing to the quarter-finals of the singles tournament before losing to **Lindsay Davenport**. In mixed doubles competition, Venus teamed with Justin Gimelstob to win the title. It proved to be an upbeat start for a year in which Venus further demonstrated her promise on the court. At the IGA Tennis Classic, she won her first singles title by beating South Africa's Joannette Kruger 6-3, 6-2. In the wake of this victory, her ranking jumped to number 12. Venus took her second career singles title in an all-teen final at the Lipton Championships when she defeated **Anna Kournikova**. She beat Patty Schnyder 6-3, 3-6, 6-2 to win the Grand Slam Cup and advanced to the semi-finals of the U.S. Open, where she was defeated by Lindsay Davenport.

In 1999 singles competition, Williams won titles at Oklahoma City, Miami, Hamburg, the Italian Open, New Haven, and Zurich. Teaming with younger sister Serena, she won doubles titles at both the French and U.S. Opens and also at Hannover, Germany. The following year, Venus and Serena teamed up to win the dou-

Related Biography: Coach Ric Macci

One of the most influential forces in shaping the careers of Venus and Serena Williams, apart from their father, has been Ric Macci, who runs a world-famous tennis academy in Florida. Since 1980 Macci has been coaching some of the most promising young tennis players from around the world including Jennifer Capriati and Any Roddick.

In the summer of 1991, Richard Williams contacted Macci and asked him to come to Compton to meet Venus and assess her potential as a tennis player. In an interview with David Higdon of *Tennis* magazine, Macci recalled Williams' request and his subsequent trip to California. "I hear it all the time: 'I've got the next Jennifer [Capriati].' Richard said he'd like to meet me but the only thing he could promise me was that I wouldn't get shot. All I could think of was: 'Who is this guy?'" Upon his arrival in Compton, Macci was driven by Williams to the local municipal park where Venus and sister Serena practiced tennis under their father's guidance. "There must have been 30 guys there already playing basketball and another 20 lying on the grass passed out."

After playing a few games with Venus, Macci remained unimpressed. But then, as he told Higdon, Venus asked "to go to the bathroom and as she walks out the gate, she walks at least 10 yards on her hands. Then she went into these backward cartwheels for another 10 yards. I'm watching this and the first thing I thought was: 'I've got a female Michael Jordan on my hands.'" Soon thereafter Venus and Serena, who had moved with their family to Palm Beach Gardens, Florida, began training at Macci's academy in Delray Beach. The academy has since been relocated to nearby Pompano Beach.

bles title at Wimbledon and the gold medal at the Summer Olympic Games in Sydney, Australia. In 2000 singles competition, Venus won titles at Wimbledon, the U.S. Open, the Sydney Olympics, Stanford, San Diego, and New Haven. In 2001, Venus successfully defended her Wimbledon and U.S. Open singles titles, while also winning titles at Miami, Hamburg, San Diego, and New Haven. She again teamed with Serena to win the doubles title at the 2001 Australian Open.

Serena Dominates in 2002

In 2002, it was Serena's turn to shine. Although she had to skip the singles competition at the Australian Open because of a sprained ankle, Serena won the other three Grand Slam tournaments—the French Open, Wimbledon, and the U.S. Open—that year. Venus also did well, but all her wins came at second-tier tournaments, including the Gold Coast, Paris Indoors, Antwerp, Amelia Island, Stanford, San Diego, and New Haven. The sisters teamed up to win the doubles title at the 2002 Australian Open, a feat they duplicated again in January 2003, marking the sixth Grand Slam doubles win by the Williams sisters. In the Australian Open's singles final, Venus faced off against Serena, but once again Serena triumphed, taking the last four of the Grand Slam tournaments to complete what fans were calling the "Serena Slam."

Away from the tennis court, Venus studies interior design at the Art Institute of Florida. She's already opened her own interior design company—V Starr Interiors—with branches in both Palm Beach Gardens and Jupiter, Florida. When not playing tennis or tending to her business, Williams likes to visit art galleries, particu-

larly enjoying the work of young, emerging artists. In addition to her interior design business, Venus designs a line of women's leather apparel, called the Venus Williams Collection, for Wilson's Leather. She shares her Florida home with a pet dog named Bobby. When she leaves tennis, Venus hopes to continue her careers in interior design and fashion design and also try her hand at choreography.

A tennis phenom since she was a pre-teen, Venus Williams continues to thrill tennis fans around the world. She and sister Serena have each held the number one ranking back and forth between themselves, clearly dominating the women's tennis scene. Asked about her personal formula for success, Venus told *Sports Illustrated*: "I think you have to believe in yourself and never give up and one day you'll make it."

CONTACT INFORMATION

Address: c/o Women's Tennis Association, 133 First St. NE, St. Petersburg, FL 33701.

FURTHER INFORMATION

Books

"Venus Williams." *Contemporary Black Biography,* Volume 34. Gale Group, 2002.

"Venus Williams." *Newsmakers 1998,* Issue 2. Gale Group, 1998.

"Venus Williams." *Sports Stars,* Series 1-4. Gale Group, 1994-1998.

Periodicals

Gardenour, Jeff. "Macci Named Coach of the Year." *Winter Haven News Chief,* (May 24, 1992).

Venus Williams

Reilly, Rick. "Double Whammy: You Just Know Serena and Venus Will Trade the No. 1 Ranking Back and Forth Like a Dress That Fits Both. "*Sports Illustrated,* (July 15, 2002).

"Sisters Grand Slam Matches." *AP Worldstream,* (September 8, 2002).

Other

"Players: Venus Williams." WTA Tour. http://www.wtatour.com/index.cfm?section=players&cont_id=player&:personnel_id=238&roster_id=12 (January 24, 2003).

"Ric Macci." TennisONE. http://www.tennisone.com/Bios/biomacci.html (January 24, 2003).

"Venus Starr Williams." WilliamsSisters.org. http://venusandserena.homestead.com/VenusBio.html (January 24, 2003).

"Venus Williams: Career Highlights." ESPN.com. http://espn.go.com/tennis/s/wta/profiles/vwilliams.html (January 24, 2003).

Sketch by Don Amerman

Alison Williamson
1971-

British archer

British archer Alison Williamson is a world champion, four-time Olympian, and Olympic and European record holder. Beginning archery at a young age, she went on to compete in the women's individual event around the world consistently placing in the top ten and ranking first in the Tournament of Nations and the Arizona Cup International. She achieved a world record score of 651 in seventy-two Arrows, and won the Moet and Chandon Young Sportwoman of the Year award in 1992. The first Briton to win an archery scholarship to an American university, she graduated from Arizona State in 1995.

Young Hopeful

Williamson seemed to be born to practice archery. Both her parents were archers, and her father gave her her first bow when she was seven. By age nine she had entered her first competition. At fourteen she became a junior international representing the British Junior Team while still attending school in Church Stretton. Her long streak of successful results was soon to emerge in international competition. She made her senior BG Team debut in 1988 and a year later ranked third in the Junior European Championships.

Alison Williamson

Chronology	
1971	Born November 3 in Melton Mowbray, Great Britain
1986	Represents the BG Junior Team
1988	Makes her senior BG Team debut
1991	Granted scholarship to Arizona State University in the US
1995	Graduates from Arizona State with a degree in social work

In 1991, she received a sports scholarship to Arizona State University and became the first British athlete to win an archery scholarship to an American university. She would graduate four years later with a degree in social work.

The first of Williamson's Olympic appearances was Barcelona in 1992, where, at age twenty, she was billed as Britain's young hopeful. Reaching the quarter finals, she placed an overall eighth. That same year she ranked second in the European Championships and was awarded the Moet and Chandon Young Sportwoman of the Year. Two more competitions followed in 1993: the World Indoor Championships in which she placed fifth, and the Arizona Cup International where she came in at the top.

Breaking records and improving her skills, in 1994 she again ranked first in both the Vegas Shoot and at the US Collegiate Championship where she won with a score of 579 in singles 18m. In the Olympic round competition of 1994, Williamson broke the world record with a score of 651 in seventy-two arrows, and achieved a European record score of 165 in eighteen arrows.

Although Williamson ranked only tenth at the Atlanta Olympics of 1996, she continued to shine in European competition. She placed first in the Tournament of Nations in Germany, and second place at the European Grand Prix. Two years later in 1998, she achieved a British record at the European Indoor Championships,

and came in at a European record ninth place at the Czech Republic Grand Prix that same year.

Her best year was 1999 with a silver medal win at the World Championships in Riom, France, a gold medal at the Cyprus European Grand Prix, a European record performance at the Grand Prix in Turkey, and third place in the team competition at the European Field Championships in Slovenia. At the Cyprus games, she performed her best twelve arrows score of 113. In 2000, she placed second at the Arizona Cup USA.

Dashed Hopes in Sydney

Williamson approached her fourth Olympics, the 2000 Sydney Games, with high hopes. Having been briefly ranked top in the world before the Olympics but going into the Games officially listed as third, the near 30-year-old again represented Team BG. She started out with superb results, shooting a perfect ten with her final arrow to attain the last sixteen of the archery competition. She won 157-154 against Turkish player Elif Altinkaynak, hitting the 12.2 cm bull from a distance of 70 meters.

Competition intensified when Williamson faced off against South Korean favorite Kim Soo-Nyung, called by some the best archer in history. Kim had won gold at both the 1988 Seoul and 1992 Barcelona Games. Ironically, it was another South Korean, 17-year-old Yun Mi-Jin in the women's individual archery event who knocked medal hopeful Williamson out of the last sixteen with an Olympic record score of 173 for eighteen arrows. Williamson scored her best total of 164 in the Games and placed an overall tenth, while Yun, Kim, and fellow teammate Kim Nam-Soon took a Korean sweep of the medals.

Williamson is an intense competitor. She has a habit of waiting until the last moment before shooting her arrows in quick succession. To focus on her craft, Williamson employs a sports psychologist with whom she communicates frequently, and listens to tapes to help her concentrate and visualize matches. She is also an avid reader, and once was photographed nude in half-light for an exhibition in the National Portrait Gallery. Williamson is an honorary life member of the Long Mynd Archers society.

Alison Williamson excelled in archery throughout European competition and four Olympic games. She attributes her success in the demanding sport to concentration and establishing a balance between the physical and

Awards and Accomplishments

1989	Junior European Championships, 3rd
1992	Barcelona Olympics, 8th
1992	European Championships, 2nd
1992	Won the Moet and Chandon Young Sportwoman of the Year award
1993	World Indoor Championships, 5th
1993	Arizona Cup International, 1st
1994	Vegas Shoot, 1st
1994	US Collegiate Champion, 1st
1994	European Grand Prix in Poland, 2nd
1994	World record score of 651, 72 Arrows, Olympic Round
1994	European record score of 165, 18 Arrows, Olympic Round
1994	European Championships, 12th
1996	European Championships, 5th
1996	European Grand Prix Rankings, 2nd
1996	Tournament of Nations (Germany), 1st
1996	Atlanta Olympics, 10th
1996	Best FITA 70m round score - 648, Atlanta, USA
1996	Best FITA Round - 1337, Eggenfelden
1997	Best 18 arrows - 169, Kyong Ju, Korea
1998	European Indoor Championships, British record
1998	Czech Republic Grand Prix, European record, 9th
1999	World Archery Championships in Riom, France, 2nd
1999	Cyprus European Grand Prix, 1st, best 12 arrows-113
1999	Grand Prix, Turkey, European record
1999	European Field Championships, Slovenia, 3rd place team
1999	Golden Targets, 2nd
2000	Sydney Olympics, 10th
2000	Arizona Cup, 2nd
2000	World ranking, 2nd place

psychological. She noted in an article for *Sports Illustrated for Women* that archery requires patience, precision, and purity of movement—qualities she has mastered as evidenced by her many victories.

FURTHER INFORMATION

Periodicals

Carol, Caroline. "World Class." *Sports Illustrated for Women* (September/October 2000): 104.

Other

Angus Achievers Award. http://www.angus.gov.uk/ angusahead/awards/2000/sport2000.htm (January 28, 2003).

Biography Resource Center Online. Gale Group. http:// www.galenet.com/servlet/BioRC (January 15, 2003).

Bownet. http://www.bownet.com/gallery/alison.html (January 15, 2003).

FITA International Archery Federation. http://www. archery.org/sydney/participants/GBR_WR_ Williamson.htm (January 15, 2003).

Guardian. http://www.guardian.co/uk/sydney/story (January 15, 2003).

Olympics. http://www.olympics.org.uk/press/pressdetail. asp?boa_press_id=44 (January 28, 2003).

Online Archery. http://www.onlinearchery.org.uk/ news_start.html (January 28, 2003).

Sports Illustrated. "Athletes Set Sights on Sydney." http://sportsillustrated.cnn.com/olympics.news/ 1999/10/04/plans_williamson (January 15, 2003).

Sports Illustrated. "For Alison the goal is clear, although somewhat blurred." http://sportsillustraged.cnn.com/ olympics/newswire/2000/09/06/226250104202_afp (January 15, 2003).

Times. "Perfect 10 Keeps Williamson on Target." http:// www.times-olympics.co.uk/archive/archerys17o.html (January 15, 2003).

Trading Standards. http://www.tradingstandards.gov.uk/ shropshire/validate15.htm (January 15, 2003).

Sketch by Lorraine Savage

Helen Wills
1905-1998

American tennis player

Helen Wills revolutionized the face of sports for American women. At a time when women were not thought capable of athletic achievement, Wills played some of the best tennis in the world, with a strength and ferocity that was far more typical of the male athletes of her time than of the female ones. She was not only dominant in women's tennis, winning thirty-one Grand Slam events over the course of her career, but she also played and beat some of the top-ranked men of her time, including the ranking Italian men's champion and the best player at Stamford University.

Early Years

The story of how Wills learned to play tennis has always been a part of her legend. Her father, a prominent surgeon in Berkeley, California, gave her her first racket when she was thirteen, and at age fourteen he got her a membership at the Berkeley Tennis Club, which was a prestigious institution. Wills never took formal lessons; instead, she learned by watching and playing against other members, both men and women. Hazel Wightman, women's tennis champion of the 1910s, was also a member of the club. Wightman worked with Wills on her game, trying especially to improve her speed. It was less than two years after she joined the club that Wills became a tennis champion, winning her first U.S. girls' singles championships at the age of fifteen. At age seventeen she became the youngest person ever to win the U.S. women's singles title.

Helen Wills

Chronology

1905	Born October 6, in Centreville, California
1919	Joins the Berkeley Tennis Club
1921	Wins first tennis championship
1925	Graduates from the University of California at Berkeley
1926	Plays famous match against Suzanne Lenglen
1929	Marries California stockbroker Frederick Moody
1937	Divorces Moody
1938	Retires from tennis
1939	Marries Irish polo player Aiden Roark
1998	Dies January 1, in Carmel, California

Wills and Wightman eventually went on to become a formidable doubles team, winning the U.S. Open, Wimbledon, and the Olympics in their best year together, 1924. They were never defeated when playing together. Despite this record, Wightman never ceased trying to improve Wills's speed, which plagued her throughout her career. In fact, when the two played in doubles together, Wightman often shouted, "Run, Helen!" However, Wills was so dominant at the baseline, and was so good at anticipating where the ball would go next, that she was not often required to run very fast.

Center Court

Wills's most famous tennis match was played against Suzanne Lenglen in Cannes, France on February 16, 1926. Wills was only twenty, but she had already won two Olympic medals and three U.S. singles championships. Lenglen, the twenty-six-year-old Frenchwoman, was a six-time Wimbledon champion who provided copious fodder for the tabloids with her flamboyant personality. Wills, who was known for her demure attitude and chaste starched cotton clothes, provided quite a contrast to Lenglen in her silks and furs, although tennis-wise the rising star and reigning champion appeared closely matched.

The match was hyped relentlessly by newspapers from around the world. Reporters followed both Wills and Lenglen about as they played in other matches in January and early February, searching for any new angle

on the story. For Wills, who had come to France, accompanied by her mother, ostensibly to continue her studies in painting, this must have been particularly frustrating. By the time that the two actually met on the court, word had spread so far that a Russian grand duke, the Swedish king, and an Indian rajah and ranee were among the 6,000 spectators in the hastily erected stands. The crowd was rowdy, and Lenglen seemed rattled. She took sips of cognac between points, perhaps to calm her nerves. Despite play that was not her best, Lenglen won the first set, but Wills made a comeback in the second. Errors in line judging in that set, not helped by fans who shouted out their opinions on the proper calls, hurt both women's concentration, but Lenglen more than Wills. Wills took the second set, but Lenglen won the third set and the match, then broke down in tears as fans surrounded and congratulated her. Wills and Lenglen played each other in doubles again that afternoon—Lenglen won again—and never again faced each other on the court. Wills missed the French championships that year due to appendicitis, and Lenglen turned professional around the time that Wills returned to competitive play.

Wills's time in Cannes was not a complete loss. A stockbroker from San Francisco named Frederick Moody had noticed Wills, and after her loss he approached her to congratulate her on her good play. They were married in 1929, and thereafter Wills played as Helen Wills Moody. The two divorced in 1937, but by 1939 Wills had remarried, this time to an Irish polo player and Hollywood screenwriter named Aiden Roark. For the rest of her life, Wills would be known as Helen Wills Moody Roark.

Retirements and Comebacks

For six years, from 1927 until 1933, Wills did not lose a single set in competition. Then, in 1933 Wills came to Wimbledon nursing an injury: she had strained her back helping her husband, Moody, to build a stone wall. Wills lost one set to Helen Hull Jacobs, who was often dubbed "Helen the Second" due to her continual overshadowing by Wills, and did not play any more that day: she left the court and announced her retirement. Wills returned to the sport in 1935 just long enough to

Awards and Accomplishments

1921-22	U.S. girls' singles
1922	U.S. girls' doubles
1922, **1924-25,** **1928**	U.S. doubles
1923-25, **1927-29,** **1931**	U.S. singles
1923-25, **1927-32,** **1938**	Wightman Cup
1924	Olympic singles
1924	Olympic doubles
1924, 1927, **1930**	Wimbledon doubles
1924, 1928	U.S. mixed
1927-30, **1932-33,** **1935, 1938**	Wimbledon singles
1928	French singles
1929	Wimbledon mixed
1929-30, **1932**	French singles
1930, 1932	French doubles
1935	Named Female Athlete of the Year by the Associated Press
1959	Inducted into the International Tennis Hall of Fame
1980	1926 match against Suzanne Lenglen named one of the top twenty tennis matches of all time by *Tennis* magazine
1996	Inducted into the Intercollegiate Tennis Association Women's Hall of Fame

Related Biography: Tennis Player Hazel Wightman

Hazel Hotchkiss Wightman thoroughly dominated American tennis at the height of her career. She was best known for her famous triple threepeat—winning the singles, doubles, and mixed doubles at the U.S. championships three years in a row, from 1909 to 1911—although her scandalous (for the time) tennis uniform of an ankle-length skirt and a short-sleeve shirt that bared much of her arms also brought her some attention. Like Wills, Wightman was from Berkeley, California, but in 1912 she married a man from Boston, George Wightman, and moved to Massachusetts. Wightman slowed down a bit after 1912, since bearing and caring for five children took much time and energy, but she did not abandon competition entirely. She was U.S. singles champion again in 1919, and in 1924, at the age of thirty-eight, Wightman, playing with Wills, won in doubles at the U.S. championships, at Wimbledon, and at the Olympics. Wightman continued to play tennis well past the age when most athletes retire: she dominated the U.S. women's over 40 doubles championships for much of the 1940s and '50s, winning her final title in that event in 1954, at the age of sixty-seven. In all, Wightman won forty-five U.S. championships in her forty-five year career.

Today, Wightman is best remembered for instituting the Wightman Cup, which was intended to be the women's equivalent of the men's Davis Cup. Wightman died in 1974, at the age of eighty-seven.

play Jacobs again at Wimbledon, defeating her and winning the title. Wills retired again, but returned once more in 1938. She played Jacobs at Wimbledon again, won, and then retired permanently.

"Little Miss Poker Face"

Wills's presence, on and off the court, was legendary. On court, whether winning or losing she displayed no emotion at all, only a fierce concentration. This concentration prompted a young *New York Evening Mail* columnist named Ed Sullivan, before the as yet unknown medium of television made him famous, to nickname her "Little Miss Poker Face." Other nicknames, including "Queen Helen," also spoke to this imperial presence. Artists and poets noticed it as well. In perhaps her most famous artistic representation, painter Diego Rivera placed her at the center of his mural at the former San Francisco Stock Exchange. When asked why he had featured her so prominently, Rivera explained by saying, "Because of that woman, California is known to the rest of the world." Wills was also featured in a sculpture by Alexander Calder, who was famous for his wire creations. Another often-repeated compliment came from silent film star Charlie Chaplin, who, when asked what the most beautiful thing he'd ever seen was, once replied, "The movement of Helen Wills playing tennis." Some women flattered by imitation, adopting Wills's trademark white eyeshade as part of their own tennis uniform.

Wills was a very public figure for much of her life; even when she was not playing tennis, she stayed in the public eye by writing newspaper and magazine articles and books, including a tennis guide, an autobiography, and a mystery. Wills was also a painter, and she exhibited her artwork in London, Paris, and New York. However, she became something of a recluse later in life. She rarely appeared in public, but she continued to follow sports on television. She particularly enjoyed watching **Martina Navratilova**'s matches. "[Wills] admired Martina Navratilova greatly," tennis historian Jeanne Cherry said in Wills's obituary in the *Houston Chronicle*. This admiration lasted through Navratilova's ninth Wimbledon championship, in 1990, which broke Wills's long-standing record of eight Wimbledon wins. "I once asked her how she felt about Martina breaking her record," Cherry continued, "and she said, 'Well, you know she pumps iron.'" Wills passed away in 1998; her ashes were scattered at sea.

"Every Woman Who Goes into Athletics Owes Something to Her"

Although Helen Wills may be nearly forgotten today, her influence lives on in the many female tennis champions who have come after her. "I think every woman who goes into athletics owes something to her," her biographer Larry Engelmann, told Dennis Akizuki of the *Knight Ridder/Tribune News Service*. "She revised popular estimations and I would say scientific evaluations of what a woman could do."

SELECTED WRITINGS BY WILLS:

Tennis, with illustrations by the author, Scribner's, 1928.
Fifteen-Thirty: The Story of a Tennis Player, Scribner's, 1937.

(With Robert Murphy) *Death Serves an Ace,* Scribner's, 1939.

FURTHER INFORMATION

Periodicals

Akizuki, Dennis. "Helen Wills Moody Dies at Age 92." *Knight Ridder/Tribune News Service* (January 2, 1998): 102K5693.

Akizuki, Dennis. "Moody Played Tennis with Entrancing Style." *Austin American-Statesman* (January 3, 1998): E1.

"An American Original." *Sports Illustrated* (January 12, 1998): 32.

Blue, Adrianne. "Obituary: Ice-Cool on Court: Helen Wills Moody." *Guardian* (London, England) (January 3, 1998): 17.

"Died, Helen Wills Moody." *Time* (January 12, 1998): 31.

"Hard Hitter Who Ruled in Golden Era for US." *Birmingham Post* (January 3, 1998): 18.

"Helen Wills Moody: Obituary." *Times* (London, England) (January 3, 1998): 25.

Lidz, Franz. "Tennis Everyone?" *Sports Illustrated* (fall, 1991): 90-95.

Matson, Barbara. "She Was Queen of Court: Wightman Had Regal Reign in Women's Tennis." *Boston Globe* (October 8, 1999): F06.

"Miss Helen Wills on Lawn Tennis; 17 May 1928." *Times* (London, England) (May 17, 1999): 23.

"Queen of the Court Dies, 92." *Sunday Mail* (Adelaide, Australia) (January 4, 1998): 21.

"Tennis Greats Memorialize Legendary Helen Wills Moody." *Houston Chronicle* (January 3, 1998): 14.

"Tennis: Last Link with the Days of Chiffon and Cognac." *Independent* (London, England) (January 6, 1998): 26.

"Tennis: Wills-Moody Dies at Age of 92." *Guardian* (London, England) (January 3, 1998): 11.

"Whatever Happened to Helen Wills Moody?" *Independent* (London, England) (August 31, 2002): 7.

Other

Intercollegiate Tennis Association Women's Hall of Fame. http://www.wm.edu/tenniscenter/ (October 11, 2002).

International Tennis Hall of Fame. http://www. tennisfame.org/ (October 11, 2002).

Sketch by Julia Bauder

Dave Winfield
1951-

American baseball player

Baseball player Dave Winfield is one of only a handful of players to achieve 3,000 hits and 400 home runs in his career, joining other Hall of Famers **Hank Aaron, Babe Ruth, Willie Mays, Stan Musial, Mel Ott, Frank Robinson,** and Carl Yaztrzemski. Winfield also won seven Gold Glove awards for his outfield skills during his twenty-two-season career. A 6'6", 220 lb. giant at the plate, he ranks among the top twenty all-time leaders in home runs, extra bases, and runs batted in. He remains the only athlete to be drafted in college by pro baseball, basketball, and football clubs. He became the first professional athlete to form a charitable organization when he founded the David M. Winfield Foundation in 1977 to help inner-city children.

Close Family

David Mark Winfield was born October 3, 1951, the son of Frank Winfield, a waiter on passenger trains, and Arline Winfield, a public school employee. His parents separated when Dave was three, and his mother raised him and his brother, Steve, alone. They lived in a black community in St. Paul, Minnesota. The three were a very closely knit family, and the boys never strayed farther than a nearby playground. There, director Bill Peterson, who was white, encouraged the neighborhood children to play baseball and basketball. Winfield later said of Peterson, "He gave more to that community than anyone I know. To me . . . he was coach, friend, father, all rolled into one."

Small for his age, Dave did not try out for the baseball team at St. Paul's Central High School until his junior year. A tremendous growth spurt helped him achieve All-City and All-State honors in both baseball and basketball by his senior year, and after graduation he was offered a scholarship to the University of Minnesota. He continued to live at home and majored in political science and black studies. During his freshman year, he was arrested as an accomplice in the theft of a snowblower from a store. When his mother came to escort him from an overnight stay in jail, she was crying, and Winfield was ashamed and remorseful that he had hurt her. He remained on probation throughout college.

Blossoming Sports Career

At the University of Minnesota, Winfield's career in sports began to blossom. As a sophomore, he was a starting pitcher who won eight out of eleven outings. In his junior year he moved to the outfield and played both baseball and basketball. He pitched again during his senior year and hit .385. The Minnesota Gophers won both the Big Ten basketball and the Big Ten baseball championships during Winfield's senior year. He was named Most Valuable Player in the National Collegiate Athletic Association tournament and received collegiate All-American honors.

On graduation, in 1973, Winfield was drafted by the San Diego Padres baseball team, the Atlanta Hawks and

Dave Winfield

the Utah Stars basketball teams, and the pro football team Minnesota Vikings, even though he had never played football in college. He chose the Padres and received a $50,000 signing bonus plus $18,000 a year in salary. At San Diego, he gave up pitching and became an outfielder. His batting was both brilliant and lagging during his rookie years. With consistent coaching, however, by 1978 he batted .308 and was named team captain. He also played his second All-Star game, and in 1979 he won his first Gold Glove award.

Winfield Foundation

In 1977, Winfield established a charitable foundation designed to mentor and guide inner-city youths, much as Peterson had done for him and his brother. The David M. Winfield Foundation has since expanded to include health and nutrition, literacy, sports and fitness programs, community holiday celebrations, and a drug abuse prevention program. Although many sports figures have since become involved in charity work, Winfield was the first to do so when he founded his organization during the 1970s.

Difficult Decade with the Yankees

In 1978, Winfield met the aggressive Albert S. Frohman, a retired businessman who would become his agent. Frohman encouraged Winfield to leave the Padres and move up to the New York Yankees. He managed to

get Winfield a ten-year contract with the Yankees, a $1 million signing bonus and regular contributions to the Winfield Foundation. The deal also included a cost-of-living pay increase, which Yankee owner **George Steinbrenner** later said he had not fully understood at the time of the contract. The deal was signed on December 15, 1980. Things seemed to go wrong from the time Winfield signed it.

Unhappy with the costly contract, Steinbrenner began to insult Winfield in the media. When he failed to perform well in the 1981 World Series, Steinbrenner called him "Mr. May," in contrast to former Yankee **Reggie Jackson**, whose World Series game hits were so outstanding he had earned the nickname "Mr. October." Steinbrenner also stopped making his agreed-on contributions to the Winfield Foundation, but Winfield sued his boss to get the money owed the organization.

In addition to these actions, Steinbrenner tried several times to trade Winfield, but his contract gave him the ability to veto the trades. Managers and coaches were fearful of praising Winfield's performance in the media, believing it would anger Steinbrenner. The fans, however, were pleased with the fact that Winfield got at least 100 runs batted in every year for five years. He was the first to do so since **Joe DiMaggio.** Winfield's struggle later came out in his autobiography, *Winfield: A Player's Life,* which is said to have infuriated Steinbrenner.

Career Statistics

Yr	Team	AVG	GP	AB	R	H	HR	RBI	BB	SO	SB
1973	SD	.277	56	141	9	39	3	12	12	19	0
1974	SD	.265	145	498	57	132	20	75	40	96	9
1975	SD	.267	143	509	74	136	15	76	69	82	23
1976	SD	.283	137	492	81	139	13	69	65	78	26
1977	SD	.275	157	615	104	169	25	92	58	75	16
1978	SD	.308	158	587	88	181	24	97	55	81	21
1979	SD	.308	159	597	97	184	34	118	85	71	15
1980	SD	.276	162	558	89	154	20	87	79	83	23
1981	NYY	.294	105	388	52	114	13	68	43	41	11
1982	NYY	.280	140	539	84	151	37	106	45	64	5
1983	NYY	.283	152	598	99	169	32	116	58	77	15
1984	NYY	.340	141	567	106	193	19	100	53	71	6
1985	NYY	.275	155	633	105	174	26	114	52	96	19
1986	NYY	.262	154	565	90	148	24	104	77	106	6
1987	NYY	.275	156	575	83	158	27	97	76	96	5
1988	NYY	.322	149	559	96	180	25	107	69	88	9
1990	NYY	.213	20	61	7	13	2	6	4	13	0
	ANA	.275	112	414	63	114	19	72	48	68	0
1991	ANA	.262	150	568	75	149	28	86	56	109	7
1992	TOR	.290	156	583	92	169	26	108	82	89	2
1993	MIN	.271	143	547	72	148	21	76	45	106	2
1994	MIN	.252	77	294	35	74	10	43	31	51	2
1995	CLE	.191	46	115	11	22	2	4	14	26	1
TOTAL		.283	2973	11003	1669	3110	465	1833	1216	1686	223

ANA: Anaheim Angels; CLE: Cleveland Indians; MIN: Minnesota Twins; NYY: New York Yankees; SD: San Diego Padres; TOR: Toronto Blue Jays.

In addition to troubles with his boss and the team, Winfield faced personal assaults during the Yankee years as well. In the mid-1980s a woman took him to court for support of her daughter, of whom Winfield did not deny paternity. He later came to establish a good relationship with the girl. In 1985, another woman sued Winfield, claiming he had given her venereal disease; this was settled out of court. Around the same time, an investigation was launched into the Winfield Foundation's finances, for alleged wrongdoing.

Through the troubles, Winfield continued to play his best baseball, batting .322—the fourth highest in the American League—in 1988. Rarely succumbing to injury, Winfield in 1989 had surgery for a herniated disk in his back and missed the entire baseball season. The following year, after a decade with the Yankees, he was traded to the Anaheim, California, Angels.

A New Lease on His Career

Winfield did well with the Angels, leading the team in runs batted in and batting .290. *Sporting News* named him "Comeback Player of the Year." In early 1992 he signed with the Toronto Blue Jays as a free agent. In Game Six of the 1992 World Series, with the score tied 2-2, men on first and second and two outs, Winfield hit a double down the third base line, bringing two men home and helping Toronto to a 4-3 victory over the Atlanta Braves, Toronto's first ever World Series championship. Winfield told *Sports Illustrated* that if his career had ended before Toronto, he "wouldn't have been really happy" with what baseball had dealt him. "I would have had no fulfillment, no sense of equity, no fairness," he said. "I feel a whole lot better now about the way the things have turned out."

In 1993, Winfield signed with the Minnesota Twins, returning home for a time. There he achieved his 3,000th hit. He played forty-six games for the Cleveland Indians in 1995 but retired as a player the following year.

Winfield was inducted into the Baseball Hall of Fame in 2001, his first year of eligibility for the honor. He chose to wear the San Diego Padres cap for his likeness on the enshrinement plaque. In his acceptance speech, he acknowledged **Jackie Robinson**, the first black player in the major leagues, for making a career in baseball possible for African Americans. He also had a word for young people: "Life and baseball are littered with all kinds of obstacles and problems. You have to learn how to overcome them to be successful."

Dave Winfield remained a calm, focused player throughout his career, in spite of numerous scandals and difficulties. In 1991, with the Anaheim Angels, he had the first three-home run game of his career. Surprisingly free of injuries throughout his twenty-two seasons in baseball, he was the oldest player ever to have 100 runs in a season, at age forty-one, with the Toronto Blue Jays. In addition to his record-breaking playing, Winfield has been a generous and caring member of society and one who has passed on the gift of guidance in youth through the Winfield Foundation.

Awards and Accomplishments

1972-74, 1976-78, 1980-82, 1985, 1991	Named to All-Star Team, seven times as a starter
1973	Most Valuable Player in National Collegiate Athletic Association Tournament; Collegiate All-American
1979	Received Young Men's Christian Association's (YMCA's) Brian Piccolo Award for humanitarian service
1979-80, 1982-85, 1987	Gold Glove Award
1990	Named "Comeback Player of the Year" by *Sporting News*
1992	Toronto Blue Jays won World Series; received Rotary Club of Denver's Branch Rickey Award for community service; received Arete Award for courage in sports
1993	Achieved 3,000th hit; won American League's Joe Cronin Award for significant achievement
2001	Inducted into Baseball Hall of Fame

CONTACT INFORMATION

Address: Dave Winfield, c/o San Diego Padres, P.O. Box 122000, San Diego, CA 92112-2000. Phone: 619-881-6500 or 888-MY PADRES. Email: fanfeedback@padres.mlb.com. Online: http://sandiego.padres.mlb.com.

SELECTED WRITINGS BY WINFIELD:

(With Eric Swenson) *Turn It Around!: There's No Room Here for Drugs,* Paperjacks, 1987.

(With Tom Parker) *Winfield: A Player's Life,* Norton, 1988.

(With Eric Swenson) *The Complete Baseball Player,* Avon Books, 1990.

Ask Dave: Dave Winfield Answers Kids' Questions about Baseball and Life, Andrews and McMeel, 1994.

FURTHER INFORMATION

Books

Contemporary Black Biography. Volume 5. Detroit: Gale Group, 1993.

Periodicals

"Dave Winfield Is New Padres Vice President." *Jet* (March 11, 2002): 53.

"Dave Winfield Named Baseball Program Analyst on FOX-TV." *Jet* (April 1, 1996): 46.

"Ex-Yankees Slugger Dave Winfield Selling Home and Buying Bigger One in L.A.'s Beverly Crest." *Jet* (March 29, 1999): 57.

"Winfield, Puckett Head Baseball's Class of 2001 Hall of Fame Inductees." *Jet* (August 20, 2001): 52.

Other

Baseball-Reference.com. "Dave Winfield." http://www.baseball-reference.com/ (November 1, 2002).

Where Is He Now?

Soon after retirement, Dave Winfield signed on as a baseball analyst for FOX-TV sports, in a show that premiered June 1, 1996. This position allowed him to remain close to baseball. In 1999 he and his wife, Tonya, then the parents of four-year-old twins, sold their 5,000-square-foot home in a posh section of Los Angeles and bought a 9,000-square-foot home in the same section. He had also invested in Burger King restaurants and owned some fifteen franchises. In 1998 he opened a company specializing in exterior lighting for commercial buildings. In 2002, Winfield returned to his original team, the San Diego Padres, as vice president/senior advisor, a position in which he handles business, marketing, and player development for the team.

CBS SportsLine.com. "Dave Winfield Bio." http://CBS.SportsLine.com/ (August 5, 2001).

Poole, Tracy. "Dave Winfield at a Glance." *Knight-Ridder News Service.* (January 3, 1994).

San Diego Padres Official Web Site. http://sandiego.padres.mlb.com/ (November 1, 2002).

Sketch by Ann H. Shurgin

Katarina Witt
1965-

German figure skater

Known as "Fire on the Ice," Katarina Witt emerged from the former East Germany to become the winningest figure skater since Norway's **Sonja Henie**. Witt made an enormous splash onto the international scene in the 1988 Olympic Games in Sarajevo, Yugoslavia, where she took her first gold medal. Sexy and charming as well as technically astute and creatively expressive, she instantly became a media darling. All told, she earned two Olympic gold medals, four World Championship gold medals, and was European champion eight times.

Witt (pronounced "Vitt") was born December 3, 1965, in the city of Karl-Marx-Stadt, in the former East Germany, which is now known as Chimnitz, Germany. Her father, Manfred, managed an agriculture factory and her mother, Kathe, was a physical therapist. She has an older brother, Axel. Witt started kindergarten when she was five, and her walk to school took her past the Kuchwald ice arena. She became fascinated with watching the figure skaters, and soon insisted to her parents that she be allowed to join them. Every detail of Witt's first wobbly steps onto the ice would remain in her memory. "I made my way out to the middle of the ice and I remember thinking, 'This is for me,'" Witt is quoted as saying by author Evelyn B. Kelly in *Katarina Witt.*

Katarina Witt

Witt emerged as a natural talent, and was approached by an East German athlete training school. In former Communist nations like East Germany and the Soviet Union, promising athletes were hand-picked by the government, and then were provided training so that they would grow up to perform favorably for their country in competition. Standards for these programs were rigid, and once entry into a state school was gained, the training regimen was strict and demanding. Before a child was offered a place in a training program, every detail of her and her family's physical and behavioral nature was measured and calculated to determine their champion potential. A child who showed a tendency toward heaviness would not be allowed into the program, so Witt's parents were weighed and measured. Officials observed Witt during practice to determine her ability to resist signs of stress or nerves. Witt stood up to the testing with remarkable poise and was accepted into the sports school.

Gave Her Life to Skating

Skating took over Witt's life. She left for practice at seven in the morning and did not return home until dinnertime. When she was nine years old, Witt caught the attention of Jutta Mueller, East Germany's most successful skating coach. Mueller took over the girl's training, and Witt was soon spending more time with her coach than she did with her parents. In addition to perfecting her technical and athletic abilities, Mueller worked with Witt to develop her showmanship. Mueller drew out a sense of seductiveness in the skater, which made her an engaging performer. Witt learned how to maximize her natural beauty with makeup and glitzy costumes.

Witt executed her first triple salchow—a complicated leaping, rotating jump—when she was eleven years old and Mueller decided she was ready for competition. Headstrong Witt was weakest in the compulsories category, where skaters must complete simple but exact figure eights, circles, and loops on the ice to display their control. The young skater found herself much more suited to the free-skating programs, where skaters must perform a number of required moves, but do so to music and creative choreography. The score for each category is an average of the scores from nine judges, with 6.0 being the highest. Witt skated in her first European championship in 1979 at age 14 and placed tenth. The next year, she placed fifth. In 1982, she won both the short and long programs, and finished second overall.

Witt entered her first Olympic competition in 1984 in Sarajevo, Yugoslavia. She placed third in the compulsories. Witt was nonplussed by the cheering American crowd, and skated confidently onto the ice wearing a traditional Hungarian costume. Skating fans used to the stern and masculine character of most Eastern bloc athletes were not prepared for Witt's personality and charm. A virtually perfect performance gave her 5.8s and 5.9s among the judges in the long and short programs. American Rosalyn Sumners scored almost as well. The fight ended narrowly: Witt won the gold

Awards and Accomplishments

1983	Silver medal, World Figure Skating championships; European champion
1984	Gold medal, Sarajevo Winter Olympics; European champion
1985	Gold medal, World Figure Skating championships; European champion
1986	Silver medal, World Figure Skating championships; European champion
1987	Gold medal, World Figure Skating championships; European champion
1988	Gold medal, World Figure Skating championships; Gold medal, Calgary Winter Olympics; European champion
1990	Emmy Award for *Carmen on Ice*
1994	Golden Camera Award for Olympic comeback
1995	Jim Thorpe Pro Sports Award; inducted into the World Figure Skating Hall of Fame in Colorado Springs, Colorado
1999	Voted "Favorite Female Athlete" in the United States by the American Opinion Research Institute and "Female Skater of the Century" in Germany

Where Is She Now?

Witt left competitive skating behind in 1994 to indulge her love for the audience, touring with *Stars on Ice*. She also indulged her love for American culture, buying an apartment in New York City, and becoming a fan of Madonna, blue jeans, and Michael Jordan. She took a break in 1995 to recover from back injuries, and received the Jim Thorpe Pro Sports Award for outstanding performances and efforts in the Olympics. She also was inducted into the World Figure Skating Hall of Fame in Colorado Springs, Colorado. She was nominated for another Emmy Award for *The Ice Princess* in 1996. Witt's star turn off the ice also included several cameo roles in Hollywood productions. She appeared in the hit features *Jerry Maguire* with Tom Cruise in 1996 and *Ronin* with Robert DeNiro in 1998. She appeared on television in *Frasier* in 1993 and *Everybody Loves Raymond* in 1996. She played herself on TV's *Arliss* in 1997 and 1998, and appeared as "Greta Krantz" in 1998 on *V.I.P* alongside Pamela Anderson. A multi-year contract with Germany's ARD put Witt in front of the cameras as a commentator for international skating. She also launched a sports marketing and promotion company called With Witt. The 1998 *Playboy* magazine she appeared in was a huge seller.

medal over Sumners by just one-tenth of a point on one judge's scorecard.

With Gold Came Celebrity

The eighteen-year-old East German skater became an instant celebrity, with a lot of attention paid to her sex appeal. Witt took it in stride, embracing the attention while training for the World Championships, which took place weeks after the Olympics. She even apologized publicly for not responding to each of the 35,000 fan letters she received after the Olympics, many of which included marriage proposals. Witt went on to win her first World gold medal in Ottawa, Canada, and repeated her gold success at the 1985 World Championships, in Tokyo, Japan. She also won the European Championships in 1984 and 1985.

Because Witt was such an accomplished athlete, and had become so because of her nation's Communist government, at no cost to her parents, she became a proud representative of the Communist system. In East Germany, she was known as "Katarina the Great." Unlike American or European skaters, skaters from Communist countries were indebted to their governments and were not allowed to perform publicly or accept endorsements that were not government approved. Communist athletes were even prohibited from traveling with their families to discourage defection. Witt's parents never saw her skate in competition.

Witt's Olympic and European and World Championship gold medals had firmly established her as the skater to beat. American skater Debi Thomas had placed fifth in Sarajevo, but took the 1986 World Championship from Witt. The upset began a determined rivalry between the two champions. It also stoked fires between East vs. West, Communism vs. Capitalism, among fans. Thomas was considered the better athlete, but Witt's showmanship, paired with her technical prowess, made

it an even match. In a program choreographed to music from *West Side Story,* Witt regained her World Championship title from Thomas in March 1987.

The Witt-Thomas rivalry was a media focus of the 1988 Olympic Games in Calgary, Canada. Ironically, each skater had unknowingly chosen the same music, from the opera *Carmen* for her long program. Witt skated a conservative program forsaking several triple jumps for doubles, and focusing more on flirting with the audience, and did not receive exceptionally high marks. Thomas skated an incredibly ambitious program, but not well enough. A few technical mistakes made way for Witt take the gold once again. A few weeks later, at the World Championships in Budapest, Hungary, Witt regained the World gold from Thomas.

Held Back by Her Government

Witt came head-to-head with her beloved government in 1988, when she wanted to skate with the American *Holiday on Ice* tour. Only after months of pleading by Witt did the rigid bureaucracy allow her to accept the offer—under the condition that 80 percent of her $3.78 million contract be paid to the East German Sports Federation. She went through the same tiresome process to appear in *Canvas of Ice* in December 1988 and to film HBO's *Carmen on Ice,* which earned her an Emmy Award. She skated with friend and American skater **Brian Boitano** in both. The government wanted Witt to pursue her education, and revoked her travel privileges to discourage her aspirations abroad. Her government lost its hold on Witt in November 1989, when the Berlin Wall was brought down and Germany was reunited as one democratic nation. The collapse of her government left Witt free to perform as she liked, but she was practically reviled in her own country for having been so favored by the government.

Witt quickly adapted to freedom. She toured North America in *Katarina Witt & Brian Boitano—Skating* in

1990. She appeared off the ice during the 1992 Olympics in Albertville, France, as a commentator for CBS-TV. In 1993, she covered the World Championships in Prague, Czechoslovakia, for NBC-TV.

Witt decided in 1993 to begin training for the 1994 Olympics in Lillehammer, Norway. Many scoffed at the decision; at age 28, she was almost twice as old as her competitors. An eighth-place finish at the European Championships did not bode well for her Olympic chances, and was a blow to her confidence. Witt dedicated her 1994 Olympic performance of "Where Have All the Flowers Gone?" to war-torn Sarajevo, where she had won her first gold a decade earlier. The performance also marked the first time her parents had ever seen her skate. Though she finished seventh, the performance was as important to Witt as any that had earned her the gold.

CONTACT INFORMATION

Address: Katarina Witt, c/o Parenteau Guidance, Gail Parenteau, 132 East 35th St., Ste. 3J, New York, NY 10016.

FURTHER INFORMATION

Books

Kelly, Evelyn. *Katarina Witt*. Philadelphia: Chelsea House, 1999.
Smith, Pohla. *Superstars of Women's Figure Skating*. Philadelphia: Chelsea House, 1997.

Other

Katarina Witt Official Web site. http://www.katarina-witt. com (January 15, 2003).
"Katarina Witt," Skating Source. http://www.skating source.com/witt.shtml (January 15, 2003).

Sketch by Brenna Sanchez

Lynette Woodard
1959-

American basketball player

Considered one of basketball's greatest female players, Lynette Woodard excelled in the sport during her professional career in the 1980s and 1990s. A two-time Olympic Game basketball player, Woodard served as co-captain of the United States' gold medal team in 1984. She became the first female member of the famed

Lynette Woodard

Harlem Globetrotters in 1985, and was named Big Eight Player of the Decade for the 1980s. In 1996 Woodard was named best female player in Big Eight Conference history, having set career records for scoring and rebounding. After a four-year retirement in the mid-1990s, Woodard returned to join the new Women's National Basketball Association (WNBA), playing for the Cleveland Rockers and the Detroit Shock. A worldwide basketball star, Woodard is known equally well in her native United States as in Italy and Japan, where she has also played professionally.

Born on August 12, 1959, in Wichita, Kansas, Lynette Woodard was one of four children born to Lugene, a fireman, and Dorothy, a homemaker. When Woodard was five years old, a U.S. Air Force jet crashed in her neighborhood, killing 30 residents and just missing the Woodard house. By 1970 an area of destroyed homes had been transformed from a vacant lot into a public park with a full-size basketball court. This was Piatt Park, where Woodard developed her talent for the sport. "We played pick-up games every day," she told the *New York Times*. "Soon the guys would pick me before their friends."

Woodard's fascination with basketball had begun when she was eight years old, when her cousin Hubert "Geese" Ausbie, a player with the Harlem Globetrotters, paid a visit during a tour. Ausbie mesmerized his young cousin, spinning a basketball on his finger and demonstrating other signature 'Trotters skills. Woodard never

Chronology

1959	Born on August 12 in Wichita, Kansas
1978-81	Dominates women's basketball, University of Kansas
1981	Becomes women's university basketball's highest scorer, with 3,649 points
1981-82	Plays professional women's basketball in Italy
1982-84	Trains with U.S. Olympic women's basketball team
1984	Co-captains Olympic team
1985	Becomes first female Harlem Globetrotter
1990-93	Plays professional women's basketball in Japan
1993	Becomes Kansas City's first district athletic director
1995	Becomes a registered stockbroker on Wall Street
1997	Joins Cleveland Rockers (WNBA)
1998	Joins Detroit Shock (WNBA)
1999	Retires from basketball
1999	Becomes assistant women's basketball coach at University of Kansas

Awards and Accomplishments

1977	Named All-American high school athlete
1978-81	Named All-American athlete, University of Kansas
1981	Awarded Wade Trophy
1982	Won NCAA Top Five Award
1984	As co-captain, led U.S. Olympic women's basketball team to gold medal victory
1989	Inducted into National High School Hall of Fame
1989	Named Big Eight Player of the Decade (1980s)
1993	Won Flo Hyman Award
1996	Awarded Globetrotters "Legends" ring
1996	Named best female player in Big Eight Conference history

dreamed then that she would one day join the Globetrotters, which was then an all-male team. With her older brother, Darrell, Woodard played "sockball" around their house, shooting rolled-up socks over open doors and using a timer on the stove as a game clock. "We used to play all kinds of games and pretend it was the Olympics," Darrell told Liz Robbins of the *Plain Dealer*. "Two pieces of candy would be the gold medal. Lynette would always win. I knew then she was ready for the Olympics."

Set Records in University Basketball

As a tenth grader, Woodard joined the varsity basketball team at Wichita North High School, leading her school to the state championships in 1975 and 1977. Also in 1977 she was named an All-American high school athlete. In just 62 high school games she had scored 1,678 points and collected 1,030 rebounds.

Woodard attended Kansas University, where she dominated women's basketball, setting national and school records that she still holds today. The highest scorer in university women's basketball, Woodard amassed a total of 3,649 points. She also tops the university charts in career field goals (1,572) and field goal attempts (2,994). Woodard was a four-time Kodak All-American college athlete and a two-time Academic All-American player. She also excelled academically, making the dean's list and majoring in speech communication.

When Woodard graduated in 1981, professional opportunities for female basketball players were few and far between. She had made the U.S. Olympic team in 1980, but a boycott had prevented the team from participating. Instead she went on to play professionally in Italy, relocating to the northern town of Schio. During the 1981-1982 season she was the only English-speaking player on her team. Since there was no language school in the town, Woodard struggled to communicate and was often left to fend for herself. "I thought when I first got there, 'Lord,

what have I done,'" she told Malcolm Moran of the *New York Times*. But the experience ultimately strengthened her character. "I think it really helped me grow as a person," she said. Woodard returned to the United States to coach at her alma mater and to train with the 1984 Olympic team, which she co-captained. At the Games in Los Angeles, she led her team to a gold-medal victory.

Joined Globetrotters

Over the years, Woodard had kept in touch with her Globetrotter cousin, and had asked him if the team would consider taking women. The answer was always no—until 1985, when an advertisement in *USA Today* announced tryouts for a female player. "I got chills," Woodard recalled to Robbins of the *Plain Dealer*. "I just shook my head, and I said: 'It's me, I know it's me.'" When Woodard showed up for the tryouts, the Globetrotters knew she was the one, too. She joined the Hollywood-based team as its first female player in October of 1985, when she was 26 years old.

Woodard toured with the Globetrotters for two years. It wasn't long before she made it to the team's Magic Circle, where chosen players dribble to the beat of "Sweet Georgia Brown." When the team's management changed after her second year, however, she parted ways with the Globetrotters. In recognition of her historical contribution, the team presented her with a "Legends" ring in 1996. The ring has been given to only eight players in the team's 70-year history.

With few opportunities in the United States, Woodard returned to play in Italy, and then in Japan. She became fluent in both languages, and gained a following in both countries. Woodard played professionally in Japan's basketball circuit for three seasons (1990-1993).

In 1993 Woodard returned to her home state to accept a position as Kansas City's first district athletic director. Through this position she met stockbroker Pat Winans, who was handling the district's retirement fund. Winans, who had started her own Wall Street brokerage firm, took an instant liking to Woodard and offered her a job at Magna Securities Corp. Woodard relocated to New

Career Statistics

Yr	Team	GP	PTS	FG%	3P%	FT%	APG	SPG	BPG	TO	PF
1997	CLE	28	217	.399	.000	.672	2.4	1.64	.36	2.46	1.60
1998	DET	27	95	.387	.000	.575	.8	.81	.11	1.15	1.20

CLE: Cleveland Rockers; DET: Detroit Shock.

York City and became a registered stockbroker in the spring of 1995.

Yet Woodard was not entirely finished with basketball. When the new Women's National Basketball Association (WNBA) was created in 1996, Woodard came out of retirement at age 37 to play for the Cleveland Rockers in the first season (1997). She didn't quit her Wall Street job, which was bringing in an annual salary of nearly $250,000. Instead, she worked out in the early mornings before work, and took leave from the office to practice and play. Her position on the team brought in a salary of $40,000. In 1998 Woodard left the Rockers to join the Detroit Shock. She played one more year of professional basketball, retiring for the second time in May of 1999, four months shy of her 40th birthday.

Woodard is an assistant coach for the Jayhawks, the women's basketball team of her alma mater, the University of Kansas (KU). Prior to becoming assistant coach, Woodard served for one year as KU's special assistant for external relations and women's basketball, where her job was to enhance and build community and alumni relations. She became assistant coach in May 1999; her responsibilities include helping with practice sessions and scouting and recruiting student-athletes. Woodard has also continued working in finance, holding a position as an independent representative of Primerica Financial. She will become eligible for induction into the National Basketball Hall of Fame in 2004.

Woodard will be remembered not only for her basketball prowess but also for her winning temperament. "She is a wonderful soul," University of Kansas women's basketball coach Marian Washington told Robbins of the *Plain Dealer*. "She is so pure at heart that anyone who gets to know her, they are touched by her."

FURTHER INFORMATION

Periodicals

"A Disappointing Game for Miss Woodard." *New York Times* (December 20, 1980): 20.

Moran, Malcolm. "Olympic Profile: Lynette Woodard Now a Role Player." *New York Times* (July 27, 1984): A18.

Robbins, Liz. "Hoops, There She Is." *Plain Dealer* (June 19, 1997): 1A.

Vecsey, George. "The Newest Globetrotter." *New York Times* (October 13, 1985): 3.

Other

"Harlem Globetrotters Legends: Lynette Woodard." HarlemGlobetrotters.com. http://harlemglobetrotters. com/history/leg-woodard.php (November 13, 2002).

"Lynette Woodard." Kansas Sports Hall of Fame. http:// www.kshof.org/inductees/woodard.html (November 13, 2002).

"Lynette Woodard Reached for the Hoops in Kansas." Kansas State Historical Society. http://www.kshs. org/people/woodard.htm (November 13, 2002).

"Lynette Woodard." University of Kansas Athletics. http://www.kuathletics.com/womensbasketball/coach es/woodard.html (November 13, 2002).

"1997 Rockers Regular Season Statistics." WNBA.com. http://www.wnba.com/rockers/stats/stats_1997.html (November 30, 2002).

"1998 Shock Regular Season Statistics." WNBA.com. http://www.wnba.com/shock/stats/stats_1998.html (November 30, 2002).

Sketch by Wendy Kagan

John Wooden
1910-

American college basketball coach

He always described himself as merely a teacher, but John Wooden was much more than that. The self-effacing "Wizard of Westwood," college basketball's most successful coach, led UCLA to 10 NCAA men's basketball championships, including seven in a row, and once led the Bruins to eight consecutive victories. He is one of two individuals to be enshrined in the Basketball Hall of Fame as both player and coach. As a college coach, his record was 620-146 at UCLA and 667-161 overall, including two seasons at Indiana State in the 1940s.

"Sometimes, when the Madness of March gets to be too much—too many players trying to make SportsCenter, too few players trying to make assists, too many coaches trying to be homeys, too few coaches willing to be mentors, too many freshmen with out-of-wedlock kids, too few freshmen who will stay in school long enough to become men—I like to go see Coach Wooden," Rick Reilly wrote in *Sports Illustrated.* "I visit him in his condo in Encino (California), 20 minutes northwest of L.A., and hear him say things like 'Gracious sakes alive and tell stories about teaching 'Lewis' the hook shot. Lewis Alcindor, that is. **Kareem Abdul-Jabbar**." Wooden never had a losing season as a high school or college coach. His top players included Abdul-Jabbar, **Bill Walton**, Keith Wilkes (later Jamaal Wilkes), Gail Goodrich, and Sidney Wicks. Wooden got such headstrong players as Abdul-Jabbar and Walton to buy into his system. Many ex-players regularly stay in touch with him.

"Indiana Rubber Man"

Wooden took interest in basketball around the age of eight, when he would shoot at a tomato basket with a makeshift ball consisting of his mother's hosiery stuffed with rags. Wooden, known for his playmaking and defensive abilities, went on to lead Martinsville, where he was raised, to the Indiana state high school championship in 1927. At Purdue University, where he sparked the Boilermakers to the 1932 national championship, he was called the "Indiana Rubber Man," because he would bounce right back up after diving on to floor. He was 1932 national collegiate player of the year.

He built a scholastic coaching record of 218-42 at Dayton, Kentucky and South Bend, Indiana before taking the head job at Indiana State. His record there was 47-14 over two seasons.

The Wooden Way at UCLA

He took over at UCLA for the 1948-49 season, and while the first national championship did not arrive for another 15 years, the Bruins were successful right away under his tenure. UCLA won 20 or more games six times in his first 15 seasons.

Wooden, according to the Basketball Hall of Fame's Web site, "began laying the groundwork for what would become the dynasty of all dynasties. He believed in lengthy practices for conditioning and endless drills to perfect fundamental skills." He even lectured his players about putting socks and sneakers on properly, to avoid blisters. Many of his players shot "bank shots," off the backboard. In addition, Wooden was ever the teacher at home, frequently writing slogans on his sons' lunch bags: "Be quick, but don't hurry" (later the title of one of his books).... "Failing to prepare is preparing to fail.... Never mistake activity for achievement."

The coach outlined his philosophy on coaching and life in his Pyramid of Success, which puts conditioning, skill,

John Wooden

and teamwork at his core. He also preached that basketball is a game of threes: forward, guard, center; shoot, drive, pass; and ball, you, man. Years later, well into retirement, Wooden admitted the one thing he missed about coaching was the practices. "(I miss) the teaching; where you establish a rapport with players. I loved to teach."

Early Championship Years

Ironically, given how UCLA rode such big men as Abdul-Jabbar and Walton to dominance, the Bruins' first championship team had no player taller than 6-foot-5. The Bruins raced to an undefeated season in 1963-64, but skeptics said the two teams ranked right behind ULCA, Michigan and Duke, did not have the necessary size and experience to flourish.

UCLA compensated for its smallness with a stifling zone press defense—Wooden's players had the conditioning to handle it effectively. The NCAA tournament semifinals, the zone press enabled the Bruins to score 11 straight points to erase a 75-70 Kansas State lead with 7:28 remaining, and UCLA prevailed 90-84. In the championship game, the zone press was UCLA's trump card again as the Bruins erased a first-half deficit and beat Duke, 98-83.

That title gave the Bruins national visibility in an era that preceded all-sports cable networks, 24-hour access to game stories and the Internet. West Coast results seldom made the following day's morning newspapers in

Chronology

1910	Born in Martinsville, Indiana
1928	Graduates from Martinsville High School; enrolled at Purdue University
1932	Marries Nell, his high school sweetheart
1932-34	Coaches at Dayton (Ky.) High School
1932-39	Plays for four professional teams in the Midwest
1934-43	Coaches at Central High School, South Bend, Ind.
1943-46	Lieutenant in U.S. Navy
1946-48	Coaches at Indiana State
1948-75	Coaches at UCLA
1985	Wife Nell dies

Awards and Accomplishments

1927	As a player, leads Martinsville High School to Indiana state championship.
1930-32	Three-time Helms Foundation All-America at Purdue
1932	Helms Foundation Player of the Year; Big Ten Medal for Proficiency in Scholarship and Athletics
1932-43	Overall high school coaching record 218-42
1947	Coached Indiana State to conference title
1948-75	Coached UCLA to 620-147 record, four undefeated seasons, an 88-game win streak and 10 national championships, including seven straight
1961	Enshrined in Basketball Hall of Fame as Player
1964	NCAA College Basketball Coach of the Year 1964, 1967, 1969, 1970, 1972, 1973
1970	The Sporting News Man of the Year
1973	Sports Illustrated Man of the Year
1973	Becomes one of two persons enshrined in Hall of Fame as player and coach (other is Lenny Wilkens)
1977	Los Angeles Athletic Club establishes John R. Wooden Award for college basketball player of the year
1994	John R. Wooden Classic basketball tournament established in his honor
1995	Receives Reagan Distinguished American Award
1999	ESPN names him Greatest Coach of the 20th Century

the East. Two seasons after repeating as champions in 1965, the Bruins corralled the nation's most prized recruit, Alcindor, out of Power Memorial High School in New York. With Alcindor in the middle, the Bruins sported an 88-2 record from 1968 through 1970 and won three consecutive national titles. One of the losses was a memorable 71-69 defeat to the University of Houston and its standout player, Elvin Hayes, before 52,693 at Houston's Astrodome (basketball games in domed stadiums are commonplace today, but were a rarity in the late 1960s). But UCLA avenged its defeat later that year, routing the Cougars 101-69 in the NCAA semifinals.

Stood His Ground

"He believed in hopelessly out-of-date stuff that never did anything but win championships. No dribbling behind the back or through the legs. 'There's no need,' he'd say. No UCLA basketball number was retired under his watch. 'What about the fellows who wore that number before? Didn't they contribute to the team?,' he'd say. No long hair, no facial hair. 'They take too long to dry, and you could catch a cold leaving the gym,' he'd say." Reilly wrote, "You played for him, you played by his rules. Never score without acknowledging a teammate. One word of profanity, and you're done for the day."

Wooden held his ground during the protest era of the 1960s and 1970s, even with All-American players such as Alcindor and Walton. Walton, a counter-culture figure who once suggested to Wooden that smoking marijuana might alleviate pain in his chronically injured knees, showed up at practice one day with a full beard. "It's my right," Walton said, to which Wooden responded, "That's good, Bill. I admire people who have strong beliefs and stick by them. I really do. We're going to miss you." According to Reilly, Walton "shaved it right then and there. Now Walton calls once a week to tell Coach he loves him." Wooden explained that, "[a]t one time, I required players to wear slacks and a sport coat while traveling. But then our university president at UCLA, and the professors, too, started wearing turtlenecks and jeans, so I changed my expectations. I only required that they be clean and neat. I

never relaxed my feeling about beards or goatees, but I did relax a little bit about the hair. I never wanted it too long, but as time went by I let them wear it a little longer than I had before."

Wooden also had to handle the constant presence of athletic booster Sam Gilbert. The late Gilbert, a Los Angeles-area businessman, was considered a father figure to many players and sat courtside during Bruins' home games at Pauley Pavilion. "Gilbert did plenty," Rob Miech of *CBS SportsLine.com* wrote in March of 2000, "... to befriend key players from the juggernaut program of the land in a relationship that has been described as mutually beneficial to himself and UCLA." Rival coaches such as **Jerry Tarkanian** and Dale Brown called UCLA's program corrupt, citing cash and gifts from Gilbert to players, though the NCAA investigated and cleared Wooden's program. "I had no relationship with him (Gilbert) and I tried to make sure my players tried to be very, very careful," Wooden told Miech. "Wooden's bosses," Miech wrote, "... must have been pleased that the dynasty wasn't prematurely dismantled because of player unrest with the strict and stern coach. It's that father-figure image the players found in Gilbert, not Wooden."

Win Streak, Dynasty Over

UCLA, meanwhile, kept racking up championships. One of Wooden's favorite teams was the team of 1969-70. "The team without," he said. "People ask, 'the team without what?' No, the team without whom? Without Kareem." Regular-season losses were rare, and after an 89-82 defeat to Notre Dame midway through the 1970-71 season, the Bruins would not lose another game for more than three years. The winning streak ended at 88 in January of 1974, when Notre Dame, ironically, defeated the Bruins 71-70 at South Bend, Indiana.

Then, in the 1974 Final Four at Greensboro, North Carolina, the championship run ended. North Carolina State, which had lost to UCLA by 18 points during the regular season, overcame a seven-point deficit in the second overtime of a semifinal game and the Wolfpack eliminated the Bruins, 80-77. UCLA's title streak ended at seven. Wooden, however, had one last hurrah. In his final game as coach, the Bruins defeated Kentucky 92-85 at the San Diego Sports Arena for the 1975 title, making it 10 championships in 12 seasons. Looking back to the start of the season, Wooden said: "To say I thought we would win (the title) back then would be stretching a point." UCLA had advanced in the semifinals by beating Louisville 75-74 on Richard Washington's basket with four seconds remaining. Louisville Coach Denny Crum was a former Wooden assistant.

In Memory of Nell

Wooden's home in Encino is also a shrine to his late wife, Nell, who died on March 21, 1985—the first day of spring after a lengthy bout with cancer. According to Jack Wilkinson of the *Atlanta Journal-Constitution,* some relatives and friends worry that Wooden has never fully recovered. According to Wilkinson, the one-bedroom condo is essentially the same since Nell died. "I've never changed anything," Wooden said. "Not even the furniture. I should," he smiled. "The furniture's wearing out." Wilkinson also writes, "John Wooden, continues to sleep on the left side of the bed, as he did when Nell was alive. On the right side lies Nell's robe, along with two framed photos of her, some flowers and a figurine. At the foot of the bed is a gold-and-blue UCLA blanket, inscribed with 'John' and 'Nell.' Atop it sits Nell's old California blue license tag: Ma Ma 7. That's what the seven Wooden grandchildren—and the 10 great-grandchildren—called her. Ma Ma, to John's Pa Pa. And on Nell's robe rests a stack of dozens of letters. 'I write her a letter on the 21st day of each month,' Wooden said. Handwritten love letters on the monthly anniversary of Nell's death. 'I might say, 'It's been 16 years, nine months and so many days since you were released from pain and taken to heaven. But you are with me always," Wooden said. 'Then I'll talk with her about some of the children and grandchildren, what they're doing, what's new.'"

"To an outsider," Wilkinson writes, "Wooden's behavior might seem obsessive, almost macabre. But spend three hours in the home he once shared with Nell, and it's clear this great man was blessed with what everyone craves: The one true love of his life." Wooden wrote in his 1997 book, *Wooden: A Lifetime of Observations and Reflections on and off the Court,* "I had a successful basketball career, but I believe I had an even more successful marriage."

Where Is He Now?

John Wooden, a widower since 1985, lives in a condominium in Encino, California, and occasionally attends UCLA home games. Chronic knee pain has limited his mobility.

Wooden, who has always disdained showboating, says the dunk has encouraged such behavior and favors banning it. Ironically, the NCAA had prohibited the dunk for a few years after Kareem Abdul-Jabbar's first varsity season, in a move many felt was aimed at the dominant Abdul-Jabbar. He also favors moving back the 3-point line.

Asked if he were coaching today, Wooden said: "You have to adjust as time goes by. I certainly know that I adjusted as time went by. But my basic philosophy of the game would not change at all. I never taught under the shot clock. I never taught under the 3-point goal. Those things would make me make changes in my style of play, but my basic philosophy would not change one bit. "I'm often asked what I would do about tattoos. I'm glad I don't have to [decide]. They say you have to change with the times. The way some players [look], I wouldn't even recruit them."

Wooden, after retiring, did not attend another Final Four until 1995, in Seattle, when UCLA won its only post-Wooden championship. He frequently speaks to the UCLA team. Among his favorite contemporary coaches are Roy Williams of Kansas, Mike Montgomery of Stanford and Mike Krzyzewski of Duke.

Wooden's Legacy

"Modesty may be Wooden's most enduring quality (He loathes the moniker Wizard of Westwood—'I'm no wizard,' he states emphatically.)," David Greenwald wrote in *UCLA Today,* a staff and faculty newsletter. "John Wooden stands out as a stalwart man of integrity, someone who taught his players first and foremost to respect themselves, their opponents and each other."

"When I left UCLA in 1974 and became the highest-paid player in the history of team sports at that time, the quality of my life went down," wrote Walton, who played on National Basketball Association championship teams in Portland and Boston during an injury-plagued pro career. "That's how special it was to have played for John Wooden and UCLA."

Wooden cast such a huge shadow over UCLA that successors found the coaching job too much of a hot seat. None of his first five successors—Gene Bartow, Gary Cunningham, Larry Brown, Larry Farmer and Walt Hazzard—held the job more than four years. Jim Harrick coached eight years and produced the one post-Wooden title in 1995, but left a year later amid a scandal. Steve Lavin, who succeeded Harrick, feels comfortable in the position. "Lavin is reminded every day of Wooden because 10 national championship banners hang inside Pauley Pavilion," the Associated Press wrote in November, 2002. "Instead of shying away from Wooden's legacy, Lavin has embraced it."

SELECTED WRITINGS BY WOODEN:

(With Bill Sharman and Bob Seizer) *The Wooden-Sharman Method: A Guide to Winning Basketball,* New York: Macmillan, 1975.

John Wooden

(With Jack Tobin) *They Call Me Coach: The Fascinating First-person Story of a Legendary Basketball Coach.* Revised edition, Waco, TX: Word Books, 1985.

(With Steve Jamison) *Wooden: A Lifetime of Observations and Reflections on and off the Court,* Lincolnwood, IL: Contemporary Books, 1997.

Practical Modern Basketball, new introduction by Bill Walton, 3rd. ed. Boston: Allyn and Bacon, 1999.

(With Andrew Hill) *Be Quick, but Don't Hurry—Learning Success from the Teachings of a Lifetime,* New York: Simon & Schuster, 2001.

Quotable Wooden, Nashville: TowleHouse, 2002.

FURTHER INFORMATION

Books

Biro, Brian D. *Beyond Success: The 15 Secrets to Effective Leadership and Life Based on Legendary Coach John Wooden's Pyramid of Success,* New York: Berkley, 2001.

Chapin, Dwight and Jeff Prugh.*The Wizard of Westwood; Coach John Wooden and his UCLA Bruins,* Boston: Houghton Mifflin, 1973.

Heisler, Mark. *They Shoot Coaches, Don't They?: UCLA and the NCAA since John Wooden,* New York: Macmillan, 1996.

Periodicals

Reilly, Rick. "A Paragon Rising Above the Madness." *Sports Illustrated* (March 20, 2000): 136.

Other

"10 Burning Questions for John Wooden," ESPN.com, http://espn.go.com/page2, (January 4, 2003).

Basketball Hall of Fame, John Wooden Biography, http://www.hoophall.com/halloffame/Wooden.htm, (January 4, 2003).

Greenwald, David. "Happy Birthday, Coach John Wooden," UCLA Today, http://www.today.ucla.edu,(January 4, 2003).

"John Wooden, Coaching Legend," Reference.com, http://www.reference.com, (January 4, 2003).

"John Wooden Fact Sheet," Sports America, Inc., www.sportsamericainc.com, (January 4, 2003).

Walton, Bill. "John Wooden, Simply the Best," UCLA Today, http://www.today.ucla.edu, (January 4, 2003).

Wilkinson, Jack. "Visiting the Wizard of Westwood," Atlanta Journal-Constitution, http://www.access atlanta.com, (January 20, 2002).

"Wooden's Influence Seen in Tradition Field," Sporting News, http://www.sportingnews.com/cbasketball, (November 29, 2002).

Sketch by Paul Burton

Tiger Woods
1975-

American golfer

Tiger Woods may prove to be the best professional golfer in history. Although he is not yet thirty, he is already well on track to break **Jack Nicklaus**'s record of eighteen career victories in professional majors. In a sport where victory is often decided by only one or two strokes, Woods has had several double-digit wins. Because of his domination of the game, and perhaps also because he is a young minority in a sport that had previously featured mostly white, middle-aged stars, Woods has achieved a popularity that extends far beyond typical golf fans.

A Golfing Toddler

Woods has been playing golf since he could walk, and studying the game even longer. His father, Earl Woods, a retired Army officer, took up golf only a year before Woods was born, but he quickly fell in love with the sport. Earl set up a miniature driving range in his garage

Tiger Woods

Chronology

1975	Born December 30 in Cypress, CA, to Earl and Kultida Woods
1978	Appears on the *Mike Douglas Show,* where he wins a putting contest with Bob Hope
1978	Wins first golf competition, a ten-and-under
1980	Begins working with first coach, Rudy Duran
1981	Appears on *That's Incredible!*
1982	Plays a two-hole tournament with Sam Snead
1987	Undefeated in junior tournament competition
1994	Begins attending Stanford University
1995	Competes in his first Masters
1996	Turns professional and quits Stanford
1996	Makes a hole in one during his first professional event
1996	Starts Tiger Woods Foundation in December
2000	Becomes youngest golfer ever to complete career Grand Slam
2000	Appears on the cover of *Time* magazine
2001	Becomes first golfer ever to hold all four major titles at once
2002	Undergoes arthroscopic knee surgery December 12

with some carpet and a net, and while he practiced Woods would sit in his high chair and watch. Earl cut some clubs down to Woods's size for him to play with, and one day, when Woods was nine months old, he climbed out of his chair when Earl took a break and tried to imitate Earl's activity. He did so almost perfectly, and the ball flew expertly into the net. "I was flabbergasted," Earl told biographer John Strege. "I almost fell off my chair."

When Woods was eighteen months old, Earl took him to a real driving range for the first time and started letting him play the occasional hole on Earl's home course, the Navy Courses at Los Alamitos, California. When he was two Woods won his first competition there, playing against boys who were as old as ten. The same year Woods appeared on the *Mike Douglas Show.* He had an on-air putting contest with Bob Hope and won. When he was three, he shot a forty-eight over nine holes on one of the Navy Courses from the front tees, and then at five he appeared on national television again, on the show *That's Incredible!*

People across the country marveled when they heard about this tiny golfing protégé, but Woods didn't want to be just a curiosity. He wanted to be a winner. He started working with his first professional coach, an assistant club professional from Long Beach, California named Rudy Duran, when he was four, and throughout his elementary school years Woods dominated junior golf in his age bracket in southern California. Although Woods was patient during this time, honing his skills and slow-

ly preparing himself for the next level, he always had his sights set on higher things. A chart of Nicklaus's records and milestones, going back to when Nicklaus was a child, hung on Woods's wall, and he was determined to surpass them all.

High School Years

When he was fifteen, Woods set out to become the youngest golfer ever to qualify for a PGA Tour event, the 1991 Los Angeles Open. He played excellently in the qualifying event but, with a bogey on the last hole, he had three strokes too many to make it to the Open. However, later that year Woods broke another record when he became the youngest person ever to win the U.S. Junior Amateur Championship.

Woods successfully defended his U.S. Junior Amateur championship in 1992, becoming the only person ever to be U.S. junior amateur champion more than once. He then won the event for an unheard of third time in 1993. Earl Woods later attributed his success to his training methods during that time. "Every year he would take the week before his major to mentally and physically fine-tune," Earl told *Sports Illustrated* reporter Jaime Diaz. "We'd drive to the site and play practice rounds, and after we got home, I'd find him lying on his bed with his eyes closed. He told me he was playing the shots he was going to need in his head."

Woods was invited back to the Los Angeles Open in 1992 on a sponsor's exemption. It was thought at the time that he was still the youngest person to play in a Tour event, but it was later discovered that a fifteen-year-old had played in the Canadian Open in 1957. Woods shot one over par on the first day and four over on the second, missing the cut by six strokes, but he still called the experience "the two best days of my life." Not until the spring of 1994, at the Johnnie Walker Asian Classic in Thailand, would Woods make the cut in a professional event.

Awards and Accomplishments

1991-93	U.S. Junior Amateur Championship
1994-96	U.S. Amateur Championship
1996	Las Vegas Invitational
1996	Walt Disney World/Oldsmobile Classic
1996	Named PGA Tour Rookie of the Year
1996	Named *Sports Illustrated*'s Sportsman of the Year
1997	Asian Honda Classic
1997	Byron Nelson Classic
1997	Motorola Western Open
1997	Named Player of the Year by the Golf Writers Association of America
1997	Given Sports Star of the Year award
1997-2002	Named PGA Tour Player of the Year
1997, 1999-2000	Named PGA of America Player of the Year
1997, 2000	Mercedes Championship
1997, 2000	Named the Associated Press's Male Athlete of the Year
1997, 2001-02	Masters
1998	BellSouth Classic
1998, 2000	Johnnie Walter Classic
1999	Deutsche Bank Open
1999	Memorial Tournament
1999	National Car Rental Golf Classic
1999	The Tour Championship
1999	World Cup of Golf (with Mark O'Meara)
1999	Wins Vardon Trophy
1999	Buick Invitational
1999-2000	PGA Championship
1999-2000	Named Player of the Year by the Golf Writers Association of America
1999-2001	WGC-NEC Invitational
1999, 2002	WGC-American Express Championship
2000	AT&T Pebble Beach National Pro-Am
2000	British Open
2000	Bell Canadian Open
2000	EMC World Cup (with David Duval)
2000	Named *Sports Illustrated*'s Sportsman of the Year
2000-01	Won Vardon Trophy
2000-01	Memorial Tournament
2000-02	Bay Hill Invitational
2000, 2002	U.S. Open
2001	Deutsche Bank-SAP Open
2001	Players Championship
2002	Buick Open

The Nike Golf Ball Juggling Commercial

Woods's skills were clearly demonstrated, even to those who couldn't tell a birdie from a bogey, in a famous Nike commercial from 1999. The original plan for the commercial was for Woods and several other people on a driving range all to be swinging in unison, but the director was having trouble getting everything to come together. The commercial was being filmed at the Orange County National Golf Club in Orange County, California, in the middle of the summer, and it was deathly hot. Woods, trying to lighten the mood, started to juggle a ball on the face of one of his clubs during a break. The director saw this and decided that it would make a better commercial than the original idea.

It only took four takes to shoot the final thirty-second commercial, which featured Woods dancing the ball on his sixty-degree sand wedge forty-nine times. He bounced the ball behind his back, between his legs, and even caught and balanced the ball on the club face's grooves. Then Woods bounced the ball into the air, wound up, and hit it like a baseball, 120 yards out on the driving range. No camera tricks were used, and the footage was not digitally altered. "It's really not as hard as you might think if you grew up playing baseball," Woods told the media after the commercial aired. "Hand-to-eye coordination—same principle."

than that he had achieved all of the goals that he had set for himself as an amateur. He had been playing in professional events, including the U.S. and British Opens and the Masters, for several years. He had not performed up to his expectations in any of them, but the amount of time that he was forced to spend studying in the spring cut into his practicing time and, he thought, left him ill-prepared for those competitions. Although he had promised his parents that he would finish college, in August of 1996 Woods withdrew from Stanford and turned professional.

Rookie Season

Woods got sponsor's exemptions to play in seven tournaments in 1996, between the time he turned professional in August and the end of the season. In order to be a member of the PGA tour in 1997, he needed to win enough in those seven tournaments to place him among the top 125 money winners on the tour for the year, or to win at least one event outright. He finished sixtieth in his first competition as a professional, the Greater Milwaukee Open, but from there his performances only improved. The next week he finished eleventh in the Canadian Open. The week after that, he was ahead by one stroke in the Quad City Classic going into Sunday. Golf reporters from across the country abandoned the more prestigious Presidents Cup, which was being held the same weekend, and flew to Illinois to cover what they expected to be a Woods win, but Woods had two bad holes on the last day and fell to fifth. In his next competition, the B.C. Open, he finished third, which placed him 128th on the money list with four more events to go.

Woods caused a major controversy the next week when he withdrew from the Buick Open and skipped a dinner that had been planned to honor him there. Woods said that he was exhausted from his rough schedule—even before turning professional, Woods had played in several challenging amateur events that summer. When he realized

On to College

Stanford University started recruiting Woods in 1989, and in the fall of 1994 he enrolled there and joined their golf team. The eighteen-year-old Woods was still the best amateur golfer in the country: that summer he became the youngest winner of the U.S. Amateur Championship in the event's ninety-four year history. Woods hoped that year to become only the third player to win both the U.S. Amateur and the National Collegiate Athletic Association (NCAA) Championships in the same year (the others were Phil Mickelson and Nicklaus), but he was suffering from several injuries and performed poorly.

Woods repeated his U.S. Amateur Championship victories in 1995 and 1996. By the summer of 1996, Woods had still failed to win an NCAA championship, but other how many people his decision had inconvenienced, Woods apologized profusely, but many people still criticized his decision. However, when Woods came back from his week off he silenced many of his critics by winning the Las Vegas Open in a playoff against David Love III. Amazingly, Woods won another event that season as well, the Walt Disney World/Oldsmobile Classic. With a third place finish in San Antonio the week between Las Vegas and Walt Disney World, Woods became the first player to finish in the top five in five straight tournaments since 1982.

Establishing a Legacy

Golf fans expected great things out of Woods in the 1997 season, and he did not disappoint them. Woods won four tournaments that year. His most prestigious win, the Masters, was also his strongest: he finished twelve strokes ahead of his closest competitor, setting a new scoring record on the Augusta National course of eighteen under par. However, in 1998 Woods slumped. Despite his successes in the previous two years, Woods knew that there were still aspects of his game that needed improvement. Although he has always been one of the longest drivers in golf, prior to 1998 he had difficulty controlling those long drives. Sometimes he overshot his mark, and even when he didn't he was often left or right of where he wanted to be. Throughout the 1998 season Woods worked on correcting this, as well as on improving his putting consistency. He only won one event on the PGA Tour that season, but in the coming years his hard work would pay off.

Woods's 1999 season was legendary. It might have been remembered as one of the best seasons in golf history, had Woods not surpassed himself in 2000. In 1999 he won seven events on the PGA Tour. In 2000 he won nine, including a victory in the U.S. Open by a record-breaking fifteen strokes, and another in the British Open by eight. That year Woods also became the youngest person ever to complete the career Grand Slam, by winning the U.S. and British Opens and the PGA Championship all in one season. Only **Ben Hogan** had ever won three majors in one year, and only four other people, including Nicklaus and Hogan, had ever completed the Grand Slam. Then, when Woods notched his second Masters win in 2001, he became the only golfer in history ever to hold all four major championship titles at once.

That Masters victory was one of only five wins for Woods in 2001. He was still the best player on the tour, winning two more events than his closest competitor, raking in well over $5 million in winnings, and winning the Vardon Trophy for the lowest stroke average on the tour, but he was not as dominant as he had been in previous two years. After Woods won the first two majors, the Masters and the U.S. Open, in 2002 many people expected him to win the single-season Grand Slam, but he was foiled by foul weather at the British Open. He shot an eighty-one in thirty mile-per-hour winds and

Tiger Woods

a pouring rain on Saturday at that event, which put him out of contention.

The Best Golfer, Period

In the complicated world of American race relations, Woods has often been frustrated by others' attempts to pigeonhole him neatly into one racial category, African-American. Woods is in fact more Asian than anything else: his mother is half Thai, one-quarter Chinese, and one-quarter white, and his father is half black, one-quarter Chinese, and one-quarter Native American. Woods identifies strongly with his mother's Thai heritage, and is offended that others insist on overlooking it. He is also annoyed that some people believe that, by virtue of his background, he owes anything to any particular ethnic group. Early in Woods's career, when interviewers would ask him questions about whether he saw himself as a role model for young black or minority golfers, he would reply that, no, he saw himself as a role model for *all* young golfers. For Woods, racial politics are nothing but a sideshow to what he really has to offer the world: his skill as a golfer. As a teenager, when many in the media dubbed him the "Great Black Hope" of the golf world, he often declared, "I don't want to be the best black golfer. I want to be the best golfer, period."

Now that Woods has achieved his goal of being the best golfer in the world, his immense popularity is bringing a diverse crowd of new fans to a sport that was previously perceived as being only for well-off white men. Although Woods does not want social issues to overwhelm his athletic achievements in the public mind, he is happy to see the love of golf extend to more segments of the American public. This is the goal of the Tiger Woods Foundation, to introduce to golf children who might otherwise never have tried the game. As Woods explained at a press conference in 2000, "America is the melting pot of the world. We have all the different ethnic races, religious choices. I just want to make golf look like that. If that's one thing I can have, that's one thing I really want to have happen."

CONTACT INFORMATION

Online: www.tigerwoods.com. Online: www.twfound. org (Tiger Woods Foundation).

FURTHER INFORMATION

Books

Rosaforte, Tim. *Raising the Bar: The Championship Years of Tiger Woods*. New York: Thomas Dunne Books, 2000.

Strege, John. *Tiger: A Biography of Tiger Woods*. New York: Broadway Books, 1997.

Periodicals

"All About Winning." *Maclean's* (June 10, 2002): 50.

Bamberger, Michael. "Not So Fast." *Sports Illustrated* (July 29, 2002): G48.

"Black America and Tiger's Dilemma: National Leaders Praise Golfer's Accomplishments and Debate Controversial 'Mixed Race' Issue." *Ebony* (July, 1997): 28-32.

Brown, Joseph H. "What Tiger Does Best Is Golf." *Tampa Tribune* (November 24, 2002).

"Changing Stripes." *Time* (August 14, 2000): 62.

Crothers, Tim. "Golf Cub." *Sports Illustrated* (March 25, 1991): 56.

Diaz, Jaime. "Masters Plan." *Sports Illustrated* (April 13, 1998): 62-67.

Diaz, Jaime. "Why Tiger Is So Bland." *Golf World* (August 16, 2002): 40.

Garrity, John. "Spoiled by Success." *Sports Illustrated* (November 26, 2001): G4.

Hawkins, John. "Survivor." *Golf World* (August 25, 2000): 18.

Jenkins, Dan. "Broken Record: Tiger Woods Does It Again for a Career Grand Slam at 24." *Golf Digest* (September, 2000): 103.

Jenkins, Dan. "Grand Slam, Anyone? It's Tiger's to Take." *Golf Digest* (August, 2002): 57.

McCleery, Peter. "The 'Tiger Effect's' Downside." *Golf World* (September 22, 2000): 40.

Morfit, Cameron. "Head to Head." *Sports Illustrated* (July 15, 2002): G21.

Morfit, Cameron. "The One and Only." *Sports Illustrated* (November 11, 2002): G28.

Nordlinger, Jay. "Hunting Tiger: Everyone Wants a Piece of Him." *National Review* (September 16, 2002).

Rosaforte, Tim, and John Hawkins. "A Star Is Worn." *Golf World* (November 10, 2000): 28.

Russell, Geoff. "History Maker: How Nike Deal Makes Woods Highest Paid Athlete of All Time." *Golf World* (September 22, 2000): 2.

Sirak, Ron. "Breaking Away?." *Golf World* (November 17, 2000): 20.

Smith, Gary. "The Chosen One." *Sports Illustrated* (December 23, 1996): 28-43.

"Tiger Juggles Ball, Nike Juggles Ad." *Holland Sentinel* (Holland, MI) (July 7, 1999).

Verdi, Bob. "Winner and Still Champion." *Golf World* (August 16, 2002): 18.

Other

Kamiya, Gary. "Cablinasian Like Me." Salon.com. http://www.salon.com/april97/tiger970430.html (February 5, 2003).

Official Site: Tiger Woods. http://www.tigerwoods.com (February 5, 2003).

"Tiger Woods." CNNSI.com—GolfPlus. http://sports illustrated.cnn.com/golf/pga/bios/2002/bio184.html (February 6, 2003).

"Tiger Woods." PGATour.com. http://www.golfweb. com/players/00/87/93/bio.html (February 5, 2003).

Sketch by Julia Bauder

Charles Woodson
1976-

American football player

The first primarily defensive player to win the coveted Heisman Trophy, Charles Woodson has never suffered from a lack of self-confidence. When pollsters seemed unable to agree on the national college champion after the 1998 bowl games, Woodson, whose brilliant defensive play had cemented the University of Michigan's 21-16 Rose Bowl victory over the Washington State Cougars, made it clear he harbored no such doubts. "National champs, no doubt," he told the *St. Louis Post-Dispatch*. "That's the way the whole team

Charles Woodson

Chronology

1976	Born in Fremont, Ohio, on October 7
1992-94	Plays on varsity football team at Ross High School
1995-98	Plays football at University of Michigan
1998	Makes professional football debut with Oakland Raiders

By the time he entered Ross High School as a freshman, Woodson had honed his gridiron skills so well that coach Rex Radeloff wanted to play him on the varsity team. But Georgia Woodson put her foot down, declaring that her son was too young to play with the bigger boys. Never one to disobey his mother, Woodson played freshman ball. He joined the varsity team as a sophomore and won All-State honors for the next three years. As a senior, Woodson rushed for a school-record 2,028 yards on 218 carries and was named Ohio High School Player of the Year. Over his three years on the varsity team, he rushed for a total of 3,861 yards and 466 points.

Begins Playing Defense

While in high school, Woodson first began to play on defense, having previously focused on offense. "Once I started playing it, it just started growing on me," he later told the *Los Angeles Times*. "I liked it a lot. I think it's a lot more aggressive. You have 11 people running to the football, trying to get there at the same time. There's a big celebration after the hit. It's kind of hard to describe."

Woodson's impressive performance as a high school football player unleashed an avalanche of college offers from all over the country, but Woodson had always dreamed of playing for the University of Michigan, so his decision was easy. Only two weeks into football training camp at Michigan, Woodson had won the job of starting cornerback. In Michigan's big game against arch-rival Ohio State, freshman Woodson intercepted a pass from Buckeyes quarterback Bobby Hoying in the first play of the second half. Michigan took the ball and scored the go-ahead touchdown. Woodson repeated the feat during the final minutes of the game, helping to power Michigan to a 31-23 upset victory over the Buckeyes.

Before the start of his sophomore season, Woodson was approached by Michigan coach Lloyd Carr who asked if the player would consider playing on offense as well as defense. Woodson agreed to work out at wide receiver. Throughout his sophomore season, he ran about 10 plays each game on offense while holding on to his defense duties as cornerback. The crowning glory of Woodson's college football career came in his senior year, when Michigan ended the season undefeated and went on to defeat Washington State, 21-16, in the Rose Bowl. Woodson contributed some key plays toward the Wolverines' victory, intercepting an underthrown pass from the Cougars quarterback in the second quarter, and late in the game gaining some first downs that helped to

feels. Nobody gave us a chance to be in the Rose Bowl. Everybody expected us to have another 8-4 season, but we all felt we could go undefeated. It was just a matter of going out and playing hard every week." Earlier in the same season, Woodson made it clear he had no doubts at all about his own ability. At a press conference before Michigan's game against Penn State, according to *Sports Illustrated,* Woodson told reporters: "Best player in the country standing before you." It might have been laughable had Woodson not proceeded to back up his boast with an amazing 37-yard touchdown reception to help lead Michigan to a lopsided 34-8 victory over the Nittany Lions.

Born in Fremont, Ohio

Charles Woodson was born in Fremont, Ohio, on October 7, 1976. The son of Solomon (an amateur boxer) and Georgia Woodson, he was born with clubbed feet and wore leg braces for a year beginning when he was six months old. When he was about 18 months old, the braces were replaced by corrective shoes, which he wore until he was four. His mother, who divorced her husband shortly after Charles's birth, later told the *Los Angeles Times:* "He didn't want to wear them. He fought it." His childhood health problems did nothing to impede Woodson's progress as an athlete. Introduced to football by his older half-brother, Terry Carter, he displayed a natural talent for the game, prompting his mother to send him to the local YMCA to play flag football.

Career Statistics

| Yr | Team | GP | Tackles | | | | Fumbles | | Interceptions | |
			TOT	SOLO	AST	SACK	FF	BK	INT	TD
1998	OAK	16	64	62	2	0.0	2	0	5	1
1999	OAK	16	61	53	8	0.0	0	1	1	1
2000	OAK	16	79	67	12	0.0	3	0	4	0
2001	OAK	16	53	42	11	2.0	1	1	1	0
2002	OAK	8	37	36	1	0.0	4	0	1	0
TOTAL		72	294	257	37	2.0	10	0	12	2

OAK: Oakland Raiders.

Awards and Accomplishments

1992-94	Wins All-State honors at Ross High School
1994	Named Ohio High School Player of the Year
1995	Named Big Ten Conference Freshman of the Year
1997	Named College Player of the Year by *Sporting News*
1997	Wins Heisman Trophy
1998	Named NFL's Defensive Rookie of the Year

clinch Michigan's victory. Both Michigan and Nebraska ended the season undefeated and were each touted as the national champion in different polls.

Wins Heisman Trophy

Only a couple of weeks before the Rose Bowl, Woodson made history when he became the first primarily defensive player to win college football's most prestigious award, the Heisman Trophy. It was a controversial decision, protested by some who felt that University of Tennessee quarterback Peyton Manning was more deserving of the honor. Shortly after Michigan's Rose Bowl win, Woodson announced that he would forgo his senior year of college in order to be eligible for the 1998 National Football League (NFL) draft. He was picked fourth overall in the first round of the draft by the Oakland Raiders, becoming the seventh Heisman Trophy winner to play for the team. Others have included **Marcus Allen**, **Tim Brown**, Billy Cannon, Desmond Howard, **Bo Jackson**, and Jim Plunkett.

Woodson, who had signed a six-year, $20 million contract with the Raiders, enjoyed an outstanding rookie year in pro football, winning the NFL's Defensive Rookie of the Year Award at season's end. He finished the 1998 season with five interceptions and was named an alternative to the postseason Pro Bowl. Of Woodson, teammate Albert Lewis, a 16-year veteran cornerback, told the *St. Louis Post-Dispatch:* "He's an outstanding athlete with ability and confidence, and he doesn't get rattled. Most guys don't come into this league looking as good as he does at that position, and he may be the best I've seen at his age. He'll experience some adversity, but for him to be playing at that level this early is a rare occurrence." Asked to grade himself on his rookie season, Woodson told the *Dallas Morning News:* "I'd give myself a B-minus. I played pretty good, but I didn't do a lot of the little things I could have done, as far as watching more film, doing a lot more studying. I pretty much played off athletic ability."

Early in the 2002 season, Woodson fractured his right shoulder in a game against the Pittsburgh Steelers. As a result he missed several games but was back in action later in the season. Commenting on the loss of Woodson to injury, coach Bill Callahan said, "He will be missed. It's a blow, because he's a four-time Pro Bowl player. When you a quality corner of Charles' caliber, who's played at an all-star level, that's hard to replace. It's something we have to overcome." With only five seasons under his belt, the final chapter to the story of Woodson's football career is unlikely to be written for another decade or so, barring serious injury. For now, he is doing what he loves.

CONTACT INFORMATION

Address: c/o Oakland Raiders, 1220 Harbor Bay Pkwy., Alameda, CA 94502. Phone: (510) 864-5000.

FURTHER INFORMATION

Books

"Charles Woodson." *Sports Stars,* Series 5. Detroit: U•X•L, 1999.

Periodicals

"For Heisman, Good Defense Beats Best Offense." *USA Today* (December 16, 1997): 14A.

Layden, Tim. "College Football: Double Threat Michigan's Charles Woodson Is a Dazzling Two-Way Player, and He's Not Alone in His Versatility." *Sports Illustrated* (November 18, 1996): 44.

Peterson, Anne M. "Raiders Sign Heisman Trophy Winner Charles Woodson." *AP Online* (July 21, 1998).

Related Biography: Football Coach Lloyd Carr

An important influence on Woodson was University of Michigan coach Lloyd Carr. Together the two led the Michigan Wolverines to their first national championship in nearly half a century.

Carr, who was born in 1945, joined the Wolverine coaching staff in 1980 as defensive secondary coach to Bo Schembechler. Over the next 15 years he was promoted first to defensive coordinator and finally to assistant head coach under Gary Moeller from 1990 to 1994. On May 16, 1995, he was named interim head coach after Moeller resigned. In November 1995 the "interim" was removed, making him the 17th head football coach in the school's history. Carr led the Wolverines to victory in four straight bowl games from 1998 to 2001.

After three years at the University of Missouri, he earned his bachelor's degree from Northern Michigan University in 1968. Carr began his coaching career at Detroit's Nativity High School (1968-69). He next moved on to Belleville (Michigan) High School from 1970 to 1973 and John Glenn High School in Westland, Michigan, from 1973 to 1975. Carr's collegiate coaching career began with two seasons at Eastern Michigan University (1976-77), followed by two seasons at Illinois (1978-79).

Rosenblatt, Richard. "Woodson Picks Off Heisman; Michigan Star First Defender to Win Award." *Denver Rocky Mountain News* (December 14, 1997): 1C.

"Woodson Shows Why He Won the Heisman Trophy." *St. Louis Post-Dispatch* (January 4, 1998): F1.

Other

"Charles Woodson." *Biography Resource Center Online.* Farmington Hills, MI: Gale Group, 1999.

"Lloyd Carr, Head Coach." Michigan Football. http://www.mgoblue.com/coach_bio.cfm?bio_id=299&section_id=257&top=2&level=3 (January 30, 2003).

"#24, Charles Woodson." ESPN.com. http://sports.espn.go.com/nfl/players/stats?statsId=4271 (December 3, 2002).

Sketch by Don Amerman

Rod Woodson
1965-

American football player

In a sport where an average pro career lasts just under four years, Woodson's 15 and counting NFL seasons make him a legend as much for his longevity as for his daring on the field. Named to the Pro Bowl at three different positions—cornerback, free safety and kick-returner—and one of only five active player to be named to the NFL 75th anniversary all time team, Woodson stands undeniably among the best players in league history. As cornerback he faced the best wide receivers in the game and years of experience taught him that con-

Rod Woodson

sistency is paramount. He told *Sports Illustrated,* "You've got to resign yourself to the fact that you can't stop the perfect pass. Let the receiver catch the ball but then tell him, 'I'll be here all day. I'm not going anywhere. Next time you are going to have to pay.'" It is just that mix of good sense and stubbornness that has gotten Woodson so far in football and has made him one of the most feared defensive players in the NFL.

Facing Racism

The youngest of three boys, Woodson grew up facing racism head on. His father, James, was African American and his mother, Linda Jo, is Caucasian. Both white and black racists targeted the Woodson family in their hometown of Fort Wayne, Indiana. Members of the Black Muslims attacked Linda Jo, pushing her and knocking her down. The Klu Klux Klan made threatening phone calls and sent disturbing packages through the mail to the Woodson home. Yet even while James worked two jobs and Linda Jo kept many part-time jobs to make ends meet, the Woodsons taught their boys to be proud of their mixed heritage and to use humor to deflect racism. Rod explained to *Sports Illustrated,* "When you are mixed, you have three options; stay in the middle, pick a side or stand on your own. My parents let me know I didn't have to pick a side, because I always had a friend in the family."

Playing football was a way to stay close to his brothers and out of trouble. Woodson told *Sports Illustrated for Kids,* "There is nothing good in the streets for a young kid. I never knew who my true friends were, so I had to stick with my own. The only people I knew who were mixed, like me, were my brothers and that made us a very close and protective family." Woodson confessed that he, ". . . started playing football because [he] wanted to play with [his brothers]."

Athletic Prowess

In high school, Woodson was a three sport athlete playing football, basketball, and running track. The high school football coaches were tough on him and in the tenth grade he almost abandoned the sport altogether. Fortunately, Woodson's track coach convinced him to give it another try, telling him that there was nothing worse than quitting. During his senior year, *Parade* named Woodson an All-American football player at both the cornerback and running back positions. He also earned high honors as part of the all-conference basketball team and twice took the state championship in low and high hurdles.

College football coaches pursued Woodson at graduation time and he chose Purdue University, staying close to his family. At Purdue, he was a four year starter for the Boilermakers, played 44 consecutive games and setting 13 team records, including 320 solo tackles and 11 interceptions.

On the football field Woodson could go anywhere and do anything. He played various positions and excelled in them all. Woodson's coaches switched him around right up until his final game at Purdue, in which he played tailback, cornerback, returned kickoffs and punts, and covered kicks on the special team units. In that game he rushed for 97 yards, caught three passes for 67 yards, made 10 tackles and returned three punts for 30 yards. At the end of his college football career Woodson earned All-American honors and was the runner up in votes for the **Jim Thorpe** Award, which honors the nation's best collegiate defensive back.

Learning to Play Well

The Pittsburgh Steelers chose Woodson with the tenth overall pick in the NFL draft of 1987. The biggest challenge to Woodson in his first year in the NFL was mastering one position. He had to buckle down and take the time to learn the cornerback position in earnest. "I was a nervous wreck," he admitted to *Sports Illustrated*. "I'd relied too long on my speed and physical talents, and I didn't understand the game." The Steelers played Woodson as a defensive backup and as a kick returner in that first year. He revealed to *Sporting News* magazine, "I had to make myself play well." And play well he did. By 1989 he led the NFL in kick returns with a 27.3-yard average. That year he won the respect of his fellow players who elected him to play in the Pro Bowl as a kick return specialist.

Playing from the Shoulders Up

Woodson intercepted eight passes in 1993 and earned the title NFL Defensive Player of the Year. The honor was hard earned. That year Steelers Coach Bill Cowher had decided to push Woodson to engage the ball more in each game. Cowher explained to *Sporting News*, "He kind of thrives on that and has taken his game to another level. You have to get him around the football as much as you can. If you leave him in one spot, they can scheme away from him. We want him involved." Woodson told the *Sporting News*, "I am just trying to play more from the shoulders up this year and let my abilities take over. I am trying to think about what I am doing. In the past, I'd have two or three great games and two or three bad ones. I've eliminated those lapses." In part because of Woodson's increased contact with the football, The Steelers entered the 1993 play-offs as a wildcard team but were soon eliminated by **Joe Montana** and the Kansas City Chiefs.

The Steelers defensive lineup finished second in the NFL in 1994. While the linebackers and defensive linesmen increased pressure on quarterbacks, Woodson went man to man with receivers. He had 83 tackles, three sacks, four interceptions and 23 pass defenses and was named the AFC Defensive Back of the Year. Because of their outstanding season record, Pittsburg was set to enjoy home-field advantage throughout the play-offs. Believing the hype that predicted an easy victory over San Diego, the Steelers' overconfidence even extended to plans for a victory Super Bowl rap video. They were on the verge of becoming the first franchise to win five

Career Statistics

Yr	Team	Tackles					Interceptions		
		TOT	SOLO	AST	SACK	BK	INT	YDS	TD
1987	PIT	20	15	5	0.0	0	1	45	1
1988	PIT	88	78	10	0.5	0	4	98	0
1989	PIT	80	67	13	0.0	0	3	39	0
1990	PIT	66	54	12	0.0	0	5	67	0
1991	PIT	71	60	11	1.0	0	3	72	0
1992	PIT	100	85	15	6.0	0	4	90	0
1993	PIT	95	79	16	2.0	0	8	138	1
1994	PIT	83	67	16	3.0	0	4	109	2
1995	PIT	1	1	0	0.0	0	0	0	0
1996	PIT	71	62	9	1.0	0	6	121	1
1997	SF	48	45	3	0.0	0	3	81	0
1998	BAL	88	80	8	0.0	2	6	108	2
1999	BAL	66	54	12	0.0	0	7	195	2
2000	BAL	77	68	9	0.0	0	4	20	0
2001	BAL	76	58	18	0.0	0	3	57	1
2002	OAK	58	49	9	0.0	0	4	198	2
TOTAL		1084	909	175	13.5	2	65	1438	12

BAL: Baltimore Ravens; OAK: Oakland Raiders; PIT: Pittsburgh Steelers; SF: San Francisco 49ers.

Super Bowls when the San Diego Chargers bested them, 17-13 with only two long touchdown passes.

Healing Power

An early knee injury took Woodson out of the 1995 season but the Steelers managed to reach the play-offs with an incredible eight game winning streak near the end of the season. Coach Cowher played Woodson in Super Bowl XXX against the Dallas Cowboys less than a year after reconstructive knee surgery. Experts were surprised at the speedy recover Woodson made but he told the *Orlando Sentinel*, "God blessed me with some good talent, but with some good recovery period, too, and healing powers or whatever you want to call it to come back from this. I did all the rehab our doctors and trainers said to do." Woodson, covering **Michael Irvin** man-to-man, and the Steelers' defense shut down the Dallas offense in the second half but it wasn't enough to overcome the Cowboys, who won 27-17.

Woodson continued to be a strong player during the 1996 season and returned to the Pro-Bowl with a team leading six interceptions. However, he suffered a blow out early in the post season and underwent knee surgery a second time. Newly a free-agent, Woodson was looking for a chance to get back to the Super Bowl. To this end, he signed for the 1997 season with the San Francisco 49ers. "I came here for one reason—to get a ring," explained the newest member of the San Francisco powerhouse. Unfortunately, the 49ers let Woodson go after the 1997 season without winning that longed for ring. The Baltimore Ravens signed the legendary defensive player in time for the 1998 season. As a defensive player for Baltimore, Woodson could have a great game with-

out getting near the ball. He told *The Sporting News*, "They've stopped throwing much my way and it can get boring after awhile." It's also bad for a player's stats. Woodson isn't much concerned with his stats these days. He declares, "What you learn in this league is that as long as you win, interceptions don't matter."

When Brian Billick became the Raven's coach in 1999, he moved Woodson from cornerback to safety. After 12 years as one of the league's all-time great cornerbacks, Woodson made the switch to safety with finesse and continued to victimize offenses with game-turning interceptions, tying for the most interceptions in the NFL that season with seven grabs. "It's definitely a different challenge," Woodson told NFL.com. "Corners and safeties are different. Corners are on an island and at safety you're controlling a lot of things from different angles." Billick saw the change as a way to work in young cornerbacks Chris McCalister and Duane Stark while keeping a veteran teacher in the secondary. "What situation has Rod Woodson not been in or seen?" Billick asks, rhetorically. "And he passes that on to other guys." Though he had lost some of his dazzling speed, Woodson leveraged his experience and knowledge of NFL offenses to great effect as a safety. The change proved to pay off big. He has gone to the Pro Bowl every year as a free safety since the switch in 1999.

On January 28, 2001, Woodson finally got what he was after. The Ravens defeated the New York Giants, 34-7, to capture their first-ever World Championship in Super Bowl XXXV played at Raymond James Stadium in Tampa, Florida. Woodson was key to the furious defensive campaign waged by the Ravens that save for Ron Dixon's 97-yard kickoff return nearly kept the Giants scoreless in the game.

Related Biography: Football Player Rich Gannon

Rich Gannon is living proof that some things only get better with age. When he was drafted into the league in 1987, the New England Patriots did not even expect Gannon to quarterback. After knocking around the league—often as a back-up quarterback, playing for Minnesota, Washington and Kansas City, the late bloomer finally hit his stride when he signed as a free agent with the Oakland Raiders in 1999.

Amazingly, in 2002 the 37 year-old Gannon may have had his best year so far. He led the league in passing yards, was named the NFL MVP for the season and took the Raiders all the way to the Super Bowl.

When asked in a December 2002 interview to explain his success late in his career Gannon praised his teammates. "I'm surrounded by a great supporting cast. We have some great players — three great receivers, a young tight end who is really coming on and a veteran tight end and electrifying backs who can make plays." Interestingly, Gannon credits his lean years as key to present success, "It's a position where experience is critical, and unfortunately in this day and age, some of these young quarterbacks have come into a situation not very conducive to learning. They have to play right away, and sometimes that experience can be damaging to a player's future. When young players have had an opportunity to watch for a couple of years, (they) are more prepared."

When he signed with the Oakland Raiders for the 2002 season, the 38-year-old Woodson joined perhaps the most aged NFL team in history. Among the Raiders starting players there were 6 veterans 35 years old and above, including League MVP quarterback Rich Gannon. The veterans led the Raiders to a Super Bowl showdown against the Tampa Bay Buccaneers. Though they lost 48-21, the Raiders remarkable season was a testament to the leadership and endurance of veterans like Woodson.

Hope for the Future

Woodson stays close to his roots in Fort Wayne by sponsoring a non-profit football camp at, Snider, his high school alma mater. The camp hosts up to 600 young players ages 8-18. "It's important for kids to be able to rub elbows with players," explains Woodson, who brings teammates and opponents alike to the camp. "It builds up a dream, a dream of hope, and that is what our society is built on for young kids. They need dreams; they need hope for the future." Woodson lives with his wife and children in Wexford, Pennsylvania, a suburb of Pittsburg. He earned his degree in criminal justice from Purdue University and serves on the board of the Leukemia Society.

FURTHER INFORMATION

Other

Galenet.com. http://galenet.galegroup.com/ (December 3, 2002).

"It's For the Kids." Rodwoodsonfootballcamp.org. http://www.rodwoodsonfootballcamp.org/bio.html (December 3, 2002).

"Q&A with Rich Gannon Late bloomer says he's surrounded by great cast" Sacramento Bee http://www.sacbee.com (December 1, 2002).

"Woodson Remains at the Top of his Game." USATODAY.com. http://www.usatoday.com/ (December 3, 2002).

"Woodson Still a Big-Play Man for Ravens." CBSsportsline.com http://www.nfl.com (December 13, 2001).

Sketch by Paulo Nunes-Ueno

Mickey Wright
1935-

American golfer

One of the greatest woman golfers of all time, Mickey Wright dominated the Ladies Professional Golf Association (LPGA) in the late 1950s and early 1960s. With a total of 82 victories, she ranks second only to **Kathy Whitworth** in career LPGA wins and in 1999 was named Female Golfer of the Century by the Associated Press. Long admired for the fluidity, grace, and power of her golf swing, Wright is the only woman in golfing history to have held four major American titles (the U.S. Women's Open, LPGA, Western Open, and Titleholders) at one time. Forced to cut back sharply on her golf in the late 1960s by bad feet and the lingering effects of an earlier wrist injury, she has played occasional tournaments and special events in the years since but spends most of her time today in retirement at her home in Port Saint Lucie, Florida.

Looking back on her distinguished career, Wright observed: "Golf has brought me more rewards, financially and personally, than I ever could have earned had I become the psychology teacher I set out to be. I feel as if I've earned my own version of a master's degree in psychology in study and experience, trial and error, on golf courses throughout the United States. For psychology . . . is as integral a part of good golf as an efficient swing."

She was born Mary Kathryn Wright in San Diego, California, on February 14, 1935. The daughter of an attorney and a homemaker, Wright was raised in the enclave of La Jolla. She began hitting golf balls with her father when she was only 4 years old and had her first lesson in golf at the La Jolla Country Club when she was 11. Her game improved rapidly and within a year she had broken 100. Wright won her first major victory the Southern California Girls Junior Championship when she was only 13. Three years later she won the U.S. Girls Junior Championship, paving the way for her entry into women's amateur competition. In 1954 she finished fourth in the U.S. Women's Open. When she wasn't playing a tournament, Wright practiced, working with her coaches to perfect her golfing technique. All the hard work paid off handsomely for Wright, as she developed one of the best technical swings of any woman golfer.

Mickey Wright

Emboldened by her success as an amateur, Wright in 1955 turned professional. Joining the LPGA tour, she announced to the world at large that she planned to be "the best woman golfer in the world some day." Wright quickly made it clear that hers was no idle boast. From 1958 through 1964 she dominated women's golf in America, winning four U.S. Women's Open titles, four LPGA championships, a Western Open title, and two Titleholders victories. Between 1960 and 1962, Wright became the only woman in golfing history to hold four major titles at once. Her titles during this period included the U.S. Women's Open, the LPGA championship, the Western Open title, and the Titleholders.

Averages 7.9 Wins a Year

In the 10 years between 1959 and 1968, Wright captured 79 of her 82 career victories, averaging an almost unbelievable 7.9 wins per year. She was a four-time winner of the U.S. Women's Open Championships, taking the titles in 1958, 1959, 1961, and 1964. Wright also was the only woman to win the LPGA Championship four times (1958, 1960, 1961, and 1963). In 1963 alone, she won slightly more than 40 percent of all LPGA Tour events, winning 13 of 32 events.

Extremely popular with her fellow golfers, Wright began to come under increasing pressure to perform in the early 1960s. Looking back on this tumultuous period, fellow golfer Kathy Whitworth, the only woman golfer with more career wins than Wright, recalled:

"The pressure was so great. Sponsors threatened to cancel their tournaments if she [Wright] didn't play. And, knowing that if they canceled, the rest of us wouldn't be able to play, Mickey would always play." It was a recipe for burnout. In 1962, Wright played 33 tournaments, followed by 30 in 1963, and 27 in 1964.

Serves as LPGA President

Because she also served as president of the LPGA during this period, Wright was duty-bound to promote the LPGA tour by presiding at scores of press briefings and doing every imaginable interview related to the tour. Despite her popularity, Wright was not comfortable with this kind of spotlight, and these promotional demands on her time took their toll. She later said: "I'm not good as far as wanting to be in front of people, glorying in it, and loving it. I think you have to love that to make that kind of pressure tolerable to me."

During the height of her career, Herbert Warren Wind, one of the country's best-known golf writers, described Wright as "a tall, good-looking girl who struck the ball with the same decisive hand action that the best men players use; she fused her hitting action smoothly with the rest of her swing, which was like **[Ben] Hogan**'s in that all the unfunctional moves had been pared away, and like **[Bobby] Jones**'s in that its cohesive timing disguised the effort that went into it." Wind was not alone in his glowing assessment of Wright. Betsy Rawls, a championship golfer who joined the LPGA four years before Wright, told the *Illustrated History of Women's Golf*: "She set a standard of shot-making that will probably never be equaled. Mickey's swing was as flawless as a golf swing can be smooth, efficient, powerful, rhythmical, and beautiful. Her shots were something to behold. . . . She contacted the ball at precisely the right point in the arc of the swing and with such clubhead speed that no shot was impossible for her. She was a spectacular golfer to watch."

Frantic Pace Takes Its Toll

By the second half of the 1960s, the frantic pace began to tell on Wright. After another in a series of wrist injuries in 1965, she briefly dropped out of the tour. She returned in 1966 to finish second in the LPGA championship. Increasingly hampered by chronic bad feet and the wrist injury, Wright dropped out as a regular on the LPGA Tour in 1969. A decade later she played in the Coca Cola Classic and took part in the competition's

---

Awards and Accomplishments

1949	Wins Southern California Girls Junior Championship
1952	Wins U.S. Girls Junior Championship
1958	Becomes first LPGA player to win LPGA Championship and U.S. Women's Open the same year
1959	Wins U.S. Women's Open
1960	Wins LPGA Championship
1961	Wins three of the four LPGA majors (U.S. Women's Open, LPGA Championship, Titleholders Championship)
1962	Wins Titleholders Championship, Western Open
1963	Wins Western Open, LPGA Championship
1963-64	Voted Associated Press Woman Athlete of the Year
1964	Wins U.S. Women's Open for the fourth time
1966	Wins Western Open
1967	Inducted into the LPGA Tour Hall of Fame
1979	Finishes second to Nancy Lopez in Coca-Cola Classic
1995	Finishes third at the Sprint Senior Challenge
1999	Named Female Golfer of the Century

---

five-way playoff, finishing second to **Nancy Lopez**. In the years since, she has played occasionally on the Seniors Tour, last competing in the 1995 Sprint Senior Challenge in Daytona Beach. It was at that contest that Wright played her last round of golf in competition.

Looking back on that last tournament, Wright told *Sports Illustrated*: "On the last hole, a par-5, I hit a pull-hook drive into the rough. The ball was way above my feet. There was water left of the green and traps on the right. I used a four-iron. I wanted to work the heel of the club through the ball and hit the inside part of the ball. The ball sailed, nice and high. I liked to hit the ball high. I two-putted for a birdie. It was a wonderful way to go out."

Wright lives today in Port St. Lucie, Florida, in a modest white stucco house on property adjoining the Club Med Sandpiper Sinners Golf Course. She lives there with longtime housemate, Peggy Wilson, who played with her on the LPGA tour. Although Wright retired from competitive golf in 1995, she continues to practice every day, hitting 40 or 50 balls from a mat on her back patio onto the nearby fairway. Of her reputation as a perfectionist, Wright said: "The perfectionist bit in golf doesn't have as much to do with doing it perfectly as the total rejection and horror of doing it badly. And I don't know which comes first, or which is more important. Winning really never crossed my mind that much. It's trite, but I knew if I did it as well as I could, I would win. If I did as well as I could, it would have been better than anybody else did it, and therefore it would win. I look back on it like it's somebody else. It's like a dream, another life. What amazes me is that I could have done it as long as I did."

CONTACT INFORMATION

Address: 2972 Treasure Island Rd., Port Saint Lucie, FL 34952.

Related Biography: Golfer Betsy Rawls

A champion golfer in her own right, Betsy Rawls was both a contemporary and an admirer of Mickey Wright. The winner of 55 LPGA events, Rawls played on the LPGA tour during the late 1950s and 1960s, the years of Wright's greatest glory in the game. Rawls first joined the tour in 1951 and retired in 1975. Both Rawls and Wright were early inductees into the LPGA Tour Hall of Fame.

She was born Elizabeth Earle Rawls in Spartanburg, South Carolina, on May 4, 1928. She grew up in Texas and didn't take up golf until she was 17. Only four years after taking up the game, Rawls won the 1949 Texas Amateur. She repeated that feat the following year and also won the 1949 Trans-National and 1950 Broadmoor Invitational as an amateur. In 1951, she joined the LPGA Tour, and led the tour in victories in 1952 (six), 1957 (five), and 1959 (10). In 1960 she won her fourth U.S. Women's Open to become the only LPGA player to win the competition four times. Four years later, Wright duplicated her feat.

After leaving the professional tour in 1975, Rawls was named tournament director of the LPGA. During her tenure, the tour experienced dynamic growth. After leaving her LPGA post in 1981, Rawls took over as executive director of the McDonald's LPGA Championship. During the LPGA's 50th anniversary in 2000, both Rawls and Wright were recognized as among the LPGA's 50 greatest players and teachers.

SELECTED WRITINGS BY WRIGHT:

Play Golf the Wright Way, Taylor Publishing, 1993.

FURTHER INFORMATION

Books

Almanac of Famous People, 6th ed. Detroit: Gale Research, 1998.
Great Women in Sports. Visible Ink Press, 1996

Periodicals

Bamberger, Michael. "Where Are They Now?: The Queen of Swing: After Dominating Golf Like No One Else, Mickey Wright Took Her Leave." *Sports Illustrated,* (July 31, 2000): 128.

Other

"Betsy Rawls." LPGA.com. http://www.lpga.com/players/index.cfm?cont_type_id=1681&player_id=31473 (January 6, 2003).
"Mary Kathryn "Mickey" Wright (1935—)." Golf Europe.com.http://www.golfeurope.com/almanac/players/wright.htm (January 6, 2003).
"Mickey Wright." PGATour.com. http://www.golfweb.com/u/ce/feature/0,1977,839856,00.html (January 6, 2003).
"Mickey Wright: Professional." LPGA.com. http://www.lpga.com/players/index.cfm?cont_type_id=1681&player_id=31552 (January 6, 2003).
"A Profile of World Golf Hall of Famer, Mickey Wright." World Golf Village. http://www.wgv.com/hof/members/mwright.html (January 6, 2003).

Sketch by Don Amerman

Kristi Yamaguchi
1971-

American figure skater

Kristi Yamaguchi

Just over a decade after Californian Kristi Yamaguchi walked away from the 1992 Winter Olympics with figure skating gold, she temporarily abandoned skating in favor of spending more time with her new husband and possibly starting a family. In the decade since her surprise victory in Albertville, France, Yamaguchi had skated professionally with Stars on Ice, touring extensively around the United States. "I love it," she told USA Today. "It's great what we do every night, and it is a thrill. But it is time to get off the road a bit."

In July of 2000, the gold medal-winning skater had married professional hockey player Bret Hedican on the big island of Hawaii. Although she still makes occasional appearances with her pals from the Stars on Ice tour, for now Yamaguchi is spending most of her time with Hedican. What made Yamaguchi's 1992 Olympic victory even sweeter was the fact that she won it in an upset victory over the favorite, Midori Ito of Japan, who had to settle for silver when the skating competition was over. A good deal of credit for her victory must go to her attitude. Yamaguchi had arrived at the Winter Games with one goal in mind—enjoying the games. She clearly hoped to perform as well as possible on the ice, but she wasn't burdened by high expectations or a need to win. She made good on her plan to enjoy the Olympics, marching in the opening ceremonies, partying with other athletes, and focusing on her skating during practice sessions. Her relaxed, laid-back approach worked wonders for Yamaguchi, who handily won the short skate competition and, despite a fall during her long program, managed to make fewer errors than her closest competitors, securing the gold medal for the United States.

She was born Kristi Tsuya Yamaguchi in Hayward, California, on July 12, 1971. One of three children of Jim, a dentist, and Carole Yamaguchi, a medical secretary, she grew up in nearby Fremont. Both of Yamaguchi's parents were among the 120,000 Japanese Americans who spent time in internment camps during World War II. Father Jim was 4 years old when his family was removed from its California ranch and transported to a camp in Arizona, where they spent the next three years. Kristi's mother, Carole, was actually born in a Colorado camp. Years later, Yamaguchi told the *Chicago Tribune* that her maternal grandfather "didn't talk much about World War II, but he let me know how proud he was to see me make it as an Asian American representing the United States. My parents let us know how fortunate we are now. Otherwise, they really don't look back on [internment] too much. It was just a time of a lot of fear in the country."

Yamaguchi was born with a deformity that caused both of her feet to point inward. To force her feet into their proper position, the infant was fitted with plaster casts reinforced with metal bars. Yamaguchi learned to walk with the casts, which were eventually removed and replaced with corrective shoes. Her mother encouraged

Chronology

1971	Born in Hayward, California, on July 12
1976	Begins taking skating lessons
1982	Starts pairs skating, teaming with Rudi Galindo
1990	Withdraws from pairs skating
1992	Launches professional career, skating with Stars on Ice
2000	Marries pro hockey player Bret Hedican
2002	Pulls out of Stars on Ice tour to spend more time with family

Awards and Accomplishments

1986	Wins bronze medal in pairs (with Rudi Galindo) skating at World Junior Figure Skating championships
1987	Wins gold with Galindo at World Junior championships
1988	Finishes fifth in adult pairs competition at national championships
1989	Wins gold in pairs and silver in singles at national championships
1989	Finishes fifth in pairs competition at world championships
1989	Named Amatuer Skater of the Year by *Skating* magazine
1990	Wins silver in ladies' singles competition at U.S. national championships
1991	Wins silver in ladies' singles competition at U.S. national championships
1991	Wins gold in ladies' singles competition at world championships
1992	Wins gold in ladies' singles competition at national championships
1992	Wins gold medal at Winter Olympics in Albertville, France
1995	Chosen by U.S. Olympic Committee as one of the "Top 100 Olympic Champions in History"
1996	Named Skater of the Year by *American Skating World*
1998	Inducted into U.S. Figure Skating Association Hall of Fame

her to become involved with hobbies and pastimes that involved her feet and legs, particularly dancing and skating. When Kristi was only 4 years old, she watched on television as **Dorothy Hamill** won a gold medal in figure skating at the 1976 Winter Olympics. Captivated by Hamill and her sport, Yamaguchi began taking skating lessons, during which she discovered a natural talent for the sport. Recalling those childhood lessons, Yamaguchi years later recalled in the *San Jose Mercury News*: "When I look back on it, I worked incredibly hard for a little kid. I would not get off the ice until I did some particular move right or until I did something! a certain number of times. From the time I was six, I kept bugging my mom, 'Let's go skating, let's go skating.'"

Takes Lessons Six Days a Week

Yamaguchi took lessons six days a week, starting at 5 in the morning and lasting five hours. After completing her daily studies with a private tutor, she either took dance lessons or trained in pairs skating. In 1982, at the age of 11, Kristi was paired with 13-year-old **Rudy Galindo** (he later changed the spelling of his first name to Rudi to match Kristi). The two were well matched in height and strength, and both were good technical skaters and showed style on the ice. Four years later, the two took bronze medals in pairs competition at the World Junior Figure Skating championship. The following year Yamaguchi and Galindo skated to gold at the world juniors competition. In January 1988, competing against adult skaters for the first time, the duo finished fifth in the pairs competition at the U.S. national championships. A year later, they'd improved enough to take the gold medal at the nationals. However, that same year the pair lost the only coach they'd ever had when Jim Hulick died of cancer. Although Yamaguchi and Galindo continued to skate together for awhile, the loss of Hulick was the beginning of the end for the pair. Shortly after the two won gold at the nationals and finished fifth in pairs competition at the worlds, Kristi announced her intention to leave pairs skating and concentrate on her singles career.

All through the years of pairs skating with Galindo, Yamaguchi had continued to compete in the ladies' singles and in 1989 had won silver at the nationals competition in Baltimore, Maryland. She skated to silver again at the nationals in 1990 and 1991 and began to worry

that she'd reached her peak and would never attain that elusive gold medal. Reassurance came in the form of a gold medal in singles skating at the 1991 worlds. In early 1992 she won a matching gold medal at the nationals in Orlando, Florida.

Despite her gold medals, however, most skating experts expressed doubt that Yamaguchi could overcome the brilliance of Japanese skater Midori Ito at the 1992 Olympics. Ito, the first woman to perform a triple axel jump in competition, had been hampered by an injury at the 1991 worlds but arrived at the Olympics in excellent shape. However, Ito's hopes for gold were dashed when she fell while attempting a triple Lutz jump. During her long program, Yamaguchi took a spill on a triple loop jump but still made fewer errors than her competitors. In the end, the gold medal went to Yamaguchi, and Ito was forced to settle for silver.

Joins Stars on Ice Tour

Shortly after her smashing success in Albertville, Yamaguchi retired from amateur competition to tour professionally with Stars on Ice. For the next 10 years, she toured throughout the country, also competing professionally. In July of 2000, Yamaguchi married professional hockey player Bret Hedican. A decade after joining Stars on Ice, she left the group, looking to spend more time with her husband and hopefully start a family. At the time she announced her retirement from Stars on Ice, Yamaguchi made it clear that she wasn't retiring from her sport but hoped to stay close to the ice, participating in skating specials on television. She said she was wary of touring but not of her sport. Whether or not she ever returns full time to skating, Yamaguchi will forever be remembered for her gold-winning perfor-

---

Related Biography: Figure Skater Midori Ito

The biggest obstacle on Yamaguchi's skate to Olympic gold was diminutive Japanese skater Midori Ito. A mere 4 feet, 9 inches tall, Ito was the odds-on favorite to win the gold medal at the 1992 Winter Games in Albertville but ruined her chances to finish first with disastrous (and surprising) falls during both her short and long programs. The first woman ever to land a triple axel jump in competition, Ito fell attempting the first of two triple axels in her long program at Albertville and also during a triple Lutz in her short program. Although she became the first woman ever to land a triple axel at the Olympics when she successfully completed the second scheduled triple axel in her long program, Ito had to settle for silver. She was so disappointed by her Olympics performance that she publicly apologized to her countrymen for not winning the gold.

Born in Nagoya, Japan, on August 13, 1969, Ito began skating when she was 5 years old and was entering competitions by the time she turned 6. Her first big wins came in 1980 when she won both the All-Japan Juniors and the All-Japan Junior Freestyle. In November 1988, Ito landed her first triple axel jump in competition at the Aichi Prefecture Championship, winning the gold medal. Although she didn't attempt a triple axel jump at the 1988 Winter Olympics, she landed a number of other triple jumps and finished fifth. Shortly after taking the silver medal at the 1992 Olympics, Ito retired from amateur skating and turned professional. She was reinstated as an amateur in June 1995 but in November 1996 she again retired from eligible skating, citing health problems that made it difficult for her to withstand the rigors of amateur competition. Ito continues to skate professionally, performing 11 months of each year in Prince Ice World shows. She worked as a commentator for Japanese television during the 2002 Winter Olympics in Salt Lake City.

mance at Albertville in 1992, bringing home the women's figure skating gold for the United States for the first time in 16 years.

CONTACT INFORMATION

Address: Kristi Yamaguchi, c/o International Management Group, 1 St. Clair Avenue East, Ste. 700, Toronto, Ontario M4T 2V7 Canada.

SELECTED WRITINGS BY YAMAGUCHI:

Pure Gold, HBJ School, 1997.
(With Greg Brown) *Always Dream,* Taylor Publishing, 1998.

FURTHER INFORMATION

Books

Great Women in Sports. Detroit: Visible Ink Press, 1996.
Notable Asian Americans, Detroit: Gale Research, 1995.
Sports Stars, Series 1-4. Detroit: U•X•L, 1994-1998.

Periodicals

Lynch, Jason, and Susan Horsburgh. "Melting the Ice Skating Back into the Limelight, Five Olympic Champions Star in TV Specials and Talk Up the Joys of Love and Marriage." *People,* (January 13, 2003): 125.

Parrish, Paula,. "A Fairy Tale Life: Ten Years Since Winning Olympic Gold, Kristi Yamaguchi Is Happier Than Ever." *Denver Rocky Mountain News,* (February 4, 2002): 16S.
Pedulla, Tom. "Yamaguchi Takes Act Off Road, Heads Home." *AP Worldstream,* (December 3, 2002).

Other

"Awards and Recognitions." Amy's Kristi Yamaguchi Fan Site. http://www.geocities.com/amyc521/awards.html (January 23, 2003).
"Kristi Yamaguchi: A Biography by Stuart." The Kristi Yamaguchi Web Page. http://www.polaris.net/~shanhew/biography/biography.html (January 21, 2003).
"A Midori Ito Biography." Midori Ito. http://www.mountaindragon.com/midori/mibio.htm (January 23, 2003).
"Profile of a Champion." Amy's Kristi Yamaguchi Fan Site. http://www.geocities.com/amyc521/profile.html (January 21, 2003).

Sketch by Don Amerman

Cy Young
1867-1955

American baseball player

Two achievements have made Cy Young an immortal name in baseball, even as other stars of his time disappear into obscurity. His record of 511 career wins, set at a time when pitchers pitched more often than today and completed most games they started, is untouchable now. And soon after his death in 1955, the Cy Young Award was created to honor the two major leagues' best pitchers of each year. Young deserves the award. He dominated the game for the twenty years of his major league career. He bridged the era of baseball's beginnings in the 1800s and the start of its modern era in the 1900s. The star of the first modern World Series, he defined pitching excellence for his time.

His Early Years

Denton True Young was born in rural Gilmore, Ohio, on March 29, 1867, to a farmer who'd been a private in the Union army in the Civil War and his wife. Educated through the sixth grade, Young and his brothers quickly took to the game of baseball, which became popular throughout the country in the 1870s. They'd travel up to twenty miles, probably on foot or horseback, to play. Young's strong arm made him a natural pitcher early on;

Cy Young

he'd practice by throwing balls and walnuts at a target on his father's barn door.

He was still a teen when he and his father moved to Nebraska; he spent two years working as a farm hand and playing in semi-pro baseball games on Saturdays. In 1887, father and son moved back to Ohio. Young spent two more years playing semi-pro ball, pitching and playing second base in 1889 for a team in New Athens that won its local championship. His talent caught the attention of a minor league team in Canton, which signed him in 1890.

The Cyclone

Young acquired his nickname right away. Worried that his new Canton teammates were skeptical of his abilities, he started throwing balls against a fence to show off. "I thought I had to show my stuff," he was quoted as saying in the 1965 book *Kings of the Diamond*. "I threw the ball so hard I tore a couple of boards off the grandstand. One of the fellows said the stand looked like a cyclone struck it. That's how I got the name that was later shortened to Cy." The local newspaper was calling him "Cyclone" by April 1890. (An alternate tale, less kind, suggests that his teammates took to calling him Cy, then a common nickname for someone who seemed like a country hick. That may have been part of the reason the name "Cyclone" was eventually shortened.)

Reporters were impressed with Young's fastball and curve ball, and he soon became known as the best pitcher in the Tri-State League, even though he was playing for an awful team. In July, Young pitched a no-hitter against McKeesport, striking out eighteen. A fierce competition for talented players that year, brought on by the creation of a third major league, made Young attractive to Cleveland's major league teams. The Cleveland Spiders paid Canton $300 to release Young, and he signed a contract with the Spiders that increased his monthly salary from $60 to $75.

Young pitched his first major league game on August 6, 1890. The press had raved about the arrival of the "Canton Cyclone," Reed Browning recounts in his book *Cy Young: A Baseball Life,* but the visiting Chicago Colts' player-manager, Cap Anson, is said to have taken a look at Young and dismissed him as "just another big farmer." Upset over the remark, Young gave up only three hits to the Colts, none to Anson himself. The Spiders won 8-1. Afterward, Anson tried to offer Spiders secretary Davis Hawley a thousand dollars to get Young on the Colts. Hawley said no.

By the end of 1890, Young had amassed a record of 9-7, respectable for a rookie. In 1891, he was Cleveland's winningest pitcher, with a 27-20 record, despite a slump toward the end of the year. He was a bright spot on the Spiders, who finished below .500 both years. The next year, Young proved to be the best pitcher in the National League, winning thirty-six games and losing only eleven. That year, the league split its schedule into two seasons, and the Spiders won the Fall Series pennant race, led by Young, who went 21-3. Young won the first game of the championship series against Boston, the spring champs, but the Spiders lost the rest of the games. In December, he was featured on the cover of the *Sporting News.*. That fall, he married 21-year-old Robba Miller, a neighbor he'd grown up with in Gilmore.

<table>
<tr><td colspan="2">Awards and Accomplishments</td></tr>
<tr><td>1895</td><td>Won Temple Cup, forerunner of World Series, with Cleveland</td></tr>
<tr><td>1901</td><td>Led American League in wins, strikeouts, and ERA</td></tr>
<tr><td>1903</td><td>Won first modern World Series, with Boston</td></tr>
<tr><td>1911</td><td>Earned his 511th win, an all-time record</td></tr>
<tr><td>1937</td><td>Inducted into National Baseball Hall of Fame</td></tr>
</table>

Strength and Stamina

In 1893, to generate more offense, baseball owners increased the distance between the pitcher and home plate by five feet to the current 60 feet, 6 inches. The change ended the careers of many pitchers, who found their pitches ineffective once batters had more time to see them, or who threw too hard and wore out their arms. Young was one of the few pitchers who did as well after the change as before. His thirty-two wins in 1893 were the second highest in the league. His 1894 record of 25-22 was decent, though weighed down by an end-of-season slump. In 1895, his thirty-five wins led the league, and the Spiders finished in second place. In the post-season Temple Cup championship, Young posted three wins as the Spiders beat the first-place Baltimore Orioles, four games to one.

His strength gave him a stamina few other pitchers had. At 6 foot 2 and 210 pounds, he was one of the league's strongest men. Every year, when baseball season was over, he'd go back to his farm to milk the cows and chop wood. He claimed he never had a sore arm. Early in his career, Young was a wild thrower, but over the years he acquired more and more control, and walked fewer and fewer batters. He had a great fastball, and he could fool hitters too. "What very few batters knew was that I had two curves," he once said, according to Rich Westcott's book *Winningest Pitchers*. "One of them sailed in there as hard as my fastball and broke in reverse. It was a narrow curve that broke away from the batter and went in just like a fastball. The other was a wide break."

Young was one of three pitchers who dominated the 1890s, along with Kid Nichols and Amos Rusie. His statistics dropped a bit in the late part of the decade as the Spiders' fortunes declined, but he still turned in his first major-league no-hitter in 1897, a 6-0 victory against Cincinnati.

At the end of 1898, after the Spiders suffered from falling attendance and a dispute with Cleveland authorities over playing home games on Sundays, team owner Frank Robison moved Young and all the Spiders' other top players to his other team, the St. Louis Cardinals. Young compiled a record of 26-16 in St. Louis in 1899, but the Cardinals finished fifth in the league. In 1900, at age 33, Young had a mediocre year, with a 19-18 record. Speculation spread that his career was almost over.

<table>
<tr><td>Related Biography: Baseball Player Kid Nichols</td></tr>
</table>

Charles (Kid) Nichols, Cy Young's rival for the title of best pitcher of the 1890s, won thirty games in seven different seasons, a record no one has ever equaled. His career began soon after the 1884 rule change allowing overhand pitches, and he became one of baseball's first fastball pitchers. For most of his career, in fact, his fastball was his only pitch. It was enough, because he also had great control. He rarely walked anyone unless he meant to.

Born in 1869, Nichols started pitching for the Kansas City Cowboys of the Western League at age seventeen. He compiled an 18-13 record, yet team management released him because they thought he was too young. Stuck with the nickname "Kid," he bounced around the minors for a few years, until his amazing 39-8 record with Omaha of the Western League in 1889 earned him a place on the major-league Boston Beaneaters' roster. He won twenty-seven games his rookie season, and went on to lead Boston to three straight pennants in 1891-93 and two more in 1897 and 1898. He won 297 games in all during the 1890s, and the *Sporting News* named him that decade's best pitcher.

During 1900 and 1901, his winning percentage dropped to about .500, and Nichols left Boston rather than accept a small contract offer. He became co-owner and player-manager of the Kansas City Blue Stockings in the Western League. He returned to the National League in 1904 as player-manager of the St. Louis Cardinals, and he amassed a 21-13 record that year, but his team finished fifth, and he was fired early in the 1905 season. He finished his career with the Philadelphia Phillies, retiring in 1906 at age thirty-six.

Nichols moved back to Kansas City, got involved in several businesses, and became a champion bowler. He was elected to the National Baseball Hall of Fame in 1949 and died in 1953.

Star of the American League

When the American League declared itself a major league in 1901, Young left St. Louis and signed with the Boston Pilgrims, who offered him several hundred dollars more than the National League's salary cap of $2,400. Young dispelled the talk that he was washed up, and became one of the new league's biggest stars. He led the league in 1901 with thirty-three wins, 158 strikeouts, and an earned run average of 1.62. The next two years, he also led the A.L. in wins. In 1903, he pitched three straight 1-0 shutouts, including the game that clinched the pennant for Boston. That year, Boston played Pittsburgh, the National League champions, in the first modern World Series. Young lost the first game of the series, but won the fifth and the seventh, and Boston went on to win the series, five games to three.

In 1904, he was just as good. He pitched the first perfect game in the 1900s on May 5, beating the Philadelphia A's 3-0. It was part of twenty-three consecutive hitless innings, still a record: six innings in two relief appearances, the perfect game, and the first six innings of the next game he pitched. He shut out Boston's opponents ten times that year, including three toward the end of the pennant race with New York, which Boston won on the last game of the season.

The Pilgrims slipped from contention for a few years, and Young's record suffered. In 1905, he struck out 208 batters, the most of his career, but his record was only

Career Statistics

Yr	Team	W	L	ERA	GS	CG	SHO	IP	H	ER	BB	SO
1890	CLE-N	9	7	3.47	16	16	0	147.7	145	57	30	39
1891	CLE-N	27	22	2.85	46	43	0	423.7	431	134	140	147
1892	CLE-N	36	12	1.93	49	48	9	453.0	363	97	118	168
1893	CLE-N	34	16	3.36	46	42	1	422.7	442	158	103	102
1894	CLE-N	26	21	3.94	47	44	2	408.7	488	179	106	108
1895	CLE-N	35	10	3.26	40	36	4	69.7	63	134	75	121
1896	CLE-N	28	15	3.24	46	42	5	414.3	477	149	62	140
1897	CLE-N	21	19	3.80	38	35	2	333.7	391	141	49	88
1898	CLE-N	25	13	2.53	41	40	1	377.7	387	106	41	101
1899	STL	26	16	2.58	42	40	4	69.3	368	106	44	111
1900	STL	19	19	3.00	35	32	4	321.3	337	107	36	115
1901	BOS-A	33	10	1.62	41	38	5	371.3	324	67	37	158
1902	BOS-A	32	11	2.15	43	41	3	384.7	350	92	53	160
1903	BOS-A	28	9	2.08	35	34	7	341.7	294	79	37	176
1904	BOS-A	26	16	1.97	41	40	10	380.0	327	83	29	200
1905	BOS-A	18	19	1.82	33	31	4	320.7	248	65	30	210
1906	BOS-A	13	21	3.19	34	28	0	287.7	288	102	25	140
1907	BOS-A	21	15	1.99	37	33	6	343.3	286	76	51	147
1908	BOS-A	21	11	1.26	33	30	3	299.0	230	42	37	150
1909	CLE-A	19	15	2.26	34	30	3	295.0	267	74	59	109
1910	CLE-A	7	10	2.53	20	14	1	163.3	149	46	27	58
1911	CLE-A	3	4	3.88	7	4	0	46.3	54	20	13	20
1911	BOS-N	4	5	3.71	11	8	2	80.0	83	33	15	35
TOTAL		511	316	2.63	815	749	76	7354.7	7092	2147	1217	2803

BOS-A: Boston Pilgrims (American League); BOS-N: Boston Braves (National League); CLE-A: Cleveland Naps (American League); CLE-N: Cleveland Spiders (National League); STL: St. Louis Browns (National League).

18-19. His performance dropped off for a couple of years, but in 1908, at the age of forty-one, he posted a 21-11 record and an ERA of 1.26—a career best—and pitched his third no-hitter, beating the New York Highlanders 8-0 on June 30.

Boston traded Young to the Cleveland Naps (who later became the Indians) before the 1909 season began. He won nineteen games that year, but by 1910 his age was finally overtaking his famous stamina. After spending most of his career in great shape, he'd developed a paunch. He started only twenty games and won only seven. Cleveland released him in August 1911, and he signed with Boston. Late in the year, he pitched against Philadelphia's rookie, **Grover Cleveland Alexander**, and lost 1-0 in twelve innings. "When the kid beats you, it's time to quit," he said, according to Westcott's *Winningest Pitchers*. He still came to spring training in 1912, but batters were bunting to reach base against him, since his portly figure made it hard for him to field. He retired before the season started.

Retirement

Young went back to his farm in tiny Peoli, Ohio, near Newcomerstown. He stayed close to baseball all his life, going to several Indians games a year and often showing up at old-timers' events. He felt hurt when he didn't get into the National Baseball Hall of Fame in the first round of voting in 1936, but he was voted in a year later. When Young turned eighty, Cleveland Indi-

ans owner Bill Veeck invited him and the entire population of Newcomerstown—about a thousand people—to an Indians game to celebrate. On November 4, 1955, he died of a heart attack in his rocking chair. He was eighty-eight.

"His record of 511 victories in 912 games will never be surpassed," Young's gravestone asserts. It's true. He averaged forty starts a year, while today's pitchers average about thirty-three, and he pitched before relief pitchers were common, so ninety-two percent of his starts were complete games. But his record isn't just the result of pitching at the right time. No other pitcher from his era managed more than about 360 career wins.

At the end of his biography of Young, Reed Browning asks whether Young can be considered the best pitcher of all time. On one hand, Young's contemporaries seemed to consider him "very good but not the greatest," Browning notes. When they were asked to name the best pitcher they'd ever seen, or to choose their all-time pitching staffs, other pitchers, such as Kid Nichols, often beat out Young. On the other hand, Browning points out, Young's long career spanned very different eras of baseball, when rules and strategies changed significantly. "Cy Young lasted as long as he did not simply because he was blessed with a tough body and durable arm," he wrote, "but also because he used his intelligence to study, adapt, and learn." However one defines "greatest pitcher," Browning wrote, "Cy Young is clearly a candidate for the honor."

FURTHER INFORMATION

Books

Allen, Lee, and Tom Meany. *Kings of the Diamond: The Immortals in Baseball's Hall of Fame.* New York: G.P. Putnam's Sons, 1965.

Benson, John, and Tony Blengino. *Baseball's Top 100: The Best Individual Seasons of All Time.* Wilton, CT: Diamond Library, 1995.

Browning, Reed. *Cy Young: A Baseball Life.* Amherst, MA: University of Massachusetts Press, 2000.

Cy Young Centennial, 1867-1967: July 14 & 15, New Philadelphia & Newcomerstown, Ohio. Newcomerstown, OH: Cy Young Centennial Committee, 1967.

Players of Cooperstown: Baseball's Hall of Fame. Lincolnwood, IL: Publications International, Ltd., 1998.

Westcott, Rich. *Winningest Pitchers: Baseball's 300-Game Winners.* Philadelphia: Temple University Press, 2002.

Periodicals

"Baseball's Cy Young Dies at 88." *Cleveland Press* (November 4, 1955): 1.

Other

Baseball-Reference.com: Major League Baseball Statistics and History. http://www.baseball-reference.com

Sketch by Erick Trickey

Sheila Young
1950-

American speed skater

In the 1970s and early 1980s, American Sheila Young was a dominant force in two sports—speed skating and cycling—though she did not receive much recognition for her accomplishments in the United States. She won world championships in both sports in 1973 and 1976. Young was also the first athlete to win three medals in one Winter Olympic Games in 1976.

Young was born on October 14, 1950, in Birmingham, Michigan, the daughter of Clair and Georgia (McCluskey) Young. Her father worked in the traffic department of an automotive parts plant in Detroit and later founded the Wolverine Sports Club. He was also a state champion in cycling in Michigan and competed in skating. Young's mother also competed at cycling (once tying for the national championship) and skating.

Sheila Young

From a young age, Young was exposed to both sports. She was skating at two, and riding a bike at four. After her mother died when Young was 12, she became more serious in sports. Her father used athletic pursuits as a way of entertaining his family, which included three other children. (Young's older brother Roger was a competitive cyclist and an older sister was a competitive speed skater.)

Becomes Competitive Speed Skater

Young first began competitive speed skating when she was nine years old. She trained on area outdoor lakes and in public rinks, with her father serving as her coach until she was 20 years old. While still in high school, Young took a second place at the U.S. National Speed Skating Championship and was also a national junior champion. She nearly made the U.S. Olympic speed skating team in 1968.

After Young graduated from high school, she moved to Milwaukee, Wisconsin, to train at the only Olympic size speed skating training rink in the country. The move paid off when, in 1970, she won her first two championships: the U.S. National Outdoor championship and the North American Outdoor Championship. She repeated as the latter in 1971.

In this time period, training for speed skating was considered unsophisticated in the United States as compared to Europe. In the early 1970s, Young hired Dutchman Peter Schotting as her coach. He used cycling as

Chronology

1950	Born October 14, in Birmingham, Michigan
1971	Hired Peter Schotting as her speed skating coach
1972	Competed in Winter Olympics
1976	Competed at the Winter Olympics; married cyclist Jim Ochowicz; briefly retired to have child, Kate
1980	Began training intensely in both sports again
1981	Placed seventh at the World Speed Skating Championship
1982	Placed second at the World's Cycling Championship
1983	Retired from competition; gave birth to Elli on December 15

Awards and Accomplishments

1970	Wins U.S. National Outdoor championship in speed skating; wins North American Outdoor Championship in speed skating
1971	Wins U.S. National Outdoor championship in speed skating; wins ABLA (Amateur Bicycle League of America) National Sprint title in bicycling
1972	Wins both 500-meter races at World Sprint Championships (speed skating)
1973	Wins U.S. Speedskating Championships in 500-, 1000-, and 3000-meters; wins 500- and 1000- meters at the World Sprint Speed Skating Championships; wins 500-meter gold at the Women's World Speed Skating Championship; wins women's sprint title at the World Cycling Championship; wins women's sprint title at the ABLA national track championships in cycling
1974	Wins ABLA Women's National Sprint title in cycling
1976	Competes at the Winter Olympics, winning gold in 500-meter race, bronze in 1000-meter race, and silver in 1500-meter race; wins the Women's World Speed Skating Championship in both 500- and 1000-meters; wins the 500 meter GKWS (speed skating), setting world's record; wins the U.S. Sprint Championship and the World Sprint Championship (cycling); named USOC's (United States Olympic Committee) sportswoman of the year
1981	Wins women's sprint gold medal at the National Track Cycling Championships; wins World's Cycling Championship; named USOC's sportswoman of the year

part of her year-round training program, which also included running and skating.

In 1972, Young competed in her first Winter Olympics, in Sapporo, Japan. She finished fourth in the 500-meter race, missing the bronze by 8/100 of a second. That same year, she won both 500-meter races at the World Sprint Championship. Young continued to modify her training, increasing the intensity and focusing on strength and endurance. She also decided to do longer races, not just sprints.

In the mid-1970s, Young was a dominant force in speed skating. In 1973, she won the U.S. Speedskating Championships in the 500-, 1000-, and 3000-meters. She also won the 500- and 1000- meters at the World Sprint Speed Skating Championships, and the 500-meters at the Women's World Speed Skating Championships. In 1975, she won the 500-meters at the World Sprint Speed Skating Championships.

Wins Olympic Medals

All her success in the mid-1970s helped prepare Young for the 1976 Winter Olympics in Innsbruck, Austria. At the games, she first won a silver in the 1500-meters, then strained a ligament in her left foot. Despite the injury, she won gold and set an Olympic record in the 500-meters and took the bronze in the 1000 meters. Later that year, she also won the Women's World Speed Skating Championships in both the 500- and 1000-meters.

Competes as Cyclist

When Young was 20 years old, she began competing as a cyclist, during the speed skating off-season. As with speed skating, her first coach was her father. Young won her first titles at the 1971 ABLA (Amateur Bicycle League of America)'s National Sprint Championships.

Young did not really become serious about cycling until 1973, when she decided to see how she would fair against international competition. She did well. In 1973, Young became the first American to win an international cycling event in more than 50 years when she won the women's sprint title at the World Cycling Championships. She won despite the fact that she had crashed twice and had injuries that should have knocked her out

of the race. Young also won the ABLA's women's national sprint championship that year.

Young wanted to quit competitive cycling, but was talked into staying by Mike Fraysse, the U.S. team manager. In 1976, Young won two more titles—the U.S. Sprint Championship and the World Sprint title—after the Winter Olympics. Despite her success as a cyclist, speed skating remained her first love. She told Nan Nelson of the *Milwaukee Journal,* "Even though I try not to have too much of a preference, I think that skating is more graceful, and I think there is more technical skill involved in it."

FURTHER INFORMATION

Books

Hickok, Ralph. *A Who's Who of Sports Champions: Their Stories and Records.* Boston: Houghton Mifflin, 1995.

Johnson, Anne Janette. *Great Women in Sports.* Detroit: Visible Ink Press, 1996.

Layden, Joe. *Women in Sports: The Complete Book on the World's Greatest Female Athletes.* General Publishing Group, 1997.

Porter, David L., editor. *Biographical Dictionary of American Sports: Outdoor Sports.* New York: Greenwood Press, 1988.

Sherrow, Victoria. *Encyclopedia of Women and Sports.* ABC-CLIO, 1996.

Woolum, Janet. *Outstanding Women Athletes: Who They Are and How They Influenced Sports in America.* Oryx Press, 1998.

Where Is She Now?

In 1976, Young was married to cyclist Jim Ochowicz and soon became pregnant. She did not compete for several years, until she resumed intensive training in both sports in the spring of 1980. In 1981, she placed seventh at the World Speed Skating Competition. Young did better in cycling, winning the national women's sprint championship and the World's Cycling championship in 1981, and placing second in 1982. Though she was aiming for speed skating at the 1984 Winter Olympics, she retired fully in 1983 when she again became pregnant.

After Young retired, she primarily focused on her family, but also completed her bachelor's degree in physical education at the University of Wisconsin at Milwaukee. She later became a physical education teacher on the elementary level for 13 years. Young remained connected to her sports by serving on the U.S. Cycling Federation board of directors and the executive board of U.S. Olympic Committee. She helped set up the 1980 Winter Olympics at Lake Placid, New York. Young was also a founding member of the Women's Sports Foundation and on the board of Special Olympics International. Young's daughter Elli became a competitive speed skater who was a member of the U.S. Olympic speed skating team in 2002.

Young told Mark Beech of *Sports Illustrated,* "I had done everything I wanted to do. I can understand people who compete into their 30s, but there are other things in life."

Periodicals

Beech, Mark. "Sheila Young, Speed Skater: February 2, 1976." *Sports Illustrated,* (February 4, 2002): 18.

Chapin, Dwight. "Elli Ochowicz; Teen is fulfilling a speedskating legacy." *San Francisco Chronicle,* (January 27, 2002): B12.

"Ex-Skating Star Wins Cycling Title." *New York Times,* (August 17, 1981): C7.

Green, Jerry. "Young a Pioneer in Women's Sports." *Detroit News,* (July 5, 2001): 1.

Johnson, William Oscar. "On Came the Heroes." *Sports Illustrated,* (February 16, 1976): 10.

Kirsch, Bernard. "Sheila Young: Dedication." *New York Times,* (February 6, 1976).

Matthews, Christopher. "She Was the Young of Old." *Sports Illustrated,* (September 20, 1976): 57.

McDermott, Barry. "Fastest Legs in Two Leagues." *Sports Illustrated,* (August 13, 1973): 20.

Nelson, Nan. "Skating Still 1st with US Biking Champ." *Milwaukee Journal,* (June 19, 1974).

Radosta, John. "Sheila on a Roll." *New York Times,* (April 11, 1983): C2.

Smith, Pohla. United Press International, (July 23, 1981).

Snider, Steve. "Speedskate Star Trains for Olympic Comeback." United Press International, (April 16, 1983).

Other

"Athlete Profile—Sheila Young Ochowicz." http://www. usolympicteam.com/athlete_profiles/s_young_ ochowicz (January 13, 2002).

Sketch by A. Petruso

Steve Young

Steve Young
1961-

American football player

Steve Young, one of professional football's greatest quarterbacks, had to wait his turn for fame, operating for a number of years in the shadow of **Joe Montana**, his predecessor as starting quarterback of the San Francisco 49ers. In the end, Young had to lead his team to a victory in the Super Bowl to prove himself a worthy successor to the legendary Montana. Clean-cut, handsome, and a little on the straitlaced side, Young compiled an impressive record during his 15 seasons in the National Football League (NFL), all but two of them with the 49ers. On a statistical basis, Young stacks up very nicely indeed against Montana. In fact, compared on the basis of the percentage of career passes completed, Young even edges out Montana with a completion rate of 64.3 percent, compared with Montana's 63.2 percent. For four straight years-1991, 1992, 1993, and 1994-Young was the highest rated quarterback in the NFL, an unprecedented feat, and in 1992 and 1994 he was named the league's most valuable player. Despite all these accomplishments, it was still difficult for Young to win the respect he so richly deserved, even after Montana had left San Francisco and taken up quarterbacking duties with the Kansas City Chiefs.

Chronology	
1961	Born in Salt Lake City, Utah, on October 11
1980-84	Attends Brigham Young University in Provo, Utah
1984	Picked by the Los Angeles Express in first round of United States Football League draft
1985	Joins Tampa Bay Buccaneers of NFL
1987	Traded by Buccaneers to San Francisco 49ers
2000	Retires from football on June 12

Awards and Accomplishments	
1983	Leads Brigham Young to Holiday Bowl victory over University of Missouri
1985	While in USFL, becomes first pro player to pass for 300 yards and rush for 100 in the same game
1990	Becomes only second 49ers quarterback to pass for more than 100 yards in a single game
1991	Leads NFL in passing efficiency
1992	Leads NFL in passing with 3,465 yards
1992, 1994	Named most valuable player in NFL
1993	Becomes only 49ers quarterback to pass for more than 4,000 yards in season
1995	Leads 49ers to victory over San Diego Chargers in Super Bowl XXIX
1996	Leads NFL in passing efficiency

Born in Salt Lake City

He was born Jon Steven Young in Salt Lake City, Utah, on October 11, 1961. One of five children of LeGrande (an attorney) and Sherry Young and a great-great-great grandson of Brigham Young, one of the founders of the Church of Jesus Christ of Latter-day Saints (the Mormon church), Young grew up in Greenwich, Connecticut. He was raised as a Mormon, adhering closely to the strict rules of his faith. After high school, where he played quarterback for the varsity football team, Young decided to attend Brigham Young University, his father's alma mater. Following in the footsteps of his father, who had been a college football star, he joined the Brigham Young football team, only to find himself playing eighth-string quarterback.

Young grew so disillusioned that for a while he considered quitting football altogether but was persuaded by his father to hang in there. Looking back on his years in college football, Young told *Sports Illustrated:* "I really didn't know how to throw back then. I learned to throw at Brigham Young, mostly from Jim McMahon [who later played for the Chicago Bears]. We were about the same size and had the same athletic abilities." Despite his inauspicious start in college football, Young worked his way up to starting quarterback by his senior year. That year he completed 306 of 429 passes for 3,902 yards and 33 touchdowns, and was a runner-up for the Heisman Trophy.

Bidding War Erupts

In 1984 Young became the object of a spirited bidding war between the Cincinnati Bengals of the NFL and the Los Angeles Express of the United States Football League (USFL). When the Express offered a contract that would pay him more than $60 million over 44 years, Young could no longer resist. He signed with the Express and in his two seasons with the team passed for 4,102 yards and 16 touchdowns. Unfortunately, the USFL was on its last legs, so in 1985 Young bought out his contract and signed on with the Tampa Bay Buccaneers of the NFL. It proved an unhappy match for both Young and the Buccaneers, who seemed unable to successfully tap the quarterback's potential.

Bill Walsh, coach of the 49ers, was convinced that Young was capable of greater things, and in 1987 San Francisco negotiated a trade with Tampa Bay. In his early

years with the 49ers, Young saw only limited action, for Montana, the team's starting quarterback, was still at the top of his game. In the early 1990s, Young began to assert himself more and more. His big break came in 1991 after Montana was injured in preseason action. Although Young himself was injured later in the season and sidelined for several games, he managed to lead the NFL in passing efficiency with a pass-completion rate of 64.5 percent.

Young Comes into His Own

Montana's injury kept him out of action for most of the 1992 season, giving Young further opportunity to showcase his talents. As starting quarterback, Young passed for 3,465 yards with an impressive pass-completion rate of 66.7 percent, earning him honors as the league's most valuable player. Although Montana played well in the second half of the last game of the regular season, 1992 belonged to Young. Forced to decide whether Montana or Young would start as quarterback in the 1993 season, San Francisco coaches went with Young, prompting Montana to ask to be traded to the Kansas City Chiefs.

Although the legendary Montana was no longer playing in San Francisco, Young found that his predecessor still had a firm grip on the hearts and minds of 49ers' fans. No matter what magic Young produced on the gridiron, it seemed somehow to pale in comparison to the feats of Montana, at least in the view of most fans. Young turned in a brilliant performance in 1993, passing for 4,023 yards with a completion rate of 68 percent. Equally spectacular were Young's 1994 statistics: 3,969 yards with a pass-completion rate of 70.3 percent. But most importantly of all, Young led his team to a National Football Conference championship with a decisive 38-28 victory over the Dallas Cowboys. The stage was set for the high point of Young's football career: Super Bowl XXIX.

Passes for Six Super Bowl Touchdowns

Although San Francisco was heavily favored to win in the Super Bowl against the San Diego Chargers, the game was even more one-sided than predicted by the

Career Statistics

Yr	Team	GP	ATT	COM	YDS	COM%	AVG	TD	INT
1985	TB	5	138	72	935	52.2	6.8	3	8
1986	TB	14	363	195	2282	53.7	6.3	8	13
1987	SFO	8	69	37	570	53.6	8.3	10	0
1988	SFO	11	101	54	680	53.5	6.7	3	3
1989	SFO	10	92	64	1001	69.6	10.9	8	3
1990	SFO	6	62	38	427	61.3	6.9	2	0
1991	SFO	11	279	180	2517	64.5	9.0	17	8
1992	SFO	16	402	268	3465	66.7	8.6	25	7
1993	SFO	16	462	314	4023	68.0	8.7	29	16
1994	SFO	16	461	324	3969	70.3	8.6	35	10
1995	SFO	11	447	299	3200	66.9	7.2	20	11
1996	SFO	12	316	214	2410	67.7	7.6	14	6
1997	SFO	15	356	241	3029	67.7	8.5	19	6
1998	SFO	15	517	322	4170	62.3	8.1	36	12
1999	SFO	3	84	45	446	53.6	5.3	3	4
TOTAL		169	4149	2667	33124	64.3	8.0	232	107

SFO: San Francisco 49ers; TB: Tampa Bay Buccaneers.

Where Is He Now?

Since stepping down as the star quarterback of the San Francisco 49ers in June 2000, Steve Young has devoted the bulk of his time and energy to running his Forever Young Foundation. The foundation, founded by Young in 1993, is a non-profit public charity that works to promote the development, security, strength, and education of children. It is funded entirely by corporate and public contributions and the proceeds from fund-raising events, including the annual Steve Young Classic Golf Tournaments held in Arizona and Utah. Young maintains homes in Palo Alto, California, and Provo, Utah.

game's most knowledgeable observers. The first time the 49ers got the ball, Young hit **Jerry Rice** for a touchdown. It was to be only the first of a record six touchdown passes thrown by Young in San Francisco's 49-26 rout of the Chargers. In all, Young passed for 325 yards, winning him Super Bowl most valuable player honors. It took one of the greatest performances in Super Bowl history, but finally Young had won the hearts of San Francisco fans everywhere.

Injury began to take its toll on Young. In 1995 he missed five games of the regular season after injuring his left shoulder, but he still managed to pass for 3,200 yards with a completion rate of 66.9 percent. Young missed four games in 1996 because of injury but again acquitted himself well, passing for 2,410 yards with a completion rate of 67.7 percent. In the eyes of many observers, Young enjoyed his greatest season as a pro in 1998, passing for 4,170 yards with a completion rate of 62.3 percent. But the cumulative damage from multiple injuries-including a number of concussions-began to take its toll. In 1999 Young played in only three games, passing for 446 yards.

Citing the numerous concussions he had suffered, Young, on June 12, 2000, announced his retirement from football. It had taken him a long time to win the respect of 49ers' fans, but in the end he was able to walk away from the game with his head held high. In his assessment of Young's career, New York Giants coach Jim Fassel told *Sporting News:* "Steve kind of set the tone for the way the game is played. Everyone saw how he ran the offense, how effective he was. Now everyone is looking for a guy that mobile."

CONTACT INFORMATION

Address: c/o Forever Young Foundation, PO Box 527, Park City, UT 84060. Phone: (800) 994-3837.

SELECTED WRITINGS BY YOUNG:

(With Greg Brown) *Forever Young.* Dallas: Taylor, 1996.

FURTHER INFORMATION

Books

"Jim McMahon." *Contemporary Newsmakers 1985,* Issue Cumulation. Detroit: Gale Research, 1986.
"Steve Young." *Newsmakers 1995,* Issue 4. Detroit: Gale Research, 1995.
"Steve Young." *Sports Stars,* Series 1-4. Detroit: U•X•L, 1994-98.

Periodicals

Barber, Phil. "Young Wins His Way into Heart of San Francisco." *Sporting News* (June 12, 2000).
Knisley, Michael. "Steve Young vs. Joe Montana." *Sporting News* (September 19, 1994).

Other

"8, Steve Young, QB." CBS.SportsLine.com. http://cbs.sportsline.com/u/football/nfl/players/1061.htm (November 29, 2002).

"Steve Young: Career Notes." ESPN. http://espn.go.com/nfl/profiles/notes/0128.html (November 29, 2002).

"Steve Young: Career Statistics." ESPN. http://espn.go.com/nfl/profiles/stats/primary/0128.html (November 29, 2002).

"Steve Young: Profile." ESPN. http://espn.go.com/nfl/profiles/profile/0128.html (November 29, 2002).

Sketch by Don Amerman

Babe Didrikson Zaharias
1911-1956

American golfer

B abe Didrikson Zaharias was one of the most versatile and talented athletes of all time; there were few sports she did not play, and she excelled at all those she tried. An Olympic gold medalist and world-record-holder in track and field, Zaharias was also an All-American in basketball, and competed in tennis, baseball, bowling, and most notably golf, ruling over the professional golf circuit in the late 1940s and early 1950s. Zaharias, a tomboy since childhood, also challenged gender stereotypes of her time, refusing to act in traditionally "feminine" modes and proving that women could and should compete widely in sports formerly reserved for men.

Mildred Ella Didrikson, known as "Babe" Didrikson and later as Babe Didrikson Zaharias, was born in 1911 in Port Arthur, Texas, the daughter of Norwegian immigrants Ole Didriksen and Hannah Marie Olsen Didricksen. She was the sixth of seven children. Her mother was a former skier and skater, and her father worked as a ship's carpenter and cabinetmaker.

Port Arthur was largely devastated when a hurricane hit the area in 1914, killing 275 people, and the family moved 17 miles inland to the rough south end of Beaumont, Texas to make a new start when Zaharias was four years old.

The family was not well-off, and Zaharias, who changed the spelling of her family name from Didriksen to Didrikson so that people would know she was Norwegian, not Swedish (the "-sen" suffix is more common among Swedes; Norwegians favor "-son"), worked various part-time jobs while she was still in school; one of her jobs involved sewing gunny sacks, earning a penny per sack.

"To Be the Greatest Athlete That Ever Lived"

The young Mildred, often called "Baby" by her family, was active, strong, and competitive, and was interested in sports from an early age, playing with and usually beating her older brothers and the boys in her neighborhood. She learned to run by racing against streetcars. In

Babe Didrikson Zaharias

sandlot ball games, she was a powerhouse hitter and a strong pitcher. She wore her hair short and wore boys' clothes. In her autobiography, *This Life I've Led,* she wrote, "I played with boys rather than girls. I preferred baseball, football, foot-racing and jumping with the boys, to hop-scotch and jacks and dolls, which were about the only things girls did." When she hit five home runs in one baseball game, her brothers renamed her "Babe" after famed slugger **Babe Ruth**; she would keep this nickname for the rest of her life. Early on, she wrote, she decided that her ambition was "to be the greatest athlete that ever lived." Zaharias' father encouraged her interest in athletics, and made her a barbell out of a broomstick and two heavy flatirons.

Although she did poorly in school, passing only enough subjects to keep her eligible to play on the sports teams, Zaharias made up for it with her accomplish-

Chronology

1911	Born in Port Arthur, Texas
1915	Moves with family to Beaumont, Texas
1929	Stars in volleyball, tennis, baseball, basketball, and swimming teams at Beaumont High School
1930	Recruited by the Golden Cyclones basketball team in Dallas; drops out of high school in her junior year to play with the team
1930	Joins Golden Cyclones track team in Dallas
1930	Wins two firsts at National Women's Amateur Athletic Union (AAU) meet, in javelin and baseball throw; wins second place in long jump
1930-32	Selected as an All-American women's basketball player; led the Cyclones to the national championship in 1931
1931	Wins national AAU meet; enters eight events and wins gold medals in six; sets world records in the high jump, 80-meter hurdles, javelin, and baseball throw
1932	Singlehandedly wins Texas AAU meet
1935	Wins Texas Women's Amateur Championship in golf
1938	Marries professional wrestler George Zaharias
1940	Wins Texas and Western Open golf tournaments
1946-47	Wins 17 golf tournaments; becomes the first woman to win the British Women's Amateur championship
1948	Wins All-American Open, World Championship, and U.S. Women's Open
1950	With 12 other women, Zaharias founds the Ladies Professional Golfer's Association
1950	Meets companion Betty Dodd at an amateur golf tournament
1953	Diagnosed with colon cancer and undergoes surgery to remove the tumor; wins Ben Hogan Comeback of the Year Award
1953	Babe Zaharias Open is founded in her honor in Beaumont, Texas; she wins the first event
1954	Wins five tournaments, including the U.S. Women's Open
1956	Dies in Galveston, Texas

ments on the athletic field. She was the high-scoring forward on the girls' basketball team at Beaumont Senior High School during both her junior and senior years, and during her tenure on the team, they never lost a game. Her obvious talent attracted the attention of Melvorne J. McCombs, who coached the Golden Cyclones, a women's basketball team sponsored by the Employers Casualty Company of Dallas, Texas; in addition to sponsoring teams, the company promoted the idea that athletes were more efficient workers. Zaharias, who in addition to her athletic ability was a skilled typist and stenographer, signed with the company as a secretary in 1930. Because she was paid $75 a month for her secretarial services, she was officially still an "amateur" athlete, an important distinction at that time; athletes who made money from their sport were barred from many competitions, including the Olympics. However, Zaharias' main focus was playing on the company's basketball, baseball, diving, tennis, and track and field teams. She soon became a star athlete. The company's basketball team won the national championship in 1930, 1931, and 1932, and Zaharias was a National Women's Amateur Athletic Union (AAU) All-American forward for the Women's National Basketball League for all three years. She often scored thirty or more points, even though at the time, it was considered respectable for an

entire team to score twenty. On the softball team, she was a power-hitter, with a batting average of over .400. In track and field, she often practiced her skills all day long; when she matched the women's high jump record of five feet, three inches, her coach bought her a chocolate soda. In *The Life and Legend of Babe Didrikson Zaharias,* Susan Cayleff described Zaharias during those years: "We don't see a young athlete striving solely for steady improvement or personal bests. We see a woman with a consuming hunger attacking—and determined to conquer—world records."

In 1931, at the national AAU track meet, which was the qualifying meet for the 1932 Olympics, Zaharias competed in eight of ten events, winning gold medals in five and tying for gold in a sixth. She set world records in the javelin (139 feet, 3 inches), 80-meter hurdles (11.9 seconds), high jump (5 feet, 5 inches, tying for first with Jean Shiley), and baseball throw (272 feet, 2 inches). At the 1932 AAU championships, Zaharias competed as a one-woman team, and singlehandedly won the team championship with 30 points; in contrast, the second-place Illinois Women's Athletic Club, which included 22 athletes, accumulated only 22 points. Zaharias's performance was the most amazing feat by any athlete, male or female, in track and field history.

Sets Records and Wins Gold at 1932 Olympics

Not surprisingly, Zaharias was a favorite to win at the 1932 Olympic Games at Los Angeles, and she did. Although women were only allowed to enter three Olympic events at that time because they were considered too weak to compete in more than that number, she broke four world records. She won the javelin throw with a toss of 143 feet, 4 inches, and won the 80-meter hurdles, breaking the world record twice during the competition; her best time was 11.7 seconds. Zaharias also made a world-record high jump, but because she went over the bar headfirst instead of leading with her feet, the jump was disqualified by two of the three judges for the event. (This rule is no longer used, and current high jumpers all lead with their heads; Zaharias was later given credit for tying for first place in the event and setting a world record in the jump.) In the press reports of the time, she was nicknamed the "Iron-Woman," the "Amazing Amazon," and "Whatta Gal Didrikson." Amazingly, during that year, male athletes only set Olympic records, leaving the world records untouched; Zaharias, on the other hand, broke both Olympic and world records in her events.

Although Zaharias's athletic talent could not be denied, she was often resented by other athletes, who felt that she was aggressive, overbearing, and a braggart, and that she would do anything to win. According to Larry Schwartz in *ESPN.com,* **Jackie Joyner-Kersee**, a track-and field phenomenon in the 1990s, reflected on these traits, "It wasn't that she was cocky or aggressive.

She was actually speaking the truth [that she was the greatest]. And some people probably didn't like it at that time because it was coming from a woman."

A skilled self-promoter, Zaharias often changed her birth date, making herself appear younger than she was. This deception was intended to make her seem even more of a star than she already was—for example, on her application for the 1932 Olympics, she wrote that she was born in 1914. As Susan E. Cayleff noted in *Babe: The Life and Legend of Babe Didrikson Zaharias,* "If a twenty-year-old excelling at the Olympics in 1932 was heralded, then an eighteen-year-old—or better yet a seventeen-year-old—might be worshipped!" Her gravestone and her baptismal certificate corroborate the earlier 1911 date.

In the early 1930s, Zaharias also began playing golf. By her eleventh game, in 1932, she drove the ball 260 yards from the first tee and played the second set of nine holes with a score of 43. She entered her first tournament in 1934, and won the qualifying round with a score of 77. At the Texas State Women's Championship in April of 1935, she carded a birdie on the par-5 31st hole and won the tournament two-up. In 1935, she was making $15,000 a year from endorsements and golf matches.

Gender Backlash

Despite her success, or because of it, a backlash against her swelled up in the press and in popular opinion, fueled by her refusal to fit typical stereotypes of womanhood. According to William O. Johnson and Nancy P. Williamson in *Whatta Gal: The Babe Didrikson Story,* she was "seen by many reporters and members of the public as a freak . . . an aberration . . . a living putdown to all things feminine." Zaharias herself expressed scorn for traditionally "feminine" clothing and mannerisms, and according to a writer in *Gay and Lesbian Biography,* once told a reporter that "she did not wear girdles, bras, and the like because she was no 'sissy.'"

The common male response to her was summed up by Joe Williams, a contemporary reporter for the *New York World-Telegram.* According to Larry Schwartz in *ESPN.com,* Williams commented, "It would be much better if she and all her ilk stayed at home, got themselves prettied up and waited for the phone to ring."

Schwartz also noted that contemporary sportswriter Paul Gallico, who lost a golf match to Zaharias and Grantland Rice in 1932, called Zaharias a "muscle moll" in one *Vanity Fair* article, and commented in another *Vanity Fair* article that she was neither male nor female, and wrote dismissively that she was a lesbian. And according to Cayleff, it was not unusual for her to be accosted in the locker room by other female athletes who demanded to know whether she was a man or a woman.

In addition to her androgynous personal style, Zaharias defied gender stereotypes of women's need to be

Awards and Accomplishments	
1930-32	All-American Basketball Player
1931	Gold medals in long jump, baseball throw, and 80-meter hurdles, National AAU meet
1932	Overall winner, Texas AAU meet
1932	Overall winner, national AAU meet in Evanston, Illinois; she enters eight events and wins gold medals in six; sets world records in the high jump, 80-meter hurdles, javelin, and baseball throw
1932	Associated Press Woman Athlete of the Year
1932	Gold medal, javelin throw; gold medal, 80-meter hurdles; silver medal, high jump, 1932 Los Angeles Olympic Games
1945	U.S. Women's Amateur
1945-46	Associated Press Woman Athlete of the Year
1946	Wins Women's Trans-Mississippi Amateur
1947	Wins Women's North and South Amateur
1947	Associated Press Woman Athlete of the Year
1947	Wins British Women's Amateur Championship
1948	Wins All-American Open, World Championships, and U.S. Women's Open
1948-51	Leading money-winner on the LPGA tour
1950	Wins U.S. Women's Open
1950	Associated Press Female Athlete of the Half Century
1951	Wins All-American Open, World Championship, Ponte Verda Open, Tampa Open, Fresno Open, and Texas Open
1951	LPGA Hall of Fame
1953	Wins first event of Babe Zaharias Open
1954	Associated Press Woman Athlete of the Year
1954	Wins U.S. Women's Open and Tam O'Shanter All-American
1954	Vare Trophy
1954	Texas Sports Hall of Fame
1974	World Golf Hall of Fame
1976	National Women's Hall of Fame
1980	Women's Sports Foundation Hall of Fame
2000	Sports Illustrated Female Athlete of the 20th Century
2001	National Women's Baseball Hall of Fame

financially dependent on men by remaining single, supporting herself, and earning a great deal of money through endorsements, stunts, and appearances. Her Employer's Casualty contract alone paid her three times as much as the average American man of her time made, and six times as much as the average American woman earned.

In time, Zaharias grew tired of defending her personal style and choices to reporters and curious fans, and made some concessions to conformity, wearing more frilly clothing than she had in the past, telling reporters that she was looking for a husband, and occasionally saying that perhaps women's participation in sports should be limited. According to a writer in *Gay and Lesbian Biography,* she also made up stories about past boyfriends for the press, and uncharacteristically advised women athletes, "Get toughened up by playing boys' games, but don't get tough." Golf promoter Bertha Bowen encouraged her new "feminine" style, and took her to Neiman-Marcus to buy new clothes, taught her how to put on makeup, and even—but only once, and only under pressure from the Texas Women's Golf Association—got her to play golf while wearing a girdle.

Babe Didrikson Zaharias

As Cayleff noted, Zaharias did not adopt this false persona without pain: "Babe's successful ascension to femininity is [falsely] hailed as an applaudable accomplishment, not the tumultuous, contrived, and limiting self-molding that it really was . . . the toll taken on self-esteem, individuality, and difference is ignored."

A few observers were able to dismiss popular notions of femininity and appreciate Zaharias's talent. According to Schwartz, sportswriter Grantland Rice wrote, "She is beyond all belief until you finally see her perform. Then you finally understand that you are looking at the most flawless section of muscle harmony, of complete mental and physical coordination, the world of sport has ever seen."

Meets George Zaharias

In 1935, Zaharias lost her amateur status in the U.S. Golf Association (USGA) because she had accepted money for an automobile endorsement and had competed professionally in other sports. For the next several years she traveled widely, playing exhibition golf. She also entered the vaudeville circuit with a variety of acts, most notably the Babe Didrikson All-American basketball team (on which she was the only woman), which traveled the country playing against local teams, and the House of David baseball team, which did the same; the House of David players were noted for their long beards, and as with the basketball team, she was the only woman among them. Zaharias could easily throw a baseball from deep center field to home plate; in an exhibition game with the House of David, she struck out famed Yankee hitter **Joe DiMaggio** with three overhand fastball pitches. Through all these activities, Zaharias was able to earn several thousand dollars a month during the Great Depression, a time when many people had no work at all.

In 1938, she met George Zaharias, a professional wrestler known as "The Crying Greek from Cripple Creek," at the Los Angeles Open. They were married on December 23, 1938, and had no children. According to Cayleff, their marriage was not based on love at first sight, as they claimed, but had a certain element of calculation. Zaharias's exaggerated manliness, she wrote, "contrasted favorably with Babe's attempted womanliness. They were working-class sports entertainers who reflected mainstream sensibilities: individualism, the will to succeed, and materialism. The two performers had found each other. There was more than a little of each in the other."

From 1938 to 1950, Zaharias, with George as her manager, traveled widely on the golf circuit; during World War II, she gave golf exhibitions to raise money for war bonds, and she agreed to stay out of professional athletics for three years in order to reinstate her amateur standing in the USGA.

George Zaharias had encouraged her to try and reinstate her amateur status, and in January of 1943 she succeeded. As a newly restored amateur, she could compete in golf's greatest tournaments, but first she had to practice. She devoted all her considerable energy to golf, driving as many as a thousand balls a day, taking lessons for four or five hours, and playing until her hands bled. This hard work paid off: between 1946 and 1947, she won seventeen of eighteen golf tournaments, and in 1947, Zaharias became the first American woman to win the prestigious British Ladies' Amateur Championship, held at Gullane, Scotland. In August of that year she decided to return to professional status, and entered the professional golf circuit, which she reigned over for the next six years. She played with celebrities, including Katharine Hepburn and Cary Grant, as well as with noted athletes of the era. She also signed a lifetime contract with Wilson Sporting Goods to represent their equipment.

In 1950, Zaharias and twelve other women, including famed golfers Louise Suggs and Patty Berg, co-founded the Ladies Professional Golf Association. They found corporate sponsors in order to hold more professional tournaments and offer larger cash prizes to winners. Zaharias quickly became the star player of the LPGA, winning more tournaments and taking home more prize money than any other golfer; her success brought publicity and credibility to the young organization.

Meets Her Toughest Competitor

In 1950, Zaharias and her husband bought the Tampa Golf and Country Club and moved into the large converted clubhouse there. However, they seldom saw each other, as he traveled widely and was rarely home. In that same year, Zaharias met youthful golfer Betty Dodd. The two quickly became inseparable, and Dodd moved in with Zaharias and her husband, living with both of them until Zaharias' death. Although neither Zaharias nor Dodd ever openly acknowledged that they had a lesbian relationship, according to a writer in *Gay and Lesbian Biography,* "it was common knowledge that they were primary partners," and the two had a strong emotional bond. Dodd later told Johnson and Williamson, "I had such admiration for this fabulous person. I never wanted to be away from her even when she was dying of cancer. I loved her. I would've done anything for her."

By the end of the golf season in 1952, Zaharias was feeling extremely fatigued, and eventually went to the doctor to find out why. In April of 1953 she was diagnosed with colon cancer, and although her doctors warned her that she might never compete again, she proved them wrong. In her autobiography, she wrote, "All my life I'd been competing to win. I came to realize that in its way, this cancer was the toughest competition I'd faced yet." She eventually underwent surgery for the colon cancer. By this time Dodd had become her full-time caregiver, and told Johnson and Williamson that George Zaharias "couldn't afford to be [jealous] anymore. Because he wouldn't do anything for Babe. . . he needed me."

Six months after her surgery, she returned to competition, placing sixth in the United States in 1953. In 1954 she tied as winner of the U.S. Women's Open, despite

---

Babe Zaharias Dies; Athlete Had Cancer

Mrs. Mildred (Babe) Didrikson Zaharias, famed woman athlete, died of cancer in John Sealy Hospital here this morning. She was 42 years old.

Mrs. Zaharias had been under treatment since 1953, when the malignant condition was discovered after she had won a golf tournament. The tournament was one named for her—the Babe Zaharias Open of Beaumont, Tex., where she was reared.

Mrs. Zaharias had fought valiantly against cancer for the last several months. She remained confident almost to the end that she would get well. Her final weeks were relatively free of pain, although the malignancy was general. Physicians here had performed a cordotomy—a severing of certain nerves—to relieve her of pain.

A funeral service is scheduled for tomorrow afternoon at the Bethlehem Lutheran Church in Beaumont.

Source: *New York Times,* September 28, 1956.

---

the fact that she had to play while wearing a colostomy bag. Because of her performance, she won the **Ben Hogan** Comeback Award for that year. In that same year, she established the Babe Zaharias Fund to benefit cancer treatment centers and clinics.

"I Just Wanted to See a Golf Course One More Time"

In 1955, however, the cancer returned, and the woman who won so many other competitions eventually lost the battle with her toughest foe. Shortly before she died, however, she showed her deep love of golf during a visit to friends in Fort Worth, Texas. One night she asked her friends to drive her to Colonial Country Club. At the club, she walked alone in the dark to one of the greens, where she bent down, ran her hands over the ground, and kissed the grass. "I just wanted to see a golf course one more time," she said, according to an article by Don Wade on the Golf Society Web site.

Zaharias died a few months later, on September 27, 1956, at the age of 45. President Dwight Eisenhower, moved by her death, began his press conference that day with a tribute to her achievements. She is buried in Beaumont, Texas; the epitaph on her gravestone in Forest Lawn Cemetery reads "Babe Didrikson Zaharias, 1911-1956, World's Greatest Woman Athlete."

Zaharias's life was portrayed in a made-for-television movie on the CBS network in 1975. Starring Susan Clark as Zaharias and Alex Karras as George Zaharias, the movie was directed by Buzz Kulik.

Zaharias left a lasting legacy in sports, a result of her lifelong challenge to stereotypes about the roles and abilities of women. She had a lucrative career in areas traditionally held open only to men, and refused to conform to ideas about "ladylike" clothing, mannerisms, and speech. At a time when, as Nick Seitz wrote in *Golf Digest,* "young women were expected to be home minding their manners and the stove," she pursued her own goals and ideals of athletic achievement. As a founding member of the LPGA, she laid the foundation for women's golf to become a respected and rewarding profession. She became a role model for active, athletic woman for decades to come, proving that women could play hard and play to win. As Larry Schwartz noted in *ESPN.com,* when a reporter asked Zaharias if there was anything she didn't play, she answered dryly, "Yeah. Dolls."

SELECTED WRITINGS BY ZAHARIAS:

Championship Golf, A.S. Barnes, 1948.

This Life I've Led: My Autobiography, A.S. Barnes, 1955.

FURTHER INFORMATION

Books

Cayleff, Susan, *Babe: The Life and Legend of Babe Didrikson Zaharias,* Champaign, IL: University of Illinois Press, 1995.

Gay and Lesbian Biography, Detroit: St. James Press, 1997.

Great Women in Sports, Detroit: Visible Ink Press, 1996.

Johnson, William O., and Nancy P. Williamson, *"Whatta-Gal" : The Babe Didrikson Story,* Boston: Little, Brown and Co., 1975.

Periodicals

Dure, Jane. "Female Athlete of the Century," *Texas Monthly,* (December, 1999).

Lemon, Del. "Unsung Heroes of Texas Golf," *Texas Monthly,* (December, 2000): S28.

Mickey, Lisa D. "In the Beginning: Unfazed by a Failed Attempt to Sustain a Tour in the '40s, Some Brave Women Hit the Road and Pursued a Dream," *Golf World,* (November 24, 2000): 12.

Seitz, Nick. "The Babe: Golf's Greatest Athlete," *Golf Digest,* (August, 2000).

Other

Babe Didrikson Zaharias Foundation, http://www.babedidriksonzaharias.org/ (September 23, 2002).

"Babe Didrikson Zaharias," Glass Ceiling Biographies, http://wwwtheglassceiling.com/biographies/bio38.htm (September 25, 2002).

"Betty Dodd Award," San Antonio Junior Golfers' Association, http://www.sajga.net/ (October 1, 2002).

"The First Fabulous Sports Babe," ESPN, http://espn.go.com/ (October 1, 2002).

Ladies' Professional Golf Association, http://www.lpga.com/ (October 1, 2002).

Schwartz, Larry, "Didrikson Was a Woman Ahead of Her Time," ESPN, http://espn.go.com/ (September 25, 2002).

Schwartz, Larry, "The Terrific Tomboy," ESPN, http://www.espn.go.com/ (September 25, 2002).

Wade, Don, "What a Babe!," Golf Society of the U.S., http://www.golfsociety.com/ (October 1, 2002).

Sketch by Kelly Winters

Zinedine Zidane
1972-

French soccer player

French soccer superstar Zinedine Zidane, "Zizou" to his fans, is a hero for the international age. Born in France of Algerian parents, Zidane has led the French national team and professional teams in Italy and in Spain to soccer championships. His impact on the culture of his native France, where immigrants-especially North African ones-and their children are often treated with distrust or outright hostility, has been particularly profound.

From Marseille to Cannes

Yazid Zidane, as Zinedine Zidane was known as a child, was one of five children born to Smail and Malika Zidane, Algerian immigrants who came to France in 1953. The family lived in the La Castellane housing project, which is notorious throughout Marseille for its high crime rate. Zinedine Zidane's father had a steady job, as an overnight security guard in a department store, so they lived a reasonably comfortable life compared to many of their neighbors. Still, the family's apartment was so small that all seven of them could not sit down to eat at the same time.

By the time he was five, Zidane was joining in the soccer games that the neighborhood's children play on the Place Tartane, an 80-by-12-yard plaza that serves as the main square of La Castellane. When he was a little older he began playing with a club, US Saint-Henri, in Marseille. His next step was the Septemes Sports Olympiques, where he began playing before the age of 11. In 1984 Zidane earned the job of ball boy at the Stade Vélodrome in Marseille, for a semifinal game in the European Cup between France, the winner, and Portugal.

Unlike in North America, France has a large system of professional soccer teams for children under the age of 19. Promising young players often join these teams very young, and Zidane was no exception: he left Marseille to

Zinedine Zidane

Chronology

1972	Born June 3 in Marseille, France
1986	Joins the Cannes junior team
1989	Plays in his first First Division soccer game
1991	Scores first goal in a First Division soccer game
1992	Signs a four-year contract with the Bordeaux team
1994	Begins playing for the French national team
1996	Bordeaux makes it the to Union of European Football Associations Cup finals
1996	Signed by Juventus of Turin
1999	Becomes Christian Dior's first male model
2001	Signs a record four-year, $68.6 million contract with Real Madrid

join the Cannes junior soccer team at the age of 13. The Cannes adult team was a prestigious, First Division team at that time, and Zidane began playing in First Division games with them when he was 17. In 1991, at the age of 18, he scored his first goal in a First Division game. As the president of the Cannes club had promised, he gave Zidane a car, a red Clio, for scoring that first goal.

Moving Up

The Cannes club had a good season that year, finishing fourth in the rankings and qualifying for the Union of European Football Associations (UEFA) Cup, but in 1992 the team finished so poorly that they were relegated to the Second Division. Zidane and his wife, Veronique, moved to Bordeaux and Zidane joined their club. Zidane played for Bordeaux for four seasons. The Bordeaux club was a solid if not an outstanding team in those years. They qualified for the UEFA Cup every year, and in 1996 they made it all the way to the finals, where they lost to Bayern Munich in two games.

Zidane's performance in Bordeaux brought him to the attention of an Italian team, Juventus of Turin, which recruited him after the 1995-96 season. With this team, Zidane would finally become a champion. Under his leadership Juventus won five titles in the next three years. In 1998 Zidane's role in these victories was honored with two prestigious awards: the Golden Ball and the "Player of the Year" designation by the Fédération

Internationale de Football Association (FIFA). As these judges and others have noticed, Zidane has outstanding ball-handling skills. He can spin 360 degrees while balancing the soccer ball on top of his foot, a maneuver that he often uses in games to avoid a tackler.

Cultural Impact

Zidane also became a hero in France for helping to lead the French national team to victory in the World Cup in 1998, for the first time in 68 years, and the Euro Cup in 2000. His success was especially important to other Beurs, as second-generation North Africans are called in France. Zidane is one of the only Beurs to be widely visible in French culture, which is often hostile to Arab and other immigrants, and he is by far the most successful one. Zidane's influence has encouraged thousands of young French Arabs to join soccer teams, and Zidane even sponsors a team in his old neighborhood of La Castellane himself.

In 1999 Zidane became arguably the sexiest man in France when he became Christian Dior's first male model. To the very happily married Zidane (he kisses his wedding ring as he steps onto the field at the beginning of each match as a gesture of love to his wife and their two sons), the sack loads of fan mail he receives from women who appreciate his good looks and athletic prowess have become a source of consternation. As John Lichfield reported in the *Independent,* "'Some say they are in love with me,' he told an interviewer, with touching confusion, as if he was expected to reciprocate in some way. 'But I'm married.'"

Another Club, Another Country

Zidane became the best-paid soccer player in history on June 9, 2001, when he signed a $68.6 million, four-year contract with Real Madrid, one of the strongest clubs in the history of European soccer. He was given the number five jersey, the number that had, until he retired at the end of the 2000-01 season, belonged to Real Madrid's star Manuel Sanchez for 18 years. Real Madrid's fans expected the same level of stardom out of Zidane, and he did not disappoint them. Less than a year

---

Awards and Accomplishments

1996	European Super Cup (with Juventus of Turin)
1996	European/South American Cup (with Juventus)
1997	League Super Cup (with Juventus)
1997-98	Italy Champion (with Juventus)
1998	World Cup (with French national team)
1998	Awarded the Golden Ball
1998, 2000	Named the Player of the Year by the Fédération Internationale de Football Association
2000	Euro Cup (with French national team)
2001	Spanish Super Cup (with Real Madrid)
2002	Champions League (with Real Madrid)
2002	Named Most Valuable Player of the 2001-02 Champions League
2002	European Super Cup (with Real Madrid)
2002	European/South American Intercontinental Cup (with Real Madrid)

---

after joining the team Zidane scored the goal that won the 2002 European Cup for Real Madrid with only seconds remaining in the final match. This was Real Madrid's ninth victory in that tournament, a record, and their win filled in a large hole in Zidane's résumé: despite his success in other venues, up till this point, Zidane had not yet won a European Cup. Fans can only hope that Zidane will continue to perform as well for the rest of his time in Madrid.

CONTACT INFORMATION

Online: http://www.zidane.fr.

SELECTED WRITINGS BY ZIDANE:

(With Dan Franck) *Zidane: le roman d'une victoire.* Pocket, 2000.

FURTHER INFORMATION

Periodicals

Lichfield, John. "In the Footsteps of Zidane." *Independent* (London; May 24, 2002): 4.

———. "A Striking French Icon: Profile: Zinedine Zidane." *Independent* (London, England) (July 1, 2000): 5.

Saporito, Bill. "Zidane Makes the French Connection: Can the World's Most Expensive Player Produce Two in a Row for Les Bleus?" *Time International* (May 27, 2002): 67.

Wahl, Grant. "Coup de Grace." *Sports Illustrated* (July 20, 1998): 28-33.

"ZZ Is Back on Top. "*Soccer Digest* (November, 2001): 34.

Other

McGarry, Ian. "Madrid Hail Wonder Goal from Zidane." ESPN.com Soccernet. http://www.soccernet.com/championsleague/news/2002/0516/20020516bayervrealrep.html (May 16, 2002).

Real Madrid Official Web Site. http://www.realmadrid.com (January 11, 2003).

"Zidane." Real Madrid, Updated News, Information, Chatroom, Forum, and Much More (unofficial fan site). http://www.fortunecity.com/wembley/trafford/555/zidane.html (January 16, 2003).

Sketch by Julia Bauder

Appendix of Sports Abbreviations

GENERAL ASSOCIATIONS/UNIONS

AAAA	Amateur Athletic Association of America
AAU	Amateur Athletic Union of the United States
NAGWS	National Association for Girls and Women in Sport
NCAA	National Collegiate Athletic Association
NJCAA	National Junior College Athletic Association
WAAA	Women's Amateur Athletic Association
WSF	Women's Sports Foundation

AUTO RACING

AMI	American Motorsport International
ASCA	American Sprint Car Association
CART	Championship Auto Racing Teams
CMS	Charlotte Motor Speedway
DIS	Daytona International Speedway
DOP	Driver's Open Practice
F1	Formula One
FL	Fastest Lap
FTD	Fastest Time of the Day
IMS	Indianapolis Motor Speedway
IMSA	International Motor Sports Association
IRL	Indy Racing League
MIS	Michigan International Speedway
NAPS	North American Pro Series
NARA	Northern Auto Racing Association
NART	North American Racing Team
NASCAR	National Association for Stock Car Auto Racing
NCRA	National Championship Racing Association
ODS	Old Dominion Speedway
PSR	Professional Sportscar Racing
STARS	Short Track Auto Racing Series
SWC	Sportscar World Championship
URC	United Racing Club
USA	United Stockcar Alliance
USGP	United States Grand Prix
USHRA	United States Hot Rod Association
WSC	World Sportscar Championship

BASEBALL

1B	First Base
1B	Single
2B	Second Base
2B	Double
3B	Third Base
3B	Triple
AA	American Association
AB	At Bats
AL	American League
ALCS	American League Championship Series
ALDS	American League Division Series
AVG	Batting Average
B	Bunt
BA	Batting Average
BB	Bases on Balls
BK	Balks
BL	Bats Left-Handed
BP	Batting Practice
BR	Bats Right-Handed
BS	Blown Save
C	Catcher
CF	Center Field
CG	Complete Games
CS	Caught Stealing
CWS	College World Series
DH	Designated Hitter
DL	Disabled List
DP	Double Play
E	Errors
ER	Earned Run
ERA	Earned Run Average
F	Flyout
FA	Fielding Average
FC	Fielder's Choice
FF	Foul Fly
FL	Federal League
FO	Fouled Out
FP	Fielding Percentage
GA	Games Ahead
GB	Games Behind
GIDP	Grounded into Double Plays
GO	Ground Out
GP	Games Played
GRD	Ground Rule Double
GS	Games Started
GSHR	Grand Slam Home Runs
H	Hits
H	Hits Against
HB	Hit by Ball
HBP	Hit by Pitcher
HR	Home Runs
IBB	Intentional Bases on Balls
IF	Infielder
IL	International League
IP	Innings Pitched
K	Strikeout
KC	Strikeout, Called
KS	Strikeout, Swinging
L	Losses
LCS	League Championship Series
LDS	League Division Series
LF	Left Field
LHB	Left-Handed Batter
LHP	Left-Handed Pitcher
LL	Little League
LOB	Left on Base
LP	Losing Pitcher
ML	Major League
MLB	Major League Baseball

MLBPA	Major League Baseball Players Association
MVP	Most Valuable Player
NAL	Negro American League
ND	No Decision
NL	National League
NLCS	National League Championship Series
NLDS	National League Division Series
NNL	Negro National League
OB	On Base
OBA	On-Base Average
OBP	On-Base Percentage
OF	Outfield
P	Pitch
PA	Plate Appearance
PCL	Pacific Coast League
PCT	Percentage
PH	Pinch Hitter
PO	Putout
PR	Pinch Runner
R	Runs
RBI	Runs Batted In
RF	Right Field
RHB	Right-Handed Batter
RHP	Right-Handed Pitcher
RP	Relief Pitcher
SA	Slugging Average
SAC	Sacrifice
SB	Stolen Base
SF	Sacrifice Fly
SH	Sacrifice Hit
SHO	Shutout
SO	Strikeouts
SP	Slugging Percentage
SP	Starting Pitcher
SV	Saves
TA	Total Average
TB	Times at Bat
TL	Throws Left-Handed
TP	Triple Play
TR	Throws Right-Handed
U	Umpire
U	Unassisted Putout
USABF	United States Amateur Baseball Federation
USBF	United States Baseball Federation
W	Wins
WHIP	Walks plus Hits Divided by Innings Pitched
WP	Wild Pitch
WP	Winning Pitcher
WS	World Series

BASKETBALL

3P%	3-Point Percentage
3PA	3-Pointers Attempted
3PM	3-Pointers Made
ABA	American Basketball Association
ABBA	Amateur Basketball Association
APBA	American Professional Basketball Association
APG	Assists Per Game
Ast	Assists
Bl	Blocks
BPG	Blocks Per Game
C	Center
D	Defense
DNPCD	Did Not Play, Coach's Decision
EBL	Eastern Basketball League
F	Forward
FG	Field Goal
FG%	Field Goal Percentage
FGA	Field Goals Attempted
FGM	Field Goals Made
FT	Free Throw
FT%	Free Throw Percentage
FTA	Free Throws Attempted
FTM	Free Throws Made
G	Guard
GP	Games Played
IBA	International Basketball Association
MVP	Most Valuable Player
NBA	National Basketball Association
NBL	National Basketball League
OER	Offensive Efficiency Ratio
PF	Personal Fouls
PTS	Points
REB	Rebounds
RPG	Rebounds Per Game
SPG	Steals Per Game
St	Steals
TO	Total Turnovers
USBL	United States Basketball League
WABA	Women's American Basketball Association
WBL	Women's Basketball League
WNBA	Women's National Basketball Association
WPBL	Women's Professional Basketball League

BIATHLON

IBU	International Biathlon Union
USBA	US Biathlon Association

BOWLING

/	Spare
G	Gutter Ball
NBA	National Bowling Association
USSBA	United States Seniors Bowling Association
WIBC	Women's International Bowling Congress
X	Strike

BOXING

FLYWT	Flyweight
IBF	International Boxing Federation
KO	Knockout
KO'd	Knocked Out
LD	Decisions Lost
LF	Lost on Foul
PR	Prize Ring
RSC	Referee Stops Contest
TB	Total Bouts
TKO	Technical Knockout
TW	Technical Win
USA/ABF	USA Amateur Boxing Federation
WBA	World Boxing Association
WBC	World Boxing Council
WBO	World Boxing Organization
WD	Decisions Won
WF	Won on Foul

CRICKET

B	Bowled
B	Bye
C & B	Caught and Bowled
C	Caught
COV PT	Cover Point
DEC	Declared
DNB	Did Not Bat
DRN	Drawn
ht wkt	Hit Wicket
LB	Leg Bye
LBW	Leg before Wicket
NB	No Ball
NCCA	National Club Cricket Association
PLD	Played Matches
R	Runs
ST	Stumped

CURLING

CC	Curling Club

USCA	United States Curling Association	FB	Fullback	SK	Sack
WCF	World Curling Federation	FD	First Down	SOLO	Solo Tackle

USCA	United States Curling Association
WCF	World Curling Federation

CYCLING

CC	Cycling Club
USCF	United States Cycling Federation
USPRO	US Professional Cycling Federation

DISABLED SPORTS

DS/USA	Disabled Sports USA
SOI	Special Olympics International

EQUESTRIAN

IEF	International Equestrian Federation
USET	United States Equestrian Team

FIGURE SKATING

USFSA	United States Figure Skating Association

FOOTBALL

ACC	Atlantic Coast Conference
AFC	American Football Conference
AFD	Automatic First Down
AFL	American Football League
AST	Assists (Tackles)
ATT	Attempts
AVG	Average
BB	Blocking Back
BCS	Bowl Championship Series
BJ	Back Judge
BK	Blocked Kick
C	Center
CB	Cornerback
COM	Completions
COM%	Completion Percentage
DB	Defensive Back
DE	Defensive End
DG	Defensive Guard
DT	Defensive Tackle
E	End
EFC	Eastern Football Conference
EP	Extra Point

FB	Fullback
FD	First Down
FF	Forced Fumble
FG	Field Goal
FG%	Field Goals Percentage
FGA	Field Goals Attempted
FGM	Field Goals Made
FL	Flanker
FS	Free Safety
FUM	Fumble
G	Guard
HB	Halfback
IN20	Punts Inside the 20
IN20%	Punts Inside the 20 Percentage
INT	Interception
K	Kicker
LB	Linebacker
LCB	Left Cornerback
LG	Left Guard
LJ	Line Judge
LNG	Long
LOS	Line of Scrimmage
LS	Left Safety
LST	Lost Ball
LT	Left Tackle
M	Field Goals Missed
MAC	Mid-American Conference
MLB	Middle Linebacker
MVP	Most Valuable Player
NFC	National Football Conference
NFL	National Football League
OC	Offensive Center
OE	Offensive End
OG	Offensive Guard
OLB	Outside Linebacker
OT	Offensive Tackle
P	Punter
PAT	Point after Touchdown
PF	Point of Foul
PK	Place Kicker
PLS	Point of Last Scrimmage
PPK	Punt, Pass, and Kick
PTS	Points
QB	Quarterback
R	Referee
RAT	Quarterback Rating
RB	Running Back
RCB	Right Cornerback
REC	Receptions
RET	Number of Punts Returned for Touchdowns
RG	Right Guard
RS	Right Safety
RT	Right Tackle
S	Safety
SE	Split End
SEC	Southeastern Conference

SK	Sack
SOLO	Solo Tackle
SS	Strong Safety
T	Tackle
TB	Tailback
TB	Touchback
TB%	Touchback Percentage
TD	Touchdown
TE	Tight End
TOT	Total
TP	Touchdowns Passing
WAC	Western Athletic Conference
WFC	Western Football Conference
WR	Wide Receiver
XP%	Extra Points Percentage
XPA	Extra Points Attempted
XPM	Extra Points Made
YDS	Yards
YG	Yards Gained
YNG	Yards Not Gained

GOLF

LPGA	Ladies Professional Golf Association
ODS	Overall Distance Standard
PGA	Professional Golfers Association

GYMNASTICS

USGF	United States Gymnastics Federation

HOCKEY

+/-	Plus/Minus Rating
A	Assist
AGP	Average Goals Against per Period
C	Captain
D	Defenseman
ENG	Empty Net Goals
G	Goal
G	Goalie
GA	Goals Against
GAA	Goals-Against Average
GF	Goals For
GP	Games Played
GTG	Game-Tying Goals
GWG	Game-Winning Goals
IHF	International Hockey Federation
L	Losses
LW	Left Wing
MP	Minutes Played
MVP	Most Valuable Player

NHA	National Hockey Association
NHL	National Hockey League
OHL	Ontario Hockey League
OT	Overtime
PIM	Penalties in Minutes
PM	Penalty Minutes
PP	Power Play
PPG	Power-Play Goal
PTS	Points
RW	Right Wing
Sh	Shot
SHG	Short-Handed Goal
SHO	Shutouts
SOG	Shots On Goal
SPCT	Shot Percentage
SV	Saves
SV%	Save Percentage
T	Ties
TGA	Total Goals Allowed
TPR	Team Power Rating
TSA	Total Shots Allowed
USAFHA	USA Field Hockey Association
USHL	United States Hockey League
W	Wins
WHA	World Hockey Association
WPHL	Women's Professional Hockey League

HORSE RACING

ALW	Allowance Race
AQHRC	American Quarter Horse Racing Council
B	Blinkers
B	Breezing
B	Brought Down
BF	Black Filly
BG	Black Gelding
C	Course Winner
CH	Chestnut
CLM	Claiming Race
D	Disqualified
D	Distance Winner
DD	Daily Double
DIST	Distanced
E	Entry
F	Fell
F	Mutuel Field
FM	Firm
FST	Fast
G	Workout from Starting Gate
H	Handily
H	Head
HCP	Handicap Race
HG	Workout Handily from Gate

LTB	Light Bay
MDN	Maiden Race
NS	Nose
P	Pulled Up
PN	Program Number
RIG	Ridgeling
S	Slipped Up
S	Spurs
SF	Soft
SLY	Sloppy
SSI	Standards Starts Index
STK	Stakes Race
STR	Stretch
TC	Turf Course
TFP	Total Finish Positions
TQ	Three-Quarter Midget
TYC	Two-Year-Old Course
TYO	Two-Year-Old
U	Eased Up
U	Unseated Rider

LACROSSE

A	Attack
C	Center
CP	Cover Point
D	Defense
FA	First Attack
FD	First Defense
G	Goal
IH	In Home
LAW	Left Attack Wing
LDW	Left Defense Wing
LF	Lacrosse Foundation
M	Midfield
NLL	National Lacrosse League
OH	Out Home
P	Point
RAW	Right Attack Wing
RDW	Right Defense Wing
SA	Second Attack
SD	Second Defense
TA	Third Attack
TD	Third Defense
USALA	United States Amateur Lacrosse Association
USCLA	United States Club Lacrosse Association

LUGE

ILF	International Luge Federation
USLA	United States Luge Association

MOTOCROSS

BMX	Bicycle Motocross
MX	Motocross

RUGBY

IRB	International Rugby Board
RFL	Rugby Football League
RFU	Rugby Football Union
RL	Rugby League

SKATING

B	Backward Edge
I	Inside Edge
ISA	International Skating Association
ISSL	International Speed Skating League
O	Outside Edge
R	Right Edge
USFSA	United States Figure Skating Association
USISSA	United States International Speed Skating Association

SKIING

E	Expert Slope
I	Intermediate Slope
N	Novice Slope
XCS	Cross-Country Skiing

SOCCER

CB	Center Back
CF	Center Forward
CH	Center Halfback
DFK	Direct Free Kick
G	Goal
G	Goalkeeper
IFK	Indirect Free Kick
IL	Inside Left
IR	Inside Right
ISL	International Soccer League
LF	Left Fullback
LH	Left Halfback
MISL	Major Indoor Soccer League
MLS	Major League Soccer
NASL	North American Soccer League
OL	Outside Left
OR	Outside Right
PK	Penalty Kick
RC	Red Card
RC	Right Center
RF	Right Fullback
RH	Right Halfback
USB	Unsporting Behavior
USSF	United States Soccer Federation

USYSA	United States Youth Soccer Association
WUSA	Women's United Soccer Association
YC	Yellow Card

SOFTBALL

ASA	Amateur Softball Association
ASA	American Softball Association
ISF	International Softball Federation
NSA	National Softball Association
USSF	United States Softball Federation
USSSA	United States Slo-Pitch Softball Association

SURFING

APS	American Professional Surfing Association
ASA	American Surfing Association
IASF	International Amateur Surfing Federation
ICAS	International Council of Associations of Surfing
ISA	International Surfing Association
ISF	International Surfing Foundation
ISL	International Surfing League
USSF	United States Surfing Federation
WISA	Women's International Surfing Association

SWIMMING

| USSF | United States Swimming Foundation |
| USSS | United States Synchronized Swimming |

TABLE TENNIS

ITTA	International Table Tennis Association
ITTF	International Table Tennis Federation
ITTL	International Table Tennis League
USTTA	United States Table Tennis Association

TENNIS

ATA	American Tennis Association
ATF	American Tennis Federation
IPTPA	International Professional Tennis Players' Association
ITF	International Tennis Federation
LGW	Love Games Won
NTF	National Tennis Foundation
NTL	National Tennis League
USLTA	United States Lawn Tennis Association [Later, USTA]
USPTA	United States Professional Tennis Association
USTA	United States Tennis Association
WLTC	Wimbledon Lawn Tennis Championship

TRACK AND FIELD

NTFA	National Track and Field Association
TFA	Track and Field Association
TFAA	Track and Field Athletes of America
USATF	U.S.A. Track and Field

VOLLEYBALL

| IVBA | International Volleyball Association |
| IVBF | International Volleyball Federation |

WEIGHTLIFING

| IWF | International Weightlifting Federation |
| USWF | United States Weightlifting Federation |

WRESTLING

USAWF	United States Amateur Wrestling Foundation
USWF	United States Wrestling Federation
WCW	World Championship Wrestling
WWE	World Wrestling Entertainment
WWF	World Wrestling Federation

Cumulative Geographic Index

This index covers all four volumes of *Notable Sports Figures*, and includes birthplaces, places of death, and places where major work was done. States within the United States are listed alphabetically, subdivided by city name where available. Country names follow the list of states; countries are subdivided by city name where available. Subjects are listed alphabetically under each geographic name

Banks, Ernie, 1:83
Butkus, Dick, 1:228
Chelios, Chris, 1:281
Conner, Bart, 1:318
Ditka, Mike, 1:403
Grange, Harold "Red," 2:573
Halas, George, 2:617
Hamill, Dorothy, 2:624
Hardaway, Tim, 2:638
Henderson, Rickey, 2:668
Jordan, Michael, 2:790
Mikita, Stan, 3:1065
Payton, Walter, 3:1214
Pippen, Scottie, 3:1247
Puckett, Kirby, 3:1258
Sharpe, Sterling, 3:1464
Sosa, Sammy, 3:1503
Thomas, Frank, 4:1594
Thomas, Isiah, 4:1597
Weissmuller, Johnny, 4:1739

East St. Louis
Connors, Jimmy, 1:322
Joyner-Kersee, Jackie, 2:797

Highland
Rubin, Barbara Jo, 3:1359

Joliet
Mikan, George, 3:1062

Maywood
Granato, Cammi, 2:571

Waukegan
Graham, Otto, 2:567

Wheaton
Grange, Harold "Red," 2:573

INDIANA
Elkhart
Kemp, Shawn, 2:821

Evansville
Griese, Bob, 2:593
Knight, Bobby, 2:853

Fort Wayne
Woodson, Rod, 4:1807

Gary
Robinson, Glenn, 3:1321

Indianapolis
DeFrantz, Anita, 1:376
Weber, Dick, 4:1731

Martinsville
Wooden, John, 4:1796

Nyesville
Brown, Mordecai, 1:209

Richmond
Ewbank, Weeb, 1:461

South Bend
Rockne, Knute, 3:1338

West Baden
Bird, Larry, 1:147

IOWA
Burlington
Warner, Kurt, 4:1713

Des Moines
Robinson, Shawna, 3:1327

Iowa City
Guthrie, Janet, 2:606

Waterloo
Gable, Dan, 2:523

KANSAS
Wichita
Mears, Rick, 3:1052
Sanders, Barry, 3:1402
Sayers, Gale, 3:1416
Woodard, Lynette, 4:1794

KENTUCKY
Ekron
Reese, Harold "Pee Wee," 3:1270

Lexington
Man o' War, 3:996

Louisville
Ali, Muhammad, 1:32
Hornung, Paul, 2:710
McKinney, Tamara, 3:1048
Meagher, Mary T., 3:1049
Murden, Tori, 3:1113

LOUISIANA
Collinston
Brock, Lou, 1:198

Monroe
Russell, Bill, 3:1366

New Orleans
Fault, Marshall, 2:473
Stewart, Kordell, 3:1541

Shreveport
Ashford, Evelyn, 1:68
Belle, Albert, 1:127
Bradshaw, Terry, 1:191

Summerfield
Malone, Karl, 3:990

MAINE
Cape Elizabeth
Samuelson, Joan Benoit, 1:135

MARYLAND
Baltimore
Alomar, Roberto, 1:41
Bogues, Tyrone "Muggsy," 1:165
Flutie, Doug, 2:496
Kaline, Al, 2:806
Ripken, Cal, Jr., 3:1302

Robinson, Brooks, 3:1311
Ruth, Babe, 3:1369
Unitas, Johnny, 4:1661

Gaithersburg
O'Connor, David, 3:1149

Havre de Grace
Ripken, Cal, Jr., 3:1302

Palmer Park
Leonard, Sugar Ray, 2:921

Silver Spring
Dawes, Dominique, 1:367

MASSACHUSETTS
Kerrigan, Nancy, 2:823

Boston
Auerbach, Arnold "Red," 1:71
Bird, Larry, 1:147
Cousy, Bob, 1:348
Fisk, Carlton, 2:486
Gibb, Bobbi, 2:537
Havlicek, John, 2:652
Russell, Bill, 3:1366
Sullivan, John L., 3:1563
Vaughn, Mo, 4:1680
Williams, Ted, 4:1775

Brockton
Davis, Al, 1:362
Marciano, Rocky, 3:1004

Brookline
Kirby, Karolyn, 2:846

Cambridge
Butcher, Susan, 1:226

East Brookfield
Mac, Connie, 3:977

Georgetown
Thompson, Jenny, 4:1605

Lincoln
Golden, Diana, 2:550

Newton Center
Albright, Tenley, 1:25

Northampton
Berenson Abbott, Senda, 1:138

Springfield
Naismith, James, 3:1123

West Springfield
Durocher, Leo, 1:423

MICHIGAN
Benton Harbor
Krone, Julie, 2:873

Birmingham
Lalas, Alexi, 2:890
Young, Sheila, 4:1819

Detroit
Anderson, Sparky, 1:46
Cobb, Ty, 1:303

WASHINGTON

Port Angeles
Elway, John, 1:442

Seattle
Akers, Michelle, 1:20
Devers, Gail, 1:389
Largent, Steve, 2:900
Ohno, Apolo Anton, 3:1156
Payton, Gary, 3:1212
Suzuki, Ichiro, 3:1569

Spokane
Stockton, John, 3:1545

Tacoma
Anthony, Earl, 1:53

White Pass
Mahre, Phil, 3:986

WASHINGTON, D.C.
Baugh, Sammy, 1:97
Baylor, Elgin, 1:103
Monk, Art, 3:1086
Sampras, Pete, 3:1396

WEST VIRGINIA

Bluefield
Martin, Christy, 3:1021

Cheylan
West, Jerry, 4:1743

Fairmont
Retton, Mary Lou, 3:1275

Rand
Moss, Randy, 3:1108

WISCONSIN

Green Bay
Favre, Brett, 2:476
Hornung , Paul, 2:710
Lambeau, Earl, 2:893
Starr, Bart, 3:1518

Madison
Heiden, Eric, 2:661
Riddles, Libby, 3:1295

Milwaukee
Aaron, Hank, 1:3
Abdul-Jabbar, Kareem, 1:10
Selig, Bud, 3:1462
Sprewell, Latrell, 3:1513

Wausau
Hirsch, Elroy, 2:686

West Allis
Jansen, Dan, 2:756

ARGENTINA

Balcarce
Fangio, Juan Manuel, 2:470

Buenos Aires
Maradona, Diego, 3:1002
Sabatini, Gabriela, 3:1383

AUSTRALIA

Albury, New South Wales
Court, Margaret Smith, 1:344

Ayr, Queensland
Webb, Karrie, 4:1723

Barellan, New South Wales
Goolagong, Evonne, 2:554

Cootamundra, New South Wales
Bradman, Don, 1:189

Mackay, Queensland
Freeman, Cathy, 2:516
O'Neill, Susan, 3:1175

Milperra
Thorpe, Ian, 4:1607

Mt. Isa, Queensland
Norman, Greg, 3:1145

Queensland
Gorman, Tom, 2:562

Rockhampton, Queensland
Laver, Rod, 2:908

AUSTRIA

Altenmarkt
Maier, Hermann, 3:988

Pfarwerfen
Kronberger, Petra, 2:872

AUSTRIA-HUNGARY

Freidorf
Weissmuller, Johnny, 4:1739

BELARUS

Grodno
Korbut, Olga, 2:859

Osetcheno
Karsten, Ekaterina, 2:817

BRAZIL

Florianopolis
Kuerten, Gustavo, 2:876

Sao Paulo
Da Silva, Fabiola, 1:359
Fittipaldi, Emerson, 2:489

Tres coracoes, Minas Gerais
Pele, 3:1218

BULGARIA

Kircali
Suleymanoglu, Naim, 3:1560

CANADA
Bedard, Myriam, 1:115

Almonte, Ontario
Naismith, James, 3:1123

Belleville, Ontario
Hull, Brett, 2:723

Biggar, Saskatchewan
Schmirler, Sandra, 3:1431

Brantford, Ontario
Gretzky, Wayne, 2:588

Calgary, Alberta
Sale, Jamie, 3:1388

Chicoutimi, Quebec
Vezina, Georges, 4:1687

Comox, British Columbia
Neely, Cam, 3:1133

Edmonton, Alberta
Messier, Mark, 3:1055

Floral, Saskatchewan
Howe, Gordie, 2:713

Humboldt, Saskatchewan
Hall, Glenn, 2:621

Islington, Ontario
Dryden, Ken, 1:417

Lac Beauport, Quebec
Rheaume, Manon, 3:1279

Lloydminster, Saskatchewan
Bailey, Garnet "Ace," 1:81

London, Ontario
Lindros, Eric, 2:939

Manitoba
Belfour, Ed, 1:118

Montreal, Quebec
Alou, Felipe, 1:44
Blake, Toe, 1:160
Bossy, Mike, 1:180
Bowman, Scotty, 1:183
Lemieux, Mario, 2:913
Pierce, Mary, 3:1242
Richard, Maurice, 3:1285
Vezina, Georges, 4:1687

Newmarket, Ontario
Stojko, Elvis, 3:1548

Oakville, Ontario
Bailey, Donovan, 1:79

Perth, Ontario
Smith, Billy, 3:1491

Point Anne, Ontario
Hull, Bobby, 2:719

Quebec City, Quebec
Roy, Patrick, 3:1353

Saint Catharines, Ontario
Mikita, Stan, 3:1065

Sault Ste. Marie, Ontario
Esposito, Phil, 1:448
Esposito, Tony, 1:451

Sayabec, Quebec
Pelletier, David, 3:1388

Shaunavon, Saskatchewan
Wickenheiser, Hayley, 4:1753

Shawinigan Falls, Quebec
Plante, Jacques, 3:1250

Cumulative Occupation Index

Cumulative Subject Index

Page references to main entries for individuals appear in boldface. Page references to illustrations appear in italic.